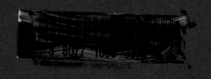

PUSHCART

THE LITTLE MAGAZINE
IN AMERICA:
A MODERN
DOCUMENTARY HISTORY

THE LITTLE MAGAZINE IN AMERICA: A MODERN DOCUMENTARY HISTORY

edited by Elliott Anderson and Mary Kinzie

PUSHCART

Printed in the United States of America.

For information address
The Pushcart Press, P. O. Box 845, Yonkers N. Y. 10701

Library of Congress Card Number: 78-69929
ISBN: 0-916366-04-9

First printing, November, 1978

Also from
THE PUSHCART PRESS

THE PUBLISH-IT-YOURSELF HANDBOOK:
Literary Tradition and How-To
(tenth printing)

THE PUSHCART PRIZE: BEST OF THE SMALL PRESSES
(1976–77 edition)

THE PUSHCART PRIZE II: BEST OF THE SMALL PRESSES
(1977–78 edition)

THE PUSHCART PRIZE III: BEST OF THE SMALL PRESSES
(1978–79 edition)

THE PUSHCART PRIZE IV: BEST OF THE SMALL PRESSES
(1979–80 edition)

This book was produced for the publisher by
Ray Freiman & Company, Stamford, Connecticut.

This book is for
its contributors

PUBLISHER'S NOTE

THE LITTLE MAGAZINE IN AMERICA: *A Modern Documentary History* is the product of a unique cooperation between two small presses— *TriQuarterly* and *Pushcart*. I would especially like to thank Elliott Anderson, Mary Kinzie and the *TriQuarterly* staff for their superb job in editing and collecting this book over a four year period, and Cynthia Anderson for her art direction. Thanks also to Michael McDonnell for his Index, created specially for this book edition of *TriQuarterly*'s history, and to Russell Maylone, Special Collections, Northwestern University, for his help in assembling the photographs and documents.

Bill Henderson
PUSHCART PRESS

THE LITTLE MAGAZINE IN AMERICA: A MODERN DOCUMENTARY HISTORY

PREFATORY NOTE

The Little Magazine in America: A Modern Documentary History was conceived as a companion to a study by Frederick J. Hoffman, Charles Allen, and Carolyn F. Ulrich, *The Little Magazine: A History and a Bibliography,* published by Princeton University Press in 1946. The Hoffman-Allen-Ulrich volume offered a twelve-chapter history of the various movements, themes, causes, and types of little magazines, as well as a 150-page bibliography. Frederick Hoffman's interest in the relationship between psychoanalysis, the literary imagination, and the avant-garde informed the book's structure and focus, although there were chapters on political movements, regionalism, and the critical and eclectic magazines as well. What was missing, and what we have tried to include in the present volume, is a sense of the living reality of the publications. Rather than offer a historical overview, or even a collaboration between historians, we have assembled a large collection of essay-memoirs by prominent and representative little magazine editors, publishers, and contributors, including a generous selection of photo-documents and an annotated bibliography of 84 important magazines of the period. Although such a documentary project inevitably lacks the integration of more conventional histories, our basic concern has been for the *phenomenon* of little magazines—for the curious and oftentimes eccentric processes of the field—not for one or another interpretation of their collective merit, however congenial. The field today is so large, the kinds of magazines and the attitudes of their editors so diverse, that no literary historian could hope to offer more than a gloss.

It is a commonplace now to say that commercial magazines and publishers no longer offer the full range of literary services that they once did, and that as a result the little magazines offer newer writers—as well as more difficult or "literary" authors—their only publishing opportunity. Little magazines generally put experiment before ease, and art before comment. They can afford to do so because they can barely "afford" to do anything; in other words, as a rule they do not, and cannot, expect to make money. Consequently, the ways in which they appeal to their readers need

3

not be coercive, stylistically uniform, or categorically topical, as the ways of commercial presses must be.

There is something edgy, something peculiar and asocial, about a great many little magazines. Those who write for them are in some sense the disadvantaged, at least by commercial standards: people who have a bone to pick, people who are writing against the grain, but who nevertheless want recognition. Not content to wait until the new sensibility of which they may be the harbingers has proven itself in time, they insist upon a revolution in taste now.

In important respects, the meaning and value of the contemporary little magazine exists between the lines of this volume, in the spoken and unspoken alliances and antagonisms that exist between the various contributors, and in the larger differences that should be perceived between past and present, between magazines of the pre–World War II period and those published since the war. It may be that the modern world is no longer as receptive to intelligent meditation as it may have been through the 1940s, and that our culture will no longer support the literary judgments of a relatively small number of literate commentators. It may be that the advances in publishing technologies and the conglomerations of their economies militate against the cultural coherence of the past. Or it may be, too, that such coherence is an inevitable function of nostalgia and that commercial publishers were no more representative and supportive before 1950 than they are now.

When a historical survey of the more recent period is written, what will be elusive about the literature of the postwar period will not be just the moment of personality—which is, after all, hard to chart in any history—but, more narrowly, the determination of the little magazine enterprise to resist any such systematic re-creation. What becomes clear, in other words, from the memoirs and documents here is the determination of many editors and writers from the fifties to the present to reject all paraphrase, to insist on the absolute inviolable idiosyncrasy of their endeavors, not simply as writers but also as editors. Oddly enough, this is often just as true of the academic editors as it is of the avant-garde and polemical-mimeo editors. The history of this period in little magazine editing is one of egregious and splendid bias. Not the least among the causes are the effort, the cost, and the fatally meager rewards of small publishing ventures—and the change in the audience for literature suggested by those diminishing returns.

4

As for the process of compiling such a history, little need be said. It took four years. Many people have contributed advice; many more have volunteered practical assistance. Once the decision was taken to assemble a documentary history, it became first a matter of establishing a shape, a profile, then of backing and filling to provide substance. Our concern from the beginning was to be comprehensive—that is, representative—including work not only about the most significant magazines but about each of the kinds as well. Whom have we left out? In quantity a great many. In kind, not many at all. We would have preferred a broader representation of ethnic and minority publications, and we would have preferred a coherent, linear view of the reasons for magazine proliferation during the sixties and seventies. Nevertheless we believe that the documents which follow—the essays, memoirs, annotations, and photo-materials—constitute a comprehensive measure of the past three decades of little magazine history.

We owe special thanks to Hanna Gray, formerly dean of the College of Arts and Sciences at Northwestern University, and to Richard Press, formerly assistant librarian for collection development at Northwestern University Library, who originally encouraged this project; to contributing editors Robert Alter, John Hawkes, Tony Tanner, and Nathaniel Tarn, for conferring with us in the early stages of planning; to Thomas R. Buckman, Joseph Epstein, Melvin J. Friedman, Bill Katz, Robie Macauley, Nicholas Nyary, Felix Pollak, Ishmael Reed, Walter B. Rideout, Frances Steloff, and Robert Wilson for their advice and suggestions; to John Jacob and Marjorie Smelstor, S. C., for substantive information and materials on little magazines; and to Russell Maylone, curator of special collections at Northwestern University Library, for his generous support. We would like to acknowledge our particular debt to Marvin Malone, poet, editor, and bibliophile, for making available to us not only his extensive private collection but also his considerable knowledge of little magazines. We would also like to thank the Illinois Arts Council, the Coordinating Council of Literary Magazines, the National Endowment for the Arts, and Charles Newman and the Huston Foundation for financial assistance without which publication of this volume would not have been possible.

E. A.
M. K.
July 4, 1978

OF LIVING BELFRY AND RAMPART: ON AMERICAN LITERARY MAGAZINES SINCE 1950

Michael Anania

Michael Anania contends that where many magazines of the fifties still exhibited strong ties to the modernists, especially Pound and Williams, such historical consciousness is largely absent from the magazines of the past two decades. As a result, a proper historical appreciation of them requires not only the scrutiny of the literary historian and the literary critic, but that of the social psychologist and perhaps the political scientist as well. Among the magazines founded since 1970, the field of true experimentation has been limited to fiction, while poetry has been excused from polemic to retreat into a licensed narcissism.

As president of the Coordinating Council of Literary Magazines from 1975 to 1976, Mr. Anania was in a good position to gauge the paradoxical politics of the little magazines, especially those of editors who styled themselves populists yet sought government money. In one of the few attempts that have been made to gain for literature the kind of massive support given by federal, state, and local governments to opera and theater companies, symphony orchestras, and ballets, Mr. Anania was instrumental in obtaining Ford Foundation money to finance distribution and promotion grants to little magazines of all kinds.

Michael Anania edited the little magazine Audit/Poetry *at SUNY-Buffalo from 1964 to 1967, and served as poetry editor and then literary editor of Swallow Press in Chicago from 1967 to 1974. He has also been an adviser to the New York State Council on the Arts and the Illinois Arts Council. His second volume of poetry,* Riversongs, *has just been published by the University of Illinois Press. Forthcoming is a book of nonfiction,* The Red Menace—*about, among other matters, growing up in the fifties, the Bomb, the ritual uses of peyote, and radical street politics.*

1

A number of years ago the editor of *Young Guard,* the principal literary magazine for Soviet writers under forty, visited my office in Chicago. He and several companions were touring the United States west to east—Hollywood, Disneyland, the Grand Canyon, a Kansas wheatfield, an Iowa cornfield, Chicago's Michigan Avenue, and, by sheer social accident, the Swallow Press: a dusty, chaotic loft, half a block from police headquarters, south of the Loop in the natural habitat of marginal commerce and the half-pint bottle. We drank coffee, exchanged cigarettes, and through a translator talked about literature and publishing. We toured the offices and the warehouse. It must have been a strange experience for the Soviet editor—that gaping old structure, with wooden beams exposed above pallets of unsold poetry books, the busy disarray of the offices, the blare of WVON Soul Radio from the packing table in the back room, classical FM in stereo from atop the file cabinets in the office space in front, the regular thud of falling objects in the Senior Citizens' Workshop one floor up. State Department tours do not, as a matter of course, feature sight-seeing at the raffish edges of capitalism. I couldn't tell whether he thought we were dilettantes or lunatics, but it was clear that our experience had very little in common with his. Back in my office, he browsed through the shelves of literary magazines on the wall beside my desk. "What are these things?" he asked, holding an early copy of *Toothpick, Lisbon and the Orcas Islands* until the translator finished the question in English.

"Literary magazines."

The answer made its way to him in Russian. He glanced at the shelves again, then at his companion, an agricultural economist in amber-tinted glasses, and asked that the answer be repeated. The shelves held three or four years' worth of fifty or so literary magazines. "How can there be so many?" I explained that what I had was barely a sample of the number of magazines being produced across the country. Again he questioned the translator about my answer. "And do they all have many readers?" I told him that some had very few readers. "How many?" He was doing arithmetic in his head, trying to figure the enormity of a literature that could sustain all this, I suppose. His magazine in Russia had a circulation of more than 200,000, with regional and ethnic supplements. It was the point of entry for most young writers into the writers' union, and so was essential to employment. It was also the key to publication by the magazine's book publishing affiliate.

"A few—just two or three—have circulations of about 10,000," I said. "Most are printed in runs of less than 2,000 copies, and many have fewer than a hundred readers." The translation reached him like a cool breeze, and he relaxed a bit. If this was to be the day on which the literature gap was discovered, at least he would be on the high side. He was still puzzled. What was the point of having so many magazines with so few readers? Wouldn't it be better to have just a few magazines that everyone interested in literature could read?

He pulled more magazines down from the shelf: an *Antioch Review*, thick as an anthropology textbook in paperback; *Kayak*, bantamweight in rough paper with untrimmed edges, on the cover an old engraving demonstrating the use of an antique prosthetic device; a yellowed *Floating Bear* in uncertain mimeograph; *Extensions*, deliberately international and tidy as a French suitcoat; a more ample *Chicago Review* with a busy post-psychedelic drawing of a tree on the cover; *Goliards* in high-gloss newsstand format and disjointed graphics, like a top hat decked out with fishing flies and campaign buttons; *Poetry*, as thin, sedate, and costly as a dowager empress. There was a last question—unasked, perhaps unformulated. He shuffled through the pile of magazines he had moved to my desk, confused and a little embarrassed. I tried hard to explain the kind of diversity the magazines represented and said something, oft-repeated during years of fund-raising, about their place in the history of modern literature. The translator worked away at this like a tireless journeyman with a bad set of blueprints and knotted lumber. The Russian listened, trying to arrange the magazines at hand into a pile that would not fall over. I wanted to convey something of the romance of little magazines, their individuality and the deep personal commitments that sustain them—something, that is, of my own attachment to them. My interrogator nodded at the translator's version of my flourish, but without conviction. He was acquiescing, not agreeing.

I consoled myself with the notion that in riffling through those magazines in a disheveled Chicago editorial office he had seen more of American literary publishing than most literary visitors, and I confess to a certain perverse pride in the irregularity of it all—the odd idiosyncrasies of magazines so intent on individuality that they refuse to share a format that will make a neat stack or an orderly shelf. But where I saw freedom (or, at least, license), he saw ineffectual diffusion, yet another Disneyland where the illusion of choice is the disguise of limitation and fidgeting activity replaces movement. His questions were clearly rooted in Soviet literary and political bureaucracy, but they are not easily dismissed. *Why are there so many magazines? Who reads them, anyway? Wouldn't it be better to have fewer magazines with larger resources and more readers?* I have heard the same questions asked by U.S. government officials, foundation executives, and little magazine editors.

> Go in for scribenery with a satiety of
> arthurs . . . malady of milady made
> melodi of malodi.
>
> —James Joyce

2

In the introduction to *The Little Magazines: A History and a Bibliography,* authors Hoffman, Allen, and Ulrich estimated that six hundred little magazines had been published in English between 1912 and 1946. Informed guesswork—not much else is possible— suggests that at least fifteen hundred such magazines are being published in the United States right now. The figure is approximate because so many magazines exist so briefly. The Coordinating Council of Literary Magazines, a nonprofit organization that distributes state, federal, and private funds to magazines nation-wide, has a current membership of over six hundred publications, and the organization requires that each member magazine must have published three issues and have existed for at least a year before applying for membership or financial support. *The Directory of Little Magazines and Small Presses* poses neither of these restrictions and offers a longer list, nearly a thousand; and it has to be assumed that magazines are published that do not find their way onto either list. A great number of magazines die before the appearance of a second issue. Three issues, the CCLM requirement, is a tough distance for most beginners. A modest first issue is likely to consume all the ready cash its editors can muster; with luck and a fair-sized circle of friends, donations and subscriptions can support a second number; but the third issue has no natural

9

resources. It is the one that naive editors suppose will be supported by sales, but it is a rule of literary magazine publishing that there are no sales, certainly none sufficient to sustain publication. Each year hundreds of magazines are born and die with one or two issues that never find their way onto lists or into copyright registry.

So the numbers are conjectural but extremely high—twice as many magazines in print at any moment in the mid-seventies as existed altogether in the first thirty-five years of little-magazine history. An explosion in little-magazine publication occurred in the late sixties and continues. It is supported in part by the availability of grants—from CCLM, state arts councils, and the National Endowment for the Arts—but depends, as well, on a growing population of writers and on access to various kinds of printing technology. Nearly 67 percent of the magazines in CCLM's most recent catalogue (May 1977) have come into existence since 1970; less than 9 percent existed before 1960; and only eight magazines from Hoffman, Allen, and Ulrich's extensive bibliography survive. The world of little magazines is characterized not only by growth but by incessant change. Magazines die, not only because they lack funds but because their editors, often quite deliberately, allow them to die—sometimes out of frustration or exhaustion and sometimes because they feel that the task of the magazine has been accomplished. This last is especially true for magazines with a closely defined literary point of view and a tightly knit group of writers.

Little magazines have always functioned primarily for writers. Readers are desirable, sometimes even actively sought out, but the impulse behind most magazines is the writer-editor's conviction that there are writers who are not being served by existing publications. At their best, little magazines draw together groups of writers and, however marginally, find them an audience. In contrast, commercial magazines find audiences and financial support and then, almost incidentally, find their writers. Because of their attention to writers the little magazines register, in their numbers and shifting variety, the literary activity in the country. The modern quarterly emerged from a period of intense interest in criticism in the late thirties and forties and seemed to dominate the literary scene well into the fifties. Yet we see the fifties in retrospect as an intense period of activity, particularly in poetry, supported by a number of remarkable small magazines—*Ark, Contact, Folder, Circle, Measure, Poetry New York, Big Table,* the *Black Mountain Review,* and others—that deliberately set themselves against the larger magazines' reliance on criticism. More important, they had an entirely new group of writers to publish, among them Creeley, Duncan, Ginsberg, Merton, Olson, Levertov, Merwin, O'Hara, and Snyder. None of these magazines survive; of the "Chief Periodicals" listed by Donald Allen in *The New American Poetry, 1945–1960,* only two magazines are still publishing: *Poetry* and *Chicago Review.* The interplay between eclectic quarterlies and highly individualistic smaller magazines continued into the sixties; but the sharp line between critically buttressed work in quarterlies (once called *academic*) and newer work faded quickly as the numbers increased and as writers of all kinds found their way into expanded versions of academe.

In the sixties and seventies, the audience for serious literature has not grown nearly as fast as the number of writers. Some have claimed that the actual number of readers has diminished. Nonetheless, writers' workshops proliferate in colleges and universities (the final redoubts of failing English departments), and poets and fiction writers in increasing numbers enter the world in search of publication. For the first time in history, we may have more writers than readers. Editorial offices of established magazines are drifted over with manuscripts, and new magazines are born to meet the writers' needs for print. Increasingly, magazines seem to reflect a sociological circumstance as much as an aesthetic one.

Aesthetically most new magazines declare themselves to be avant-garde. Very few are. The declaration is ritualistic, a part of the magazine's acknowledgment of its lineage among the magazines of the first part of the century. Many of the recent magazines are really involved in the eccentric use of literary precedents—a useful procedure, but one that is more cautious and traditional than most editors would like to admit. Typically, a magazine will be generated out of a sense of common interest—even of immediate community—among writers. The editors write to one or two prominent figures they admire, asking for contributions. Sometimes, in less coherent groups, all that is being sought is a little authority with which to launch the project, that and some validation of the less notable writers the magazine will include. In more carefully

11

organized groups, the figureheads define the magazine's aesthetic precedent. Thus the magazine's orbit is in perigee around its most notable contributor. Usually the writers chosen for these roles are not broadly accepted national figures—never a Lowell or a Berryman, Roth or Cheever—but are the distinguished vestiges of previous new waves. Modern American literature has seen a succession of avant-gardes; very few have captured an enduring authority. For all the ballyhoo, the center of American letters has remained fairly conservative since the 1930s.

An example of a magazine that started in this way is *Milk Quarterly,* a Chicago publication that emerged from a group of writers which met regularly. The magazine began as a forum for writing done by members of the group, but declared at the outset an allegiance to the New York School with regular appearances by Ted Berrigan. Berrigan gave precedent to much of what appeared in the magazine, though very little of what was published was directly generated from Berrigan's work. This kind of situation can be seen in magazines with precedent-figures as different as Thomas McGrath, Thomas Lux, Charles Bukowski, Harold Norse, and Ed Dorn. In the almost totally decentralized literature of the late sixties and early seventies, these associations are measures of what was once called influence. Magazines of this sort can be seen as developmental. What's going on is an experiment with the possibilities of a fairly well-articulated aesthetic; the play is outward from, then back to, a source, like a game of hide-and-seek—furtive, sometimes daring, but always in sight of home base. When the exploration of possibilities is especially thorough or eccentric, the magazine can be very exciting.

In their attachment to the very recent past (the day before yesterday, in some cases), many magazines reflect a general trend in the society; in America, after all, nostalgia has replaced history. The association of literary movements with precedents is obviously not new. The magazines that presented the "new poetry" of the 1950s all exhibited strong ties to the modernists, to Pound and Williams most firmly; they looked to a tradition of experimentation in the twenties and before, and beyond that to Whitman. What is peculiar to the contemporary use of literary precedent is that it is willing to take its masters from so close at hand. With few

12

exceptions, history, at least literary history, is largely absent from newer magazines. In addition to their role as adversaries to popular literary trends, the magazines of the early part of the century exhibited a number of broad historical and critical concerns. In *The Little Review, Dial,* and *Hound and Horn* there appeared regularly essays by modern writers that treated historical figures— reclamation, even conscription for the movement of Dante, Homer, Blake, Shelley, the Elizabethans, the Metaphysicals, the French. Ezra Pound's brief essay, "The Tradition," first appeared in *Poetry* (III, 3, December 1913); essential essays by Eliot and Joyce first appeared in *The Little Review* and *The Dial,* along with essays by Santayana and Bertrand Russell. If the modern movement was intent on reinventing the past to suit its own purposes, contemporary writing seems preoccupied with knitting up the tattered edges of the present. Few contemporary magazines take a critical stand; essays, even book reviews and correspondence, are less and less common, especially in newer magazines. Perhaps the weight of criticism that filled the quarterlies is still being counteracted, or it may be that the excesses of academic, scholarly criticism are now too apparent. There are exceptions. *Io,* which is involved primarily in myth and cosmology, is full of prose discourse by poets, but by design none of it is what would traditionally be called critical. At the other end of the scale is *Parnassus,* a magazine composed entirely of critical reviews of books of poetry. Some quarterlies still attempt a traditional balance of fiction, poetry, and criticism, but few of these have much critical authority among writers. *Partisan Review* sustains itself but with far less of the political and cultural focus it once had. *American Poetry Review* includes a great deal of commentary through a number of regular columns, and *Salmagundi* and *Massachusetts Review* are noteworthy for the consistently high quality of their critical essays. There are also some notable smaller magazines that have reserved space for closely focused commentary. *Kayak,* an exemplary smaller magazine in a number of ways, still includes letters and comments that have a clear relationship to the concerns of the magazine. Robert Bly's magazines (*The Fifties, The Sixties,* and *The Seventies*) have been models for idiosyncratic editing and highly personal critical commentary. Somewhere between the larger magazines with balanced content and these smaller, more personal publications is *Field*, a magazine with particular interests in translation and in surrealism, which has engaged a number of important writers in important theoretical discussion.

There are broad literary differences among the magazines of the last three decades: university-based reviews with eclectic interests; quarterlies with distinct critical frameworks; independent eclectic magazines that have invariably served the centrist literature nobly and well (*Poetry Northwest* and *Beloit Poetry Journal* are just two examples of this type of magazine); and adversary magazines, those quicksilver enterprises that hold much of the romance of the little magazines in their invariable insistence that everybody in print is wrong about nearly everything literary and cultural except the few people published in their thirty-two saddle-stitched, untrimmed pages. Distinctions among very recent magazines—the 69 percent founded since 1970—are less easily drawn. Obviously, the field is too big and too crowded. Differences are also confused by quarrels about size and funding. In the clamor for grants and the squabbling that has ensued, literary matters have been entangled with financial statements. "Hard-pressed" has been taken to include experimental; "independently owned" in some circles is synonymous with avant-garde. Except for the activities of a few publications involved with conceptual art, like *Vile* or *Northwest Mounted Valise*, most experimentation in magazines seems internecine or elaborately involved with the play of precedents discussed earlier. Concretism came into American magazines late and was introduced here by a university magazine (*Chicago Review*). As far as I know, there was never a magazine in this country comparable to Ian Hamilton Finlay's *Poor. Old. Tired. Horse.* or a publishing program like Agenzia in France. The most intense literary experimentation in the last decade has been in fiction, and the economics of magazine publication kept most of the little magazines out of the center of these activities. There was also an area of conflict between the new fiction and small pressmanship. In addition to demanding increased expenditures for typesetting and paper, the new fiction's antirealism became the focus for charges of social elitism that poetry—its mantle of sentimental individualism and licensed narcissism still intact—was spared. Fiction, it seems, invokes a politics from which (sadly) poetry has been excused.

14

When I was a director of CCLM, I was accused in public of being antirealist, and therefore elitist, by a small-magazine editor who in the previous breath had proclaimed himself a member of the avant-garde and one of the few true heirs of the modern magazine tradition. If the new fiction wanted magazines, it would have to make its own.

In the 1960s little-magazine publishing, like much of the rest of the culture, was suffused in politics. Poets who would never have spoken to one another on literary grounds were allied in reading against the war in Vietnam, and there was a companion solidarity among magazines. As in the general culture also, there remains in the magazine world a residual leftism, focused occasionally on conservation or on a particular struggle, which surfaces in literary discussion here and there. Institutions are still distrusted. A populism never required of poetry is frequently demanded of fiction, and experimental fiction is seen as dangerously self-involved. The editor's inherent interest in production and distribution veers dangerously close to capitalism. With all the cosmological froufrou of the Whole Earth Movement, do-it-yourself printing and binding is often raised from its place as economic necessity to a level of singular and unassailable virtue. As I suggested before, the magazine boom requires sociology as much as it does criticism or literary history. There are basic contradictions between the obvious goals of most magazines and the political sentiments that seem native to meetings of little-magazine editors, and are part of the relationship of literature to the society as a whole. Magazine editors, as much as any group, are concerned about the dangers of growth. There is a sense among them that whatever it is that makes literature most valuable and vital cannot survive corporate climates and the manipulations of large amounts of money and resources. The problems are quite real, but the emotional recoil from them frequently results in limits set so close at hand that they make any development impossible. I have attended meetings at which any editor who talked about professionalized production or energetic distribution was hooted down as a sellout.

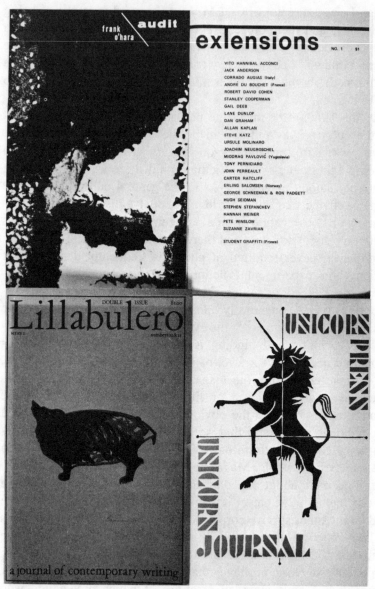

audit, *Vol. 4, No. 1, 1964, edited by Michael Anania and Charles Doria;*
extensions, *Vol. 1, No. 1, 1968, edited by Suzanne Zavrian and Joachim
Neugroschel;* Lillabulero, *double issues Nos. 10/11, 1971, edited by Russell
Banks and William Matthews;* Unicorn Journal, *Vol. 1, No. 1, 1968, edited
by Teo Savory (courtesy Michael Anania).*

Transatlantic Review, *No. 58/59, 1977, edited by J.F. McCrindle;* Antaeus, *No. 27, Autumn 1977, edited by Daniel Halpern;* The Hudson Review, *Vol. 31, No. 1, Spring 1978, edited by Paula Deitz and Frederick Morgan;* Chicago Review, *Vol. 22, No. 1, Autumn 1970, edited by Harry Foster (courtesy Michael Anania).*

*Where there are angels, there are
wrangles, where there are editors,
there are creditors . . . it is as
simple as that.*
—Cyril Connolly (1964)

3

Literary magazines are all failing business propositions. That any
survive at all is a tribute to editors skilled at everything from
typesetting to down-home flimflam. Traditionally, magazines were
supposed to be supported by angels, creatures as implausible in
contemporary literature as they are in modern theology. There
are some magazines that still have benefactors left over from the
fall of the patronage class. Some rely on university support—a
financial base that has grown less dependable as universities themselves have lost much of their financial stability. It was once
assumed that a university-based editor was on easy street; now
he has to be seen as someone deftly juggling a small morsel above
a tank of piranha. The majority of contemporary magazines are
supported almost entirely by their editors—in cash and labor.
Even with the infusion of editorial labor, most magazines have
fairly high unit costs; magazines with cover prices of a dollar to a
dollar and a half frequently cost two or three dollars to produce
and distribute. Some larger magazines can manage better cost
figures because of larger print runs, but distribution barriers seem
to exist that keep them from taking advantage of favorable numbers. Simply put, all magazines need money, and money for literature is hard to get. Foundation support for literature nationally is
less than 1 percent of all grants made, and the National Endowment
manages less than 2 percent. Literature is altogether too private,
both in its production and consumption, to gather the support given
to operas, orchestras, theater companies, and ballets. There are no
opera house overheads, no unions, no guarantees, no advance ticket
sales, and, finally, no grand openings to ooze social prominence
and drip jewelry.

Since 1967 the Coordinating Council of Literary Magazines
has served as a grant-giving agency for literary magazines, distributing funds from the Endowment and a few private sources.
Because the organization deals in funding magazines and has a
large membership, it is a good context in which to test the
possibility of cooperation suggested by my friend the Russian

18

editor. If the total consolidation of production, distribution, and editorial judgment he had in mind are both impractical and undesirable in our situation, some sense of common purpose once seemed possible through CCLM. The grants program brought the magazines together, however churlishly. The initial notion was to fund quality magazines according to their needs. The idea never sat well with the small-magazine editors, who argued that because of large costs of big magazines, they would get all the money. Figures sailed back and forth between CCLM and COSMEP, a coalition of small magazine and small-press editors, with attendant accusations. Grants committees were elected from among the editors and writers involved with the magazines, but since the amount of money available in grants was never large enough, no one was ever really satisfied. No big magazine could ever hope to get a grant that would make a useful dent in its deficit; the smaller magazines were never persuaded that deficits were anything more than the numerical record of the capitalistic vices of larger magazines.

The fracture between large and small, in many ways unjustifiable on hard evidence, was fairly permanent. Also, the Endowment seemed eager to be swayed by the quarreling that went on, largely because the CCLM grant represented a large portion of Literature Panel funds that had gone out of the Panel's control. The arena for charges, accusations, and threats simply expanded. Eventually the Endowment established two grants programs for magazines independent of the CCLM program.

The future of CCLM in the midst of such fractured funding is uncertain. Certainly the sort of magazine unity I had once thought possible has been foreclosed. The grants procedure has always posed a threat to the independence of the magazines, though it was hopelessly exaggerated by all the quarreling. If judgments were made on the basis of quality, then marginally, at least, the organization was monitoring the editorial content of the magazines. It was presumed that the elected grants committees would disarm this concern. They did not. The degree of distrust was so high that everyone involved was suspect. The final stage in the grants committee system was reached in 1977, when an elected committee decided that it would not make qualitative judgments of any kind. The funds were simply divided equally among all the applicants,

19

giving each a grant of about $900. In this gesture some of the grantees received more than a year's total budget; others were stuck with far less than a meaningful sum of money. The organization, which had spent years building assurances of noninterference into the rules governing committee procedures, was forced to sit by and watch its basic assumptions about magazine funding fall victim to a single committee. Unity had come to mean equity, and equity finally became equivalency.

Quite apart from issues of literary quality, but in keeping with the populist attitudes within the organization, CCLM has undergone another set of strains on its potential unity. Along with the society as a whole, the organization has been forced into an awareness of minority needs. A program was established to bring minority magazines into the grants procedure early by waiving the three-issue rule. Affirmative action resolutions were passed. The scenario is a familiar one, but CCLM, more than most institutions, is ill suited to the situation. Its history has been completely involved with independent, highly individualistic operations, the literary equivalent of Jefferson's American frontiersman, nervous when anyone else has settled within ten miles. For political and social reasons, minority magazines tended to be the work of coalitions. A very nearly atomized pluralism that had just been served by replacing judgment with long division was being asked to deal with a series of collectivist groups. Although the goals of ethnic literary magazines were acceptable, the nature of their demands was dangerously close in dollars to the amounts requested by larger magazines, but in this instance accusing the magazines of rampant capitalism seemed implausible.

Because CCLM had been involved primarily with editors and their magazines, their needs came to overshadow the concern with writers and their work. Magazines can easily become their editors' primary form of self-realization—peculiar monads of intense self-reflexivity. The tendency is probably endemic and not altogether bad, for it carries some of the essential brave lunacy that keeps editors and magazines going. Still, it is hardly conducive to organizational strength. When self-realization is a primary goal, then one self-realization is as good as any other; the more liberal sanctity a demand has, the less likely it is to be treated in any sort

20

of measured way. The alternatives are simply capitulation or self-serving retreat.

Like the welfare system, CCLM has identified a community it has neither the resources nor the will to serve. It has made enough effective grants at lower levels to insure the marginal survival of much of its burgeoning population, but in the process has generated a new range of expectations that it cannot fulfill. All this could be an incentive to positive action if some sense of common purpose could be agreed upon. A Disneyland without Disney's resources, my Russian friend might argue—a system of illusions at the point of collapse, praising its own tatters as signs of virtue.

> *Nothing much then in the way of sights for sore eyes. But who can be sure who has not been there, has not lived there, they call that living, for them the spark is present, ready to burst into flame, all it needs is preaching on, to become a living torch, screams included.*
> —Samuel Beckett

4

The questions posed by my Russian friend—*Why are there so many magazines? Who reads them? Why aren't there fewer magazines with more readers?*—are troublesome because they sit so readily among the anxieties I have had about them as a writer, editor, and . . . what's a good term for a CCLM director? . . . strategist (perhaps). They also play evil tricks with the deformations of my own nostalgias. I have a fondness for the magazines of the first half of the century. I keep them around—not a collection, nothing so orderly as that, just a scattering of things: a few *Poetry*s from 1913, a *Horizon* from 1944, some early *Partisan Review*s, some few *Botteghe Oscure*s, a *Dial* from 1929. What I do have in sequence begins in the 1950s when I started subscribing. The earlier things are talismans, magical remnants of a world made orderly, even heroic, in retrospect. The great magazines of that era seem so singular that, taken one by one, they suggest an overall clarity of literary purpose that could never have existed.

Of course, the Russian did not understand the import of that stack of magazines he could not keep upright. How could he? Their significance so easily eludes *us*. The answers to his questions are

21

altogether too simple to give us much comfort. *Why are there so many?* Because that's how it is for a literature committed to change. Literary magazines today fill the same functions they filled at the beginning of the century. They give a place to writing for which no other place has been made. Criticism is slow and cautious; popular taste, as important as it is in other contexts, has nothing to do with the development of writing; commerce is too cautiously trying to pace a slow criticism to quixotic popularities. The world of literary magazines is raffish and irregular because nothing else will do in a setting in which the best hope of every serious writer is to undermine every notion of what makes a piece of writing good and durable.

Of course there are too many magazines. The genius that magazines have shown for graceful dying has not been entirely lost, and it should be cultivated. Yet the magazine explosion, finally, is not the fault of editors or national endowments but of writers. More and more we have drawn the magazines to our various isolations, instead of moving on, as we should, into riskier associations. If the magazine community is past fragmentation and nearer atomization, so are its writers. The magazines have always moved with writers. In our fear of any authority we have accepted a certain protective diffusion, and the magazines have responded by replicating and amplifying that diffusion in ways which make authority nearly impossible. In a symbiosis refined to neural complementarity, they serve our fears as well as our more cogent desires.

Who reads magazines, anyway? Again the answer is too simple. Editors and writers, mostly, and a few stray fans. Some of the larger magazines have enormous impact. Most small magazines are communications among contributors. In a CCLM survey of magazine subscribers, we found the readers are largely writers, then teachers, followed by librarians and students. Most are highly educated and underpaid, not the sort of community that would make for a good advertising sales campaign. Perhaps magazines that have very small readerships are occasionally read by editors of magazines with larger readerships; it's hard to know. In some instances, magazines serve largely as the medium through which writers give their work its public gesture—that crucial, if phantom, reader out there who is often important chiefly as a hypothesis.

The Russian's last question is the one I have spent the most time

22

puzzling over, here and elsewhere. I became involved with CCLM in the conviction that some unity among magazines could be fashioned which could be a service to them without getting in their way. Obviously, we cannot have a *Young Guard* taking the place of our fifteen hundred magazines. Throughout the century, American literature has taken its vitality from its own extreme edges, since its center is too often lifeless and boring. This last is not only a corollary of the tradition of the new; it has to do, as well, with the desperation with which status is held onto in a society that claims not to value status. Without the graduated steps of a writers' union and an official publishing bureaucracy, we cling to our little tracts of notoriety with all the tenacity and imagination of suburbanites. American letters can survive only by confronting change, and the magazines serve as both belfry and rampart in this essential confrontation.

THE CULTURE IN WHICH
MUST MAKE ITS WAY IS
AS WE ARE SO OFTEN RE
TO IMAGINE WHAT POSSI
A JOURNAL'S ATTEMPTING
VARIETY OF MODELS, IMAG
FOR ATTENTION AGA
OF LIMITLESS

THE LITTLE MAGAZINE
A NOVELTY CULTURE,
MINDED, AND IT IS HARD
BLE GOOD CAN COME OF
TO ENCOMPASS THE SHEER
ES, ARTIFACTS COMPETING
NST A BACKGROUND
POSSIBILITY.

—ROBERT BOYERS

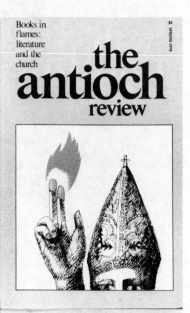

New Fiction by Ralph Ellison, Hilary Masters, James McPherson ● Interviews with Toni Morrison and Ralph Ellison ● R. Yarde, *paintings*; L. Sykes, *photos*; Poems and Essays by Michael Harper, Robt. Stepto, R. F. Thompson, Sherley Williams, Robert Hayden, Frederick Turner, Richard Frost, Mary Berry, John Blassingame, and George Rogers Taylor

Books in flames: literature and the church

DENIS DONOGHUE: "Trilling, Mind, and Society"

Fiction by WILLIAM HOFFMAN AND SUSAN THALER

Poetry by WILLIAM VIRGIL DAVIS, JOHN R. REED, LARRY RUBIN, BARRY SPACKS, AND OTHERS

LITERATURE, SCIENCE, AND TECHNOLOGY
ROBERT BEUM: "Literature and *Machinisme*"
DAVID J. GORDON: "The Dilemma of Literature in an Age of Science"

Reviews by J. A. BRYANT, JR., MALCOLM GOLDSTEIN, PAUL RAMSEY, H. L. WEATHERBY, AND ULRICH WEISSTEIN

GERALD WEALES: The State of Letters

WALTER SULLIVAN: Fiction Chronicle

CALVIN BEDIENT: Poetry Chronicle

Spring 1978

VOLUME LXXXVI, NUMBER 2   Each Copy $2.50

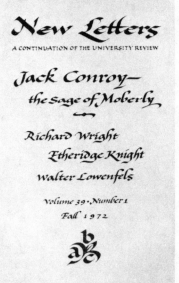

New Letters

A CONTINUATION OF THE UNIVERSITY REVIEW

Jack Conroy—
the Sage of Moberly

Richard Wright
Etheridge Knight
Walter Lowenfels

Volume 39 · Number 1
Fall 1972

The Massachusetts Review (*Amherst, Hampshire, Mount Holyoke, and Smith Colleges, and the University of Massachusetts*), *Vol. 18, No. 3, Autumn 1977, edited by Lee Edwards, John Hicks, Mary Heath, Robert Tucker;* The Antioch Review (*Antioch College*), *Vol. 36, No. 2, Spring 1978, edited by Robert S. Fogarty;* The Sewanee Review (*University of the South*), *Vol. 86, No. 2, Spring 1978, edited by George Core;* New Letters (*University of Missouri, Kansas City*), *Vol. 39, No. 1, October 1972, edited by David Ray (from* TriQuarterly).

ACADEMIA AND THE LITTLE MAGAZINE
Charles Robinson

According to the late Charles Robinson, little magazines no longer offer the unified resistance to the forces of popular taste that they once did. He contended that university-based magazines have adopted a peculiar academicism as sterile as the policy of popular magazines turning out formula pieces and have thus divided the field. Mr. Robinson saw the proliferation of little magazines in the 1960s as responsible for the division of loyalties, and maintained that independent and university magazines alike publish far too much material. As a result, the material is often imitative and mediocre at best. He concluded that unless little magazines impose their own restraints they will lose much of their vitality.

Mr. Robinson was born in 1939 in Scranton, Kansas. He grew up in Waseca, Minnesota, and was graduated from Waseca High School. He attended the University of Minnesota and Mankato State College, Mankato, Minnesota, where he received his B.A. degree in 1965. He received an M.A., with a thesis on poetry, from Colorado State University in June 1967. He was killed in an automobile accident on August 16, 1967.

Little magazines, which have always pursued a kamikaze course, are now confronted by a new peril: the encroachment of universities which, for reasons of prestige, have started publishing their own little magazines with unimaginative gusto. The perennial suicidal tactics of operating on shaky finances while heralding the avant-garde writers are still part of the pose struck by little magazines; but the creeping influence of university reviews and quarterlies is usurping their unique position. Unlike the independent littles, university-based magazines have secure financing that ensures them a longevity which the independents have never had, seldom have desired, and often have scoffed at. In addition, they can afford posh formats the independents seldom approach.

Originally published in *Trace*, ed. James Boyer May, no. 64 (1967).

The psychological value of a tidy periodical of ninety-six or more pages, replete with drawings, engravings—often vari-colored printing—is devastating. The majority of independent magazines are hand-set or mimeographed (often from incomplete or mixed fonts) and shoddy by comparison. They may be more ingenious and experimental with layouts; but, on the bookshop magazine shelf, the university magazine is immediately more appealing. Prospective readers are drawn to the university magazine's attractive cover just as prospective auto buyers are drawn to the sleek-line car with a plush interior. In both cases external appearance is a more decisive influence than relative horsepower or performance.

But the predecessors of the university magazines, the little magazines that got their start from 1912 to 1925, demonstrated their capabilities, careening into the calm highways paved by Howell's middle-classism and insipid realism with a candor and brazen self-assuredness which most Americans weren't ready for and couldn't accept. The new generation of writers—from Frost, Pound, and Eliot to Anderson, Joyce, Hemingway, and Faulkner—found sympathetic editors, not at the publishing houses, but in the little magazines: *Poetry, The Little Review, transition,* and the *Double-Dealer.* America's roving literary impresario, Ezra Pound, forwarded manuscript after manuscript to *Poetry* editor Harriet Monroe, *Little Review* editor Margaret Anderson, and others.

The thirties brought several changes: many of the magazine editors had served their literary cause and, like Margaret Anderson, decided to stop publishing, while many were forced to stop publishing by lack of funds. Though other little magazines were beginning to fill the void, most of them switched emphasis from literature to politics, filling their pages with left-wing treatises—the intellectual's answer to the depression. And the universities began to publish little magazines—*Prairie Schooner* at the University of Nebraska, *Kenyon Review* in Ohio, *Southwest Review* at Southern Methodist University—many of them to provide markets for inland writers who were finding it difficult, if not impossible, to publish in the East, the center for both magazine and book publishing.

After a temporary lapse during War II, the late forties saw a revival of interest in little magazines which has continued through the fifties and into the sixties, particularly at the universities. Almost every major university has now placed an entry in the little-magazine field, but the results have not been altogther favorable.

The reasons for starting a literary magazine at a university are not in accord with the idealism that prompted the independent magazines to crusade for the new writers with the unorthodox forms, confusing syntax, and obscure symbols. For the most part the universities is interested in establishing its own reputation and image via the literary magazine much as Kenyon College has with the influential *Kenyon Review*. Although there are editors, like John Crowe Ransom, who are involved with and concerned about literature and might use a magazine as a vehicle to carry out their own particular concerns and involvements, they are handicapped because the magazine is also a vehicle for the school. Most editors recognize this dilemma, even though they do not feel it as a handicap. The editors of one university review, for example, have said: "We are grateful for the support given the magazine by the University. . . . In return we hope to add to the‘prestige of the University by publishing a good magazine. There are no disadvantages that we can now discern." The editor of *Trace,* James Boyer May, has noted: "No matter what may be *said* [about university attempts] . . . to alter policies and/or bring influence to bear with . . . contributors—I believe personal independence of the editor is vital. If a conscientious person, he [the university editor] will be bound to modify more or less his decisions—even though no *actual* pressures may be brought to bear. . . ."

Intervention and/or censorship by university administrators has been more direct, however. Last year the University of Oregon withdrew its support from the *Northwest Review* (later restored). Karl Shapiro, who has edited two of America's most distinguished little magazines, *Poetry* and *Prairie Schooner,* elaborated upon university administrative meddling with both, during a Library of Congress symposium on Literary Publishing in America, held last spring. He had this to say about his dismissal from *Prairie Schooner:*

I edited the Prairie Schooner, *said to be the oldest campus literary magazine in the country, also for about six years, and was forced to resign (or was fired) over a question of censorship. Evidently a chemist who had become a Dean was informed by a telephone operator at the university press, who read proof in her spare time, that I was printing irreligious and obscene literature. I took to the radio and read it to the citizens of Lincoln, Nebraska. No one objected to the story.**

Shapiro's conclusion was:

In every campus literary venture there is a chain of command that runs from the magazine itself, through the English and other Humanities Departments, through the university press, the administration, and on to public opinion. In extreme cases, . . . the controls can go as high as the governors of states and involve the expression of historical fact itself.

This control, whether subtly oblique, as May suggested, or overt, has resulted in university magazines which are conservative, even staid. And, quoting Shapiro again: ". . . magazines that may develop a stylistic expertise that is amazing, but that is all they can do." Thus, university-based little magazines tend to establish coteries of writers who reappear with boring frequency. Only token, if any, attempts are made to "discover" new writers; and often when new ones are published, there is a surprising similarity between their stories and poems and those of the established coterie. All of which suggests that it is virtually impossible for the university magazines to cause any upheaval in current literary practice or tradition—one of the most important functions of the genre.

Some of the independents of course are still crusading for the new writers and schools and publishing avant-garde and experimental stories and poetry. R. R. Cuscaden, editor of *Midwest,* has pointed out that "none of them last very long and perhaps their real function is not to outlast *Poetry* but to provide, however temporarily, the loyal opposition." And: "Thank God for the mimeograph machine, anyhow. There is a kind of rise and fall in editorial direction and purpose in little mags that is no doubt inescapable. *Midwest* is probably now at its apex; I hope to maintain the present plateau, but the laws governing all this are immutable. . . ." And here is the real problem and issue: are the independents furnishing the opposition, and, if

*See the interview with Karl Shapiro, p. 197. (Editor)

30

they are, will they be able to withstand the surge of the university magazines and offer them continued opposition?

Because of their financing, universities have the advantage not only of offering a better-looking product but of being able to peddle their product more effectively. For instance, libraries, which are a valuable source of income for any little magazine, are more likely to subscribe to the university magazines, since they will continue publishing (the independents probably will not) and they will be publishing reputable writers (the independents may not be—at least, not from the contemporary perspective); yet it is the independent magazine which is in dire need of the libraries' financial support. Too, universities often provide their magazines with enough money to conduct subscription drives; if they do not, the magazines can continue at a loss (such periodicals, independent and university alike, rarely operate in the black) and build subscriber lists. Though they would like to conduct subscription drives, the independents do not have the necessary finances or, in most cases, enough money to let them continue appearing until their subscription lists can be built up. In addition, the university magazines can pay for secretarial and editorial help, pay contributors, purchase advertising, and in other ways function much like commercial magazines—if on a smaller scale. All these advantages—the combination of good packaging, marketing, and respectability— will eventually result in the university magazines' accumulating the bulk of the little magazine readers. Or—considering the other face of the process—independent little magazines will not be able to perpetuate themselves because they are no longer reacting solely against the mass-circulation magazines (as they were twenty or thirty years ago), but also against members of their own family, the university little magazines.

Thus, the whole battle has changed. Where once there was a unified force of little magazines and supporters fighting for recognition against popular tastes, today the forces have split. The independents feel that not only have the popular magazines sold out, but that the university magazines have followed suit—that, although the latter may not appeal to popular tastes, they have adopted a peculiar academicism as sterile as the policy of popular magazines turning out formula pieces. The university magazines, of course, deny the charge. And while this ordinarily might be a healthy literary fight, the overwhelming advantages commanded by the latter will eventually destroy the "loyal opposition."

For the most part, university magazines are unconcerned with this situation. Involved with assembling their select coteries and enhancing their magazines' literary prestige—and, tangentially, that of their benefactors—the overall state of literary publishing is of little or no concern to them. Being academically oriented, many of them deemphasize creative literature, with scholarly criticism, reviews, and articles taking up two-thirds or more of their pages. This is not altogether surprising. The insistence upon teacher-publishing necessitates more and more outlets—and, since a university is footing the bill for a magazine, it is not unreasonable to expect the magazine to be an outlet for academicians. What is surprising is that such a magazine should also attempt to be a literary showpiece. Not that the two aims are incompatible, but that this schizoid ambivalence seems to have resulted in the mediocrity of these journals.

If the university magazines would abandon their ambivalent role and concentrate on criticism and reviews, their relative value and position would be considerably enhanced. Criticism, for instance, has been the forte of the *Kenyon Review;* and it is with the criticism—not the stories and poems—that *Kenyon Review* has established its reputation.

And if little magazines are to remain a vital literary force, they will have to reassess their positions and attitudes. In the past, they largely refrained from attempting to play a dual role. When criticism was part of their content it was relevant to the original work being published. Margaret Anderson and the readers of *The Little Review* carried on a steady dialogue about the arts, a dialogue that was both stimulating and pertinent to many of the works being published therein, such as Joyce's *Ulysses.* Now there is a trend toward the type of criticism found in the university magazines—of late, concerned with such recently current authors as Hemingway and Faulkner.

This, of course, isn't the entire story. There are other reasons why the present bumper crop of little magazines generally lacks the vitality of its illustrious predecessors. If, for instance, university magazines are guilty of functioning primarily as public relations

32

enterprises for their benefactors, then far too many independents, under the guise of grandiose proclamations, are founded and maintained solely to satisfy the egos of their editors and the editors' friends. The result of such an objective is as staid a type of magazine, printing as repetitiously boring and uniform kinds of material and names as any academic university-oriented magazine with its coterie. Far too often an independent magazine is begun because a group of friends want an outlet of their own; and it remains just that, not attempting to expand either its contributions or its quality.

And as Robert Bly and others pointed out in "something like a symposium" (*Carleton Miscellany*, Spring 1966), most little magazines, university and independent alike, are publishing far too much material; and, consequently, the material is imitative and mediocre at best. Perhaps the present proliferation of little magazines does not permit selectivity; faced with filling X number of pages four times a year, an editor has to take what is available. If true, this in itself is antithetical to the expressed aims of most editors: ". . . to print the best poetry being written today, . . ." etc. And in the final analysis, indiscriminate editing results in self-annihilation—usually an early death for an independent magazine and nothing more than an innocuous, inane life for a university magazine.

Unless, then, little magazines begin to be more discriminatory and impose restraints upon themselves, their vitality and ultimate worth will be negligible. The independents will have to expand their coverage and actually attempt to print the best—not just the best that the editor's friends are writing. And only if the university magazines recognize their relative strengths and weaknesses—which are so intimately connected with their academic umbilical cords—can they be an effective force. Were they to limit themselves to criticism and reviews, their academic forte, they would then avoid the control problem. Regardless of where the support is coming from, little magazines will have to become more selective and begin to publish what is deserving and exciting rather than what simply fulfills a coterie—academic or otherwise—requirement. When these things happen, little magazines can once again join forces to bring *Kultur* to America.

magazine is. But definitions are difficult. It is easier to recognize a little mag when you see it than to describe it. A man who should have known better, a librarian, once asked me, "What do you mean by little magazines? Little vertically or little horizontally?" Of course I was appalled and indicated that it was a matter of small circulation. And smallness is not only a matter of necessity but also a matter of choice. Now, when you are limiting yourself by choice you tend toward what I call the "elitism" of little magazines. But that's another subject and maybe another question.

Are little magazines an art form in themselves, purveyors or conveyors of art, or both?

I would say both. Little magazines are certainly here to convey art, but they are shaping it too. Every little-magazine editor who is worth his salt knows that he's creating a work of art and, in the aggregate, creating a new genre. Every title, if it runs for any length of time, takes on some character and voice of its own and becomes a work of art as well.

It seems that a great number of taboos so many of the little magazines were trying to break down have now become the mulch of the commercial garden. Does a little magazine still characteristically have an iconoclastic function?

When you consider European magazines, and particularly some of the German magazines like *Der Querschnitt* and even *Der Sturm,* and when you think of some of the little French magazines that started in the nineteenth century and incidentally were called *revue avant-garde* and not *petite revue,* you are talking about general-interest magazines that simultaneously show a lot of the spirit that characterizes little magazines. These magazines suggest there was no need for little magazines in the American sense because these bigger magazines themselves were open to new ideas, experiments, new modes of saying things—and also open to new writers who didn't have to be already proven before they could find entrance. So actually the American little magazine comes out of a special need to say things that our big commercial magazines will not accept.

It is perhaps correct to say that, since our taboos have broken down—sexual taboos, for instance, have been practically eliminated even in the bigger magazines—the little magazine thereby loses its original iconoclastic function. But there are many other features that make little magazines necessary and viable. First, the bigger magazines and the commercial magazines are not accessible to new writers per se. They like names that have already been established, whereas little magazines are usually wide open to newcomers. Second, advertisers still control our big commercial magazines, and that is where the real censorship comes in. In America we don't have state censorship or governmental censorship as in Russia, in Nazi Germany, and in many of the authoritarian states. The state itself doesn't censor news. Of course, we might not get the whole news, or we might get slanted news, but content isn't really censored from above. It is the advertisers who are the real censors in our magazines, and if anything in a story or poem or essay displeases a major advertiser because of its language, because of the views expressed, because it is pro-abortion or anti-abortion, or what have you, he will simply tell the editor, "Listen, cut that stuff out or else I'll withdraw my ads." And naturally the ads are what make those big magazines flourish. Without advertising, they would probably go under, because newsstand sales and subscriptions alone cannot take care of those big, expensive publications. So, many publishers and editors are subject to the advertisers' whims and will give in to them. This the little magazine will never do. In the first place, it carries no advertising or only a minimal amount.

Furthermore, little magazine editors typically resist any indebtedness to patrons, even patrons who don't want to dictate taste. They are always afraid that if they are paid by somebody, they will be beholden. Most editors don't even want school sponsorship, because once a board of regents, a college president, or a department head puts his hand into the pie, he's likely to make demands or set restrictions. There have been such cases of censorship.

Could you mention any?

Oh, for example, there is the celebrated case in which Paul Carroll and his whole editorial staff resigned from the *Chicago Review* in 1958 because the University of Chicago objected to their printing of a chapter from William Burroughs' *Naked Lunch*. Carroll thereupon printed the chapter in his new magazine, *Big Table*,

37

which was launched through a benefit reading by Allen Ginsberg, Gregory Corso, Peter Orlovski, and William Burroughs. Earlier than that was the split-up of *The Beloit Poetry Journal* and Beloit College because of a falling out between the editors and the college administration over an "underground issue" of West Coast poets. This took place around 1957, I'd say, after eight years of the magazine's publication by the college. Thereafter the editors financed the magazine out of their own pockets and have been doing so ever since. Other college cases pertained to the secession of *Coyote's Journal* from *Northwest Review,* also because of "filthy and way-out" material. That must have been in the late sixties. And there were other cases in which the censorship was not exerted by a college but actually through the police. I'm thinking of the magazine of the fifties, *The Miscellaneous Man,* and the alleged obscenity of a gay short story. Those are examples of the little magazines' obstinate and rambunctious independence and their determination to brook no interference from whomever. And this distinguishes them very essentially from all other types of publication.

There is even a sense in which little magazines resist the imposition of standards. Editors may take the risk of printing work that isn't so hot but shows a certain new trend, or at least a will to try something new, and that's valor in itself. The experiment may fail, but at least it gives somebody the opportunity to experiment. The big magazines cannot afford to do this because they have to go with the proven, the staid and stable and acknowledged. I don't deny that *Harper's, The Atlantic Monthly, The New Yorker,* and so on have high standards. There's no question that they publish very good stuff, but it is safe stuff. It is the stuff that is already recognized as being good. Little magazines can afford to print trash and frequently use this liberty to excess. It's quite true that many of the people who publish in little magazines couldn't get into the big ones because their work is not good enough. But there's always the chance that something exciting will happen in little magazines that cannot happen in the bigs.

What did a magazine such as Der Sturm *do to remain big and yet have the focus of a "little"?*

38

Well, its time was the nineteen-tens and twenties. What its editors did was to espouse isms. They were interested in new movements, new ideas, and they had that same kind of excitement about new art, new writing—for instance, the *Neue Sachlichkeit* (which means a new kind of realism), or surrealistic experiments, or dadaism, whatever. They were not really big circulation magazines. But they were read not only by the people who wrote for them; they were read by a general group of artists in different fields— sculptors, musicians, painters and photographers, etc. This was the *Sturm Gruppe,* a focus for new, younger artists who had something new to say and who were against the established modes, whatever they had been. In that sense *Der Sturm* was a little magazine. In format it looked a bit more like the *New Republic* or like a tabloid, but it had the little-magazine spirit.

Do you think a magazine could exceed a circulation of 15,000 and still have a little-magazine spirit?

Well, I don't know about that figure exactly. There is certainly nothing precise about it, but I believe, for example, that the *Evergreen Review* had the little-magazine spirit when it started out, though its circulation far exceeded what is normal for a little magazine, which I would say is between 200 and 1,000. But when its editors started out, they had a starry-eyed, excited interest, a willingness to print new things and be literary-minded, and they published a lot of translations to show what was going on in other countries. It was really a literature-oriented magazine, and it published people like Ionesco, Beckett, Albee, etc. Then it became a kind of whore, publishing soft-core pornography, titillating its readers with pictures—not *Playboy* girlie pictures, but smirkier and dirtier in some way. I have nothing against girlie pictures, but the more recent *Evergreen* didn't have anything to do with litera- ture or with its spirit. It was just out for the buck. So the *Evergreen Review* wilted and became very brown around the edges and finally folded, after changing format several times. When I was in charge of the Sukov collection at the University of Wisconsin, I incor- porated the original *Evergreen Review* into the little-magazine collection, but gave up on it when it became a different magazine. That's what I mean by a spirit that is usually more important than anything else, but that spirit is usually connected with a certain limitation in means and a certain willingness to stay small. The larger little magazines are exceptions to the rule. Those fat ones like *TriQuarterly* or *The American Review,* formerly *New American Review,* can still be considered little magazines. Many of the larger quarterlies can likewise be considered little magazines because they have that particular feature of bringing in new writers. Many publish foreign work in translation and most, if not all, would be willing to print a story that was different from others. If a new James Joyce should suddenly turn up on the horizon, these magazines might still be willing to print him.

The *Paris Review* would, I assume, be one of those that have a bigger circulation and is still a little magazine.

Reed Whittemore once asked, "Does the little magazine of today occupy as important a place as those founded by William Carlos Williams, Margaret Anderson, and Harold Loeb?" I'd like to ask you the same question.

I don't think so. When the *Little Review* was being published, Ezra Pound was scathing about it. He thought the editors accepted an awful lot of trash, and that Margaret Anderson in particular was some kind of scatterbrain who didn't know what she was doing. And it's true; I think Jane Heap was more intelligent than Margaret was. Margaret had the enthusiasm and the naiveté. Now, of course, the *Little Review* is something of a legend, a holy cow, and it's only spoken of in capital letters. But I still think it had something. Also, there were fewer magazines then; they were more centered; they were the meeting places of the important writers, who today are more scattered. And I think that in many ways they had different roles from the little magazines of today, although I would say that something like *Kayak* has a place. *Kayak* has a face among fairly recent magazines, as—for another example—has *Poetry Northwest,* and a number of other contemporary mags, which in retrospect might be considered quite important. Among less recent magazines, the *New Orleans Poetry Journal* stands out in my mind as a gem.

In general, I would say the earlier magazines were more important. They had a bigger role to play, and we must not forget those were the twenties, the so-called golden age of the little magazine, a time of great excitement and of great innovation and of many isms, and schools, and movements.

Do you think that it made a difference, too, that little magazines then were centered in the East, where the input from Europe was more continuous?

I would think that had something to do with it. The *Little Review*, for instance, started in Chicago, then moved to New York, then moved to Paris. However, one really doesn't have to be on the spot in order to know that a Sartre may be writing something interesting. If you're looking for things, you can also send a correspondent abroad, if you have the means, or you can utilize people already living abroad as correspondents. So when a magazine moved to New York or Europe, that was probably indicative of its interest in the place, but I think the openness to new ideas came first.

It seems that magazines today don't have that openness. Would you agree?

Well, there's Robert Bly, who brings out a lot of translations, except that he doesn't print regularly. *The Sixties* appeared sporadically, and *The Seventies* has come out with one issue so far. But whatever he does publish has translations from the Spanish and Portuguese of South American writers. *Paris Review* and *Quarterly Review of Literature* publish translations, as do *Mundus Artium, Field, Bitter Oleander,* and *Modern Poetry in Translation, Moons and Lion Tailes*, etc. And among a number of magazines there is also a great interest in the American Indian. So I wouldn't quite say that there's no openness, but there is a certain chauvinism, a certain American nationalism in many magazines that are not interested in writers from the rest of the world. Many have a regional emphasis. Many are provincial, local even. I have heard Kenneth Rexroth say in San Francisco that "all we need are California poets; we don't care about anybody else." The New York poets have their New York School and are only interested in that. In these cases, writers put themselves under a voluntary limitation based mostly on chauvinism or ignorance, which runs contrary to the example of men like Robert Bly, who has many foibles but in this case is right in complaining that we are closing our eyes to important things going on outside this country.

When we read about the literary movement of the nineteen-tens and twenties, we sense that there was a lot of input from other arts. The movements weren't formed just by literature, but by theater and painting as well.

True. Kindred spirits were collaborating then, and the same ideas were at work in all the arts. People who formed little-theater groups, which were very much the spiritual twins of the little magazines, worked closely with writers. Clifford Odets had a group of actors around him. He wrote his plays for them, but they all worked on the plays as they rehearsed. In Germany, there were groups of artists—*die Brücke, der Blaue Reiter*—that consisted primarily of painters but drew in sculptors, writers, musicians, and also dancers, set designers, mimes, in later years even filmmakers, satirists, political celebrities, poster artists, etc. The composer Ernst Krenek, for instance, who was one of the disciples of Schoenberg, was also interested in literature. So is Kokoschka, the painter, who is still alive. What they accomplished is illustrated by the movement "Secession," after which one of our American magazines was named. In Vienna, the painters moved out of a museum that wanted only to show rehashes, the same old paintings over again. They wanted to work in a new mode so they built a new museum in Vienna called the *Sezession*. The editors of *Secession* thought theirs was a brilliant title, and of course, having this same outlook and being avant-garde, they said, "We are going to do the same thing in our own way."

You mentioned in "Elitism and the Littleness of Little Magazines" that Margaret Anderson had considered the term "little review" a badge of honor and an expression of defiance. Regarding Secession and the mixing of media, is the genre of the little magazine still viable? Does it shape anything new in literature? Or is it time to look to a newer type of display form? Is the whole foundation of the little magazine bankrupt?

I am an adherent of the printed word, and I believe in writing, and

I believe language will go on as long as the human spirit goes on. So while you may have tape recordings instead of print, and while you may have TV performances and movies and visual aids of all sorts, I still think that the printed word is of primary significance— in the end you come back to the book. In the end it's also the easiest way of carrying words around, carrying ideas around. And only if we raise a generation that is illiterate, educated solely by television—a deplorable kind of education, I should think—only then will the word have disappeared. As long as you have print, I think the little magazines will be an important part of that method of expression. All the music of the world is contained in the keys of a piano, and it is inexhaustible. All the literature of the world— past, present, and future—is contained in the keyboard of a typewriter. All the possible games of chess that can be played are contained in the squares of a chessboard, and yet the moves and combinations are inexhaustible. So I'll take the *word* over "input" and "feedback," and *print* over "printout" any day. In the same way, I would say that the little magazine, as an idea and as a way of communication, is not obsolete and cannot be supplanted by anything else.

Have the isms of the fifties—eclecticism, academicism, and so on— disappeared? Is the time of these schools over? And would their passing be to the detriment of the little magazines?

Yes, I believe the time of isms is over. There are no more flaming manifestos in little magazines. This is to the detriment of the little magazines insofar as it takes away the intensity, the commitment, the involvement, the passion with which those magazines originally set forth their particular programs. "Schools" acknowledged a sense of mission: they knew the Truth, not only about substance but about form. The imagists knew that there was no other writing but imagism, and they were passionate about it. Of course they were not right, but they were *passionately* wrong— which in the domain of art is close to being right. Actually, the *Little Review* people bragged, I think, that in its span the magazine had supported twenty-three different isms; that is, systems of art. They were always sailing with the wind. Margaret Anderson was always eager for the new because that was her philosophy. She always had her ear to the ground, or to the air, or wherever. But at least she had an enormous enthusiasm for certain kinds of writing, and that, I think, is missing in what we have now.

However, I don't think one has to be committed to just one kind of school in order to be good. If it is a matter of real taste, and of real creative instinct, and of the ability of an editor to pick out the best, the result can have great merit even without any particular ism.

What about regionalism in little magazines, in the Midwest particularly?

Well, of course, I'm the wrong guy to ask about regionalism because I have never quite distinguished it from provincialism. Perhaps I'm wrong, but I've always felt that one has to be somewhere, like the little man in the closet. When the husband came home and smelled cigar smoke in the house, he said, "Who was here?" And his wife said, "Nobody," and he didn't believe her, so he went searching around the house, and when he opened his clothes closet there was a little man hiding between the coats, and the husband thundered, "What are you doing in my closet?" And the little man said, "Well, sir, everybody has to be someplace." That's what I feel about regionalism: you have to be someplace, and so you write about what you see, which doesn't necessarily make you a regional writer. I don't know how it works to pick one region and be committed to it, nor whether that is a virtue in itself. I certainly have my childhood memories connected with Vienna, and I write about Vienna occasionally. But I don't think that makes me a regional Austrian writer, and nobody can call me a Wisconsin writer now.

Was Mark Twain a regionalist? Hardly. He wrote a lot about Hannibal, Missouri, and life on the Mississippi; yet he is understood and admired all over the world, particularly in Russia, curious to say. And what about Faulkner? You know what *he* wrote about. If anything, his region is perhaps the only place where he is *not* read. And how about Dickens? Or Dreiser? Or Thomas Wolfe? Or Sinclair Lewis? Or Thornton Wilder? (*Main Street* and *Our Town* are everywhere.)

[There followed a lengthy discussion between John Judson and Felix Pollak, interspersed with remarks by Richard Boudreau and Mark Olson, touching on urbanization, the hippie movement, back to the soil, and the real or alleged regionalism of little magazines. The South Dakota Review *and the* Little Farm *were mentioned by John Judson as true regional magazines, while Felix Pollak pointed out that the* Minnesota Review, *for one example, was for a long time published in Milwaukee, and is now being published in Indiana and may some day be published in California, and will still be called* Minnesota Review *while really not having any local or regional ties at all. It was finally decided that the problem would need a greater in-depth treatment and Mark Olson continued with his next question.]*

Another question: In a symposium held in the pages of the Carleton Miscellany *in its Spring/Summer 1966 issue, the editors largely agreed with the statement attributed to Bly and Duffy that most of today's poetry is too old-fashioned. But none of them seemed to spell out ways of updating the magazines of poetry. "Make it new" is just a phrase credited to Pound, who is now a solid member of the kulchur he despised. Do you see this as a time of experimentation, or are the younger writers having such difficulty understanding what happened in the first half of the century that it seems impossible to come up with anything new? The question probably boils down to asking if we are in a time of playing catch-up ball.*

Well, I think that anything new, any kind of experimentation, is an organic thing that has to grow out of somebody's mind and out of the conditions of the time; it has to evolve organically, not synthetically. Nobody can get it by sitting down and saying, "That was the old. Now I'm going to do something new." That isn't what Pound meant at all. What Pound meant was that you must see as a child sees for the first time. Look at things as if you were seeing them for the first time, and you can talk about them—even the moon in June when you first experience it—in ways that will be new and fresh.

Newness, in any case, is merely a new way of using old materials. I don't think even the surrealists can really create something new without using real (old) materials. We always have to work with age-old motifs—pain, grief, joy, ambition, envy, lust for power,

45

etc.—emotions that have come to us from the time of Homer or before. We just present them in new costumes and different words. That's why I think that anything which tries to be so original that it disregards tradition and believes it can start from scratch is bound to fail. Even the surrealist has to use birds' wings to put them on frogs so as to create a creature that normally has no wings.

Would you say that writers come out of schools of thought rather than that schools of thought come out of writers?

Well, I don't think writers come out of schools of thought at all. Schools of thought come later. We are influenced, however, by our environment and the socioeconomic, political, and technical conditions of our period, and now there is no way of not writing about them. Certainly no subject in poetry or fiction is taboo and some subjects are imperative for a contemporary writer. After all, we live in a time of computers, nuclear fission, pollution, racial tension, population explosion, and so forth, which previous ages have not had.

In the "Elitism" *article, you said that the mimeo revolution has brought about a proliferation of titles unmatched before, and thus an abundance of the mediocre. Robert Bly has said that too much is published, and he goes on to state that the best thing that could happen to American literary publishing would be for editions of little magazines to voluntarily reduce their numbers. Do you think that the sheer numbers of littles today is detrimental to them?*

I'm not sure. I think it certainly would be more convenient and more comfortable to have just a few places where you know all the important writers are congregating in writing. Then you wouldn't have to go through too many little magazines in order to find what is going on and what is good. But convenience and comfort are not the main objects of the game. The mere fact that every type of expression can find a forum is more important, I think, than to have a few recognized littles, which are already in danger of becoming establishment. If you don't somehow conform to *them* then you can't get in anywhere again, and that is the grave danger. The great antidote against this is the variety and the large number of outlets. Even if they are not so good, and even if readers have to go around searching for good material in innumerable magazines

46

and find it embedded in a great amount of junk, you still have a better chance of giving a hearing to everybody who is important. Therefore, I think that the very vitality which is expressed in a high death rate and a high birthrate is an essential feature of the little-magazine scene and a value in itself.

Can a little magazine create an audience? This question brings to mind the work of the CCLM. I'm sure you've heard about their efforts to put magazines in libraries and set up distribution co-ops and things like that.

Well, I think that only a little magazine, only an individual magazine, can create its own audience. I think all the mechanical ways of trying to get an audience, of increasing circulation, of getting new outlets that will store the little magazines and put them out for sales, are all very well but all artificial. Nobody's going to buy a magazine just because it hangs on a newsstand somewhere or sits on a shelf. I think what does build audiences is a commitment to this kind of magazine, a conviction that whatever is in that magazine will be of interest and quality and appeal to somebody. In that way, slowly and surely, circulation is built. Of course, it doesn't hurt to make the mags widely available, and if distribution schemes by organizations like CCLM and COSMEP can advance that cause, I'm all for it. However, this is all secondary to the magazines' own efforts.

When I think about the magazines that flourished in the heyday of the littles, it seems to me their editors would be appalled that anyone but themselves would be distributing them.

True. There's also the idea of staying small—not wanting to compete, say, with the underground presses that are on all the newsstands and all over the supermarkets. To become a mass medium would be so foreign to a little magazine that the genuine little would shy away from it. There is also the hassle of putting magazines into bookstores on consignment, as many editors have told me. The bookstores don't bother to pay, and the editors have to run after their money. The booksellers sometimes assert the mags were not sold but stolen, and sometimes issues are found tucked away in a corner, looking much the worse for wear. The whole thing is cumbersome, the kind of machinery the editors would rather do without. I think they would rather have their subscription lists, however small, and know that whoever wants to subscribe will be interested in getting the magazine. Whether the public of a little magazine consists primarily of its contributors is another question.

Another thing that happened in the fifties and the sixties was that writers tried to make their living by also being teachers. How strong, how good or bad have been their effects as members of the academic institutions? Is it only natural that there would be an increase of academic quarterlies growing out of the Fugitive group emphasis and the New Criticism? Or is this an unnatural phenomenon forced by people who want to get into publishing?

I don't know whether it has really to do with the Fugitive group or with the New Criticism—which certainly was, as the name itself says, interested mostly in criticism rather than in creativity. I think what it has to do with is simply economics. Most people who are interested in writing are likely to study English in college and then become college teachers, and I don't see why somebody has to be a bad poet just because he makes his living as a teacher of literature. I don't see why it would make him a good poet to dig ditches, or sell vacuum cleaners, or live on handouts, or push dope, or whatever. I don't understand the academy baiting that is carried on primarily by people who make their living in academies and have an inferiority complex about it. They feel that they are really catering to the establishment or that they are bourgeois or that teaching in colleges makes them somehow pale and academic (in the sense of anemic, acad-anemic, so to speak). I don't feel that way about it. When I was a librarian, just the mere fact that I couldn't really do anything particularly interesting during the day made me feel that writing in the evening was what made my life meaningful. I suppose an English professor might also feel that he could be only partially creative in his daily teaching and that he must draw on his own creativity to fulfill himself. I think there is a certain openness and a freewheelingness in being a vagabond, but this kind of romanticism is first of all overrated and, second, good only for people under thirty. After thirty, if you're a hippie, you're a bum, and then it isn't so funny or so good any more. This whole question has many specious facets to it. I firmly believe that the mere fact of teaching cannot make a bad poet out of a good poet, or that by

48

not teaching a bad poet will turn into a good one. One can experience life even if one is employed in a college.

Many editors of true littles have said that we're being overwhelmed by quarterlies and reviews and that they're corrupting the whole idea of the little magazine. Do you believe that?

The academic quarterlies are, in my opinion, relatives of the little magazines, and they are, as you'll remember, included in Fred Hoffman's book. When he and I, just before his sudden death, contemplated a new book on that subject, we decided that they must be dealt with in a chapter by themselves. They may lack the irresponsibly free and unfettered spirit that characterizes the genuine little mags, but the best of them—like the old *Accent,* to name just one—contain very creative materials: stories and poems by new writers, translations of foreign authors, and criticism usually so original and lively that it is just as creative as poetry and fiction. The pages of *The Little Review,* of *Hound and Horn, Broom, The Seven Arts,* etc., have exposed the prejudice that criticism per se is dull and uncreative, and names like Edmund Wilson or Lionel and Diana Trilling in themselves bear witness against that bias. I'll admit that the publications devoted to the New Criticism of the forties and fifties were usually dull and pedestrian and pedantic, but these no more constitute a threat to the little magazines than do the slicks and pulps, the girlie mags, and the astrology mags, etc., against which the complaint you mention is *not* made. The very fact that some little-mag devotees appear paranoid about the academic quarterlies would seem to prove that the best and liveliest of them—*Prairie Schooner, New Letters, Ohio Review,* etc.—are indeed of a kindred genre. But some competition is good for standards, and the true littles have unique positive features which their more stable and respectable rich relations lack. Incidentally, the writers who appear in the best of the littles and in the best of the quarterlies are frequently the same, which confirms what I just said.

One final question. Do you think you could summarize in one or two sentences the most important characteristic of a little magazine?

If I would have to put it into one sentence, I would say that a little magazine is much more than a small magazine that would like to be big.

THE LITTLE MAGAZINE IN ITS PLACE: LITERARY CULTURE AND ANARCHY
Robert Boyers

Robert Boyers' essay explores the dangers of an indiscriminate love of experiment, of manic eclecticism, and of anti-intellectualism in little magazine editing. His attitude suggests a consistent adversary relationship between editor and reader in the presentation of criticism and original poetry and prose.

Mr. Boyers began Salmagundi *on the model of* Partisan Review *as a left-wing journal without parochial commitments, but soon became less topical and current where contemporary fiction and poetry were concerned. He decided to promote contemporary arts primarily through the publication of critical essays, interviews, and combative book reviews. Probably the likeliest models for the issues of* Salmagundi *during the past decade would, Boyers says, be the intellectual quarterlies of the nineteenth century,* The Westminster Review *and* The Edinburgh Review, *with their long theoretical and practical essays. In its hospitality to the outsized essay,* Salmagundi *has undertaken a job of critical inquiry no other intellectual quarterly of the period has continued to do. Among the topics engaged by some of the magazine's writers are the Frankfurt school's critical theory, pornography, the family, the psychoanalysis of lying, the aesthetics of the dance, and the major cultural historians (Gershom Scholem, Max Weber, Ortega y Gasset, Havelock Ellis, and Herbert Marcuse). The favored contributors to the magazine include Henry Pachter, Philip Rieff, George Steiner, Christopher Lasch, John Bayley, Erich Heller, Barry Targan, Martin Pops, John Peck, Ben Belitt, and Howard Nemerov.*

Mr. Boyers is the author of more than seventy essays on contemporary poets and novelists, film, politics, psychoanalysis, and contemporary culture. He has written and edited nine books, among them anthologies of essays on Robert Lowell and R. D. Laing, original monographs on Lionel Trilling and F. R. Leavis, and a collection of essays on the writer and contemporary culture, Excursions *(1976). Boyers is also the editor of the newly founded arts magazine* Bennington Review *(1978+), in which he attempts to reproduce contemporary arts graphically as well as critically.* Bennington, *like* Kulchur *and* Partisan *before it, publishes continuing columns on the art scene by critics, poets, and art historians.*

The little magazine as a general subject has been talked almost to death, and it is an unavoidable fact that, while so many specimens currently exist, only a handful are worth examining. There are, though, several worthwhile distinctions yet to be made without which it is difficult to understand the situation of our literate culture and the function of little magazines in that culture. It is not necessary to read through large numbers of little magazines to discover these distinctions, but familiarity with the appropriate publications should certainly bear out our experience in other areas—as filmgoers, classroom teachers, conference participants, or readers of popular monthlies with substantial circulations. To describe this experience is inevitably to speak of the audience for serious works of literature and art; for when we are speaking of so intimate a phenomenon as the little magazine we cannot but dwell upon the quality of its appeal to a particular readership. To put it bluntly, the audience for serious works of contemporary literature has fallen prey to an appalling and undiscriminating habit of alternating cynicism and enthusiasm: cynicism about intelligence, about critical thinking, about the premises and uses of evaluation; enthusiasm about creative energy (no matter how obviously misdirected), about anything politically a la mode (new styles in feminist ideology, for example), and about the "good sentiments" (liberality, love, innocence, simplicity).

There is at the same time, of course, a strangely modish attraction to writers like Borges and Pynchon, neither of whom is the chanticleer of a new dawn of liberality, love, innocence, or simplicity. Clearly the cultural situation, while unmistakable, is anything but monolithic. It is surely possible to cultivate an appetite for

Borges while spending much of one's time touting phony nativist verses or singing the praises of naked poetry. No doubt it is the professional literary academic who is most susceptible to this division of loyalties. With one foot in the youth culture—combing the pages of *Rolling Stone, Village Voice,* and some variant of *Poetry Now*—and the other in the college classroom, the with-it literary professor is bound to find value in maintaining flexible sympathies. Writers like Pynchon and Nabokov are, after all, creators of eminently teacherly volumes, spawners of soon-to-be-accredited "texts" whose interpretation provides busywork for employable professors, most of whom—with-it or not—wouldn't know a genuine little magazine from a cardboard box. In a culture that, as Lionel Trilling recently remarked, "fosters a form of assent which does not involve actual credence," it is fully possible to look in two opposite directions at once without feeling committed to choose between them or to consider seriously their relative merits.

The little magazine, then, finds itself in a precarious position. Massed on one side of the potential literary market are the professors, with their specialties, their linguistic codes, their heavy-artillery apparatuses. The appetite here is not a literary appetite but a hunger for publishing outlets, for interpretive gimmicks, for professional status accreditation. The magazines that cater to this predictable hunger are not little magazines or literary journals, but professional journals with a card-carrying readership that is anything but loyal or intelligently committed. After all, if these journals represent nothing to speak of, if their business is simply to promote professional careers and to accumulate research materials for use by prospective Ph.D. candidates, they are not likely to develop identifiable profiles or to work out positions on living issues. The libraries are stacked with such journals, and a recent survey records that fewer than one hundred persons may be supposed actually to read through any single item in a particular issue. Want to know what Borges really had in mind in *Tlön?* Answers are readily available. Need to trace the possible sources of tag names in Pynchon? Help is not far away.

Massed on the other side of the potential market are the inevitable camp followers of one fashion or another: the naked-poetry crowd, feminist ideologues, back-to-nature freaks, even the insistent structuralists with their diagrams and their programmatic rigidities. Each camp following will have its own favorite journal, or several, which participant members study more or less carefully, swear by, and aspire to publish in. From these phalanx formations various cult figures are born and, if they are lucky, quickly fade to be replaced by others, usually less interesting and less given to the possibilities of accommodation to other angles of vision.

What, then, constitutes a favorable profile by which to measure and recognize a little magazine, and what sort of audience may be expected to support "the real thing"? Perhaps as good a place as any to begin an investigation is the volume *A Return to "Pagany": The History, Correspondence, and Selections from a Little Magazine,* by Stephen A. Halpert with Richard Johns (Beacon Press, 1969). The volume opens with a statement from the poet William Carlos Williams which, though probably responsible for some of the inane crap promoted in little magazines, accurately represents the sentiments of many creative artists and legions of would-be creators:

The little magazine is something I have always fostered; for without it, I myself would have been early silenced. To me it is one magazine, not several. It is a continuous magazine, the only one I know with an absolute freedom of editorial policy and a succession of proprietorships that follows a democratic rule. There is absolutely no dominating policy permitting anyone to dictate anything. . . . It must be a person who does it [edits a little magazine], a person, a fallible person, subject to devotions and accidents.

Williams's statement belongs at the front of the *Pagany* volume, for in the years of its brief life, from 1929 to 1932, it managed to be very much what Williams wanted. It published a wide range of writing, was frequently brash and opinionated, and found room for writers who in time went on to great influence and achievement. If, as one correspondent wrote in 1930, it "struck a fine balance between extreme experimentalism and the rather rigid *Dial* standard," it was not averse to trying out unfamiliar work by unknown writers, nor to irritating members of its potential readership by taking unpopular positions on this or that. Though *Pagany* did print a good deal of criticism, it tended less and less to see its mission in terms of evaluation and precise analytic discrimination.

53

But what could Williams have meant when he wrote of the little magazine's "absolute freedom of editorial policy," of "democratic rule," of the absence of a "dominating policy"? To impose a literal reading on any one of these earnest formulations is to recognize at once how fuzzy Williams could be when he wrote outside the formal constraints of a poem, or novel, or story whose self-generating conventions he respected even as he worked to free himself from what he took to be the burdens of inherited form. In fact, Williams could not have responded favorably to any magazine that had no discernible policy or canons of taste. He liked *Pagany,* as he intimates, because it was a vehicle for his own work in progress—including his first novel, *White Mule*—and because in its editor, Richard Johns, he recognized a companionable spirit committed to vitality and experiment rather than to closure and caution. And though Williams staunchly supported *Pagany,* he could acknowledge its important deficiencies, some surely implicit in his own muddleheaded conception of the little magazine in general. In a letter to Johns dated May 1, 1930, Williams wrote that *"Pagany* is and must be a miscellany, a true, even a realistic picture of the rather shabby spectacle America still makes from the writer's viewpoint. At least you are not 'decent' even though you are not organized—as perhaps you should be." He even agrees with critics of the magazine that some of its material is "especially poor," "punk stuff," and though *"Pagany* seems not to be taking any stand [especially on political issues] at all . . . it is better than some of the stands that have been taken." Surely a dubious apology at best. Williams's concession to the claim that *Pagany* might usefully get itself organized only confuses still further our sense of his call for "absolute freedom of editorial policy," and we come increasingly to feel that he really didn't know what he thought, much as he felt intermittently in his blood what he liked.

Now there is no doubt that the happy accident is as desirable in the editing of a magazine as it is in the composition of a poem, and Williams's predilection for finding things by the way, picking them up, and making them work for him somehow did surely account for special and valuable qualities in his verse. But one may be forgiven for expressing some suspicion of a method which is no method at all, and which when freely indulged is as likely to defeat as to enhance one's prospects for genuine accomplishment. *Pagany* surely meant a great deal to the various writers who found a home in its pages, but it seems likely that Williams and other ambitious figures would have gotten their writing done even had they never met Johns or heard his clarion calls for material. More important, what about the various people who never amounted to anything as writers, who were encouraged by their appearances in *Pagany* and other little magazines to think of themselves as destined for literary careers, when in fact their talents were less than meager and their ambitions preposterously inflated? Is it ungenerous to suppose that such people might in the long run have been better off had they never been so encouraged, had there been some marginally definable criterion of professional competence by which hopeful contributors to *Pagany* might plausibly measure their chances of acceptance? Perhaps it is unreasonable to suggest as much, and surely no editor owes it to potential contributors to explain to them the limits of their ability and the precise nature of professional achievement. Besides which, there aren't many aspiring writers who tend to listen to chastening advice, no matter how well intentioned, and editors are usually wise to avoid comment altogether when they have nothing flattering to say.

The issue at hand is larger, though, than we've yet been able to suggest. If Williams was somewhat incoherent when he spoke of a program for *Pagany,* he and others who spoke like him came to have great influence—both on the development of little magazines and on the shape of literary experiment in America. When Williams spoke of democratic rule, of freedom, and of happy editorial accidents, he was already moving in the direction of a creative bias which has come increasingly to dominate American cultural life. This bias has it that, when you come right down to it, there is only one real enemy to creative inspiration and achievement. Although it is called by many names—caution, timidity, hairsplitting, and compulsiveness—it is best known by one: critical thinking. And if critical thinking has often been known to align itself with such characteristics as analytic scruple, concern for detail, organizational coherence, insistence upon clarity and reasonableness, these are then to be the characteristics most despised by creative spirits.

Erskine Caldwell to Richard Johns, July 12, 1930: "Personally, I like anything that has the utmost in vitality, no matter the style, subject, or point of view—God, as long as you don't grind any axes [Take a position? Discriminate severely?] or let some scented paper drive you off your wheels, I'm with you.—I hope you don't change your mind about having done with pieces-about-pieces. Criticism wears out the best of creative work, after a time."

Not all of *Pagany's* influential correspondents shared Caldwell's views. Ezra Pound, for example, wrote in *Pagany* itself that "the function of the critic (benevolent and beneficent) is to select"; more, that "critical writing is ancillary. It is the shoe-horn not the foot. The attempt to pass it off as peer to creative writing is rooted in inferiority complex, the jealousy of the eunuch for Don Juan." Though there are at present several important academic critics who continue to press the latter argument, from a position distinctly opposed to Pound's, the issue has never seemed to me of compelling interest. Whether or not criticism is "peer to creative writing" is less important than the fact that at its best it serves a variety of purposes which no one interested in language and literature ought entirely to overlook. One does wonder, though, how a critic may be asked to be benevolent and also to select, for of necessity to select means also to reject, to discriminate better from best, good from bad. Pound, like Williams, was of two minds on how to organize a magazine and to promote standards of genuine literacy, but his sympathies were clearly with those who wanted to keep criticism well in its place, to keep the world safe for the more unruly and exciting creative energies.

Why should the critical enterprise have come so to dominate the anxious reflections of editors and poets in the early years of this century, and why should it remain at present more a threat than a promise? The writers in the *Pagany* circle are not, after all, easily distinguishable, in some of their attitudes, from contemporary literary people—including directors of federal humanities endowment programs and other artsy-craftsy bureaucrats who believe that the word is sacred only if it's patently poetical, less than referentially precise, and oh, so sincere. The road from Williams to such governmental spokesmen for the arts is long and tortuous, of course, and no one will suppose that similarities in their attitudes toward critical thinking reflect other and more crucial similarities. Williams was not only a great poet; he knew better than the rest of us, in his verse at least, how to be at once precise and passionately sincere while largely avoiding the more obvious sentimentalities in behalf of which the government is told it must support the arts. Chief among these sentimentalities is the absurd notion that hairsplitting damages the brain, that poets walk about under a divine spell which dissolves upon contact with analytic rigor even when directed by other friendly creators. At a time when most of our best poets and novelists manage to do superb work while teaching in the academy, beset on every side by critics and hairsplitters, the government agencies and their "informants" still think it especially useful to protect artists wherever possible from abrasive contact with what Pound found it easy to call the community of "eunuchs." No wonder so much government money has lately been spent in support of virtually worthless little magazines, the main function of which is to prevent their editors and contributors from discovering what they are and are not suited to do. How often in recent years have I winced while reading grant printouts from one agency or another, discovering their continuing support of magazines whose editors have proven time and again their inability to distinguish a poem from a bit of self-congratulating nonsense.

We have not the leisure here to trace in detail the process by which all this came originally to pass, but it is clear that the relative marginality of poetry—and, to a lesser extent, of serious fiction—in the reading habits of otherwise serious people has had significant effect in converting vague tendencies to firm predispositions. In the twenties and thirties, when Pound and Williams were young and the little magazine seemed full of promise, it was no doubt appealing to think of a publication directed mainly to one's peers in the community of letters. In time one might expect to win a range of other readers, and very few artists actually believed it might be possible to produce important work without ever passing beyond that original little-magazine readership. In our time the literary situation has decidedly altered such expectations. One needn't have precise figures to know that the wider readership earlier anticipated by the poets does not exist; that volumes of poetry, even by established and clearly "successful" older poets like Stanley Kunitz, will find readers only in the tiny community which reads and aspires to publish in this little magazine or that; that a brilliantly accomplished and not impossibly difficult novelist like William Gass will be lucky to find ten thousand readers for his book over a period of ten years. Nor do exceptions to the rule tell us much, except that the publicity apparatus in American publishing and reviewing circles is unstable and occasionally subject to unpredictable whims. Contemporary writers, when they are not themselves subject to delusions of grandeur, come early to recognize that what now passes for the little magazine may be as much as they can aspire to succeed in; that they may be more certain of a genuine readership, though small, for periodical publication of a poem or story than for subsequent book publication. They will not on this account forgo the modest advantages of book publication, but will understand that more often than not the only fate of a good volume is to stand virtually unread on the shelves of a university library, while books of an entirely journalistic and ephemeral character are widely reviewed and disseminated. These are facts of life, and one would be foolish indeed to grow indignant over so trifling a matter. There are innumerable opportunities in this country for writers to break into print, and there is always the chance that a writer with fine talent will be discovered by the media and permitted to "make it" as fully as he deserves.

In the face of all this, it is not surprising that writers should be jealous of the limited advantages they have; that poets and other self-conscious keepers of the sacred flame should want to bar critical voices from the sanctuary; that questions of the relation between authority and revelation, as it were, be all but denied. Criticism does tend frequently to confuse matters which had once seemed to enthusiasts perfectly clear. If one is determined to admire "anything that has the utmost in vitality," in Caldwell's phrase, one will not like to be told that vitality in itself may constitute an insufficient virtue, or that what seems vital to one reader seems merely shrill and arbitrary to another. The little magazine, unfortunately, has had an important role in encouraging writers to think of themselves as somehow beyond criticism and as working in the service of goals to which only they and their creative peers may suitably testify. Nor does the mere presence

58

of a critical essay or two guarantee that a little magazine will perform its function better than publications restricted to poetry or fiction. Much that passes for criticism in the little magazine is no better than a plug for an aspiring local boy, or a species of coterie commentary which certifies that a given figure belongs among the circle of writers and readers associated with that journal. Besides, no one would be so foolish as to require a magazine to publish a particular quota of critical articles. Critical thinking is what we must care about, and it can as well be present in a little poetry magazine as in a journal predominantly committed to the publication of literary essays. The critical function is performed whenever a magazine editor severely discriminates among the MSS submitted to him, and indicates by his selection of material for publication that he knows what he is doing and could more or less readily account for his choices in a way that would do credit to his judgment and interpretative faculties. Is this the case where most little magazines are concerned? Surely it is not possible to discern a consistent pattern of taste or judgment in the selections from *Pagany* printed in the recent volume. And *Pagany* was, by all odds, a distinguished little magazine.

We are back, then, to what Williams called organization, and to issues raised by his calling for a little magazine that is at once miscellaneous and realistic in representing the spectacle of the culture to which it is addressed. The central question raised has to do with the relation between the magazine and its audience. At its best, I would contend, the little magazine always cultivates something of an adversary relationship with its readers. It is, by intention, at least occasionally upsetting, always provoking, and eager to remain a step ahead of most of its readers in recalling to them their obligations as literate persons. None of this is possible without organization, for if readers are to be genuinely provoked, if they are to submit to literary experiences which are often unfamiliar, difficult, or unpleasant, they will have to trust their editors to provide consistently valuable provocation. Otherwise readers will simply resist what they read, or turn their attention elsewhere at the first sign of difficulty. The trust in editorial judgment required to sustain a fruitful adversary relationship between reader and journal is a function of an organized vision of literary possibility to which every item in the magazine implicitly subscribes. Confronted again and again by this organized vision, the reader has a developing basis on which to evaluate individual items against the broader pattern, and to consider the effectiveness of the pattern in promoting particular literary projects which might not otherwise have been conceived. This experience can be a good deal more complicated than the observation that a certain film critic would never have written a given essay had he not been commissioned to do so by a given journal. The issue is, what *kind* of essay was conceived, and how would the essay have had to be different were it conceived for the pages of another journal, or written into the void with no thought of context, format, or audience at all? Similar questions may even be asked about poems or stories; for it is an undeniable fact that many younger writers cultivate an ideal of themselves as adequate to a certain kind of literary expression largely because they have been responsibly and critically encouraged by one or more editors. While writers of major talent, even when young, may not be susceptible to that kind of encouragement, most of what appears in any magazine will be something less than major work, and most writers will surely consent to be "brought along" by gifted and helpful editors.

The little magazine as miscellany, though—in the sense of the word "miscellany" intended by Williams—is not a good bet to provide professional help, or to attract a serious audience willing to be challenged at the very heart of its ideas, self-images, and aesthetic predilections. If the journal is miscellaneous only insofar as it reflects the obscene pluralism of a democratic ethos gone awry, it cannot concern itself with differences in quality, scope, and moral tone that make the selection of one item rather than another an interesting and fully significant decision. The culture in which the little magazine must make its way is a novelty culture, as we are so often reminded, and it is hard to imagine what possible good can come of a journal's attempting to encompass the sheer variety of models, images, artifacts competing for attention against a background of limitless possibility. The miscellaneous quality of *Pagany* was a function of a particular kind of abdication for which editor, contributors, and readers may be said to share responsibility. We know what the abdication amounted to, and signifies still, when we try to bring ourselves to speak without embarrassment of such things as quality and standards in a magazine. The words seem somehow—do they not?—to compromise our allegiance to vitality, to the experimental and courageous. We do not like to think ourselves hung up on narrow loyalties, and we take as humanly offensive the very idea of a code or tradition of standards which may be legitimately applied to works of literature. No matter the esteem in which Eliot and other spokesmen for a traditional culture are said to be held in academic circles: what is genuinely prized, by most academics as by writers and editors, is the individual talent. We have, in fact, the full realization of what Philip Rieff has called an experimental ethos, according to which every man is fruitfully creative in the degree that he expresses his feelings without undue restraint, and uncritically opens himself to the music of his creative peers, most of them blithely sawing away on tuneless instruments.

How little aware of the situation I was when, in 1965, I began to conceive the publication of a little magazine may be surmised from the fact that my friends and I chose to call it *Salmagundi*. As the original designation of a stew consisting of various and sundry oddments, yet not without a certain spice, the name was bound to conjure up an entirely miscellaneous phenomenon; and though for thirteen years now *Salmagundi* has published a wide assortment of materials, it cannot be said to have spoken for that various and protean spirit all too casually announced in its name. As I think of our first issues, however—of the promise others saw in them and the particular satisfaction they gave us then—I think it fair to claim an early intuition of what *Salmagundi* was intended to accomplish. I'd hesitate now to promise anyone "a unique reading experience" such as we promised readers on the covers of early issues; still we have always thought it useful to consider what we could enthusiastically provide which no other magazine would be likely to publish, or at least to feature. Editorial emphasis in the early years had more to do with the mix of materials than with the tonal thrust of individual items. When, on the basis of three published issues, Lionel Trilling wrote in May 1966 that *"Salmagundi* gives every promise of becoming one of our truly distinguished intellectual quarterlies," we thought the expression "intellectual quarterlies" caught precisely the kind of little

A Quarterly of the Humanities & Social Sciences / No. 41, Spring 1978/$3.00/£2.

Salmagundi

Lionel Trilling

Essays on Trilling by Joseph Frank, Helen Vendler, Robert Langbaum, Mark Shechner — Also, a *Sincerity & Authenticity* symposium with contributions by Trilling, Irving Howe, Leslie H. Farber, and others.

Books and Films in Review:

Alan Spiegel, Film-Flam / Peggy Boyers, Girard & Freud Adrian Kuzminski, Professionals / Eduardo Gonzalez, Fuentes

New poems by Wagoner, Keane, and others

Salmagundi, *No. 41, Spring 1978 (courtesy Robert Boyers).*

magazine we were in process of creating. Nor were we resistant to Irving Howe's 1966 description of *Salmagundi* as "a magazine run by young people who are struggling to develop a serious critical relationship to American life and writing." "Struggling" was—in some sense still is—quite right, and though by now we have surely indicated many times over a profile of our "critical relationship to American life and writing," we have never managed to be more than ambivalent about many cultural issues to which some journals respond with almost perfect ideological consistency. The critic Robert Alter, in a letter responding to our first issue, remarked on the "good range of subjects, writers and viewpoints—little threat of the stifling coterie quality one feels in so many of our intellectual publications." Also, he went on, "I much preferred the pieces that argued a viewpoint rather than being merely expository—Sagarin's sharply written statement on hatewhite, and your own attack on the sentimentalizing of Negro folk culture." It was possible, so it seemed to us, to make *Salmagundi* at once various and sufficiently organized to present an identifiable profile. We could print articles with widely differing views without compromising our devotion to critical care and responsible political commitment. While our political sympathies were decidedly leftist—they still are—there was no reason to buy the ongoing cultural revolution as though one had no choice if one's radical credentials were to be kept in order. And finally, granted that the magazine was to be directed primarily to the literary community, there was good reason to suppose that our readers would especially benefit from just the sort of social and political commentary that other literary publications had narrowly excluded.

Where *Salmagundi* was concerned, the necessary adversary relationship with readers was to depend on our steady introduction of unfamiliar perspectives on materials that were, with few exceptions, at least marginally familiar. There were "discoveries," of course, but we tended not so much to insist upon priority as to beg patience for what often seemed—even to us—intimidating. While we were the first general American journal to run extended articles on writers like T. W. Adorno, Walter Benjamin, R. D. Laing, Philip Rieff, and Witold Gombrowicz, we were not averse to printing essays in cultural history which focused upon "classical" writers like Sartre, Ortega y Gasset, Nietzsche, William James, and Havelock Ellis. Though we devoted entire issues in 1967 and 1977 to appraisals of Robert Lowell—hardly a stranger to the American literary community—we assiduously promoted the work of other poets with little or no reputation. We never went out of our way to cultivate controversy, but we knew how to get trusted contributors to press and probe in places that proved frequently more susceptible to analytic attack than anyone had yet imagined they would. Finally, we made room for a kind of literary display which, when less than perfect, is apt to strike readers as compromising that standard of high seriousness to which we had unashamedly dedicated the journal. In ambitious works by Martin Pops, by Edward Said, even in portions of Philip Rieff's "Fellow Teachers," we published a rare and splendid sort of item which C. S. Lewis, speaking of More's *Utopia,* once described as the "holiday work," reflecting an "overflow of intellectual high spirits, a revel of debate, paradox, comedy and (above all) of invention, which starts many hares and kills none." Happily, most *Salmagundi* readers have understood precisely in what spirit such works were intended to be read, and have been satisfied to search out the thread of intermittent practical comment or serious theorizing wherever it might be found. Fortunately, too, many other works we have featured, including several which could never have been conceived with anything approaching comic intention, have taken heart, as it were, from our "holiday works," and have thereby been able to poke and prod readers as no sober academic treatise is likely to do. In the past few years alone, in such pieces as Leslie H. Farber's "Lying on the Couch," Robert Weisberg's "Civility and Its Discontents," John Lukacs's "The Future of Historical Thinking," Tony Tanner's "Games American Writers Play," and others, we have given readers sometimes dizzying speculative displays about which they could naturally speak in tones of real enjoyment.

As editor of *Salmagundi,* I have found that the literary situation in this country is as open to influence from within as one has any right to hope. Where powerful institutions are concerned, changes are likely to occur slowly, if at all, and the fact that one is listened to with a degree of respectful attention does not ensure that one's views will be taken seriously. Acknowledging as much, I have tried to worry as little as possible about the views of this contributor or that, and have thought instead to present an attractive model of mind doing its appointed work: inventing, evaluating, interpreting, establishing necessary priorities, filling in obscure backgrounds, and so on. Though I have been accused of willfully turning my back on experimental writing, of virtually ignoring the feminist revolution, of (God forbid!) actually promoting the work of stodgy or reactionary figures like Philip Rieff, John Lukacs, even Saul Bellow, I have made decisions out of the conviction that, as editor, I know what best represents and tries the parameters of literate discourse. The verse collected in the magazine *Unmuzzled Ox* may be someone's idea of experimental writing, but it is not mine, and I am quite willing to settle for "traditional" verse if it can do consistently more exciting and exacting things than what passes for the new. Besides, common designations really do not serve very well to describe our experience of particular books or poems. Howard Nemerov, known to many observers as an academic poet, has done more to extend the language of poetry than any dozen self-conscious avant-garde litterateurs. And Philip Rieff has, from a "reactionary" position, done more to strengthen the critique of late capitalist consumer culture than any of the popular self-styled radicals who write for *Rolling Stone* or *The Village Voice*. The point is made with devastating accuracy in a 1975 *Salmagundi* essay by Charles Molesworth, in which he argues that "only by whoring after the new and the experimental can capitalism maintain its cultural grip on people." Recommending a careful reappraisal of Herbert Marcuse's theory of "repressive tolerance," Molesworth goes on to describe a "confused 'public' badgered by a thousand spokesmen and faddists and practitioners of universal brotherhood all trying to shape taste and influence history. This unfortunately remains true in the 'fields' of academic learning, pop music, pharmaceutical sales, high-fashion designing, and women's liberation, as well, all fields that reflect in exaggerated and distorted ways the structure and mores of monopoly capitalism."

But let us press the analysis a little further, particularly as it affects our account of literary culture and the function of little magazines. Contemporary literary culture, in its commitment to

65

the new, in its amiable pluralism and openness, has proven more repressive in its impact than most of us are willing to acknowledge. As it wants so badly to accept everything, to impugn no credential and erect no barrier to any ambition, it stands, really, for nothing, and may be said to furnish no whit of guidance to anyone concerned with elementary canons of taste, decorum, wit, or intellectual acuity. While all are encouraged to create, to think themselves "liberated" to self-expressive experimentalism, there is finally little sense of gratifying achievement, of limitations absorbed and fitfully overcome, of instruments finely honed to register particular elusive scales. The debasement of discourse consequent upon the unlimited expansion of literary possibility is quickly apparent in the contents of the most energetic and widely distributed literary magazines, including several whose tabloid formats clearly announce their intention to be done with pretension and the "scented paper" syndrome. In these current versions of the little magazine, one is likely to find a fine poem buried at the foot of page 47, and an absurdly mawkish little power-to-the-people exercise proudly emblazoned on the front cover; or, following a careful, discriminating piece of criticism, a bit of self-promoting propaganda for immediacy and self-exposure. No one is honor bound to stand firm against immediacy or self-exposure or experimental intensity, but it is surely obvious that unless we grow somewhat more skeptical of such qualities, and resistant to their allure, we shall be in a good deal of trouble. Unable to resist anything new or vital, we shall succumb with all due speed to that condition in which all we can comfortably manage is to lie still, smiles idiotically fixed on our faces, while the dance of creation spins frantically about us.

The answer to what Marcuse and his colleagues called repressive tolerance is not, of course, repressive intolerance, and it would be foolish indeed to expect anything hopeful by closing off the legal freedoms literary people were for years avid to win. No one is forgetting *Lady Chatterley* or *Tropic of Cancer* or *Lolita,* and we all know of gifted writers who have died of neglect. All the same, it is time we spoke of censorship, more particularly those powers of rejection and discrimination which literary editors are especially suited to exercise. The only possible way that literary people can address the human and intellectual challenge of a commodities culture is by insisting again and again that there are fundamental differences between one object and another; that judgments are not simply and irrevocably arbitrary; that there are viable standards whose perpetual application enables resistance to just those spurious appeals that a commodities market will make to each of us—whether the object peddled be deodorant, pop music, books, or new styles in humanist ideology.

The little magazine has an important role to play in this. Directed as it is to an audience presumed to have some feeling for genuine literary values, and to be at least somewhat disaffected from the mass media and its staple literary outlets, it has a basis on which to cultivate a creditable countercultural profile. By promoting in its selection of materials a bracing, elusive notion of literary value, by being less open to innovation and more respectful of literary and intellectual traditions that have generated undeniable achievements, the little magazine may come in time to stand for something, to suggest in what degree it may be worth fighting for and against. The function of the little magazine is, must be, to serve to erect and stand by principles of intelligent and imaginative discourse. Its function is not to serve the professors, or to provide indiscriminate encouragement to poets, or to build an audience responsive to particular experimental forms. Any of these objects may incidentally be realized as the little magazine does its appropriate work, but its primary object will always have more to do with providing a living model of the literary mind struggling to nurture and preserve—in Arnold's tainted words—the best that has been thought and said.

IN OUR LORD'S HO
THERE HAD BETTER
THE WHOLE MULTIFARIOU
ITS SIDESHOWS. THE ON
TO DO WAS TO DEP
OURSELVES OF THE
SHAPE IT MIGHT

E OF LITERATURE
ROOM ENOUGH FOR
HOW, INCLUDING SOME OF
HING WE DID NOT WISH
VE LITERATURE OR
ENUINE, WHATEVER
APPEN TO TAKE.

←—THEODORE WEISS

The Kenyon Review, *Vol. 18, No. 1 (courtesy Michael McDonnell).*

THE KENYON REVIEW, 1939-1970
Robie Macauley

Robie Macauley, now senior editor at Houghton Mifflin, edited
The Kenyon Review *from 1959 to 1966, and was the fiction editor
of* Playboy *magazine from 1966 to 1977. He owes his education in
editing to Ford Madox Ford, once editor of* The English Review
and later The Transatlantic Review, *and to John Crowe Ransom,
who edited* The Kenyon Review. *Macauley has been a longtime
admirer of book editors Maxwell Perkins, Saxe Commins, and
Albert Erskine, and, among magazine editors, of H. L. Mencken,
Kerker Quinn, Reed Whittemore, and William Phillips. His
favorite little magazines are* Hound and Horn *and* The Southern
Review *when it was edited by Robert Penn Warren and Cleanth
Brooks.*

*Mr. Macauley was educated at Kenyon College and the Uni-
versity of Iowa. He has taught at Bard College, the University of
Iowa, the University of North Carolina, Kenyon College, and the
University of Illinois at Chicago Circle. He is the author of a novel,
a collection of short stories, and two books of criticism. His work
has appeared in* Esquire, Playboy, The Partisan Review, The New
York Times Book Review, *and* The New Republic, *and a number
of his stories were selected for the* O. Henry Prize Stories *and* Best
American Short Stories.

In 1939, Kenyon College was a small liberal arts college with
about three hundred students. Hidden on a green hilltop in rural
Ohio, it was noted—when noted at all—for having produced a
number of Ohio politicians and Episcopalian clergymen. John
Crowe Ransom was a fifty-one-year-old professor of English who
had just arrived, after becoming unwelcome at Vanderbilt University for his modernist views about literature. He had published
four first-rate books of poetry and had recently taken to criticism

with *The World's Body*. He had begun to feel that a revaluation of literature by new critical methods was the important work of the time. Gordon Keith Chalmers, former Rhodes scholar, was the ambitious young president of Kenyon. Roberta Teale Schwartz (Chalmers), his wife, was a poet. Mrs. Chalmers suggested that what Kenyon—and the country—needed was a literary-critical review in the grand style of the nineteenth-century *Edinburgh Review* and *Blackwood's*. I was an uneasy sophomore. Like my friends Robert Lowell, Randall Jarrell, and Peter Taylor, I had been drawn there because I'd heard that Ransom was a great teacher.

Like all literary magazines, the *Review* was the combination of a lot of enthusiasm, a little money, and high intentions. Its chief assets were the talents of Ransom and his associate editor, Philip Blair Rice, and an innocent assumption that one could produce a major literary magazine in a sleepy village in Ohio, far away from the vortex of New York. Ransom was, by philosophy, a confirmed provincial, and he believed that as long as the postal system existed, no place was better than any other. He thought of the *Partisan Review,* then the leading magazine of the literary metropolis, as a little flashy and curiously Trotskyite. For him, the Republic of Letters existed in no particular geographical place and Gambier, Ohio, with its good garden space and croquet lawns, was better than most.

In almost every observable normal way, Ransom was conservative—a soft-spoken, smiling, elaborately courteous southern gentleman with a classical education and a high regard for all the most proper traditions of life and letters. But he had one dangerously subversive idea. He felt that the whole matter of writing about literature, and thus of teaching it, had been loose, ill considered, and largely irrelevant. For him, psychological or biographical studies of writers, historical examinations of their times, descriptions of their sources and influences, scrutiny of their moral values were satellite affairs that revealed only vague intimations of the real thing—the work itself. A study of the work itself could show that an author sometimes wrote better than he knew, sometimes wrote counter to the culture that produced him or counter to his most ostensible meanings. This, I think, is what the New Criticism (his book gave the school its name) was largely about. *Kenyon Review* was to be an instrument for bringing to

72

bear the kind of criticism he believed in. (Later on, the New Criticism was to become such a widely accepted—and mechanical —part of academic study that Ransom himself shuddered at it.)

I think that I made a fair general statement of Ransom's and Rice's intentions in a foreword to the *Review*'s twenty-fifth anniversary issue:

Although it never published a manifesto, credo, or formal statement of editorial policy, what the Review *stood for was always perfectly clear. It stood, first of all, for the discussion of values in literature. As Mr. Ransom said, "One of the saving gifts of our age, against the many ways it has devised for being wretched, is its turn for literary criticism, and for a literary criticism evidently so enterprising and acute, and so grounded in good conscience, as can scarcely be predicated of the other periods of literary history." He thought of the era in which the magazine appeared as one of evaluation and critical comprehension rather than one of high creation; it was a time of literary conscience rather than of literary passion. The function of the* Review *was to express that new capability.*

Indeed, it was new. The writers who have recently been deploring "the age of criticism" and writing essays "in defense of ignorance" ought to remember that there was very little American criticism of any value before the 1930s. We were almost totally lacking in what Edmund Wilson described as the "interest of the intelligence fully awakened to the implications of what the artist is doing, that is to say, to his responsibility." Literary journalists often repeat the falsism that the Review *was simply an organ of the New Critics. The truth is that, in 1939, almost any kind of intelligent critic was new—and over the years the* Review *has been hospitable to all varieties of them.*

I suppose that in the history of American literary magazines Ransom's volumes of the *Review* will always be labeled, a journal of criticism that published R. P. Blackmur, Lionel Trilling, William Empson, Richard Ellmann, Robert Penn Warren, Irving Howe, Cleanth Brooks, Kenneth Burke, and many other eminent critics of the time. But that ignores the fact that its pages also included a brilliantly creative collection. Dylan Thomas, Delmore Schwartz, James Dickey, George Seferis, John Berryman, Robert Lowell, Robert Fitzgerald, Wallace Stevens, Randall Jarrell, W. H. Auden, and Robert Graves are just a few of the poets who appeared in the *Kenyon Review.* Some of Bertolt Brecht's plays were printed there for the first time. Boris Pasternak—then quite unknown in this country—contributed a story. But lists of names are not very revealing. It is sufficient to say that the *Review,* in Ransom's time, represented some of the best imaginative writing of the 1940s and 1950s. Some, but not all. It had its shortcomings and omissions. T. S. Eliot did not appear (until much later, just

73

before his death, when I published an interview with him). Saul Bellow was given a cold shoulder. The French existentialists were ignored. The remarkable group of Italian fiction writers who appeared just after World War II went almost unnoticed. Lorca was there, but Neruda was not. There was one story by John Wain, but the "angry young men" in postwar England—Braine, Osborne, and Amis among them—were never represented. Nor was Graham Greene or Frank O'Connor.

Fiction was always one of John Ransom's blind spots. He considered it an interesting semi-art, necessary but usually tedious, and he did not read it often. Once, in the 1950s, he told me that he had discovered a new, clever, young English fiction writer who for some reason had taken the name of a Japanese drink for a pseudonym. I refrained from telling him that "Saki" was not "sake" and that H. H. Munro had been killed in World War I. It was this lack that had something to do with my interest in becoming the second editor of the *Review*.

I respected criticism and wanted to keep up that *Review* tradition—but with rather more maverick critics than John Ransom had printed. I also wanted to do well by the poets, though knowing that my editorial insight could never equal his. But chiefly I hoped that the *Review* could display some of the new talents in fiction. The late 1950s and early 1960s were a promising time for fiction writers. Bellow, Cheever, and Updike had established themselves. Isaac Singer and Bernard Malamud were doing fine work. Ralph Ellison's *Invisible Man* seemed to be the forerunner of new accomplishments by black writers. Kerouac and other Beat generation writers were getting much attention.

Under Ransom's editorship, the *Review* had tended to favor southern fiction: Robert Penn Warren's, Flannery O'Connor's, or Andrew Lytle's. My theory was—and is—that a good literary magazine ought to be about ten years ahead of general acceptance, as experience has proved. This is what avant-garde really means, although the term is often confused, in the minds of editors, with pure experiment for experiment's sake. The chief work of a literary journal is to print the early writing of Hemingways, Faulkners, Marianne Moores, and W. H. Audens rather than the literary curiosities of, say, Gertrude Stein, Eugene Jolas, or Donald Barthelme. That, of course, is not its only obligation but it is a central one.

So in the 1960s I hoped to find the unknown generation of the 1970s—or at least some worthy part of it. Most literary magazine editors share this hope and almost all of us are doomed to half-success. My first teacher and editorial mentor had been Ford Madox Ford who, through the luck of good connections, excellent taste, and the ability to be in the right place at the right time, had produced two excellent magazines. His *English Review,* published in London just before World War I, prospered with such writers as Henry James, D. H. Lawrence, Joseph Conrad, Ezra Pound, and Wyndham Lewis. The *transatlantic review,* edited by Ford in postwar Paris, rode with a generation of writers like James Joyce, Ernest Hemingway, e. e. cummings, and John Dos Passos. In two relatively brief spans, Ford had brought out the best English magazine of its time and the best Paris magazine of the 1920s. That kind of success is difficult, perhaps impossible, to repeat.

When John Ransom turned the *Review* over to me, he said simply, "Now I can get a good night's sleep for the first time in years." One of the reasons for an editor's insomnia is the thought of talented writers he may have rejected, overlooked, or failed to

Robie Macauley, editor of The Kenyon Review *(right), with Assistant Editor Irving Kreutz (left) and John Crowe Ransom,* circa *1959. Photograph by Thomas B. Greenglade.*

75

find. I don't mean that later reputation and acclaim are the sole, or even the most important, criteria; there are a number of now well-known writers I'm glad I rejected and would reject again today. But one does have long-lasting feelings of regret about having turned away or left unnoticed quite a few of the writers who have since proved themselves. With such hindsight, one could produce the most brilliant literary review of its time—but every editor, even the best, is granted no more than his share of foresight.

Still, there are satisfactions. Among fiction writers in my volumes of the *Review* appeared the then unfamiliar names of Joyce Carol Oates, Thomas Pynchon, John Barth, V. S. Naipaul, Doris Lessing, R. Prawer Jhabvala, Mordecai Richler, and Julia O'Faolain. More familiar were Nadine Gordimer, Frank O'Connor, J. F. Powers, Christina Stead, Jessamyn West, and Flannery O'Connor. Sylvia Plath, James Dickey, John Berryman, William Stafford, Robert Lowell, Randall Jarrell, and James Wright were just a few of the poets.

In the mid-1960s, I began to have a sense that the purely literary review was becoming outmoded. It was rather like a Conestoga wagon in the day of the automobile. It arrived four times a year, two hundred pages heavy, and demanded some long evenings of attention. It carried no news—literature is very seldom a matter of news. That was perfectly suitable for Victorian readers but not for modern Americans. We are conditioned to a life of instants: fast food, quick travel, speed reading. Along with that, there was the plain fact that Americans, even the most intelligent, were concerned far less with imaginative writing than with politics, social questions, factual writing of all sorts. It was natural, then, that the most widely read literary journal in the country should be replaced by reviews in a newspaper format. *The New York Review of Books* was full of news (or pseudo news)—the newest reputations in New York, who was savaging whom, what Mary McCarthy thought about Vietnam. The days when crowds waited on the New York docks for the ship carrying the latest installment of *Oliver Twist* and when the backwoods Ohio store of William Dean Howells's boyhood was the scene for debates about *Don Juan* were over. Readers wanted to know immediately what Norman Mailer had felt at the peace march last week in Washington.

All of this, happily, has no effect on the "little" literary magazine (as distinct from the quarterly review). That kind of magazine has the freedom of its enthusiasm and its poverty. It is published for a small group of like-minded readers with enormous tolerance for the worst and the best. It can ignore every rule of current taste and fashion, pay no attention to a hydrogen bomb dropped on Washington, be as eccentric as it wishes, and—this is its reason for being—occasionally find a genius.

The quarterly review, however, in its responsible role as culture-bearer, is constantly encroached on. Its news value is gone. Its function as a developer of new talent has been lessened by the quicker receptivity of the commercial press. I once published in the *Kenyon Review* sections of a novel that became a Literary Guild selection by the next year—and, in different ways, this happens frequently. Once upon a time the *Saturday Evening Post* and *Hound and Horn* were totally different worlds of writing. That is not true of their successors, and, for better or for worse, there are no longer strict highbrow-middlebrow-lowbrow lines in publications.

For these reasons and some personal ones, I left Kenyon in 1966. The *Review* continued for four more years under the editorship of George Lanning until, at last, an economy-minded president of the college decided to end it. There was a little show of mourning when the *New York Herald-Tribune* and the *Times Literary Supplement* deplored its passing, but every publication has its given life span and many of the best die young. In its thirty-one-year history, the *Kenyon Review* did contribute a good deal to the "interest of the intelligence fully awakened to the implications of what the artist is doing, that is to say, to his responsibility," among American readers and teachers. And by that, all John Crowe Ransom's long labor is rewarded.

THE SOUTHERN REVIEW AND A POST-SOUTHERN AMERICAN LETTERS
Lewis P. Simpson

"After Louisiana nothing has been real," Robert Penn Warren said about the early days of The Southern Review *at Louisiana State University in the Huey Long era. Mr. Warren and Cleanth Brooks had been brought to Baton Rouge by a young and remarkably intelligent dean, and encountered a flamboyant university president who, before he was put in jail for misusing college funds, asked the two professors to edit a literary quarterly. Both Brooks and Warren were graduates of Vanderbilt; both had been Rhodes scholars in the early thirties; both were Agrarians and involved with the New Criticism. The magazine they edited tried to interpret the South to the nation, and to relate national issues to the southern literary scene.*

Lewis P. Simpson places their Southern Review *(old series) in the context of the history of southern magazines, both after the Civil War and after World War I. He then relates the magazine's new series (since 1965) to the dialectic between history and tradition carried over from the earlier phase. The main focus of the magazine during the past eighteen years has been, he admits, "retrospective," looking back to the issues of modernism and to the great modernist writers. Speaking as the co-editor of* The Southern Review, *Mr. Simpson writes: "We have said, if mostly by inference, that the sixties and seventies are not a time of literary origination but a time of falling off from the literary intelligence." He sees a contraction of what he calls "the public space of literature."*

Lewis P. Simpson, William A. Read Professor of English at Louisiana State University, is a literary historian with a particular interest in the history of the literary profession in America. This interest extends to the history of American periodicals, especially those published in New England and the South. The present essay is part of a work-in-progress on the continuity of the southern literary expression from colonial times to the present.

Mr. Simpson is the author of The Man of Letters in New England and the South *and* The Dispossessed Garden: Pastoral and History in Southern Literature. *He has also written a history of* The Monthly Anthology and Boston Review *(1803-1811), published together with selections from its pages as* The Federalist Literary Mind. *He has edited the writings of Cleanth Brooks in* The Possibilities of Order, *which contains a long theoretical and retrospective conversation between Brooks and Warren. Mr. Simpson is the editor of the Library of Southern Civilization series of the Louisiana State University Press; has served on the editorial board of* American Literature; *and has received fellowships for his scholarly work from the Guggenheim Foundation and from the National Endowment for the Humanities.*

The historical character of the literary periodical is immutable. It cannot for a moment be separated from its context in the accumulative literary record. Unlike a play by Shakespeare, an ode by Keats, a lyric by Wordsworth, a novel by Joyce, a periodical never achieves—in a single issue, in a single volume, in its whole serial run—even a quasi transcendence. Its historicity is germane to its origins in the seventeenth and eighteenth centuries, when the extension of the printing technology brought literature and printing into an absolute relationship and literature became identified primarily with what is made public in printed form. The periodical became the answer to the need for conveying literary news and argument. Its historicity was greatly reinforced when it took the form of the review journals of the nineteenth century, like the *Edinburgh Review* and the *Quarterly Review*. It then became the record of a critical debate or dialectic about the nature and influence of literature as an institution. It became a record of the struggle of literature for self-interpretation and historical definition in a civilization that, in embracing science, technology, and industrialism, had entered into a state of continuous revolution. Today when we pick up, say, a forty-five-year-old number of an American literary quarterly (often a hybrid form, a mingling of the critical quarterly and the general literary magazine, containing not only essays and reviews but stories and poems), we may find in it a poem, a story, or an essay that we have long regarded as speaking with its own luminous autonomy. We are slightly shocked to see it in a magazine. Marked by periodicity, it seems to bear the aspect of mortality. It assumes the appearance of an artifact of literary history; and we are averse to relics, sharing as we do the inclination of men over the last two centuries to be so historical that we are impatient with history. Nothing is so old as yesterday's news, and this includes the literary news. Many of us have probably not heard of the journal or the editor, but the archetypal literary periodical is Pierre Bayle's *Nouvelles de la République des Lettres* (1684–1718).

I set down these observations not for what they may be worth as summary wisdom, which is no doubt very little, but because they have grown out of my effort to inquire into a seemingly small and specific question: the circumstances under which the publication of the *Southern Review* at Louisiana State University was renewed in 1965 after a lapse of twenty-three years. The circumstances—I realize now far more than I did ten or twelve years ago—were something more than adventitious. Indeed the historical connection between the *Southern Review* of the 1960s and 1970s and the *Southern Review* of the 1930s and 1940s is absolutely fundamental to our place in the present-day spectrum of American literary quarterlies. I shall not only dwell on this connection but expand upon it—at the expense of ignoring other important aspects of the present *Southern Review* which would be included in a longer discussion, as, for instance, our publication of a variety of young poets, fictionists, and critics.

1

A preface to the first number of the new series, in January 1965, recognizes the outward circumstances of the resumption. These were quite regular. Certain persons who were strongly interested in renewal were located in the right niches of power, including the late Nathaniel M. Caffee, professor of English and dean of the Baton Rouge campus of the university; the president of the university system, John A. Hunter; the dean of the Graduate School, Max M. Goodrich; and the chairman of the English

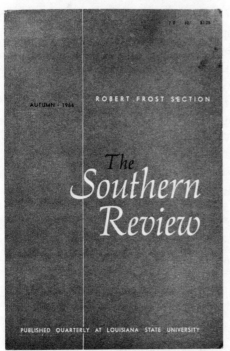

The Southern Review, *Vol. 2, No. 4 (N.S.), Autumn 1966 (courtesy Northwestern University Library).*

department, Thomas A. Kirby. In 1963 an administrative decision to renew publication was implemented by the appointment of a faculty committee to assist in planning the resumption. This prepared the way for appointment of the present staff. Donald E. Stanford and Lewis P. Simpson, of the Baton Rouge campus, were made co-editors; and Rima Drell Reck, of the New Orleans campus (now called the University of New Orleans), was named associate editor. Patt Foster Robertson was appointed the first business manager. (Subsequently Karen R. Paterson served as business manager, succeeded by Sarah E. East and Susan Polock.) Temporary office space was secured in the administration building of the College of Agriculture. (This had nothing to do with the association between the original series of the *Southern Review* and the Agrarian Movement.) By mid-1963 we were in business, and before long had arranged to engage the services of Franklin Press, Baton Rouge, printers of the 1935–1942 series. Save for an alteration of the cover design, the editors decided that the second series of the *Southern Review* would appear in a format identical with that of the original series. Later, when the William

Byrd Press of Richmond, Virginia, took over the printing of the magazine (in 1975), the paper and typeface were altered, but the general resemblance to the original series has been maintained.

There was an element of the purely fortuitous in the printing arrangements, yet they were symbolic of a continuity between the original and the new series of the *Southern Review* that was deeper than appearance. The continuity was not sought as a matter of deliberate editorial policy. When Cleanth Brooks—who, with Robert Penn Warren, served as managing editor of the original series—was questioned about the direction a reinstituted *Southern Review* should take, he remarked that it should take one as different from that of the magazine of 1935–1942 as the literary situation demanded; and this, he thought, might mean a quite different direction. But the road taken by the new series of the *Southern Review* has not been a different one, because its editors have found that the literary situation requires a sequential direction. A divergent road *might* have been taken in the new series if its co-editors had been younger. But their literary education was primarily shaped by the age which nurtured the original series—that of the southern renaissance or, more broadly speaking, of the second American renaissance. Their response to literature at any time could not fail to be governed, in considerable part, by the powerful sensibility of an age that seemed to be revolutionary but is to be understood in perspective as one which found an often contradictory, though massive and brilliant, motive as it struggled to recover the use of letters as a functional arena of civilization, as an arena of discourse, as a public space—the literary *res publica*—in which the drama of existence is portrayed and the proper relation and separation of the elements of order is discussed.

2

The reconstruction of the public space of literature in the post–World War I situation notably involved the relation between history and tradition. Nothing had so decisively manifested itself in the eighteenth and nineteenth centuries as the concept of the historicity of man, society, and the world. All concepts of permanence were abandoned; all forms of order, including all forms of transcendent order, seemed to become irreversibly subject to

82

the process of historical transformation. The modern historical sensibility began to appear in the disappearance of the corporate sensibility of Christendom—at that point marked, T. S. Eliot says, by a "dissociation of sensibility." In the vacuum left by the separation of sensation and intellect, poets and philosophers perceived with uneasy and increasing conviction the total historicity of perception itself.

And yet it seemed—and has not yet seemed too late—to defy such a closure of vision by the truth of tradition: to assert the past in the present, not as integral to ongoing process, but as integral to the ongoing incorporation or assimilation of literature to the mystery of existence, which is, properly speaking, the reference of all history.

The effective representation of the arena of discourse, of the literary order, has depended on the portrayal in poetry, fiction, drama, and essay of the struggle that, myriad in its definition of issues, has fundamentally assumed the form of a conflict between history and tradition as modes of existence. But as the struggle in most respects has become more and more weighted on the side of historicism—on the side of scientific determinism in the interpretation of the consciousness of man, society, and the world—the historicist interpretation has tended to close around the public space of letters. This tendency could result, we may suppose, in the absolute alienation of literature from existence, and hence the destruction of the peculiarly modern realm of moral and spiritual literacy.

The American republic has a significant source of origin in an unprecedented extension of the public space of literacy. In America it has been assumed that the existence of the state is synonymous with the lettered condition of its citizens. In actuality, the autonomy of the Republic of Letters has been modified, if not disposed of, by the American assumption that this realm could be incarnated in history. An American destruction of the literary realm, to be sure, was seen to be a distinct possibility by the Federalist literati during the first two decades of the new nation. One of the early nineteenth-century New England periodicals, the *Monthly Anthology and Boston Review,* expresses the fear that the American attempt to be the historical embodiment of the Republic of Letters may convert the literary order into an amorphous "democracy of letters." From this time on, we can trace a quarrel in American magazines between an endorsement of the prescriptive custody of literacy and the advocacy of its democratization. In mid-nineteenth-century America the issue gets rather neatly dramatized in the opposition between the *Whig Review* and the *United States Magazine and Democratic Review*. But it is too simple to say that the one magazine supported a traditionalist view of culture and the other the historically determined rise of democracy. Writers were often pulled different ways. It was not always easily possible to belong either to the movement or the establishment—to employ the Emersonian terms, to the "Party of the Past" or the "Party of the Future." Neither Emerson nor Thoreau, although denying the past at their backs, divested themselves of classicist attitudes. While they internalized the dialect of tradition and history, it is a major force in the works of both. In spite of their vision of an anti-traditionalist, autonomous self triumphing over history, they were participants in the literary dialectic and helped to prevent the realm of discourse from closure, either by assimilation to the democratic state or to the compelling historical determinism which culminated in a Henry Adams.

The literary situation in the nineteenth-century South was not the same as that in New England and the East. In the South the realm of public literacy was virtually closed by the defense of slavery. The dialectic of history and tradition ceased.

Chattel slavery, as it existed in the American South, was not a traditional but a novel institution. It began in historical contingency and was perpetuated first as an expediency and then as a singular historical necessity in the planting states. When the "peculiar institution" came under attack, its defense ultimately demanded its identification with the state. The assimilation of slavery to the state meant also that the realms of both religious and literary expression were assimilated to the state. Before this finally happened, a notable tendency in the southern literary mind was to evade the relationship of literature to slavery by isolating literature in a classical piety. This motive is implied in Hugh Swinton Legaré's depiction of the holy commonwealth of secular letters in the leading essay of the first number of the first quarterly to bear the title *The Southern Review* (published in Charleston,

84

South Carolina, 1828–1832). Legaré says that a classical literary education will let a young man "into that great communion of scholars throughout all ages and nations—like that more awful communion of saints in the Holy Church Universal," and he will "feel a sympathy with departed genius, and with the enlightened and the great minds of other countries, as they appear before him, in the transports of a Vision Beatific, bowing down at the same shrines and glowing with the same holy love of whatever is most pure and fair and exalted and divine in human nature." As the assimilation of letters to the state proceeded in the Old South, the purity of the literary realm began to be defined in prescriptive terms—which is to say in terms of whether or not literature in any way questioned the institution of slavery. When the editor of the *Southern Literary Messenger* was accused of "injudicious leniency towards Northern books and authors," Paul Hamilton Hayne of *Russell's Magazine* offered a curious defense of his fellow editor:

Now, it seems that when a work is purely literary, interfering in no way with the "peculiar institution," or our rights under it, common honesty requires that it should be reviewed without reference to the birth-place of its author, or the locale of its publication. A true literary spirit is essentially liberal, and the Editor who should arraign Irving's "Washington" or Hawthorne's Tales, upon the charge that their authors were Northern men, would be guilty evidently of the grossest absurdity.

That a young southern man of letters could make such a statement in the late 1850s indicates the extent to which the literary order and the world of the slaveholders had been joined.

The reopening of the public space of literacy in the South after the Civil War was signified by the inauguration of the second quarterly to be named the *Southern Review*. Published in Baltimore from 1867 through 1879, the second *Southern Review* was edited by the aging Albert Taylor Bledsoe. Known in the antebellum South as a proslavery advocate and in the Reconstruction as an unreconstructible fire-eater, Bledsoe was a man of letters and mathematician of very considerable learning. In the first essay in the initial number of the Baltimore *Southern Review*, taking as his point of departure the works of Vico, Lessing, Hegel, and Schlegel, Bledsoe anticipates the disposition of the twentieth-century southern literary mind to enter into the deeper levels of the relationship of tradition and history. "The history of civilization," he says, "is nearly, if not absolutely, the same as the Philosophy of History, or the Education of Mankind." (This statement is prefaced by the remark, "The Philosophy of History is one of the creations of modern genius.") The sense of history as the symbol of civilizational existence, expressing itself in one way in the formation of an Old South–New South opposition, was embodied in William Porterfield Trent's founding of the *Sewanee Review,* a magazine which has had continuous publication since its inception and is justly entitled to its claim to be the nation's oldest literary quarterly. A few years later, a similar sense of history was embodied in another continuing periodical venture, the *South Atlantic Quarterly,* which was launched in 1902 by John Spencer Bassett at Trinity College (now Duke University) in Durham, North Carolina. Other significant periodical ventures responded to the impulse of the southern literary mind to reconstruct the literary polity. Among these were the *Texas Review,* established at the University of Texas in 1915 (transferred to Southern Methodist University in 1924 and renamed the *Southwest Review*), and the *Virginia Quarterly Review,* established at the University of Virginia in 1925. Meanwhile the reopening of the literary realm in the South evidenced itself in the appearance of several independent little magazines, among them the *Double-Dealer* in New Orleans and the *Fugitive* in Nashville. The last (published from 1922 through 1925), like the *Dial* of Emerson and Margaret Fuller in New England eighty years earlier, has exerted a lasting literary power. The *Fugitive* of John Crowe Ransom, Donald Davidson, Allen Tate, and Robert Penn Warren not only expanded the realm of literary discourse in the South but pushed its boundaries outward to embrace the modernist discussion of history and tradition.

Poetry, the oracle, is gone. Our time cleaves to no racial myth, its myth is the apotheosis of machinery. Perhaps Oswald Spengler is right: a man is a fool to be an artist or a poet in this age. But at least our poet is aware of his own age, barren of any art though it may be, for he can't write like Homer or Milton now; from the data of his experience he infers only a distracting complexity.

Thus Allen Tate in the *Fugitive* in 1924. He is continuing a "discussion of the future of modern poetry" begun by Ransom in the preceding number. Within a few years several of the more prominent Fugitives would inaugurate the Agrarian Movement—

86

which, although it has been widely misinterpreted as a political movement (a misunderstanding promoted by the agrarians' own misinterpretation of their basic motives)—was a literary movement. As the Transcendental Movement opened the New England mind fully to nineteenth-century literary discourse, the Agrarian Movement opened the southern mind fully to the discourse of the twentieth century. In so doing, it substantiated the modern realm of letters in the South and provided for the southern literary renaissance. The third southern quarterly to be called the *Southern Review* (1935–1942) was the most effective critical expression of this flowering. It appeared at the point when the dialectic of history and tradition, focused and developed by the *Fugitive* group and the agrarians, was ripe for consolidation on a broader, more reflective, and more sophisticated level.

The story of the publication of the *Southern Review* at Louisiana State University in the years of the Louisiana hayride has acquired an aura of legend. Looking back on that time, Robert Penn Warren commented, "After Louisiana nothing has been real." He was no doubt thinking about the strange improbability of certifiable circumstances in the Louisiana of the Huey Long epoch. Among these was Warren's reunion at LSU with the slightly younger Cleanth Brooks. Both graduates of Vanderbilt, both fresh from the experience of being Rhodes scholars at Oxford (Warren, B. Litt., 1930; Brooks, B. Litt., 1932), both close to the Agrarian Movement (although Brooks had not been a contributor to *I'll Take My Stand*), they were joined in academic destiny as though by happenstance. But it was, in good measure, owing to a greater improbability of the time: the appointment of Charles Wooten Pipkin to the deanship of a fledgling LSU Graduate School. Pipkin, a native of Arkansas, was thirty-two years old when he became the graduate dean at LSU. He too had been at Vanderbilt; he too, after a short period at Harvard, had been at Oxford. A political scientist whose fame in his field made him a full professor at twenty-eight, Pipkin exemplified the recrudescence of Jeffersonian cosmopolitanism in the post–World War I age. He was a twentieth-century *philosophe,* a forceful advocate of the League of Nations and of the "redemption of the South through education." Alex Daspit, who knew Pipkin both as a student and a colleague, has recently said of him:

He [Pipkin] criticized university programs which "had grown from catechisms of denominational colleges to the vast catholicity of curricula which mean nothing . . . [,] this animated academic circus of mediocrity and miscellany." He derided the "righteous contentment of many college professors who are embalmed within the shroud of a Ph.D." and, surveying the result of much of what has passed for academic research, observed that if Dr. Johnson were alive, "he would not overlook the vast possibilities of the word 'research' as the last refuge of the scoundrel."

Pipkin set as the minimum objective of the LSU Graduate School (in his own words) "a greater immediate realization of the inherent capacities of the southern regions and a more vital reintegration of the regional culture in the national scene." Neither his emphasis on employing graduate education in the pursuit of, as he said, "the optimum conditions of the good society," nor his contention that "the American is a world citizen inheriting his internationalism from the great power of the industrial potential of the United States," was compatible with the agrarian perspective. But Pipkin's stress on the southern intellectual as a cultural redeemer fell within the ambience of literary modernism. While his outlook was directed toward historical necessity (industrialism) rather than traditionalism (agrarianism), Pipkin had the vision to allow for the marshaling of all "the skills necessary to utilize the existing resources of the [Southern] land and the people." Robert Penn Warren and Cleanth Brooks, opponents of the industrialization of the South though they might be, were among its promising cultural resources. Pipkin brought them to LSU, as he did Albert R. Erskine, Jr., a student at Vanderbilt during Warren's brief teaching stint there following his Oxford days. Erskine was the first business manager of the *Southern Review*. (In 1940 John Palmer, another Rhodes scholar, replaced Erskine.)

Another person in the improbable mix of the times at LSU was the president of the university, James Monroe Smith, whose flamboyant misuse of university bonds eventually resulted in his incarceration in the state penitentiary at Angola. (A photograph in *Life* shows Smith in striped prison garb at work in a prison sugarcane field.) Fortunately, Smith had a regard for the university as well as for himself. Somehow (on this point the record seems to be obscure) he saw, or was made to see, the attractive possibilities of a first-class literary quarterly at LSU. Emulating the administrative style of the Long era, on one improbable Sunday afternoon in late February 1935 he drove up to Robert Penn Warren's residence in Baton Rouge and invited Warren and his guest, Albert Erskine, to go for a ride. The story is told by Brooks and Warren in their introduction to *Stories from the Southern Review*:

> While the official black Cadillac crunched the gravel of the back roads, President James Monroe Smith revealed the motive of his invitation. Was it possible, he wanted to know, to have a good literary and critical quarterly at the university. Yes, was the answer he got—yes, if you paid a fair rate for contributions, gave writers decent company between the covers, and concentrated editorial authority sufficiently for the magazine to have its own distinctive character and quality. There was one more stipulation: that quality must not be diluted or contravened by the interference of academic committees or officials. How much would it cost? Toward $10,000 a year.

Smith suggested that Warren and Erskine confer with Pipkin and Brooks and promised to authorize funds for the magazine upon receiving a statement of the plans for it. He received this the next day. In June 1935 the first issue appeared, the masthead carrying Pipkin as the editor and Brooks and Warren as the managing editors. So in an improbable time and place—in a time of bizarre political corruption mingled with intellectual and literary excitement, in a provincial state university in the Deep South—a distinguished literary magazine came into its improbable being. A few years later, when the scandals broke at LSU and Smith went to prison, the unlikely circumstances which had created the *Southern Review* disappeared. The entrance of the United States into World War II was sufficient reason for an institution still affectionately known, in tribute to its origin, as the "Ole War Skule," to remove the *Review* from its budget.

3

The first number of the Pipkin-Brooks-Warren *Southern Review* had been preceded by a prospectus which avowed that the chief aim of the quarterly would be "to define large issues" and "to attempt interpretation of the contemporary scene." To this end it would publish essays on "social, economic, political and literary topics, fiction, poetry, and reviews of current books"—these to be written by a cosmopolitan authorship which would include not only established writers but new ones, their works to be judged uniformly on the basis of "significance and artistic excellence." It was within the amplitude of such intentions that the *Southern Review* would "aim at presenting and interpreting Southern problems to a national audience and at relating national issues to the Southern scene."* To the extent that the original series of the *Southern Review* carried out its ambitiously broad editorial policy —and this was to a considerable degree—the new series is obviously not continuous with it. Our policy, set down early in the planning stage of the resumption, was more narrowly literary. That policy, however, represented more decisively the editorial practice in the original series: to make literature the most prominent subject. It may be observed, too, that the continuity of the original and the new series does not lie merely in subject-matter emphasis; it lies in similarity of tone and temper.

Some of our readers have remarked, as a matter of fact, that our endeavor is chiefly retrospective, and their criticism is not without justification. The first issue of the new series begins with an essay on Ransom and includes essays on the agrarians, Yeats, Céline, Faulkner, and D. H. Lawrence. Throughout the first eleven volumes of the new series, and in the two numbers of the twelfth volume published by the time of this writing, similar attention is given to writers who had their beginnings in the twenties and thirties. No special number has been devoted to writing during the sixties or the seventies. Special numbers or special sections of the magazine have been devoted to Frost, Wallace Stevens, Yeats, Caroline Gordon, Faulkner, and Mark Twain. Other special issues deal with such general subjects as the French literature of the past 150 years and the literature of the 1920s. Five numbers given over to the subject of writing in the South have mostly looked backward.

I may be giving the impression that the continuity between the original and the new series of the *Southern Review* has the character of a pietistic response to a brilliant past. Yet I would say that whatever piety there is in our inclination to retrospection is dominated by a more complex impulse toward continuity: the

*I am indebted to Ronda Cabot Tentarelli for the quotations from the prospectus, which she discovered in the files of the LSU student newspaper, *The Reveille* (April 16, 1935). See Tentarelli, "The Life and Times of the *Southern Review*," *Southern Studies* 16 (Summer 1977). This essay places the first series of the *Southern Review* in the context of the thirties.

perpetuation of the dialectic of history and tradition. This motive has never been formally recognized by the editors. They have accepted its presence as implicit in the historical act of resuming the publication of the *Review*. Because it is a policy statement as well as an advertisement, a few words from a brochure prepared by the editors during the fourth year of the new series are worth quoting. Addressed to potential contributors and subscribers, this states in part:

The new Southern Review *is maintaining the original high standards [of the 1935–42 publication] by drawing on the resources of writers from the South and other regions of the USA and abroad. It continues to bring the readers a variety of poetry, fiction, critical essays and book reviews of lasting merit. The editors believe that a serious interest in literature starts from the present and that contemporary literature matters because it is the consciousness of our own age. Emphasis is on the twentieth century, although criticism that furnishes fresh insights into the literature of the past and essays that deal with the culture and history of the South are also published. There are frequent bilingual poems and essays dealing with contemporary European literature. Emphasizing technical discipline in fiction and poetry and clear thinking in critical essays,* The Southern Review *invites you to recognize new talents and rediscover established writers.*

After the passing of another eight years or so, I find this statement both puzzling and illuminating. (Of course I do not speak for the other editors.) What is meant by the declaration that "a serious interest in literature starts from the present"? What present? What is meant by the term "contemporary"? By the phrase "the consciousness of our own age"? What, in fact, is meant by "our own age"? And why are readers and/or other writers invited to "rediscover established writers"? In 1968, when the above statement was published, had established writers become so disestablished that they needed "rediscovering"? Who are "established" writers anyway? Our advertisement of our virtues in 1968, it seems to me by hindsight, is ambivalent. If we attempted to devise a similar advertisement today, would it be less so? I doubt it. In its uncertainties the 1968 statement reflects a longterm situation in America, one in which an unprecedented degree of literary activity is accompanied by an unprecedented literary eclecticism. It is a time when not only a great literary movement—modernism—is ending, but a time when the very power of literature as a civilizational order seems to be suffering depletion.

As can be seen in the light of eleven years of publication, the

Southern Review, new series, has assumed a certain editorial mission of continuity through retrospection. In doing so we have possibly thought to influence the literary future. In the 1930s the modernist recovery of tradition often bore the paradoxical guise of an avant-garde mission (T. S. Eliot being the exemplary instance); and the original series of the *Southern Review,* in its association with the "new criticism," seemed prospective instead of retrospective. Its editors believed that a "serious interest in literature starts from the present," for the present comprehends the past and in this comprehension implies the future. The *Southern Review* of the sixties and seventies has remained within the aura of modernism: seeing contemporary writing not as postmodern but as related to the continuity of modernity, seeing our immediate age as still giving literary expression to the sense of history and tradition as conflicting modes of existence. The original series of the *Southern Review* commented on this conflict in the leading essay of the first number in 1935. Entitled "Culture Versus Colonialism in America," the essay is by Herbert Agar, who a year before had won the Pulitzer Prize in history for his book *The People's Choice.* Accepting the Spenglerian cyclical view of history, Agar questions whether the struggle between "the deep instinctive faith which is the essence of the Culture and an abstractly rationalizing self-destructive element which is a feature of man's mind" must necessarily be resolved in favor of doubt, disillusionment, and death. America's large cities, he contends, are colonial outposts of Europe; in them America imitates an "alien . . . old age." The saving native American tradition lies in the provinces. Agar expresses the general hope of the agrarians: the redemption of America by a provincial assertiveness, particularly in the South. But the fundamental significance of his essay is more general. Projecting the dialectical drama of history and tradition in the initial essay in the Pipkin-Brooks-Warren *Southern Review,* it suggests this drama as the contextual image of the magazine.

We have sought to perpetuate this image. We have said, if mostly by inference, that the sixties and seventies are not a time of literary origination but a time of falling off from the literary intelligence. We have said, if only by implication, that the falling off from the literary establishment—which has included the dis-

92

avowal of Eliot and Hemingway, though not so much of Joyce and Faulkner—has left a vacuum. In contrast to the disassociated personalism of post–World War II poets and novelists, the writers of the "second flowering" (Malcolm Cowley's term) represented the tradition that literature is integral to the corporate structure of civilization. Their thrust was toward the restoration of this structure; they aspired to contribute to the literature of civilization. The *Southern Review* of recent years, aspiring to recover the impulse of the second flowering, has represented a critical effort that might be dubbed the recovery of a recovery. Like our most direct competitor, the *Sewanee Review,* we have affirmed the validity of the great literature of restoration created by the "traditionalist moderns." Underlying this critical redundancy is the concept that the literary quarterly functions, as Allen Tate said in the *Southern Review* in 1935, through the "conviction of being a part of literature."

In the late twentieth century the best news the literary journal can report from the failing Republic of Letters is the feasibility of its restoration and perpetuation. Approaches to this subject in the new series of the *Southern Review* include (as a result of the editorial energy and acumen of Donald E. Stanford) essays both by and about Eric Voegelin, whose monumental *Order and History* is becoming recognized as one of the key works of the twentieth-century restorationist movement. Other *Review* essays pertinent to this movement are those by and about Brooks and Warren; several essays by Cowley should be mentioned, including one in the Winter 1976 number on the concept of literary generations. Then, too, there are the writings of younger authors who may be referred to as neo-restorationists; prominent among them is Wendell Berry, the Kentucky poet-novelist-essayist, whose search for a relation to the land is at once a repudiation of agrarianism and a quest in its own right.

But it must be admitted that the restorationist motive is haunted by the suspicion of its mere redundancy. This is especially so in the South, where the twentieth-century literary flowering has been not truly a second flowering but more nearly a first one, which moreover, holds no promise of a second. Moving into the last quarter of the twentieth century, we may well have reached the point from which we can look back on southern writers from

1920 to the 1960s as belonging to a distinct phase of modern literature—as, in spite of their diversity, having made in sum a literary movement, one distinguishable from the cosmopolitan modern movement by its own historical coherence, yet deeply identified with it as a symbol of the corporate activity of the literary order. By the sixties the southern movement, like the New England movement of 1820–1860, was reaching a stage of exhaustion. Unlike the New England movement, the southern movement is not, it would seem, to have a long aftermath continuous with a still unfolding literary modernity. The southern E. A. Robinsons, Robert Frosts, Robert Lowells will not appear; for the southern movement (continuous with Proust, Yeats, Joyce, Mann, Kafka, Pound, Eliot, Ford, Auden) has symbolized literary modernity in its finality, and itself has been one of the final phases of modernity.

When it is hinted that the postmodern world—announced by Hiroshima but struggling to be born long before Hiroshima—may take the shape of a nonliterary world, we are extremely resentful of such a notion and are helpless before it. We cannot discuss a nonliterary world, for a world in which the public space of literacy has disappeared is undiscussable. Standing in the evanescent margins of the dialectic of history and tradition, we seek the shape of postmodernity by trying to imagine a world without the antithesis of history and tradition. The shape of such a world may already have formed; it may be familiar now in existentialist interpretation. We are inclined nonetheless to see existentialist concepts as versions of historical interpretation and to oppose these to traditionalism. We want desperately to hold onto the tension between history and tradition as modes of existence; for in this tension we have defined the modern mode of existence we call literature. But the tension is no longer a vitalizing experience, a ratification of being—even in the literary mind of the South, which recently knew it strongly and intimately. The lapse of the literary dialectic is variously recorded in the *Southern Review*: one powerful instance is Walker Percy's essay "The Delta Factor"; other striking instances are Walter Sullivan's essays "Death by Melancholy" and "The Decline of Myth in Southern Fiction." The dialectic of the secular realm of letters provided a context for the discussion of the opposing theories of man as organism (physical and social) and man as soul; for the drama of the false divinization of secular letters (Hegel called this the "secularization of spirituality") and the rise of the writer as pseudo priest. In the void left by the depletion of the literary dialogue, we have the anguish of Percy and Sullivan about the meaning of language and about the status of the literary vocation. In different ways, Percy and Sullivan intimate a reunification of church and letters in a reclamation of the religious view.

In the broadest sense, the significance of the *Southern Review,* new series, has been its continuation of the argument between history and tradition as modes of symbolizing existence. But the very act of continuation has constantly insinuated the question, is the continuity meaningful? Have we entered a completely historical age—an age so possessed by history as process that it has no past at all? If so, there is no need for literary journals. There is no news from the nonexistent Republic of Letters. Yet, locked in the history it depicts, a literary quarterly like the *Southern Review* cannot predict the end of the literary world, but only record it. So far, it seems to me, the *Southern Review* has in the past twelve years recorded—a century after the lapse of a New England American letters—the coming of post-southern American letters. And this may be a less conclusive situation than I have indicated. Academic insolence compels one to prophecy; but if we can detach ourselves from the dialectic of history and tradition, we may find that we have scarcely imagined the possibilities of literature under the conditions of a fully realized historical existence.

A note on the Southern Review authors

The *Southern Review* (1935–42) was a young person's enterprise. Writers in their fifties, like John Crowe Ransom and Wallace Stevens, constituted a minority of its authorship, which included several poets (among them W. H. Auden, John Berryman, and Randall Jarrell) and a number of fiction writers (among them Andrew Lytle, Peter Taylor, and Eudora Welty) who were barely beyond apprenticeship. Robert Penn Warren was only a slightly older presence among the poets and storytellers of the original series; "How Willie Proudfit Came Home" introduced the memorable character subsequently to appear in Warren's first novel,

Night Rider. The original series also included several youthful critics, notably R. P. Blackmur ("Humanism and the Symbolic Imagination") and Cleanth Brooks ("Three Revolutions in Poetry"). Allen Tate, whose career as poet and critic was fully mature by 1935, was thirty-six years old the year the original series commenced. His contributions to it included "Literature as Knowledge," a key essay in the southern movement.

The *Southern Review* series beginning in 1965 displays a numerous and diversified authorship. But among its important contributors are more than thirty writers who appeared in the original series. These include Ransom (who died in 1975), author of three essays, one being his significant revisionary estimate of Eliot; Warren, the author of no less than seven essays, the latest being a portion of his recent book, *Democracy and Poetry;* and Brooks, the author of five essays, one of them (Fall 1976) being an interesting appraisal of "Allen Tate and the Nature of Modernism." Other contributors to the present series who had been associated with the southern movement of the twenties and thirties are Eudora Welty, Katherine Anne Porter, Caroline Gordon, Donald Davidson (died 1968), Jarrell (died 1965), Lytle, and Tate. Of course numerous writers of non-southern origins appeared in the 1935–42 *Review,* and several have reappeared in the new series. Kay Boyle, Mary McCarthy, Josephine Miles, Kenneth Burke, Howard Baker, and Arthur Mizener may be mentioned. Nor should we fail to mention Joseph Frank (distinguished studies of Chernyshevsky and Dostoevsky), the late Yvor Winters ("Forms of Discovery" and "The Poetry of T. Sturge Moore"), and James T. Farrell (an evocative prize story, "An American Student in Paris"). Malcolm Cowley, who appears in the original series only as a correspondent but whose acquaintance with the American literary scene of the twenties and thirties is unparalleled, has been an outstanding contributor to the *Southern Review* in the past ten years. His essays—on Conrad Aiken, on the concept of literary generations, on a visit with the agrarians in the depression years—are rich in literary history and in critical suggestion. Cowley's contemporary, Matthew Josephson, has also contributed valuable reminiscent views.

Writers of first importance in the new series whose careers originated in the twenties and thirties but who cannot be conveniently categorized are the emigrés René Wellek and Eric Voegelin. Voegelin is especially to be noted, for when he left his homeland in the thirties he came to LSU; there (although not a contributor to the original series of the *Southern Review*) he wrote much of his monumental *Order and History*. The impact of Voegelin's mind on historical, political, and philosophical studies is beginning to be grasped; the relation of his thought to literary studies is scarcely yet appreciated, but its relevance to literature is cogently suggested in his essay on Henry James's *The Turn of the Screw* (new series, VII, Winter 1973).

While the prevalence of an older generation of writers in the new series indicates its restorationist quality, a mingling of generations is evident in most numbers. A good many writers whose careers originated in the late 1940s and in the 1950s appear: Louis D. Rubin, Jr., Thomas Parkinson, Sherman Paul, Elizabeth Spencer, Walter Sullivan, Thomas Daniel Young, John Hazard Wildman, Walker Percy, Charles East. More significant, possibly, is the presence of a considerable number of writers whose careers are more or less contemporary with the new series. Joyce Carol Oates has made repeated contributions, not only as storyteller but as poet and essayist. H. E. Francis, Philip O'Connor, Gordon Weaver, and John Gardner (a part of the novel *Nickel Mountain*) are in the pages of the new series. Reynolds Price ("The Knowledge of My Mother's Coming Death" and other stories), David Madden ("Traven" and "No Trace"), and John William Corrington ("Pleadings") are among new series fiction writers who are associated with southern writing. The more recent poets in the current series make up a large and eclectic group, including W. S. Merwin, James Seay, Daniel Hoffman, Robert Hollander, James McMichael, Mona Van Duyn, Stanley Plumly, Turner Cassity, Catherine Savage Brosman, besmilr brigham, Wendell Berry, William Heyen, and Miller Williams (a group of his poems was featured in the Summer 1976 issue as he prepared to leave for a year abroad on a Prix de Rome fellowship). Younger critical voices heard in the new series include George Lensing, Ronald Moran, Kenneth Fields, Marion Montgomery, George Core, and Maureen Henry.

An analysis of categories of authorship in the new series should include foreign authors. The bilingual publication of such poets as Osip Mandelstam, George Seferis, Pablo Neruda, and Eugenio Montale has been a feature in many numbers. British and Irish writers (George MacBeth, Kathleen Raine, Patricia Hutchins, Graham Hough, W. W. Robson, Mary Lavin, Denis Donoghue) have often been present.

Significant articles reflective of American literary life

Wendell Berry, "The Regional Motive," *Southern Review,* n.s. 6 (Fall 1970).

Cleanth Brooks, "The Current State of American Literature," *Southern Review,* n.s. 9 (Spring 1973).

Malcolm Cowley, " 'And Jesse Begat . . . ': A Note on Literary Generations," *Southern Review,* n.s. 12 (Winter 1976).

William C. Havard, "The New Mind of the South," *Southern Review,* n.s. 4 (Fall 1968).

Andrew Lytle, "The State of Letters in a Time of Disorder," *Sewanee Review,* 79 (Autumn 1971).

Walker Percy, "The Man on the Train: Three Existential Modes," *Partisan Review,* 23 (Fall 1956).

_____, "The Delta Factor: How I Discovered the Delta Factor Sitting at My Desk One Summer Day in Louisiana in the 1950s Thinking about an Event in the Life of Helen Keller on Another Summer Day in Alabama in 1887," *Southern Review,* n.s. 11 (Winter 1975).

John Crowe Ransom, "Art and the Human Economy," *Kenyon Review* (Autumn 1945).

_____, "The Concrete Universal: Observations on the Understanding of Poetry," *Kenyon Review,* 17 (Summer 1955).

Adrienne Rich, "The Kingdom of the Fathers," *Partisan Review,* 43, No. 1 (1976).

Louis D. Rubin, Jr., "The South and the Faraway Country," *Virginia Quarterly Review,* 38 (Summer 1962).

_____, "Southerners and Jews," *Southern Review,* n.s. 2 (Summer 1966).

_____, "Uncle Remus and the Ubiquitous Rabbit," *Southern Review,* n.s. 10 (Fall 1974).

Walter Sullivan, "Death by Melancholy: Southern Writers in the Modern World," *Southern Review,* n.s. 8 (Fall 1972).

_____, "The Decline of Myth in Southern Fiction," *Southern Review,* n.s. 12 (Winter 1976).

Allen Tate, "The New Provincialism, with an Epilogue on the Southern Novel," *Virginia Quarterly Review,* 21 (Spring 1945).

_____, "Our Cousin, Mr. Poe," *Partisan Review,* 16 (December 1949).

_____, "To Whom Is the Poet Responsible?" *Hudson Review,* 4 (Autumn 1951).

_____, "The Man of Letters in the Modern World," *Hudson Review,* 5 (Autumn 1952).

_____, "A Southern Mode of the Imagination: Circa 1918 to the Present," *Carleton Miscellany,* 1 (Winter 1960).

Lionel Trilling, "Art and Neurosis," *Partisan Review,* 12 (Winter 1945).

_____, "The Kinsey Report," *Partisan Review,* 15 (1948).

_____, "William Dean Howells and the Roots of Modern Taste," *Partisan Review* (September–October 1951).

Eric Voegelin, "A Letter to Robert B. Heilman [on Henry James's *The Turn of the Screw*]," *Southern Review,* n.s. 7 (Winter 1971).

Robert Penn Warren, "Faulkner: The Negro and the South," *Southern Review,* n.s. 1 (Summer 1965).

_____, "Democracy and Poetry," *Southern Review,* n.s. 11 (Winter 1975).

_____, "Homage to Theodore Dreiser on the Centenary of His Birth," *Southern Review,* n.s. 7 (Spring 1971).

_____, "Mark Twain," *Southern Review,* n.s. 8 (Summer 1972).

ON EDITING <u>FURIOSO</u>
Reed Whittemore

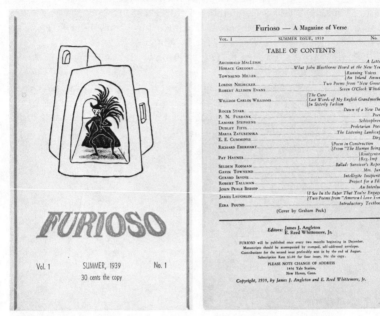

Furioso, *Vol. 1 No. 1, Summer 1939 (courtesy Reed Whittemore).*

Reed Whittemore has edited Furioso *(1939–1952) and* Carleton Miscellany *(1960–1964), and was literary editor of* The New Republic *from 1969 to 1973. He was one of the founders of the Association of Literary Magazines of America (ALMA), which later became the Coordinating Council of Literary Magazines (CCLM). He is also the author of a pamphlet in the University of Minnesota's Little Magazines series. Mr. Whittemore finds magazines with a political edge more interesting than "pure ones" like* Poetry. *The wild ones like* Big Table *and* Neurotica *are, he says, always good: "We need them, although sometimes their arrogance is oppressive." To the question, "Have you been able to support yourself by editing and publishing?" he answers, "Has anybody?" He lost about $4,000 a year when he edited* Furioso. *Losing money is, in his view, a "given"; the problem is to lose for some grand cause.*

Reed Whittemore has taught at Carleton College, the University of Maryland, and Princeton University. In 1971 he was the recipient of an award from the American Academy of Arts and Letters. Numerous volumes of his poetry have been published, as well as William Carlos Williams: Poet from Jersey *(1975) and* The Poet as Journalist: Life at the *New Republic (1976).*

The magazine *Furioso* that James Angleton and I began at Yale in 1939 was a late showing of the odd twentieth-century art beast, modernism. I say it was a late showing because in 1939 Jim and I were undergraduates, yet the modernism that we latched onto was middle-aged. Or maybe old-aged. Looking back now, I have the impression that we were much more antiquarian, at least in our first issues, than we knew. We were, if inadvertently, putting together in each issue an anthology of poets mostly a generation or more older than ourselves—and doing well at it too, printing Pound, Williams, cummings, MacLeish, Stevens, and Auden as well as dozens of other lesser known figures. All our teachers were impressed by our industry but must have understood that the industry was not matched by wisdom. Publishing the magazine became a big part of our college education, but there were qualities in most of the poetry we published that I didn't understand until later.

I didn't understand, for instance, the dimensions of the modernist war we had jumped into. I knew that the war existed; I had read "Don'ts for Imagists." I had begun to struggle in my own verse (none of which, luckily, was printed in *Furioso* during the early years) with the curious modernist game of avoiding the poetic in order to be poetic; and I had been indoctrinated in who the important modernists were. I knew also that the war was going on throughout the whole of literary Yale, faculty as well as students. But what the fuss was finally about was another matter.

I received a number of clues from my parents, though I didn't recognize them then as clues. Both Mother and Father took the position that *Furioso* was a strange and marvelous invention that was quite beyond them. I think I was pleased it was beyond them, pleased to be able to play snob with my Book-of-the-Month Club elders, but I don't think I imagined myself going so far as to become what they must have thought I was becoming—incredibly arty. No, I had democratic yearnings mixed in with my snobbery. I thought I was disposing of old cultural and artistic pretensions and reaching down to fundamentals. The elders knew better but they didn't mind, and Mother was a great help, selling subscriptions to her friends—who also kept insisting that *Furioso* was beyond them. Even when we had Ezra Pound himself as guest in my parents' apartment for a night and he was very pretentious about his cultural accomplishments, I did not think of him as representing *us* and what *we* were doing. He was just EP, the great eccentric.

Do I now know better? I think so. I think I now know that modernism, though one of the most confused of isms, was at least steady and clear in being a long conspiracy against the middle class. It produced few Marxists, it produced few artists who had social interests of any kind, but it was a social rebellion all right, a rebellion against the likes of my parents. In other words, it was beyond my parents because it was meant to be. Though Pound reading Rihaku in our living room was beyond the beyond, he had as attendant lords a great many poets who were also thoroughly capable of his kind of cultural snobbery— in the name of the modernist cause. For instance, e. e. cummings was (I realize now) a cultural snob. So, for all his democratic gesturing, was MacLeish. And Eliot surely was, Eliot by reputation the greatest snob of all—but we never met Eliot, nor printed him, but only dreamed of doing so and walked about New Haven quoting "Prufrock." Instead we met Williams, Eliot's mortal enemy, and Williams told us to steer clear of Eliot. We printed, in our second issue, a Williams letter to me that was full of anti-snob advice, but we didn't listen really, and we were not at the time even aware of how deep were Williams's feelings. His letter dealt with the role of ideas in poetry, especially political ideas, but had a paragraph about Eliot that should have tipped us off about the war:

Take an extreme case, take the concepts that walk around as T. S. Eliot. We know that they are completely worthless so that aside from Eliot's being a poet we do not have to pay much attention to him. He is strictly limited even as a poet but for all that we may speak of him as a good poet, good, that is, far beyond his other limitations.

Of course Williams himself was less of a snob about the middle class than any of the others—which may be a reason for his popularity in the new anti-Eliot age of poetry around us—and he lived the middle-class life as most of the others didn't. Yet even he had his troubles living that life and being a modernist. Early in his doctoring career he sometimes didn't think he could stick it out in doctoring, didn't think he could continue to live in Rutherford, New Jersey, and at the same time write the poetry that he knew he had to write. Later on, when he was mostly reconciled to the town and the life, he was still unusually sensitive to the relationship of the poetry to that life, was thoroughly aware that his neighbors thought the poetry beyond them. So though he hated Eliot for having, as he conceived it, taken modern poetry off in the wrong direction —the direction we might now call elitist—he couldn't finally escape such a tag himself. He could merely try to, by swearing, playing tough, telling dirty jokes—only to have a neighbor come up to him and say, "Well, Doc, how you doin' with your shitty little verses?"

We turned out only four issues in the era of our undergraduate ignorance, but they may have been the best of all of *Furioso's* thirty-two issues because we kept our mouths shut and drove around in my Ford picking up works by the masters. The issues were also handsomely printed, though for the first two or three we were plagued by the typos of a drunken linotypist. Jim was interested, as I was not, in format and makeup, and he insisted on good, heavy, expensive paper for these remarkable productions (for which we charged 30 cents a copy, $1.00 for four issues). We put too much poetry on a page, and we allowed insufficient margins for the prose in the back, but otherwise we did our publishing chores pretty well. Our editing was another matter.

We had a large cardboard box into which we threw manuscripts. We kept the box in a closet in our college room and didn't allow it, sitting there in the dark, to disturb us much. Every month or so we would haul it out, reject a few poems that could have been rejected by an illiterate, then put it back in the closet with all the problematic poems unsullied—that is, the poems that might be good. We kept being annoyed by plaintive notes that arrived in the mail asking about those poems, but there was one poet, *Oscar* Williams, who sent us an envelope of his verses almost daily for a period of months without once complaining. One night we spent several hours struggling with all those envelopes, then sent them all back in a bundle by parcel post. Two days later we received a curious one-line communiqué from him: "This will teach me never again to try to fuck a rathole."

With no other poet were we, I think, so undiplomatic, but then no other poet so flooded us with verses. Later, much later, I was to learn that with poets like Oscar Williams speedy rejection didn't work either. They would tirelessly ship poems to the magazine anyway, and become slowly aggravated, whether the rejection slips were polite or surly, at anything but acceptance. They believed they could wear an editor down. They believed an editor was an editor so that he *could* be worn down. When he didn't wear down he was a bad editor.

Of course it is not beyond possibility that while we were in college we were in fact bad editors. Anyway we emerged from college finally with four issues behind us, went off to war, returned from war, and resumed the magazine with all our new maturity. Or rather, I resumed the magazine with new editors, since Jim stayed in the intelligence work he had entered during the war.

I now had a different vision of what the editing act should be. I was as anxious as ever to avoid looking middle class, but I had been out in the big world now and thought I knew what my middle-class targets were. They were chiefly two. They were the commercial publishers, who were evil because they published bad literature that drove out the good literature (the good literature that at the time I mistakenly thought was being written), and they were the cultural pussyfooters in the English departments, the ones who turned out scholarly monographs about minor matters in old literary works, and read no new literary works. I was in the process of becoming an English teacher myself, but I thought I could distinguish English teachers of the pussyfoot variety from myself and my teacher allies. Meanwhile I was about to start a golden age of poetry on my own, but was ready to share the golden age with Howard Nemerov, John Pauker, Ambrose Gordon, W. R. Johnson, and Irwin Touster. They joined me in editing the sheet for a bit and proceeded, as I did, to fill it with their own work. When that set of editors tired, I gathered together my colleagues at Carleton College to make up the staff: Arthur Mizener (Arthur's wife

104

Rosemary served as managing editor for a time), Scott Elledge (Scott's wife Liane did the managing-editor thing too), Charles Shain, Edwin Pettet, and John Lucas.

But it was not a golden age (I see now). It was not as foolish an age in its pretensions as the age just around the corner—the apocalyptic age that would descend upon us in the fifties just as *Furioso* was folding; but it was an age of withdrawal, an age of a greater cynicism than some ex-GIs and young teachers should have been able to muster. We knocked off the publishers in a single blast in 1946, then moved on to the pussyfooters in our reviews, but in our poems and stories we did not display such activism. My own aesthetic inclination at the time, shared in some measure by the other editors, was to write about the futility of action. My most-read poem then was "A Day with the Foreign Legion," a narrative describing the incapacity of aging, alcoholic legionnaires to do battle with the enemy in the desert. And despite its campaigns, *Furioso* was, after the war, a magazine oddly dedicated to incapacity.

Put it that the writers closely connected with *Furioso* in the years 1946–53 were a small-scale lost generation, a lost generation of World War II. Our trouble was that we had no Paris to go to and be lost in. Instead we had a legacy of literary ideals that we were unable to put wholly aside, even though the evidence around told us that the legacy had depreciated. We had the legacy and we had responsibilities to it—which no lost generation ought to have—and we also had enough self-confidence to think we would make a go of our own writing; but we had no home, no real home, for either our legacy or our talent. We were lost in that sense, and my own private lostness was aggravated by the death of both my parents, in 1943 and 1946. I was alone in the world with a little capital. I bought a cabin in the woods— what else?—and my lost writer-friends joined me there irregularly, and the magazine emerged from those woods. Its isolation seems now its most poignant feature. For even when I determined for myself that I could not just live and write in the woods but had to be *something* in the world to survive, the woodsiness of the magazine remained. That is, it remained essentially a product of cultural and social isolation, even when it was moved to the offices of an English department.

Perhaps I should blame my own private withdrawal tendencies for the magazine's fate; yet there was more to that fate than my troubles. The legacy of modernism that I had partaken of so ignorantly while at college was now, in its depreciated state, thoroughly a part of my writing consciousness—and of Nemerov's, Pauker's, and the others'—and it gave us depressingly conflicting instructions about what we had to do with our writing lives. It instructed us, for example, to cultivate and preserve our isolation (else we would turn into stockbrokers and the Word would not be saved); but it also instructed us, with great ambiguity, in all the lessons of the thirties, lessons we were too young to know except vicariously, lessons about commitment *and* the dangers of commitment, lessons tending to cancel each other out, but still lessons. In the very first issue of *Furioso* Jim and I had been treated to at least three thirties' lessons, all different. There was, first, the lead article—put forth as a letter—by Archibald MacLeish, which represented well what has been called his "American front" period and advised young poets to avoid being little aesthetes, advised them to walk out into the big world and write for people (the way to do this in 1939, thought MacLeish, was to write radio drama). Then in the back of the magazine there was a blast at usury by Pound, presented in the form of an "introductory textbook" and representing Pound's own frenetic and unheeded way of removing himself from *his* aestheticism. And third, there was the very funny "Proletarian Poem" by Dudley Fitts that was a satirical answer to all the Marxist literary activists of the thirties, perhaps the first of the *in*activist recommendations we were to print. It described a momma and poppa trapped in the industrial mess, sitting around in the parlor and, with true prole realism, doing little else—just sitting there "darkling" as the rich got richer. It ended:

> *When Momma came home from work Poppa was waiting.*
> *Poppa was waiting. When Momma came home from work*
> *Poppa said* Darkling I hear thee.—*Momma sat down*
> *Completely. Then it was afterwards. Later when*
>
> *Momma came home from. Poppa was waiting.*
> *Momma was coming. Poppa sat home from work.*
> *Momma said* We're here as on a darkling
> Plain. *Poppa sat in the dark without saying.*

I've always wished I had written that poem, especially the line, "Then it was afterwards"; but when Dudley Fitts wrote it there was a freshness of reaction to thirties' prole literature that of course could not be sustained after World War II. The postwar era was not so much one of reaction as of a vacuum, an age to start all over in, but we were not in a position to start over. We had our heritage and it kept telling us on the one hand that our literary mission was a high and lonely one in a world that had gone to hell, and on the other that we should forget about missions and save ourselves. We would have been better off, perhaps, as members of the other, earlier lost generation. We worked too hard. We were uptight. I remember a dreadful summer when Nemerov was in the living room of the cabin trying to write a novel, and I was in a bedroom of the cabin trying to write a novel, and on weekends there would be other writers, there would be wives and guests and partying, but always the typewriters sat there making their demands. They were vicious, those typewriters.

And though the missionary spirit in us kept being aborted, it should not therefore be ignored in favor of looking at the poems and stories we printed. We did print some good ones, and the magazine came to stand for a kind of literature that I would still like to imagine could be preserved—a literature of the mind, of intellectual awareness and spaciousness—but beyond the works there was always the missionary thing and I was dead set on it, wouldn't let it go. I imposed it steadily on the review section in the back, and when that wasn't enough I started a regular column, called "The Department of Culture and Civilization," in which I tried, over a period of several years, to make our (my?) mission clear. The mission? Somehow, despite the modernist failures, to keep literature from being as isolated as we were.

The Department went at that mission backhandedly because we could see no other way. When we prattled about culture and civilization, we took potshots at the glib ones who thought they had a handle on culture and civilization. In fact, what we meant by the title of the column was that the culture and civilization out beyond our woods were neither civilized nor cultured. We aimed some of our shots at popular culture but some at the highbrows too, some in our own backyard. We ranged from complaints about corrupt cigarette advertisements and dishonest reportage, to annoyance at the *Hudson Review* and the Keats- Shelley Society. Most of the editors tried their hand at writing for the Department, but the steadiest contributors were Wayne Booth and I. (Later Wayne was to work at it solo for the *Carleton Miscellany,* calling it "The Department of American" and concentrating on jargon and miscellaneous verbal nonsense, especially in the social sciences.) We were not nearly solemn enough to win the war against the solemnities around us, but if we *had* been solemn we would have lost the war within ourselves, that war being between our solemn high mission and our deep awareness of what happened, in empty places, to solemn high missions. I think we did well with the Department, and if I were ever to start another magazine (I won't) I would want to have another one; but the Department was not a success. It was largely misunderstood by those it attacked, and it did not get out into the big world as it was supposed to. When we started it, we were uncertain about the title and called it tentatively (in an advertisement in *College English*) "The Department of Culture, Agriculture, Forestry and Housekeeping"—and sure enough a number of agricultural schools rushed to subscribe. Everybody out in the world wanted us to be specialists at something, wanted us to be a trade magazine. And because we didn't want that, we ended up being considered— as one confused reader conceived us—*Curioso.* Surely that is the end of modernism?

Each writer has to work his way out of the box he grows up in, and for a remarkable number of American writers that process has involved editing a little magazine. A little magazine is not, normally, the kind of enterprise that Jim and I began at college but the kind of enterprise that the postwar *Furioso* was—an enterprise where the editors of the thing are also its chief writers and where the editors' own literary destinies are muddled away at. After the war we certainly did muddle, and so we were then in the great tradition of little magazines. The results of the muddling are now in: we slowly discovered that we couldn't make a living, or a life, out of muddling.

But there was a happier result, too. We found that though we had muddled we had at least sometimes muddled at something of consequence, something beyond ourselves, something that made

108

the literary act also an ideological act, a moral act, an act with some (we were never sure what) social meaning. At least I know that I personally, looking back on the muddling, think that our lost generation was not as lost as the present one.

There have been, according to my mathematics, two literary generations now since ours: the apocalyptic Beat generation, with what the social scientists call its alternative life style, and the new quiet generation, with its attentiveness to its poetry and its poetry only (or its art and its art only). I had no time for the Beats when they were around, but I grant that they achieved a measure of social success in their writings—success of the wrong kind, but success; and I grant also that the success was not inadvertent. The Beats were *interested* in culture and civilization, wanted to change it, thought that literature had a role in changing it, and were even annoyed with our generation because they found us too literary and inactivist. *Big Table* in Chicago was a good example of a lively magazine of that generation, busy printing Burroughs, busy disturbing the peace. And of course the Ferlinghetti publications out of San Francisco were good examples too, at the center of the action, thoroughly social in their belligerently antisocial way. But when their day was done—and it was not done really until Allen Ginsberg began doing funny little Eastern chants (accompanying himself on his one-handed accordion) rather than poems —they were replaced by a generation of literary isolationists who were, I see now, a natural development out of the frustrations of my generation. These new young writers learned that culture and civilization were not, after all, to be saved by blue jeans and drugs and the open road, and so they lowered their sights, concentrating on their poetry, renewing their faith in it as an art. The trouble was not simply that they took it on alone in the woods, as we had, but they took it on without the past that we had, took it on essentially as an art of isolation, an art of the solitary sensibility, an art determined to stay in the woods and like it.

The result? Maybe something or somebody wonderful will happen soon, but I can't imagine what it (or he, or she) could be. The best magazine that I have seen lately—and I know there are dozens and dozens I have not seen—is *The American Poetry Review,* which must have a fairly large circulation and is certainly an ambitious venture that attracts poets of different shapes and destinies. I think the editors should be happy with their creation, but I do wish that the creation, as it poeticizes, would also make gestures out of, away from, poetry. My experience tells me that such gestures are the only way literature can survive. A literature as narrowly conceived and practiced as the current woods-poetry makes of literature at best a craft, at worst an indulgence.

Maybe there is no alternative to woods-poetry. Maybe culture and civilization do indeed need to be run, from here on, by the journalists and social scientists, who certainly want to run them. But if that is so, then there would seem to me to be little reason to trouble with literature at all.

Looking at the young writers around me, and their magazines, I keep asking myself questions about them: What do they want? Where do they think they are going with their craft? And the best answers I find are that they don't know what they want, and don't want to answer for themselves where they might be going. They know only what William Carlos Williams knew when he couldn't write; they know only that when they cannot write they are unhappy and sick. To know this much about writing is fine and important, of course, but it is not enough. Williams at any rate knew something else too, something beyond the private imperative. He knew—because such knowledge was conventional knowledge in his time—that poetry was important to culture and civilization as well as to the self. Unfortunately we now seem to have constantly less and less reason to know this.

Reed Whittemore, circa *1948 (courtesy* **Poetry** *magazine).*

ON ANVIL
Jack Conroy

Jack Conroy's interest in little magazines began at an early age, stimulated by the Haldeman-Julius Little Blue Books and by their weekly magazine, and then by his association with Charles J. Finger and his All's Well, *a continuation of Reedy's* Mirror. *In 1927, while living in Hannibal, Missouri, Mr. Conroy joined David K. Webb in editing* The Spider, *an American "college radical" magazine. Later, he visited Noah Whitaker in Springfield, Ohio, where Whitaker was editing* Pegasus *and printing it in his basement. He admired* The Double Dealer *in New Orleans during the early 1920s, and* The American Mercury, *whose editor, H. L. Mencken, published a number of his stories.*

Mr. Conroy founded Anvil *in 1933. In an appeal for funds for the* New Anvil, *written in collaboration with Nelson Algren and John T. Frederick, state director of the Illinois Writers' Project, he describes his little magazine as follows:*

"The Anvil *is recalled for the success with which it tapped new veins of realism. It was publishing such novelists as Nelson Algren, Benjamin Appel, August Derleth, Harriet Hassell, Josephine Johnson, Karlton Kelm, Edward Newhouse, Joseph Vogel, Richard Wright, and Louis Zara before these had yet emerged from obscurity. More* Anvil *fiction found its way into the established anthologies than from any other magazine of approximate scope. It consistently rejected all mystical aesthetic formulae, and much of its meaning derived from this rejection. From its first issue, it sought the work of the affirmers of life against death, of progress against reaction, of struggle against acquiescence. Miners, mill hands, and factory workers gave it their confidence because of the accuracy with which it expressed ideas and emotions relevant to their own lives, because in its pages they felt themselves at last becoming articulate. College students and instructors began subscribing to the unprepossessing little journal. Established writers contributed stories representative of their finest efforts. Erskine Caldwell's 'Daughter,' for example, was turned down by half the*

111

slick magazines in the country before its publication in Anvil, *and its subsequent republication in several anthologies. Its theme was too bold for conventional editorial tastes."*

Mr. Conroy has made his living at literary pursuits since 1935. He worked on both the Missouri and Illinois Writers' Projects. In Chicago he was an editor for Nelson's Encyclopedia *and the* Universal World Reference Encyclopedia, *and from 1947 to 1966 was senior editor of the* New Standard Encyclopedia. *His published work includes two novels,* The Disinherited *(1933, reissued in 1963) and* A World to Win *(1935), and a history of Negro migration entitled* They Seek a City *(1945, with Arna Bontemps). In 1966 Mr. Conroy returned to his home town, Moberly, Missouri. In partial recognition of his contributions to the literary arts, the University of Missouri, Kansas City, awarded him the degree of L.H.D. in 1975.*

When I was a lad of eight or so, with a little learning acquired from infrequent attendance in the one-room Sugar Creek schoolhouse, I decided there was a decided lack in the reading material available for the miners and their families who lived in Monkey Nest coal camp, clustered in a ragged semicircle on the hillside beneath the somewhat more pretentious story-and-a-half house we occupied. There was too little that gave their side of the social situation—that invested them with the dignity and importance they deserved.

Mother was a subscriber to *Comfort,* which ran serials written by such practitioners of the ultrasentimental school as Mrs. E. D. E. N. (standing for, I learned years later, Emma Dorothy Eliza Nevitte) Southworth and Bertha M. Clay. The latter was a pseudonym used by a number of English and American novelists, both male and female. The Clay novels frequently dealt with a lovely but lowly born maiden (often the lodgekeeper's daughter) who aspired above her station and fell in love with the young lord of the manor (like as not a wine-bibber and rakehell before her love redeemed him). We also read *Hearth and Home,* one of those monthly periodicals having a subscription price of only about 25 cents per year, but, as I recall, its stories—though customarily

112

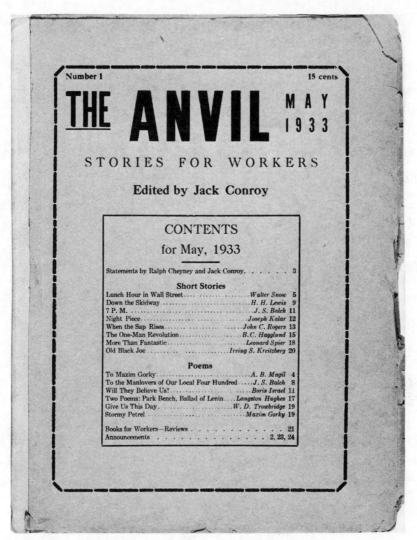

Number 1   15 cents

THE ANVIL

MAY 1933

STORIES FOR WORKERS

Edited by Jack Conroy

CONTENTS
for May, 1933

Anvil, *Vol. 1, No. 1, May 1933 (courtesy Jack Conroy).*

more American in locale—were no better when it came to dividing the classes into upper and lower.

Mother, who had literary ambitions and was well read for a miner's wife, deplored this tendency. One of her favorite complaints was a song that emphasized the baser traits of miners but wound up charitably, "It's not the collier's heart that goes astray." For one thing, I don't think any Monkey Nest miner ever would call another a "collier" unless he was prepared to fight. I suppose there was some writing with a proworker emphasis in circulation at that time, but it was unknown to us.

Hardbound editions of the juvenile novels of Horatio Alger and the prolific Englishman G. A. Henty could be had for two bits at Robinson's bookstore in Moberly. By retrieving bottles from trash piles left near the camp (the offal of more prosperous town dwellers), stealthily gathering walnuts and hickory nuts from farmers' trees, and snagging gunnysacks that had held hog or cattle feed for farmers and were left behind or lost by them, I managed to collect a sizable library of Algers and Hentys. In the Algers, the poor boy who escaped to a higher social level usually did so more by fortuitous accident, such as saving the local banker's daughter from a runaway horse, than by dint of long, faithful, and unquestioning service. The lesson, nevertheless, was clear: the poor will always be with us, dependent upon the bounty and wisdom of their betters, the well-to-do. In the Henty historical novels, the class lines were even more sharply delineated. The boy miners who thwarted a strike in *Facing Death* were depicted as heroes and examples for their fellows rather than as finks or scabs, as they would have been regarded in Monkey Nest camp.

So on fine large sheets of yellowish butcher paper, with only a fleck of blood on it or a spot of grease now and then, I laid out the *Monkey Nest Monitor* and printed it with lead pencil. There were news sections in addition to stories and poems and even a cartoon strip—I think an imitation of the Katzenjammer Kids with miners' children substituting for the mischievous little Deutschers. The stories were about miners in heroic roles, not relegated to the menial roles assigned to workingmen in *Comfort* and *Hearth and Home*. I printed only one copy of each issue of the *Monkey Nest Monitor,* but it circulated around the camp so that quite a few people read it.

114

A good many years later, traveling around the country as a free-riding boxcar passenger and working at all sorts of muscle-straining and low-paying jobs, I learned that the workers engaged in such tasks often have something vital to add to the body of American literature—something rarely tapped by more aesthetic and more insulated authors who operate in more rarefied realms of experience. After I came to Chicago in 1938 to establish *The New Anvil,* with the help of Nelson Algren, I collected a number of stories and recalled others for an "industrial folklore" collection for the Illinois branch of the Federal Writers' Project. But this is anticipating a bit.

I was a young married man with a wife and two children to support when I moved to Hannibal, Missouri, in 1927 to work in a rubber-heel plant and write poetry and letters at night. Soon I was in touch with Ralph Cheyney, an anarchist poet who had been jailed during World War I for resisting the draft and who, with his wife Lucia Trent, also a poet, had organized Rebel Poets, the Internationale of Song. Both had strong anticapitalist and antiwar sentiments, and had just edited *America Arraigned,* a collection of poems protesting the execution of Sacco and Vanzetti. The Rebel Poets organization was truly international, with members in a dozen countries, but mainly in the United States, England, and France. Since its membership represented about every variety of rebellion, it was not long in inviting the reproach—but not at first the active condemnation—of Marxist theoreticians who deplored its lack of the correct revolutionary direction.

The first official organ of the Rebel Poets was a bulletin turned out on a hectograph by its secretary, Hugh Hanley (pseudonym of Emerson Price), in Columbus, Ohio, where Price was a bank clerk soon to have a story, "Ohio Town," published in the *American Mercury.* (His 1939 novel, *Inn of That Journey*, was republished in 1977 by Southern Illinois University Press in its "lost novel" series.) Shortly after I moved to Toledo, Ohio, to work in the Overland automobile plant, I called on fiery old Jo Labadie in his Bubbling Waters sylvan retreat near Detroit. The spunky old anarchist printed booklets of his own verse on an antiquated hand press at very little cost. An excellent collection of radical literature called the Labadie Collection was later gathered at the University of Michigan in Ann Arbor. I realized then that good

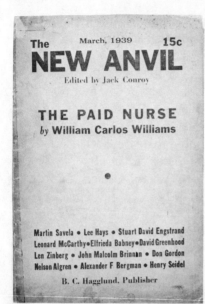

Top: The New Anvil, *March 1939; Nelson Algren,* circa *1939. Photograph by Robert McCullough. Bottom: Jack Conroy outside Ed Nyquist's Chicago studio on Rat Alley, April 1940. Photograph by John G. Rogers (courtesy Jack Conroy).*

poets need good printers and that rebellious poets (and publishers) need self-sacrificing printers who will print for whatever sums you can rustle up for them. If *The Anvil,* in its period of greatest circulation, had been conducted on that principle . . . but again I anticipate.

Such a printer, to be sure, was Ben Hagglund from the Minnesota muskeg country. He was still setting type by hand for another issue of his quarterly *Caravel* when he died on December 18, 1975, in Thief River Falls, Minnesota. He had come home after working and printing in many sections of the country. His native village, Holt, no longer existed, so he settled as near to its site as he could. While I was living in Hannibal, Ben began printing and distributing his *Western Poetry* (later *Northern Light*) when he could spare time from hay baling or working on a railroad section crew. Most new magazines began with a statement of policy or manifesto. In his first (December 1928) issue Ben deplored the lack of social expression in current verse and demanded that poetry "come into its own again, as the militant foe of injustice." A month earlier, D. Maitland Bushby had launched a new quarterly out in Arizona with the declaration: *"Tom-Tom* is conventional in form and spirit. We rarely use free verse and have no time for radical or sex poetry." During the same month, *Janus* ("a quarterly review of letters, thought, and the new theology") surfaced in Washington, D. C., and Solon Barber, its editor and publisher, emphasized that the periodical "is sincerely and honestly devoted to the policy of having no policy. It symbolizes individualism gone loco and ideational freedom carried to a licentious excess."

With a growing membership (in the New York chapter, at least), it was felt that the Rebel Poets needed a somewhat more ambitious organ of expression than Hugh Hanley's hectographed bulletin. A call went out to the Minnesota muskeg country, and Ben Hagglund answered. Therefore, the first issue of *The Rebel Poet* appeared on four 8½" x 11" pages of rough paper in January 1931. B. C. Hagglund was listed as both publisher and editor, but he protested that he was only printer-publisher while Conroy actually was the editor, and thereafter the masthead indicated that. The front page was occupied by a manifesto that dwelt at some length on the tribulations of insurgent literary magazines, and the final paragraph read:

Nothing but general sympathy with our aims is required of members. Affiliated with no political party, we stand unequivocally for the defense of the Soviet Union against the enemies that are massing for attack, we champion the cause of the weak and defenseless, we combat the greed of industrial barons who are converting American laborers into abject serfs, we decry the spirit of intolerance that endeavors to abrogate the inherent rights of free speech as demonstrated in the recent Marcus Graham case and in the raiding of union halls in the South and the attempted electrocution of four workers in Georgia for the crime of striving to better the conditions of the textile slaves. We ridicule the musty echoes of the fin de siècle *slogan "Art for Art's Sake," and inscribe on our banner:*

ART FOR HUMANITY'S SAKE.

The Rebel Poet, *Nos. 1, 16, 17 (courtesy Jack Conroy).*

The manifesto was a joint effort of Cheyney and myself, and reflected, I fear, a shared tendency toward floridity and flamboyance. But the spirit and fervor were genuinely sincere. It was a time for choosing sides. Since the publication of *Writers in Revolt: The Anvil Anthology, 1933–1940,* edited by Curt Johnson and myself and published by Lawrence Hill and Company late in 1973, I have discovered that I am a "Populist" and always have been—or so a number of critics have deduced from the contents of the anthology, which were gleaned from the three magazines I edited, and my introduction thereto.

While *The Rebel Poet* prospered moderately, all was not harmonious in the New York chapter of the Rebel Poets organization. Some time earlier I had asked a young Russian-Jewish immigrant named Philip Rahv to take part in its activities, after he had done some translations for the magazine. Walter Snow, a Connecticut Yankee, poet, and journalist, was also an active member; the two

118

soon were at loggerheads and leaders of rival factions. The all-inclusive policy of *The Rebel Poet* irked the superrevolutionary Rahv, who was fond of pyrotechnic tirades against the capitalists and glowing prophecies of the imminent triumph of the class-conscious proletariat. Here is a sample of his customary manner in what may be called his Stalinist period, taken from a review of *Scottsboro Limited*—four poems and a play by Langston Hughes—in the August 1932 issue of *The Rebel Poet:*

The sophisticates and the Montparnasse Brahmins are fond of asserting that the Negro knows how to laugh beautifully; they go into raptures over the urban Negro's bluesongs and the country Negro's "spirituals." With characteristic cruelty they sadistically exploit the colored people's "picturesqueness" as an aid to their attempt to cover up and conceal the misery of the Negro masses sweltering in the hell of bourgeois rule in the city and on the farm. But the halcyon days of culture by immaculate conception, unrelated to the economic bases of existence, are now a thing of the past. The Negro may know how to laugh beautifully, yet on the day when together with his white fellow-worker he will come into his own in the new Socialist society, the lackeys of the moneybags will not enjoy it so much. . . .

The gruesome specter of death awaiting the Scottsboro boys in Alabama is routed by the overwhelming joy of proletarian brotherhood—"together, black and white, up from darkness into light."

Soon Editor Conroy was beleaguered in his Moberly isolation with demands for a more definite revolutionary affirmation in the magazine, demands that it unequivocally identify itself with the avant-garde of the proletariat, as represented by the Communist party cultural apparatus. The militant Rahv assumed command of a faction which eventually outvoted Snow and his two (and sometimes three) followers. Then it was demanded that Conroy yield the editorial reins to an editorial board composed of Rahv, Walt Stacy (a Rahvite), Fred R. Miller (another Rahvite), Edwin Rolfe (a neutralist), V. J. Jerome (the CP's cultural commissar), and (as a Conroy representative) Leonard Spier. Another demand was that the magazine's name be changed to something more assertive, such as *Red Dynamo, Pen and Gun, Advance Guard, Red Express,* or *Class Front.* I decided with some misgiving that the last of these names might not be too obnoxious if it meant keeping the magazine afloat. To Spier's suggestion that all members take a bundle of magazines, say ten, and hawk them at meetings, Rahv replied that somebody should be hired to do this. With no money in the till, that idea seemed impractical to

119

Spier, to say the least. He had handled distribution to bookstores and newsstands and had collected accounts (when he could) while, he complained, the Rahvites spent most of their time in polemicizing and planning the rearrangement of the magazine.

Before the transformation could be effected, Snow and Spier had seceded—taking with them the only other Conroy loyalist, the poet George Jarrboe. The junta had decided to fire Hagglund, his printing not being classy enough. (They were to learn that altruistic and philanthropic printers were hard to find.) So with no printer to work for whatever measly sums he could get, and no workhorse Spier to distribute the magazine and cajole bookstores and others to stock it (and pay for the copies sold!), *The Rebel Poet* died of malnutrition. I had by this time succeeded Cheyney as president of the Rebel Poets organization, he being alarmed at the turmoil in the New York chapter and the growing leftward turn of the magazine. So I exercised my executive privilege and declared both the magazine and the organization kaput.

Walter Snow had discussed with me on several occasions the possibility of publishing a magazine devoted to fiction—with some verse but no theoretical articles such as those so dear to the hearts of most left-wing editors in those days. Hagglund, the nonpareil printer, once more signed up for the duration. He had turned out seventeen issues of *The Rebel Poet,* often receiving little more than the cost of the paper; its size had increased from four pages to twelve long before the final issue of October 1932. I chose to call the new magazine *The Anvil,* with the subtitle "Stories for Workers." Our motto was declared to be, "We prefer crude vigor to polished banality." Friction between socialists and communists had become more intense, and, upon being told of the plans for the magazine, Cheyney offered this statement for the first issue:

Please let me urge you to support The Anvil *if you are a Communist or broad-minded enough and financially able to be interested in a Communist poetry magazine.*

I believe that The Rebel Poet *accomplished much good but that the change of name and the fearless acceptance of a role in the Communist movement is probably an inevitable development. The Rebel Poets, the Internationale of Song, was founded as a non-sectarian comradeship embracing Socialists, Communists, Anarchists, and those without definite affiliations but on the side of labor in the class struggle. The* Unrest *anthologies represent pinks, reds, many shades. Some of us felt that poets could serve the social revolution best by not being affiliated in our poetic capacities with any political or industrial group. But the logic of events seems now to be indicating that each rebel poet should align himself actively, openly, specifically, with the general organization with which he is most in accord.*

I am not a Communist. Neither is Lucia Trent. Both of us are left-wing Socialists. As such, we reach a parting of the ways with The Anvil. *We are not deserting. They are not deserting. Simply a new chapter of more intimate integration with life has been opened in social poetry. May it speed social revolution!*

Emphasis should not be on personalities but social movements, yet in closing I want to say that, though Jack Conroy may regard me as a double-dyed villain, I admire him as a gifted author and self-sacrificing rebel who should have the utmost loyalty of Communists. Other charges that may be brought against me ever I shall be glad to answer, but there is one to which I must plead guilty. I should have rendered more aggressive service to those ideals I always have served and always shall serve. That I have done my best under the financial circumstances is no alibi for not having accomplished more. But what are you *doing?*

Ralph Cheyney

This was my reply:

I've no intention of denouncing Cheyney as a double-dyed villain. On his part, he seems determined to warn everybody that I am a wicked Communist and if you have aught to do with me, you're not only aiding and abetting the Reds but are renouncing the world and the flesh in the manner of a nun taking her vows. I've never attempted to disguise my belief that the literary movement revolving around The New Masses *is the only one in this country possessing any degree of vitality. Furthermore, I deny that there is any "Socialist" (left-wing or right-wing), Anarchist, Syndicalist or any other radical movement of any consequence standing in opposition to and clearly distinguished from the bourgeois tradition other than the movement of which* The New Masses *is the pole-star. Cheyney himself, writing in* Poetry World, *has mourned that the League for Industrial Democracy (which he characterizes as an admirable organization) has absolutely no use for verse as propaganda. "Social Vision verse is mostly bad verse, and who wants to encourage bad verse," an official of the L.I.D. said.*

Contributors to The Anvil, *successor to* The Rebel Poet, *and members of the Proletarian Writers' League, successor to the Rebel Poets, need not be Communists, of course. My associate editors and I are going to try to present vital, vigorous material drawn from the farms, mines, mills, factories and offices of America. We'll not devote much space to theoretical problems. For theoretical guidance, we refer you to* The New Masses *and* International Literature.

I cannot think that the polite evasions used by Cheyney to mollify timorous readers have any positive effect in bringing about and fostering a revolutionary literary movement—rather they help to nullify its beginnings. We shall never

121

bring the revolution inside the walls of literature within a Trojan horse camou-flaged by such euphemistic phrases as "social vision" (a pleasant substitute for the harsher "revolutionary") or by soothing reformist publication by advocating "the revolution of the spirit."

I don't think that many playboys "broad-minded enough or financially able" to support a Communist magazine will come to our aid. Communists are being taken too seriously. Whimsical wealthy people sometimes toy with radicalism by subsidizing "social vision" or bohemian periodicals that care more about sexual freedom than industrial freedom—but whenever one strikes vigorously at the roots of private property, these synthetic radicals howl louder than J. Hamilton Fish himself.

"You want to keep the Communists out of your unions. They will cause you trouble," said a representative of Illinois' governor to a delegation from the "radical" Progressive Miners' Union. Apparently the editor of this union's official organ is willing to take the reactionary politician's advice, for every issue of the sheet contains vicious vituperation directed against the Communist Party and its press and sarcastic references to "Big Joe Stalin."

While I am assuredly not asking every contributor or reader of The Anvil *to become a member of the Communist Party, I wish to make it clear that it will never give aid or comfort to any publication, individual or organization that joins in the wolf pack yelps against the only Workers' and Farmers' government in the world. I believe that every honest intellectual should be able to say with the liberal author, Waldo Frank:*

"What is taking place in Russia is the most precious social event, the most precious social life, of our crucial epoch. . . . We must defend the Soviet Union with our spirit; if need be, we must defend it with our lives."

The publisher, several comrades and myself have kept The Rebel Poet *going for several years, often at the cost of severe personal sacrifice. And other friends have helped when they could ill afford it. I should be very sorry, indeed, to lose the esteem and confidence of these friends, some of whom may not see exactly eye to eye with me. Cheyney's reasons for indiffer-ence toward the magazine since it turned more sharply leftward are best known to himself. I believe he was once a Syndicalist and suffered persecution for his courageous stand against the imperialist holocaust beginning in 1914. For that he deserves credit. But his classification of himself as a "left-wing Socialist" I hold to be a retreat. It is perhaps inevitable that, with the sharpen-ing of the crisis, some will travel in one direction—to the right—while others will veer to the left.*

We'll publish The Anvil *as frequently as we can. We are issuing it tenta-tively as a quarterly. But with any appreciable degree of support we hope to issue bi-monthly or monthly. I've learned that it is useless to plead trumpet-tongued for support. Those who can help us and want to help us will do so without excessive urging. You may be sure that every penny donated, every subscription (new or renewal) will be appreciated tremendously.*

Jack Conroy

Since *The Anvil* intended to publish only creative works, I hoped to avoid ideological disputes. At the same time, the only movement with a great deal of vitality or potential for distributing

122

a magazine without any other source of revenue than its circulation, with no advertising income, with no fairly generous angels such as those enjoyed by some other periodicals voicing revolt of a less explosive nature, was support that used the Communist party cultural apparatus as its polestar. Having never been east of the Hudson, I was still full of naiveté as to the theories and practices of New York's coffee shop revolutionaries.

Ben Hagglund knocked out the first issue of *The Anvil,* and in 1933–34 he journeyed down to Newllano Cooperative Colony in Leesville, where he had the help of Marvin Sanford, a veteran socialist printer, and the use of a much larger press, including a linotype. Sanford was for some time listed as publisher. The Anvil Press in Newllano printed a number of other left-wing journals, among them *Blast, The Little Magazine, Scope, Left Review,* and *Pollen.*

Walter Snow, the New York editor, began to take a vigorous hand in the magazine's editing and distribution. A skilled public relations man (he had served in that capacity for several New York publishers), he put a large share of his somewhat meager earnings as a newspaper editor into a campaign to make the magazine acceptable to the New York Seaboard CP pundits. I was then almost oblivious to the partisan disputes raging among the various factions in New York, each of which professed to expound the only true and valid gospel of Marxism.

My awareness was sharpened after I ran a story called "On the Sea," by Robert Whitcomb, which later formed part of his novel *Talk United States.* This seemed to be pretty good proletarian fare, though the slangy, breezy talk was a bit affected. According to Snow, when Philip Sterling, a writer of true Stalinist faith and allegiance, beheld the story in *The Anvil,* he recoiled in horror. It seemed that Whitcomb, once on the staff of *The Daily Worker,* had turned Lovestoneite and was hence beyond the pale. Philip Rahv and a new disciple, Wallace Phelps (soon to change his name to William Phillips), were just about solidifying their de facto control of *Partisan Review,* official organ of the John Reed Club of New York, and were quick to announce piously that if Snow had aught to do with this heretical outrage, he should be brought up on charges before the John Reed Club.

"Out in Missouri," Snow wrote me, "you probably don't realize the war-to-death waged against Lovestoneites, Trotskyites and other renegades. No United Front proposal ever includes such elements. How can I impress this fact on you strongly enough? Maybe in this way: if Whitcomb or any other renegade ever appears again in *Anvil,* I will be compelled to sever all connections with the magazine and publicly dissociate myself from you—even you!"

Heywood Broun proclaimed in his newspaper column that, after reading the first issue of *The Anvil,* he had decided not to make his next book a proletarian novel. Some of the stories, he complained, put Horatio Alger's Ragged Dick in reverse: from riches to rags, rather than the familiar formula. Left-wing critics in general were more lukewarm than were conservatives. Harry Hansen of the *New York World Telegram,* for example, usually managed to give us some publicity in every issue of his column, which was syndicated rather widely. He said this of the November–December 1933 issue:

It would be great to turn Erskine Caldwell loose in a mob and have him come back with a report of what he has heard. At San Jose, California, he would have collected some remarkable exhibits in the vernacular.

This comment is prompted by my reading his very short tale, "Daughter," which opens Jack Conroy's paper, The Anvil, *for December. Here Caldwell tells the story of a Negro sharecropper who killed his daughter because she complained constantly of hunger. The Negro had been robbed of his share by the wealthy landlord. The technical adroitness of the author is revealed in his description of the crowd which gathers outside to free the Negro, and which slowly makes up its mind.*

None of the other stories in The Anvil *quite come up to this, but several invite interest. Paul F. Corey, of New York City, shows office clerks at the mercy of shifts and changes, and Louis Mamet describes a factory tragedy in a new technique. Joseph Kalar's "Funeral" is given a star by Thomas Uzzell, who will reprint it in his next* Short Story Hits. *Other contributors are Helen Koppell, John C. Rogers, Eugene Joffe, and Joseph Vogel.*

Jack Conroy edits The Anvil *in Moberly, Mo. He wrote the other day:—"I live here like Thoreau beside his pond and you can throw a cat through the walls of my shack in a dozen places." A few subscriptions might help Conroy to plaster up the holes; besides, it would make life easier for the cat.*

A ripple of response did result, with a handful of welcome subscriptions. When "Waldo Tell" reviewed the January–February 1934 issue in the first (February–March) issue of *Partisan Review,* official organ of the John Reed Club of New York, he spoke with

124

condescension of the fiction and dismissed the verse as "painfully sincere, but, with the exception of two poems by Walter Snow and Edwin Rolfe, of little value as poetry." It was several years before I learned that "Waldo Tell" was a pseudonym for Edwin Rolfe.

When I arrived in New York City in 1935 to attend the first American Writers Congress, *The Anvil* had, as the song about Kansas City puts it in the musical *Oklahoma,* "gone about as fur as it could go." A printing of 4,000 had been ordered for the October–November issue, the final one as it turned out. The fancy printing of the Liberal Press had been more expensive than the Hagglund-Sanford issues turned out at Newllano, which cost only about $52 for 200 copies on cheap paper. Snow felt he could no longer underwrite the debt of about $100 on each issue, and thus was receptive to a suggestion from Alexander Trachtenberg that *The Anvil* merge with *Partisan Review,* now under the complete control of Philip Rahv and William Phillips. Recalling the coup engineered in the New York Rebel Poets chapter, I became suspicious as to the nature of any "merger" that might be effected. I wrote to Snow:

I understand your discouragement about The Anvil. *It does seem impossible to keep it going alone. I had been hoping that Mike Gold and Trachtenberg would be able to suggest some way to keep it afloat independently. Trachtenberg, especially, seemed enthusiastic about its possibilities and the desirability of keeping it going. . . . It might be possible to call the merged magazine* The Anvil, *since it is undoubtedly the stronger of the two. It has more circulation, has had more recognition, and has appeared steadily, while almost no issue of* Partisan Review *has been on time.*

Snow, bone-weary and broke, still saw the merger as our only salvation. I would always be honored as a founder-editor, have a voice in selecting material. The magazine's name was to be *Anvil and Partisan Review.* When it actually did surface (February 1936), its name was *Partisan Review and Anvil.* The editorial board consisted of Rahv, Phillips, Alan Calmer (a polemicist in the Rahv-Phillips orbit), Ben Field (a short story writer), Edwin Rolfe (a. k. a. "Waldo Tell"), Clinton Simpson (a New York editor and critic friendly to Conroy), and myself. Simpson soon informed me that Trachtenberg wanted the new magazine ". . . to be more or less a counterpart of the French *Commune,*

125

the literary magazine which holds fairly close in critical attitude to the CP, points out divergences and welcomes sympathizers among the writers and acts as a literary and ideological journal representing the Party."

Alas for Trachty's grandiose dream, as we shall see!

In a long review entitled "Papa Anvil and Mother Partisan," printed in the February 18, 1936, issue of *The New Masses,* Michael Gold saluted the new hybrid:

Partisan Review and Anvil *is a curious name for a literary magazine. Like many such compound names, it means that a shotgun wedding has taken place. It represents a merger of two magazines: that spunky pioneer of mid-west proletarian literature, Jack Conroy's* Anvil; *and* Partisan Review, *organ of the New York left-wing intellectuals.*

Well, the child of roughneck Father Anvil *and his thoughtful college bride has at last appeared. It's a vigorous male, retaining the best features of both parents; papa's earthy directness and mama's erudition and sensibility. Handsome and clear-cut in appearance, pulsing with revolutionary life,* Partisan Review and Anvil *is now on the newsstands and as a magazine promises to be a success.*

News of the impending merger had inspired Malcolm Cowley's muse, as follows:

> *I'm glad to hear the* Partisan Review
> *Will soon appear in an almost wholly new*
> *Format, combined with the fiction-flaunting* Anvil
> *And print young writers, so people will know that Granville*
> *H. and Isidor S. and Michael G.*
> *Joe F. and Robert F. and Robert C.*
> *And others of us graybeards aren't the only*
> *Prose proletarian pundits, and the lonely*
> *Young poets won't be lonely any longer*
> *And stories can be shorter, sharper and stronger*
> *And critics lay a heavier barrage*
> *And all reporting can be reporting*
> *And talent flourish, And in short I mean*
> *Hurrah, Red Front, hats off to your new magazine.*

It soon became obvious that not a merger but a takeover had occurred, as I had anticipated. Rahv and Phillips and the compliant Calmer regularly vetoed any suggestions of Clinton Simpson after Ben Field and Edwin Rolfe retired from the editorial board. I, far away beyond the Mississippi, was never consulted even before the *Anvil* was dropped from the title in the October 1936 issue—the final one. After six issues, the magazine had suspended publication. The irrepressible duo, Rahv and Phillips, hibernated for a year and then launched a new *Partisan Review* with a slightly Trotskyite, surely anti-Stalinist flavor. The sacrifice of *The Anvil* had been in vain from a CP standpoint, and V. J. Jerome (the cultural commissar selected from the editorial board to displace Conroy as editor of *The Rebel Poet*) cried out in anguish:

Who in the world of bourgeois letters had ever heard of or given a hoot for Rahv and Phillips, for example, amateur literati who mishandled a magazine that started out with all the auspices and forces to make it a success.

Papa Anvil, as personified by Conroy, had never been privileged to share the nuptial bed with Mother Partisan, so did not feel too completely disillusioned or bereft. At about that time, some who remembered the old *Anvil* wondered whether it might not, like Lazarus, be made to rise again. One of these was Nelson Algren in Chicago, some of whose very early stories had appeared in *The Anvil*. I had previously met with Nelson in Chicago on several occasions. He and Richard Wright, another *Anvil* contributor, were working in the Chicago office of the WPA Writers Project, and Nelson had thought that project director John T. Frederick, with whom I had been in touch when he edited *Midland,* might find a place for me on the project. Frederick agreed that he could.

So when Nelson managed to get me a bus ticket to Chicago in return for an article to be written for the *Midwest Daily Record,* I set out to plan with him a revival of *The Anvil.* He put me up in his pad in one of the storefront studios that once had housed shops catering to visitors to the World's Columbian Exposition of 1893. This was in March 1938, and a year passed before we were able to put out the first issue of *The New Anvil.* In the meantime we had begged, cajoled, thrown benefit parties, and sponsored lectures by Richard Wright, Peter DeVries, Shaemas O'Sheel, and others to raise funds. Our most effective source of revenue was a music-hall style melodrama named *The Drunkard's Warning, or Chicago by Gaslight,* with Algren and myself assuming leading roles. This and other of our activities caused some left-wing condemnation of Algren and myself as bohemians. Frank Myers, a cultural attaché of the CP then stationed in Chicago, asked us to come in to discuss the magazine. He kept us waiting in an anteroom for about an hour, then delivered a stern lecture about the necessity of publish-

127

ing material that made explicit a Marxist moral. Myers, as has been the case with several gung-ho Marxist authoritarians of that period, later swung to the other extreme of the spectrum and became a right-wing doyen in the Buckley camp.

Hagglund printed 2,500 copies of the first issue, of which about 2,200 were sold. William Carlos Williams contributed the feature story. John Malcolm Brinnin, Don Gordon, and Nelson Algren were among the five poets represented.

For a time we were able to rent from the Institute for Mortuary Research, a public relations service for undertakers, a cubicle just vacated by Sidney Justin Harris, whose liberal magazine, *The Beacon,* had had to give up the struggle. We had access to a large quantity of stationery bearing the Institute's imprint, of good quality but a rather depressing shade of blue. On these Nelson and I often tried to offer suggestions that we thought might help the authors. One Jerry Salinger (a. k. a. J. D. Salinger) thanked me for my "warm note" which had taken "the chill off many a rejection slip." *The New Anvil* by then was on its last go-round and I had been compelled to tell him so. Algren's kindly and shrewd rejections, too, left lasting impressions, as he learned years later from Joseph Haas after Haas had been made literary editor of the *Chicago Daily News.* Frank Yerby told us when he submitted his story, "The Thunder of God" (published in the April–May 1939 issue), that it was his first published piece, aside from poetry in college magazines. Yet most biographical sources date his career from the short story "Health Card," which won the O. Henry Memorial Award in 1944. This was characteristic of the not-so-benign neglect accorded *The New Anvil* by east-of-Hudson arbiters.

The retreat from the Burnham Building cubicle to Algren's studio on Cottage Grove Avenue began a steady decline in sales and revenue. An urgent appeal, "Look into the Future with Us," in the final (May–June 1940) issue evoked only a small ripple of response. The squelching of Hitler then seemed to be the main order of business for progressives.

I often wonder what became of the zeal for human betterment that inspired so many writers in the thirties. The Korean "police action" and the Vietnam adventure disillusioned many poets in particular. Al Masarik, a Korean vet, wrote a collection of poems

128

called *Invitation to a Dying* (Vagabond Press, 1971) with an introduction by Charles Bukowski, who observes:

I feel that the breakoff of real poetic talent began with World War II and that it never returned. What the causes were (are) I don't know. But from the beginning of World War II and up to 1971 it has been a very barren time for poetic production, not only that form of production but, I feel, creation in other art forms and originality outside of the art forms.

The sort of material *The Anvil* pioneered in publishing is now diffused throughout the "little magazine" community. In Minneapolis, whimsically named *Moons and Lion Tailes* welcomes Meridel LeSueur, Thomas McGrath, and other former contributors to *The Anvil* and *The New Anvil*. The revolutionary note is still sounded by *TRA (Toward Revolutionary Art)* in Los Angeles, where an edition of 5,000 can be distributed by its non-professional staff, to bookstores, at meetings. etc. College-based reviews such as *New Letters* (University of Missouri at Kansas City) and *The Chariton Review* (Northeast Missouri State University) do not even blanch at the once-dreaded word "proletarian." In Kansas City, *The Foolkiller* magazine, organ of the Folk University there, has borrowed the *Anvil* slogan, "We prefer crude vigor to polished banality."

Even the name of *The Anvil,* as well as its insurgent spirit, survives in *North Country Anvil,* a sort of *New New Anvil* edited, published, and printed by Jack Miller in Millville, Minnesota. Miller, following in the footsteps of Ben Hagglund, managed to establish his own print shop and has survived for nineteen issues. Now and then he reprints something from the original *Anvil.* Today, of course, there are different things to worry about: ecology and abuses of our natural resources, for example. In the thirties we didn't have nuclear waste to pester us.

ON <u>PARTISAN REVIEW</u>
William Phillips

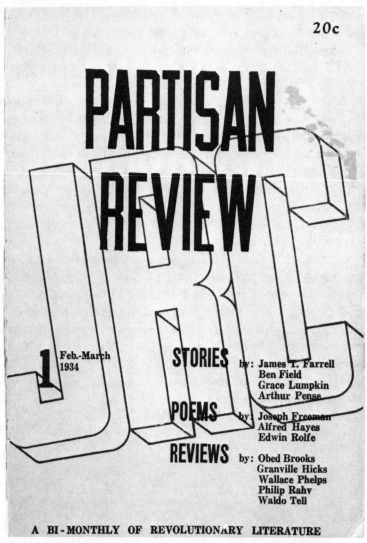

Partisan Review, *Vol. 1, No. 1, February–March 1934 (courtesy Northwestern University Library).*

"We were cocky kids," writes William Phillips about himself and Philip Rahv in the early thirties. "We had the idea of launching a new literary movement, combining older with younger talents, and the best of the new radicalism with the innovative energy of modernism." Intellectually, Mr. Phillips says, he was born in the thirties: "Perhaps it is egocentric to identify one's formative years with the beginnings of this era. But I think it can be said that the thirties were the cradle of our entire epoch, and that we are all living out of the unsolved problems—intellectual as well as political—first posed at that time." For Mr. Phillips, the contemporary mind, as well as the past three decades of Partisan Review, *had their origins in the traumatic shift of consciousness that took place then.*

William Phillips has edited Partisan Review *since 1934. He has also served as a consulting editor at Dial Press, Criterion Books, and Random House, and has taught at Columbia, the New School for Social Research, Sarah Lawrence College, and Rutgers University. He has published numerous articles in literary quarterlies and is the author of* A Sense of the Present *(1967). Mr. Phillips is a member of President Carter's Task Force for the Arts and Humanities.*

I have been asked how *Partisan Review* has weathered so many political and literary storms. As far as I know, it is one of the few magazines of its kind that have spanned several different periods, and still occupy a central place in the literary scene. Literary publications, unlike journals of opinion that reflect the changing intellectual climate, usually have their moments of glory, after which, if they survive, they carry on like old soldiers. Literary magazines, like writers, appear in a certain time and place, out of some literary current or sensibility. Thus *Partisan Review* was born in the thirties, actually twice-born, and originally bore the stamp of that era. If it has not been restricted by its origins, if it has defied all the pressures of a time and a country that has celebrated youth, novelty, and escape from tradition, I think this is mainly because of the continuity between the thirties and the following decades.

Of course, when *Partisan Review* was started in the thirties, first as an organ of the John Reed Club and then as an independent journal, the concept of the future to me and the others was nothing more than a personal and historical abstraction. None of us thought of the magazine as anything but an instrument for dealing with the pressing literary and political problems of the time; we never dreamed that *Partisan Review* would not only influence writing and thinking but would also set a pattern for literary publication in the following decades.

But in retrospect it can now be seen that our idea of the magazine provided an approach to new situations as well as a response to the immediate one. The problems to which we addressed ourselves at first partially, then more fully, turned out to be the main concern of the period. Essentially our aim was to reconcile the modernist spirit, which was often conservative and antihistorical, with a political consciousness that emphasized the radical and historical dimensions of art. Since the thirties, definitions of literary modernism have been shifting, as has our political thinking, but the fate of modernism and the relation of writing to the pressures of the culture as a whole have been key questions throughout. Of course, our prime concern has been with literary quality, new talent, and new ideas. But the criteria for judging originality as well as accomplishment obviously have to do as much with literary direction as with taste.

Anyway, it was with the most blatant and extreme form of these matters that *Partisan Review* was concerned in the beginning. The magazine started out as the organ of the John Reed Writers' Club, an organization within the orbit of influence and control of the Communist party. Since the Communists fell far short of state power, such control consisted not in following strict orders, as it did in the Soviet Union, but in setting the limits of dissent. In practice, this meant that members of the club could hold a variety of literary beliefs as long as they did not question the authority and the general line of the Communist party. One could even be cynical and somewhat disaffected (as I understand Soviet intellectuals can be) so long as one did not write about it or make it too public in any way. And while the Communists in that period supported the idea of proletarian literature and took the position that art was a weapon in the class struggle, there was some latitude in interpreting these doctrines or even in questioning them—especially

132

since they were soon to be abandoned entirely as the party shifted to the new popular front policy, which was geared to recruiting writers who might balk at such sectarian views of literature.

The *New Masses,* the official cultural organ of the Communists, was the stronghold of those who had the strictest and most vulgar interpretation of the "party line" in literature. The John Reed Club, however, had some writers who came out of a bohemian and a more freewheeling literary tradition—though, in keeping with the spirit of the times, they were willing to go along with what they thought the Communist party ultimately stood for, however disillusioned they were with its current practices. Philip Rahv and I were the most dissident members of the John Reed Club, and we were most concerned with keeping literature free of illegitimate political pressures. But others were also interested in countering the factional approach of the *New Masses,* which converted all literary questions into political ones, and they agreed to join Rahv and myself in starting a literary magazine in opposition to the *New Masses.* The *New Masses,* however, was subsidized by the party, while we had to scrounge for money. Fortunately, a fund-raising lecture by John Strachey, a suave British literary Marxist, brought in $800, enough to finance a magazine for a year at depression costs. We had no rent or staff, and, as I recall, Rahv got twelve dollars a week to do the production, though I helped too.

From the outset, the policy of the newborn *Partisan Review* was rather clearly defined. Our outlook was Marxist, and our sensibility had a radical bent, but we stressed the relative autonomy of writing and were open to work that had been influenced by the experimental currents of the twenties. The magazine lasted a little more than a year as the publication of the John Reed Club, but from the beginning Rahv and I felt more and more hemmed in by the restrictive atmosphere of the Communists. Many gifted writers were on the Communist index, and thus the range of exploration in fiction and poetry, as well as in criticism, was limited. Even more important, we were finding it impossible to live with the corruption, the lies, and the authoritarian structure of the party. And it was becoming clear that the Communists, to whom many people stuck because they believed their ends were more important than their means, were themselves the main obstacle to the realization of a socialist society.

133

Still, our discontent was concrete. It came not so much from a yearning for some abstract ideal of freedom, of the kind conservative rhetoric celebrates (though that was there too), but from the feeling that we were cut off by the doctrinaire and factional policies of the party from the free play of the critical mind and from the modernist trends and experimental talents to which we were drawn by our radical ideas and sensibility.

The next phase of the *Partisan Review,* our second birth, began in the late thirties, when the magazine broke with the John Reed Club and with the Communist party and started up again as an independent, radical literary journal. Rahv and I, the surviving editors of the old *PR,* were joined by Mary McCarthy, Dwight Macdonald, F. W. Dupee, and George Morris to put out the new *PR.* We were a jaunty, raucous, quarrelsome group, always disagreeing about something, but all of us were intent on printing the best and most advanced writing and on maintaining a radical, anti-Stalinist intellectual and political position. I think the essence of our stand was that we assumed both aims went together. One might say there was a simultaneous widening and narrowing of focus, which is at the heart of any effective critical stand; our concern with the most advanced forms of modernism brought an enormous variety of talents to the magazine, while our social and historical bias gave it direction and influence. This double vision, as it were, sometimes seemed to lead to contradictions—as in our publishing of the leading New Critics, who certainly did not represent our more historical sense of literature. However, it did indicate a more fundamental principle: that only ideologues conceive of the culture as a monolith.

It might be interesting to quote from the editorial statement in the first issue of the new *PR* and to cite some of the contributors in the first couple of years, who ranged from Leon Trotsky to T. S. Eliot. It would also serve to illustrate how a policy that combined a radical but anti-Stalinist politics with a modernist sensibility was translated into the contents of the magazine. The issue included Delmore Schwartz's famous story "In Dreams Begin Responsibilities," poems by Wallace Stevens and James Agee, essays by Edmund Wilson and Lionel Abel, reviews by Sidney Hook, Lionel Trilling, Arthur Mizener, and William Troy.

134

The editorial statement was not free of the ponderous political rhetoric of the period, but it did introduce for the first time the combination of social concerns and literary standards that guided a new creative and critical movement. And it is interesting to quote from it at length, if only to see how well some of its formulations have stood up.

> As our readers know, the tradition of estheticism has given way to a literature which, for its origin and final justification, looks beyond itself and deep into the historic process. But the forms of literary editorship, at once exacting and adventurous, which characterized the magazines of the esthetic revolt, were of definite cultural value; and these forms Partisan Review will wish to adapt to the literature of the new period. . . .
>
> But Partisan Review aspires to represent a new and dissident generation in American letters; it will not be dislodged from its independent position by any political campaign against it. And without ignoring the importance of the official movement, as a sign of the times we shall know how to estimate its authority in literature. But we shall also distinguish, wherever possible, between the tendencies of this faction itself and the work of writers associated with it. For our editorial accent falls chiefly on culture and its broader social determinants. Conformity to a given social ideology, or to a prescribed attitude or technique, will not be asked of our writers. On the contrary, our pages will be open to any tendency which is relevant to literature in our time. Marxism in culture, we think, is first of all an instrument of analysis and evaluation; and if, in the last instance, it prevails over other disciplines, it does so through the medium of democratic controversy. Such is the medium that Partisan Review will want to provide in its pages.

The energy of the magazine in its early years might be said to have come from the unusual combination of modernism, a radical sensibility, critical intelligence, and a variety of talent that had not yet been siphoned off by the larger and the commercial publications. And though this coalition seemed to last until the fifties, the fact is that it was gradually being split apart. On the political side there was a slow movement to the right, due partly to disillusionment with the Communists, but mainly to the increasing prosperity of the country and the feeling that the youthful radicalism of the thirties had been outgrown. A number of anticommunists left their radical base and became more and more conservative, to the point where they were not only more critical of all socialism but also less critical of the status quo. Anti-Stalinism first turned into anticommunism and then into antiradicalism. In addition, those who remained on the left were being splintered by all kinds of ideological and tactical differences. Some opposed World War II on the old Marxist grounds; some became pacifists;

135

but most shifted to support of the war in the belief that fascist totalitarianism represented a new kind of barbaric society. There was also a strong pull toward anarchism, which came from the feeling that the answer to communism lay not in another variety of Marxism, however much it might profess to be dedicated to the ideals of democracy, but in a stand that elevated morality over expediency and decentralization over discipline.

By 1944 the other members of the board had left, leaving Rahv and myself as the editors, and shortly after this William Barrett and Delmore Schwartz joined us as associate editors. Mary McCarthy and Fred Dupee had left for personal reasons. Dwight Macdonald resigned mainly because of political differences, and he subsequently founded *Politics,* which was less literary than *Partisan Review* and leaned toward a more anarchist and moral view of politics.

It is impossible to reduce editorial policy to a single definition, but it might be said that we had several aims, partly conscious, partly unconscious. Basically, I suppose, we tried as much as possible to sustain the grouping of ideas and talent that was brought together originally by the magazine. We also tried to maintain the earlier combination of literary modernism and political radicalism, though our own beliefs and perspectives were also shifting. We too were part of the swing away from the doctrinaire positions of the thirties. As I look back, it would appear that we swung too far, though I must say that we always dissociated ourselves from the conservative anticommunists and the magazine always remained critical of the culture and politics of our country. In fact, as the temper of the nation became more conservative, the magazine became more critical of the adjustments to the new political and literary mood. But our primary aim, as it had been even in the earlier, more homogeneous period, was to keep that difficult balance between representing new ideas and talents and maintaining our own sense of values and direction. By trying to uphold what we thought were the highest standards of quality, we felt we were not only representing the best of contemporary writing and thinking, but we were also promoting and illustrating our own views about the current state of culture and politics.

During this period we published most serious writers who were

136

either already established or who became known later, but always in a context that indicated the policies of the magazine. At this point, it might be informative to list some of the contributors to indicate both the range and the accent of the poetry, fiction, and criticism published in those years, and to note the shift in the accents of the magazine.

The early issues included: André Gide on the Soviet Union, Edmund Wilson on Henry James, Meyer Shapiro on Lewis Mumford, James Burnham on American capitalism, William Phillips on Marxist aesthetics, F. W. Dupee on Malraux, Philip Rahv on contemporary fiction, Max Brod on Kafka, Harry Levin on Heine, William Troy on Thomas Mann, Leon Trotsky on art and politics, Clement Greenberg on avant-garde and kitsch, Harold Rosenberg on myth and history, Eliseo Vivas on John Dewey, R. P. Blackmur on current poetry, W. H. Auden on Yeats, Louis MacNeice's diary; fiction by John Dos Passos, James T. Farrell, Franz Kafka, Ignazio Silone, Eleanor Clark, William Carlos Williams, Charles Jackson; poetry by Elizabeth Bishop, Louise Bogan, e. e. cummings, D. S. Savage, Julian Symons, Theodore Roethke, John Berryman, Randall Jarrell, Dylan Thomas, R. B. Fuller, George Barker, David Gascoyne, Wallace Stevens, Allen Tate, Robert Fitzgerald; also theater criticism by Mary McCarthy, *Letters from Prison* by Rosa Luxemburg, and a symposium on *The Situation in American Writing,* with John Dos Passos, Allen Tate, James T. Farrell, Kenneth Fearing, Katherine Anne Porter, Wallace Stevens, Gertrude Stein, W. C. Williams, John Peale Bishop, Harold Rosenberg, Henry Miller, Sherwood Anderson, Louise Bogan, Lionel Trilling, Robert Penn Warren, Robert Fitzgerald, R. P. Blackmur, and Horace Gregory.

Among the contributors to later issues were Leslie Fiedler, Stephen Spender, George Orwell, Vladimir Nabokov, Arthur Koestler, John Berryman, Irving Howe, Saul Bellow, W. H. Auden, Cyril Connolly, James Baldwin, Hannah Arendt, John Crowe Ransom, Elizabeth Bowen, Tennessee Williams, Graham Greene, Albert Camus, André Malraux, H. L. Mencken, Robert Lowell, Jean Genet, Alfred Kazin, Jean-Paul Sartre, Simone de Beauvoir, I. A. Richards, Henry Miller, Paul Goodman, Ignazio Silone, Arthur Schlesinger, Jorge Luis Borges.

In the fifties, the divisions that were tearing apart the earlier coalition were becoming clearer and sharper. Neoconservatism was in full swing, as former radicals began to sing the praises of the country and the culture. The conservative anticommunists no longer regarded the Soviet Union as an obstacle to socialism; it was now simply a threat to the existing system, which suddenly became full of newly found virtues. The slogan of the new conservatism was "the end of ideology," by which was meant the end of radical ideology. To speed up the end of ideology, the new conservatives mounted a high-powered attack not only on Marxism but on all other forms of radicalism. That some of these attacks were justified is beside the point, for the impulse was polemical, not open-minded.

The fifties, which have become the favorite arena for revisionist history, were of course memorable for the exploitation of the anticommunist position—originally kept within bounds by radical opponents of the totalitarian turn Stalinism had taken—by reactionary and chauvinist ideologues. The culmination was reached in the wild, irresponsible, and pathologic campaign of Senator McCarthy who, besides persecuting innocent as well as guilty people, not only succeeded in distorting the issue of communism, but also set back the cause of genuine radicalism in this country. *Partisan Review* again, in this muddled and unsavory situation, saw its task as that of opposing both the crackpot politics on the right and the lies of the Communist left.

Culturally, the spirit of retrenchment showed itself in a turn against experiment and avant-garde attitudes in the arts, and in a general reaction against the idea of modernism. It meant, too, that the mass media were looked at more indulgently; conventional writing became more acceptable; and academicism became the dominant mood, particularly in poetry and criticism.

In the fifties, too, the assault on the idea of a minority, or adversary, culture—the idea that had sustained the modernist movement—gained respectability. Before that, it had been the philistines and the commercial writers who had acted as the apologists for the mass culture. But in the fifties many of the young, serious writers began to appear in the more popular magazines and to propound a number of ingenious theories rejecting the old division of high, low, and middle culture—theories that could

138

be used to obliterate the difference between publications like *Playboy* and journals like *Partisan Review*. And although the magazine had addressed itself earlier to these questions, most notably in Clement Greenberg's famous essay "Avant-Garde and Kitsch," we now felt it necessary to emphasize the old distinctions that separate entertainment and literary packaging from the less popular forms of serious writing. Ironically, it should be added, the populist strain in the vulgar Marxism of the thirties helped prepare the ground for the later reconciliation with the commercial pressures of the mass market and its need for more conventional forms of art.

In fact, *Partisan Review* was also swayed by these powerful currents, but I think only in a small way. The main effort of the magazine was to counter the conservative push, yet without giving in to those radicals in politics and in the arts who had resisted the tide but had swung to a nutty or sectarian extreme. The problem, however, was further complicated by the radical-conservative polarization that affected writing as well as politics, though it might be said that in the fifties the culture was still mostly on the side of tradition. In this situation we saw that our role was to maintain literary standards while being open to new work, and to reexamine liberal and radical positions while being critical both of the new Right and the lunatic Left. We were, of course, subjected to pressures from both sides: from the Left for having abandoned our radical heritage, from the Right for not being anticommunist enough or for being tolerant of youth and their half-baked experiments and ideas. At this time, for example, we published an assault on the new conservatism by Irving Howe, which—excessively, I think—also accused the magazine of giving in to it. At the same time, I myself wrote several pieces critical of the move to the right, politically and culturally; the title of one of them, "A Portrait of the Artist as a Middle-Aged Man," clearly indicated our bias.

But it was the sixties that brought the earlier tendencies to a head—and sharpened the dilemmas of the magazine. The blossoming of the New Left and the counterculture not only drove the conservatives more to the right but further splintered the remnants of the Left. And the hostility of the New Left to the so-called Old Left further complicated the role of the magazine. Politically, the problem was to steer a course that was, on the one hand, sympathetic to the innocence and idealism of youth, who were trying to escape from the system without getting caught in the rigid ideologies of the communists, and, on the other hand, was critical of the counterculture and the New Left for converting their ignorance, their petulance, and their self-indulgence into an infantile left in politics and a pop culture that managed to be both alienated and modish. Culturally, the polarization tended to highlight the celebration of experience, sexual freedom, and half-cocked experiments at one extreme, and a devotion to order, rationality, and tradition at the other. But there was a good deal of sanity and talent in between, which was ignored by obsessive polemics on both sides. *Partisan Review*—acting on the assumption borne out by cultural history that ideological extremes play themselves out and that in the long run only talent and genuine ideas survive—tried to foster the kind of writing that was not affected by either conservative or radical postures. To be sure, this was not easy, since distinctions are not as clear-cut in practice as in theory, and I must admit the magazine was swayed by the crosswinds as it tried to stay on its cultural course. But in the overheated atmosphere of the sixties the magazine got it from both sides, as it was accused both of swinging with the youth and of holding the line with the old guard.

Where are we now? The frenzy of the sixties has cooled off. But if some of the nonsense has gone, so have the energy and the restlessness that come from a refusal to adapt to things as they are. The dominant mood is one of confusion. The plastic arts, particularly, are in a state of chaos, as fashionability and experiment are mistaken for each other. Even though a good deal of serious poetry, fiction, and criticism is being written, an air of uncertainty about our relation to the modernist tradition and to the mass culture hangs over us.

In four decades the face of the country has changed. Wars, revolutions, and liberation movements have torn apart traditional politics and have eaten away at the idea of an elite culture. Disaffection and the feeling that America is going down are wide-

140

spread; and earlier radical impulses have been supplanted by the mushrooming of cults, breeding an optimism of political and psychological self-realization. These dislocations have naturally had their effect on writing. And though many strong talents have emerged, on the whole the current moods have not so far been transformed into a literature which has outgrown its peripheral and eccentric origins.

Perhaps it is my bias that leads me to hear echoes of the thirties in the issues we face today, issues that basically have to do with the relation of literature to politics. But it is the bias that has, I believe, kept *Partisan Review* on top of what is going on.

William Phillips, editor of Partisan Review, circa *1977 (courtesy William Phillips).*

W A K E

the creative magazine

Seymour Lawrence

Jose Garcia Villa

editors

WAKE EDITIONS
Copyright 1950
New York City

Wake, *Vol. 1, No. 1, September 1944 (courtesy Seymour Lawrence).*

MEMOIR OF A 50-YEAR-OLD PUBLISHER ON HIS VOYAGE TO OUTER SPACE
Seymour Lawrence

The magazines Seymour Lawrence took as models when he edited Wake *from 1945 to 1953 were* transition, Hound and Horn, This Quarter, *and* The Little Review. *He has worked in the field of publishing for thirty-three years: for the D. Van Nostrand Press, the Atlantic Monthly Press, Alfred A. Knopf, and the publishing house of Seymour Lawrence, Inc., which he founded in 1965 and which has published the work of Kurt Vonnegut, Jr., J. P. Donleavy, Katherine Anne Porter, Tillie Olson, Richard Brautigan, Dan Wakefield, John Malcolm Brinnin, Robert Coles, Robert Musil, Jorge Luis Borges, and Miguel Angel Asturias. Mr. Lawrence is also indebted to the editorial and literary manners represented by Gordon Cairnie of the Grolier Book Shop, Frances Steloff of the Gotham Book Mart, Maxwell E. Perkins, and Alfred A. Knopf. He belongs to the Harvard Club, the Century Association, the Signet Society, and the Union Boat Club.*

Harvard during World War II and the postwar years was a marvelous place to be an undergraduate. Many of the students came on the GI Bill—highly motivated, career-bent veterans who had seen combat. Among them were decorated war heroes, former colonels, fighter pilots, OSS paratroopers still in their early twenties who as a generation were regarded as tough-minded idealists. To the incoming eighteen-year-old freshmen from high schools and prep schools these older veterans, in their uniforms of J. Press tweed jackets, khaki chinos (or officer "pinks"), and combat

143

boots, represented experience and romance. But Harvard remained Harvard. In 1944 it still had the quality of a self-contained New England community, rather than the *rive gauche* scene of coffee-houses, bistros, boutiques, street musicians, and astrological head shops that it is today.

The faculty was extraordinary. F. O. Matthiessen, in nervous staccato sentences, conveyed the achievement of the American writer—Melville, Hawthorne, Emerson, Thoreau, Dreiser, Sherwood Anderson—and the American loneliness. Theodore Spencer urbanely discussed the comedies and tragedies of Shakespeare. Harry Levin lectured brilliantly on Proust, Mann, and Joyce, each lecture a carefully wrought essay. Walter Gropius spoke from direct experience of the Bauhaus School. I. A. Richards dazzled and mystified audiences with Seven Types of Ambiguity and the Meaning of Meaning. The great anarchist-scholar Gaetano Salvemini lyrically re-created the Italian Renaissance and the Risorgimento. ("History is *never* black and white, only grays. History is not made of wars and generals and tyrants. History is the story of the common people.") The world-renowned German classicist Werner Jaeger inspired overflowing lecture halls with his pure vision of the plays of Aeschylus and Euripides and the Golden Age of Pericles.

And at dusk on warm spring evenings, Harvard and Radcliffe lovers would stroll along the banks of the Charles. Groups of students sat and gossiped while a solitary oarsman silently rowed by.

It was in this setting that *Wake* was born. The magazine was founded by Harvard freshmen in 1944 as a wartime measure to fill the vacuum left by Mother *Advocate* (the oldest American undergraduate literary magazine) who had "folded her wings for the duration in November 1943, leaving a definite gap in the undergraduate literary world" (from an unsigned *Wake* editorial in Volume I, number 1). Without the war there would have been no *Wake*.

The first issue of *The Harvard Wake* appeared in September 1944. There was no masthead. The stories and poems were typical of any undergraduate magazine anywhere: introspective, soul searching, entirely undistinguished and unmemorable. Not one of the contributors is known today as a professional writer. Nor was there any indication of how the name *Wake* originated. I later learned, perhaps apocryphally, that it was christened by the novelist John Hawkes (Class of '47), but to this day I still have no idea what *Wake* stands for. An Irish wake? The verb wake? A ship's wake? You pays your money and you takes your choice. This pilot issue ran to 36 pages. The cover, on coated stock, was illustrated with a black-and-white drawing of a unicorn, a harp, and a tree sprouting leaves and naked young men (the kind you might see on Muscle Beach in Southern California) minus their private parts, and in the corner was the Harvard seal inside a broken chain. The issue sold for twenty-five cents a copy and I can't imagine who would have bought it.

Number 2 appeared in December 1944. The cover, again on coated stock, was illustrated with a black-and-white drawing of two hands (male) reaching for two other hands (male). This time the editors came out of the closet and declared themselves. The masthead listed a president, an editor, a secretary, an editorial board, and a business board. Seabury Quinn was the editor, and we shall return to the mournful, moustachioed Mr. Quinn in a few moments. The only name I recognize today is Craig Gilbert, a successful television dramatist and the creator of a devastating documentary called *An American Family*. As for the issue itself, the editorial (unsigned but presumably written by Mr. Quinn) stated that the eminent Harvard sociologist Pitirim Sorokin thought the first issue was "an excellent example of the social sewerage raked around by contemporary artists." The editorial continued:

Granted that this first issue impressed many as a tour de force *in morbidity, let us remind you that the adolescent mind, to whose production the* Wake *limits itself by policy, tends in this direction anyway, and as most of us know, there's a war on. Future policy, however, will try to lean more to the healthy outlook towards life, the lack of which in our first endeavor was so widely deprecated. . . . To this end in order to get the benefit of the female viewpoint the present edition contains our first contribution from Radcliffe.*

What follows are "A Moral Tale: Honi soit qui mal y pense" by Seabury Quinn, and other stories and poems of no particular character except for a two-page exercise in slice-of-life realism titled "Washington, Southwest" by Austryn Wainhouse (who later became an expatriate in France, a superb maker of furniture and an equally superb translator of the works of the Marquis de Sade

145

and other French writers, including *Chance and Necessity* by the eminent biologist Jacques Monod, for which Wainhouse received the National Book Award for Translation in 1972). This second issue ran to 32 pages and sold for a quarter.

Number 3 appeared in March 1945 with a classier cover than its predecessors: straightforward typography on coated white stock, listing the contents and having a Harvard seal inside a broken chain in the left-hand corner. The masthead changed a bit, with Seabury Quinn now editor in chief, a business manager, and a much reduced editorial board. The Contents listed "Seven Points on Prophecy" by I. A. Richards, a poem by Theodore Spencer, and a poem by a talented Radcliffe contributor, Alison Lurie (who later achieved success as a novelist and as the author of a remarkable novel, *The War Between the Tates*). The editorial for this issue opened on a note of despair:

The Wake *has fallen on comparatively evil days. As yet the prognosis is not definitely negative, but we have taken council to change our policy.*

Apparently, the editors had not been able to find enough good material from the undergraduate body to fill an issue, and decided to print contributions from "faculty members, graduates, post graduates, and anyone else we can lay our hands on." Which accounts for I. A. Richards and Theodore Spencer. The issue ran to 64 pages and included 27 pages from a novella in progress by Jay Lafferty, which concluded with the following notation: *To be continued.* Mr. Lafferty's novella was never continued.

Number 4 appeared in June 1945 with a light gray cover on uncoated stock, a Harvard seal inside a broken chain in the center, and the Contents printed in blue ink. That issue marked a turning point in the life and nature of *Wake*. A mild palace revolution had occurred on the editorial board. A group of us succeeded in pushing Seabury Quinn upstairs as president, and a troika of editors was formed, consisting of two upperclassmen and myself. We were supported by a group of associates composed of several freshmen, including my then current lady love, S. S. Phillips (now Sayre Phillips Sheldon, a member of the English department at Boston University). Gone was the self-serving editorial, and in its stead appeared a "Note on Contributors" column.

Among the contributors to this issue were Conrad Aiken,

e. e. cummings, Kenneth Patchen, F. O. Matthiessen, Harry Levin, José Garcia Villa, and ten undergraduates.

Among the noncontributors was William March, a neglected writer and the author of *Company K* and *The Bad Seed,* who had generously contributed a humorous story called "The Borax Bottle." The story concerned an old man recalling his early courtship of his wife and how they met as small children. They were playing in an open field when the little boy showed his private parts to the little girl and vice versa. A bee stung the boy's pecker and it started to swell. The little girl found a bottle of borax and told him to stick his wounded member in borax to ease the sting and reduce the swelling. But alas, it became even more swollen and got stuck in the bottle. The rest of the story described how the children hid from their parents, not wanting to explain how the boy got stuck in the borax bottle. Seabury Quinn, as president, was offended by the story and voted against publication. There were enough of us, however, who voted to publish it. An outraged Mr. Quinn took his case to A. Chester Hanford, dean of Harvard College, a gentle, kindly man of the old school.

The following morning I was summoned to the dean's office in University Hall. Dean Hanford's desk was bare except for the manuscript of "The Borax Bottle." He asked my intentions and I told him that the editors had voted to publish the story. He allowed that he had read the story, found it embarrassing, not in the best of taste, and certainly not appropriate to an undergraduate magazine bearing the name of Harvard. He went on to say that he could not prevent us from publishing the story and he had no intention of being a censor. However, if we persisted, he had no recourse but to suspend the magazine and to suspend me and my associates from Harvard College. We bowed before the crimson glove and scepter, and "The Borax Bottle" did not appear in Volume I, number 4. And Mr. Seabury Quinn did not appear in number 5 or in any issue thereafter.

Regarding the contributors to number 4, Professors Levin and Matthiessen had been approached on the basis of Harvard loyalty. The work of Conrad Aiken, e. e. cummings, and Kenneth Patchen had been acquired with the help of the Philippine poet José Garcia Villa. I had met Villa in 1943 when I was living in New York City, taking random courses at Columbia as a special student and working part time as a clerk in the Columbia University Book-

147

store where Villa worked full time. Although not actually being enrolled at Columbia College, I was allowed to audit courses: literature with Mark Van Doren and F. W. Dupee, philosophy with Irwin Edman, and *Moby-Dick* with the great Melville scholar Raymond Weaver. I also served as an editor of the *Columbia Jester Review* (a wartime merger of the humor and literary magazines). Besides knowing Villa, I had occasional escapades and encounters with Allen Ginsberg, Jack Kerouac, and the legendary Lucien Carr (who killed an older friend with a boy scout knife during that period). After a year of so-called *la vie bohème* I decided to go legal and at the age of eighteen I took College Entrance Board examinations to qualify for Harvard.

Does anyone still read the work of José Garcia Villa? When his first book of poems—*Have Come, Am Here* (announcing his arrival on the scene)—was published in 1942, it was hailed as a literary event by e. e. cummings, Marianne Moore, Mark Van Doren, and others. Villa lived alone in one room near the Columbia campus, surrounded by books of poetry and his own Modigliani-like paintings. (He was also an accomplished short story writer, and his work appeared in several O. Henry collections.) He worked all day in the Columbia bookstore, where he sold more poetry than anyone else before or after him. He was an unofficial member of the faculty, and in the evenings he would discuss modern poetry with selected undergraduates. His taste was practically flawless (he could not bear the work of T. S. Eliot), and he adhered to rigid standards and self-discipline. He knew and understood poetics, and he communicated his knowledge of poetry and his love of the English language. But he was a demanding teacher and something of a despot; like Gurdjieff, his disciples inevitably left him. It was Villa who introduced me to the work of Gerard Manley Hopkins, Rainer Maria Rilke, Hart Crane, Ernest Walsh, Wallace Stevens, Henry Miller, Arthur Rimbaud, Gertrude Stein, and D. H. Lawrence. I learned about *transition, Hound and Horn, This Quarter, The Little Review,* Harry Crosby, and the Black Sun Press. Mark Van Doren and José Garcia Villa were my essential teachers at Columbia.

Before I entered Harvard, Villa had brought me to tea with e. e. cummings and his wife, Marion Morehouse, at their tiny house in Greenwich Village. And it was Villa who conceived the idea of devoting a special number of *Wake* to cummings.

Cummings

number

A PLAY—A FAIRY TALE—A POEM

by E. E. CUMMINGS

CONRAD AIKEN

JACQUES BARZUN

JOHN DOS PASSOS

LLOYD FRANKENBERG

HORACE GREGORY

ALFRED KREYMBORG

HARRY LEVIN

MARIANNE MOORE

FAIRFIELD PORTER

PAUL ROSENFELD

KARL SHAPIRO

THEODORE SPENCER

WALLACE STEVENS

ALLEN TATE

LIONEL TRILLING

MARK VAN DOREN

WM. C WILLIAMS

MARYA ZATURENSKA

WAKE 5

Wake, *No. 5, Spring 1946, inscribed to Seymour Lawrence by E. E. Cummings (courtesy Seymour Lawrence).*

That number, *Wake* 5, was published in the spring of 1946. I was in my sophomore year, and the preparation of this issue consumed most of my spare time. I had to abandon honors tutorial work with Harry Levin, and my grades probably suffered, though I don't recall being concerned: I was learning to be a publisher. I rarely skipped classes and took every course I possibly could that was offered by F. O. Matthiessen, Gaetano Salvemini, I. A. Richards, Werner Jaeger, Renato Poggioli, and Albert J. Guérard.

The masthead of *Wake* 5 read as follows:

Editor:	Seymour Lawrence
Guest Editor:	José Garcia Villa
Associates:	Donald Berlin, Robert Creeley, Race Newton
Business Manager:	Amos L. Hopkins

Donald "Buddy" Berlin was a cool, self-contained Andover boy, son of a successful Brookline, Mass., doctor, who wrote Kafkaesque stories, played a tenor sax, and was a friend of the jazz musicians Dizzy Gillespie and Charlie "Yardbird" Parker. Last heard of, "Buddy" Berlin was running a foreign car agency in New Mexico.

Race Newton was my freshman roommate. The son of a prominent doctor in Little Falls, N. Y., Race had studied poetry at Choate with Dudley Fitts, and had read most of Gertrude Stein and the surrealist poets by the time he entered Harvard. Like Berlin, he was a skillful musician and played jazz piano. At sixteen, he had been seduced by the wife of a Choate master, a scene right out of *Tea and Sympathy*. Race Newton is now a gentleman farmer living in the west of England.

Robert Creeley, class of '47, had returned to Harvard after having served with the American Field Service as an ambulance driver in India. His family lived in Cambridge, where his mother worked as a registered nurse. Creeley had lost an eye in a childhood accident and always wore a black patch. A lean, rangy, soft-spoken New Englander, Creeley loved to listen to jazz at the Savoy in Boston. He was very much his own man, as he still is, and he has followed a true and steady course—a poet of great integrity, much admired by the young. Creeley brought back from India a knapsack full of ganjha, a hallucinatory drug which we occasionally smoked (twenty-five years before the pot scene). We would

150

empty the contents of half a cigarette, replace the tobacco with the hemplike weed, light up, and off we'd go. But this was a rare occurrence. We were a booze generation, and some of our parties lasted several days.

Amos Hopkins was my sophomore roommate, a Boston blueblood, son of a banker and a wise, widely read southern mother. Amos, or "Mouse," studied biology and irregular German verbs and managed *Wake*'s business affairs. He is now a research scientist at Case Western Reserve Medical School.

Hopkins and I shared a suite in Lowell House, on the top floor of G Entry (known as Gentry). Two floors below us lived Professor Gaetano Salvemini, who had escaped from fascist Italy after having failed in a plot to assassinate Mussolini. We each had our own bedroom, a bathroom with shower and two sinks, and an enormous sitting room with fireplace. It was a great place for parties, *Wake* and otherwise. At one of these parties the Spanish/Philippine painter Fernando Zobel, fresh from Manila and on his second day at Harvard, recalls walking into a candle-lit room and being approached by a stranger who asked, "And what do *you* think of Pavel Tchelitchew?"

Hopkins had "borrowed" a complete skeleton from the biology department, which we dressed in a dark three-piece suit, scarf, socks, shoes, an old fedora pulled down over its forehead, and a book in its lap. The skeleton was always seated in the corner of a long leather couch, with its back to the entrance of the suite. Unsuspecting visitors, on entering the room, thought a person in a hat was reading quietly, and got the shock of their lives when they looked closely. Hopkins had also tacked a huge map of the United States on one wall of the sitting room, on which he would affix red pins whenever we established a new outlet for *Wake*.

The cummings number brought us national attention—and a visitor from Vassar. One morning there was a knock on our door. We opened it, expecting the laundryman (in those days Harvard undergraduates had daily maid service—"biddies" from North Cambridge—and laundry service once a week). Standing in the doorway was a tidy, small man with glasses, correctly attired in a boy's Brooks Brothers suit. He hesitantly introduced himself as Howard Moss, a teacher from Vassar, and he wanted to know if

151

this was the place where the cummings number was edited. I didn't know what to make of him and was neither courteous nor hospitable, and he went away. In later years I came to know and respect this shy, diffident man as a superior poet and critic, the discerning poetry editor of *The New Yorker,* and someone who helped people when they needed help. (Howard, if you happen to read this monologue and have got this far, what I want to know is, What the hell happened to the laundryman that morning?)

Back to the cummings number. Villa not only conceived of this special issue, but he was instrumental in acquiring new and unpublished material from cummings himself: a fairy tale called "The Old Man Who Said 'Why,'" a poem, and a morality play called *Santa Claus.* Villa was also primarily responsible for soliciting and gathering original essays and statements in appreciation of cummings from Marianne Moore, William Carlos Williams, Allen Tate, John Dos Passos, Lionel Trilling, Karl Shapiro, Jacques Barzun, Harry Levin, Paul Rosenfeld, Lloyd Frankenberg, Alfred Kreymborg, Theodore Spencer, Fairfield Porter, Horace Gregory, and Marya Zaturenska. There was a splendid frontispiece photograph of cummings in profile, taken by Harry Dunham, and there was a brief bibliography.

The issue ran to 96 pages of which the cummings material occupied 77 pages. The remaining pages included new poems by Wallace Stevens, Conrad Aiken, William Carlos Williams, Mark Van Doren, José Garcia Villa, and the very young work of four Harvard undergraduates: Robert Creeley, Race Newton, Donald Berlin, and the author of this long-winded exercise who squirms every time he looks at his juvenilia (a word too close for comfort to genitalia).

The cummings number sold for a dollar a copy. We printed 2,000 copies and the sainted Frances Steloff—an extraordinary presence and a dedicated bookseller, as shrewd as they come (she taught me what an invoice was and how to write one)—bought 500 copies for her Gotham Book Mart at 40 cents a copy and stored most of them away in her cellar. Some years later, when there were no copies to be had, Frances had them. There was that pristine white cover on uncoated antique stock, with the words "cummings number" in bright red script across the top, selling at five dollars a copy. Lord knows what it would sell for today.

We received orders from all over this country, England, and the Continent. Amos Hopkins ran out of red pins. An exhibit of cummings' paintings was held at the Grolier Book Shop in Cambridge, whose proprietor, Gordon Cairnie, will be remembered and cherished long after most of us are gone. Much has been written about that dear man whom so many of us loved, who encouraged us to browse for hours in his bookshop (*No Textbooks!*) without ever suggesting that we buy anything or saying a word except to tell us to be sure to shut the door when we came in.

At the Grolier Book Shop I first met Conrad Aiken, in for a visit from his home on Cape Cod. He would invariably invite Gordon Cairnie to the Harvard Club for martinis and lunch. No one escaped Gordon or would want to escape him. An innocent undergraduate, sitting in the corner of Gordon's old broken-down sofa (with Gordon in the other corner writing invoices and gently complaining), would suddenly be transfixed by the appearance of T. S. Eliot or Edmund Wilson or Robert Lowell in the doorway. I may have spent as much time in the Grolier Book Shop as I did at Harvard College; I know that I spent more time there than at Widener Library.

Gordon was our friend, and to many he *was* Harvard. We are all his customers in one way or another, and all the money in Boston could never repay him for what he gave us. When I celebrated my twenty-fifth Harvard reunion in 1973, I had to wear a top hat, white tie, and cutaway because I was a marshal's aid, regarded as an honor for so-called distinguished alumni. My job in the academic procession was to carry a banner and lead the classes of 1962–1972 through Harvard Yard into the Tercentenary Theatre, where speeches are given by prominent folk and recipients of honorary degrees. After leading my flock, I returned the banner to its home, walked out of the Yard, and made a beeline for the Grolier Book Shop. I opened the door, shouting, "Have you got any textbooks on physics?" Gordon looked up, about to tell me to go to blazes or to shut the door, when he saw me in my fancy regalia. He immediately wanted someone to take our photograph together in front of his shop, so he phoned Elsa Dorfman, his friend and one of the most sensitive photographers of poets and writers I know. She took our pictures. Gordon was wearing a tweed cap (which Alastair Reid and I had bought for him in

Scotland), scruffy tweed jacket, and disreputable khaki pants. I stood next to him in my top hat, et cetera, carrying a black baton with a red ribbon around it. The pictures were never developed. Gordon Cairnie died a few months later, and since these were the last photographs ever taken of him, Elsa Dorfman, who revered Gordon, could never bring herself to print them.

It was two years before we published the next issue, *Wake* 6. Why the time lag I don't rightly remember. Studies, girls, lack of funds, an honors thesis, my senior year—it could have been any one of these reasons, but most likely it was a combination of all. Race Newton had been expelled from Harvard. "Buddy" Berlin had lost interest in *Wake* and writing, and had gotten more into jazz. Amos Hopkins was involved in research and laboratory work. Bob Creeley had married his first wife by then and was living in Provincetown.

A new staff was created, comprising myself, John Hawkes, who had already begun work on his first novel, and John Rogers, class of '49, a laconic New Englander with a painstaking sense of craftsmanship, like a good carpenter or shipbuilder.

In the intervening years, the *Harvard Advocate* had been revived, so there was no real reason to retain "Harvard" in the name of our magazine. I approached one of the deans, told him I was graduating in June, and asked if I could continue as sole owner of *Wake* after graduation. Since the university had never contributed any funds or office space to *Wake*, and since we had assumed responsibility for printer's bills from the very beginning (we rented a Cambridge post office box for mail, manuscripts, bills, etc., and the editorial office was my suite at Lowell House), Harvard had no objection to our dropping its name from the magazine. I could own *Wake* if I wished, provided I personally assumed full responsibility for any debts the magazine might have incurred while I was an undergraduate and afterward. I accepted these conditions and *Wake* 6 was published in the spring of 1948. The issue ran to 96 pages and sold for a dollar. We printed 2,000 copies, as we did with *Wake* 5; but unlike the cummings number, which sold out entirely within a few months, we were left with half the printing unsold. Printing costs had risen, there were only two ads, and we ended up with a deficit of $1,500 owed to the printer.

154

I had devoted several months to preparing the issue and had to abandon my honors thesis on Sherwood Anderson, which was no great loss to scholarship. Since I had no interest in graduate study, my not writing a thesis simply meant no *cum laude,* no *magna cum laude,* certainly no *summa cum laude.*

Wake 6 was a varied and interesting issue, with poems by William Carlos Williams, Wallace Stevens, Conrad Aiken, Richard Wilbur, Louis Simpson, Robert Creeley; a fairy tale by e. e. cummings, "A Little Girl Named I"; fiction by John Hawkes, Albert J. Guérard, Austryn Wainhouse; and the "comma poems" of José Garcia Villa, an innovation that disconcerted many readers (comma, poems, are, poems, conceived, with, commas, in, which, the, commas, are, an, integral, and, essential, part, of, the, poem, enabling, each, word, to, attain, a, fuller, tonal, value). I remain a devoted admirer of Villa's work, and some of his most beautiful poems are "comma poems" which,may,be,enjoyed,with,or,without, commas.

I graduated from Harvard in June 1948, without honors and without a penny to my name. The final thrust was having my "class poem" rejected as being unsuitable and inappropriate to the occasion—which it probably was, since the poem was against ambition, the business rat race, money grubbing, etc. On Commencement Day in Harvard Yard, class officers always lead their class; they are distinguished by red tassels on their mortarboards, while the rest of the class have black tassels. Since there was to be no class poem, I saw no point in being the class poet, a post to which my class had elected me. So I marched in black-tasseled cap and gown with a thousand other undistinguished Harvard citizens, next to Amos Hopkins, the man who helped me put *Wake* on the map in Suite G-42, Lowell House. We were admitted by President James Bryant Conant to the fellowship of educated men.

I spent the summer after graduation as an itinerant houseguest, visiting friends in Bucks County and Long Island, swimming, playing tennis, and wondering how I would get $1,500 to pay the printer and how to get even more money to finance *Wake* 7, which Villa and I were preparing.

I always knew that I would be a publisher but the question was, How and where do you begin? The previous spring I had been interviewed by Frank Taylor, then a senior editor at Random House, in his spacious *moderne* Madison Avenue office. As I sat

155

uncomfortably in a canvas sling chair, Taylor told me how *he* had begun as an advertising copywriter—or was it in publicity?—for a publishing firm. He then described his meteoric rise, first becoming editor in chief of Reynal and Hitchcock, a small, distinguished firm now defunct, and later attaining his present position. He pointed to a fancy Ronson cigarette lighter on his desk and said, "I'm now a luxury item in the industry, like that expensive lighter." The interview left me in a mild state of shock. Taylor seemed to me to be no more than a slick Madison Avenue huckster and not the image of a publisher I always had in mind. At Harvard I had read and reread the *Letters of Maxwell Perkins,* those beautiful, wise, and compassionate letters to Fitzgerald and Hemingway and Wolfe. And at the Grolier Book Shop I would constantly examine Gordon Cairnie's outstanding collection of first editions, none of which I could afford. Early on, I became aware that the Borzoi imprint of Alfred A. Knopf stood head and shoulders above every other American imprint. This was how books should be designed and made. These were the standards I wanted to maintain. This was what publishing was all about.

Wake 7 appeared in the fall of 1948 with this title page:

WAKE
the creative magazine

Seymour Lawrence
José Garcia Villa
editors

WAKE EDITIONS
New York

It was a thick issue of 104 pages and sold for one dollar a copy. I had found an excellent printer near the Bowery who was willing to extend credit.

The issue was divided into four sections: "Poetry," "Prose," "Translations," "New Writers." In the "Poetry" section were new poems by Edith Sitwell, Stephen Spender, Henry Miller, Conrad Aiken, Richard Wilbur, Walter de la Mare, W. S. Graham, Frederick Prokosch, more "comma poems" by José Garcia Villa, and an unpublished poem by D. H. Lawrence. In "Prose" there were a story by Theodore Spencer, an essay on Tristan Corbière by C. F. MacIntyre, and a treasure which Villa somehow managed to unearth from a collector he knew: unpublished notes and letters

156

of Walt Whitman. There were translations of Rimbaud, Stefan George, and Tristan Tzara. In the "New Writers" section were poems by Robert Creeley and Louis Simpson; short stories by Alan Harrington, John Lawson, and C. C. Brelis (Dean Brelis, my "blood brother" at Harvard—war hero, novelist, foreign correspondent, a fiercely loyal friend, and the most incurable romantic I know).

To pay the piper, I took a job as a college traveler with the venerable firm of D. Van Nostrand Company, publishers of textbooks in mathematics, the sciences, and engineering—which were Greek to me. After several months of training on New York's "Publisher's Row" (lower Park Avenue near Eighteenth Street), I was given my choice of a company car and chose a Chevrolet convertible. Equipped with two suitcases, catalogues, and sample books, I drove west to visit colleges in Arkansas, Oklahoma, Kansas, and Missouri. My salary was $2,600 a year plus all expenses on the road. I instructed the office manager to send my monthly paychecks to a bank in New York, and by the end of the year I had over $2,000 in savings, which covered not only the Cambridge printer's bill for *Wake* 6 but a down payment to the New York printer for *Wake* 7.

Seeing America as a college traveler was the finest graduate course I could have had. I drove and drove and drove, seeing as many as thirty or forty professors in a day, securing classroom adoptions of Van Nostrand textbooks, flooding the home office with weighty, unpublishable doctoral dissertations (and occasionally a marketable textbook). On weekends I would read manuscripts for *Wake* which Villa would send ahead to hotels in places like Chickasha, Oklahoma. I would also visit college bookstores, after a day's work, and open up new outlets for *Wake*. I was on the road four months at a stretch, returning to the home office during the Christmas recess, then going back on the road again.

Wake 8 appeared in the spring of 1949. While I traveled, Villa did most of the acquiring of manuscripts by established writers. The four categories established in *Wake* 7 continued. In "Poetry" were new poems by e. e. cummings, William Carlos Williams, Richard Eberhart, Jean Garrigue, Paul Goodman, Sir Osbert Sitwell, James Laughlin, Horace Gregory. In "Prose" appeared "The Baby Elephant," a play by Bertolt Brecht, and

157

short stories by Paul Bowles and Mark Van Doren. The translation section was exceptionally fine, containing Eluard, Baudelaire, Mallarmé, Claudel, and Bertrand. Plus poems and short stories by nine "New Writers," among them James Broughton, Barbara Deming, Jane Mayhall, Stanley Moss, and Katherine Hoskins. The issue ran to 128 pages and sold for a dollar.

My college traveling efforts were rewarded that fall with a raise in pay to $3,100 a year, and my territory was expanded to include Iowa, Nebraska, North Dakota, South Dakota, Montana, Wyoming, Colorado, Idaho, Washington, and Oregon, in addition to Arkansas, Oklahoma, Kansas, and Missouri. I saved money, paid all *Wake*'s bills, and the magazine flourished as new outlets were created on college campuses in the Midwest, Southwest, and Northwest. The magazine was always sold on consignment, and what the bookstores did not sell they would return, paying only for copies sold. Since we continued to use an uncoated antique white cover stock, the returned copies were usually soiled and unsalable.

Wake's availability on Midwestern campuses was a blessing for some. The West Coast poet Michael McClure recalls passing around tattered copies of *Wake* to other kindred souls while a student in Kansas. At the University of Missouri I was invited by William Peden to address his class in advanced creative writing, and I took an hour off from selling chemistry textbooks to discuss little magazines. One evening at dinner in a professor's house in western Iowa, I was introduced to a young Scot clad in kilts and a navy blue blazer bearing the crest of St. Andrews University. His name was Alastair Reid, and this was his first visit to the States as a teaching fellow. When Reid learned that I published *Wake,* he cried: "What on earth are *you* doing out here? I've been sending my poems to *Wake* in New York." Reid had come across *Wake* in the St. Andrews library, and more than anything else he wanted to be published alongside cummings, Stevens, Aiken, et al., whom he admired far more than their British contemporaries. At times I felt like Johnny Appleseed distributing *Wake* across the prairies.

After two years of traveling in the West, I joined the Ronald Press as field editor in the humanities. My territory was New England, and I decided to live in Cambridge. *Wake* and I were back home.

158

Wake 9 appeared in the spring of 1950 with six poems by Wallace Stevens and poems by Marianne Moore, William Carlos Williams, H. D., Mark Van Doren, Richard Eberhart, Jean Garrigue; translations of Mallarmé, Lorca, Mistral, Kästner, Rimbaud, and Villon; a fairy tale by e. e. cummings called "The House That Ate Mosquito Pie"; prose by William Carlos Williams, Theodore Spencer, and Mark Van Doren; and twelve new writers including Robert Creeley, Jackson MacLow, John Clellon Holmes, Francis Golffing, Eugene Walter, David Marcus, and James Broughton. The issue ran to 128 pages and sold for a dollar.

Although *Wake* never paid its contributors, we barely managed to break even and there was often a deficit after paying printer's bills, postage, stationery, etc. Neither Villa nor I ever received a salary. The only person who demanded payment was Vladimir Nabokov (or perhaps it was Mrs. Nabokov?), whom I visited at his apartment while he was teaching at Harvard. Since we could not pay him without paying other contributors, we parted amicably and *Wake* endured without Nabokov. I also recall being berated at length by F. O. Matthiessen while having lunch at the Signet Society, Harvard's undergraduate literary club. Matthiessen said that it was unprofessional of us to accept contributions from writers without paying for them. Several of my friends and class-mates witnessed this scene as I stammered, quite shaken and red-faced, "But, Professor Matthiessen, no one has ever asked for payment, and if we started paying there would be no *Wake* to publish." Matthiessen was, of course, entirely right, and as a professional publisher I believe that writers should always be paid when there are profits to be made; but *Wake* was never a profit-making venture. Matthiessen was also astonished that we could consistently draw first-rate work by established poets without payment. José Garcia Villa had a great deal to do with this, but I also think our contributors appreciated *Wake,* what it was trying to do and what it stood for. They may have liked its karma, aura, "vibes," or whatever it had. Fundamentally, I think they trusted *Wake* and they enjoyed being published there.

Wake 10, which appeared in the spring of 1951, was the last issue co-edited by José Garcia Villa and myself. Nothing really caused the parting of our ways except that I was mostly in New England and seldom in New York. Out of sight is out of mind, and we were also out of touch; it was a friendly geographical divorce. Villa's final coup was a sequence of eight original drawings by Saul Steinberg, which served as a preface to the issue. There were poems by Mark Van Doren, Richard Eberhart, John Hay, H. D., Brewster Ghiselin, William Jay Smith, Michael Hamburger, and Jean Garrigue; prose by e. e. cummings, David Cornel DeJong, and Kenneth Lash; translations of Hölderlin, Laforgue, Novalis, Mestrovic, and an ode by Dante translated by Howard Nemerov. In the "New Writers" section were poems by Daniel G. Hoffman, Alastair Reid, Denise Levertov, Barbara Gibbs, Gene Baro. The issue ran to 112 pages and again sold for a dollar.

I had known Conrad Aiken since my undergraduate days, when Gordon Cairnie introduced us at the Grolier Book Shop. Aiken invited me to visit him and his wife at their house in Brewster on Cape Cod. He said, "Come for orange blossoms." I had no idea what they were. I went down by bus, and five or six orange blossoms later I staggered out into the night and got lost in the woods. I never did get back to Cambridge and ended up spending the night at their house, "41 Doors." I had long admired Conrad Aiken as one of the few true men of letters in America, and the totality of his work was impressive: poetry, novels, short stories,

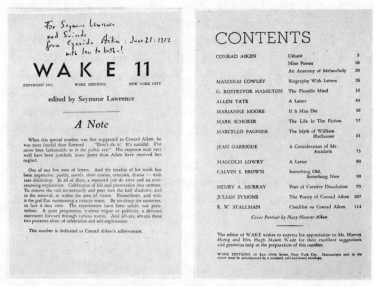

Wake, *No. 11, Spring 1952, a special Conrad Aiken number inscribed:* "For Seymour Lawrence and Suicide from Cyanide Aiken" (courtesy Seymour Lawrence).

criticism, drama. But he had never been fully appreciated and always stood in the shadow of his Harvard contemporary, T. S. Eliot. When I first suggested to Aiken the idea of a special number of *Wake* devoted to his work, he was more fearful than flattered. "Don't do it! It's suicidal. I've never been fashionable or in the public eye." All the more reason for doing it, I told him.

Wake 11, the Conrad Aiken number, was published in the spring of 1952. I had corresponded with Aiken and with many of the contributors from a villa in Positano, where I lived for several months during the fall and winter of 1951. After three years of selling and acquiring college textbooks, the honeymoon was over. I had learned a great deal about marketing but not about the kind of publishing I was interested in. I quit. And in the summer of 1951 I drew all my savings out of the bank, packed all my clothes, all my books, and with a trunk full of *Wake*s sailed on the *Île de France*. I spent a few weeks with my future wife in England and Wales, went on a walking trip with Alastair Reid in Scotland, and distributed copies of *Wake* to London bookshops. I then went to Paris, where I opened up new outlets for *Wake* on the Left Bank and on the rue de Rivoli. From Paris I went to the south of France and spent a week at St. Paul de Vence, where I met the poet Jacques Prévert in the bar at La Colombe d'Or. Prévert was the village character, a Rabelaisian figure in a bright red shirt, bursting with life, constantly talking and gesturing. I could understand only a fraction of what he said, but I enjoyed his company immensely.

After traveling to Florence, Venice, Rome, and Naples, I reached my final destination—Positano on the Amalfi Drive, where a Harvard classmate, the composer Douglas Allanbrook, was living on a Fulbright. Allanbrook and piano occupied the lower half of a villa, and I, with trunk loads of books and *Wake*s occupied the upper half. My plan was to live there a year, reading, writing, and editing *Wake*. But I became restless after several months and sailed home.

The Conrad Aiken number appeared a few months after my European interlude and around the time I was hired as special assistant to Edward Weeks, editor of the *Atlantic Monthly* (referred to by Aiken as the *Atlantic Weakly*). The issue ran to 128 pages and sold for $1.50. It included a section from Aiken's autobiographical novel *Ushant,* nine new poems, and his brilliant essay on T. S. Eliot's *The Waste Land* which originally appeared in the *New Republic* in 1923. There were essays on Aiken's work, letters and personal memoirs by Malcolm Cowley, Allen Tate, Marianne Moore, Mark Schorer, Henry A. Murray, G. Rostrevor Hamilton, Malcolm Lowry, Jean Garrigue, Julian Symons, Calvin S. Brown, Marcello Pagnini; and a comprehensive Aiken bibliography by R. W. Stallman. The cover drawing of Conrad Aiken in profile was by his wife, Mary Hoover Aiken.

The final issue, *Wake* 12, was the contemporary foreign number and was published in the fall of 1953. After that I felt it was time to close shop. I had other commitments, personal and professional, which occupied me. Moreover, *Wake* was primarily a magazine of poetry, and I had become increasingly concerned with publishing good fiction, which I did at the *Atlantic* and which I do to this day under my own imprint. Finally, and quite seriously, I am superstitious, and I did not want to publish *Wake* 13.

The foreign number was devoted to the work of writers from France, Italy, Germany, and Greece. A leading authority on each country wrote a literary and cultural overview. The issue was not meant to be comprehensive or a world anthology. It was a selection of contemporary writing abroad, and the main criterion was well-translated material. If a particular author's work, no matter how historically important it might be, was ill served by the translator, it would not pass. I had hoped that this special issue would serve as an introduction to show American writers and students what was being done abroad. It was one of the most satisfying numbers to publish.

The section on Italy included an essay titled "The Italian Success Story" by Renato Poggioli (whom I'd studied with at Harvard), followed by the poems of Morarte, Penna, Ungaretti, Scotellaro, Montale, and Quasimodo; and fiction by Pirandello, Natalia Ginzburg, Tecchi, and Alvaro. The section on Greece was prefaced with an essay, "The Greek Tradition," by the anthologist Kimon Friar; he selected and translated all the material, which included "The Odyssey" by Kazantzakis, with illustrations by Ghika, and poems by Seferis, Papatzonis, Elytis. The section on France included a general essay on the intellectual and cultural climate of postwar France by the poet and Resistance leader, Pierre Emmanuel. There were translations of work by Valéry,

Cocteau, Michaux, Larbaud, Emmanuel, Segalen, Claudel, Jarry, Reverdy, Apollinaire, Jouve, Prévert, and Rousselot. The section on Germany had a long essay on German postwar literature by Edgar Lohner, a brief essay on the poet Christian Morgenstern by E. M. Valk, and translations of the poetry of Morgenstern, Trakl, Benn.

The contemporary foreign number ran to 148 pages and sold for $1.50 a copy. Next to the cummings number, it was the most successful issue of *Wake*. Three of the poets—George Seferis of Greece, Eugenio Montale and Salvatore Quasimodo of Italy—received the Nobel Prize for Literature in later years.

Since this was the farewell number, I felt it might be appropriate to say a few words about *Wake* and what we tried to achieve during its ten-year span. I put it in the form of a "Note," and I will quote the opening paragraph and the final sentence.

Wake *has never been a crusading magazine in a partisan sense. What it has attempted to do during its life is present the finest possible poetry and fiction. If it has taken any* anti *position, it has been against the constricting effect a certain kind of critical-academic thinking has had on the minds and work of young writers.* Wake *has been primarily* for *things—for good poetry, for good prose, for unknown writers and for their recognized elders.* Wake *has served, more than crusaded. The search for distinguished writing has been its sole and guiding force. . . .*

This final issue is dedicated, with pleasure, to young writers everywhere.

163

QRL: HALLELUJAH ON A STRAW
Theodore Weiss

By the time poetry had become Theodore Weiss's chief interest in life, he had discovered a number of magazines whose work he considered important. Among these were The Kenyon Review, Partisan Review, The Sewanee Review, *and* Poetry. *He also valued* The Nation *and* The New Republic *for their literary sections. None, however, seemed quite so exciting as* Accent, *which— although it had been founded in 1940, only three years before QRL —served as both model and challenge. Mr. Weiss considers the influence of Pound and Williams on QRL, as well as on his own poetry, to have been greater than that of the New Critics, whose criteria for excellence in poetry he found dissatisfying.*

Mr. Weiss is the author of eight books of poetry, among them The World Before Us: Poems, 1950–1970 *(1970);* Fireweeds *(1976); and* Views and Spectacles: Selected Poems *(1978), as well as numerous poems, articles, and reviews in a variety of little magazines and anthologies. He has received fellowships from the Ford and Ingram Merrill foundations and has twice been a member of the National Book Award jury for poetry.*

Three issues of the Quarterly Review of Literature *showing format changes. Left to right: Vol. 2, No. 4; Vol. 12, No. 4; Vol. 19, Nos. 3–4; (courtesy Theodore Weiss).*

The first ten years or so of the *Quarterly Review of Literature* might well have satisfied us. As little mags go (and of course they usually have the good sense and tact, if not exhaustion, to go quickly), had we not, from 1943 to 1953, without any help or support from foundations, good angels, etc., carried out an adequately honorable tour of duty? By the very nature of the little mag, a ten-year life span already far exceeded the normal, decent run of the best of them. For people who had never expected or wanted to be editors, let alone sole custodians, of a magazine, we had certainly proved ourselves. We had done what we could to forward the cause of the writing we believed in; we had published unknown or little-known young writers on whom, at least in part, the future of literature would depend, and older ones—like cummings, Williams, Stevens, Pound, Marianne Moore, Rexroth—not yet acknowledged or read in anything like the degree their work deserved. Thus Williams wrote us in September 1944:

I feel very grateful to you for your support, you'd be surprised how isolated one feels at times and how many small irritations one must face to keep writing. I was sixty-one a few days ago, let's hope that in the next twenty years I shall find more ease.

Also, as every magazine and literature must—not alone to fill out pages but to provide a larger context in which writing might thrive—we had published writers who produced only a few things, failed their promise, or simply fell silent. More than that, we had attended to our sense of the importance of importations: the way, subtle and otherwise, foreign writing (either of other lands or other times) can enrich local products, add exotic spice to them, or show them new directions. So the pages of our first ten years had sported translations of Andrade, Stefan George, Heredia, Sappho, Broch, Ramon Sender, Alberti, Corbière, Juan de la Cruz, Yvan Goll, Jiménez, a collection of recent Japanese poets, and a host of others.

Early on, Robert Bly had rebuked us for our editorial policy. Polemics, he assured us, was what was most needed. We countered by remarking that polemics already filled *his* magazine and one such was quite enough for us. Furthermore, our choices of material entailed criticism and judgment of, as far as we were concerned, the best kind: in action. But, as though to give personal point, a sense of program and commitment, to a magazine otherwise rarely overtly polemical or manifesto-minded, I had engaged in a doughty set-to with Yvor Winters, especially for his all-out attacks on writers like Pound, Eliot, and Stevens. This vehement flurry of fisticuffs attracted very considerable attention. What sympathy I might have had, even then, for many of Winters's reservations anent modernism was dissipated by the absolutism of his position. Meanwhile all kinds of correspondence occupied us from every corner, it seemed, of the United States and from distant parts of the world as well. Indeed we began to feel like some sort of international central. Writers like Williams and Rexroth, in their generous warmth yet hotly asserted and guarded stands, reassured us even while they kept us happily hopping. Williams, by his spontaneous enthusiasm no less than by his complaints about himself and his work, gave us a sense of importance, a fundamental reason for being editors. Rexroth peppered away at us in a Poundian style, with impatient yet affectionate pedagogic ukases. One could not want more entertaining, irritating, ingratiating communiqués; this was truly avant-gardism at its most exuberant, and we were in the middle of it.

Nonetheless, whatever our cordial participation in the views of both men, we held out, as we most fervently wished to, against the sirenic seduction of one voice, no matter how alluring, as against another; we skirted the Scylla of one extreme: all-out experimentation, say—and the Charybdis of another: constricted formalism. For in the felicitous example of Pound at his best we meant to serve literature itself, considered it more important than any one of its most persuasive practitioners. We wanted to keep the writing in our pages as open and various as possible. Thus, already anticipating the civil (and not so civil) war of the different camps-to-be—among the poets and fictionists shortly after, among critics and/or academics naturally later—we could present with similar enthusiasm the floribund work of a Stevens, the international (if not inter-epochal) complexities of a Pound, and the much sparer poetry, with its passion for the plain and the local, of a Williams. A poet friend told me that in my own work I was attempting to combine the two Bills: Shakespeare and Williams. Much as both meant to me, this formulation did not have an entirely implausible ring. Certainly I had read, loved, and taught both of them for many years. Yet lest this seem impossible

166

and egregious even to me, let's propose the likelier combination of Williams and Stevens, something like the language of the former and the syntax and reach of the other. So we hoped to have them and their like living happily cheek by jowl in our magazine.

As writers no less than as editors we inclined to one style, especially when it seemed to us unfairly or unfortunately neglected, rather than to some other immensely popular style (such checking-and-balancing has always been our impulse). We wanted to encourage and to urge the lost-sight-of and to challenge the acclaimed—not out of simple perversity or anti-joinerism, but out of an abiding sense of the costliness, to writing and to us, of such exclusiveness. The writer in ourselves well understood the monomania creative people often have to entertain to justify their own practice. But editorially we resisted such restrictedness; we printed work we might not fundamentally and personally care for but in which we recognized, given the writer's premises (these we felt, if they were serious, we must not quarrel with), its legitimate accomplishment. In our Lord's house of literature there had better be room enough for the whole multifarious show, including some of its sideshows. The one thing we did not wish to do was to deprive literature or ourselves of the genuine, whatever shape it might happen to take. Already, as in 1950, we had displayed our appetite for gamut by featuring Giraudoux's lovely, suave memoir "From My Window" and (in two issues) Louis Zukofsky's extraordinary novella, "Ferdinand"; a selection of Gongora's hermetic poetry and Paul Goodman's heel-kicking three playlets, "Theory of Tragedy," and of "the Pathetic." All this we followed with Lorca's essay on Gongora, the ultramodern on the remote but highly relevant; slices of *Paterson;* and a three-act play, "Stevie Guy," by Gil Orlovitz, a writer of mammoth ambition and boundless energies who, becoming a close friend, increasingly wrested from us editorial comments like, "You have great guts, as good as any in the business; now if only you could find a belly to put them in!" And an issue later we ran "Amphion," a play by Valéry, and a suite of poems by the exciting young avant-gardist Robert Duncan, already as devoted as Pound to past and recent greatness in the arts.

Accordingly, in 1953, with ten years completed and with

my first year off from teaching—made possible by a Ford Foundation fellowship which suddenly and blessedly descended on us—the cessation of the magazine might have seemed sensible, even judicious, especially since my own writing had become increasingly urgent. But beyond letters like Williams's which helped to keep us editing, my chief goddess, Inertia, scorned such an obvious, sane course. And before leaving for a year in Europe, we readied—what now strikes us as quite incredible—three issues. Their contents ranged from Seferis and cummings to the young short-story writer George P. Elliott, from Williams to eight young Dutch poets. When we left Yale for Bard College in 1947, Stevens had written, "You carry the *Quarterly Review* around with you the way a Chinaman carries his bird." He was right, right perhaps beyond his intention; for this bird—even as it provided us, in our moving about, with a kind of home, a nest full of incessantly hungry mouths (mouths of those who somehow never grew up or left)—tried to warble out the whole summer of literature. Or hallelujah on a straw!

One feature in Volume VII, number 3, had particular resonance for us: three essays that were the consequence of a poetry conference some years earlier at Bard College on "Experimental and Formal Verse." Williams and Louise Bogan, each holding forth on his and her specialty, were the main speakers. To give the occasion additional éclat, we invited younger poets, most of whom had appeared in *QRL*, to participate. To our delight almost all—Elizabeth Bishop, Richard Eberhart, Robert Lowell, Jean Garrigue, Lloyd Frankenberg, James Merrill, Kenneth Rexroth, and Richard Wilbur—accepted. The conference, one of the great-grandfathers of a later frequent kind, went off with a bang. Aside from the initial formal session in which Williams and Bogan delivered their papers and the younger poets as well as the audience responded, parties and impromptu readings followed, with the poets sometimes reading their own work, or that of other poets present, or of someone else. Robert Lowell was an enthusiastic, large presence. The second evening, clearly moved by the whole affair, he held a group of us captive while he delivered a several-hour monologue on what now seems to have been the whole of English literature. In fact, he liked Bard and its countryside enough to spend some time after the conference in the nearby house of Fred Dupee. As exhilarated as he had been at the conference, so mild, gentle, quietly kind was he afterward. Kenneth Rexroth wrote on November 30, 1948:

Look honey—you don't want my report on what the poets did. . . . I am much more interested in other things—some blonde, some brunette. Me, I had a very good time—and it was wonderful, sitting & singing all night. And I was very happy meeting you & Renée & Senior—and Wilbur whom I hadn't met before. My only regret is that I didn't bring down my girl at Smith—who would have transferred to Bard right then. When I teach Bard is where. Told my wife all about it—and it fascinated her, too.

Among the writers and artists in the audience was Mary McCarthy, who had taught at Bard the year before. She found the conference fruitful enough to inspire some considerable part of her novel *The Oasis.*

The conference did now provide *QRL* with three essays. The first consisted of a brief, fairly typical, staccato, if not impatient piece by Williams. In his words—even as he denied "that impertinence," poetry, for his true interest, the poem—"I would be the poet, not the one to talk about it [poetry]." But he did make much of the fact that modern poetry, since "it had gone back to the roots," was

a baby art, a screaming, brawling brat. It is in a primary phase and needs to be understood lest we be tempted to strangle it—for relief. We can get little adult pleasure from it as yet. . . . We catch only a longing glimpse of what it might be—hopefully desired by all. It is not finished.

He also stressed "poetic structure," "a field of action worthy of masculine attack," and deprecated the valuing of a poem for "what is *said* in the poem" rather than for "what we *make* of it, in what it stands to be as a metrical invention, something new in the world that once more asserts the world as real for us." And he named "the really great names of the past . . . Sappho, Sophocles, Dante, Villon," who "seem comparable in our day to the great inventors." Then he reached his basic theme: American, a "dynamic" language, versus English, with its "static nature" and remote from us. So too its prosody.

Louise Bogan's paper began by agreeing with Williams's, "If a poem has measure it is a poem." But then, by way of experimenters like Baudelaire, Rimbaud, Mallarmé, Laforgue, she maintained, ". . . as we look back on 'modern' poetry as a whole, we find as much experimentation *in* form as out of it." In the not so distant past, it is true, if we wished to praise a poet for his daring, his experimentation, it was for his ability to exercise his art in a great variety of forms, some of them his own or extensions of, departures from, established ones. Today many poets seem to mean by experimentation no form at all. As a consequence, a shapelessness, an anonymity, settles on most of their writing. Pointing out how rhyme "became necessary . . . as rhythm weakens," Bogan quoted Gilbert Murray to good effect:

Greek and Latin could do without rhyme because they had clear meters. Rhyme is needed to mark clearly the end of the line, and to provide the ear with fixed resting places. Without such divisions the metrical form would become dull and obscure. The hearer would not be sure where one line ended and the other began; he might not even be sure whether he was listening to prose or to verse. It is worth noticing that Latin took to rhyme when it began to lose the sense of quantity. Chinese insists on rhyme because it has no meter.

In recent times, rhyme having disappeared for most poets, and other features of poetry as well, rhythm has been in increasing trouble. Thus a growing number of writers, once declared poets, have understandably and sensibly abandoned the line about which they had long been uneasy, its arbitrariness, in their work. We have, then, that hybrid called the prose-poem, often not poetry, not prose, a poor, wingless, footless bird that can neither fly nor walk. Such writers, I would suggest, have abandoned the teachings and the example, not only of Pound, but of Williams as well, who was deeply concerned with shape, structure, especially "measure." Recognizing the exhaustion that can set in in meter and the need for change, Bogan says aptly that free verse "becomes as hampering as any rigid meter when it rules out *any* return to form."

Some time after the conference, Richard Wilbur sent us his reflections on the subject in a paper entitled "The Bottles Become New, Too"—as cogently reasoned an apologia for formal verse as we have seen. Praising Williams's work and the theory he needed for it, Wilbur finds that theory "not judicial but strategic" and Bogan, not Williams, critically right. He maintains: "In each art the difficulty of the form is a substitution for the difficulty of direct apprehension and expression of the object. . . . If you respect the reality of the world, you know you can only approach that reality by indirect means." He admits that "any basic rhythm . . . is a perfectly artificial and abstract thing." He shares none of the modern illusion that art, by being spontaneous outbursts,

170

can be life or, for that matter, art. He considers rhythm "as time-less and noncommittal as the triangle. The horses of the nineteenth century did not run in iambs, any more than the Studebakers of the twentieth do." Like Bogan he calls on one of the most basic arguments against free verse: "Another point in favor of formal structure is that there is no way of noticing certain subtleties and stresses and variations unless there is a norm, an apparent regular structure from which divergences are made." It is the touching desire of the modern artist to capture the uniqueness of each moment, not realizing that if it is indeed preciously unique it cannot be repeated without losing that very quality and, alas, often having no other. Beyond that, one might wonder where free verse will be when it is altogether triumphant and common-place, with no formal work to react to, nothing to resist or over-come. Perhaps out of a sense of insurance, the free-versifiers ought to see to it that a real measure of formal verse be kept going!

I have gone into all this because—late though the day may be for such arguments, with the almost total capitulation of the bulk of poets to free verse—the relevancy of the issues raised may prove precisely all the more urgent. In many ways prose is winning another battle, here perhaps a fundamental if not final one, over poetry in poetry's own bailiwick, not to say nature, and by its own consent. It is one thing to see how close poetry can come to prose without losing itself, to reclaim material from prose, and to learn—as Pound urged—the best lessons of great prose; it is another to succumb to it completely and often at its sloppy worst.

As though in answer to all this—and so we did see it—the fol-lowing issue featured Williams's very lovely, very important trans-lation, "Dactyls—from Theocritus," composed in the triads that Williams had recently discovered for himself. It reflects his splen-did, usually unerring ear; at the same time its being a translation of an ancient classical poem in a traditional, highly artificial genre, the pastoral, demonstrates the exciting freshness available in the past and shows Williams for what he fundamentally was, even in grimy, Manhattan-shadowed Rutherford: a bucolic poet. The same issue also presented eight Dutch poets, very clearly the able heirs of modern foreign influences, and went back to the rigors, still with us, of Gottfried Benn, translated by Edgar Lohner with a modernist, Cid Corman.

171

We had an extraordinary year abroad, living at Iffley, a tiny village outside Oxford; sharing a house with Mrs. Collingwood, the tart old Scottish wife of the former eminent philosopher and aesthetician R. G. Collingwood; visiting T. S. Eliot at Faber and Faber; and spending a most memorable afternoon and evening pub-crawling at Swansea with Dylan Thomas, Vernon Watkins (a frequent contributor to *QRL* whom we had come to see), and their childhood friend, the painter Fred Janes. On our return we continued our devotion to the liveliness of the best parts of the past, properly confronted. We published an all-Leopardi issue— this after our Kafka, Valéry, Marianne Moore, and Pound issues. A poet still little known in this country, Leopardi is surely one of Italy's and his time's major poets, and in mood and spirit most pertinent to our age. We appealed to a number of people for help in translating some of his poems and were fortunate in their response, as we were in William Fense Weaver's translations of various examples of Leopardi's extraordinary prose. We wanted some critical intelligence to accompany his work. Despairing of finding anyone to supply it, late in our stay in Iffley I girded myself for an all-out effort and, ensconcing myself in the Bodleian, I read in several all-day sessions whatever Leopardi, in whatever translation and comment, I could find. Then I batted out a brief article on him, chiefly valuable, perhaps, for the absence of any preconceptions or prejudices. Bard's program in its freedoms had no doubt helped to encourage me toward such sudden sorties.

An issue later, we were delighted to publish a one-act play, *The Bait,* by one of our regular contributors and now our friend, the immensely talented James Merrill. From the start, his gifts had been conspicuous and astonishing, gifts that fortunately were superbly managed. We had never met anyone quite so precociously capable. In 1949 we had published a group of Merrill's poems, and the year before we had been involved in his becoming a special instructor at Bard for one year—and at the advanced age of twenty-two. James or Proust was already the atmosphere he seemed to carry around with him, and Proust was what he taught at Bard. (In that 1949 issue we had also featured another extraordinary poet and man of letters, Ben Belitt, with his "School of the Soldier," a most imaginative memoir to which we gladly gave our first annual award for fiction.) At this time we also printed poems by young writers like John Ashbery and Jean Garrigue, David Galler and Jane Mayhall, who soon became good friends and *QRL* regulars, and Lorine Niedecker.

The third number of Volume VIII opened with "Poetic Acts," a speech that Wallace Stevens, recently dead, had delivered at Bard College in accepting an honorary degree. Williams, a recipient of a degree a year earlier through Bard's emphasis on creativity, was supposed to speak on that occasion, but a few days before the ceremony Flossie Williams phoned to inform us that Bill had just had a stroke. Then, to my amazement and consternation, she said, "Here's Bill. He wants to talk to you." And in broken, scarcely intelligible syllables Bill apologized for letting us down and launched a long, doctorly explanation of his illness. After a day or two of depression, with the event almost on us, I aroused myself and decided to phone Stevens to ask him if he would replace Williams. An older man, Stevens agreed with cheerful alacrity to make an acceptance reply. That weekend, involving Stevens, Kenneth Burke, and Glenway Wescott, was an awesome one, especially the first evening, when Stevens, imposing yet tiny-voiced, read his paper to the obbligato of thunder and lightning, and the stentorian clatter of rain on the tin-roofed gymnasium (Bard's only large auditorium). He could not be heard beyond the first row or two, but the sight of him and the surrounding accompaniment were quite enough to keep the audience spellbound. As Wescott told us, "I came down on the same train with Stevens, but though I watched him all the way, I didn't dare approach him." Other events paled beside this one. Burke, however, after a faltering start, forgot or abandoned his announced subject when he happened to mention the *Oresteia*. Taking off like a rocket, for well over an hour he filled the hall with crackling Greek and Trojan fire; the whole trilogy, Furies and all, came crashing down on us. That issue, along with Stevens's speech, also had fourteen poems by René Char; three remarkably commodious poems by a recent Bard student, Raphael Rudnik; and a selection of Louis Zukofsky's poems including a long extract from section 12 of his most ambitious work, *A,* and an essay on his poetry by Lorine Niedecker.

Up to now I have failed to mention the fiction writers given houseroom in *QRL;* as with the poets, quite a few of these came to Bard to teach. So a congenial company, in print as in person, was cultivated. Among the most striking was William Humphrey. A young goat-herder with his painter-wife Dorothy (that is, they tended a weekend commuter's fantasy of a farm), he had come to our attention with his first story in *Accent,* now sadly neglected but at the time as exciting a little literary magazine as existed. Humphrey's distinction was at once evident. When we met Charles Shattuck (an editor with Kerker Quinn, the magazine's prime mover), visiting Vassar for a year, he informed us of Humphrey's proximity and fairly desperate situation. We got in touch with him, arranged for visits, and promptly saw that we must bring him to Bard. A special one-year writer's fellowship was established, since he had no degrees and no teaching experience. The closest he had come to literature, beyond his own work, was a stint at the New York Gotham Book Mart, but we felt that a term with Mrs. Steloff should more than adequately prepare one for the ardors of Bard. That summer Humphrey, with his customary ravenousness for books, prepared for a course by ramming through the eighteenth century. Like a true autodidact, he shamed most of his well-degreed colleagues. His seriousness, his fiery enthusiasm made him an instant success as a teacher. A fellowship at Bard, it should be said, meant doing at least as much work as anyone else carried—a superhuman load of three different classes, plus many faculty meetings, plus meeting ten to twelve students for an hour or more each week in individual, substantive tutorial, or actually thirteen to fifteen courses a week! It soon became obvious that we must keep Humphrey, so he became a regular teacher until his first novel enabled him to go off to Europe for a long spell and a career of writing.

In short, Bard's Language and Literature Division had a heavy preponderance of fiction writers and poets alike. Among the former, at one time or another, were Warren Carrier, Jack Ludwig, Saul Bellow, Ralph Ellison, Robert Coover, and Mary Lee Settle. And the division was probably as lively, as dedicated to literature, the making and the keeping thereof, as one could find in the United States.

In 1957, with the arrival of poems by Theodore Enslin, another intense correspondence began. Enslin was already something of an underground figure in poetry. A man altogether devoted to his

174

work, he anticipated the physical as well as spiritual retreat from the modern "established" world that later became quite common. (He lived in Temple, Maine: "Have you ever tried 50° below in a drafty old farmhouse?") After many compatible years we hit a snag. In a letter I had remarked on "the broken-down, beat-up character of much that tries to pass itself off for poetry." He agreed in part, then went on, "But if you mean the jagged bright edges that are a part of our speech, which is from our life, then emphatically no." He praised those who had been "known as beat a few years ago. They really did clear the air of a lot of old heraldic hangings that ought to go." I had no quarrel with this; it was the hot air or simple flatulence frequently substituted to fill the emptied spaces that disturbed me: my awareness that a new academicism, at least as rigid as the old, was hardening into place. Enslin continued, "I think a poem should be in plain sight, plain workaday dress for the most part, although there are times for fancy dress balls, too." Whatever our shared enthusiasm for Williams, I maintained that style should be free to change with the occasion; that the so-called plain style, usually serviceable and apt for much of our world and time, should not be allowed to outlaw other "changes of clothes." Poetry, by its nature as by ours, ought to enjoy as various a wardrobe as possible. Even the plain style, not to say nakedness, if exclusively insisted on, could become as drab, limited, imprisoning a uniform as any. Beyond the poet's own deepest impulse and intelligence, no one could tell him what to do, but there would be a moment now and then when inversions, multiple adjectives, etc., might be useful and expressive, if not also natural and necessary. Fortunately one could find plenty of these in Pound and Williams; as practicing poets they were too good to be bound by rules, even their own and even those dedicated to freedom.

In his next letter Enslin countered:

But the "plain workaday dress" I must insist upon. It is a constant—always has been in good poetry, I think—I do not put on a cutaway coat when I go out to cut weed. It doesn't need to become plain. It does with many, I know, but I'm talking about well-made things, not the drab, or shoddy . . . no prescriptions before the poem, O.K., but that has its limitations too, as anything else.

It was not cutaway coats I was after, though I might have demurred at cutting weeds as a norm of conduct. But I feared the puritanism the plain style often tended to bring with it, and the diminution of wit, gaiety, and rich variety that might ensue.

In addition to cummings and Williams and Horace Gregory, a poet at present inadequately attended to, *QRL* in 1957 printed, sometimes twice, memorable young poets like Nemerov, Finkel, Leonard Nathan, Goodman, Golffing, Gibbs, and James Wright. The second issue we gave over to an early long poem by Rexroth, "The Homestead in Damascus," and an article on Rexroth by Lawrence Lipton. At this time also our relationship with M. L. Rosenthal, John Simon (who later taught at Bard), and James Dickey began. Simon, as one might expect, produced tight, witty, brilliantly acerb poems. Rosenthal, on his way to being one of the principal critics of modern poetry, already revealed the feeling, the tenderness that were to characterize his work as a poet. We had carried on a considerable correspondence with the young James Dickey, encouraging him in his obviously distinctive, powerful poetry and advising him—foolishly, as it turned out— to continue (since he and his poetry were doing so well) as an advertising writer rather than take a teaching position. He had told us he required $25,000 a year, his then salary. Out of our long academic experience we believed the expectation of such a salary in teaching was pure fantasy. We had not reckoned with Dickey's personality, did not know his talents as a public reader and performer. In good American style, he proved that even poetry can be made to pay.

QRL opened 1959 with a Hölderlin issue. This we especially valued. Not only did it make available a very great poet, one little known in the United States, but it brought together the labors of many people we admired and were very fond of: our close colleague and dear friend Heinrich Bleucher, and his wife, Hannah Arendt, powerful critic and splendid person; the acute, engaging Paul de Man (teaching at Bard College then); friends from our University of North Carolina days—Earnest Morwitz, once an important member of the Stefan George circle, and his collaborator Olga Marx (we had been delighted to print their superb Sappho, which Williams praised most enthusiastically); the sharp, capable John Simon; and a brilliant student at Bard, Alice Gladstone. Add to this list Vernon Watkins, a poet often in our pages, plus Erich Heller and Willard Trask, and one had a happy company indeed. Volume X, number 3, followed, with a section from Ralph Ellison's novel-in-progress (we would be fortunate enough to print more from it later) and a suite of poems by W. D. Snodgrass, among them "A Flat One," perhaps his most powerful poem. We devoted Volume XI, number 1, to the prize-winning work from our competition for a long poem, story, or play. Two zany, free-for-all plays by Holly Beye had been chosen by our judges, F. W. Dupee and Randall Jarrell, and ourselves.

We began 1962 with a double issue that gave us additional space for longer work and the good material now pouring in. Double issues would become our practice. This one featured a fascinating two-act play, *Faustina*, by Paul Goodman—a "ritual tragedy," he called it. Accommodating most modern interests and dramatic devices, it seemed to us one of the most successful ventures in modern theater. Here too we printed Denise Levertov and Richard Hugo for the first time. Denise Levertov's ten poems splendidly exhibited her strength out of lyrical delicacy, already fully at her command. She soon became a good friend. Hugo, at that time working at Boeing, sent us some memorable observations, applicable to his work and to the poetry of our time:

I have developed several elaborate theories, but my poet-friends tell me that the best thing about my poems is that when I write them, I ignore my own theories. This much is not theory: Often I start a poem with a place or scene in mind and then work to leave the place and arrive at the poem—to "get off" the subject and "onto" or "on to" the words. In such poems, the most common cause of failure seems to be my inability to leave the scene. It helps to love the scene or place. When you love something, you can leave it because you know it will be there when you return. . . . I have no objection to any "kind" of poetry—Campus NeoClassical, Beatnik, etc., but I do consider a clamor for originality a mistake. Originality cannot be willed. The original poet will be original even if he tries to write like somebody else—he will mis-hear other poets [foreshadowings of Harold Bloom's "strong" poet!], because his obsessions interfere with his hearing. So, when he tries to imitate, he really has it all wrong. . . . [And then a comment that seems even more pertinent today:] Technique seems to come a little too soon for many young American poets. When a 22 year old poet appears to have as good a command of rhythm as did Yeats after 25 years of writing, I can't help but wonder if something isn't missing. It's hard to believe that we are a nation of poetic geniuses.

No doubt there are people who, following the most highfalutin notions of Blake and Whitman, do so believe. All you have to do is abandon all standards, at best pesky things, and we *are* a nation of poetic geniuses. The amount scribbled today in the name of

177

poetry would certainly indicate that the scribblers think so. That issue also contained four short works by Robert Musil, for us a major modern much neglected in the United States.

In 1962 our all-Montale issue, guest-edited by Irma Brandeis, close friend and colleague, favored Montale with what he deserved, the best translators we could find: the poets Lowell, Merrill, Belitt, Nims, Corman, English, and Raiziss, with de Palchi, and such Montale experts as Brandeis and Cambon. We also ran some of Montale's short fiction and two essays on him. The third issue of Volume XII (1963) was enhanced by four elegies from Ovid's *Amores* translated by Horace Gregory, four poems by Robert Duncan, a long poem by Louis Simpson, nine poems by David Ignatow, and a story by a young fictionist, soon to emerge as one of our best, John Gardner.

Our large twentieth-anniversary poetry issue of 1964 opened with eight hitherto unpublished Whitman poems, in their brevity and point particularly apposite to our day's poetry. Michael Hamburger's translation of Hölderlin's play *The Death of Empedocles* appeared prominently, and four later Alberti poems, translated by Belitt. In addition, the issue printed many of our regulars and, for the first time, Ammons, with seven poems; six poems of Anthony Hecht; a long poem by Carolyn Kizer; and five poems each by Christopher Middleton, Josephine Miles, and William Stafford. Next, our twentieth-anniversary prose issue featured a difficult, stunning story, "The Death of Martin Presser," by H. D.; Ralph Ellison's "Juneteenth," one of the most extraordinary black sermons ever delivered; and William Humphrey's timely "A Job of the Plains," about a poor white boiled in his own oil, discovered on his land. Three other distinguished writers present were the ubiquitous, astonishing Joyce Carol Oates and two English fictionists, the experimentalist Christine Brooke-Rose and Hilary Corke. In the next issue, besides running many poems of *QRL* familiars, we offered for the first time poems by the coruscating, sophisticated Richard Howard, Michael Benedikt's translations of Max Jacob, and six poems of the ingenious, profoundly searching Mona Van Duyn. One suite we were especially pleased to present in translation: fifteen poems by the German poet Johanness Bobrowski, who had died a little while before. Volume XIV, number 3/4 was remarkable for the brief extract from Dostoevsky's notebooks, his reflections on death and immortality, written at the bier of his first wife (brought to our attention by our good friend and Princeton colleague, the distinguished critic Joseph Frank); *The Tower,* a Peter Weiss play translated by Michael Hamburger; and three stories by Robert Coover, a young writer emerging as one of our more notable, more inventive fictionists, then teaching at Bard.

In 1965 I was invited to be writer-in-residence at Princeton University, and we spent a delightful 1966–1967 in Princeton, though of course *QRL* continued to appear under our Bard address. Volume XV, number 1/2, announced that henceforth *QRL* would appear twice a year with double issues (each over 200 pages), one of poetry and one of fiction and drama, each "a yearly anthology of new creative work." That issue offered Helen Barolini's translation of eleven new Montale poems, "Xenia," in memory of his wife—poems that were personal, immediately and poignantly available, unlike much of his earlier work, in their often wry feeling. We printed four Seferis poems and his diary account of his meetings with T. S. Eliot, translated by Edmund Keeley (the director of the Creative Arts Program at Princeton and eventually my chief colleague and friend), Philip Sherrard, and Mary Keeley. And there was a long monologue of my own, "Caliban Remembers." I had read the poem, just newly finished, for the first time and as my sole offering—perhaps half-defiantly, very possibly desperately, but at least with the excitement of its writing still on me—at the New York YMHA Poetry Center after hearing my co-reader James Dickey deliver himself of a series of poems on adultery. Whatever the effect of my disclaimer—"After Mr. Dickey's poems mine, I fear, must seem a little like post-coitum triste"—no doubt many members of the crowded audience, even if they had read *The Tempest,* must have been baffled by my unabating assault.

Asked to remain permanently at Princeton, we moved with *QRL* to Haslet Avenue, our private as well as editorial address. In the double prose issue, Volume XV, number 3/4, still bearing the Bard address, we announced the removal and *QRL*'s affiliation with Princeton's Creative Arts Program. The issue reflected the change by featuring two early Borges stories translated by one of my Princeton colleagues, the important Borgesian James E.

Irby. These stories, with the earlier Keeley-translated Seferis, marked the beginning of a fruitful collaboration with Princeton University faculty members, accomplished writers, translators, and critics like Clarence Brown, John Peck, Robert Fagles, and visiting writers in the Creative Arts Program. Even as, in our twenty years at Bard, we had been involved in the establishment of a literary community, so now at Princeton we were happy to call on the company of gifted people available.

Our twenty-fifth anniversary poetry issue, appropriately the first under our new address, rounded up many of the poets familiar to *QRL* readers and, in addition, for the first time exhibited work by Amichai, Ted Hughes, Enzensberger, Saint-John Perse (translated by Richard Howard), Sylvia Plath (a section of her radio play, *Three Women*), Adrienne Rich, and Anne Sexton. We were also delighted to present Wallace Stevens's chief play, *Bowl, Cat and Broomstick,* and a most engaging "Conversation with Marianne Moore," recorded by Grace Schulman. Our twenty-fifth anniversary prose issue ranged widely indeed—with the first general publication of Walt Whitman's "Notes from a Train Journey" (from Camden, New Jersey, to Colorado and back); Richard Howard's translation of Jean-Paul Sartre's preface to a volume of Mallarmé's poems; and the third section of Ralph Ellison's novel-in-progress to appear in *QRL*. Robert Coover and W. S. Merwin, *QRL* oldtimers, further enriched the issue with samples of their highly original, experimental prose, which was close to poetry yet preserved the virtues of prose.

In our double poetry issue, Volume XVII, number 1/2 (1970) two of our poets—W. S. Merwin with seven prose poems and James Wright with six poems—shared top billing with Francis Ponge's "The Parti Pris of Things (II)," translated by Lane Dunlop. Also prominent were such distinguished poets as Donald Davie, Richard Eberhart, and Günter Eich, whose nine poems were translated by David Young. In his introduction, Young remarked Eich's unique importance to postwar German literature: his making poetry possible again after Hitler. Young cited Celan and Enzensberger, two very considerable contemporaries of Eich, on this fact. In Enzensberger's words:

After the entry of the Allies, Germany was mute . . . a speechless country. There is a poem in which this paralysis has itself become language and which simultaneously describes and overcomes the situation: it has become famous and is regarded today as the birth certificate of the New German literature. Günter Eich wrote it: "Inventory." . . . The poet is staking a claim to the absolute minimum that remains. . . . The text sounds like a man learning to speak; it is with such elementary sentences that language courses begin.

Lane Dunlop translated one of René Char's surrealistic playlets, "The Man Who Walked in a Beam of Sunlight," and John M. Gogol translated three prose poems by Solzhenitsyn as well as a large group of poems by the contemporary German poet Reiner Kunze. Beyond our usual company, other poets—represented, when possible, by a group of poems—appeared for the first time: Galway Kinnell, Reginald Gibbons, Greg Kuzma, Linda Pastan, Stanley Plumly, Dabney Stuart, Brian Swann (who also provided us, in collaboration with Ruth Feldman, with a selection from Lucio Piccolo's poetry), and Karen Swenson. The double prose issue, completing the volume, printed a moving, painful novella by the gifted Greek writer Kay Cicellis, and stories again by John Gardner and Joyce Carol Oates.

The next volume (XVIII, number 1/2) concentrated on three major poets: Cavafy, translated by Keeley and Sherrard, and two tragic figures—Paul Celan, translated by Michael Hamburger (one poem, "Afternoon with a Circus and Citadel," addressed Mandelstam), and one of the greatest Russian poets, this same Osip Mandelstam, fourteen of whose poems were translated by W. S. Merwin and Clarence Brown. Jean Garrigue (our contributor column called her one of our "prize perennials") also appeared with "Studies for an Actress," the title poem in what would become her last book. One other unusual entry was the work of Charles and Raphael Rudnik. Charles, the father of Raphael, after retirement "became interested," as our note says, "in poetry with his son's work"; eventually, for the first time, he began to write poetry himself—becoming, in a sense, his son's son. The poems we printed were Charles Rudnik's first to be published and later, with others, were included in his first volume. Also noteworthy were the fifteen poems of John Peck, soon to be collected in a splendid first volume, *Shagbark*. The prose issue that followed reinforced the Mandelstam poems with an astounding fireworks of a "travelogue" by Mandelstam: "Journey to Armenia," also translated by Clarence Brown. In Brown's words, Mandelstam's "highly placed protector, Nikolai Bukharin, arranged for the poet / and his wife to be sent off to distant Armenia in order to be out of harm's way"; thus the commission to write this piece, surely one of the most amazing to come out of Soviet Russia. Robert Coover, an old friend and a writer-in-residence for the year at Princeton, supplied the issue with a modern racy version of Snow White, and Wright Morris, writer-in-residence at Princeton the year before, appeared with a matter-of-factly sinister New York story. Three other unusual works in the issue were a remarkable exchange, involving the painter C. D. Friedrick, between Kleist and Brentano, edited and translated by a former Bard student and Princeton colleague, Philip Miller; Howard Moss's play, "The Palace at 4 A.M."; and Stratis Tsirkas's "Seferis' Last Days," translated by Minas Savvas.

Now, with our thirtieth anniversary upon us, we decided to celebrate in a large way with several commemorative retrospectives. The celebration, once it began, exceeded our expectations. We had thought preparations would be easy, but the physical job of cutting up issues and arranging the pages proved enormous. Even before that, plunging into the Herculean process of selection (easy!), we discovered to our dismay (and pleasure too) that we could not possibly limit our choices to two volumes—one poetry, one prose. And gradually, as the work proceeded, we saw that even three would not satisfy us, let alone the thirty years of *QRL's* contents. So, the poetry issue having appeared and the prose already in preparation (these almost 600 pages each), we realized that two more issues lay before us: one devoted to the special issues—Kafka, Valéry, Pound, Leopardi, etc.—that we had published over the years, and another containing the magazine's miscellaneous criticism. The poetry issue, presenting 146 poets, elicited a gratifying response. Princeton University Press decided to bring out a second edition of it as *Contemporary Poetry* in its paperback series. The prose issue, despite its size, had to be limited to only thirty-one writers, and selecting them proved excruciating. But eventually the Special Issues Retrospective and the all-criticism issues came out. Surely all four issues constitute the biggest little mags in the history of little maghood! But in America one might take it for granted that even the small must be large.

Now we look to the future with a possibly somewhat different publishing program in mind. After the criticism issue we intend to devote an issue to the complete poetry and whatever else we can find of the poet David Schubert. We hope to include memoirs of him by friends and statements from poets who have recognized his unique worth and benefited from his brief yet signal practice. And after that? What notions we have so far entertained require brewing (brooding?) time. After thirty years of experience we count on being overtaken by surprise. Let the straw be ready when the music comes along.

Postscript

Now, many months later, we are happy to be able to say that the music has declared itself. We plan to undertake something we consider fairly novel—namely, to cross the border between books and magazines. Many little mags are already devoted to miscellanies of poems. And, despite the great amount of poetry being written, commercial publishers are printing fewer books. We have therefore decided that, starting with our next volume, we will present, within a two-issue-per-volume subscription, several collections of poetry in each issue. These may consist of a single long poem or a suite of connected poems, a group of miscellaneous poems, a poetic play, a work of poetry translation. Since we know the trouble even well-established poets often encounter, the manuscripts need not be first volumes. Each accepted work will receive a prize. This fellowship of several books together, and the fact of our subscriptions, should ensure each collection a readership much exceeding what individual books of poetry can normally expect. At some later date, as times and our mood change, we may devote our pages to prose instead, possibly long stories or novellas. Meantime, we feel we can most usefully employ our energies and *QRL*'s space in this fashion. We have, it seems, decided to attempt our hallelujah on a larger scale.

James Boatwright, editor of Shenandoah *(courtesy James Boatwright).*

A MANIFESTO
(SOTTO VOCE)
James Boatwright

James Boatwright has taught at Washington and Lee University since 1961, where he began editing Shenandoah *in 1962. He has served on the Coordinating Council of Literary Magazines and the Literature Panel of the National Endowment for the Arts, and has been a fiction judge for the National Book Awards.*

When he is not in Lexington, Virginia, Mr. Boatwright travels in Greece and around Key West, Florida. He has published essays and reviews in The New Republic, The New York Times Book Review, The Kenyon Review, Carleton Miscellany, *and* Revue des lettres modernes.

> *Not you, lean quarterlies and swarthy periodicals*
> *with your studious incursions toward the pomposity of ants ...*
> —Frank O'Hara

I come to this job of writing about *Shenandoah* with an almost paralyzing diffidence, and one of the strategies it decrees is to examine the diffidence itself. What's behind this hesitation, this inability to be straightforward? Is it fear? Am I reluctant to be explicit about editing because deep down I'm afraid I'll be found out, the old fraud at long last exposed? Or is it mere timidity, passivity, absence of purpose, waffling? Or is there some nobler, more honorable buried motive, growing out of the vague feeling that certain things (e.g. magazines) had best be left to speak for themselves, an uneasy impatience with those brave manifestos that often promise the world but deliver something less.

The manifestos are fresh in my mind (this past spring I gave a short course on the literary magazine), their voices ranging from Wyndham Lewis's *Blast* to Lincoln Kirstein's elegantly sounded *Hound and Horn* and the opera buffa tomfoolery of Reed Whittemore's *Furioso*. Even more daunting than these manifestos are the essays that appear every seven years or so to pontificate

185

on serious matters with a positively Arnoldian weightiness: "The Idea of a Literary Review" (Eliot); "The Function of the Critical Quarterly" (Tate); "The Present Function of the Literary Quarterly" (Monroe Spears); "The Intellectual Quarterly in a Non-Intellectual Society" (Philip Blair Rice).

These essays and manifestos are daunting to me because they so little reflect my own experience with a magazine. I read them admiringly and with envy, on the one hand, the suave or fiery assurance of the manifestos, and, on the other, the essays' clarity of purpose, their coherence of thought, their loftiness of ideal. I come away chastened but somewhat puzzled. None of these pieces has much to say about the *personal*—about how much accident and serendipity may have to do with an editor's becoming an editor and with his work as an editor, about the less exalted circumstances and ambitions that are part of the editor's life (at least *this* editor's life). By now we've pretty much accepted the notion that writers write because they have to; it's a secular calling. Do editors edit because *they* have to? Am I being too Hobbesian and small-minded in suggesting that these questions about personal history and motive are too often glossed over, the editor springing before us full grown as spokesman for culture?

When faced with the rhetoric of *TriQuarterly*'s prospectus for this issue, I see something not far different from the rhetoric of those essays and manifestos, and I have the same response: a testy determination to play Peck's bad boy, to lower the tone of discourse about certain literary institutions. (This deflation is desperately needed in our new literary bureaucracies where the language has gone berserk: witness the solemn designation of *master poets* for hundreds of unknown poets in the schools, or the shy-making prose and poems issuing from the office of the director of literary programs for the National Endowment for the Arts.) I intend to do this by looking at my own career with what I hope is a sufficiently cold and skeptical eye. It may be that mine is a unique history, in which case it could have at best only a mild clinical interest, but I'm obviously convinced that it's in some ways representative.

. . . the fundamental ideology of little magazine editing since William Dean Howells took over at Harper's Monthly, *the syncretic enthusiasm for a mixture of high and low. . . .*
—TriQuarterly prospectus

186

What's mainly missing in my character, I think, is the kind of historical sense well demonstrated in the preceding quotation. William Dean Howells, syncretic enthusiasm, fundamental ideology! What editing a literary magazine provided me with was an escape from such language, the kind of language I associate most vividly with exams in graduate school. I began working with *Shenandoah* when I was twenty-eight, two years out of Duke, still fondly expecting to complete a doctoral dissertation (a critical edition of one of James Shirley's plays; no doubt some one *has* edited the play by now). In my early years at Washington and Lee I was teaching freshman English, the British survey, seventeenth-century poetry, getting up for eight o'clock classes six mornings a week, grading mountainous piles of papers, serving on the Registration Committee (i.e., doing what the computer does now)—when suddenly the job of editing *Shenandoah* dropped into my lap. Douglas Day, who had arrived at W. & L. the same year I did, had been offered that job and refused it. (Instead, he left for the University of Virginia, went on to write the biography of Malcolm Lowry and win the National Book Award.) I leaped at the chance to edit a magazine; I knew that in some obscure fashion it was what I had always wanted and been working toward. I had no preparation, no particular qualifications other than an intense interest in contemporary literature, no training, no experience.

As early as my grammar school years, when one of my friends would take me to his grandmother's print shop, I had discovered in myself this peculiar, almost erotic interest in papers and inks, in watching the operations of the presses. In high school I did better in English than in any other subject, and when I reached the University of Georgia I studied journalism; I thought that was the way you became a writer. I tried working for the college paper but quit when they turned down my first story and put me to writing headlines. One summer during my college years I "interned" for a weekly paper in a small north Georgia town, and learned then that I didn't want to be a journalist. The only other literary job I had as an undergraduate was editing my fraternity "rush" pamphlet. But I was also taking creative writing courses, turning in tortured stories that all ended in suicide, reading Oscar Williams's anthology of modern poetry and the paperbacks of Gide and Moravia and Hemingway and P. G. Wodehouse—any novel written in the twentieth century.

My closest hometown friend, a student at Washington and Lee, had as a fraternity brother a boy named Tom Carter, who edited a magazine called *Shenandoah*. I had seen copies of it; there was nothing like that at the University of Georgia. The *Georgia Review* (the only academic magazine I'd heard of in high school; an uncle sent it to us) was a (literally) gray magazine devoted to tales of the Old South and to an annual bibliography of Georgia authors. *Shenandoah* was remarkable because it was edited by a contemporary of mine (how could that be?) and featured exotic writers (e. e. cummings, Wallace Stevens) whom I knew were important even though I didn't know much about them. I had even met Carter when I went to W. & L. one party weekend, and I was surprised to find that he seemed only a little different from your ordinary KA. But the difference was significant.

Shenandoah had been started by some young instructors in the English department, who within a couple of issues had selected Carter to be the editor, a job he held until he graduated. Carter *made* the magazine; he gave it a stamp. He had edited a magazine when he was still in high school, and he was a great letter writer to the famous, including Pound. In the early years of the magazine—in addition to cultivating student talent like T. K. Wolfe, Jr., the contributor of several stories and now better known as Tom the Scourge of Mere Fiction—he pushed Pound and related magi and hierophants like Wyndham Lewis, Peter Russell, Hugh Kenner, and Kenner's colleague Marshall McLuhan. After Carter graduated but continued to serve as adviser, there was also, perhaps inevitably, a strong Agrarian bias in the magazine; it was too late to *be* Agrarian but not too late to act as the historian of the movement. I think what this all means is that the early *Shenandoah* had a real, if not altogether clear, ideology and identity. In retrospect it looks like an amateurish, smaller, somewhat more single-minded version of the *Sewanee Review* or *Southern Review*.

Carter, following graduation, went to graduate school and taught; he also wrote criticism, receiving one of the *Kenyon Review* fellowships in criticism during these years (not very long after that came his untimely death at thirty). At the magazine he was followed by other student editors, who published early

Flannery O'Connor and a Dylan Thomas issue. But none of them was a Tom Carter, and by the late fifties the editorship of the magazine had slipped into the hands of the faculty, where it lost whatever sense of identity it had made for itself.

There it remained. Until I was made editor, for several years each issue was edited by a different member of the board of publishers, drawn from the various academic departments: thus the magazine had issues devoted to contemporary German literature, to Robert Graves, to Sherwood Anderson, etc., which made for great variety but not much continuity. Behind the placid and simple exterior of those slim issues, all was chaos. A student more or less handled the meager subscription list (there was no secretary); manuscripts were dutifully opened but, because most issues were special ones, they mostly got returned unread. In my first year or so, I found myself stuffing envelopes and licking stamps (the magazine didn't have second-class mailing privileges since it had been coming out only three times a year) and wondering what I was doing.

What *was* I doing? What was I up to sixteen years ago? I was only a little fuzzier on these matters then than I am now. I had and have no program, no plan, no easily articulated cause. As I've said, it was a job I simply wanted to do, from whatever obscure motives. Over the years, though, I have *discovered* something of what I've been up to.

I didn't know it when I started, but editing *Shenandoah* would be a way for me to beat the system, to move on up the academic ladder without getting the sacred Ph.D. It would make my life more complicated, more interesting than the life of teaching and scholarship that graduate school seemed to be preparing me for. The editor of an academic literary magazine not only teaches (and basks in the security of tenure and dependable paychecks), but he works directly with writers and becomes the friend of some. And he has unmediated access to the world of literature— raw, not yet anthologized—where he is able to taste some of the bohemianism and anarchy, the freedom from tacky academic domesticity which that world promises (although it doesn't always come through on its promises). If he gets drawn into the burgeoning literary bureaucracies, he even experiences the *frissons* of dabbling in the hard-nosed world of business and money. (Literary magazines don't have enough money; they are the victims of the vast commercial system; they deserve money. The magazine editor likes dropping by the Ford Foundation; he appreciates more than just the comedy as he sinks into a plush sofa and expatiates on these themes in the steely-eyed presence of a Foundation executive.)

But the most important thing I learned about editing is that it was the surest way of my being close to a life I knew to be irreproachably desirable. It seems plain to me that there are basically two kinds of editors of literary magazines: (1) those who first find themselves as *writers* and then go on to act as editors for a variety of reasons (to use up excess energy, to fulfill an authentic desire to mold taste, to shape the course of the art) and (2) those who first find themselves as *editors,* the next best thing to being writers. (Here, I guess, should also be included most editors in publishing houses.) These editors may go on to actually become writers as well. In the first group are such obvious examples as Pound, Eliot, Tate, Marianne Moore; in the second, Harriet Monroe, Margaret Anderson, George Plimpton, Ted Solotaroff, and (humbly, humbly) myself. I see myself as being further representative of an at least numerically significant subgroup, the would-be writers who became teachers of literature (how many unpublished novels lie in the dark recesses of otherwise respectable filing cabinets: "English 2: Notes," "English 254: the British Novel from Richardson to Dickens"?) but I find this an insufficient gesture toward that luminous icon, the writer's life. Teaching *and* editing is a more intimate tactic, a multiplying of intensities, as the supplicant presses nearer the flame.

We are interested in direct statement of some of the political issues which inevitably arise in publishing a magazine, and which took particular form where the publishing of Shenandoah *is concerned* (a letter from the editors of TriQuarterly).

I've been surprised by what I've learned about politics—that for me it's interior, not exterior; personal, not public. My first response to the above was, "What politics?" The only conventionally political incident happened a couple of years ago. The trustees of the university receive the magazine as a courtesy, and one day I had a telephone call from a dean asking if a certain trustee's name

190

Shenandoah

FALL 1976 $1.50

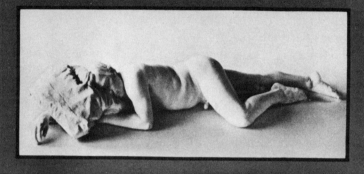

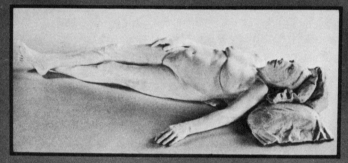

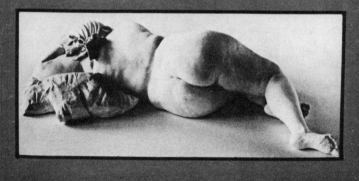

Shenandoah, *Vol. 28, No. 1, Fall 1976 (courtesy James Boatwright).*

was still on our mailing list. Yes, it was. Unfortunately the trustee's brother was receiving the magazine (the trustee having died without the magazine's taking notice of that fact); he was a "friend of the university" and he didn't like what he saw. Would we kindly remove that trustee's name from our mailing list? We would and did. Otherwise, nothing.

As far as I can tell, the powers-that-be approve of the magazine, although there's little direct confirmation of this. The indirect confirmation is the continued approval of our modest budget, which has been allowed gradual increases similar to those granted to departments. I have never been directly criticized by anyone within the university for anything I've published (although there was some criticism in the early years for failing to review books by faculty members, but that has died down). The conclusion I draw is that it's largely unread on campus; certainly there aren't many faculty subscribers. I suspect that some of my colleagues disapprove of the magazine, see it as a waste of money or worse, but they don't tell me these things themselves. They might say them to the chairman of the board of publishers, but he and I have always had friendly relations. He has always seemed to respect, if he didn't necessarily admire, what was going on. It's been a marvel to me how little trouble there has been. Of course I realize the situation could change overnight if there were a new president or other powerful figure who actively disliked or disapproved of the magazine, or if I suddenly had grandiose notions for expanding it. Washington and Lee is a small private university; it has nothing to fear from outraged state legislators; and it probably sees *Shenandoah* as a relatively inexpensive means of certifying its interest in the arts, both within the university and in the outside world.

But I know there *is* a political question, a personal one, disturbing to me and many other southerners: what are my allegiances, how southern *am* I? And what is the relationship between my sense of being a southerner and the magazine? One thing is clear: a magazine in the South is expected to be southern. The only really nasty letters the magazine has received came several years ago when two reviews in the same issue were less than favorable to some fellow Southerners. My credentials as a southerner are in order. I was born and bred in the South, and my ancestors fought on the right side in the War. But I've already admitted to a deficient

192

historical sense, and I have no more than a passing interest in southern history. Although Flannery O'Connor and Eudora Welty are two of the writers I most admire, although the magazine has gratefully published and interviewed writers like Peter Taylor, Reynolds Price, and James Dickey, although the last two have generously served as advisory editors for many years, I keep telling myself that it's not necessarily their being *southern* writers that draws me to them, and I bridle at the idea of *Shenandoah* as a southern magazine. What's the origin of these renegade feelings of mine, this fatal flaw? I am caught in that famous ambivalence of attitude toward this place, simultaneously grateful for what it gives me and offended by what it demands of me. I have consciously tried to reject the Calvinist, family-obsessed, bear-huntin' Faulknerian world for reasons fairly pure and desperately simple: I don't see how I can have my life *and* be a good ol' boy.

I was criticized some time ago when I wrote a piece saying that I found *Gone with the Wind* a bore now, twenty years after I first read it, and the criticism came both from expected sources (a columnist in an Atlanta paper) and from a surprising one—an exceedingly intelligent and gifted writer friend who has, I think, less clay between his toes than I have but who expressed dismay that I had sold my birthright. *Sold* it? I'm still here, forty-five years on; I can't write an account of the *dispossessed* southerner, crouching ironically in a Manhattan cave or discovering in a chic Long Island resort touching reminders of his southern boyhood. I've stayed here, willy-nilly. For sixteen years I've edited a magazine in a place where Robert E. Lee is not altogether humorously referred to as St. Robert, and I've more or less kept my wits about me as I walk a thin line between those who see me as a betrayer of the motherland and those who see me and the magazine as her embodiment. What I've done as an editor or reviewer has never proceeded from a coherent, well thought-out position on Being a Southerner. Far from it: it has been truly reactionary—an uncertain, faltering effort not to *use* my being southern, not to exploit it and make a career of it, not to sing those Rebel Blues. Alas, it's likely to end up one more lost cause. When I read *Portnoy's Complaint,* it struck home like a hammer blow. For *Jew* I had only to substitute *southerner:* Sophie and Scarlett are kissing cousins, and not many of their kin escape their loving clutches.

They were right, my dear,
all those voices were right
And still are. . . .
—W. H. Auden

And there have been other discoveries, some surprising, some not. I've been chagrined to learn how unoriginal I am, how dependent I am on other magazines for my conceptions of what *Shenandoah* ought to be, how much plain envy and *Schadenfreude* I'm capable of. The most obvious case: the *Paris Review*. I've always admired inordinately the format, the artwork, the fiction (the poetry is another matter), and the interviews (how shamelessly I've imitated those!). I liked the air of gentlemanly diversion the magazine sported, and Styron's introductory note in the first issue (it adamantly refuses to be a manifesto) struck a sympathetic chord, with its emphasis on fiction, its potshots at academic criticism, its blithe indifference to politics. A few years ago, Plimpton became involved in a complicated controversy with the National Endowment for the Arts, and many of his fellow editors (myself included, I'm ashamed to say) self-righteously accused him of censorship. It seems clear to me now that envy of Plimpton's worldliness, assurance, and *success* had as much to do with our attack as any more virtuous motives. In other words, I don't think I'm alone in my uneasy, ungenerous feelings about the competition, but this isn't a sentiment that I've often heard expressed.

Nor does anyone say much about the limitations of his magazine, those limitations imposed not by the philistinism of the culture or the stinginess of foundations but by the paucity of worthwhile manuscripts. Am I the only editor who has no backlog of fiction, who has never been an issue ahead, who wonders if there will *be* a next issue? (This doesn't hold true, I assume, for poetry, poetry magazines, poetry editors. The poetry editor of *Shenandoah,* Dabney Stuart, recently resigned after ten years of hard work, and he always had more poems on hand than we could publish.) This particular problem is no doubt closely linked to other defects of my character, including my inability to hustle; I'm shackled by my nice southern-boy politeness and dilettantism. Even my best friends (especially my best friends) have chastised me for not doing more with the magazine, for being lazy, haphazard, unimaginative, for not giving it enough time—and they

194

are right, my dear, all those voices are right. It's significant, isn't it, that when someone asks me how the magazine is doing, I invariably say, "Oh, it's limping along." That poor invalid.

And yet, despite the *mea culpas,* the perhaps overly masochistic inspection of the soft underbelly of the creature, despite the fact that I'm still bemused by all the larger questions, I *do* know why I edit. I believe there are reasons neither trivial nor self-serving, but they are still relentlessly personal, private: to celebrate and . . . what? Disseminate? Promote? (Ah, the stiffening rhetoric!) I have wanted to celebrate those writers whose work has figured strongly in my life—Yeats, or Welty, or Auden. On two occasions not long ago I was moved to celebrate a place—Greece—and its literature, because coming to know that place has been as momentous for me as encountering "Among School Children," or *Losing Battles,* or "In Praise of Limestone." These passions are joined with a third, more general one: a passion for prose, fiction or nonfiction (did anyone else lament the disappearance of that surpassingly beautiful magazine *Prose?*)—regardless of length, or style, or subject matter, the authors famous or unknown—any prose that interests and moves me, heightens my sense of things. Dabney Stuart's dedicated and exacting work excepted, whatever value *Shenandoah* has had stems, I believe, from these passions. When I've been good at my job, I've acted freely; I've made unfettered choices and published them without any consideration other than their quality. A rare transaction, the real thing.

Poetry

vol. 85 no. 2 • NOVEMBER 1954 • $5.00 a year

PRIZE AWARD NUMBER

FRANK O'HARA   ROSALIND LEVINE

WILLIAM SAUNDERS   TOM SCOTT

CID CORMAN   DONALD JUSTICE

LOUIS ZUKOFSKY   JOHN J. GILL

HOLLIS SUMMERS   MERRILL MOORE

WILLIAM PILLIN   MARY FRASER WALKER

LAWRENCE P. SPINGARN RICHARD EBERHART

Reviews by LEONIE ADAMS, REUEL DENNEY,

ANTHONY KERRIGAN, BYRON VAZAKAS & ROSS WURM

50 cents

Poetry *Prize Award Number: winners for 1954 included William Carlos
Williams (The Levinson Prize); Anne Ridler (The Oscar Blumenthal
Prize for Poetry); Reuel Denny (The Eunice Tietjens Memorial Prize);
Reed Whittemore (The Harriet Monroe Memorial Prize); Hayden Carruth
(The Bess Hokin Prize); and Dorothy Donnelly (The Union League Civic and
Arts Foundation Prize).*

KARL SHAPIRO
AN INTERVIEW ON POETRY
Michael Anania & Ralph J. Mills, Jr.

Of Karl Shapiro's generation of poets, "the generation of Jarrell, Wilbur, myself, Roethke, Lowell, Schwartz, Bishop, Ciardi, Berryman, Kunitz, Nemerov, Whittemore—one is almost inclined to add Merrill Lynch, Pierce, Fenner and Smith," Mr. Shapiro has written: "Our generation lived through more history than most or maybe any. We lived through more history even than Stendhal, who fell, as he says, with Napoleon. We were reared as intellectuals and fought World War II before it happened and then again when it did happen. We witnessed the god that failed and helped trip him up. We predicted the Alexandrianism of the age, and like everybody else, we throve on it. We drove our foreign cars to class to teach. And we bit the hand that fed us, but not very hard, not hard enough. The hand went on signing papers. Once upon a time we were all revolutionaries of one stripe or another, but when we got married and settled down, with tenure, we talked technique instead of overthrow. Half of us stopped rebelling and not because of middle age. The age made it so easy to be a poet, or to survive on lobster, the age gave in so sweetly to our imprecations, the age so needed us to help it hate itself, this spineless age ended by softening the backbone of poetry."

Karl Shapiro has been connected with libraries and universities most of his life. He was awarded the Pulitzer Prize for Poetry in 1945, served as the Librarian of Congress from 1946 to 1947, and has edited the following magazines: Poetry, *from 1950 to 1956;* the Newberry Library Bulletin, *from 1954 to 1955; and* The Prairie Schooner, *from 1956 to 1966. He is currently serving on the editorial board of* The California Quarterly *at the University of California, Davis, where he teaches. Random House has published Mr. Shapiro's* Collected Poems 1940–1978.

This interview was held in Chicago in November 1976, when Karl Shapiro was the featured poet on Poetry Day. In attendance were Michael Anania (see his essay, the first in this volume) and Ralph J. Mills, Jr. Mr. Mills, who was a member of the board of trustees of Poetry *in the early sixties, has written about numerous contemporary poets and is the author of several volumes of poetry. He teaches at the University of Illinois at Chicago Circle.*

Karl Shapiro, Summer 1954 (courtesy Poetry *magazine).*

In 1950, the first year you were editor at Poetry, *you wrote an editorial which answered a letter from T. S. Eliot. There you agreed with Eliot that* Poetry *was not a little magazine but an institution. Eliot had said that little mags should have short lives and should exist under only one editor, and even referred to* Criterion *as a little mag of that kind. In the editorial you said* Poetry *had several functions. One was to discover and encourage new talent; a second was to print the new work of poets already known; and a third was to represent current tendencies in poetry.*

I remember that shortly after I came to *Poetry, Time* magazine sent a reporter over to Erie Street, and he said, "What is your policy?" I was sort of horrified because I never thought of a literary magazine having a policy in *Time*'s sense. I just said that well, we wanted to print the best poetry we could find, and new poets, and so on, and that I consciously tried to publish people who had never been published in a magazine before. Now, I may have over-done that. I don't know. Some of those poets I've never heard of since. But some I have, like Frank O'Hara and Tomlinson.

Hayden Carruth was your predecessor. How long had he been editor—just a year or so, wasn't it?

A very short time. There was a philosophical crisis then, and I have never really got to the bottom of it. (I think it was some factionalism over the New Criticism.) I don't want to get into a fight with Allen Tate, but Allen was living here at the time and Hayden was his protégé and had been made the editor of *Poetry*. Allen, I think, believed that this could be another organ of the New Critics. But anyhow, the old-timers got rid of Hayden. People couldn't get along with him.

Was that the period when they were doing those critical supplements, which were like teacher's guides to Poetry?

That's right. I couldn't understand the New Critics, so I thought it would be a good idea to get a glossary. The William Elton supplement, "A Glossary of the New Criticism," sold like crazy. Really esoteric. I knew that *Poetry* magazine carried a great deal of critical weight, and so—in the same way Harriet Monroe used Ezra Pound as her foreign correspondent—I got Wallace Fowlie, who was a friend of mine and wrote some very good stuff, to get

199

good translations. And I didn't know Hugh Kenner, but I was leaning over backward to take away some of the obloquy or whatever it was that I had heaped on Ezra Pound, and I leaned over backward to get Kenner to be the critical editor. He wrote a lot of stuff there. He played some awful dirty tricks on me too, like the attack on Delmore Schwartz, which was completely uncalled for. And I think I did get an article to sort of balance that, a kind of a pro-Schwartz article.

You published eleven of Schwartz's poems in one issue.

Well, I was an admirer of Schwartz, but Kenner was out to get him. That happened to me several times. Probably the best piece of prose I published was an essay on Sandburg that William Carlos Williams did at my request. Maybe I was critically naive not to know what Williams was going to do—although it is one of his best essays—but it was a bad blow for Sandburg, who was never friendly to me after that. I can't blame him.

There was also a great fuss over the Dahlberg piece on Aiken.

Edward Dahlberg. Photograph by Gerard Malanga.

Now that was another thing. Dahlberg, I think, is a kind of nut. He asked me if he could review Conrad Aiken's autobiography *Ushant,* a beautiful book, and I was naive enough to think, well, if a man asks to review a book, it's because he likes it. How wrong I was. And Aiken wanted to sue *Poetry.* He made us reprint parts of his original text—there were so many errors. I lost his friendship over that.

But you used Dahlberg?

I tried to avoid him, but he was so persistent. And I must say I do admire the cranky kind of prose he writes, with a sort of Old Testament nuttiness. And I admire the beautiful books that New Directions used to make out of it.

You did an issue on two poetry workshops. Paul Engle presented some of his students from the University of Iowa workshop, and Theodore Roethke presented some of his from the University of Washington. I don't think there's ever been another issue like that. Roethke wrote that piece "The Teaching Poet" for it.

Another thing I tried to do was publish special issues of foreign poets in translation. We did a Greek one with Kimon Friar. In my last year as editor I was in India, getting translations. (I'd already left *Poetry* but was collecting material for it.) I think Henry Rago did publish an Indian issue later on. But that material was very hard to get because most people in India write what I call Anglo-English—weird English.

You published that issue which Wallace Fowlie edited on the postwar French poets, and you usually published translations. You did six poems of Max Jacob's and some of Marianne Moore's La Fontaine fables. Did you feel that American readers ought to know more about European literature?

I published all those translations partly because of my interest in foreign poets and partly because I was a bad linguist. I was very much in love with poets like Rilke and Lorca, but I could read them only in translation. In my own work I relied very heavily on foreign poets as well as contemporary English and American ones, so I liked to get as much of them as possible—when the translations were good and had some life in them.

201

People like Robert Bly have maintained that in the forties and fifties there was a tendency to block off American literature from foreign influences, that only a few poets like Valéry or Rilke were translated, and that therefore American poets became somewhat insular.

Well, I wasn't aware of that then because I was publishing translations of Rilke and Stefan George and so on. It seemed to me there was quite a lot going on in translation of foreign poets.

Wasn't there an issue of Poetry *that was mostly devoted to Juan Ramón Jiménez?*

Yes, I guess so. Shortly after he had won the Nobel Prize.

What do you think about the business of a magazine's being an institution?

I've thought a lot about that over the years, and I really do believe this isn't just a puff. I really believed then, and I do now, that *Poetry* could not have been founded anywhere but in Chicago, and it could not have survived in any other place. I can't see that magazine in New York or London or Paris. It wouldn't work there. It rose out of the Middle West poetry movement, which was the big authentic American poetry movement in the country, and it was a perfectly natural flowering of the whole Chicago renaissance. When I lived in Chicago and the Middle West I always felt that I was somewhat protected from what is nowadays called the New York/eastern establishment. In those days I didn't believe in what some people have called the Jewish literary Mafia in New York— you know, the *New York Review of Books* and all that stuff. New York was not so coordinated then, literarily speaking. It was mostly just a center of publishing. The literary magazines were not published in New York; they were published in other parts of the country and in universities, except for commercial ventures like the *Saturday Review*. I felt very strongly that Chicago had the right kind of insulation for *Poetry* magazine to flourish and survive. In that sense I think Eliot was right: *Poetry* did become a Chicago institution. But in another sense, as I soon discovered, it really was an institution because of being a part of other institutions— the Newberry Library, the University of Chicago, the opera, the Arts Club, the Art Institute—because the magazine was backed

202

by the same people who were backing the big institutions in Chicago. For a while I thought, well, that's a bad thing. It's a kind of a gang. There were some people who said it was terrible for all of these aristocrats to be running this magazine. But then I began to see that this was *why* it existed.

Yes. It's still that way, I think. Look at the patrons and the members of the Modern Poetry Association; they're essentially the same people—or members of their families, or relatives—who back the Art Institute and are trustees of the University of Chicago.

I think that's great. Except for a kind of cornball city like San Francisco, this is really the only city in the United States where that kind of patronage works well—as it might in, say, a European city.

In the early sixties, I guess, I was at a meeting in Washington which was conducted by the Carnegie Foundation. You were on the panel, talking about the disaster of magazines' being funded by universities and eventually, as it turned out, by the government.

Well, you know, I do these redneck things. That meeting was at the Library of Congress, on the little magazines. Well, I was telling the little magazines to stay away from government money. That was my position and everybody said, get rid of him. In fact Allen Tate and Wayne Booth very carefully planned an attack on me, to cut me to ribbons. They said, don't pay any attention to him. He's just an entertainer.

I don't think Allen Tate ever got over the shock of In Defense of Ignorance.

That book made me lose practically all my friends. It was the end of my friendship with Allen. I had a bitter experience at the *Prairie Schooner,* where I was fired—or, rather, urged to quit. (Now, that was interference, academic interference.) I had wanted to publish a story that mentioned a homosexual. It was set in galley proofs, but I went away, probably to Europe, and the acting editor held the galleys for a whole year. When I came back I demanded that the story be published. The staff went to the chancellor, who used to look over the galleys of the *Prairie Schooner*—which I didn't know—and his decision was to cut the story. So I resigned from the magazine and began to look for a job elsewhere.

Ezra Pound shown shortly after his release from St. Elizabeth's Hospital, Washington, D.C. (the Bettmann Archive).

T. S. Eliot diagramming a play at Princeton University (the Bettman Archive).

Then you said you were going to go on the radio and read the story.

Oh, I did.

And they said if you did that, they would have you arrested.

I did that heroic thing. They had a nice little FM station there in Lincoln, Nebraska, and I said, I'm going to read the story on the radio. The university said that if I did (they had a sheriff's car there), they were going to arrest me and also the guy who owned the station. But they didn't. I read the story and everybody in Lincoln listened to it. You wouldn't believe how innocuous that story was. What got the university administration was that it mentioned homosexuals in an English department.

Nobody interfered with anything when you were at Poetry *magazine?*

Never. No, wait a minute. As a matter of fact, there was one thing I tried to do that I shouldn't have done because *Poetry* was not the right place for it. I had a friend at the Newberry, an ex-German who was very aware of all the Nazi business. He was also an editor at the University of Chicago Press; Fred Wieck, his name was. The Press was going to publish a book by Morton Grodzins that was the first really good sociological study of the Japanese concentration camps out west. The University of Chicago Press had accepted it and it was going to be published; but here's where we get into big politics. Hutchins was persuaded by Governor Earl Warren of California to suppress the book. So one of the editors from the Press came to me for help. He said, "Will you publish in *Poetry* a letter that I will write exposing this suppression?" I said yes, and he wrote the letter. I was going to have it set—maybe it was set—when the magazine's board got wind of it. Now, there was some interplay between the trustees of the University of Chicago and the board of *Poetry* Magazine. They got wind of the letter and they persuaded me not to publish it—I forget how, but I knuckled under. Maybe *Poetry* was not the place for it, or maybe it was. I don't know.

In general, though, do you think that dealing with an institution, one guided by the kinds of culturally concerned people who exist in Chicago, was much better than dealing with a university?

206

Yes, because I was let alone. You know, as editor of *Poetry* you really did have autonomy. Maybe I was conditioned to a certain extent. For example, I remember that Paul Goodman once sent me a group of obscene poems. Now, I had published some of Paul's poetry, and some of it was very good. But I couldn't print these. You know, you couldn't use "shit" and "fuck" in *Poetry*; it had never been done, and back in the fifties it would have meant the suppression of the magazine. Wouldn't it? In the fifties? Anyway, Paul wrote back a huffy note, saying I was a prude.

Do you recall that the first issue of Big Table *was originally set as an issue of the* Chicago Review? *The problem there was the material by Ginsberg, Burroughs, Kerouac, and others which offended some people.*

I've often asked myself what I would have done. I left *Poetry* magazine just at the time that "Howl" was about to be published. Well, I was a great admirer of "Howl," but if Ginsberg had sent me that poem, would I have put my life on the line? I don't know the answer to that.

You did publish it in your anthology.

I was the first one to publish it in an anthology. I told Bill O'Connor, who was the general editor of that series, that I would do an American anthology on one condition—that he would let me publish that poem in it. And O'Connor said fine. A secretary at the publishing company, Crowell, actually went out of her mind. She had to be put away because of reading that poem.

You never got poetry manuscripts from any of the Beats?

I was going to Japan about that time. I was in San Francisco, and I got in touch with Ferlinghetti. The trial was going on, the "Howl" thing, and I told him that if I could be of any use, as a favorable witness or something like that, I'd be glad to appear. But the trial went very well and I was never asked to do anything. I think they considered me a sort of friendly enemy—or not really that; they considered me a sympathizer, but somebody from the other world, which they had long since dropped out of. Even Rexroth used to say that whenever he went across the bridge to Berkeley he needed a passport. That was when Berkeley was a university, and not a nest.

I think I was a very terrible business manager, and still am. I mean, if it weren't for Teri I'd be on welfare. But financially at *Poetry* magazine we went from bad to worse. We were supported for three or four years, secretly, by the Bollingen Foundation. They did not want it to get out because a lot of other magazines would say, well, help us, too. Without Bollingen we wouldn't have survived, and when that support ran out, we were really in trouble. That was when Ellen Stevenson remodeled the house she lived in, the castle she was born in across from the Drake Hotel, and we moved our offices there. There were other cultural things going on in there, too.

Didn't they have something like a poetry club?

Well, the idea was sound, but the papers ridiculed it out of existence for political reasons. They were out to get Adlai through his ex-wife, whom they delineated as "this crazy woman." But the idea was sound. The Modern Poetry Association Club, or whatever it would be called, was to have a public membership. You paid something like twenty-five dollars a year and you could use the bar, which was a beautiful bar, and also attend the poetry readings, and other stuff went with the membership, too. If we had had a good business manager, which we didn't—Mrs. Stevenson's business manager didn't give a damn about poetry and thought it was a waste of time because there were better things she ought to be doing with her money—it might have worked. When I precipitated a crisis on the board, in which she was forced to resign and so was I—at that point the magazine collapsed. And so we had to move to the attic of the Newberry Library, which we got rent free. In the wintertime we almost froze to death. We drank vodka to keep warm. But we got the magazine out. Those issues are interesting; they're printed on butcher paper—you know, very cheap paper, the cheapest paper there was. That went on for about a year, and then I got this job at Berkeley.

What was the circulation of the magazine then?

Well, I'm just guessing, but I don't think it was over 5,000. I don't know what it is now.

Oh, it's about 10,000. I think it runs between 8,000 and 10,000. One of the problems with editing the magazine now is that there are so many poets and the weight of manuscripts is just incredible. I don't know what Daryl's [Daryl Hine, editor] numbers are . . .

He told us the other day. They're getting something like 5,000 poems a month.

When I edited poetry for Partisan *for a while, they were getting 26,000 poems a year and published only fifteen or twenty. And the whole period when I was at Swallow we got about 3,600 book-length manuscripts a year. That's like ten a day.*

What do you make of that?

I think there are too many poets now. There was a kind of Arcady back there in the fifties when there were fewer poets and a more coherent sense of who was who.

I've now come back to what I call the B-S-K Theory of Poetry— there can be only three poets at a time, such as Byron, Shelley, and Keats.

At least two of them died early. Well, now there are a thousand magazines in America that publish poetry.

And dictionaries of names, addresses, and phone numbers of poets which the taxpayers are paying for because they are covered in part by the National Endowment for the Arts. That's really funny. Somebody's got to write a poem about that. I've tried. I'm *going* to. And the supplements . . . I think it's all part of this whole sick bureaucracy we're living in. Everything else has been bureaucratized; now it's poetry. Look at all these new generations of people who've taken creative writing classes.

What was your sense of the world of people writing poems and contributing to Poetry *in the fifties?*

We used to complain then that there were too few places for poets to get published and that there were too few readers of poetry, but we certainly did not feel that we were being overwhelmed by paper. We had three or four or five readers. I discovered Isabella Gardner. She sent some poems to me, and I thought they were very good. I published them and asked her to come and be a reader. She was the most faithful one I had in five years. She was there every morning at nine o'clock and would stay all day long, reading, weeding out the bad stuff. I think it must have been easier in the fifties to weed out bad poetry than it is now, because now everybody who takes a creative writing course has a bag of tricks which can fool you.

Louis Simpson says they write one damned thing after another. They can't bring a poem to a conclusion; they just keep going at a certain momentum; they don't know how to stop.

The *Sorcerer's Apprentice.* . . . I'm thinking of another thing that didn't happen then. There were some classic bohemian bum poets, like Bodenheim and Dylan Thomas, living out a kind of nineteenth-century Bloomsbury style. But there were only a few of those. Nowadays "poet" also means what they call a life style. You may or may not write poems, but you can call yourself a poet, and you have a set of values which you can throw at anybody at any time. There are millions of those people running around loose in California.

The English have a certain fascination with Bukowski and Norse and people like that.

Now Bukowski, I think, is an authentic poet He was over at our house and threatened to tear it apart. A wonderful artist had loaned us a couple of his paintings, beautiful abstractions. Bukowski sat down on the sofa, and somebody said to him, "What do you think of that painting?" He said, "Vulgar bourgeois shit."

The idea of Bukowski's using the word "vulgar" is priceless. He gives readings and a lot of people you'd never associate with poetry come to the readings in leather jackets, carrying six-packs of beer and bottles of whiskey, to egg him on, and then he sits there and belches through a reading. The British, though, love this. London Magazine, *which has a publishing subsidiary, has published two or three of Bukowski's books over there, and they got big reviews. People talk about him as if they were talking about Hemingway.*

The multiplication of poets—it sort of leaves my mind blank. I don't know what to do with them. I get all these magazines—they just come flooding in—and they all sound the same. Now and then there's a good one. *Kayak* is a good one; Hitchcock knows what he's doing. It's consistent and it's amusing. It's a lot of fun sometimes, but that's pretty rare nowadays. The other day somebody sent me a copy of *Sewanee Review,* which I hadn't seen for years. I was amazed—such big beautiful black type, and poems in stanzas, and serious articles about Elizabethan plays. So I guess the old tradition persists in pockets. Am I mistaken? I have a feeling that *Poetry* magazine is still holding its own, and is still strong. It's always been lampooned by the avant-garde from the day Harriet Monroe started it. But I always have the feeling—I get it every month, and sometimes I can't stand it when the poems are kind of dead—that it is still the touchstone. When Henry Rago was editing the magazine, I was kind of bewildered. I could never quite grasp Henry's poetry, and the poems he published seemed to be of his kind. I mean, they had a certain diffuseness, which could have been in some European symbolist tradition or something like that.

He also had a strong feeling for the Black Mountain people— Duncan, Creeley, and Levertov—and also for the neglected objectivists. He gave a whole issue to Louis Zukofsky, and a whole issue, or almost a whole issue, to Basil Bunting. And he published David Jones. But then he had a set of extra-poetic interests, which were theological and mystical.

Maybe I'm getting mellow or something, but I like the physical appearance of the magazine. I think Daryl Hine has done something with it, and I like whatever that artwork is. It's interesting— certainly more so than just printing names. And it does seem to me that, whenever I get it, it is a magazine I read through. I don't do that with many literary magazines, at least with many poetry magazines. I can't bear most of the stuff; it seems so ill written and so ill conceived.

Would you want to be editing a magazine now?

No, and I often thank God I'm not. We started a magazine called *California Quarterly,* but it's partly a teaching tool. It's not a great magazine, but it helps us in our creative writing program. We're now using it to teach our graduate students how to edit, which I think every writer should know. When I was editing, I did like it —it's exciting. But I think you have to be younger than I am to want to do that now.

What was the atmosphere around the Poetry *offices during the time you were editing? Were there lots of people who came in from out of town? Was it a place people would visit when they came through?*

It was rather exciting, because poets from all over the world would come through Chicago, and when they came to Chicago they would always come to the office. We'd take them out for martinis. Once there was an English poet who, I found out later, hadn't eaten for three days. And all we gave him were martinis! Then he got on a bus and went to Seattle or some place. There were literary get-togethers, and we gave T. S. Eliot a cocktail party, which was a kind of highlight. And we had good relations with English department people at the University of Chicago. But then, of course, there was the Hayakawa crisis. Marge, his wife, was associate editor and, I believe, was still associate editor when I arrived. There was a South Side poetry magazine faction that centered around Hayakawa—not around his wife Marge. I think Hayakawa wanted to be the editor. He was editing *Etc.,* the semantics magazine, and he had a strong interest in *Poetry*. As far as I know, he himself did not write poetry, but he always had poets at his house. Anyway, I did a terrible thing, I fired Harriet Monroe's secretary. She'd been there since the magazine started and was a very close friend of Hayakawa's. This was a shock to them. First Don tried to get me fired, but I was too new, and I had allied myself with the North Side faction. So I was protected. It was kind of a civil war. Everybody who was on his team resigned from the board.

There were also literary quarrels at the mag during that time. The essay Williams did on Sandburg, for one; and then that brief exchange between Carruth and Yvor Winters.

It had something to do with new critics, or maybe with Winters' peculiar ideas of what was a good poet. You know he would say things like "the four greatest poets in English literature are Milton, Shakespeare, Spenser, and Marilyn Schmiddling" (who was sitting in the first row). He came to a poetry reading of mine once. I didn't want him to come, but he came and sat in the first row. Afterward he didn't say one word about my poems. We just talked about Airedale dogs, which he was raising.

I think the Carruth thing had to do with poets who were teachers. Carruth was down on the idea of poets' teaching.

He had had a very bad experience with teaching. I'm glad to see that he's now writing and reviewing. I think he would have made a very good editor, but he might have been too limited and maybe his tastes were too sharp. A poetry magazine's got to have some play in it, some flexibility. The *Poetry* editor I liked best was George Dillon in the late forties. He was the one who originally printed my poems in *Poetry* and really got me going. And under his editorship the magazine was printing those early Auden poems and beautiful MacNeice lyrics, and it was very fresh and bouncy.

You published one of the important Auden poems, "The Shield of Achilles."

We gave him a big special prize for that, in 1954. Sort of a cooked-up deal, in a way. I think Auden knew about the prize and knew he would win it.*

Do you remember all those auction dinners? When the auction started, after dinner, waiters would go around with trays of champagne. All the librarians would come, and they kept drinking the champagne and raising their hands and, of course, my God, some beautiful items were auctioned off. The time Auden was there, they had one of his manuscripts to auction off. I think it was just a fine copy, a handwritten manuscript, of "The Shield of Achilles." Beforehand Auden said, "I have to get the hell out of here." John Ciardi was the auctioneer, and Auden said, "Ciardi's going to make me come up there, and stand there while they auction off this poem."

Poor Auden, I was really shocked when he died. I don't think he had lost his touch at all. It reminds me so much of Augustan poetry. I mean Roman poetry. All that beautiful indirection and sophistication . . .

Looking back, I am rather pleasantly surprised to see that I did publish so many good poets.

*Editor's note. As announced in *Poetry* (May 1954), the award was made to Auden " in consideration of his entire lifetime's work." The statement of the award committee said in part: "Auden is a man who expresses himself acutely, and with poetic vivacity. In his identity as an American he has become a permanent part of American poetry."

You did those nonsense poems, the children's poems—and a whole group of Roethke's.

And then I got Roethke to do a review of a Dylan Thomas book (*In Country Sleep*), which he wrote under an assumed name.

Yes, "Winterset Rothberg." He called it "One Ring-Tailed Roarer to Another."

And I published John Logan.

Ben Belitt. And Merwin, very early Merwin.

Marianne Moore, Patchen, Stevens, Viereck . . .

And a chunk of Williams' Paterson.

At the same time, I think the magazine itself has got to take credit for a lot of this. How many places were there for poets to send their stuff to? What other place was there to send it? Maybe there were half a dozen suitable magazines around, but *Poetry* was the most dignified.

Was The New Yorker *competing, in the sense of publishing good verse at that point?*

I think so, although I've always been a little bit puzzled by *The New Yorker's* literary policy. I sometimes think they were publishing the not-quite-best poems of the good poets—not Roethke's really good poems, or Auden's, because the readers had their own limitations too. I mean, the guys who ride the New York New Haven and Hartford trains to Westport are not going to read "The Shield of Achilles." But they'll read a poem about Central Park.

Were there any other magazines you thought of as being your competition? Some that would want to get a poem before you got it?

I don't recall that we had that problem. How many purely poetry magazines were there? The good magazines, like *Partisan Review*, and *Kenyon*, and so on, had some poetry, but they came out only three or four times a year. I think we had the pick. For one thing, *Poetry* magazine was and is in every university library. English professors read it. Critics read it, no matter what they say about it. They look at it, they're aware of it. And having been published in *Poetry* is a good mark, a plus that counts when they're up for a promotion. You know, *Poetry* has authority.

The reviews were interesting because they came from so many different directions and because there was no policy governing them, so you could always be surprised by the position some reviewers would take. I think Paterson *got a negative review in* Poetry.

That might have been Randall Jarrell's review. He liked books 1 and 2, but he didn't like 5. I loved Jarrell's prose.

There are some other poetry magazines that would like to take a general eclectic course, like American Poetry Review *and* Poetry Now. *I like* Poetry Now *better because there are more poems in it.*

I do too. I really read it through, because it does print lively, good writing.

I'd be interested in what you thought of APR *when Stephen Berg was doing it all by himself. He was making the choices, and doing bold and, I think, exciting things. Now what has evolved is a board of editors—six editors—whose personal taste I can't figure out.*

I agree with Eliot. I think the editor of a literary magazine should be an autocrat. It should be one guy. I once sent a poem to one of those tabloid poetry magazines; they rejected it. (I don't know whether you noticed, in *Poetry* magazine, that long translation from *Metamorphoses* about Philomel.) I sent it to Daryl, and put at the bottom of my letter, "A certain magazine (that looks like a newspaper) sent this back saying the plot was weak." I think he liked the poem for that reason.

One of these days I'm going to write a novel (I think it's got to be a novel) of that period when I was at *Poetry* because of all the weird involvements, even including national politics.

THE CARE AND FUNDING OF PEGASUS
Joseph Parisi

Poetry *Prize Day, November 1958. Left to right: Henry Rago, W. H. Auden, Karl Shapiro; (right foreground) Marion Strobel and Mrs. A. Bowe; (in doorway) Robert Mueller and John Bowe (courtesy* Poetry *magazine).*

As associate editor of Poetry *magazine, Joseph Parisi has numbered among his duties the first reading of the 60,000 unsolicited poetry manuscripts received each year, the production of the magazine's monthly issues, fund raising, and liaison between the magazine and its board of trustees. Houghton Mifflin has just published* The Poetry Anthology: 65 Years of America's Most Distinguished Verse Magazine, *co-edited by Mr. Parisi and former* Poetry *editor Daryl Hine.*

Mr. Parisi has been the associate editor of Poetry *since 1976. He is a specialist in eighteenth-century literature, has a doctorate from the University of Chicago, and is writing a book on his period called* Mobs and Lords. *He has published several articles in the* Contemporary Poets, Novelists, and Dramatists *series edited in London by James Vinson, and has written numerous reviews on poets and novelists for* The New Leader, Poetry, *and the* Chicago Tribune.

Poetry in a sense ceased to be a little magazine almost two decades before 1950. Conventionally defined, as T. S. Eliot wrote Karl Shapiro in that year, the little magazine has a single editor, a small circulation, and a short life span, rarely exceeding that of the founding editorship. *Poetry,* Eliot continued, was no longer a little magazine but an Institution.

How the magazine achieved its special status in literary history is well known. Less familiar are the financial and administrative affairs of the magazine—a complex, evolving story often as entangled as its literary correspondence and relationships. If, as Stephen Spender has written, *Poetry* is unique in having published virtually every important poet in English of the century, it is also singular in its economic resourcefulness. For all its years of continuous monthly publication, and even with its illustrious roster, its existence has been precarious. Had the magazine been forced to depend solely upon poetry lovers or literati, it would have gone the way of so many of its fellows and rivals who had equally distinguished contributors and even better known editors. It has survived to become an internationally recognized forum because it has been a Chicago institution. *Poetry* is still very much the magazine Harriet Monroe founded.

217

Anyone acquainted with the history of *Poetry* cannot help being struck by its continuous adherence to the first principles of its founding editor. From the beginning, Miss Monroe declared that *Poetry* would have an "open door"; it would not be a factional organ or the mouthpiece of a coterie or currently fashionable movement. (That is why, when she frustrated his attempts to campaign in the prose section, Ezra Pound resigned as her first foreign correspondent.) Nor did she want it to be an academic or scholarly journal; the magazine would avoid critical and theoretical biases. Only in its most desperate hours did her successors consider university affiliation. Thus, whatever the disagreements about the particular tastes of individual editors—and there have been plenty —their integrity has not been in doubt. Miss Monroe knew that to establish the magazine and keep it going with editorial freedom required money, without strings. To their credit, her first supporters not only gave generously—they never interfered with editorial policy. This pattern of private philanthropy with editorial independence has continued to the present.

In 1912 the annual budget for the magazine was $5,000, much of it going to pay contributors. Harriet Monroe was not rich herself, but she was well known, at least in Chicago. She was also well connected, since her father, H. S. Monroe, had been a prominent lawyer. On the advice of well-placed friends she made her rounds to the socialites and to the leading industrialists, bankers, and lawyers. Appealing to their civic pride—these were, after all, the people who funded the Art Institute, the Chicago Symphony Orchestra, the University of Chicago, the museums— she got 108 backers to pledge fifty dollars apiece annually for five years. Her list of guarantors reads like a social register of Chicago in the teens of this century: Ryerson, Lathrop, Moody, McCormick, Insull, Palmer, Pullman, Field, Burnham, Borden, Blair. Beyond the listing in the magazine, and the personal satisfaction of helping the "experiment," the guarantors got little else, not even good publicity. Literary magazines do not offer the glamour that other, more highly visible cultural enterprises can afford.

Poetry at this time had no board of trustees, nor would it have one for almost thirty years. Miss Monroe did select an advisory committee, but it was only advisory. (Even in awarding

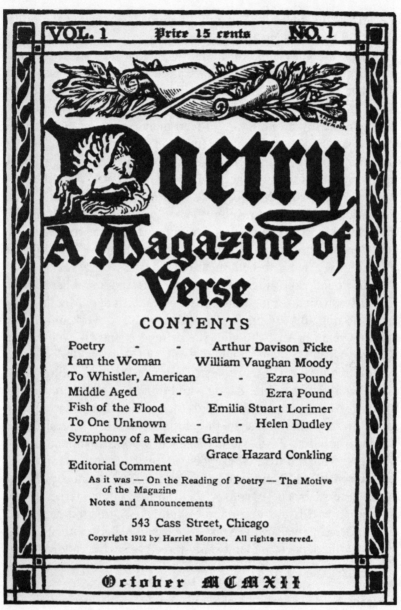

VOL. 1   Price 15 cents   NO. 1

Poetry
A Magazine of Verse

CONTENTS

543 Cass Street, Chicago

October MCMXII

Poetry, *Vol. 1, No. 1, October 1912 (courtesy* Poetry *magazine).*

the prizes, the committee merely confirmed whomever the editor chose.) There was no doubt about who ran the magazine. But *Poetry* in those days, and for many years after, was a very informal organization. The atmosphere at Cass and Erie streets was more like that of a club than an editorial, let alone business, office. Poets and friends (but only a very select group of guarantors) were continually dropping by to read manuscripts, argue, listen to chief assistant Alice Corbin Henderson's witty remarks, and to eat Miss Monroe's candy and the impromptu meals she whipped up over a bonfire out back. Many of the poets were literally starving, and Miss Monroe was known as a soft touch. The custom of entertaining traveling poets was important not only for indigent rhymesters but also for support of the magazine. It kept *Poetry*'s sponsors "involved"; thus Miss Monroe could always count on her friends to help meet the deficits.

With Pound exporting material from England and Alice Corbin Henderson sifting through the daily domestic sludge, Miss Monroe had little difficulty filling *Poetry* with interesting work during the first five years or so. Although she printed poems by well-known figures such as William Vaughn Moody and William Butler Yeats, she discomfited the literary establishment by presenting then-radical work in vers libre. Along with Pound's so-called Imagists— Richard Aldington, H. D., Ford Madox Hueffer (Ford), and James Joyce—she published the earliest works of several future standard authors: T. S. Eliot, Wallace Stevens, William Carlos Williams, Robert Frost, Marianne Moore. Ever the populist, she also presented and continued to champion Carl Sandburg, Edgar Lee Masters, Vachel Lindsay, and other midwesterners, and devoted several issues to American Indian, Negro, southern, and "folk" poetry, as well as to cowboy songs and ballads. Other special issues featured poets under twenty-three, verse by children, and war poems.

When costs doubled after the First World War, she found it increasingly difficult to balance the books. Like the poets, she had to keep knocking on doors. In the 1920s she lent her pages to the Objectivists (edited by Louis Zukofsky), to a Spanish-American number and an English number (edited by Basil Bunting and Michael Roberts), and to the "social poets" (edited by Horace Gregory). But as financial problems grew, editorial quality diminished. Along with the guarantors, she was losing important contributors to rival publications which had sprung up after her pioneering success. Luminaries were being replaced by ladies with three names; a distressing number of dull issues in the twenties and thirties are filled with mediocre and parochial verse.

Harriet Monroe did not believe the magazine could continue after her death. With typical generosity, she stipulated in her will that all of *Poetry*'s papers and books should go to the University of Chicago. An anonymous donor also provided a fund to buy books, to add to what became the Harriet Monroe Collection. Had the magazine been able to retain and eventually sell this treasury, it would, of course, have been financially secure, perhaps indefinitely. After her death in Peru in 1936, tributes poured into the office, along with protests from writers, editors, and friends around the country that a magazine with such an unprecedented history should not be allowed to die. Despite the depression, staff and supporters decided to persevere.

Morton Dauwen Zabel, who had been acting editor during Miss Monroe's trip, took over, staying for a year. The high point of his brief tenure was the famous English Issue (January 1937), which he invited W. H. Auden and Michael Roberts to edit. Zabel too became occupied with raising money and put together a brochure featuring all the poets whose works had appeared in *Poetry* during the past twenty-four years. When he returned to teaching, George Dillon, with Inez Cunningham Boulton as first reader, took over the gravely ailing magazine. Things continued touch and go, then became critical when the second of two emergency grants from the Carnegie Foundation ran out in 1940.

As it happened, that year Inez Boulton had introduced the young Dillon to Augustine Bowe, later chief justice of the Chicago Municipal Court, and his wife Julia, who were staying at their summer place in Palos Park. They were immediately charmed, especially Julia, who shared Dillon's knowledge and love of French poetry. This meeting, along with Gus Bowe's love of poetry of all kinds, helped form one of the most important relationships the magazine has had. In the evenings the judge argued politics but wound up discussing poetry with a Palos Park neighbor—industrialist and financier J. Patrick Lannan, who more than anyone was responsible for rescuing the magazine in later years.

Since current fund-raising was ineffective—and especially difficult

221

because of the war—Judge Bowe suggested the magazine try the same techniques that the Art Institute and other Chicago cultural institutions used, and immediately had his nephew and law partner, John Casey, draw up papers of incorporation. (Through the years, lawyers have played prominent roles at *Poetry*.) The papers arrived in August 1941, giving the Modern Poetry Association not-for-profit status. At the same time Julia Bowe and Marcia Masters (the poet Edgar Lee Masters' daughter, who volunteered as a reader at the magazine) decided that, to get anywhere or anything, the backing of Chicago's "old guard" was essential. They asked Marion Strobel Mitchell, herself a poet long associated with *Poetry,* to help. In Washington, ex-Chicagoan Archibald MacLeish read at a benefit whose list of sponsors was headed by Mrs. Eleanor Roosevelt. Leading writers and editors in California and on the East Coast also contributed. Within six weeks, $3,000 was raised, enough to get the magazine through the current year. Earlier, Dillon had had to print an announcement that the June 1942 issue might be the last; in October he was able to list 180 sponsors.

Since the magazine continued to need money, Julia Bowe, who chaired the Committee on Funds, organized a lecture series on modern art. Frank Lloyd Wright, David Daiches, Arthur Meeker, Jr., Daniel Catton Rich, president of the Art Institute, and Rudolph Ganz, president of the Chicago Musical College, enlightened good crowds at the Arts Club in 1943—and broadened the support of *Poetry*. Peter DeVries, who was editor with John Frederick Nims, Marion Strobel, and Jessica Nelson North while Dillon was in the service, also invited James Thurber to speak; Thurber provided *Poetry* with a new drawing of the Pegasus. (DeVries eventually joined *The New Yorker*.) Thus began the benefits and other ventures that have helped sustain *Poetry* until now.

Important as they were, the Committees on Funds at first had no formal standing. Indeed, the most important contributors often weren't members of the Board; even today, many of the most generous patrons have no official connections with *Poetry*. In 1941, the Board of Trustees was composed of staff only; there were just four members. In 1945, the Board grew to eleven; the staff, as officers, were joined by William Monroe, Judge and Mrs. Bowe, Arthur Leonard of the Continental Bank (business expertise was

222

sorely needed), sometime staffer Katinka Loesser (Mrs. DeVries), S. I. Hayakawa, then an assistant professor of linguistics at Illinois Institute of Technology, and circulation manager Margedant Peters (Mrs. Hayakawa). In 1947, the Board was further enlarged to thirteen, and the bylaws were changed to admit sustaining, but nonvoting, members (i.e. sponsors).

Bylaws notwithstanding, a casual atmosphere still prevailed. All the trustees were old friends, and the social and literary aspects of *Poetry* were pleasantly combined, particularly on Saturdays when staff, trustees, and visiting poets, many returning from the war, formed a kind of Algonquin Round Table West at Mike Fish's Restaurant. In 1946 Julia Bowe organized a "Purse for Pegasus" benefit at the Casino Club, at which Thomas C. Lea, a retired businessman, expressed an interest in *Poetry*. He soon became treasurer of the Modern Poetry Association. (The treasurer, who had no discernible literary expertise, also came by the office to read manuscripts.) He lost no time in writing the Bollingen Foundation and getting a $10,000 grant for 1947, which was renewed for 1948 and 1949. It looked as if no more benefits would be required, at least until 1950. Fanny Butcher, book editor of the Chicago *Tribune,* also joined the Board and saw to it that *Poetry* got good press coverage. In 1947 the magazine brought out its first Critical Supplements, edited by John Frederick Nims, who with Marion Strobel continued to help edit the magazine. In 1949 the magazine also reprinted, in pamphlet form, William Elton's *Poetry* articles on the New Criticism, and the *Glossary* (and later *Guide*) proved popular enough for four more printings.

Dillon, upon his return to civilian life in 1947, had resumed the editorship. But soon his parents required him at home in Virginia, and early in 1949, with the Bollingen funds running out, he decided to resign. He felt, as he wrote Paul Mellon in May, that his own fund-raising resources were at an end (he had always been shy about soliciting money), and without further funding—the deficit now stood at $20,000—the magazine would also come to an end. *Poetry* was now known worldwide, he continued; it would be hard to replace. Inez Boulton, then living in Washington, also wrote Mellon. Meanwhile Don Hayakawa inquired whether the English department at Northwestern University would take over, but nothing came of this idea for educational sponsorship.

223

Hayden Carruth followed Dillon, ostensibly as editor in chief; Nims and Strobel (who was by now president of the Board) remained editors as well. Selections were to be made by mutual agreement of the three and, somewhat redundantly, of the Executive Committee—at least for Carruth's first six months, until the Board "knew his abilities better." The old communal arrangement proved less than satisfactory—perhaps inevitably, considering Carruth's tentative status. He had made known some "Observations on Direction of Editorial Policy" when he took the post: more and longer poems by established poets should be presented; publication of younger poets should be more selective; the prose section should be expanded, especially if there were not enough good poems. Eventually some issues contained more prose than poetry. By late fall of 1949, as the money problems remained unsolved, the office grew tense because of "the mutual lack of respect between Miss Strobel and Mr. Carruth." By December the situation became intolerable.

Although the Board decided, by a very close vote, that Carruth should have complete editorial authority, he resigned at the beginning of 1950. Marion Strobel became editor pro tem, and Julia Bowe was instructed to ask Karl Shapiro to assume the editorship. Formal policies now replaced the previous casual procedures. The Executive Committee would select the editor, who in turn would select the staff and determine the contents of the magazine. On January 14, Shapiro accepted the job. He also became secretary of the Board, a position he, and later Henry Rago, kept throughout their tenure.

Though relatively short, Shapiro's four-year term as editor was very active, not to say controversial; and it was significant not only because of the caliber of the content of *Poetry* but also because of a change in policy. Steering away from the critical and academic direction the magazine had recently taken, Shapiro reasserted the traditional editorial policy of printing "the best new and unpublished poetry . . . regardless of school or clique." His report to the Board in 1952 continued: "Because of the tendency of little magazines today to become semi-scholarly journals of literary history and aesthetics, *Poetry* must keep its pages open to writers outside the universities and orthodox critical circles." In a detailed "History and Summary of Activities of

Poetry Magazine," he reminded the Board that, "Because of its long reputation for high standards and complete integrity, *Poetry* is the magazine to which all serious poets turn for publication of their work. . . . Poets can obtain a considerably wider audience by publishing their work in *Poetry* than they can publishing in books."

Among those poets who began appearing during the 1940s and continued to appear during Shapiro's editorship were David Wagoner, James Merrill, John Berryman, Leslie Fiedler, Paul Goodman, Vernon Watkins, e. e. cummings, Delmore Schwartz, George Barker, Richard Wilbur, Anthony Hecht, Randall Jarrell, and Robinson Jeffers, with occasional appearances by Robert Graves, Muriel Rukeyser, R. P. Blackmur, Weldon Kees, W. S. Merwin, W. H. Auden, and Wallace Stevens. Equally impressive was the prose section under Shapiro—perhaps the most distinguished and lively in the history of the magazine. There were regular contributions by Hugh Kenner and Wallace Fowlie; historical and critical articles on Baudelaire, Apollinaire, St.-John Perse, Mallarmé, Jean Cocteau; a history of Imagism; an interview with Auden; Schwartz on Eliot and on "The Vocation of the Poet in the Modern World"; Cleanth Brooks on F. O. Matthiessen; Eric Bentley on the Abbey Theatre; Theodore Roethke on writers' workshops; Dudley Fitts on Ezra Pound; Horace Gregory and Edouard Roditi on Cavafy; Jacques Maritain on "The Poetic Sense."

In a sketch of the magazine prepared for the Board, Shapiro also clearly outlined the respective duties of the Executive Committee and the branches of the staff, editorial and business. The new bylaws establishing the editor's authority were soon put to the test. Shortly after arriving in Chicago, Shapiro fired Harriet Monroe's old secretary, Geraldine Udell. Though a "faithful employee of *Poetry* for twenty years," he explained in a confidential letter to the Bollingen Foundation, he had found her inefficient. Money and time were being wasted, especially as Miss Udell's friends and certain trustees had made the *Poetry* office "headquarters for their own interests," chiefly general semantics. There was a suspicion that the Hayakawas had personal designs upon the magazine; perhaps their efforts to "save" it during the Carruth crisis were not wholly selfless. In any case, they and their faction

225

on the Board resigned en masse. This cleared the way for a new Board.

In its ten years of existence the Board had been composed of a rather close-knit group, dominated by the staff and the literary old guard. It was defined geographically, and hence socially, by the Near North Side, which centered on Astor Street, and to a lesser extent by Hyde Park, the environs of the University of Chicago. (Today this pattern still holds, though the change in social history since the fifties has been reflected in a sizable shift to the North Shore, particularly Lake Forest. As in the past, many trustees also sit on the boards of the Art Institute, Chicago Symphony, and various museums and universities.) Although some of the old trustees expressed reservations about the possible "literary sympathies" of any prospective new members, several "influential" and "well-known Chicagoans, actively engaged in businesses related to literature," were recruited, bringing the Board membership up to twenty trustees. With the addition of these business leaders, the Board's fund-raising improved and civic interest increased, as did publicity in the Chicago papers and around the country. Even *Time* ran a story.

While recognizing the value of individual donations from long-time friends as well as benefits, lectures, and other activities, Shapiro told the Board that such contributions were no longer sufficient and were "always of a problematic success." He soon found, however, that the alternatives were perhaps more problematic. His wife Evalyn took over the business side of the magazine, until the greatly increased duties proved too great for her. (When the magazine found it could not afford to replace her, an accountant was hired.) After the first detailed annual budget was prepared, revealing a $20,000 deficit, letters and trips to the Bollingen Foundation followed, and eventually an unpublicized grant of $15,000, to be divided over two years, was promised. To develop a broader base of support, Shapiro wanted to increase memberships in the M. P. A. Associates program. (For $10 members received a year's subscription, special publications, and reports of the Proceedings of the Board.) For the same reason, the Associates program was reactivated as late as three years ago, but while the extra income has been welcome, it has amounted to less than 4 percent of the total budget.

To cut costs, the magazine was redesigned. Julia Bowe recruited a dozen volunteers to do clerical chores. Isabella Gardner also came in to read manuscripts. Circulation went up, more advertising appeared. Shapiro later solicited, and got, letters of endorsement from prominent poets—Eliot, Spender, cummings, Williams, Edith Sitwell, MacLeish, Graves—which ran monthly in 1954 and 1955 on the inside front cover of the magazine.

After the Bollingen money ran out in 1952, descendants of the original guarantors were asked to contribute to a special fund for the fortieth anniversary. The most grandiose plan was to persuade Robert Maynard Hutchins, in his capacity as head of the Ford Foundation, to build a poetry center in Chicago. For this, John Nef of the Committee on Social Thought at the University of Chicago submitted a draft proposal to the Board: *Poetry* and the Committee would request $250,000, which they would split, to support them both, set up the center, and use to "sustain people of artistic talent" through fellowships awarded by the editor. Dylan Thomas came to read; publicity was good, but receipts were not. Readings from the magazine were broadcast over radio station WFMT. Despite these efforts, it appeared in August 1952 that unless more money were forthcoming, the magazine would soon go out of business.

That was not the time for strained relations to develop with the Board. But Shapiro created a flap by "firing" the wife of a Board member. Disturbed by what he felt was damaging in the public relations work she had been doing, voluntarily, for the magazine, he dismissed her without consulting the Board. Word had got out to her friends in the Chicago press, who were already curious about the doings at *Poetry,* especially its relationship and possible political connections with Mrs. Ellen Borden Stevenson, another Board member. In a heated meeting, Daniel Catton Rich, the Board president, rebuked the editor and wanted to know why he had taken such action. Shapiro cited the bylaws that granted him control over editorial policy. Rich denied that public relations fell under the editor's jurisdiction. As arguments intensified, tempers flared, Rich threatened to resign, and eventually Shapiro agreed to consult the Board on public relations matters in the future: a small concession, since the situation was not likely to come up again. Rich stayed until the end of the year, when Mrs. Stevenson became president.

Early in the summer of 1953, the magazine was forced out

of its Erie Street offices by another great Chicago tradition, the creation of parking lots. Mrs. Stevenson had recently converted the old family mansion into what was now termed the 1020 Arts Center, where she offered to rent space to the magazine. Ensconced in their new home on Lake Shore Drive, sharing quarters with several service organizations and station WFMT, the staff and the Board could contemplate Lake Michigan—and the $6,000 deficit. As the usual fund-raising measures proved insufficient and the financial situation became grim, new sources of revenue had to be explored. The magazine arranged to sell the papers in its files from 1936 to 1958 to the University of Chicago for the surprisingly modest sum of $3,000. *Poetry* also entered into negotiations to have the University of Chicago become its printer. Besides doing the printing, the university would keep the subscription lists (at that time taped to the office walls), fill orders, do the advertising, and handle promotion. (This was the first serious effort in its history to sell the magazine itself.) Despite a clause stipulating that the Board of University Publications had to approve of the editor, the contract was signed, to go into effect in January 1954.

When the University of Chicago printing department began production, the M. P. A. Board, all of whose members had examined the contract, discovered that a detail had been overlooked: the new arrangement effectively froze all the magazine's operating capital. Already in debt to the old printer (the paper company had graciously wiped out its bill), the Board would have to borrow to meet day-to-day expenses. Mrs. Stevenson hoped that her Arts Center would generate income, but until it did she made two $1,000 loans to the M. P. A. What happened next is not entirely clear. However, Julia Bowe, in her unpublished memoirs, remarks, "The meals were wonderful, but we had no money coming in and Ellen refused to raise any funds." When the magazine hit rock bottom—by June there was only $100 on hand—the Board met in an emergency session chaired by Stanley Pargellis, director of the Newberry Library. Amid upset, confusion, and misunderstanding—among other things, Shapiro and the Board had mistaken Mrs. Stevenson's loans for gifts—several trustees threatened to resign. Although she had said she would assume financial responsibility for the magazine until the end of the year, Mrs. Stevenson changed her mind. Then she resigned.

228

Dr. Pargellis became president of the Board and offered *Poetry* space in the Newberry attic.

Late in 1954 Karl Shapiro moved to California, where he offered to edit *Poetry* without pay. But of course *Poetry* had always originated in Chicago, and Shapiro suggested that Henry Rago be made editor. At the Board meeting of November 29, 1954, the trustees voted that Rago be given a temporary appointment, with the understanding that "his position [was] not to be regarded as a succession." He stayed on for fourteen years, the length of his reign second only to Harriet Monroe's. (Here it may be noted that although it is clearly written in the M.P.A. bylaws that the Board of Trustees will appoint the editor, since 1954 each new editor has been chosen by his predecessor, then confirmed in the position by the Board.) Besides the change of editorship, November 1954 marks another turning point in the fortunes of the magazine. From the lowest point in its financial history, the Modern Poetry Association climbed to its highest and most stable period of fiscal health. This happy and unprecedented state resulted chiefly from the efforts of J. Patrick Lannan. Though not on the Board, he had been a faithful contributor for years, and now promised to underwrite deficits for the first quarter. Then, like his friend Judge Bowe, he became an active but unofficial adviser, suggesting first of all a professional approach to the management of the Association.

While volunteers were useful, it appeared that *Poetry* should have a regular paid staff, including a public relations person. To succeed, it would have to generate more Chicago involvement and support from the rest of the country. Julia Bowe and Mrs. Clinton King (Narcissa Swift) had brought Oliver St. John Gogarty to the Arts Club to read his work in 1954. Early in 1955 Dame Edith Sitwell recited her poems, and attended a party hosted by Mrs. John Wentworth at the Casino. Both events were great social occasions and generated lots of publicity. But when Mr. Lannan saw the pitiful receipts ($109 and $1,298), he suggested a better idea.

Robert Frost was invited to read for what became the first annual Poetry Day, in November 1955. At the same time Lannan, with Dr. Pargellis and book collectors, organized the first auction, to be held in conjunction with the public reading. With Professor

229

Bergen Evans of Northwestern as auctioneer, fifty-four rare literary items went up for bid before 168 people—none of them poets, though a few were "literary": presidents and directors of several large corporations, from IT&T to Lipton Tea, as well as the directors of the new Lilly Library at Indiana University, the Museum of Modern Art, and the Morgan Library. Though not as famous then as he was to become, in part because of Poetry Day, Frost drew a large crowd, and the proceeds from the reading and auction were a great relief to the budget. A major feature in *Life* Magazine spread the fame of *Poetry,* and did not hurt Frost's career either.

Following this success, the pattern was set. Carl Sandburg, who first appeared in *Poetry* in 1913, read for the next year's Poetry Day. The 1957 benefit required more effort, since John Crowe Ransom, the featured poet, was not well known to the general public. So Mr. Lannan invited several important New York publishers to the Harvard Club and asked them to search their files for interesting items for the auction, which they did. Archibald MacLeish appeared at the benefit the following year. Then in 1959, a banner year, T. S. Eliot read in Orchestra Hall, which could have been filled twice. That year also Mr. Lannan, who, besides organizing the events, contributed substantial sums each year, finally accepted the chairmanship of the Board.

By 1961 *Poetry* was the largest little magazine in the country, and second or third among the general literary-academic group, quarterlies included, with a print order of 5,500. Costs of publication, however, had also risen—to $64,000 in that year, with substantial increments each year thereafter ($68,000 in 1965, $73,000 in 1967, and $83,000 in 1970). Thus, while Poetry Day had become a very popular attraction for the Chicago public and a tremendous aid to the magazine, as usual the funds were still not enough. Reprint rights to the magazine were sold to AMS Press. A new lecture series was inaugurated. The Board was increased to thirty-seven trustees. Further manuscripts and correspondence were sold at a very low price to the University of Chicago. *Poetry* arranged several exchange ads with other journals, while it tried to find a sponsor for the 400 foreign subscriptions to the magazine originally subsidized by the Ford Foundation but carried by the magazine since 1958.

230

Like his predecessors, Henry Rago found himself spending a great deal of time writing letters, making applications, and traveling for funds. He got the long-suffering Bollingen Foundation to provide another two-year grant to help publish the special British (May 1962), French (July 1962), and Double (October 1962) issues prepared for *Poetry*'s fiftieth anniversary. (While his taste was catholic enough to include nearly all the serious, famous, or fashionable American and English poets of the time—except the Beats, who got a negative review in November 1958—his guiding spirit was ecumenical. He had already devoted special issues to Japanese [May 1956], Modern Hebrew [July 1958], Indian [January 1959], and Italian [August 1959] poetry.) He also negotiated a more favorable disposition of the *Poetry* papers with the Lilly Library at Indiana. He attracted several new foundations and individual donors to the cause. Among them was David Rockefeller, a friend from his service days, whom he persuaded to offer a personal grant of $22,500, to be matched over a three-year period by other new contributors. The future began to look brighter. Even when the subscription price and the M.P.A. membership fee had to be raised, circulation continued to rise, until in 1966 it reached almost 9,000. By 1967, Rago was able to report to the Board that the magazine had earned all but $20,000 of its costs.

Meanwhile, back at the office, the old clubby atmosphere virtually disappeared. Karl Shapiro had already drastically curtailed casual visitations, and under Rago the shop was run in a very businesslike manner. Although he always maintained the closest and most cordial ties with the trustees, he managed, in his friendly but formal way, to run not only the editorial but also the broader administrative operations of the M.P.A. (through his office as secretary of the Board) largely according to his will. At 1018 State Street, whither *Poetry* repaired in 1957, he ran a tight ship. His penchant for orderliness manifested itself in his insistence that only new bronzette paper clips be used; and on those days when he worked at home, he was wont to call the staff at 4:55 P.M. to make certain they were still on duty. Unfortunately, this passion for detail was not foolproof. In 1968, when the first thorough audit of the Modern Poetry Association was completed, it was discovered that the corporation had been dissolved. Since 1960 the M.P.A.,

231

through a simple clerical error, had neglected to send in the annual two-dollar filing fee. (Lawyers were quickly dispatched and the decree of dissolution was soon vacated, retroactively.)

At the time of the 1968 audit, Lawrence Towner, director of the Newberry Library and recently elected president of the Board, proposed new bylaws for the Association. The number of trustees was reduced from thirty-nine to thirty, to be reelected or replaced on a regular schedule. Voting privileges were now restricted to the trustees (formerly, all M.P.A. members could vote, and often did so by proxy); old members and new contributors could, however, become nonvoting Associates. There was also some feeling that other changes were needed. Perhaps sensing this, Rago requested a year's leave of absence to permit "a more leisurely enjoyment of his teaching and reflection at the University of Chicago"—he had always kept up his ties as humanities professor in the College and theology lecturer in the Divinity School—"more time to work at his new book of poetry, and in 1969 a long summer on the Continent with his family." As Shapiro had done before him, Rago invited in a "visiting editor."

Henry Rago was not terribly familiar with Daryl Hine, but they were acquainted, since Hine had recently taken his Ph.D. at the University of Chicago, where he had started teaching. When Hine came on, in October 1968, he had had little editorial experience, but now had time to get it, since Rago had thoughtfully left manuscripts to be used. Rago would also call and drop by on occasion, to indicate typographical errors in an issue or other fine points to his stand-in. This aid was not always appreciated. After his long association with the magazine, Rago apparently had a hard time letting go. But early in May 1969 he made his leave of absence permanent, and Daryl Hine's appointment as editor was formally announced on May 18. On May 29 Henry Rago died of heart failure.

In personality, background, and tastes, Daryl Hine was quite unlike Rago. When he assumed the duties of editor, he had had little administrative experience, nor did he develop much ability along that line. He had little interest in, or capacity for, fundraising, and even less for public relations, although at first he did what had to be done and worked hard on editorial matters. The Board seems to have understood his limitations when he was

232

hired. In any case, there did not appear to be much reason for worry about the business side of the magazine, since it was now on a firm footing economically. Further, it was expected that Hine's term of office would probably last only five years. The Association had voted to pay Mrs. Rago a modest pension, but this extra expense, and even the low returns from the 1969 Poetry Day (*In Memoriam* Henry Rago), created no problem. In fact, that year income from sales and subscriptions exceeded costs by $3,000. This improbable stroke of good fortune was, of course, too good to last.

In 1970 *Poetry* was again displaced, this time by a plaza, and the office moved to its present location on North Dearborn Parkway. Along with the rent, printing and mailing costs went up drastically, while income from gifts fell sharply. A matching grant from CCLM helped soften the blow, and there seemed no immediate cause for alarm. But in 1971 circulation dipped from 9,000 to 7,400, and the magazine experienced a deficit of over $12,000. (Federal grants to universities were cut back at that time, reducing their ability to buy journals.) Dr. Towner suggested that the Board consider hiring an "executive director," who would "free the Editor from most of the burdens of fund-raising, administration, and planning of social events. . . ." One trustee pointed out that this sort of arrangement usually did not work. The motion was tabled, and nothing came of it.

In September 1972, *Poetry's* anti–Vietnam War issue appeared. In the past the magazine had carefully avoided political commentary, although during World War I Miss Monroe had presented "War Poems," and later editors had also printed many poems about war in general and the Second World War in particular by men in the service and other poets. But the Vietnam War was, of course, quite different from previous conflicts, and Rob Allen, the associate editor at the time, had suggested the idea of a special issue when anti-war feeling was high. The Board itself had already taken a step unprecedented in its history. On May 10, 1972, ten trustees approved, in a telephone vote, a proposal that the Modern Poetry Association should send President Nixon, Secretary Kissinger, Senators Stevenson, Percy, Fulbright, McGovern, and others in government a telegram "protesting recent American aggression in Vietnam." At a Board meeting later in the year, the editor was able to report generally favorable responses to the Against the War Issue, and a big demand for reorders.

Aside from the war, during 1972 there was reason, if not for excitement, at least for celebration, since that year marked the sixtieth anniversary of *Poetry*. Douglas Macdonald, proprietor of Two Hands Books and at that time a member of the Board, organized a Chicago Poetry Festival for March 5–7. This was the first time the magazine had co-sponsored such an event, and it was successful. For Poetry Day, Allen Tate was invited to read; a group of actors also gave recitations from Harriet Monroe's correspondence.

From 1973 on, editorial and managerial matters returned to fairly normal routine. In 1973 yearly subscriptions had to be raised to $15, and they were again raised, to $18, in 1976. The Board contemplated buying a building, rental income from which might help offset costs, but this plan fell through. The annual Poetry Day continued, along with other efforts at raising money, which included another sale of papers to the Lilly Library. Meanwhile printing and mailing costs rose 20 percent in two years. In 1976 and 1977 there were some months when not enough remained in the checking account to pay the printer. The Association was forced to dip into its capital reserves, already much reduced by recent downturns in the stock market, to balance the budget.

By the summer of 1977, Hine, who had considered resigning for some time, was thoroughly dissatisfied with the job. In June, somewhat precipitously, he decided to quit. He asked John Frederick Nims, whose most recent association with the magazine was that of visiting editor during 1960-61, to take over. The choice was confirmed by the Executive Committee and then the Board.

When the new editor assumed his post, in January 1978, he was immediately faced with a novel crisis: *The Readers' Guide to Periodical Literature*, which had indexed *Poetry* since 1915, decided to delete the magazine from its listings. Since the majority of *Poetry*'s subscribers are libraries, and many of them will subscribe only to publications listed in the *Guide*, this action was potentially dangerous. Supporters around the country wrote in protest, praising the magazine and pointing out *Poetry*'s important history. (Even the staff was surprised by the size and warmth of

234

the response.) The *Guide,* however, decided not to reconsider the listing until 1983.

While several former contributors have started submitting work again, the editorial course of the magazine is, at this writing, not established. The financial problems, however, are clear. They remain what they have been since the beginning, except that fund-raising is perhaps more difficult today. Ironically, the very longevity of the magazine creates the erroneous impression that *Poetry* must be well off. But, as it has throughout its history, the magazine operates at a substantial deficit and continues to depend on its friends to bail it out.

After sixty-five years of continuous monthly publication, *Poetry* would prefer not to retire. Judging from their past response, the friends of the magazine will keep it going. In the depth of loyalty *Poetry* has always elicited from its supporters, as well as its staff, one realizes how much affection exists for the magazine. In that way, too, *Poetry* is unique among cultural institutions.

SERIOUS WRITING

BETWEEN A ROCK

ONE OF ITS DUT

TO SING OUT THAT THE

SOCIAL ORDER DEPENDS

SUCH SINGING HAS ONL

UNLESS, OF COURSE, BE

IS ITS OWN

…HAS ALWAYS BEEN
…ND A HARD PLACE.
…S, AFTER ALL, IS
…MPEROR IS NAKED. SINCE
…N CULTIVATING DELUSION,
…OCCASIONAL REWARDS.
…G AN ENFANT TERRIBLE
…ATISFACTION.

—PETER MICHELSON

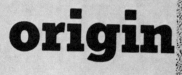

origin

A Quarterly for the Creative

featuring

Charles Olson

I

SPRING - 1951

75¢

Origin, *Vol. 1, No. 1, April 1951 (courtesy Northwestern University Library).*

ORIGIN
Cid Corman

In his first and almost only publicity for Origin, *Cid Corman announced that his magazine would be devoted to "giving adequate outlet to those new/unknown writers who have shown maturity/ insight into their medium"; "to giving the push to creative minds, to demonstrate the going concerns, (and) directions of contemporary creativity." This editorial ambition gradually extended to include work by writers "no matter their age or even if long since dead," who seemed to Mr. Corman "alive" and inadequately known in this country.*

Mr. Corman was born in 1924 in Boston. In 1954 he left the United States and has subsequently lived mostly in Europe and Japan. Of his more than forty books, the most readily available are Livingdying *and* Sun Rock Man *(New Directions), and volumes of translations of Basho, Kusano Shimpei, and Francis Ponge (Grossman).*

Perhaps Mary Kinzie's questions to me—based on the introduction to *The Gist of "Origin"* (Grossman/Viking, 1975)—can serve as a lead-in here. From them I can expatiate on a few notions about the nature of the "little magazine."

She asks me (in a letter dated 22 August 1975) "whether [I] consider T. S. Eliot's five-year run a valid restriction (since neither he, with *Criterion,* nor you have taken it *that* seriously). . . ." The question clearly has been answered by both Eliot and myself already, and MK answers her question as well—differently. A one-man operation is best paced, I feel, by such an approach, and it allows a more open attitude toward other mags. My own reasons for curtailing the 2nd series of *Origin* are amply explained and it was NOT planned—nor desired. A number of other mags—including *Caterpillar* and *L'Ephémère* (Paris)—have picked up from my stance and—I think—to good effect. On the other hand—Ted Weiss has had his *QRL* going irregularly for a long time and evidently finds it both worthwhile and effective. Each must judge for himself. There is no RULE.

The next question runs: "Can you expand on the idea of refusing to take contributions from poets not 'from any sense of connivance, but because it was a question of taking the full risk'?" I fear MK may not have grasped my point or that, in any event, the reader will miss the point in her out-of-context query. I was referring to *monetary* contributions. And it should be obvious to anyone—from Lockheed executives on down—that gifts of money bear with them certain obligations whether stated overtly or not. In the case of a little mag—say—it should be transparent that I would feel obligated to use writing from anyone who contributed notably to the magazine's existence. Perhaps other editors would not feel such an obligation. I cannot speak for others. My point was simple and clear: I preferred scraping along and being independent. As I have often had cause to note: if one means to be free in that sweet land of America, one had better be prepared to be brave.

Next: "Does the idea of the give-away journal clash at all, for you, with the marvelous $17.50 price of the anthology?"

I might add for those who may not know: *Origin* 2nd series was given away to those who wrote me regularly for it (including libraries) and indicated they genuinely wanted it. I still like the idea—though it requires enough economic support at root to allow for it. I'll expand upon this idea a little later in this article.

MK's query seems gratuitously querulous. Only someone who is being paid a regular salary and has never had to cover publishing costs could come on so. It is evident that the price of the anthology —though painfully steep to my sense of wanting it to be generally available to the younger generations—is strictly controlled by the economics of publishing. No publisher prices any book higher than he needs to—normally. Even so—if one examines *Gist*—it will be found to be worth its weight in gold.

"Do you in some way think of the magazine's three series as three different journals?" The question is like asking a novelist if he or she thinks his or her books are different works. Yes—and no. All one's works are one work—but in differing ways. And in the case of *Origin*, where the intentions have been frankly maintained through one series to the next—what happens is rather more ramification and perhaps clarification. Perhaps the novelist should be

240

regarded in the light of a trilogy: like Joyce Cary's—say. Is *The Horse's Mouth* and *Herself Surprised* and *To Be a Pilgrim*—one book or three books? Or *The Oresteia*? Pardon the excessive implications. But *Origin* has, in fact, been edited upon "large" lines.

"In what way does one's/your editing provide an unexpected context for poems?"

I believe there is no little magazine heretofore or since that has been edited with as much care for the placement of works, not only within a single issue, but within the run of a series and even from series to series. Readers who are interested can look into the matter for themselves—since *Kraus Reprint Co.* has made all the issues newly available.

Many writers who had never been aware of each other were suddenly brought into contact. And it isn't by any means the least service of a little mag. In *Origin*'s case the relationships expanded with unusual fruitfulness. And here too those who have special interest can go to the sources and find for themselves. Much of what I say will gradually become apparent through letters when they are, as they are bound to be, published. In sum, there is a great deal of mutual stimulation in such editing. For myself, of course, as well as others.

Or look at my Albers issue in the 3rd series—where many poets and writers are culled unexpectedly in reference to his work—and the reverse implications. And all this can be, and should be, done without big editorial comment. An editor should make his feelings and attitudes implicit in the very way he edits.

Messages by editors are invariably forms of self-publicity. And the heavy blurbs that editors of so many mags—big and little—allow themselves make me wonder where integrity begins in such matters.

"Are your assumptions, do you think, as an editor of poems, different from those of fiction and/or essay journals?" And the related question: "Are little magazines by definition poetry rather than eclectic?"

By "eclectic," presumably she refers to the use of other materials in addition to poetry. Again—her question makes me wonder if she has read *Gist*—or even looked beyond the introduction. Half the book is prose—including essays and fiction. *Origin* has printed a short novel—many short stories—and many essays.

I tried short book reviews early on. Yes—the clear emphasis is on or toward poetry. That is my bias. It also leads into the issue of the outlets for poetry.

Everyone who reads will be aware of the fact that poetry books by major publishers are few and far between and they rarely get much circulation—unless the author has some claims to celebrity status—which has nothing to do with poetry per se. At this point —the need for small-press poetry publication becomes crying. And there are a host of "brave" small presses that often do magnificent work and fulfill an important function in offering outlets to the increasing number of poets "around."

The little magazine—which is invariably dedicated (whatever tastes are involved and invoked) to publishing people whose outlets tend to be minimal—naturally espouses poetry.

University-affiliated "little mags" (for me a little mag is only such when independent of such clear sponsorship by an institution) usually must provide outlet for the academy and that means they MUST carry articles. Not every academician is a poet.

I do think that a little mag should have stimulating essays dealing with any work that has implications for poetry—which means— literally—ANY work. There are countless books that I have found stimulating and warranting consideration in little mags that never come under scrutiny. I think of books like Zuckerkandl's on music or Buchler's *The Main of Light* or Beckett's *The Lost Ones* or Vicker's book *Towards Greek Tragedy* or Ian Robinson's exciting books on Chaucer or various books—in various languages—on form in plants or the nature of history—plus reviews of interesting selected foreign volumes of poetry. So that even the academic little mags could be several hundred percentage points more interesting and engaging than they now are—instead of always discussing the same books and issues.

But the real crux in all this is twofold: the sense of the editor and the quality of the work received. No editor can print better work than he obtains. This truism cannot be repeated often enough. And it has its corollary in the capacity of the editor (—s: the plural added reluctantly) to recognize the excellent or valuable when received. No one is infallible. We have Gide's famous example apropos of Proust as personal caution. But there is no substitute for honesty. (As I like to point out to students of English—in shape and sense, words like "honest" and "modest" are superlatives and cannot be further inflected.)

My "assumptions," then, are no different from those of any other editor who means to be honest—and who is allowed to be independent: I will draw on the best work that comes my way or that I can elicit. And—perhaps my difference—I will edit—place —the work in such a way as to enhance it both for writer and reader within a given issue/context. To the extent that I can.

The matter of independence may perhaps warrant stress here. The little mag has as its major raison d'être—in my eyes—this very possibility of independence. And it is—I think—the hallmark of every little mag worth our attention. It means frank bias. But the very proliferation of such mags permits ample range and a full spectrum. The grab-bag mag that has one or two or three poems by many poets of many varying qualities seems to me to be "copping out." A handful of poets in any one issue is more than enough and the presentation should always be enough to give a clear sense of poetic identity—or identity of mind/spirit no matter what form the writing takes.

If a poet *is* very modestly represented, it should be as a hopeful lead-in to future extension. And—again—a look at *Origin* will reveal how many of the writers were pre-sented—pre-sentimented. And—again—errors are made and the writers don't pan out—or not for myself.

During the course of the three series of *Origin* many "rejected" writers found ample outlet and reputation elsewhere. But it isn't a matter of "rejection": it is a matter of helping to the degree that one can. Young writers often—in their greed and need for attention—fail to allow for the fact that they are dealing with human beings who have daily cares too and have many others to attend to as well as themselves.

MK asks: "How does the 'speed of transference' operate in engendering a sense of community?"

I'm not sure the question is apt. But let me discuss briefly the idea of "speed of transference" (Olson's) and "the sense of community" (in the world of poetry, etc.) separately and we'll see how and if they connect.

For myself a little mag should appear at regular intervals and thus become anticipated. If it is openly limited—say—as *Origin* has been in each series—to a five-year span—it can never be taken for granted. And its time-limit provides in advance a sense of shape and of shaping going on. The 64 pages I have espoused seems to me "just right": it isn't so heavy that it cannot be enjoyably read through at a sitting and at the same time is weighty enough to make a decisive impression as "something." A mimeo of 100 pages feels like a telephone directory. And a printed mag of 120 pp. or more seems also like a job and one only browses.

The most recent economics of time valuation makes it painfully patent that in developed countries people buy more books than ever, but the bulk of them go unread and remain as part of the interior decoration of a room/house—like art work. My own sense is to face the facts. To address the little mag to its precise audience —which is small in number though very large in spirit and which includes the finest reading audience (I believe) in existence—and not to strain the bounds of anyone's "time."

The speed—however—of a quarterly—of transferring writing to the page to the reader—while not that of a newspaper or weekly —is ideal. The material is taken out of the merely passing or fashionable and given a larger hold—while at the same time not holding up work for a year or years—as is the case with book publication generally. (*Gist*—for example—was sent to the publishers nearly 4 years ago.) I had the notion many years ago—as a graduate student at Chapel Hill—of doing film reviews AFTER the film had had its run—so that the concern should not be with its commercial success or failure—but with discussing its content and value with whatever audience it had had. Not IN ADVANCE then—but while the material was still alive in the mind.

It is never a question of the avant-garde: it is a question of keeping a community alert to its own best possibilities. Which may, in fact, be via writers whose works are in "the past," but have— for whatever reason—remained untapped. As Roussel or Bataille or Blanchot remain unknown to most readers in America, since the regular publishers haven't gotten around to them yet. Or so many of the poets *Origin* has brought over from "abroad." I have always felt that writers everywhere should be aware of and stimulated by each other—beyond camps. And beyond special issues of little mags. As if *TriQuarterly* with this issue can wash its hands hereafter with the little-mag thing and say, "We've done that now—what next?" As if French poetry or that of any other country were a package and had to be treated as such—and then forgotten.

I believe in the continuity and relation of writers. Not as competition, but AS community. As I indicated in the intro to *Gist*—much of the fiercest criticism I've received as an editor has come from those I published objecting to other work I've published. How Creeley fulminated against Paul Carroll, how Levertov blasted me for printing the Zukofskys' Catullus, etc., etc. But this is part of the life of the thing. An editor tends to receive little credit for his work and when he does he should have sense enough to realize it may be misapplied. Editing is a job and no one is forced—least of all in the little mag scene—to take it on. No one lives without more or less abuse. I am at least as sensitive as any other poet—but also—like the survivors—tough too. And no one will say I am not abusive at times in turn.

This is part of what community is all about: there is interaction on many levels and involvement. If Diane Wakoski—say—has a penchant for attacking me in public—it may relate to the fact that I often "rejected" work of hers. Not that I dislike her work—there is much of it I like—but simply that what she sent me didn't make it with me. She is—needless to say—not alone in this situation. But then my work has been even more frequently rejected by other editors. I've never been subjected to the "scratch-me-back" that Olson seemed worried about.

"Do you feel largely responsible—*are* you, in fact—for introducing Artaud in the States?"

The intro to *Gist* states the situation exactly and again those who would research the question can do so—easily. Before I left the USA in 1954 I'd already translated a fair amount of Artaud—and it was his work that I largely went into on my arrival in Paris that year. Since two of the main protagonists in America of Artaud today are Jack Hirschman and Clayton Eshleman—both of whom came to know his work via *Origin*—I'd say there is some basis for my being a key factor in the first real wedge for the man in the New (Old) World. It seems to me of minor import—however. The bulk of Artaud's work is still unknown outside of France. *The Letters from Rodez* and the bulk of his poetry. But the strength of his work may be best gauged by reading Michaux's splendid volume of poems: *Moments*.

But beyond all these questions that may seem too detailed for most—unless there is a specific concern with recent little mag history—let me examine the "field"—such as it is—during the past 25 years.

Editors of little mags often—sadly—have a sense of disproportionate self-importance. If I focus on poetry here—as I tend to do—it serves only as a focus—an extreme focus—but what I say touches on all such periodicals—whatever their contents. That is, the small mags too often have small minds running them. I find few who have any larger sense of commitment. In the university set-ups, they are often way-stations for those seeking tenure or jobs in the larger publishing world. OK. Why not? But in the native form—the little mag tends to be the effort of one person to feel more accurately what is going on with his or her contemporaries, to enlarge or enter the community, such as it is. A way of paying dues, of learning "on the job." Fine. It is an engagement.

The extremely ephemeral approach of some—one or two—issues is unfortunate. It means a poor sense of management and planning. And though the issue or two may look promising and even include something 1st rate—it serves only a very small audience IN ADVANCE of more regular publication. It can be a too early burial of fine work. *Yet*—and I score the word—everything helps.

For the writer—the young writer above all—merely seeing his work presented in a form available to others makes him or her feel like he or she exists—approaches a certain professional status—and even the least feedback can prove remarkably stimulating.

And periodical publication often gives the writer his first chance to look at his work with cold, or colder, eyes. A distance accrues. It is not "final": revision is possible. The experience of an "advance" audience is offered. And this is the writer's immediate community. Poets—like Larkin—may pooh-pooh what seems like a highly restricted public—but one has to begin somewhere. And the little mag is where most of us begin. Including Larkin.

Yes: there is a larger audience waiting to be tapped. I have unbounded faith in the power of poetry. I feel it has potentially a larger "market" (a larger audience) than ANY other form of art. And I think it will expand to that public in due time. In the meanwhile—the little mag acts as go-between. The writer may be able to wait for his wages—but he cannot get on without some response. Even Emily Dickinson had to turn to Higginson.

246

My wish to serve that audience—that inner core of audience—I have defined as "elite" is not in order to single such people out—but to be honest. In America—say—there are not more than 1,000 readers of poetry who will genuinely attend. And the figure may be no more than several hundred. I would—with *Origin*—like to put the magazine at once into the hands of this readership—without interposing an economic hangup (price). The cost is one of care and attention. And certainly for the writers involved this would be tremendous—to tap in at once upon this readership—to know that one's work would enjoy so fine a public at once. What payment can equal this?

In addition—these finer readers—mainly writers themselves—are invariably those who share their affections—so that audience would—in effect—be immeasurably larger and keep opening outward.

This can only be done—in my experience—by one's own efforts. I have enjoyed no access to special funds. *Origin* has had more lip-service than any other little mag in existence—that I am sure—but there has been little concrete support for it. My intention to do a 4th series I know already will only be realized through my own efforts. Being penniless is a steady state with me—but perhaps that may change yet and if it does—*Origin* may appear again—for five years.

A little remains a little—but a little can go a long way.

ON BLACK MOUNTAIN REVIEW

Robert Creeley

Robert Creeley with Ann Creeley on Mallorca, 1953. Photograph by Jonathan Williams.

Robert Creeley was part of the "Black Mountain group" at Black Mountain College in North Carolina, first as a student and then as an instructor. What gave rise to his own poetry and to the avant-garde poetry he published in The Black Mountain Review, *he says, was a dissatisfaction both with what was being published —and rejected—by magazines like* Hudson Review, *and with the prewar "solutions" of the Establishment, which did not relate to the postwar "global nightmare." The new poetry of the fifties and new magazines, like* Origin *and Creeley's own, were part of his generation's solution.*

By the 1960s, Mr. Creeley had begun to receive recognition from an Establishment that he in part had helped to change. He has won prizes from Poetry *magazine and fellowships from the Guggenheim and Rockefeller foundations, and has taught at a number of universities. He is the author of some twenty-five books of poetry and fiction; his* Selected Poems *were published in 1976. The following essay is reprinted without changes from Mr. Creeley's introduction to the 1969 AMS Press reprint of the contents of* The Black Mountain Review, 1954–1957.

In hindsight it is almost too simple to note the reasons for the publication of the *Black Mountain Review*. Toward the end of 1953 Black Mountain College—a decisive experimental school started in the early thirties by John Rice and others in Black Mountain, North Carolina—was trying to solve a persistent and most awkward problem. In order to survive it needed a much larger student enrollment, and the usual bulletins and announcements of summer programs seemed to have little effect. Either they failed to reach people who might well prove interested, or else the nature of the college itself was so little known that no one quite trusted its proposals. In consequence, a summer workshop in pottery, which had among its faculty Hamada, Bernard Leach, and Peter Voulkos, found itself with some six rather dazzled persons for students. Whatever the cause—and no doubt it involves too the fact that all experimental colleges faced a very marked apathy during the fifties—some other means of finding and interesting prospective students had to be managed, and so it was that Charles Olson, then rector of the college, proposed to the other faculty members that a magazine might prove a more active advertisement for the nature and form of the college's program than the kind of announcements they had been depending upon.

This, at least, is a brief sense of how the college itself came to be involved in the funding of the magazine's publication. The costs, if I remember rightly, were about $500 an issue, so that the budget for a year's publication would be about $2,000—hardly a large figure. But the college was in such tight financial condition that it could not easily find any money for any purpose, and so its support of the magazine, most accurately the decision of the faculty to commit such an amount to that purpose, is a deeply generous and characteristic act. Too, it's to be acknowledged that Olson's powers of persuasion were considerable.

The nature of the magazine itself, however, and the actual means of its publication, that is, literally its printing, are of another story which is really quite separate from the college itself. In the late forties, while living in Littleton, N. H., I had tried to start a magazine with the help of a college friend, Jacob Leed. He was living in Lititz, Pennsylvania, and had an old George Washington handpress. It was on that that we proposed to print the magazine. Then, at an unhappily critical moment, he broke his arm; I came running from New Hampshire—but after a full day's labor we found we had set two pages only, each with a single poem. So that was that.

What then to do with the material we had collected? Thanks to the occasion, I had found excuse to write to both Ezra Pound and William Carlos Williams. I didn't know what I really wanted of them but was of course deeply honored that they took me in any sense seriously. Pound very quickly seized on the possibility of our magazine's becoming in some sense a *feeder* for his own commitments, but was clearly a little questioning of our *modus operandi*. What he did give me, with quick generosity and clarity, was a kind of *rule book* for the editing of any magazine. For example, he suggested I think of the magazine as a center around which, "not a box within which / any item." He proposed that verse consisted of a constant and a variant, and then told me to think from that to the context of a magazine. He suggested I get at least four others, on whom I could depend unequivocally for material, and to make their work the mainstay of the

250

Charles Olson. Photograph by Gerard Malanga.

magazine's form. But then, he said, let the rest of it, roughly half, be as various and hogwild as possible, "so that any idiot thinks he has a chance of getting in." He cited instances of what he considered effective editing, *The Little Review* and the *Nouvelle Revue Francaise,* when its editor gave complete license to the nucleus of writers on whom he depended "to write freely what they chose." Williams in like sense gave us active support and tried to put us in touch with other young writers (as Pound also did) who might help us find a company. But with our failure to find a means to print the magazine, it all came to an abrupt end. I remember Pound's consoling me with the comment that perhaps it was wise for "the Creel" to wait for a while before "he highflyz as editor," but things seemed bleak indeed.

Happily, there was what proved to be a very significant alternative. Cid Corman, then living in Boston and having also a weekly radio program there called "This Is Poetry," had come to be a friend. I had heard the program, by some fluke, in New Hampshire, wrote him, was not long after invited by him to read on the program, and soon we were corresponding frequently, much involved with senses of contemporary writers and writing. It was Cid, in fact, who got me in touch with Olson, by way of their mutual friend, Vincent Ferrini—who sent me some of Olson's poems, with his own, for possible use in the magazine that had not yet collapsed. In returning Olson's poems to Vincent, I made the somewhat glib remark that he seemed to be "looking for a language," and got thereby my first letter from Olson himself, not particularly pleased by my comment and wanting to discuss it further, like they say. The letters thus resulting were really my education just because their range and articulation took me into terms of writing and many other areas indeed which I otherwise might never have entered. But the point now is that Cid, once Jake Leed's and my magazine was clearly dead, undertook himself to publish a magazine called *Origin.* Significantly enough its first issue includes some of the material I had collected—for example, Paul Blackburn's, whom I had come to know through Pound's agency—and features the work of Charles Olson, specifically the first of the *Maximus* sequence as well as other poems and prose.

Origin was, in fact, the meeting place for many of the writers who subsequently became the active nucleus for the *Black Mountain Review*. More than any other magazine of that period, it undertook to make place for the particular poets who later came to be called the Black Mountain School. In its issues prior to 1954, and continuingly, it gave first significant American publication to Denise Levertov, Irving Layton, Robert Duncan, Paul Carroll, Paul Blackburn, Larry Eigner, myself, and a number of others as well. Although I had, for example, published stories in *Kenyon Review* and the *New Directions Annual,* neither place could afford me the actual company nor the range of my own work that *Origin's* second issue provided. For me it was an acknowledgment I had almost begun to think impossible, and I am sure that Cid's consistent support of our writing had much to do with what became of it.

The point is that we felt, all of us, a great distance from the more conventional magazines of that time. Either they were dominated by the New Critics, with whom we could have no relation, or else they were so general in character that no active center of coherence was possible. There were exceptions certainly. *Golden Goose,* edited by Frederick Eckman and Richard Wirtz Emerson, was clearly partisan to myself and also to Olson, and it published my first book, *Le Fou,* and would have published a collection of Olson's, *The Praises,* but for a misunderstanding between him and the editors when the book was already in proof. Both men were much involved with Williams, and made his example and commitment the center for their own. There were also other, more occasional magazines, as *Goad*—whose editor, Horace Schwartz, involved me in a useful defense of my interest in Ezra Pound, just that it helped clarify my own terms of value.

But, with the exception of *Origin,* and possibly *Golden Goose* also, only two magazines of that time, the early fifties, had finally either the occasion or the sense of procedure, which served as my own measure of the possibility. One, *Fragmente,* edited and published in Freiberg, Germany, by Rainer Gerhardt—whose acquaintance I was also to make through Pound's help—was an heroically ambitious attempt to bring back into the German literary canon all that writing which the years of the Third Reich had absented from it. Rainer and his wife, living in great poverty with two young sons, were nonetheless able to introduce to the German

253

context an incredible range of work, including that of Olson, Williams, Pound, Basil Bunting, and myself. I was its American editor but its literal activity was completely the effort of Rainer and Renate. Their conception of what such a magazine *might* accomplish was a deep lesson to me. They saw the possibility of *changing* the context of writing, and I think myself that this magazine, and also the small paperbacks they were able to publish, effectually accomplished this for present German poetry—despite the bitter fact of Rainer's early death.

In like sense, a group of young writers of various nationalities centered in Paris was of great interest to me. They were led by a lovely, obdurate and resourceful Scot, Alexander Trocchi, and included the British poet Christopher Logue and the brilliant American translator Austryn Wainhouse. Others too were of equal interest: Patrick Bowles, for example, who translated the first of Beckett's French novels into English—and Richard Seaver, who was later to become a decisive editor for Grove Press. Again, what these men proposed to do with their magazine, *Merlin,* and the books which they also published with the help of the Olympia Press as Collection Merlin, was to change the situation of literary context and evaluation. I've given a brief, personal sense of my relation to Trocchi in a novel, *The Island,* where he figures as "Manus," and I was also invited by them to be an associate editor on the magazine—but by that time the funds necessary to continue publication of the magazine were not obtainable. But their translations, of Genet's and Beckett's work as well as their brilliant critical writing, which extended to political thinking as well as literary, made them an exceptional example of what a group of writers might do.

By 1954 my wife and I were already much involved with a small press called the Divers Press. We had moved from France to Mallorca, and had become close friends with a young English couple, Martin Seymour-Smith and his wife Janet. It was Martin who first interested us in publishing books, since, as he pointed out, printing costs were exceptionally cheap on the island and much might be done on a shoestring. But our initial venture together, the Roebuck Press, came a cropper because Martin's interests were not really decisively my own nor mine his. We did publish a selection of his poems, *All Devils Fading,* but our center

254

was finally in writers like Olson *(Mayan Letters),* Paul Blackburn *(Proensa* and *The Dissolving Fabric),* Irving Layton *(In the Midst of My Fever),* Douglas Woolf *(The Hypocritic Days),* Larry Eigner *(From The Sustaining Air),* and, though he comes a bit later, Robert Duncan *(Caesar's Gate).* We also published Katue Kitasono's *Black Rain,* and it is a design of his that was used for the covers of the first four issues of the *Black Mountain Review* as well as another on the credits page. What I felt was the purpose of the press had much to do with my initial sense of the magazine also. For me, and the other writers who came to be involved, it was a place defined by our own activity and was accomplished altogether by ourselves—a place wherein we might make evident what we, as writers, had found to be significant, both for ourselves and for that world—no doubt often vague to us indeed—we hoped our writing might enter. To be published in the *Kenyon Review* was too much like being "tapped" for a fraternity. It was too often all over before one got there and few if any of one's fellow writers came too. Therefore there had to be both a press and a magazine absolutely specific to one's own commitments and possibilities. Nothing short of that was good enough.

Origin had already done, in some sense, as much as one could hope for, and I remember having doubts about either the use or the practicality of simply another magazine more or less "like" it. I certainly didn't want to compete with Cid. But one possibility did seem to me lacking in *Origin,* despite occasional notes and reviews, and that was the *ground* that an active, ranging critical section might effect. I wasn't thinking of criticism finally as a judgment of whether or no this or that book might be deemed "good" or "bad." What I hoped for, and happily did get, was critical writing that would be, in Olson's sense, "prospective," a kind of writing that would break down habits of "subject" and gain a new experience of context generally. If I have any disappointment in the magazine in retrospect, it's only that this part of it does not extend as far as I had hoped. Still, Jung's "The Mass and the Individual Process" (in the fifth issue)—which I remember he sent to "The Black Mount Review," which pun, unintentional I assume, was a delight—and Borges' "Three Versions of Judas" (in the seventh issue)—which I read with absolute seriousness, not real-

255

izing it was a "fiction"—are some instances of what I was after. But, and here I was much influenced by Olson, the possible *range* of such writing as we conceived of it was never fully demonstrated.

There have been various comments and summaries published with respect to the *Black Mountain Review's* activity as a little magazine. Most lively and helpful, I think, is Paul Blackburn's account which appears in *Kulchur* (Vol. 3, No. 10, Summer 1963) called "The Grinding Down." Among other things, he identifies the initials used by reviewers in the first four issues, and also the pseudonyms used for signatures in some other instances. Too, Kent State University library, in one of its bulletins, provides an accurate and useful bibliography together with a brief note by myself. But now I think it best that the pseudonyms stay pseudonyms, and that initials, if not recognized (I used three sets, for example), be part of the present reader's experience. Often I, or some friend I could quickly get hold of, had to fill blank pages to manage our length of 64 pages, or subsequently the longer format of 220 plus. I at times had nightmares of having to write the whole thing myself.

The contributing editors listed in the first issue conform to that sense Pound had earlier made clear: get a center of people you can depend on for consistently active contributions, elsewise you'll have nothing to build with. Olson was to prove that center almost single-handedly, but Blackburn was also very helpful, with all manner of support including legwork around New York to get the magazine into stores, as well as much sympathetic and practical hand holding. Layton I had come to know through a Canadian mimeographed magazine, *Contact,* which many of us had been involved with as its contents will show. He had an intensive energy and obviously was restless with what was then the Canadian literary milieu. His brother-in-law, John Sutherland, editor of the *Northern Review,* no longer invited him to literary parties because Irving's conduct was so irascible. So he was an unequivocal cohort and wrote, happily, voluminous amounts of verse. If I remember rightly, I also asked others as well—in particular Paul Goodman, who answered he'd prefer being just a contributor, since his other commitments very possibly would not give him time to do more. Rexroth generously agreed although we had little information of each other beyond his own public figures. Less happily, by the

The Black Mountain Review

Charles Olson
Against Wisdom As ·Such

Robert Hellman
The Quay

René Laubiès
Eight Reproductions

Spring 1954
75 cents

The Black Mountain Review, *Vol. 1 No. 1, Spring 1954 (courtesy Peter Michelson)*.

time he'd read the first issue, he realized his error, and his withdrawal (as well as that of Paul Blackburn, whose reasons were happily less adamant) is noted at the back of the Fall 1954 issue along with a defensive comment by myself.

Many of the writers who became very decisive to the magazine are not so listed, however, Robert Duncan is very much one of these. His first contribution, sent at Olson's suggestion, was a poem I in turn suggested we print a section of—and Duncan's response was to the effect that if he *had* wanted a section of the poem printed, he *would* have sent it—and I learned much from him also. There was one very amusing confusion involved with a poem of his I did print, in the Fall 1954 issue, "Letters for Denise Levertov: For An A Muse Ment." Apparently Denise, for some reason, took it as a parody on her own way of writing, and was thus hurt. And Olson too thought it was some kind of attack on him. I think that poor Duncan and myself were the only ones to unequivocally enjoy it, and it remains for me an extraordinary summary and *exemplar* of contemporary possibilities in poetry.

Denise herself, Louis Zukofsky (whom I found thanks to Edward Dahlberg and also Duncan), Jonathan Williams, and Robert Hellman (a close friend first in France, who subsequently came to teach briefly at Black Mountain), all were of great help to me in that they were there to be depended on, for specific writing but equally for a very real sense of the whole act's not being merely a whistling in the dark but something making a way. God knows one often doubted it. Holding to Pound's sense of letting at least part of the magazine seem wide open, I know I printed work at times that any of them must have been puzzled by. Some things I just liked, for example, Gautier's "The Hippopotamus," which appears in the fifth issue. I still do. However, I've never found anyone to share my pleasure in "The Goat Man" by Harold Lee Drake, in the sixth issue. He wrote, to put it mildly, extraordinary prose—including one piece involved with masturbating by the seashore, which the condition of censorship in the fifties never permitted me to print. He was one of the contributors who came out of nowhere, and unhappily seems to have returned there, since I've never seen his work printed again.

Of contributors generally, I've defined, I think, the character of one group clearly evident throughout the magazine's publication.

258

These are writers who have either come together earlier, in *Origin,* or who are "found" by the same nature of attention that *Origin's* preoccupations had effected. Louis Zukofsky would be one of these latter as would be also Edward Dahlberg. There are also "occasional" contributors, as Paul Goodman, and those who simply appear with no previous or necessarily continuing sense of relationship, like James Purdy. I think we were, possibly, the first magazine to print his work in America, and that was surely a pleasure. He had found us somehow, submitted the story, and I printed it. The same is true of Sherry Mangan's story (a curious echo from the twenties) in the seventh issue, or of Alfred Kreymborg's "Metaphysical Ballad," printed there as well.

But two other kinds of contributor were particularly significant. Thus far the relation to the college itself must seem the fact that it was paying for the magazine's publication, and that Olson was the rector of the college. Although Hellman, Duncan, and myself were briefly on the faculty, this was somewhat after the fact because the nature of the magazine was determined otherwise and really prior to that fact. But if those contributors are noted who were either students at the college at the time, or had recently been so, then a relation of the college to the magazine, and particularly to Olson's influence as a teacher, becomes very clear. First there is Jonathan Williams—who is certainly not a "student" at this point, but who is much interested in the college and in Olson particularly, as his own publishing *(Jargon)* makes clear. Look at the advertisements for his press in the various issues of the magazine, for further instance. Then there is Joel Oppenheimer, who had left the college not long before the publication of the first issue and so comes into its activity by that fact. Then Fielding Dawson—also absent at this point from the college, in the army in Stuttgart, but again much involved by relation to the college and so with the magazine also. Then there are those literally there: Edward Dorn, Michael Rumaker, and Tom Field. Dorn had published one poem in *Origin,* in an issue edited by Denise Levertov, and his story in the *Black Mountain Review* is, I think, his first published prose—and a clear example of what was to be his extraordinary ability in that mode as well as in poetry. Michael Rumaker has his first publication of any kind in the magazine, with two stories I feel to be as fine as ever were published—in fact, "The Pipe" I think as exceptional a piece of writing as any of any time. Then, finally, Tom Field—actually a painter, but whose writing struck me usefully, though it has not proven of major interest to himself. But think of it—that a college having an enrollment of about *twenty* people as average during the time the magazine was published should have such gifted men as Dorn, Rumaker, Dawson, Oppenheimer, and Williams have so proven themselves to be. Hopefully, it makes excuse for the kind of eulogy these comments must now seem.

The college closed in the spring of 1956 and at that point Jonathan Williams became the ostensible publisher of the last issue—on the cover of which he put a little sticker to make this fact clear. There was hope we might continue. Some material for the next issue was in hand, some photos of Frederick Sommer for one thing, and some essays of Edward Dahlberg's. But the last issue itself was almost impossible to manage. I had left Black Mountain, had been briefly in San Francisco, and was now living in New Mexico. The printer, of course, was still in Spain, and the delays in proofing, or even getting the initial printing begun, were almost impossible to manage. However, the last issue—with the addition of Allen Ginsberg as contributing editor—defines the last group of contributors who have particular relevance. Ed Dorn had moved to San Francisco with his family after leaving Black Mountain the year previous. I was in restless state, having separated from my wife, and being really at odds with much in my life. I wanted a new condition and so went west, where I'd never been, to see if that might be an answer. So I was also in San Francisco, in the spring of 1956—and for a writer there was really no place that could have been quite like it, just at that time. The contents pages of the seventh issue make this much clearer than I can—Ginsberg, Kerouac, Whalen, McClure, Burroughs (Lee), Snyder—and another man I was deeply pleased to include, albeit from the East, Hubert Selby, Jr. It was unequivocally a shift and opening of the previous center, and finally as good a place as any to end. Other magazines had appeared as well, with much the same concerns, among them *Big Table* and the *Evergreen Review*. Whatever battle had been the case did seem effectually won.

A last note, briefly, about the divers reproductions and photographs that appear in the various issues, as well as the covers for the last three . . . I valued these especially, in that they freshened

260

everything when otherwise things seemed almost too dense. It was a particular honor to include Franz Kline, Philip Guston, Aaron Siskind, and Harry Callahan, because all had been teachers at the college, and, even more than that, had each made so actively clear a new way of seeing in their art. John Altoon I can never thank enough for so much it would be specious to try to list—and he also has made very evident how extraordinary a painter he is. Dan Rice, a close friend of those days and first met at the college—the same. Edward Corbett I met while I was editing the last issue in New Mexico, and though I'm sure he thought I was simply hysterical, his cover as well as other generosities is a lovely fact of his concern. As for Laubiès—he saw it all.

So it's finally all well in the past, either as one's own experience of something, or else the communal fact of what the writers of that situation and time seemed to have had in mind. I don't think it can ever be very different. You want to do something, to see it happen, and apparently it can't or at least can't with what then exists as possibility. So you try to change it and you do or don't as proves the case. What really now delights me is that a magazine having a usual printing of some 500 to 750 copies, about 200 of which ever got distributed, could have made any dent whatsoever. That should cheer us all.

Robert Creeley. Photograph by Gerard Malanga.

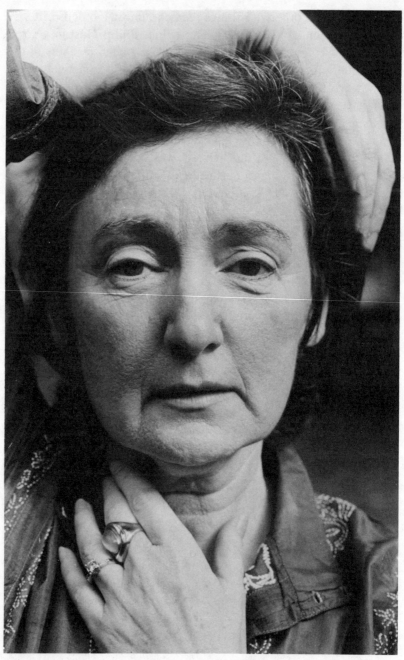

Daisy Aldan, editor and publisher of Folder. *Photograph by Gerard Malanga.*

DAISY ALDAN
AN INTERVIEW ON
FOLDER
Dennis Barone

Folder, *edited by Daisy Aldan and Richard Miller, appeared in four issues between Winter 1953 and Winter 1956. Although the New York School poets and painters appeared in the magazine, it was not limited to that school. There were poems and stories by Italian artists (Giorgio Caproni and Pier Paolo Pasolini), Ms. Aldan's translation of Mallarmé's "A Throw of the Dice Will Never Abolish Chance," silk screen prints by Grace Hartigan and others, song music, and photographs.* Folder *published the work of James Merrill, James Schuyler, Kenneth Koch, Frank O'Hara, and Charles Olson.*

Daisy Aldan has published two books of poetry. She is currently working on her second novel and on a set of translations of the poetry of Swedish-Finnish poet Edith Södergran. She lives half the year in New York and the other half in Switzerland.

Dennis Barone is a poet and editor (Tamarisk) *who has conducted interviews with a number of little magazine editors.*

This interview was conducted on February 8, 1977, in New York.

When I interviewed Gilbert Sorrentino a few months ago, he said that in the early fifties there was no environment for artists outside of Black Mountain College and that it was dreadful to live in a big city like New York or Chicago. I was wondering if it was so dreadful . . .

In the fifties?

In the early fifties. Without an environment for artists how did a magazine like Folder *emerge?*

263

Until about 1953 there were about forty-two literary magazines in the whole country, and most were controlled by the academic poets. Any so-called avant-garde poet had great difficulty having his work published. In my own work I was involved with new forms. I happened to be starting my doctoral thesis, which because of my affinity was then called *The Influence of French Surrealism on American Literature.* At Hunter College I had been an editor of the literary magazine, and that imbued in me a lasting desire to publish a magazine. I did not publish *Folder* because avant-garde poets were not being published. It was an impulse of my own nature and I happened to publish it when it was needed.

I wonder if you could say something about the technical decisions concerning Folder. *It was such a high-quality magazine.*

Yes. I was poor and I was teaching. A young student poet in my class, the only student in the school at the time writing good poetry—and, incidentally, being discriminated against for it (in the sixties there were many student poets, so the scene had definitely changed)—well, this student, Leon Hecht, and I used to put out little booklets done in calligraphy. We had a great interest in dada, and one day the idea of a magazine inspired us. We were going to call it *Any Minute Now Somebody's Going to Do It!* after a poem of mine—an unusual title for those times. We planned to get paper from the supply department (it was an art school), but when we started, nothing but the best laid paper satisfied me. I always loved beautiful books. We had to figure out a way of binding the magazine without paying exorbitant binding costs. By now Richard Miller and Floriano Vecchi were helping, and after experimenting with many forms we designed a cover into which folded sheets could fit. The form also made it possible for each writer to have a folio of his own.

I was always interested in an integration of the arts (an avant-garde idea at that time) and so attempted to incorporate serigraphs, music sheets, and photographs. In my school they had a silk-screen shop and there, sitting in with students, I taught myself silk-screening. Subsequently we rented a little studio, called it the Tiber Press, and invited artists like Grace Hartigan, Alfred Leslie, Larry Rivers, and Joan Mitchell, none well known in the

FOLDER

POEMS

JOHN ASHBERY
DAISY ALDAN
GIORGIO CAPRONI
JEAN GARRIGUE
LEON HECHT
KENNETH KOCH
JAMES MERRILL
FRANK O'HARA
ALEXANDER RANDOLPH
JAMES SCHUYLER
EDWIN TREITLER
SANDRA WOOL

1

A PLAYLET
JAMES SCHUYLER

SHORT STORIES

FREDERICK ENGLISH
GIUSEPPE PATRONI GRIFFI
ROBERT HELLMAN
WILLIAM FENSE WEAVER

THREE ORIGINAL SILK SCREEN PRINTS
GEORGE HARTIGAN

Folder, *Vol. 1, No. 1, Winter 1953 (courtesy Northwestern University Library).*

FOLDER

FRANK O'HARA

SANDRA WOOL
JOHN ASHBERY

GIUSSEPPE PATRONI GRIFFI
EDWIN TREITLER

ALEXANDER RANDOLPH
JAMES SCHUYLER

DAISY ALDAN

GEORGE HARTIGAN
FREDERICK ENGLISH
JAMES MERRILL
ROBERT HELLMAN
LEON HECHT
JEAN GARRIGUE

WILLIAM FENSE WEAVER
KENNETH KOCH

GIORGIO CAPRONI

Daisy Aldan a
William Fens
Floriano

from Folder *Vol. 1, No. 1: three original silkscreen prints by "George" (Grace) Hartigan (courtesy Northwestern University Library).*

field at the time, to come up and make their own serigraphs under the supervision of Floriano, who made himself into a silk-screen expert there. The magazine was produced with my own money, earned in teaching. The magazine *View* had suspended publication, and so *Folder* became the only good magazine in America publishing exciting new work. Poets like Frank O'Hara, John Ashbery, Kenneth Koch, Storm De Hirsch, James Broughton, Arthur Gregor, Harriet Zinnes, all largely unknown at the time, were published in *Folder*.

How did you meet that whole group?

I was involved with the artistic world. Some were friends. One told another. Later on, when I published *A New Folder: Americans: Poems and Drawings,* which included work of about fifty poets and fifty painters, I had met Allen Ginsberg and his circle. Those poets were very generous with each other, recommended each other. In those days I traveled a good deal during my summer vacations and in Paris I met many writers, and so it went.

Before long, *Folder* was being reviewed. *Arts International* gave us a good review. Stuart Preston of the *New York Times* wrote a great review. It was an exciting magazine, an exciting adventure.

I set the type by hand. I bought a Kinsey handpress for ninety dollars by mail and began to set *Folder* letter by letter. Later I had the type made in lines and did the pages by hand, line by line. This gave me a lot of leeway with layout. I also chose handset type for titles. I did this in a little print shop on 82nd Street. When someone entered the shop, I had to stop work because women were not allowed in the union then and the printer would have been suspended or fined.

What a lot of work!

I enjoyed it.

Why did Grace Hartigan go by the name of George Hartigan?

Because at that time women's work was rarely published or accepted in major art galleries. Some gave themselves male names or used initials. However, by the time *Folder* 3 appeared, the scene had begun to change.

Some say that that time was a male era.

Yes. If you look at contributor lists, you will see hardly a woman's name, but I published many women. In *A New Folder* there are at least twenty-five, if not more. In 1954, I actually made a list of women poets for an intended anthology, which I never accomplished. It was not that I wished to take up the standard for women. It was because the work of many fine women poets came to my attention, and good women poets were among my friends, and I felt they should be published.

I remember something Francine du Plessix Gray said. She said that at Black Mountain Charles Olson did not like teaching women. He said women should never write . . . .

Oh, really? I'm surprised. I met Olson. I liked him. I published his work. Yes, in the fifties there was that kind of feeling among men writers and editors. They spoke about "woman's poetry" as if it had a special sentimental romantic quality or was a kind of imitation of Emily Dickinson. I was often introduced as "a poetess" or sometimes "a poetress." An editor once said to me, "If I didn't know that you, a woman, had written these poems, I would like your work." And once an editor wrote me, "Your poems are dynamic, colorful, exciting, but too strong for a woman."

I always stated that labels were invalid. I don't believe in "old poets," "young poets," "black poets," "women poets." One is a poet, an individual; that's what is important. In the *Folder* days I followed that conviction. I still do.

You mentioned academic journals—Kenyon and so on . . . .

Yes.

Well, how, in that environment, did the change in the poetic line come about? You look at someone like Robert Lowell and then a year later you look at someone like John Ashbery.

It was the moment of transition. I often act on intuition and then find that the activity I set in motion becomes general. I'm not implying that I bring it about . . . simply that, as an instrument, I have a fore-intuition that is getting ready to become manifest.

The coming to the fore of abstract expressionism in America and poetry which had as its inspiration French surrealism and its forerunners Rimbaud, Baudelaire, Mallarmé, Apollinaire—who had been waiting in the wings—took the stage in 1953. *Folder* and the work it published helped in this attempt to liberate static forms.

I started the first big poetry readings in the city, outside the "Y." One midnight at the Living Theatre, eighteen *Folder* poets (the list now reads like a *Who's Who* in poetry)—James Merrill, Michael McClure, Ginsberg, Schuyler, O'Hara, LeRoi Jones, Garrigue, M. C. Richards, and so on—read their work to a background of projected abstract expressionist drawings which were in my book: de Kooning, Kline, Pollack, Blaine, Knaths, Freilicher, Goldberg. I could have bought a de Kooning then for fifty dollars. I meant to, but just didn't get to it.

It was a time of ferment. The Artist's Club, to which I used to go with Kiesler, was meeting in the Village, and great discussions were held there. Some of the poets and painters used to come up here to this very apartment where, incidentally, I haven't been for twenty years. I've come back here and it's interesting that you should be interviewing me about *Folder* here, where most of it came to birth and grew. We made tape recordings here; had readings. A fermentation was going on and we were part of it. *Folder* became one voice, an instrument of definition.

I always hear that the abstract expressionists and the New York school, so to speak, had a great effect upon one another.

Yes, that's so. All were friends. (Later, as they became famous enmities developed. The nature of human ambition, alas!) They met at the Artist's Club, at the Cedar Bar, at Hartigan's studio, in Westhampton or Easthampton. Poets and painters influenced each other. For example, Grace Hartigan and Frank O'Hara were close friends. Frank and Larry Rivers were friends. They did poetry-painting collaborations, and Richard Miller, Floriano Vecchi, and I were attempting to do poetry-painting collections. You know, Larry wrote poetry also. I published his poems in *A New Folder*.

Yes, I saw that. I didn't realize that till I saw his poems there.

However, *Folder* was not just a publication for New York poets and painters. I published Pasolini in America for the first time.

I was going to ask you about that.

270

A friend of mine, Bill Weaver, who became my Italian editor, was a dear friend and translator of Pasolini. He sent me his work. I published some of the first translations into English of the Greek poet George Seferis. I published other Italian poets, Haitian poets, poets from the Midwest, from the West Coast, and so on.

I like that Pasolini translation a lot. I was going to ask you, do you think Montale had a negative influence on Italian poetry? He seems so much more conservative than someone like F. T. Marinetti.

What you call "conservative" I call the *real* avant-garde. The surrealist "games" are, or should be, over. The real avant-garde is a spiritual awakening, and this is manifest in the best work of our time. As Tristan Tzara, whom I met in Paris in the fifties, said to me then, "The trouble with many of today's poets and painters is that they don't know dada is dead."

You must have met a lot of interesting people.

Yes, fascinating! The Princess Caetani of *Botteghe Oscure* . . .

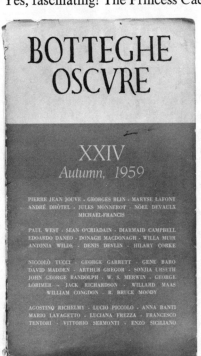

Botteghe Oscure, *No. 24, Autumn 1959, edited by Marguerite Caetani. Botteghe Oscure is the name of an ancient street in Rome which passed along one side of the Circus Flaminii, built in 220 B. C. In the Middle Ages, after the Circus had fallen into ruin, merchants began to use its dark arcades as shops, and so the street received the name of Apothecae Oscurae. Later it became known as Via delle Botteghe Oscure, from which the name of the magazine derived.* Botteghe Oscure *appeared twice a year and contained in each number five sections: French, English, American, Italian, and (alternately) German and Spanish (courtesy J&F Anania).*

That was a great magazine!

Yes. She published Ezra Pound, Dylan Thomas, René Char, hundreds of now-renowned writers. I met Caresse Crosby of Black Sun Press, whose *Portfolio* and other publications brought out some of the best writers of this century. Ruth Witt Diamant became a friend.

What about Ruth Witt Diamant?

She created the Poetry Center in San Francisco, the spawning ground for so many American poets, including the group that became known as the Beats: Kerouac, Corso, McClure, Snyder, et al. The three women have not received their due recognition. Without their taste, courage, initiative, the literary world would be much poorer.

Speaking of a poorer world, Man Ray died recently.

I read about it.

It's hard to believe that he was born in New Jersey, just about where I was born.

In New Jersey? Really I didn't know that.

It's odd to think of. I've always connected him with Paris.

The early surrealists included many geniuses, but many did not really understand what Breton was striving for—a spiritual renewal. They got waylaid into blind alleys: drugs, insanity, suicide, games which had nothing to do with the essence of real poetry. It is the same today. Some poets are just beginning to read surrealist translations and are imitating forms of the past without insight.

Did View *influence* Folder?

No. When I started *Folder,* I had not heard of *View,* but it was an excellent magazine.

I was wondering if any other magazine influenced you?

Yes—Caresse Crosby's *Portfolio.* She had published it during the war when paper was scarce and had used any paper she could find; all sizes and colors. The pages were unbound. That gave me the initial idea for the *Folder* format, when some copies came into

272

my hands in connection with my thesis. My format was made neater, could be better handled, and I used beautiful laid paper. But the inspiration came from *Portfolio.*

I think she published the first Charles Olson poem. How did you get to meet Olson? Were you familiar with Olson's Maximus Poems?

Jack Hammond, of Hammond Organ fame, had a medieval castle which he had had transported stone by stone from Italy and re-erected in East Gloucester, Massachusetts. Kenward Elmslie and Ruth Yorke were friends of Hammond, and through them I was invited to this castle. Several poets, including Olson, lived nearby and often met there for readings and discussions. They all knew about *Folder,* and so when I came it was natural that Jack would invite a group over to meet me. Olson and I liked each other at once. In the beautiful little chapel, we all read our poetry to each other, and I remember that Kenward and I did a scene from *Macbeth* on one of the galleries.

After that meeting, Olson and I started a correspondence. He was a brilliant person, a wonderful human being. His poems, though not always clear to me at the time, nevertheless impressed me as being among the better artistic works of our day, full of integrity.

Had you been aware of the Black Mountain scene?

Yes, I was aware of it because when I was graduated from Hunter College, I was invited to go there at about the same time that that famous group was there: Duncan, M. C. Richards, Olson. I was in love and wouldn't leave New York. When I think how my destiny later brought me into contact with almost everyone in that group, it seems incredible. I regret that decision.

Was it New York that brought you all together?

No. What brought us together was *Folder.* It also brought me into the literary world. Before that, I was an actress and a teacher who wrote poetry. At the point of *Folder,* a new stream entered my life. *Folder* became one of the focal points for artists and writers. There were others: Ruth Yorke's salons, Johnny Latouche's salons, the Artist's Club, Grace Hartigan's studio. Soon galleries were exhibiting works by the painters involved, and poetry readings in the city multiplied. I was the first to introduce poetry readings in the Donnell Library. I had to beg the people in charge. The participating poets had to send in the poems they would read to be approved, in order to ascertain that not one obscene word would be expressed. Times certainly have changed.

You sold Folder for one dollar. That must have entailed a great loss.

Very great. I still lose money. I publish a book a year—always a financial loss. It was fortunate that I was teaching. I gave extra classes after school so I could earn extra money for the magazine. I stinted on clothes. No one helped me financially. Ever.

Lots of times people ask me why anyone would do that.

It's creative. It's exciting. It's alive. I encourage anyone who wants to publish a literary magazine, even today when about 5,000 exist. Even if you just do it and give copies away to your friends, it's good. The only thing is, you should have an objective sense of responsibility for what you are printing. Then it becomes a definition of life. I was always interested in literature. I was interested in publishing. I was interested in magazines, in poetry. I never asked questions.

How did you put the magazine together?

It was really amusing. The poets and painters who were in the first issue—Grace, Frank, John Ashbery—they all came to this little studio and we walked around a table putting the pages together like a smorgasbord.

Why did you decide to give up the magazine and do A New Folder?

By 1959 there were more than a thousand little magazines where the avant-garde could be published. The need for the magazine, as I saw it, had ended. Then I was eager to do a book, a book that was bound and could be put on shelves without falling apart.

Who was the audience?

Writers. Painters. Dancers. Gallery people. I was getting orders from all over the country. I met Caresse Crosby through her cor-

274

respondence with me. That's how I met Anais Nin. She was, as it happens, my first subscriber. She wrote to me asking if I had bought her type from her old press, since I was also using Vogue sans-serif type, rarely used at that time. That's how I met Eugene Walter and the Princess Caetani, as well as Ruth Yorke, Kiesler, Latouche, Varese, Dlugozewski, Erich Hawkins. It is incredible to think how many are dead: Kerouac, O'Hara, Garrigue, Anais.

I traveled every summer in those days. One day in Athens I saw a notice of an exhibit of beautiful books. I went to it and to my surprise there was *Folder* on exhibit! I have no idea how it arrived there. But that's how it is. When you send something beautiful into the world, it finds its own way.

What bookstores were they sold in?

Gotham was one of the first to take it. Frances Steloff even gave us an exhibit in her windows. I appreciated that. The 8th Street Book Shop, Phoenix . . . places like that. I went around to the bookstores, loaded down with books. People who met me later said to me, "I always remember you walking around with a heavy bag full of books." I still have to do it. As I said, I try to put out one book a year, but without the same intensity. This year I published Harriet Zinnes's *I Wanted to See Something Flying*. It received an Elliston Award mention.

I went over to Gotham to see how much they wanted for Folder 4. *It was fifty dollars.*

That was cheap. Number I is difficult to find for one hundred dollars. It was printed on laid paper; it contained serigraphs made by the artists, and poems, and stories. I used to sell it to my students for fifty cents. The Museum of Modern Art awarded Grace Hartigan a Graphic Arts prize for her serigraphs in *Folder I*. I have her extra copies which the museum was selling for ten dollars each at the same time that anyone could have bought all three plus the other stuff for one dollar. Well, if you could find a copy of Edgar Allan Poe's self-published booklet, which he couldn't sell even for one cent, you'd be rich. That's the way it is!

Folder I is almost entirely set by hand. There were only five hundred copies. I had to steal my mother's not too long ago.

Concerning translations: do you feel that one should publish only American works because these need more nurturing?

I don't feel that way. I'm interested in good poetry and I don't care where it's from. I don't believe in any kind of nationalism.

What do you see as the purpose behind a magazine?

Well, it's a way of getting the defined experience, which is poetry, into the world. It brings the *book,* as Mallarmé called it, that we are all writing into definition. Even if one person alone is transformed by something he reads there, it's important. It is a record of the place people have reached in consciousness at any given time. The best will remain, will rise to the surface as the inept gets filtered out, and this will indicate mankind's path on this earth. That's part of it, but I don't think people who publish ask themselves that question. Maybe they should. Also, in our time the written word is important. In ancient times, it was not. Now we get knowledge through the written word.

Did you publish only people you knew?

No. I read every manuscript that came in. Some came on torn dirty paper, written in pencil. Sometimes these works were among the best and I published them. I remember some poems of Gregory Corso came that way. I turned down friends whose contributions didn't seem at the time to be of the standard I was seeking. For example, I love the work of Calder and Saul Steinberg, but turned down the drawings they sent in.

How does the publication of a poet's work affect the poet?

By reading the work of other poets, which published poets generally do, they are inspired to new creativity. Also, a poet is encouraged by approval. All creators have a need, even if it is unconscious, to share their work with the world. Community is created in this sharing. We poets need that—true community of individuals. One must no longer isolate oneself in a cave. Who reads poetry magazines? Mostly poets! A community of poets! Those responsible for the renewal of the word.

I noticed you published Frank O'Hara in every issue.

Yes. In those days he was my favorite. I considered him highly gifted. He had difficulty getting his poems published in the established magazines. I felt that his later work, filled with private games and personal allusions, had veered away from what poetry is meant to fulfill. Who is to know whether, if he had lived, his work would have passed beyond the trivia into new creativity? Once at a birthday party for him in Grace Hartigan's studio, I found him crying and asked him why.

"Because today I am thirty years old and have so little time left. Chatterton died at eighteen, Shelley at twenty-six."

When I made my film, *Once upon an El,* in 1955, when the city was demolishing the Third Avenue el, eighteen poets and painters participated. In Frank's sequence, he pretends to throw himself in front of an oncoming train. You know he was killed by a roving beach car, a moving machine. Amazing! He was a remarkable individual.

Some people say that O'Hara and Ashbery and the group around them had a destructive effect on poetry or at least on young people writing today.

I don't believe that. I think the Beats did, even though there were many gifted among them, but O'Hara and Ashbery cannot be considered Beats. A lot of things John does I consider unnecessary, but a poet is allowed to try everything. His good work is very good. It always was and it still is. He is a brilliant person. Those who say that group had a bad influence are not reading carefully or have little insight, and experience superficially, not with inner vision.

In my work I have almost totally ignored the Beats.

You should not. Just develop judgment to see where they were destructive and where liberating. I knew most of them and published them in *A New Folder.* I was considered one of them, although I was never a Beat. They were corrupted by fake Orientalism, drugs, license mistaken for freedom, and a malcomprehension of the ideals of surrealism. Henry Miller was God to them, and in my opinion, although at his best he is superb, he had a very destructive influence on American life and culture.

Did Mallarmé influence your own work? Blake and his vision?

Blake had no influence on my work. I just have similar ideas about consciousness. As for Mallarmé, certainly there must have been some influence, particularly in terms of *Coup de Dés,* which I translated.

I saw your translation in Folder 4.

He was perhaps the first to break up the coffin'd poem on the page and let "the light stream, not on, but through." I tried to carry that further in *Breakthrough*.

In his time he was not understood. All his friends left him. In high school, I gave a talk on T. S. Eliot, whom no one understood at that time. Now every student quotes him. That should answer your question about publication.

What do you think of some of the big magazines getting federal grants?

I think the National Endowment for the Arts has been a stimulus to the arts. I think its standards might be improved. It should help only those publications that manifest real quality. I don't find this the case now. As long as government does not attempt directly or indirectly to dictate policy, then I believe government encouragement is fine. Of course, that danger is always there.

Kelly at Bard *says magazines should not accept unsolicited work. Poets should spend more time at their work, not in the post office.*

A facile comment. Who will solicit an unknown poet's work? We do spend half our time in the post office, and also our money. A poet can't earn enough to live on with his poetry. Also, one can't deduct expenses from one's income tax, as the government says it won't support a losing business.

Do you remember how much your postage was in the fifties?

Four cents for a letter. Eight cents to send the magazine.

Sorrentino said that in the Cedar Bar in the fifties, you could get beer for a nickel and if you didn't have the money, someone would give it to you.

That's true.

Poor artist's special—thirty-five cents!

Everything was cheaper in those days. Certainly being poor never deterred a really gifted person from creating art.

What do you think is the avant-garde of today?

278

The artist who is aware of the evolution of consciousness, and recognizes that his work must heal a wounded world.

Can you name some poets who may be said to exemplify that concept?

Well, Albert Steffen, the Swiss poet, for one. Then many poets in our own country today are writing fine work which inherently follows that concept: W. S. Merwin, Galway Kinnell, Jane Randolph, Zimmer, Hine, Swenson, and many others. Some of the best poetry in the world is being written in America today.

What are you doing now?

Finishing a novel, a novel with an atmosphere of poetry in it.

Kulchur, *Vol. 1, No. 1, Spring 1960 (courtesy Northwestern University Library).*

KULCHUR: A MEMOIR
Lita Hornick

*"I have an unbroken, seventeen-year record of losing money,"
says Lita Hornick of her experience with* Kulchur *magazine. Although Mrs. Hornick began as an academic with a Ph.D. from
Columbia ("I was the only pregnant woman on the campus"), the
magazine she published in the early sixties was anything but "Establishment."* Kulchur *published writers like LeRoi Jones, Denise
Levertov, Gilbert Sorrentino, and Louis Zukofsky, who discussed
a variety of topics from film, jazz, architecture, dance, drama, and
painting to civil rights and politics.* Kulchur *was, in Mrs. Hornick's
words, "the only journal of criticism and comment in the underground then."*

*Lita Hornick began publishing volumes of poetry under the
Kulchur Books imprint in 1966; to date she has brought out
twenty-four volumes. In 1970 she founded the Kulchur Foundation, which, in addition to publishing books, also offers grants to
poets, small presses, and artists. She has sponsored poetry readings
at the Museum of Modern Art and the Whitney Museum in New
York, and the Institute of Contemporary Art at the University of
Pennsylvania.*

Kulchur was founded in 1960 by Marc Schleifer, who published
and edited the first two issues. I became the publisher in February
1961, and formed Kulchur Press, Inc. I shall not deal with the
two issues with which I had no contact, as this essay is conceived
as a personal memoir. In the first three issues under my ownership,
I was not involved in any editorial work, but devoted myself to
the business end of the magazine, struggling to find a national
distributor and to build a subscription list.

Schleifer edited *Kulchur* 3, and then took off for Cuba without
telling me where he was going or how long he would be gone.
That issue was more political than literary in orientation, but
nevertheless contained some notable pieces. Most important of all,
perhaps, was "In Search of Yage," letters to Allen Ginsberg by

William Burroughs, recounting his search for the drug in South America. There were poems by Charles Olson and Diane di Prima and "sound scores" by George Brecht. (The printing of scores and articles on music was a tradition which was to be continued in later issues of *Kulchur*.) Joel Oppenheimer wrote a very interesting piece on the obscure poet Samuel Greenberg, LeRoi Jones an essay called "Milneburg Joys (or, Against 'Hipness' as Such)," and Julian Beck an article on "The Life of the Theatre." "A Second Look at Pornography" by Donald Phelps was noteworthy. There were also reviews of art exhibitions, books, films, and records—a feature of the magazine that was to be continued.

Before Schleifer left, he appointed Gilbert Sorrentino guest editor of *Kulchur* 4, and I persuaded Gil to go ahead with the issue. Number 4 was much more concerned with literature and poetics than were previous issues, and was much more to my taste. Gil had the honor to introduce Robert Duncan into the magazine; he contributed a very important essay, "Ideas on the Meaning of Form." Characteristically, Duncan relates the poetic imagination to the forces of the cosmos and scorns conventional inorganic form. Ed Dorn, also new to the magazine, contributed an important essay, "What I See in the *Maximus* Poems (1)." His writing on poetry was the furthest thing in the world from the New Criticism, and this was what *Kulchur* was later to strive to feature: comment by poets on poetry in a vein far different from that of the academic quarterlies. Ron Loewinsohn, for example, contributed an essay on his poetics called "A Credo Sandwich."

Besides these notable essays on poetry and poetics, the issue contained a hard-hitting essay on brutality in mental hospitals by "Harry Black," pseudonym of Hubert Selby. LeRoi Jones's article on the history of African and Afro-American music was a learned piece that was never pedantic. Although Jones is known today chiefly as a black political revolutionary, the actual range of his intellect can be quickly estimated from the pages of *Kulchur*. Last but not least among the essays in *Kulchur* 4 was the first appearance in the magazine of the great but then neglected poet Louis Zukofsky, writing here on the art of Charlie Chaplin. The issue closed with reviews of books and films but none of art exhibitions or records—the only areas later featured in the magazine that did not appear in this issue.

282

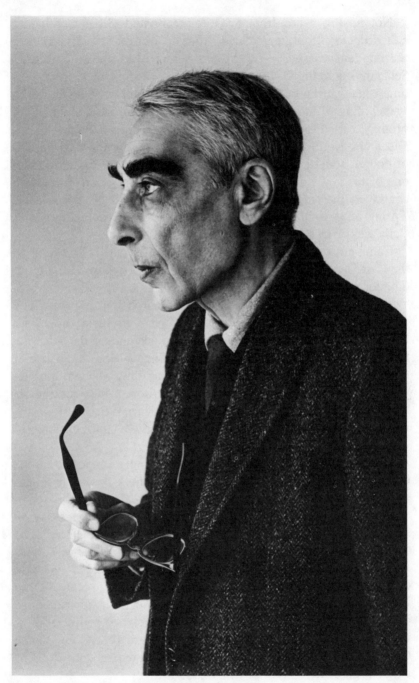

Louis Zukofsky. Photograph by Gerard Malanga.

Not having heard from Schleifer, I invited Gil Sorrentino to edit *Kulchur* 5, but he declined. Marian Zazeela (now married to the eminent composer La Monte Young, but then married to Schleifer) appointed Joel Oppenheimer as editor, with my acquiescence. Joel continued the policy of publishing Louis Zukofsky —including "Little Baron Snorck," an account of a child violin prodigy, based on the childhood of Zukofsky's son Paul. Charles Olson contributed a poem, and Kenneth Koch a hilarious parody of Pound. Jones's piece, "Tokenism: 300 Years for 5 Cents," was one of his key works and prophetic for 1962. Gilbert Sorrentino continued the tradition of literary comment with "Reflections on 'Spring and All.' " Most notable of all, perhaps, were Louis and Celia Zukofsky's translations of Catullus.

Comment on music fell to A. B. Spellman with "The Next to the Last Generation of Blues Singers." Lawrence Kornfeld, a great director who has never received the recognition he deserves, provided the theater article, "A Director's Search for a Stage." The pièce de résistance was *Kulchur*'s first "Art Chronicle" by Frank O'Hara, which I solicited. It included an account of the Abstract Expressionists and Imagists show at the Guggenheim, a defense of that controversial Frank Lloyd Wright building, and an appreciation of Claes Oldenburg's exhibition, The Store, which contradicts the commonly held opinion that Frank O'Hara hated all pop art. He also spoke well of the Rauschenberg show at the Leo Castelli Gallery. Film and book reviews followed.

Still not having heard from Marc Schleifer, I undertook the editing of *Kulchur* 6 myself. This issue presented the first publication of Louis Zukofsky's great play *Arise, Arise*. It also had a cover and picture portfolio on the Living Theatre and an essay by Julian Beck titled "Broadway and Living Theatre Polemic." The so-called "deep image poets" made their initial appearance here in *Kulchur*—the first of my continuing efforts to broaden the base of contributors and cover the whole avant-garde scene. "Deep Image" was represented by Jerome Rothenberg in an exchange of letters with Robert Creeley on the subject of poetics, and by Robert Kelly in the poem "Staccato for Tarots: I." (Of course Creeley did not belong to this group, but was receptive to Rothenberg's argument.)

An essay by Denise Levertov on current English poets was also included in number 6; it had been solicited by Joel Oppenheimer, but he had decided against printing it in *Kulchur* 5. Comment on music was presented in Morton Feldman's "Liner Notes," his first appearance in the magazine, and comment on film consisted of an article by Donald Phelps on Parker Tyler's film criticism. Frank O'Hara's second "Art Chronicle" dealt enthusiastically with the Nakian sculptures at the Loeb Study Center and at the Egan gallery, Alex Katz's cutouts at Tanager, and the Gorky exhibitions at Janis and Anderson. Film reviews by Fielding Dawson closed the issue.

When *Kulchur* 6 was in page proof, Marc Schleifer returned from Cuba and resigned from the magazine to take off for parts unknown. At that time he persuaded me to buy his back-issue inventory of *Kulchur* 1 and 2 so that I might fill the needs of new subscribers who wanted a full set.

After the resignation of Marc Schleifer, I appointed an editorial board composed of LeRoi Jones, Gilbert Sorrentino, Frank O'Hara, Joe Le Sueur, Bill Berkson, and myself. This group held together roughly from *Kulchur* 7 through *Kulchur* 12. *Kulchur* 7 was notable for the reprinting of Louis Zukofsky's "Five Statements for Poetry," which I had solicited. Two of these statements, "Program: Objectivists' 1931" and "Sincerity and Objectification," were first printed in *Poetry*'s historic objectivist issue in 1931.

Ed Dorn's "Notes More or Less Relevant to Burroughs and Trocchi" continued the precedent of unorthodox comment on literature. Bill Berkson, at Frank's request, provided the "Art Chronicle." Joe Le Sueur wrote the first of *Kulchur's* "Theatre Chronicles," which dealt with, among other things, a fine production of Beckett's "Happy Days." LeRoi provided another of his essays on black music, "Introducing Bobby Bradford."

Issue 7 was rich in reviews. LeRoi edited his first jazz record review section, written by himself and A. B. Spellman. The book review section, edited by Gil, dealt chiefly with small-press books, which went unnoted by other magazines at the time and are scarcely noted today. *Kulchur* continued to review them throughout its duration. Perhaps the most important contribution to this section was Paul Blackburn's review of Robert Kelly, "The American Duende."

At Frank O'Hara's request, the issue was dedicated to the late

Franz Kline, and a reproduction of one of his paintings, "Cardinal," graced the cover. Reproductions of paintings by De Kooning and Guston were also included.

Kulchur 8 continued the reprinting of Zukofsky's "Five Statements for Poetry" with "Poetry for My Son When He Can Read." Cid Corman, in his first appearance in the magazine, contributed an important essay on Creeley's "For Love." Paul Zukofsky, Louis's gifted musician son, presented us with an essay on the musical setting of one of his father's poems. Another first appearance was Michael McClure in an essay on Anglo-Saxon words called "Phi Upsilon Kappa"; the title was supposed to be "Fuck" spelled in Greek. At that time (winter 1962), I feared that if "Fuck" appeared as the title the Post Office would impound the issue, so McClure rather humorously agreed to "spell it in Greek."

Joe Le Sueur's always interesting "Theatre Chronicle" contrasted the Eric Bentley and Living Theatre productions of Brecht's *A Man's a Man,* and offered an appreciation of Joseph Papp's productions of Shakespeare in the Park. Gil wrote, to my way of thinking, an ill-considered attack on pop art, "Kitsch into Art: The New Realism," but unfortunately there was no "Art Chronicle." Anselm Hollo provided a report on the somewhat gloomy state of poetry and jazz in England.

A long and solid jazz review section, edited by LeRoi and written by Spellman, Jon Rappaport, and Jones himself, was included. The creditable book review section, again edited by Gil, unfortunately did not feature small-press books, but did contain reviews of important avant-garde writers such as Kerouac, McClure, and Olson, written by Sorrentino, Dorn, and Richard Barker.

Kulchur 9 was a special drama issue edited by Joe Le Sueur. Larry Rivers did the cover on which, in his own words, he "put Shakespeare behind the eight ball." Although our usual chronicles and reviews were included, there were no essays, only plays. The issue was most notable for the first publication of LeRoi's famous and savage play "The Toilet," later produced off Broadway to much acclaim. Michael Smith wrote an amusing satire of a mother and son in an oedipal situation. Arnold Weinstein contributed a two-page absurdist trifle. Douglas Woolf, a too little appreciated writer, sent us a poignant play, "The Love Letter," and Ruth

286

Krauss a charming little poem-play. Kenward Elmslie's contribution, "The Aleutians," was written in the author's well-known witty manner, and Diane di Prima's "Murder Cake" was a beautiful and funny fantasy that included such characters as Childe Harold, Richard Lovelace, and Dante. Barbara Guest contributed a short poem-play.

Frank's third and last "Art Chronicle" appeared in this issue. He only wrote three for *Kulchur,* contrary to other information: Donald Allen, in the biographical notes to his edition of Frank O'Hara's *Collected Poems,* states that Frank wrote an "Art Chronicle" for every issue of *Kulchur!*

Instead of editing a book review section for *Kulchur* 9, Gil wrote a "Poetry Chronicle," which was in most respects excellent. I was embarrassed by his attacks on Jerry Rothenberg and the "four young lady poets"—Rochelle Owens, Diane Wakoski, Carol Bergé, and Barbara Moraff—but of course he had the right to speak as he saw fit. The first of Bill Berkson's three "Film Chronicles" appeared, and the music section, in addition to LeRoi's and A. B.'s jazz reviews, included a review of a Günther Schuller concert by Morty Feldman.

Kulchur 10 featured the wonderful essay by Edwin Denby, "Balanchine Choreographing," with cover and picture portfolio from the New York City Ballet, all obtained by Frank. The issue was also rich in comment on poetry by poets, always the core of the magazine. George Oppen covered a good deal of modern poetry in his essay "The Mind's Own Place." Paul Blackburn contributed an important piece on literary magazines, and Louis Zukofsky his historic essay on poetics, "A Statement for Poetry (1950)." Michael Rumaker also sent us a piece on Melville's "Bartleby the Scrivener," and Larry Eigner a piece on Gertrude Stein's *Three Lives.*

There were three essays on music: La Monte Young's "Excerpts from 'Lecture 1960,' " Martin Williams' "Thelonious Monk: Prelude to Success," and Gil's "Remembrances of Bop in New York 1945–1950." Joe Le Sueur's "Theatre Chronicle" covered "The Milk Train Doesn't Stop Here Anymore" by Tennessee Williams, "Natural Affection" by William Inge, "Who's Afraid of Virginia Woolf?" by Edward Albee, and "Lorenzo" by Jack Richardson. Bill Berkson contributed his second "Film Chronicle."

Above: Robert Ducan; Michael McClure. Opposite: Joel Oppenheimer; Diane di Prima. Photographs by Gerard Malanga.

The book reviews were written by LeRoi, Gil, Charles Olson, and Donald Phelps, and the jazz reviews by A. B. and Joe Early. The issue also included a letter to the editors by Anselm Hollo attacking Gil for his roasting of Rothenberg, Owens, Wakoski, Bergé, and Moraff and Hollo's own translations of Russian poets, "Red Cats." For the first time, *Kulchur* became an arena for a diversity of opinion. Gil resigned as an editor after this issue, and I took over the editing of the book review section myself, striving thereafter to cover as many small-press books as possible. The reasons for his resignation were never very clear to me, but I doubt that they had anything to do with Anselm's letter. He told me he didn't like the direction in which the magazine was going, but agreed to stay on as a contributing editor.

Kulchur 11 featured a brilliant piece by W. S. Merwin, modeled on Swift's "A Modest Proposal," suggesting ways in which the mutants produced by nuclear explosions might be put to service in the army. Robert Duncan sent us a story, entitled "Love." Comment on literature was provided by Zukofsky's great essay on Pound. Ed Dorn also contributed a valuable appreciation of Douglas Woolf, and Anselm Hollo an appreciation of Jerome Rothenberg.

Musical scores and a brief essay by Morty Feldman were included. Joe's "Theatre Chronicle" was devoted to a rave notice of the Living Theatre's production of "The Brig" by Kenneth H. Brown, which Joe saw as a realization of Artaud's "theatre of cruelty." Bill Berkson's third and last "Film Chronicle" appeared, and there were book reviews by Sorrentino, Kenneth Irby, Jones, and Saul Gottlieb. Most notable was the review of Rochelle Owens' *Futz* by Saul Gottlieb, at that time unknown and unproduced and only recently published by Hawk's Well Press. The jazz reviews were written by LeRoi and A. B., and the issue concluded with a letter to the editors by Jerry Rothenberg, refuting Gil's criticism of him in *Kulchur* 9. Bill Berkson then went off for an extended stay in Europe; he never wrote for the magazine again, though he never formally resigned. However, in a recent conversation Bill told me he never formally resigned because the relationship among the editors at that time was so *casual*. This, I think, was entirely true.

Kulchur 12 was originally planned as a special issue devoted entirely to civil rights, but not enough material on the theme was submitted. As it finally turned out, the civil rights section extended only from page 2 to page 32, containing contributions from Jones, Spellman, Robert Williams, Sorrentino, Dorn, Oppenheimer, Donald Windham, and Denise Levertov. The rest of the issue contained the sort of material usually featured in *Kulchur*.

Undoubtedly the most important piece was Robert Kelly's long analysis of Zukofsky's "A 1–12." LeRoi contributed another important article, "Expressive Language," about the social implications of speech, especially black American speech. Film was covered by William S. Pechter's essay on Frank Capra. There was no "Theatre Chronicle" by Joe, but Kenward Elmslie contributed a "Chronicle of Musicals," which dealt with *How to Succeed in Business Without Really Trying, A Funny Thing Happened on the Way to the Forum, Oliver, Stop the World—I Want to Get Off, Mr. President, Hot Spot, Little Me, Tovarich,* and *She Loves Me.* Ed Dorn sent us an enigmatic little story called "Clay," and LeRoi provided a smashing post-assassination poem called "Exaugural Address (for Jacqueline Bouvier Kennedy, who has had to eat too much shit)."

The book review section included a review of John Rechy's *City of Night* by Frank O'Hara, the last thing he was to write for the magazine, and reviews of four small-press books: *Reality Sandwiches* by Allan Ginsberg, reviewed by LeRoi; *The Wake* by Andrew Hoyem, reviewed by Gil; *Residence on Earth* by Pablo Neruda (translated by Clayton Eshleman), reviewed by Gil, and *City Lights Journal #1,* reviewed by Allan Kaplan. Jazz reviews by LeRoi, A. B., and Marion Brown concluded the issue.

After *Kulchur* 12, I wrote to Frank, Joe, and LeRoi, telling them I would hold no more editorial meetings but would edit the magazine myself thereafter, inviting them at the same time to continue as contributing editors for as long as they desired. I listed them as editors on the masthead for one more issue, but the credits in *Kulchur* were never a very accurate indication of who was doing the work—more often than not only a courtesy. There was no unpleasantness between us. I was motivated merely by the fact that the poets' own work drew them increasingly away from the magazine, whereas *Kulchur* was my only interest at that time. It became more and more difficult to get them to write the chronicles they had agreed to write, to solicit material, or to read manuscripts. Therefore the last eight issues of the magazine, numbers 13 through 20, were edited by me, although LeRoi continued to handle the jazz section through number 15. After that, there was no more jazz section.

Kulchur 13 boasted a cover and picture portfolio by Andy Warhol, from his film *The Kiss*. Comment on literature was provided by two Canadian poets, hitherto unpublished in *Kulchur*: George Bowering on William Carlos Williams and Warren Tallman on Robert Creeley. Gil contributed a very important piece on "The Art of Hubert Selby." Allen Ginsberg sent me a poem, "The Change: Kyoto-Tokyo Express July 18, 1963," and Ed Dorn a story, "Rest Stop." Richard Brautigan, then a relatively unknown writer, contributed a characteristic piece of fiction called "The Post Offices of Eastern Oregon." Joe sent me his last "Theatre Chronicle," as well as some brilliant film reviews by Pauline Kael. A brief essay on music by Peter Hartman was included and, much to my satisfaction, twenty pages of book reviews covering a wide variety of opinion. The reviewers were Allan Kaplan, Joe, Jerry

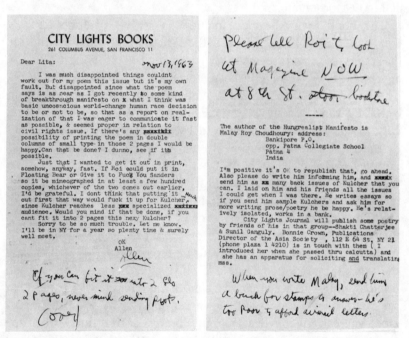

Letter from Allen Ginsberg to Lita Hornick (courtesy Lita Hornick and Kulchur).

Rothenberg, Kenneth Irby, George Economou, and LeRoi. Jazz reviews by Martin Williams, A. B., Marian Brown, Kenneth Irby, John B. Litweiler, and James Brody completed the issue.

Kulchur 14 had a cover by the wonderful young artist and writer Joe Brainard. The issue was originally planned as a Zukofsky number, but only three writers contributed pieces on L. Z.: Creeley, Jonathan Williams, and Charles Tomlinson. Clayton Eshleman's translations of Vallejo, sent to me by Gil, were, I felt, among the best things I had ever published. There was also a remarkable story, sent to me by LeRoi: "The Fable of Orby Dobbs" by Mack Thomas. Michael McClure reappeared in the magazine with his essay on "Reason" (though I cannot help thinking it was more about instinct than reason). Kenneth H. Brown, author of *The Brig,* proved in his piece "My Seed Grows Wilder" that he really could write and that *The Brig* was not merely a director's play. The extensive book review section included four small-press books: *The Moderns,* edited by LeRoi and reviewed by Gil; *Twenty Poems of César Vallejo,* reviewed by Clayton Eshleman; *Her Body Against Time* by Robert Kelly; *El Corno Emplumado,* reviewed by Kenneth Irby; and *The World of the Lie* by Ron Lowenstein, reviewed by Irby. John B. Litweiler was the only jazz reviewer.

Kulchur 15 contained the first piece on art to be published in the magazine since Frank had ceased to write his chronicles—a long and brilliant essay on Robert Rauschenberg by the eminent art critic Nicolas Calas. The Leo Castelli gallery provided the Rauschenberg cover and an eight-page picture portfolio. George Bowering contributed an important essay on prosody. Charles Boultenhouse, the distinguished underground filmmaker, appeared as our new film chronicler with a piece on film time and its relationship to real time which commented extensively on the art of cutting. Donatella Manganotti, the most devoted scholar of the works of William Burroughs, sent a very solid essay. Music and musical theory were covered by Barney Childs in "The Beginning of the Apocalypse?"; the article was a refutation of a piece by Leonard B. Meyer in the *Hudson Review.* Also published in this issue was an interesting story, "To Lie Down in Negritude," by an unknown writer, Rush Greenlee.

The book review section had the distinction of introducing

Gerard Malanga and Ted Berrigan to the magazine for the first time. The other reviewers were Gil and Rochelle Owens, and four small-press books were reviewed. The last jazz review section that LeRoi edited appeared in this issue, with reviewers John B. Litweiler, Joe Early, Frank Busto, and Mack Thomas. The issue closed with the "Hungrealist Manifestos," statements on poetry, the short story, and politics by a group of young writers in India who were very much turned on by the American avant-garde.

Kulchur 16 was graced with a cover by the distinguished artist Al Held, and a picture portfolio of his drawings, but unfortunately there was no article to accompany them. The issue opened with two of LeRoi's poems, "A Western Lady" and "Correction." These were followed by Charles Tomlinson's important interview with Creeley in which, as might be expected, the subjects dealt with were Pound, Williams, Zukofsky, Olson, the *Black Mountain Review,* and some of the action painters at Black Mountain College. Jack Hirschman contributed a very interesting essay, "Constellations," primarily concerned with Mallarmé's *"Un Coup de dés"* but ranging over a broad field of contemporary poetry and music. Nicolas Calas' brief "Exercises" was followed by Gerard Malanga's interview with Andy Warhol, in which Andy answered questions in his usual cool and cryptic manner. Martin Williams contributed an article on television and Charles Boultenhouse wrote a "Theatre Chronicle" instead of a "Film Chronicle" for this issue. This was supplemented by Wallace Thurston's essay on "The Films of Charles Boultenhouse." "Elga's Incantation," a work in progress by Rochelle Owens, was an early rendering of this gifted writer's now famous style.

The issue concluded with John Keys's interesting "Letter to Robert Kelly," which was more general philosophy than poetics, and with the book review section, which comprised reviews by Economou, Bowering, Carolyn Kizer, Allan Kaplan, Berrigan, Malanga, Irby, and Ron Padgett in his first appearance in the magazine.

Kulchur 17's startling cover was a reproduction of Robert Indiana's painting *DIE,* one of several illustrations accompanying Carl Belz's article, "Pop Art, New Humanism and Death." It is uncertain whether the many deathly images in pop art, such as Warhol's electric chairs and auto crashes, represent a criticism of

294

our society or mere deadpan cool. Nicolas Calas, a literary as well as art critic, contributed an essay on the poetic image. A poem by LeRoi, "Corregidor," was his last contribution to the magazine. Much to my satisfaction, Clayton Eshleman contributed some more of his brilliant translations of Vallejo. Ron Padgett's hilarious takeoff of some solemn discussions of poetic form struck a new and refreshing note.

The inside front cover carried an announcement that I would publish a poetry anthology edited by LeRoi, first projected as a book and later as the contents of *Kulchur* 20. Unfortunately LeRoi never did this, having by that time become completely involved in black politics.

The next three issues were to see the introduction of a whole new group of writers, who might have contributed much to the magazine had my time and energies permitted me to continue as editor. Number 17 was concluded with Charles Boultenhouse's "Film Chronicle," Matthew Andrews' "Theatre Chronicle," and the book review section, where Irby, Berrigan, Padgett, Malanga, and David Meltzer reviewed, among other things, eight small-press books.

The opening piece in *Kulchur* 18 was Morgan Gibson's interview with Paul Goodman. Charles Boultenhouse contributed his last and most important piece about film, an essay on Stan Brakhage's "The Art of Vision." Charles and I watched the film together for five hours at the Film-Makers' Cinemathèque (then near the Brooklyn Bridge), nourished by brandy and sandwiches. Margaret Randall, the distinguished poet and editor of *El Corno Emplumado,* sent me "Thoughts on the Poetic Line." Another important comment on literature was the first part of a long essay on Wallace Stevens by Armand Schwerner. Music was covered by Robert Ashley's interview with Morty Feldman.

"Poem-Plays" by Ruth Krauss was one of the delights of the issue; famous as a writer of children's books, Ruth had not yet attained recognition as a writer for adults. Joe Brainard's story "Sunday, July the 30th, 1964," was a landmark for the magazine. Felix Pollak's "Soirées" was a satire on Denise Levertov which in retrospect seems to me too harsh. At that time, however, I was interested in making *Kulchur* an arena for a diversity of opinion and anxious to prevent it from becoming a coterie magazine.

The notable "Art Chronicle," by David Antin, was his first

published piece of art criticism and dealt mainly with Duchamp. The "Theatre Chronicle" was by Matthew Andrews. The book reviews were by Fielding Dawson, Berrigan, Randall, Padgett, and John Sinclair. Ron Padgett's review of Joe Ceravolo's unpublished manuscript, "Wild Flowers Out of Gas," was included.

Kulchur 19 was distinguished by a variety of brilliant and funny contributions from the group of then-emerging young writers who are now sometimes called the second generation New York School, though none of them like the appellation. There was Ron Padgett's mad story "Bill" and Ted Berrigan's account of an academic poet on a reading tour, "A Boke." Tom Veitch's "Yoga Exercises" was hilarious and obscene. So was Ron's picture story, "Pere Ubu's Alphabet," derived from Jarry and Bonnard. Ted's "Art Chronicle" was witty and outrageous, and the illustrations were the funniest I have ever seen. Two scenes from Dick Gallup's much admired play "The Bingo" were an important contribution, while the second part of Armand Schwerner's essay on Stevens provided more sober comment on literature. The "Theatre Chronicle" by Matthew Andrews and the "Film Chronicle" by Yale M. Udoff followed. Book reviewers were Berrigan, Sinclair, Margaret Randall, Eshleman, Malanga, Bowering, Morgan Gibson, Aram Saroyan, Douglas Blazek, and Irby. This section covered a wide range of often conflicting ideas, including Ted's review of Harold Rosenberg, which was shocking to some people.

Though I don't think I was wholly aware of it at the time, looking back through the issues of *Kulchur* I realize that number 19 may have seemed to reflect a surprising change in editorial perspective. There was really no reason for this except that I felt I wanted to do something different. I was excited by the new writers' work and felt the emphasis of the modern cultural scene had shifted. I wanted the magazine to reflect that change.

In *Kulchur* 20 Ted and Ron continued their wildly funny writing with a series of letters, "Big Travel Dialogues." This was later reprinted in *Bean Spasms,* a book by them that I published after I had ended the magazine and switched to publishing books. Gerard contributed an interview with the dancer James Waring, accompanied by a cover photograph and picture portfolio, and Ron and Joe had a poem-picture series entitled "Go Lovely Rose." A selection from Ted's wonderful "Sonnets" was included and a

296

long poem by Armand, "Prologue in Six Parts." Comment on literature was covered in an essay on Creeley by Ellen Maslow, comment on art in David Antin's second "Art Chronicle," dealing with current art criticism, and comment on film by Yale M. Udoff's review of *Girl with the Green Eyes* and Margaret Randall's poem "The Ritual, Antonioni." The book review section, which included six reviews of small-press books, again presented a wide variety of opinion, provided by Fielding Dawson, David Meltzer, Margaret Randall, George Bowering, David Ross, Ted Berrigan, Tom Clark, and Ronald Caplan.

This last issue of *Kulchur* appeared while it was still at its height. There was no reason to feel that the magazine's energies were depleted and that it had to end; it was only *my* energies which were depleted. After editing eight issues myself, with quarterly deadlines, I found I had no time for my husband and children. I decided to switch to publishing Kulchur Press books, producing only two books a year and working with only one author at a time. I also felt that, after five years of publishing a magazine which focused mainly on criticism, I would like to change to publishing poetry. Since then I have published twenty-four books. My decision may have seemed confusingly abrupt to some, since *Kulchur* 20 bore an announcement promising great things for *Kulchur* 21. I'm afraid it *was* rather abrupt, but little-magazine editors have never been known for their reasonableness.

Lita Hornick. Photograph by Gerard Malanga.

NEON, KULCHUR, ETC.
Gilbert Sorrentino

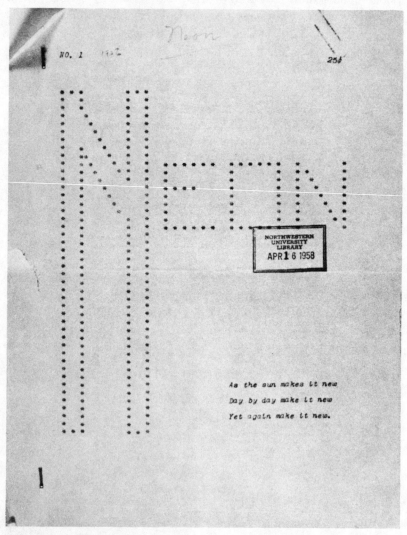

Neon, *No. 1, 1956 (courtesy Northwestern University Library).*

Gilbert Sorrentino explains that an estimated audience of two hundred readers for Neon *sufficed, because in the late fifties in New York the community of poets and writers was so tight. An editor could be absolutely certain that the people who wanted to see the magazine would see it, either by purchasing a copy at the Gotham Book Mart, the Eighth Street Book Shop, or Make It New, or by meeting someone who would lend him one. Magazines like* Neon, *the early* Kulchur, *and* The Floating Bear *were strong, independent little magazines that grew, as Mr. Sorrentino says in the following essay, out of a specific modern movement, and they were important to that movement's cohesion. As William Carlos Williams advised Mr. Sorrentino just before* Neon *began: "A little magazine's only rationale is its editor's belief that the writers he prints must be presented as a group. Anything else is just a collation of pages."*

Models for Mr. Sorrentino when he edited Neon *and worked as book editor for* Kulchur *were* The Black Mountain Review, The Exile, Contact, The Little Review, *and* Measure. *The editors whose work he admired were Ezra Pound, William Carlos Williams, John Wieners, and Robert Creeley. And the magazines that served as examples of what not to do were* The Kenyon Review, The Hudson Review, Discover, *and* Botteghe Oscure.

Although eclectic magazines serve some useful ends—and although most magazines, whatever else they may try to be, have something eclectic about them—Gilbert Sorrentino has been most drawn to those that have a bone to pick. Commercial magazines, in his view, can never be focused in this way. By definition, the editors of commercial publications must be interested in turning a profit. They must also create *an audience instead of aiming their material at an audience that already exists. For all this, Mr. Sorrentino does not believe that commercial publishing in New York is worthless. When he worked as book editor for* Kulchur, *he advised Lita Hornick not to focus all her reviews exclusively on small press publications, since there was a lot of hackwork there too. Rather, she should mix reviews of the best books from small presses with reviews of books from big houses, which produced a lot of good work to be praised and a lot of sacred cows to be slaughtered.*

Born in Brooklyn, New York, in 1929, Gilbert Sorrentino has published five books of fiction, eight books of verse, and six

299

anthologies, and has been awarded an Ariadne Foundation Grant, a John Simon Guggenheim Memorial Fellowship, a National Endowment for the Arts Fellowship, a CAPS grant, and the Samuel Fels Award for Fiction. His work has appeared in a wide range of magazines, among them Partisan Review, TriQuarterly, Caterpillar, Kulchur, Fuck You, The Village Voice, *and* Esquire.

The decade between the mid-fifties and the mid-sixties, a singularly rich one for American writing, appears, on reflection, to be complex in the extreme as far as the little magazine is concerned. It seems to me that, although there were fewer magazines in evidence at any given time during that ten-year period than there are at present, many if not most of those magazines were oddly interdependent; this gave them a presence and an influence far exceeding their numbers. Those that were involved in publishing what may be called the "new writing"—if that is not too pompous and shopworn a phrase—were possessed by a passion to print what their editors took to be writing that quite literally had no place else to go. Not surprisingly, it fell out that the bulk of this writing was done by a rather small group of writers, so that many little magazines drew on essentially the same authors as contributors. There slowly evolved a kind of network of magazines acting as a general clearinghouse for new methods, techniques, and ideas of literary composition and criticism.

I think two things should be made clear immediately. The magazines I speak of were not academic or scholarly, and had little to do with what are called quarterlies; nor were they open to anything at all, refuges for writers who wished to "express" themselves—in other words, they were not what might be termed bohemian publications. On the contrary, they had a definite literary bone to pick, and they set themselves up not as a mere *alternative* press but as a press that considered its criteria to be correct. At this remove, I sometimes detect the wild eye of the fanatic staring out from these defunct journals; yet by and large they were not fanatical, but revolutionary in a conscious, controlled, and planned way. To call them, even now, "alternative" or "experimental" smacks of the academic patronization that, not so many years ago, was made manifest as contempt, hatred, and even fear. If this seems farfetched, the reader is urged to peruse, at his leisure, the reams of nonsense written, for instance, on the "Beat generation" in the popular, slick, and academic journals of the late fifties. The new writing was bitterly maligned and insulted by all those who, as Robert Creeley has noted, "were dominant in their insistence upon an *idea* of form extrinsic to the given instance." A critical-academic structure that rigidly excluded such writers as Williams and Zukofsky did not know what hit it in the fifties.

In 1953 I was discharged from the Army and began work on a novel, the first extended piece of writing I had ever done. Concurrently I wrote poetry, which I had begun to write while in college in 1949. It became clear as time passed that there were few, if any, magazines interested in publishing the kind of work that I was doing. I don't mean to imply that my work was first-rate; on the contrary, it was the work of an apprentice, one who was casting about to find some form into which he could work his experience. Yet the writing in the magazines I read at the time seemed to be singularly stale, even though it was presented as a model of excellence. *Partisan Review, Hudson Review, Poetry,* and others were publishing writers who, for some reason, seemed to me to be people who lived at another time in another country. The poetry I read might as well have been written in a foreign language. I had begun to read Pound and had just discovered Williams; in a half-baked way I knew that what these poets had discovered and championed had not been acted upon by the poets who were at that time critically acclaimed. The concerns of the latter seemed to be those of a polite and official intellectualism. Lowell, Roethke, Berryman, Wilbur, Eberhart, Shapiro, Viereck, Schwartz, et al.—I read them all. And the more I read them, the more I wallowed in confusion. Their poetic concerns seemed oddly fossilized and rigid, and my own poems, in their crudity and ignorance, "floated," as it were, as I belligerently refused to use the poems of my celebrated masters as models. My slow understanding of Williams' work exhilarated and depressed me—the former since I saw in his writing a method of anchoring my work sans stuffiness and

301

dullness, the latter because I realized that Williams was not a peer; there was something that I "heard" that Williams did not. How was one to transcribe that sound? Was there anyone who was trying to do the same thing? In brief, who and where were my peers? Did they publish anything? If so, where?

All this seems quite extraordinary to me now, almost as if it did not happen that way, but I assure you that it did. In 1955 I returned to college, for want of something better to do. I was still almost totally ignorant of my peers, but I had, as they say, glimmerings, although I knew no other writers. At Brooklyn College I met some young men as dissatisfied as I, who also had begun, in one way or another, to write. We read each other's work; we complained of the insubstantiality of the literary establishment; we decided, in time-honored fashion, to begin our own little magazine, to be called *Neon*. (The title referred both to the ubiquitous city lights and the meaning of the word in Greek: "new thing.") I don't think any of us knew what we were doing, only that we wanted to publish our work together, to make a statement of sorts. The friends involved with *Neon* were Sam Abrams, John Richardson, Jack Freiwald, Alfred Siegel (a dedicated Poundian), and Hubert Selby, who had, as I recall, just begun to write. We were, it goes without saying, hopeful and naive. Somehow, through Hugh Kenner, Siegel had put me in touch with Pound, and I wrote to ask if he would be interested in contributing to the magazine. To my absolute amazement, he replied to me by postcard, giving me the names of two Australians, Noel Stock and William Fleming, both of whom were affiliated with an Australian magazine, *Meanjin*. Whereupon I wrote to them and they responded with poems.

At about this time, early 1956, I met Williams. I had sent him, with misgivings, a short impressionistic sketch I had written while in the Army in 1951. He replied cordially, and subsequently invited me to Rutherford for dinner. As it turned out, he wanted my permission to use a piece of the sketch in *Paterson Five,* which he was then in the process of composing. I of course granted him permission, and we began a correspondence. In the course of it, I asked him for a poem for *Neon,* but he declined, writing, as I recall, that it would be much better for us to go it alone with a first issue.

Some time in February or March, the mimeograph stencils

302

were cut for *Neon* 1, in Jack Freiwald's basement apartment in Brooklyn. The bill was paid by Alfred Siegel, and toward the end of March we had 250 copies of the first issue in hand, with work by Abrams, Richardson, Freiwald, Stock, Fleming, and myself. The price was a quarter.

Copies were placed in the Eighth Street Book Shop, Gotham, a Bleecker Street shop called the Make It New, operated by John Kasper and William Horton more as a dissemination point for right-wing political propaganda than as a bookshop, and City Lights in San Francisco. As I remember, the Make It New manager, a young woman and a rabid follower of Pound's politics and economics, seemed to think that *Neon,* perhaps because of the inclusion of "Pound's people," Stock and Fleming, was or soon would be a political broadside. At all events, the store soon closed—what happened to the copies of *Neon* that they had taken I don't know. The rest of the copies were given to contributors and friends, and a few were sold by mail.

I'm afraid that after the publication of *Neon* 1 things happened so fast—and it seems, all at once—that I doubt if I can set them down here in any true chronology. I had by this time discovered the *Black Mountain Review, Origin,* the *Chicago Review* (under Irving Rosenthal), and other magazines. *On the Road* had been published, and I had read Ginsberg, Corso, McClure, et al. Then *Neon* 2 was ready; it included Selby's first published story, "Home for Christmas," Williams' "To My Friend Ezra Pound," which he had sent me because of his pleasure in the first issue of the magazine, and some poems by Paul Goodman, whom Selby had met and requested work from. Selby paid for this issue, which was multilithed. I believe we sold it out, perhaps on the strength of Williams' poem. *Neon* 2 was much more sophisticated than the first number, since we had discovered an entire world of writers that we had not known existed just two years earlier. Everything indeed seemed to be happening at once: I had just read Creeley's poems in the *Black Mountain Review,* his book *All That Is Lovely in Men,* and in *Origin,* and began a correspondence with him; unsolicited poems were coming in to the magazine, many of them from Southern California (I was still almost completely ignorant of the writers of the San Francisco area); we had, by some means, obtained a mailing list and the magazine was beginning to receive subscriptions; and Jack

Freiwald, who had moved to the West Coast, had found a printer who said he would do *Neon* 3 for a reasonable price.

Toward the end of 1957 Selby completed a story called "Love's Labor's Lost," which would later be the first part of "The Queen Is Dead." Since his first story he had worked almost constantly at his prose, writing hundreds of drafts that were then revised, rewritten, torn apart. I don't know another writer who so swiftly mastered his statement as Selby. In any event, when I read "Love's Labor's Lost" I was certain that he was well on his way to becoming an extremely powerful and important writer. I badly wanted to publish the story in *Neon* 3, which was still in gestation, but something had happened to my financial plans insofar as the West Coast printer was concerned and Jack Freiwald was looking about for another one. I suggested to Selby that he send the story to Williams for his comment, which he did. Williams replied, almost immediately, that the story had absolutely stunned him but that it was, as far as he could see, quite unpublishable, given the subject matter and language. However, Williams went on, if *anyone* would publish it, it would be the men who edited the *Black Mountain Review* and he had taken the liberty of sending the story to Jonathan Williams.

Jonathan read it and sent it on to Creeley, who was at the time in New Mexico, and Creeley scheduled the story for what was to be the final number of the *Black Mountain Review;* the college had closed and there were funds only for that last issue.

Neon 3 was finally published, an ill-starred attempt on my part to partially represent in the magazine what I took to be the "California writers." As I look at the issue now, it seems fuzzy, unfocused, hardly cogent, although some individual pieces stand out as having merit—they are lost, however, in this issue, which is, quite candidly, an aberration. God knows how long I had waited for the publication of *Neon* 3, but in the meantime I had almost completed assembling *Neon* 4 and, once again, was looking around for a printer that I could afford—or, I should say, could afford to be in debt to. Before I write of *Neon* 4, and the circumstances of its publication, it might be useful to try to make clear to the reader the ambience that existed in New York at that time (1958).

I suppose what is fondly called by literary historians a "ferment" was occurring in the arts at this time—most of it, it seems to me, quite accidental. That is to say, a number of very diverse things all happened at the same time, all of them linked together, however tenuously, and all of them serving to create what I might call, with some misgivings, an avant-garde community in New York that had cultural and artistic ties to other communities in other parts of the country. At the risk of boring the reader with dry notation, here are a few of the things that occurred in the last three years of the fifties—none of them in itself remarkable, yet together serving to consolidate what had begun as a scattered movement. Black Mountain College had closed, its students and faculty settling in New York and San Francisco, with Creeley temporarily anchored in New Mexico, where his friends were Max Finstein and Judson Crews, among others. The Beat writers—Ginsberg, Kerouac, Corso, et al., after "electrifying" the Bay Area, had begun moving back to New York, whence they had originally come. Don Allen's "San Francisco Scene" issue of the *Evergreen Review* (number 2) had acquainted East Coast writers with McClure, Spicer, Duncan, Brother Antoninus, Rumaker. The writers who were later to initiate the "New York School"—Koch, O'Hara, Ashbery, Field, Schuyler, Guest—had come together in New York as a loosely affiliated group. Ashbery and O'Hara were deeply involved with painting and the other plastic arts as critics and general commentators (O'Hara was a curator at the Modern), and associated with painters and sculptors in a natural and easy way. This had not previously been the case in New York, where the abstract painters formed a group *sui generis*. And among the younger artists were such men as Dan Rice and John Chamberlain and Robert Rauschenberg, all of whom were alumni of Black Mountain College. Paul Blackburn had returned from France to settle in New York. And everyone—painters, sculptors, poets, and writers—used the Cedar Bar in Greenwich Village as a headquarters, base of operations, and home away from home. It was an incredible stew out of which was to come an American literature that by 1960 could no longer, even by the most benighted, be called "fanatic," "ignorant," "vapid," or "puerile." By the most curiously unintentional means, as I have said, the scattered elements of this movement became unified.

By late 1958 *Neon* 4 was in the process of being printed, but it would be a whole year until I received finished copies. Early in that year Jonathan Williams had written to Joel Oppenheimer to tell him of Selby, and they arranged to meet. Through Joel Oppenheimer, Selby met Fielding Dawson and then introduced both men to me, as the editor of a magazine that might possibly take on many of the writers who had been affiliated with the *Black Mountain Review*. Through Oppenheimer I met Max Finstein, just arrived from New Mexico, and a little later, I met Jonathan Williams, in New York for a visit. *Neon* 4 had contributions from Finstein, Oppenheimer, and a collage cover by Dawson; at the time when I met these men I had begun to read what little there was available by Louis Zukofsky, and wrote to ask him for a contribution, which he sent, telling me at the same time to write to Lorine Niedecker, Cid Corman, and Robert Duncan. The fourth issue was rapidly being filled, and contributions also came in from William Carlos Williams, Paul Goodman, and Selby, who gave me a story called "Double Feature." There were many other writers in *Neon* 4, plus a section of translations of the Chinese ideograms in *The Cantos* by Alfred Siegel.

While the issue was being made up, I received in the mail

Gilbert Sorrentino (left) and Allen Ginsberg. Photograph by Jonathan Williams.

306

one day the first issue of *Yugen*, edited by LeRoi Jones (Amiri Baraka) and Hettie Cohen. *Yugen*'s early issues focused on Beat writers—Ginsberg, Corso, Bremser—and also printed work by Phil Whalen and local Greenwich Village writers. I subsequently met Jones, and we became fast friends; through him I got to know "his" writers, and through me he got to know "mine." LeRoi Jones had a magnetic and powerful personality, and his magazine immediately began to flourish—so much so, in fact, that the poets and writers who contributed to it and who were drawn to Jones's apartment (first on West 20th Street in Chelsea and later on East 14th Street) became known as the *"Yugen* crowd." Jones had informal gatherings in his apartment for readings, discussions, talk, and drinking, and often these gatherings would turn into all-night parties. A not at all atypical party at Jones's would include Selby, Rumaker, Kerouac, Ginsberg, Bremser, Corso, Rosenthal, Oppenheimer, Finstein, and, when they were in New York, Wieners, George Stanley, Dorn, and Burroughs. There was often music played by Ornette Coleman, Archie Shepp, Wilbur Ware, and Don Cherry. About 1960 or so, Frank O'Hara, Koch, Bill Berkson, and other people of the New York School also began to frequent Jones's place. It assumed the character of a freewheeling and noisy salon.

By the time *Neon* 4 was off the press, Jones had just published *Yugen* 4. Dawson did a drawing for *Yugen*, black on white— his collage for *Neon* had been white on black—and he had suggested to Jones that his drawing be printed as a negative, so that it too would be white on black and the two magazines could therefore be displayed in bookshops as "sisters." Jones did this, and the magazines were displayed, at least in the Eighth Street Book Shop, side by side.

Some months earlier, I had complained to Dawson about the ridiculous length of time I had been waiting for *Neon* 4. Many people, incidentally, thought that *Neon* had folded, and some subscribers had canceled their orders. Dawson suggested that we do, jointly, a supplement to the magazine, to be given to subscribers as a sign of good faith and a kind of bonus. We decided to call it *Supplement to Now*. It was to be small, both in number of pages and format, and Dawson arranged to have it printed at the plant of the *Kirkwood Messenger,* his Missouri hometown newspaper, for sixty dollars. Its theme was to be, as the title implies, "now." As I look back at the magazine, the theme seems thin, tenuous at best, but it provided a hook on which we hung a number of excellent pieces. The issue had Charles Olson, Robert Creeley, Max Finstein, Hubert Selby, Jonathan Williams, Dawson, and myself. The cover, a drawing of a linotype machine by Dawson, was especially fitting. *Supplement to Now* appeared at the end of 1958 and was immediately mailed to subscribers free of charge; it was sold in bookshops for fifty cents, and has become, so I am told, a collector's item, one that is very scarce.

Neon, after the appearance of its fourth issue and the supplement, entered a period of extreme financial difficulty. Numbers 3 and 4 had been printed on the West Coast—a situation that had become impossible. There was no way to oversee the printing, there were no proofs, and the low production costs were offset by the freight bills that had to be paid upon delivery. *Neon* 5 was ready by this time, and what I needed was a New York printer who would do the issue in a month or so and at a reasonable price. LeRoi Jones had found a small printing company in East New York, the Orion Press, and used it to do a reprint of Olson's "Projective Verse" as a Totem Press chapbook (Totem was a *Yugen* book imprint). Nothing turned out well with *Neon* 5, however, and it was all I could do to get my deposit on the printing bill back from the company. I was very disappointed, since *Neon* 5 was to have included work by Duncan, McClure, and Loewinsohn, the first time that the magazine was to have Bay Area writers represented in its pages.

At this point I was just about ready to give up on the magazine. There was never enough money to bring issues out on a fairly regular basis, but, more depressing, the issues always seemed to be too slender to have any adequate selection of prose among their contents. I wanted to print Selby, Rumaker, and Douglas Woolf— I also had begun to think that it was time to use the magazine as a place in which nonfiction—criticism and reviews—might appear as a regular feature. There seemed to be no hope of doing this, and in 1960, with a gift of money from Tony Weinberger, I put together a final issue of the magazine, *Neon Obit.* Again it was to have a unifying theme—this one on dead Americans who had made a great impact on this country, or on dead currents of

Top: Neon, *No. 4, 1959;* Supplement to Now, *including work by Charles Olson, Robert Creeley, Max Finstein, Gilbert Sorrentino, Hubert Selby, Jonathan Williams, and Fielding Dawson, 250 copies printed August 1958. Bottom:* Neon Obit *(courtesy Gilbert Sorrentino).*

behavior and thought that were still in the air. The contributors were Dawson, Jones, Selby, Weinberger, Early, Oppenheimer, Loewinsohn, Olson, Finstein, and myself. The cover drawing was again by Dawson, of a Curtiss Robin that had gone out of production during the depression. If I remember rightly, 300 copies of the issue were sold out immediately.

In the same year, Jones began to run critical articles in *Yugen*. His feeling about them was much the same as mine; that is, the new writers had been appearing in magazines for about a decade, and it was time for the establishment of a critical position vis-à-vis these writers. The reader must know that, to my knowledge, not one so-called major critic had ever written a word on any of the writers I have here mentioned; indeed it was a cause for utter astonishment to be shown a review, however mindless, of one of their books. If anything did appear in print about any of them, it was usually in the nature of a jeremiad against "the destroyers of letters and culture," etc., etc., ad nauseam. It was quite apparent to Jones and to me as well (and to many others) that the writers of this new movement should have at least one outlet for their own critical commentary on their peers. It also seemed incumbent upon us to begin a counterattack against those who had set themselves up as the guardians of letters and arts. *Neon* was, for all purposes, dead, and the avant-garde community in New York had only *Yugen* as a medium for expression. And *Yugen* simply did not have the room to print anything more than short critiques.

While this was going on, a young journalist, Marc Schleifer, brought out the first issue of a magazine called *Kulchur*, with Jones as one of the contributing editors. (The others were John Fles, Charles Olson, Donald Phelps, and Martin Williams.) *Kulchur* was exactly what we had been looking for—a magazine of criticism and comment, dealing with literature, politics, art, jazz, and popular culture. Through Jones, I met Schleifer and accepted his invitation to write for the magazine, which looked as if it might indeed become that catholic yet eclectic publication which was needed. The problem, as always, was financial: Schleifer had to pay for the printing of *Kulchur* as best he could, and it seemed as if it would collapse almost before it got started. One night, Jones, Schleifer, and I sat talking in the Cedar, and discovered

310

that Schleifer had somehow met a wealthy woman who was interested in the arts, Lita Hornick. She offered to pay for *Kulchur,* oversee its distribution, and assure its appearance, right on time, every three months. Most agreeably, she wanted nothing to do with the editorial policy of the magazine, nor did she wish to exercise editorial judgment concerning its contents. It was absolutely too good to be true. If I am not mistaken, it was on this same night that we decided to bar all poetry and fiction from the magazine and devote its pages to criticism and commentary. (In later issues this policy was relaxed, but never to the extent that unsolicited poetry and fiction were considered.)

It is probably quite unfair of me to say so, but I always thought of *Kulchur* as the critical wing of *Yugen;* that is to say, *Kulchur* seemed to me to be what *Yugen* might have become had Jones had the money to continue it. The nucleus of the magazine, from the beginning, was made up of those writers who had been affiliated with *Yugen* and *Neon,* and, further back, with the *Black Mountain Review.* (Ultimately, it became the official voice of the entire new movement. Although I haven't the issues at hand, it seems to me that every nonacademic writer of value in this country either appeared or was discussed in its pages.)

At all events, *mirabile dictu,* we had a magazine of our own, one that we did not have to worry about funding. I became the poetry editor with, I believe, number 3, and then book editor. My function was to be responsible for all articles and reviews on writing and books and to contribute regularly to the magazine.

Kulchur published, over a five-year period, twenty issues. I believe it must be considered one of the great magazines of the twentieth century, an authoritative voice, as important as *The Little Review, The Dial, transition, The Criterion,* and *Contact.* It had a clear point of view, an unmistakable position, and its range of commentary was simply staggering. It was a perfect argument against the idea that a magazine is a hodgepodge of good pieces by good writers. The articles in each issue complemented and buttressed each other and lent weight and depth to the articles in every other issue. It had, in a word, a tone that was unique to itself—*Kulchur* simply did not read like any other magazine before or since.

The editors all wrote for almost every issue, so that the voice of the magazine was coherent and *located*. The regular reader knew where the editors stood, and hence their criticism made sense; it had roots. Interestingly, *Kulchur* evolved a review style that, for better or worse, has persisted in little-magazine writing to this day. It was personal, colloquial, wry, mocking, and precisely vulgar when vulgarity seemed called for. It was also "careless," by which I mean that it wore its learning lightly, was witty and, as they say, irreverent. Although in its twenty issues at least a dozen brilliant essays were printed, not one of them had the miasmal aura of the "think piece." Most pointedly, perhaps, the *Kulchur* "style" expected the reader to know what was occurring in the avant-garde community in New York; nothing was ever explained, the writing was elliptical, casual, and obsessively conversational. We had wanted a flashing, brilliant magazine that had nothing to do with the academic world and we had got one.

By 1961 Marc Schleifer, because of an increasing concern with politics, had begun to lose interest in the magazine, or perhaps he no longer had the time to edit it—it came to the same thing. He asked Mrs. Hornick for a leave of absence and requested that I be guest editor for *Kulchur* 4. I accepted, and went to work on the issue. I asked Zukofsky (whom I badly wanted to begin to use the magazine for an outlet), Duncan, Ron Loewinsohn, and Selby for contributions, and they all responded. Zukofsky gave me "Modern Times," a beautiful essay on Charlie Chaplin, written in 1936 and never before published; Duncan sent his matchless "Ideas of the Meaning of Form"; Loewinsohn sent "A Credo Sandwich," a piece on poetics that complemented Duncan's; and Selby, writing as "Harry Black," submitted "Happiness House," a bitter assault on New York State mental institutions. Jones, as an editor, gave me a chapter from his as yet unpublished book, *Blues People,* and I asked Edward Dorn if I might reprint his "What I See in the *Maximus* Poems," originally published in Gael Turnbull's *Migrant*. Paul Goodman sent a comment on material that had appeared in number 3. An oddly curious Freudian study of L. Frank Baum, and in particular the Oz books, came in unsolicited from Osmond Beckwith, of whom I have never again heard, and seemed to me exactly right for the issue. The reviews were by Dawson, Jones, Cid Corman (on Zukofsky), Oppenheimer (on Dorn), and Walter Lowenfels, who sent a review of *Tropic of Cancer,* written in Paris on the appearance of Miller's novel in 1933 and previously unpublished. Marian Zazeela, Marc Schleifer's wife, gave me a snapshot of Kerouac and Burroughs taken in Paris about 1955, and that became the cover: the title page identifies it as a photograph of Inspector Maigret and Sam Spade.

Joel Oppenheimer was the guest editor for number 5. He printed a group of the Zukofskys' Catullus translations and a chapter from Louis Zukofsky's novel *Little* (from this point on, Zukofsky was a regular contributor to *Kulchur,* all of his "Five Statements for Poetry" appearing in later issues). And he "commissioned" the first of Frank O'Hara's art chronicles, which were to become a regular feature of the magazine.

After the appearance of *Kulchur* 6, the editorial staff was set. Schleifer had not returned, and the magazine, instead of having a single editor to oversee everything, had an editorial board, each member of which had absolute autonomy in his field. Lita Hornick was listed as the managing editor; the music editor was Jones; Frank O'Hara was art editor; Joseph Le Sueur, theater editor; Bill Berkson, film editor; and I was book editor. The contributing editors were Diane di Prima, A. B. Spellman, Charles Olson, and Donald Phelps. I should mention that *Kulchur* 9 was a special theater issue of short plays, edited by Le Sueur.

By the end of 1963 my editorial relationship with the magazine was becoming strained, mostly because of editorial differences between me and Mrs. Hornick. Increasingly, she had begun to take a hand in editorial decisions affecting the contents of *Kulchur.* Pieces appeared without having been seen or approved by any editor. Writers who had very little to do with the tone or position of the magazine were asked, by Mrs. Hornick, for contributions. *Kulchur* began to assume the look and feel of just another little magazine; it rapidly began to lose its singularity, and the excellent pieces that still appeared were weakened or lost within the context of these diffuse issues. Mrs. Hornick had become not only an editor, but *the* editor.

One incident that occurred at this time stands out in my memory. Donald Phelps, as a contributing editor—one of the original contributing editors of the magazine—had sent in a film review that Mrs. Hornick rejected, I cannot remember on what grounds. I protested, as did some of the other editors, pointing out that as a contributing editor he was expected regularly to contribute to *Kulchur,* and that if his work was to be rejected, what was the point of carrying him as an editor? Mrs. Hornick did not see it that way, and by issue 11 I had asked to be relieved of my editorial duties and listed as a contributing editor. By issue 14, all the editors had been metamorphosed into contributing editors, and the masthead of number 20, the final issue, carries only Mrs. Hornick's name and represents the total change that had come over *Kulchur.* Of the old contributors, only Fielding Dawson was left.

All this happened very gradually, over a period of a year and a half or so. On reflection, it seems unfortunate to me, since I think that *Kulchur* might have gone on for at least another half-dozen issues had it retained its original focus. At precisely that moment at which the magazine found itself in the position of being without peers, it became fuzzy, off-center, and fashionable. I suspect that the reason for this was that Mrs. Hornick wanted to discover her *own* writers, and ranged all over to get them. So the magazine died—having, at its end, less energy and verve than it displayed in its first tentative issue. *Kulchur* was a remarkable publication because its strength came from the fact that its editorial position was rooted in a true artistic community, and that community was rooted in a great city. It was not the organ of a precious and isolated "artists' colony," nor was it—horror of horrors—the journal of an academic milieu's rebels. The contributors were asked to submit work on the basis of what the editors took to be relevance to the magazine's overall position, not because they were fashionable or well known. (In later issues this changed.) It was alive because it grew out of a *specific* modern movement and because it was necessary to that movement's cohesion. Williams told me, just before *Neon* began, that a little magazine's only rationale is its editor's belief that the writers he prints must be presented as a group. Anything else is just a collation of pages. I have always believed this, and the experience of the past twenty years has shown that the magazines that never really come to life are always those that reveal themselves to be little anthologies of anything at all (as long as it's "good").

I should mention, before I close, another publication that was

circulated concurrently with the last issues of *Yugen* and throughout the life of *Kulchur*. This was *The Floating Bear,* edited by
LeRoi Jones and Diane di Prima. I was not directly involved
with it but contributed to it on an irregular basis, often under
pseudonyms (the only one I can remember being "Abe Harvard").
The *Bear* was a mimeographed newsletter of about 15 to 20
pages, and distributed solely by a mailing list, free of charge. It
can best be explained by the fact that its first fifteen or twenty
numbers contained all the material that could have just as easily
gone into *Kulchur* had that magazine been a monthly. In other
words, it had "hot news"—reviews of movies, plays, recitals, jazz
clubs, and the like. It also contained poems, essays, letters to
the editors, buyer's guides, notes on trashy paperbacks, reading
lists, and an enormous amount of New York "inside" gossip.
Hundreds of people contributed to it. It was, at its best, fresh,
arrogant, and funny. After 1965 or so, it continued under, I
think, the sole editorship of Diane di Prima until about 1973,
appearing less and less frequently. Its last issues were almost all
gossip and deeply involved in an alternative politics.

The reader will have by now seen that my own view of the
little magazine of the fifties and sixties is necessarily narrow, being
severely restricted to my knowledge of the workings of my own
magazine, *Neon,* Jones's *Yugen,* and the magazine we both worked
for over a four-year period, *Kulchur*. There were many other magazines that appeared at about the time *Kulchur* was entering its
last year of publication, among them *Trobar, Poor.Old.Tired.
Horse., Poems from the Floating World, Some/Time,* etc. Many
of them were outlets for those poets who at that time had embraced
the theory, if you will, of the "deep image." I am essentially
ignorant of these magazines and never appeared in any of them.
Although I rarely agreed with any of those poets on anything,
the magazines that presented them were *absolute;* i.e., they too
had a bone to pick, and articulated a position doggedly.

When I consider *Neon, Yugen,* and *Kulchur,* they seem to me
almost of a piece. I often cannot recall what pieces I contributed
to which of them. The three of them performed a particular function at a particular time, and died, one might suppose, when
they were no longer needed. *Kulchur* most definitely reflected
the close of a literary era that had begun in about 1950 and

315

found its first voice in the *Black Mountain Review* and *Origin*. By the time it ceased publication, in the winter of 1965, that era was over and the community from which it had sprung no longer existed—it had become something else. By that time, most of the writers who appeared in these magazines were known, and some of them were beginning to be treated with at least a measure of respect; they were no longer considered ignorant beatniks by the great majority of critics and academics.

A final note. I suspect that a new magazine—perhaps even one of "criticism and comment," like *Kulchur*—will soon be necessary. The generation that had just begun to write and publish in the mid-sixties has been around more than a decade. Although the writers of this generation have published in many magazines (and published many books as well) and founded many others, they have been curiously and inexplicably uncritical of each other and of everybody else; everyone seems to like everyone else's work. The situation is oddly passive, and many of the magazines in which these writers appear read like the later issues of *The Floating Bear*—all charm, gossip, and news notes. These younger writers have never established a critical position for themselves; it seems to be beneath them. Perhaps it is. Maybe they are too close to my generation to assault it—certainly they were born, as it were, into an era that was kind to them. In comparison to the fifties, it was an era of light, air, and acceptance or, as Frank O'Hara might put it, of girls, grapes, and snow. If the next generation sees this present one as dull and empty, I'm certain we will see the birth of another literary movement that will view the present generation of younger writers as the establishment, and launch its own rebellious magazines.

Opposite: LeRoi Jones, circa 1962. Photograph by Mario Jorrin (courtesy Poetry *magazine).*

LEROI JONES
AN INTERVIEW ON
<u>YUGEN</u>
David Ossman

LeRoi Jones did not adopt the name Imamu Amiri Baraka until the late sixties. After the middle of that decade, he turned away from his literary interests and toward black theater and black politics in Newark. (He ran for community council office there in 1968 to oversee slum rehabilitation, but lost the election.) From that time on he increasingly departed from the white world, favoring even "a mathematics which would have no whiteness in it."

In 1960, when David Ossman conducted this interview, LeRoi Jones had edited his magazine Yugen, along with the Totem Press, for two years (Yugen ran until 1962). It was later in 1960 that he visited Cuba to demonstrate support for Fidel Castro. His poem Preface to a Twenty-Volume Suicide Note was published by Corinth Books in 1961, the same year that he became an instructor at the New School for Social Research and a contributing editor to Diane di Prima's The Floating Bear. In 1962 he took the post of music editor for Kulchur and continued to write his columns on jazz until 1964. It was during these years that LeRoi Jones was writing his first important plays—Dutchman, The Toilet, and The Slave (all first produced in 1964).

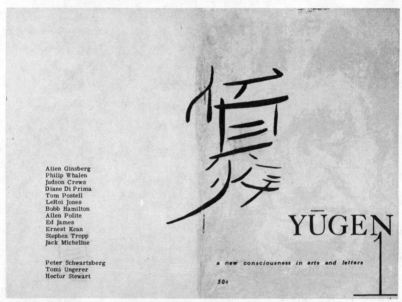

Yugen, *Vol. 1, No. 1, 1958 (courtesy Northwestern University Library).*

Yours seems to be one of the three or four "clique" magazines around today, in that it publishes a fairly restricted group of so-called "Beat," "San Francisco," and "New York" writers. Why do you publish this group—this "stable" of writers?

Well, it does seem to fall that way. But for a long time Dr. Williams couldn't get into the *Hudson Review,* and several other mature, older poets like Kenneth Patchen were never admitted there, or in magazines like the *Partisan Review* or *Sewanee.* If those editors had a literary point of view in excluding their work, then I feel I have as much right, certainly, to base my choice on my literary taste. If it seems like a coterie—well, it turns out to be that way. There are other reasons—but that's the simplest explanation, actually.

The writers that I publish are really not all "Beat" or "San Francisco" or "New York." There are various people who could also fit into other groups—for instance, the people who went to Black Mountain College—and others not affiliated with any real group. But they have some kind of affinity with the other so-called groups—their writing fits into a certain kind of broad category.

Many of the same names appear regularly in Yugen, Big Table, Evergreen . . .

It's a little different though. Most of the people whom, say, Paul Carroll prints, he wouldn't have printed if it hadn't been for a magazine like *Yugen.* And *Evergreen Review,* to a great extent, has picked up on things that I've done already and that have appeared in magazines like the *Black Mountain Review* and *Neon.* They pick them up. As a matter of fact, in Paul Carroll's case, I know of at least two poets who appear in his magazine only because of various things he saw in *Yugen* and in an essay I wrote. He said he picked up some things in that essay that enabled him to understand, or become more sympathetic with, certain people's work.

I'd like to have your thoughts on a kind of contemporary writing that could be illustrated by Frank O'Hara's "Personal Poem" in Yugen 6. *In it he describes his thoughts before and after having*

This interview is reprinted from a collection of interviews with modern poets by David Ossman called *The Sullen Art,* published by Corinth Books in 1963.

lunch with one "LeRoi." With its highly and specifically personal references, it seems to be more an anecdote of interest to future scholars than something partaking of the heightened qualities of a more traditional poetic nature. What is the validity in this kind of writing?

I didn't especially think that there was any charted-out area in which the poetic sensibility had to function to make a poem. I thought that anything—anything you could grab—was fit material to write a poem on. That's the way I think about it. Anything in your life, anything you know about or see or understand, you could write a poem about if you're moved to do it. I'm certain that if they have to footnote what the House of Seagrams was in his poem, or who the LeRoi was, that will only be of interest to academicians and people doing master's theses. Anybody who is concerned with the *poem* will get it on an emotional level—or they won't get it at all. Certainly, if I didn't like it, I wouldn't go through any book to look up those names with the hope that I would feel moved once I knew where the building was or who LeRoi was. I don't think that means anything at all. I don't think that has anything to do with the *poem*, actually. What the poem means, its function, doesn't have to do with those names—that's just part of it. It doesn't seem to me to be the same kind of stupidity that's found when you have to go to Jessie Weston's book to find out what a whole section of "The Waste Land" means. The House of Seagrams is certainly less obscure than certain Celtic rites. And I don't see what makes it any less valid because it's a casual kind of reference or that it comes out of a person's life, rather than, say, from his academic life.

I'd say that if a poem, as a whole *poem, works, then it's a good poem. . . .*

Right. . . .

You once wrote that, "MY POETRY is whatever I think I am. I make a poetry with what I feel is useful and can be saved out of all the garbage of our lives." Would you like to develop that a little more fully?

Well, it's part of what you mentioned about "traditional" poetic areas. I believe that the poet—someone with a tempered sensibility

320

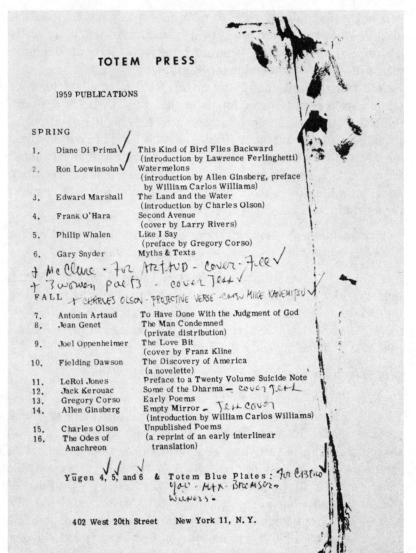

TOTEM PRESS

1959 PUBLICATIONS

SPRING

1. Diane Di Prima — This Kind of Bird Flies Backward
   (introduction by Lawrence Ferlinghetti)
2. Ron Loewinsohn — Watermelons
   (introduction by Allen Ginsberg, preface
   by William Carlos Williams)
3. Edward Marshall — The Land and the Water
   (introduction by Charles Olson)
4. Frank O'Hara — Second Avenue
   (cover by Larry Rivers)
5. Philip Whalen — Like I Say
   (preface by Gregory Corso)
6. Gary Snyder — Myths & Texts

+ McClure - for Artaud - cover - free
+ 3 women poets - cover text
+ Charles Olson - Projective Verse - cover Mike Kanemitsu

FALL

7. Antonin Artaud — To Have Done With the Judgment of God
8. Jean Genet — The Man Condemned
   (private distribution)
9. Joel Oppenheimer — The Love Bit
   (cover by Franz Kline)
10. Fielding Dawson — The Discovery of America
    (a novelette)
11. LeRoi Jones — Preface to a Twenty Volume Suicide Note
12. Jack Kerouac — Some of the Dharma *— cover text*
13. Gregory Corso — Early Poems
14. Allen Ginsberg — Empty Mirror *— text cover*
    (introduction by William Carlos Williams)
15. Charles Olson — Unpublished Poems
16. The Odes of — (a reprint of an early interlinear
    Anachreon — translation)

Yūgen 4, 5, and 6 & Totem Blue Plates: *for Castro*
you - Max - Bremser -
winners -

402 West 20th Street   New York 11, N. Y.

Totem Press, 1959 list of publications (courtesy Gilbert Sorrentino).

—is able, or should be able, to take almost any piece of matter, idea, or whatever, and convert it, if he can, into something really beautiful. I don't mean "beautiful" the way Bernard Berenson means it—but into something moving, at least.

And I don't think that there are any kind of standard ideas or sentiments or emotions or anything that have to be in a poem. A poem can be made up of anything so long as it is well made. It can be made up out of any feeling. And if I tried to cut anything out of my life—if there was something in my life that I couldn't talk about . . . it seems monstrous that you can tell almost anything about your life except those things that are most intimate or mean the most to you. That seems a severe paradox.

You've mentioned your influences as including Lorca, Creeley, and Olson. What from Lorca—a surrealist approach?

Yes, that, but at the time I got hold of Lorca, I was very much influenced by Eliot, and reading Lorca helped to bring me out of my "Eliot period" and break that shell—not so much *Poet in New York*, which is the more surreal verse, but the early *Gypsy Ballads* —that kind of feeling and exoticism.

What about the Black Mountain people, and Williams?

From Williams, mostly how to write in my own language—how to write the way I *speak* rather than the way I *think* a poem ought to be written—to write just the way it comes to me, in my own speech, utilizing the rhythms of speech rather than any kind of metrical concept. To talk verse. Spoken verse. From Pound, the same concepts that went into the Imagists' poetry—the idea of the image and what an image ought to be. I learned, probably, about verse from Pound—how a poem should be made, what a poem ought to *look* like—some little inkling. And from Williams, I guess, how to get it out in my own language.

Is there a middle ground between natural speech and formal metrics?

Oh, yes. I don't mean that I write poems completely the way I'm talking now, although I'm certain that a great deal of my natural voice rhythm dominates the line. For instance, my breathing— when I have to stop to inhale or exhale—dictates where I have to break the line in most cases. Sometimes I can bring the line out longer for effect—you learn certain tricks, departures from a set method. But mostly it's the *rhythms* of speech that I utilize, trying to get closer to the way I sound *peculiarly*, as opposed to somebody else.

Does your being a Negro influence the speech patterns—or anything else, for that matter, in your writing?

It could hardly help it. There are certain influences on me, as a Negro person, that certainly wouldn't apply to a poet like Allen Ginsberg. I couldn't have written that poem "Kaddish," for instance. And I'm sure he couldn't write certain things that have to deal with, say, Southern Baptist church rhythms. Everything applies—everything in your life. Sociologically, there are different influences, different things that I've seen, that I know, that Allen or no one knows.

I asked that because I don't find in your work the sense of "being a Negro" that occurs, say, in the poetry of Langston Hughes. . . .

That may be part of, like they say, his "stance." You have to set up a certain area in which you're going to stand and write your poems, whether you do it consciously or not. There has to be that stance. He is a Negro. It doesn't lessen my feeling of being a Negro—it's just that that's not the way I write poetry. I'm fully conscious all the time that I am an American Negro, because it's part of my life. But I know also that if I want to say, "I see a bus full of people," I don't have to say, "I am a Negro seeing a bus full of people." I would deal with it when it has to do directly with the poem, and not as a kind of broad generalization that doesn't have much to do with a lot of young writers today who are Negroes. (Although I don't know that many.) It's always been a separate section of writing that wasn't quite up to the level of the other writing. There were certain definite sociological reasons for it before the Civil War or in the early part of the twentieth century, or even in the 30s, but it's a new generation now, and people are beset by other kinds of ideas that don't have much to do with sociology, per se.

I'm always aware, in anything I say, of the "sociological configuration"—what it *means* sociologically. But it doesn't have anything to do with what I'm writing at the time.

A BACKWARD GLANCE
O'ER BEATNIK ROADS
Krim

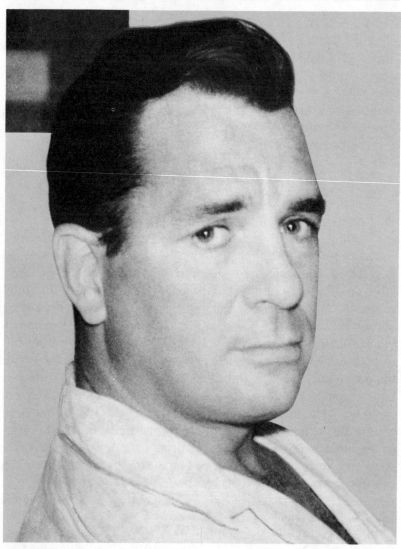

Jack Kerouac (the Bettmann Archive).

*In 1941, at the age of nineteen (Seymour) Krim worked as a re-
porter for* The New Yorker's *"Talk of the Town" column. That
magazine became his chief model for excellence—though not
necessarily for subject matter—when, twenty years later, he edited*
Swank *(specifically a "Beat Writing" section within that girlie
magazine) and* Nugget. *Mr. Krim's career as a reporter, critic,
essayist, short story writer, poet, anthologist, editor, and teacher
has been varied. Perhaps best known for his personal essays collected in three volumes—*Views of a Nearsighted Cannoneer
(1961), Shake It for the World, Smartass *(1970), and* You & Me
*(1974)—he has also edited two collections—*The Beats *(1960),
one of the most comprehensive anthologies of Beat writings ever
produced, and* Manhattan: Stories of a Great City *(1954). His
essays, reviews, and stories have appeared in dozens of magazines
and newspapers, including, among others,* Cosmopolitan, The
Evergreen Review *(for which he has served as a consulting editor),*
Playboy, The Smith, Vogue, The Village Voice, Newsday, *and the*
Washington Post. *He was awarded a Guggenheim fellowship in
1976. He lives in New York City.*

Looking back at the Beat Gen. as I puff and snort forward—for
I'm deep into a present-tense chronicle about the country called
Chaos [sic!] which, for sure, gets some of its impetus from Beat
style—I'm amused by our open-fly radical innocence in those late
fifties days but heartened by our courage. More was promised
than was accomplished, I guess, but the accomplishments themselves (still open to debate) generated much energy, passion, turn-
on, camaraderie, faith—essential human things that are good in
themselves even if your cause ends up dead on the Mexican
border as Neil Cassady did. But let me explain my relationship
to all this before editorializing.

I had been a New York Jewish satellite of the *Partisan Review*
gang up to 1955, when I had a crashing breakdown, brought on
as much by trying to parse *Finnegans Wake* and Marx's *Das
Kapital* and make some kind of amalgam as by having a lousy
emotional/sex life. As a "middle-aged young writer"—actually
thirty-three—I was kept in a constant state of anxiety and dependence by the terrifying amount of scholarship that the T. S.

Eliot/Lionel Trilling combine demanded: always reading like a desperate man instead of writing like one, which is really more interesting. My position and condition were not unique, unfortunately. One was afraid of using one's own voice at that time. More to the point, it was despairingly hard to get a hearing for that voice unless it was studded with a kind of modern formalism backed to the hilt by the most knowledgeable of the university-sponsored "little" mags, like the *Sewanee Review*, the *Kenyon*, the independent but Princeton-incubated *Hudson Review,* and of course the hiply hybrid *Partisan Review,* where my early Greenwich Village friends and gurus like Isaac Rosenfeld, Saul Bellow, Delmore Schwartz, William Barrett, Weldon Kees, Manny Farber, Anatole Broyard, Willie Poster, etc., etc., published and held sway in downtown N.Y. literary society.

Young men and women my own age who had simply wanted to be lyric, realistic U.S. novelists, as I did, were tied into knots by the inhibitions and inferiorities brought about in the mind by our uncomfortableness with Kafka, Karl Jaspers, Rex Warner—name your own nemesis!—that whole slew of tantalizing foreign intellects who were suddenly dumped on us as the Standard. I actually have come to love the pure, martyred Franz, and I'm oversimplifying the complexities of all the issues involved to get to the crucial point: that we had the bad luck to come of age in a rabidly intellectual, criticism-dominated period when our native juices wanted to pour out rather than stew. I, and no doubt others, stewed so long and so unfruitfully that we finally exploded one way or the other: I into creative paralysis, psychoanalysis, a couple of sanitariums, and the slow climb back—but up another road—and Allen Ginsberg into *Howl*, Kerouac into *On the Road*, Corso into *Fried Shoes*, and Burroughs into *Naked Lunch*.

After so much choking repression, explosion was inevitable. You would never think of tremblingly gentle, humane men like Eliot and his disciples (Trilling, Tate, Blackmur, John Crowe Ransom, et al) as dictators in any sense, but that's the way they operated in the tight little world of upper American letters until young writers more confident than myself took their own bull by the horns—even call it bullshit, in some cases, and it was still exciting!—and just threw it where it landed. Such recklessness was needed; a better word or words might be abandonment, range, expressionism, risk, all the neo-romantic qualities that had been sanitized for the preceding ten years and now broke loose like fire hydrants on a sweltering Harlem street. Well, as you can imagine, the howls at the university English departments and their surrogates, the big little mags, were loud and contemptuous, but the effect on those of us who had been held captive by these invisible mental chains of inferiority and self-denigration was immediate. We started rushing out our own work on the wave of free energy that the Four Big Beats—Ginsberg, Kerouac, Corso, and Burroughs, hottest group in town—kicked off, and we started improvising the original counterculture apparati to carry and promote that work. It was a Civil War atmosphere, and we were the outnumbered but bloodcurdling rebs.

In my own case, I could no longer go back to the kind of Thomas Wolfean fictional innocence I had once loved—after such knowledge, what forgiveness? But I did bat out a series of personal gut pieces and published them in a true home-made underground press rather than hawk them uptown. We called the book *Views of a Nearsighted Cannoneer* and actually made enough money to pay ourselves back, because the literary counterculture had by now, in 1961, created its own audience. Jack Gelber wrote *The Connection,* and the youthful, Beat-oriented, not-then-so political Living Theater put it on at 14th Street and 6th Avenue, with great Establishment-uptight success. That Bronx bull Jack Micheline wrote *River of Red Wine,* published it privately, and came out a winner. The same with many gung-ho writers of the time who found friends or instant publishers to put their work into pamphlets or broadsides, including Dan Propper, Erje Ayden, Jack Green, Tuli Kupferberg, Ted Joans, Ray Bremser, Joel Oppenheimer, Fielding Dawson, Diane di Prima, Gil Sorrentino, LeRoi Jones (his pre-black-militant handle), Hubert Selby, etc. It's also important to keep in mind that when this burst of anti-authority energy began to surface in waves between, say, 1957 and 1963, strong writers who had already made a name for themselves independent of the Beats—people like Mailer, poets Frank O'Hara and Robert Creeley, even the young newspaperman Tom Wolfe—joined in the fun as honorary members, with some of the beatnik style rubbing off on them at the time. As a matter of fact, I see the New Journalism (especially the Hunter Thompson–Tom Wolfe wing) coming out of the Beat explosion, although not on a direct route. Practically every under-forty American writer was slightly infected by the spirit and lingo, even if it didn't stick. And not only writers; the Beat assault released a new gang of amateur publishers and impresarios in a hurry.

My *Cannoneer* was published by Marty Geisler, a brash young guy who ran a chain of paperback bookshops—a handy operation when you're publishing—but he gave up after a couple of years when the Beat energy began to flag. Julian Beck's and Judith Malina's Living Theater did Gelber's play and later Ken Brown's *The Brig,* but then they went deeper and deeper into the anarchistic-political bag that's become their trademark. The dedicated Ted Wilentz, friend of literally hundreds of Beats and then co-owner of the 8th St. Bookshop, founded the Croyden Press, which is now mostly a backlist. Out on the Coast, Lawrence Ferlinghetti was a prototypical artist-publisher force of the time; one of the best of the Beat poets, he also published Allen G.'s *Howl* and then Mailer's *The White Negro,* plus a lot of other first-rate stuff, with his City Lights Books. Of course, Kerouac and Ginsberg were active all over the place as influences and lobbyists for Beat writing, with the highly imaginative Kerouac christening the dissident U. of Chicago's literary mag, *The Big Table.* It served up some exotic goodies under the editorship of Irving (*Sheeper*) Rosenthal before the university disowned it. Some of the other magazines that came and went with great fanfare were *Neon, Beatitude,* LeRoi Jones's *Yugen,* Ferlinghetti's *City Lights Journal, The Black Mountain Review,* my own ragtag *Provincetown Review* (Bill Ward was the editor, I his evil genius), and a slew of others that have momentarily gone down the drain of memory. All of them were touched by the Beat rhythm, although a number hated the name; don't forget, it was the time of "Beatnik for Hire" ads and other caricatures. I want to go into this in a moment, but first I'll point to one publication that stuck and prospered: *The Village Voice,* founded in 1955, a year before Gins's breakthrough reading of *Howl* in S. F. There would have been no *Voice,* in my opinion, without the Beat energy, just as there would have been no New Journalism. We didn't know that at the time, but as I look back they all seem to tie together at one of those pregnant points in history where a lot of forces are blindly converging to say, "Enough already! This is the direction we have to turn to for our souls' sake!"

Now that we have some perspective that we didn't have between

328

1957 and 1965, when the Beat thing had finally spent itself or at least metamorphosed into hippiedom, it's best to see the label as a looser one than we originally took it to be; or at least to make a distinction between the Beat freaks on the street and those behind the typewriter, who would share a joint with the first in a pinch but that's about all. Writers like Oppenheimer, Sorrentino, Dawson, the powerful Selby, Jones (Imamu Baraka today) refused the Beat label with indignation and thought the childishness of the primitive "like, man" beatniks was an insult to their seriousness. Yet even if they resisted the tag, they too were caught up in the special manic *doing* which was generated by the unclassifiable presence of Kerouac and the inexhaustible activities of Ginsberg, who was more strategically conscious about what he was up to than J. K. (my belief) and had the model of Ezra Pound in mind. Nevertheless, between the two of them, along with ballsy mascot Corso and guru Bill Burroughs, the time was one of almost fierce activity with a heroic attempt to erase the line between play and achievement.

Coming back to your reporter here, I was exactly Kerouac's age—born in 1922—and older than most of the turned-on writers and editors in the movement; that is, I was more interested in taking this new style and vision into the larger world and making converts. While it's true that Ginsberg and Corso were highly media-conscious, picketing Brentano's in Paris in the late fifties for not stocking their work and making such a row that they got on TV, Kerouac was really a more brooding and withdrawn guy underneath the Gary Grayson looks *(Gary Grayson Goes to Yale, etc.)*, and Burroughs was "a wheel that rolled uphill" in Bing Crosby's great autobiographical line—that is, he just got there on his own mysterious forces without pressing. And by the way, Ginsberg's smarts in handling the media were to affect young hipsters of a more political generation, like Abbie Hoffman and Jerry Rubin. Hippie media manipulation, with Abbie burning ten-dollar bills in the N. Y. Stock Exchange to the true horror of the brokers, got its virginal start with Allen and Corso; Kerouac played a tortured part—after all, he was the all-American-looking star—but my bottom feeling was that he was always ambivalent about the camera and the microphone, especially in his bitter last days; while Burroughs, the great cool freak, just did his appearances as he brushed his teeth, with no emotion and no

Above: Lawrence Ferlinghetti, poet and Proprietor of City Lights Books, San Francisco. Opposite, top: poets Gary Snyder (left) and Allen Ginsberg; bottom: poet Peter Orlovsky (standing) with brother Julius at the Ginsberg/ Orlovsky farm, Cherry Valley, N.Y. Photographs by Gerard Malanga.

Above: William Burroughs in front of Burroughs Corporation Headquarters, N.Y.C. Opposite, top: author Brion Gysin (left) and William Burroughs; bottom: Charles Bukowski (foreground), with his publisher, John Martin of Black Sparrow Press. Photographs by Gerard Malanga.

aggressive desire for attention—which Allen and Gregory definitely had.

Anyway, being older, coming from a hell of a different background, I saw my job, after *Cannoneer* came out, as one of ambassadorial negotiation from the downtown world to the uptown one. There were a couple of others who felt the same. Barney Rosset, another Taurus born within a couple days of me—however criticized in later years for making bucks out of porn when it was just that he was fascinated by sex in every conceivable shape and form—joined hands with the sharp editor Don Allen and turned *Evergreen Review* into a great forum for Beat writing. Grove Press, the parent outfit, also joined to some extent, although its commitment was not as total as the magazine's. Out in Venice, California, Lawrence Lipton, older than Rosset and myself by at least twenty years, also took up the torch and produced *The Holy Barbarians* and a lot of journalism for Art Kunkin's *Los Angeles Free Press* as pro-Beat propaganda. In my opinion his effectiveness was cut down by his personal power play with the whole thing—he's now dead—but there's no denying that he was a remarkably crisp and formidable partisan, a holy terror, right to the end. I don't think we've heard the last of Lipton. Finally there was James Laughlin, the founder of *New Directions* who had already published the great money-losing moderns when nobody else would touch them, and he too was still young enough in heart to publish Corso, Bob Kaufmann (a rare half-Jew, half-black famous in my world for the *Abombunist Manifesto*), Kerouac and even Cassady, the legendary coast-to-coast driver whose nonstop rap was word-music to two generations, Kerouac's and then Ken Kesey's.

So. To get the word out to the masses, and also to make a buck but not much more, I did the anthology *The Beats,* brought out by the hard-boiled adventure line of Gold Medal Books (half my contributors greeted the project with suspicion and I don't blame them), and we went into two editions with the writers sharing the bread. Years later I would meet members of the hippie generation who said that this gaudily packaged parcel of what I believe was the real thing had stung their Texas or Ohio eyes like a can of Mace. I want to believe them. Then—for the Cause and for a living, and they get more confused and harder to separate as you go along!—I edited a "Beat Section" for the girlie mag *Swank* and then moved my operation to the more classily tits-and-assed *Nugget* from 1961 to 1965. Along the way, right between the legs of the photos you might say, we published Kerouac, Ginsberg, Mailer, di Prima, O'Hara, Selby, Terry Southern, John Clellon Holmes, Al Aronowitz *(The New York Post* reporter most trusted by the increasingly wary, even paranoid Beat figures), Chandler Brossard—just about everybody now in their late forties or fifties who was closely or even tangentially connected with the Beat impact.

By the time 1965 rolled around, the Beat nucleus had splintered. Ginsberg bought a farm in Cherry Valley, N. Y., and tried to pump some physical and moral health back into poets like Corso and Ray Bremser who were strung out on drugs. Burroughs was living in London. Kerouac was hiding out from a new Beat/hippie world he said he'd never made, and *Nugget* went under. Casualties on every side!

That was the end of my explicit involvement with Beat publishing and editing; but the fact that the next thing I did was join the *New York Herald Trib* on a dare as a general assignment reporter (at the age of forty-three and did a pretty good job, too, until the paper folded in April 1966) has a lot to do with the entire Beat phenom, and I'd like to talk about that before winding down this very informal Remembrance of Flings Past, and certainly the Beat era was one long terrific spree that nonetheless was damn serious at the pit of it all. The Beats, wittingly or not, did a lot to break down the iron lines separating poetry from prose, and fiction from nonfiction, and the big go-for-broke book I'm finally getting around to now upholds all these experiments twenty years later. So it couldn't have been all foam and noise, unless I am a prime sucker who is just rehashing a novelty from the past. Dan Wolf, who started *The Village Voice* in 1955 and in his own way added to the new beat of the Beats, used to say with a certain amount of embattled sourness that he wasn't running a damn "little magazine" when some of the late fifties writers for the *Voice,* including myself, would take high-flying liberties with an ordinary fact piece. True, he was running a weekly newspaper with a very crackling political slant, but after the Beat radiations got into his more polemical climate you couldn't tell the difference. Journalism as well as standard literary prose was shaken with new, even previously undreamed-of, possibilities. I don't want to exaggerate, but there was a line of descent that the Beats tapped which had been squeezed out of the ordinary decent writer's thinking before then. As Dan Wakefield once said in a review of Kerouac's *Desolation Angels,* it was all repressed primary American stuff, with roots in the rebelliousness of Whitman and Huck Finn and Henry Miller, to just touch on one of the main Beat streams; the other, not as significant to me, was surrealist and French contraband brought in by Burroughs and Ginsberg from people as diverse as Céline, Gide, Rimbaud, Mallarmé, and God knows who else, but it was all pegged on very down-home American experience. The fact that I could go into daily newspaper work from my original elitist ass-licking with the *Partisan Review* crowd is a testimony (to me) of the really big democratizing influence of the Beats. When Tom Wolfe in what is probably his best book, *The Electric Kool-Aid Acid Test,* mixes poetry and prose and information and sound waves and light waves, all reduced to little ole words themselves, he is paying tender respects to the Beats. And when Karl Shapiro turned his back on his own Pulitzer Prize (I believe it was), given for the traditional rhymes of *V-Letter & Other Poems,* and paid his deeper respects to the old uncrowned king of crotch, Henry Miller, and the young swanker Tom Wolfe—catching fire for it too—he was doffing a nice, real, character-crushed fedora to the Beats and the changes they had brought about in his head.

Well, I have to turn mine back to what's right here in front of us now—more crazy experience than we can utter, I'll bet, which is fittin' for game American writers to tackle!—and let the past take care of itself. Much was done back then, I admit it, that has faded away: mags and instant publishers and half-sincere promoters and poetry-and-jazz ephemera—which owed much to the previous generation's neglected Kenneth Patchen, by the way —and even writers (among the honored dead are Kerouac, Frank O'Hara, and Paul Blackburn so far). But a lot has survived in all the underground papers in this country and abroad; in the experiments of the New Journalism, especially Hunter Thompson and Tom W.; in the New York School of poetry, some of it; in Dylan and Bruce Springsteen and Patti Smith and a good slice of white rock and even the storytelling bluegrass sound; in the best of the so-called counterculture, from *The Greening of America* (the Beats really wanted to make it bloom) to the Carlos Castenada books, which Kerouac would have loved and which actually have a precedent in Burroughs' *Yage Letters* to Allen G. from some dope-infested little mystery country in Central America where Explorer Bill went to get high and have visions—went to learn guarded knowledge, to put it simply. All these things are still alive and kicking today, what more can you ask?

As for myself, in my own lengthening years I've reached the point of being on the road in quest of honest fulfillment where I'm no longer quite the same kind of God-will-provide literary romantic as in the old days. I've paid my dues, at least for myself. I'd like to make a decent living from my work for a change and tell post-Beat truths in the likes of such commercial formats as *The New Yorker* and *Esquire* and *Time* (what could be more American?), so that every regular, literate, equally questing average/unaverage Joe and Jill can be exposed to what I was taught right off. I guess I've been popularized all the way from my underground beginnings in the trenches, but I'm not ashamed. My type is known as a survivor, I think, and we can't afford it. Hell, I look forward to what might be the Beat Gen.'s last grand illusion (we were always optimists when you get down to it) without any sense of betrayal to those who gave their best in the last twenty years to make the likes of me now.

Krim. Photograph by Sy Johnson.

ANOTHER LESSO
WAS THAT COLLECTIVE
THE GREATEST INITIAL E
DRAWBACKS. IN FACT
TO THINK THAT MOR
PUBLICATIONS H
BY THE MULTIP
IN THE LITERAR
ANY OTHER

I ALSO LEARNED
EDITORSHIP, EVEN WITH
THUSIASM, HAS DREADFUL
I SHOULD BE INCLINED
INITIALLY PROMISING
VE BEEN RUINED
CITY OF LADIES
BROTH THAN BY
NGLE CAUSE.

—GEORGE HITCHCOCK

Peter Michelson (courtesy University of Colorado).

ON <u>THE PURPLE SAGE</u>, <u>CHICAGO REVIEW</u>, AND <u>BIG TABLE</u>
Peter Michelson

When Peter Michelson began working as an assistant editor for The Chicago Review *in 1961, he says he was "in a state of inno-cence too embarrassing to describe. . . . I knew a bit of the two contending poetry anthologies: Hall, Pack, and Simpson's* New Poets of England and America *and Donald Allen's* New American Poetry. *The latter, more self-consciously shouldering its way into the poetry world, was especially significant, introducing me both to new poetry and to new critical approaches. Grove Press and* The Evergreen Review *mattered a lot. Also, for reasons now obscure to me, I recall liking* Contact, The Outsider, *and* The Tulane Drama Review." *Mr. Michelson writes that as a young editor he was "naively eclectic," and that he learned most from a study of the history of* The Chicago Review, *whose editorial range included the experimental (William Burroughs), the academic (Hazel Barnes), and "pop" (Walt Kelly).*

By the time he accepted a position at the University of Wyoming in 1969 to edit The Purple Sage, *he had assimilated a variety of ideas and approaches. His decision to produce an intermedia pub-lication was based on his interest in such diverse art forms as concretism and sound poetry, as well as in such magazines as Henri Chopin's French* Revue ou, *and Dick Higgins' Something Else Press. "We were trying," Mr. Michelson notes, "by beating the bushes worldwide, and by providing a regular, albeit irregular, forum, to keep the energy and ideas flowing on all fronts. It was in a fair way toward working, too, until the sky fell." On literary experiment, he observes that as an editor he was quite consciously interested in being experimental, but that as a writer he has no particular commitment to experiment. "As an editor, experiment might well be an end in itself (though whether to publish is a more complicated matter), but as a writer I never think of experiment as an end. The thing to be written is the end, and any experiment (just as any theft from tradition) is a means of getting the job done right."*

Mr. Michelson's published work includes a critical volume, The Aesthetics of Pornography *(1971), and two collections of poems,* The Eater *(1973) and* Pacific Plainsong I–XIII *(1978). His poems and essays have appeared in a variety of magazines, including* TriQuarterly, The Chicago Review, The Nation, The New Republic, Oink, *and* Mojo Navigator(e). *He received a poetry grant from the National Endowment for the Arts in 1976.*

They may prefer one magazine to another, or mimeo mags to printed university slicks, but when it comes to the little magazine in general, writers great and obscure will talk it up like Little League infielders. Going into an aggressive crouch, they smack their mitts and chatter shameless tropes of praise—"the very heart of contemporary literature," "the cutting edge," "the avant-garde," "the pulse," etc. But my favorite is attributed to George Hitchcock of *Kayak.* Little magazines, says Hitchcock, are "the furnace where American literature is being forged." I like his industrial metaphor; it emphasizes the real center of things and implies a connection between little magazines and the workaday world. Also, there is a sense in which the flood of literary magazines does make up a kind of industry. Or perhaps counter-industry, since for many editors and writers little magazines and presses are an alternative to the conventional business of life.

The clinker, as everyone knows, is that, though small magazines have heroic production records, they can't market to save their souls. As *Coda,* the *Women's Wear Daily* of the trade, notes, there are three to ten producers of poetry, the little magazine's heaviest staple, for every buyer of little magazines. Moreover, the poets themselves apparently aren't buying. That they may not *read* either, as some commentators on the subject claim, is a prospect too dismal to contemplate. However that may be, in most industries this problem would correct itself in the obvious ways. Not so here. Wages being few and far between and profit nonexistent, deficit spending is the very nature of things, and the notion of an expanding market is an industry-wide joke. Not only that, but the worse the market gets, the more little magazines there seem to be. So how in the name of double-entry bookkeeping do these things survive?

That they are labors of love is obvious enough. But what does that mean in a culture where love is to labor what fish are to bicycles? What, besides making application for nonprofit status and government grants something of a national pastime, do little magazines provide that we should cultivate them so? By way of proposing an answer I take the liberty of shamelessly invoking not only autobiography but racial memory as well. And I begin with my father's father, whom neither I nor my father ever met except in print. My grandfather, a poet, was a friend and associate of Harriet Monroe, the archetype of little magazine editors, founder and for twenty-four years editor of *Poetry* magazine in Chicago. In her autobiography this is what she said about him:

Now and then . . . ambition was too insistent, delight in the art too absorbing, leading to bitter disappointments or some more tragic denial. Max Michelson, for example, was a little back-street Chicago furrier whose exquisite sensibility transcended the demands of his business. Our office, and the encouragement we gave his slow-working delicate talent, became gradually a necessity of life to him, and we found his quiet presence helpful in the routine of our work, and his judgment of new poets suggestive. His fur business was neglected more and more, orders were delayed beyond his customers' endurance, his patient lovable wife became profoundly discouraged, and all his friends were extremely anxious as it gradually seemed evident that his mind was weakening under the strain. At last his wife took their little child to her parents' home in Seattle, secured work there, and sent for him. He was as gentle as ever when I took him to the station and confided him to a sympathetic porter, but soon after his arrival in Seattle a mental hospital had to be his refuge.

Max lived in that hospital—an incurable paranoid schizophrenic "haunted by voices," his records say—until he died, about 1953. For the last thirty-eight years of his life he lived quietly, it seems, tending the hospital farm, violent only when recalling the outside world. His last contribution to *Poetry* was in 1921, from the hospital. A 1925 note from Sara, his wife (who died when I was a small child), to Harriet Monroe remarks a collection of now lost manuscripts. After that there is no indication he wrote anything whatsoever. I can't say which half of his life was better, though I've always felt Lear was on the mark when he said, "I would not be mad." But then how clear are one's real-life choices? Did Max know, for example, that his "exquisite sensibility" was irreconcilable with the "demands of his business"? One story has it that, just before Max's madness came on, Ezra Pound had offered him a "job" with *The Egoist,* the magazine with which Pound and Eliot were connected in London; and that, it seems, was the straw that broke the back of sanity. If this is so—Max did review Pound's early work appreciatively in *Poetry,* and *The Egoist* did publish poems by Max—doesn't it confirm what Harriet Monroe says, that poetry became a "necessity of life to him"? And isn't Pound's own much-disputed madness a sign of the inevitable tension between aesthetic and economic necessity? On two levels, then, we may say *Poetry* gave Max a lease on life. For a time, at least, it allowed him his "exquisite sensibility," which is obviously where his real life was. And it also makes my own history—or racial memory— accessible. In this very personal sense, then, I think little magazines give life to both the individual and the collective psyche. If that seems opaque, return with me to the 1950s, the heroic age of contemporary poetry, to 1958 and the unlikeliest of places: Laramie, Wyoming.

Laramie is located roughly halfway between Seattle and Chicago —that is, between the place where Max began his life (which actually was Lithuania, a fact irrelevant to the symmetry of my story) and where he ended it. And since the University of Wyoming is located in Laramie, and it was there I first saw Max's name in *Poetry* and thus had my first tangible sense of his being, I think it was something more than accident that directed me to Laramie. This man—whose son knew only vaguely that he had written some poetry and had died in an "asylum" (I believe that he was, in fact, still alive and not more than fifty miles away at the time this information was passed on to me)—turned out to be, however minor, a historical figure. Was his historicity—my myth, if you will—a document in the life of poetry, or was poetry a document of his life? Certainly his only life for me is in *Poetry: A Magazine of Verse.* And, moreover, before then I had not even seen a little magazine. But willy-nilly my karma was upon me, at the propitious age of twenty-one. And, as if to give an imprimatur, the University of Wyoming's now long-defunct student literary magazine published a story of mine.

That story was about my brother, in reality my half-brother and no kin to Max at all. So from the beginning little magazines have been for me a romance, in which I both found and tried to shape the iconography of a complex past and present that simultaneously were and were not mine. Of course I didn't understand myself to be doing anything of the sort. Nevertheless the powers in charge sent me to North Dakota for seasoning, to teach, coach the debate team, and be the line coach for the Jamestown College football team. Even in North Dakota the contemplative life had its distractions. But a good angel, in the form of John R. Milton (now editor of the *South Dakota Review*), awaited me, a copy of *Big Table* 1 in his left hand, his own mimeographed magazine, *Plainsong,* in his right. He had a hypothesis that American writing done west of the Mississippi, the sort he preferred, tended to be Jungian, while that done east of the Mississippi inclined to be Freudian. "Here," he said with a resigned shrug, "maybe *you* can make sense of this," and handed me his copy of *Big Table.* This was 1959, and in fact I could not make much sense of Kerouac's "Old Angel Midnight" or Burroughs' "Naked Lunch," and only a little of Dahlberg's "Further Sorrows of Priapus" and perhaps a bit more of some poems by Corso. Remember, I still thought that little magazines spontaneously generated themselves in somber black bindings on library shelves. I didn't know that living people made and wrote them. *Big Table* was news to me. So I just gazed eastward across those infinite Dakota plains and wondered what the hell was going on at the far side of the horizon.

True, I had heard of Kerouac, if only to have his grammar denounced at great length by a professor of mine. Even I, however, knew that something more than grammatical finesse was at stake. I had nothing like a world view, so it suffered no rudeness at the hands of Burroughs and company, but they certainly helped me eventually to recognize that if, as F. R. Leavis (who was then very big in the academy) contended, Jane Austen was alpha and omega of "the great tradition," then the great tradition was not my dish of figs. And that, though it may not seem like much, meant there was *an alternative;* it was, when I finally caught on, as if Galileo had just invented the telescope. Bemused, I kept my own counsel and gazed eastward across the infinite Dakota plains. My naked lunch was on a back burner, simmering. Meanwhile I began experimenting with some poems, and Milton published them, crude as they were, in his magazine, *Plainsong.*

I don't know how *Big Table* made its way to the middle of North

Dakota. But its coincidence there with me had to be also more than accidental. For one thing, as if to jog my karmic recollection, the magazine was published in Chicago. Moreover, it was born out of the suppression of the *Chicago Review,* which four years later I would edit. So, while I watched the deer and antelope play on the great high plains, it was more than mere idle curiosity that made me wonder what was going on at horizon's edge. Heavy karma was coming down in Chicago.

It was a staging area for the Beat revolt from the great tradition. The Beat wars against the academy (though in fact they were against the middle-class taste for which the academy had become apologist and preserver) were fought in two ways. They began in the oblique guerrilla-like spiritual life described in Kerouac's *The Dharma Bums.* But as the Beats got more artillery—the notoriety of Kerouac's and Ginsberg's work, for example—they raised the ante and began to engage the academy head-on in the urban university areas (San Francisco, Chicago, and New York), where they had grass-roots sympathy and support. From the start the academics were at a disadvantage because they either did not know or would not admit their role, which was to help conserve social order and contentment under the guise of maintaining immutable aesthetic standards. All right, said the Great Bald Eagle, maybe in the fickle, illusory world of reality we have to allow women to vote, property taxes, social security, labor unions, habeas corpus to Bolsheviks and malcontents, blacks to live wherever they like, and so on. Unpleasant, to be sure, and our hands are tied when the people get so feisty. But *Beauty,* there we draw the line! Things were further confounded when in the courts they were reduced to "obscenity." So the academics found themselves inextricably identified with either Victorian mores or authoritarian censorship or both. The Beats consequently caricatured them as either fools or Nazis. In any event, the Beats were successful and, like good revolutionaries, even turned apparent tactical defeats into strategic victory.* The *Chicago Review*–cum–*Big Table* war is a classical instance.

*So successful were they, in fact, that by 1972—a dozen years after their official entry into American literature via Donald Allen's anthology, *The New American Poetry*—they were building their own institution, the "Kerouac School of Disembodied Poetics," in Boulder, Colorado; and, like any academy, it is now being hounded by its own harpies of orthodoxy and conservatism.

Chicago Review, *Vol. 12, No. 3, Autumn 1598. The Irving Rosenthal–edited number contained the controversial chapter from* Naked Lunch *(courtesy Peter Michelson).*

While I sat in North Dakota wondering what went on east of the horizon, a copy of *Big Table* 1 dangling in my hand, this is what was going on. Irving Rosenthal, editor, and Paul Carroll, poetry editor, of *Chicago Review* had got wind of what has since come to be called the San Francisco renaissance. They excitedly set about gathering manuscripts from writers who were getting to be known as Beat. The Spring 1958 issue of *Chicago Review* was a special San Francisco number. It included work by Kerouac, Ferlinghetti, Ginsberg, Duncan, Wieners, McClure, Doyle, Lamantia, and Whalen and the first chapter of Burroughs' *Naked Lunch*. The Autumn 1958 issue featured Burroughs' second chapter, as well as prose by Whalen, poetry by Antoninus and Oppenheimer, and two brief but significantly articulate letters about the Beat movement by Allen Ginsberg. (Five years later, when I became editor of *Chicago Review,* Richard Stern, novelist and member of the University of Chicago faculty, was still distressed about the publication of those letters.) It also presented work by Chicago writers and artists, including Paul Carroll and John Logan, and the issue included essays by David Riesman and Hugh Kenner. Those were intelligent, lively, balanced issues. Moreover, in presenting *Naked Lunch,* the magazine was making history. But a Chicago columnist, Jack Mabley, got hold of the issue and promptly wrote an attack of the most nitwitted sort, challenging the trustees of the University of Chicago to put their house in order. (Albert Podell's detailed account of this episode in *San Francisco Review* 2, Spring 1959, does an especially nice job of dissecting the stupidity of Mabley's article.) The article was run on the front page of the *Chicago Daily News* under a banner headline, "Filthy Writing on the Midway." Keep in mind that this was 1958, in the wake of McCarthyism among other things, and the University of Chicago had not long before been on the public carpet for harboring communists. The administration was in no mood to take a smut rap. Moreover, the university fund-raisers complained that the *Chicago Review* publicity was making their jobs more difficult. Meanwhile Rosenthal and Carroll were going ahead with plans for their winter issue, presenting work by Kerouac, Dahlberg, Burroughs, and Corso. The image of the university was on the line, but its principles apparently were not. Administration and faculty both took a decisive stand against common sense and freedom of the press. The winter issue of the *Chicago Review* was suppressed.

BIG TABLE 1

\$1

THE COMPLETE CONTENTS OF THE SUPPRESSED WINTER 1959 CHICAGO REVIEW

JACK KEROUAC

OLD ANGEL MIDNIGHT

EDWARD DAHLBERG

THE GARMENT OF RA

FURTHER SORROWS OF PRIAPUS

WILLIAM S. BURROUGHS

NAKED LUNCH

AND POWER, ARMY, AND POLICE BY GREGORY CORSO

Big Table, *Vol. 1, No. 1, Spring 1959. Edited by Irving Rosenthal, it contained the contents of the suppressed Winter 1959* Chicago Review *(courtesy Peter Michelson).*

The Great Bald Eagle smiled. His boys were on the job. And they kept things admirably confused, so that nobody need have an embarrassingly clear perception of what had happened. The administration, headed by Lawrence Kimpton, simply asserted its power as publisher and got off the PR hook by putting its own house in order. It left explanations to its faculty. The faculty, not wanting to be impaled on smut censorship, invoked a variety of transparent evasions. The editors, they said, were narrow-minded, fiscally irresponsible, inflexible, too limited in taste, etc. But cut it as fine as you might, the simple fact was that the *Chicago Review* had been censored, and the faculty had facilitated censorship as agents of the administration. Though I didn't know it, dreamily innocent back there in Dakota, this was a karmic paradigm that was to hang over my head like Pigpen's dust cloud on several occasions in later years.

For their part, Rosenthal and Carroll were annoyed and baffled. They had done their job as they supposed, rightly, that it should be done. They had tracked down lively new writers and were giving them a hearing, and at the same time were responsive to tradition—though not, it's true, the formalist traditions then dominant in academic circles. They were confident they had found writing that was, whatever else, vivaciously real, a literature energized by its own time and place. Here was something new that mattered, and as editors they were adding it to the spectrum of possibilities. To do that, they supposed naively, was why the university subsidized the magazine. Wrong. As Rosenthal put it, "Mr. Kimpton does not want free expression at the University of Chicago; he wants money." So Rosenthal, Carroll, and four of the five remaining editors resigned from the *Chicago Review,* and on Christmas day 1958 they decided to make their own magazine, without subsidy or censorship, using the suppressed *Chicago Review* material for their first issue. The title came from Kerouac, who wired apocalyptically, "CALL IT BIG TABLE."

If the suppression of the *Chicago Review* was a defeat in the Beat wars with academe, the inception of *Big Table* was a stunning counterattack. And the Beats regained a solid beachhead in the Second City, giving them serious artillery installations coast to coast: *Evergreen Review,* Grove Press, and New Directions in New York; *Big Table* in Chicago; *Contact* and City Lights Books

350

in San Francisco. There was also the "sleeper," *Black Mountain Review,* and there were other outlets—*Yugen, Kulchur, Beatitude,* Jargon Books, *San Francisco Review*, etc.—but the former were the big guns, partly because they were consistently in the glare of obscenity litigation. "Thank God it was banned," Carroll later said of the Post Office impoundment of *Big Table* 1; "it made the magazine known to writers, and gave it some celebrity." Conceived in the censorship of the private sector, *Big Table* was swaddled in the censorship of public institutions. But such is the energy of contradiction that the greater the crunch from the top, the greater the possibility of the sides bursting all around. How else could I have gotten in North Dakota a copy of a magazine that was banned even as it was mailed in Chicago? The Post Office, however, impounded only four hundred copies, so some slipped by them into the hinterlands where innocents like myself were waiting. The Great Bald Eagle was not happy at that turn of events, so his Post Office minions placated him in timeless bureaucratic fashion, by neglecting to tell Rosenthal (who edited *Big Table* 1; Carroll edited subsequent issues) that the magazine had been impounded.

When Carroll, who was going ahead with *Big Table* 2, found out, he went to the Post Office and then the ACLU. The Post Office demanded that copy for *Big Table* 2 and subsequent issues be sent for prepublication inspection. The ACLU challenged the Post Office's authority to either impound or preview editorial matter, and requested a public hearing. It took a year to get the hearing, which had no legal authority but was necessary—such is the de facto clout of the Great Bald Eagle—in order for the ACLU to get the case to court. At the hearing, the Post Office offered August Derleth, book editor of a Sauk City, Wisconsin, newspaper, as its sole witness against the literary merit of *Big Table* 1. The ACLU presented a host of literary eminences, including Jacques Barzun, John Ciardi, Norman Mailer, and Lional Trilling, who testified to the contrary. Nevertheless the Post Office found *Big Table* 1 obscene and unfit for the mails. Getting into court took another year.

Meanwhile *Big Table*s 2 through 5 were being sent through the mail. The Post Office's passion to either preview or impound the magazine was held off by the ACLU while the trial was pending. The trial judge, ironically, was Julius S. Hoffman, who years later presided so infamously at the Chicago Seven conspiracy debacle. In this case, however, he consulted precedent judiciously and followed Judge John Woolsey's famous decision on Joyce's *Ulysses*. Of Kerouac's "Old Angel Midnight," which had baffled me, he commented that it was "a wild prose picnic . . . which seems to be some sort of dialogue, broadly, between God and Man." Of the episodes from Burroughs' *Naked Lunch* he said that they were "intended to shock contemporary society, in order perhaps to better point out its weaknesses and flaws." He concluded by citing Judge Woolsey: "Art certainly cannot advance under compulsion to traditional forms, and nothing in such a field is more stifling to progress than limitation of the right to experiment with a new technique." The Great Bald Eagle was miffed, to say the least, and spent the next nine years clouding Judge Hoffman's mind in preparation for his rendezvous with conspiracy. But history does not forget a moment of lucidity, when a judgment is free of the talons that make "e pluribus unum."

Even though it is chronologically out of order (for I am still in Dakota, remember, contemplating the horizon), I will comment on this matter of obscenity and law. It's not out of line with my subject in any case, because during the period of the late fifties and early sixties the little magazines and small presses carried most of the burden of resisting censorship, both institutional (e.g., *Chicago Review*, *Prairie Schooner*, *Northwest Review*, etc.) and civil (e.g., City Lights Books and Grove Press/*Evergreen Review*). As reasonable as were the decisions of such judges as Woolsey and Hoffman, they were nevertheless essentially wrongheaded. Like the professors who were conscripted to rationalize for the Great Bald Eagle's supersubtle machinations, these judges were manipulated into doing business not properly theirs. And in consequence they helped distract social energy and resources from the real issue. It is quite reasonable to distinguish literary from prurient obscenity, which is the basis of these decisions. But such deliberations sanction state authority where it ought not to be. As Justice William O. Douglas put it, the First Amendment "says in words that are unambiguous, 'Congress shall make no law . . . abridging the freedom of speech, or of the press. . . .' " The legal issue is therefore simple: no law means no law, and *some* abridgment is abridgment. Obscenity is a social problem, then, not a legal one. Citing Jefferson, Douglas hits the mark directly:

The way to prevent these [errors] of the people is to give them full information of their affairs through the channel of the public papers, and to contrive that those papers should penetrate the whole mass of the people. The basis of our governments being the opinion of the people, the very first object should be to keep that right.

In short, full information being imperative, the primary business of a democratic society should be to contrive that full information penetrate the whole mass of the people—through the media, government information agencies, social services, education and continuing education, etc. But this is precisely what the Great Bald Eagle contrives *against,* what with his Watergate caperings, his secret CIA/FBI budgets, files, and carryings-on, his multinational legerdemain, etc. Why spend our time splitting hairs: is this obscenity prurient? or this other socially redeeming? We must find ways to provide ourselves with the information necessary to withstand the obscenities, vulgarities, stupidities, and immoralities with which the big birds contrive our befuddlement.

Meanwhile (just as I am preparing to leave off contemplating the horizon and resume pursuit of my myth to Chicago, quite to the satisfaction of my now restless karma), after two years of hassle and litigation *Big Table* 1 was free to walk the streets. Also in that period, Carroll had produced four more issues, presenting a spectacular roll call of "new" American writers—Kerouac, Burroughs, Mailer, Corso, Ginsberg, Ferlinghetti, Bowles, Bro. Antoninus, Blackburn, Logan, O'Hara, Ashbery, Creeley, Koch, Duncan, Rechy, Wright, Dorn, etc. But more even than publication of specific individuals—it is no small credit, for example, that *Chicago Review* and *Big Table* were midwives to the birth of William Burroughs—*Big Table* had helped give shape to the Beat and Black Mountain "revolution" in poetics. It had, in short, done a damn good job—legally, socially, and aesthetically. And there it stopped, at *Big Table* 5. The reasons were, as one might expect, money and energy. But there was also something else, something perhaps unique to little magazines, especially those that burn hard and bright and briefly: a sense of organic completion. These decisions, as Carroll says, "are more complex, more human. . . . I might have simply reached the limit of what I was about; I went on with it until it seemed to reach its termination. And then, when it was time to stop, it was simply time to stop." The announcement, in *Big Table* 5, of Carroll's next projected issue—a symposium on "Post-Christian Man"—suggests that this indeed was so. After what had been going on in *Big Table*, Allen Tate, Russell Kirk, Paul Goodman, and William Phillips writing on "Post-Christian Man" would have had to seem too much like academic filler. And so it must have seemed to Carroll himself, for the symposium never appeared and *Big Table* was laid to rest with its integrity intact.

In a recent article in the *Nation,* Gene Lyons admonishes little magazines that they must "grow or die." His position has a logic, but it is not sufficiently understanding of the kamikaze character of at least one sort of little magazine, the sort of which *Big Table* is a classical example. It exists for a particular purpose; and when that is realized, part of its function is to die rather than go moribund. The history of little magazines is larded with examples—*The Egoist, Blast, Others, The Anvil, Yugen, Big Table, The Outsider,* to name but a few that come to mind and not even touch on the hundreds of mimeo or single-shot magazines that have come and gone. Little magazines cannot support themselves any more than little grocery stores can. Their vitality in part *depends upon* a short life span. Even for relatively long-lived magazines supported by institutions there is often a regular rate of editorial turnover. However, the different purposes of institutional and private magazines are more or less complementary. The expansion of taste effected by kamikaze magazines like *Big Table* is usually reflected subsequently by the more stable magazines, or even, as was the case with the Beat revolution, in commercial publishing. Aesthetic impact makes waves beyond the point of collision only if it hits hard enough, so it should be expected that many little magazines will have resources only for the one big shot. Every magazine of high impact, like *Big Table,* draws energy directly and indirectly from dozens of transient and obscure mimeo magazines. At the time *Chicago Review* and *Big Table* were "discovering" the San Francisco Beat, for example, North Beach was buzzing with obscure, now forgotten journals being hawked in bars and coffeehouses. They helped create the environment that encouraged the writing which was more widely broadcast by ambitious little magazines, until at last commercial publishers took it on and stamped it officially into American literature. In short, as in many ecological structures, the dying, the dead, and even the stillborn are essential to the life of the system. So there's no point in our lecturing little magazine people. With a few exceptions, they don't

354

want to grow. In Boulder, Colorado, population about 70,000, there are between six and nine little magazines, depending on how the money tree grows. I once asked the editors of three of them, who were all friends of one another, why they didn't merge and, in effect, grow. They weren't even vaguely interested. About all they could say was, "Well, ah, er, you don't understand. . . ." What I didn't understand was that they'd rather do it themselves because the doing was hip by haunch with being. So far as death goes, they know they're going to die. Meanwhile, however, they're living. And working, so to speak, for themselves. Many little magazine people are as afflicted with "careersma" as anybody else, but mostly they're in business to be out of business. So of course they violate the logic of business. That's why they're in business.

Anyway, just after *Big Table* received extreme unction, I came across the plains to Chicago in a wheezy old Ford that had just enough cylinders working to deposit me on the doorstep of my birthplace, Hyde Park. I had gone from North Dakota to Mexico and then to California, but the big finger bone of fate pointed to Chicago. The University of Chicago held the archives of *Poetry* and thus more of the precious little information available about Max and my racial memory. And of course there was the *Chicago Review*. In my own head I supposed that I was after a Ph.D. in literature. Since high school, the life of a teacher had seemed to me synonymous with the good life, and I was simply following that through to its logical conclusion: being a professor. I did not presume to think of myself as a writer. Even though an editorial in *Big Table* 1 had laid out its connection with the *Chicago Review*— and I presumably had read the editorial—the information didn't stick. So when I discovered that the magazine was housed on the University of Chicago campus, I came to it as unprejudiced as I had come to the university itself. Hyung Woong Pak three years earlier had been the only editorial staff member who did not resign in protest at the university's censorship of the magazine, and he had taken over as editor. In consequence, he was profoundly distrusted not only by the literary community but also, ironically, even by the faculty of the university. Pak, a North Korean expatriate, was accustomed to that atmosphere and seemed almost to cultivate it. He was the very image of the inscrutable Oriental. His political mode was feudal, and he supposed that his survival depended on systematically playing both ends against the middle. If, for example, the faculty and the literary community distrusted not only him but one another, their double alienation neutralized both factions, which was the way he wanted it. That seems natural enough for someone who had fled to the south from North Korea during the communist coup and then, seeing General Park at work, kept on truckin' to the United States—where, of course, he was not only an alien but a yellow one to boot. Pak had no doubt earned his paranoia, but it nonetheless lent his life the quality of a continuing melodrama.

As far as the *Chicago Review* was concerned, his machinations were pretty unreal. He had little to fear from the faculty, who had been burned so badly in the censorship controversy that they were more than happy to keep hands off. Moreover, Pak was a Europhile, and his primary interests were the configurations of European intellectual history—a subject perfectly congenial to academics and sufficiently abstract to be safe from smut hunters. And if the literary community had more or less turned its back on him and the *Chicago Review* in retaliation for the censorship, that was no great matter because he was not all that interested in poesy anyway. Nonetheless, paranoia prevailed and served to widen the breach between the *Chicago Review* and the literati. Despite all this, Pak edited a good magazine. If creative writers were down on it, academic and critical writers were well served. He did impressive issues on existentialism and phenomenology, for example, and he gave space and encouragement to two young critics who have subsequently attained some prominence, Ralph Mills, Jr., and Geoffrey Hartman. Mills has since become a poet, but Hartman has hewed rigorously to the academic mainline. He had been, as I recall, dismissed at the University of Chicago and had gone on to the University of Iowa. He seemed somewhat nervous and obviously ambitious. He and Pak would rendezvous on occasion at Chicago's Midway Airport, with a kind of conspiratorial air. Pondering what new moves with which to dazzle the academy? I soon realized that my editorial interests led another way. But I did my chores and tried to learn the trade.

Pak's academic interests had given the magazine that stamp; my interest was to restore its literary character and its rapport with the literary and artistic community. Inconveniently for me, I knew nothing about how to do it. Nor, in 1962, was there anything so

356

dramatically coherent as the Beats or the Black Mountaineers to "discover." So there I was, still more or less fresh from the wilderness of the Louisiana Purchase, with a magazine to fill with something more substantial than my innocent goodwill for the arts. A year or two before I became editor, the Associated Literary Magazines of America (ALMA) had organized itself to deal with distribution, the perennial problem of little magazines. The *Chicago Review* was a charter member, and I decided to go to the second ALMA meeting in New York, partly to learn about distribution but mainly to introduce myself to New York and the whirl of the literary world. ALMA—which originated, I think, out of the energies of Reed Whittemore of the *Carleton Miscellany* and Robert Bly of *The Sixties*—was at that point a cozy group of fifteen or so members. But the idea had caught on, and people were there from all over the country to apply for membership. The rift between the established magazines—*Partisan, Quarterly Review, Hudson, Sewanee,* etc.—and the newer, smaller, less well-heeled ones began there, a rift which has seemed to widen in COSMEP and CCLM, the offspring of ALMA. With wide-eyed interest I watched not only the harangues but also the celebrities of the little magazine world, keeping what I hoped would seem a sophisticated silence. It was the only mask I had, and I was found out pronto . . . in the latrine.

Though others have ungenerously suggested malice afore-thought, I think it was mere unhappy chance that brought Gordon Lish to the neighboring urinal. He had just delivered a ringing call for support of Karl Shapiro (not present at the meeting), whose magazine, the *Prairie Schooner*, had recently been censored by its publisher, the University of Nebraska. Lish, subsequently fiction editor for *Esquire* but then editing *Genesis West* in San Francisco, was bristling with eloquence, outrage, and indignation. His oration had been enthusiastically received, and he was still trailing clouds of glory. I'm sure he had business to attend at the urinal, but before he began he said, "You from *Chicago Review?*" His tone let me know I had something to fear. Maybe I should stonewall it, I thought, or has he got the goods on me, and in my defensive agitation I nearly turned toward him in full arc. I should have. Only the most reptilian quisling, he told me, would consent to edit a censored magazine, had I no pride, no morals, all the editors in the country ought to protest, to strike, blahblahblah. . . . Standing there with my now thoroughly wilted privy part adangle, I was defenseless. My sophisticated silence became a squawk in my throat as Lish flayed me both back and side. Luckily, at that point Roger Aplon and John Logan, who then edited *Choice,* were moved by the Grand Design to relieve themselves—if design, as the poet says, govern in a thing so small. Logan ranked Lish on the matter, since he had contributed to both *Chicago Review* and *Big Table.* He dismissed Lish and his splenetic tirade, commending the direction of my editing. Lish, Logan said, would probably end up editing fiction for some goddam magazine like *Esquire.* Then Logan and Aplon introduced me to the social whirl of little magazines.

Here's how that went. George Plimpton threw a party for the assembled editors and writers. In those days Plimpton's parties were famous. A few weeks previously, *Time* had carried a story of Jackie Kennedy cavorting at one of them. High art and high society, and me all atwitter in anticipation. Aplon and Logan invited me to accompany them, Robert Bly, Carolyn Kizer, and Donald Keene. I in turn invited my old friend Ron Tavel, whose work I was trying to promote in the *Chicago Review.* We were received with Plimpton's urbane but boyish charm. His apartment overlooked the East River and was hip deep in literati. There was a lot of liquor. Wit, wisdom, and literary gossip crackled like endless strings of ladyfingers. I wandered about like a rube, gaping and eavesdropping. The convivial stream didn't look too deep. I stuck my toe in and asked Plimpton about all the pictures of him with baseball players. He was amused. He put me on for two or three sentences. What was he saying? Had he been a baseball player? He was still more amused. He gestured vaguely with his hand. Baseball, he said, was Marianne Moore's favorite sport, and sidled off to less gullible guests. Someone introduced me to Andrew Lytle, longtime editor of *Sewanee Review.* Lytle, from the old school of southern gentlemen, had precise but crafty manners. He was willing to talk to new talent. I didn't know if I qualified. I introduced him to Tavel. Tavel told him he was writing an avant-garde novel. A *what,* Lytle asked in mock ignorance. I groaned. Tavel didn't give a shit. An avant-garde novel, he repeated. There is no such thing, Lytle said; there are only good novels and bad novels. Greenwich Village girded for battle with Yoknapatawpha County.

I kept drinking and wandering through the party like the camera eye of *Last Year in Marienbad*. On every circuit I ran into Jules Chametsky of the *Massachusetts Review,* and each time we met I would say, "Remember to say hello to Joe Langland." Soon his eyes began to roll in his head when he saw me coming and we would chorus the line together. Meanwhile the party had run out of food. Logan and Kizer and Bly were getting hungry, and they were maybe a bit miffed about something. By this point I was stone high on New York literary life and could have danced all night. But they were gathering our party together to leave for dinner. Plimpton was concerned. He scurried about in his kitchen and came up with several large cans of Dinty Moore beef stew. He might as well have offered dog food; Logan, Bly, and Kizer had not come to New York to eat Dinty Moore beef stew. I dragged Tavel away from his umpteenth rebuttal with Lytle. We all left in something of a huff—with me, however, trying to smile over my shoulder to Plimpton, indicating that personally I was not at all insulted by Dinty Moore. Though I confess that until then I had never seen a can of the stuff and thought, given Plimpton's style, that it might be some New York gourmet item. Plimpton shrugged and spooned himself a bowl of stew.

Sandra Hochman joined our exodus. She was being squired by a young executive type, obviously a man of means. After our dinner he said he knew a Turkish bar complete with belly dancers. The elders declined, but the rest of us piled into his Lincoln Continental. We drank and caroused, and after a while Sandra Hochman and her swain rose to leave. He tossed a fistful of bills on the table, inviting us to stay on as his guests. We drank him a toast and then one to poetry and to Sandra Hochman, to New York, to Turkey, and finally to such largesse as was induced by our host's passion. I was pretty pleased with the style of life in New York. Finally, in the small hours, as Tavel and I were stumbling toward the street, we found ourselves behind one of the dark, exotic Turkish dancers into whose cleavage we had been stuffing our host's dollars. "We gotta hustle ta catch a cab," we overheard her say to her boyfriend in a flat, incongruous Brooklyn accent. Tavel, who was from Brooklyn, smiled. I thought of an old actor friend of mine who used to say, and perhaps still does, that theater people are all fake.

Sometimes shortly after Kennedy was inaugurated—and we thought the good guys were in office and Nixon had disappeared—

the Bay of Pigs invasion happened. This was just before we were, as you may recall, eyeball to eyeball with the Russians over some missiles in Cuba, until they blinked. That being the level of our foreign policy, I thought it right to put together a symposium on "Morality and Power Politics." I wrote to a dozen or more political theorists and theologians—Adlai Stevenson, Arthur Schlesinger, Jr., Arthur Larson, Paul Tillich, Reinhold Niebuhr, etc.—asking them to contribute. All but one declined. Stevenson wished us luck. Larson, then director of the Foreign Affairs Institute, wondered, ahem, what fee might be involved. Well, I replied, we might, ahem, be able to come up with fifty dollars. Alas, he was unfortunately too busy. A month or two later he had an article in *Harper's* or the *Atlantic* on a subject very like morality and power politics. But Reinhold Niebuhr, partially paralyzed and on what I believe turned out to be his deathbed, sent an incisive, humane article entitled "The Nuclear Dilemma," along with a very moving note in which he apologized for the condition of his manuscript, but he could only type with one hand and did not have a secretary. Our symposium never materialized as such, though the nuclear dilemma, needless to say, did. But the effort was worth it, if only to be able to encounter Niebuhr's profound humility and grace.

As an editor, one has more than his share of humbling occasions. At that time, having been a student most of my life, the energizing thing about editing was that you were always on the line. Each decision mattered because it was a public statement. Even what you didn't print was in some way public. The most humbling "mistake" during my time at the *Chicago Review* was our failure to publish Kenneth H. Brown's play *The Brig*. It is a highly theatrical piece but not especially literary, and we were all literary folk, none of us with a director's vision. The irony is that we were making special efforts to locate and publish plays as a way of helping to stimulate theater in this country, but we failed to recognize the single most arresting piece of theater we encountered. Luckily there are more magazines than one, and the *Tulane Drama Review* (now *The Drama Review*) published the play. Within a year of our rejection *The Brig* was a nationally celebrated item in the Living Theater's repertory, so we had our comeuppance even if nobody but ourselves and Kenneth Brown were the wiser.

Sometimes, on the other hand, we were right on the money.

Though we were no more Zen monks than we were directors, we had sufficient wit to publish Lucien Stryk's and Takashi Ikemoto's Zen anthology. And we had the pleasure of having helped it become a successful book, giving Stryk's careers as poet and as translator a much deserved boost. And it mattered more to me than all the Plimpton parties or Brooklynese belly dancers in New York when Robert Bly called me from Paul Carroll's apartment to say how important he thought it was that we had published those translations. Helping to secure an audience for new or little known writers is obviously the biggest satisfaction in little magazine publishing. There is also, however, the equally important job of providing space for experimental work by prominent writers. When we published his "The Boys' Magazine," for instance, William Burroughs had an international reputation. But his reputation exceeded his prerogatives. While *Esquire* or *Playboy* might contract with him for a journalistic piece, they could not publish his real work, the experimentation which had won him his reputation. But *we* could and did. In the same issue we published a piece of Tavel's "avant-garde" novel, *Street of Stairs* (subsequently published in an unhappily aborted form by Olympia Press), and when he found his name back to back with Burroughs' in the table of contents it was, he wrote, like a swig of pure oxygen. We had our downs, but we also had our ups.

Editing the *Chicago Review* was a profound turning point in my life, though I didn't get hold of its significance until three or four years later. While editing I had also been teaching at Northwestern University, playing father to two babies, and increasingly attending to my own poetry, so there wasn't much time to think about a dissertation and Ph.D. I had supposed I would get back to that. But by this time it was 1965 and Johnson had just been elected to keep Goldwater from defoliating Vietnam. The citizens of the United States were about to have a radical confrontation with both their private and their public mythologies. Mine had begun with the *Chicago Review,* where Max's legacy became my tar baby. Was I actually going to be a writer? Nearly thirty years old and obviously not precocious, I was hard to convince. And why not? Where I grew up, one could conceive of being a bricklayer or a fireman but not a poet. It wasn't in the vocabulary. And when it did enter my consciousness it came like Max, like a ghost. But the big finger bone nudged me once again, through the agency of a little magazine, *TriQuarterly*—which, so far as I am concerned, could have been invented precisely for that purpose. Some writers, perhaps the best, are born to the pen. Keats and Corso, for example, didn't need to be persuaded they were poets; they just *knew*. I don't know if that was true of Stevens, but I take heart in the fact that he didn't publish a book until he was forty-four. At any rate, *I* needed to be convinced.

So here's how a little magazine added twelve inches to my chest expansion and gave me biceps to be proud of. Do scholars kick sand in your face at the beach? Are you chagrined before your best girl as critics mock your puny thighs? Little mags can help you too! In fact, the first issue of *TriQuarterly* in 1964 featured a parody of the Famous Writers School ads. It was one of Charles Newman's first ideas for the magazine. Happily, however, it also featured the calligraphic poems of Kenneth Patchen and other items that announced it was up to serious business. Actually Newman conceived *TriQuarterly* on a grand scale (i.e. in little-magazine terms) and it has behaved itself grandly ever since. All the better for me. Newman published an early version of one of my plainsongs. (A complete volume of these, I am pleased to announce, was published by the Brillig Works in the spring of 1978. Demand a copy of *Pacific Plainsong* from your local bookstore, and if this entire parenthesis does not appear here you will know *TriQuarterly* has betrayed its heritage!) Also a couple of essays—one of them a piece on Ronald Tavel's Theater of the Ridiculous and Andy Warhol's film factory, which I wrote only at Newman's insistence. It was spotted in *TriQuarterly* by Gilbert Harrison, then the publisher and editor of the *New Republic,* who promptly wrote me what he called a fan letter, asking if I had anything in mind that I might do for his magazine. Two years earlier, I had tried unsuccessfully to get approval for a dissertation on a critical study of pornography at the University of Chicago, and now I wrote an essay on the subject for the *New Republic.* A month or so after it appeared, the editor of Herder and Herder (now the Seabury Press) called to offer me a contract for a book on the subject. I was in business, and more or less on my own terms.

From one point of view, 1968 had seemed like a very good year. Radical energy was mobilized and full of purpose. It was

362

fantasia most especially for white radlibs. Having, as interlopers, ridden the coattails of the black movement, we seemed to have found our own raison d'être in the Vietnam war. Not only had we found our voice, but it appeared we were heard. Johnson had withdrawn. McCarthy and Bobby Kennedy were laying out at least the most urgent part of our case. And if we didn't have enough power to elect a president, we still had enough to defeat and discredit Humphrey liberalism. We had to be reckoned with. Or so we thought. I thought so, and it was a cocky feeling, like one's twenty-first birthday. As if one's imagination were no longer a quixotic aberration but had at last taken on social viability. At any rate, it was in that spirit that I accepted an offer from the University of Wyoming to edit an "experimental" arts journal. I spent time at Northwestern and Notre Dame, and was pleased to reply, when the Wyoming administration asked me what I thought the focus of such a journal would be: "What is important is that we do not need another journal for its own sake. We do, however, need one that is capable—i.e. set up for the purpose— of exploring the dynamics of contemporary art and culture. I think the increasingly intermedial character of the arts, for example, is changing our sense of artistic form and aesthetics. A magazine sensitized to this evolution and willing to pay for its practice and criticism would be a valuable addition. . . ." In short, I proposed an "international journal of experiment in the arts." I also pointed out the obvious, that such a venture could not be subject to censorship of any sort. I was feeling pretty nifty, my myth well in hand, poet with portfolio. Somewhat to my surprise, and greatly to my pleasure, they agreed "enthusiastically," as the dean of academic affairs informed me. So, my head brimming with visions of sugar-plums, I once again packed myself off to Laramie, home of the Wyoming Cowboys.

But one man's meat . . . The year 1969–70 was *not* a good year for the administration of the University of Wyoming. Reality came crashing in on its mountain hideaway without so much as a by-your-leave. Its nervousness began with the October moratorium —marches, demonstrations, and vigils in Laramie as elsewhere. Nervousness blossomed into full hysteria when the administration felt obliged to support the football coach's firing of fourteen black football players from the Wyoming team, which brought national

363

notoriety and a million-dollar NAACP lawsuit. And that spring, in response to a passive, orderly demonstration protesting the Kent and Jackson State shootings, the administration became altogether unhinged. The university president, before hiding out in the Ag School's milking machine, called in the state troopers, the National Guard, and, yes, the *fire department*. The university administration, like the national one, had lurched from bungle to botch in these "crises." And having had all they could take, they brought the same calm perspicacity to the suppression of *The Purple Sage*, as I decided it should be called—*Purple* as in "purple patches" and *Sage* as in wisdom and the well-known brush. Besides, who could resist a table of contents called "The Writers of the Purple Sage"?

Specifically they suppressed *The Lover's Horoscope*, our first publication. It was an erotic poem, "kinetic" in form, printed on eight discs which are riveted at the center so as to be able to spin. Twelve verses, corresponding to the twelve signs of the zodiac, are printed on each disc. The zodiac signs are printed at the edge of the discs. The reader spins each of the eight discs separately, and the verses that randomly align with his sign provide him with an erotic poem by way of instruction for the day. A reader might come up with this: "Touch ritually / prick / to nipple kiss / her lips, or butterfleyelash / enter after soixanteneuf / meet her gaze, or moan one obscene word / come unexpectedly talk of the zodiac, crossed signs, the mysterious marriage." The wheel is in color, ranging progressively from violet, at the smallest center disc, to a bright yellow. A handsome, prickly piece of stuff. A pleasure. A good piece of art. And, alas, erotic—more than the burghers running the university could abide. Though, as it turned out, there was more to their reaction than the horoscope. As I suggested above, the horoscope came at the end of a bad year. The penny-wits running the university were frazzled. Scared and confused, they had here, at last, something they could get hold of: the horoscope was "smut" and *The Purple Sage* was "radical." One perhaps has to have had some experience in Wyoming to quite appreciate what that meant.

I have been asked, especially by editors of university-based magazines, why I began with what was most likely to terrify a university administration. First, I thought the agreements under which I took the job had settled that problem. The university had agreed to the experimental character of *The Purple Sage* and had said there would be no censorship. Second, when the issue did come up, I offered to postpone distribution of the horoscope until other issues had articulated more clearly the aesthetic range of *The Purple Sage*. But even this was a compromise I had to force myself to offer. Because the real issue was freedom, the freedom to make an aesthetic and moral statement as you think it *ought* to be made. And that was compounded by the need—as I supposed, and still do—that a journal claiming, as *The Purple Sage* did, to be "an international journal of experiment," and coming as it did out of an obscure, small state university, had to make its initial statement as precisely as possible. *The Lover's Horoscope* was perfect. It was written by a British poet. Its form was experimental. To make its format an entire issue was saying beyond any rhetoric that we were not going to be bound by the conventions of magazine publication. Its tone and subject were their own statement, and augmenting the aesthetic of *The Purple Sage*—at once graceful and obscene, lyrical and pornographic—it said something about the condition of beauty. And, goddamit, it was happy; it celebrated life. If an experimental journal can't risk celebrating vitality and energy, then it damn well better close up shop.

The X factor in editing an institutionally supported magazine is what motives the institution has. One has only to think of *Encounter's* association with the CIA to know what I mean. Where you get your money, and why, matters. Even when there are no visible strings attached, there is always that moment waiting when things will come to push and shove, and at that point motives count. Every subsidized magazine has seen it, or will. (For *TriQuarterly* it came with the publication of William Gass's *Willie Masters' Lonesome Wife*.) Which is why many editors prefer their own shoestring budget, even if it means mimeo rather than print, just because in the crunch who pays the piper always calls the tune. Moreover, in a university one is always dealing with a compounded bureaucracy. If you're doing anything at all adventurous, you're not likely to get coherent faculty support, partly because faculties have their egos, tastes, and special interests to protect and too many of them are threatened by contemporary literature or condescending to what has not yet been certified. And even if you do get faculty support it won't matter much because administrators

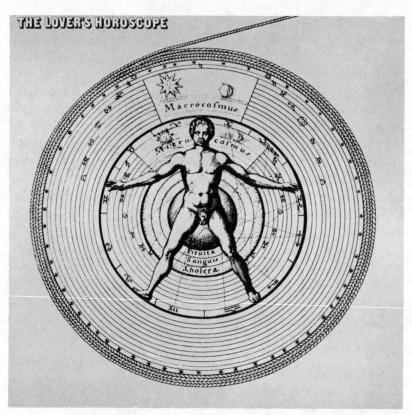

Above: cover of The Lover's Horoscope (Purple Sage)*, designed by Lawrence Levy. Opposite: poster advertising the* Purple Sage *(courtesy Peter Michelson).*

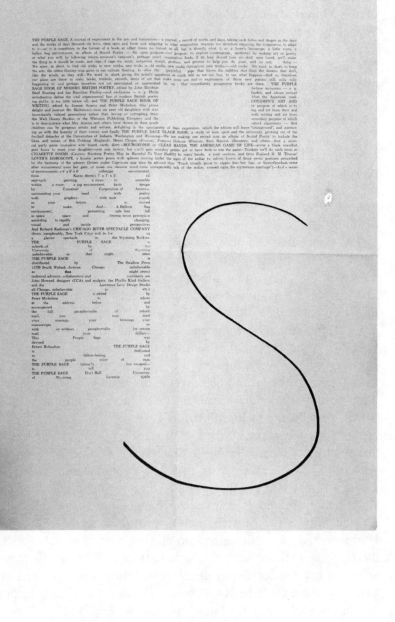

THE PURPLE SAGE, A journal of experiment in the arts and humanities—a journal, a record of works and days, taking such forms and shapes as the days and the works of days demand—its form, then open and loose and adapting to what imagination requires (or therefore requiring the imagination to adapt to it—or it is sometimes in the format of a book, at other times no format at all, but is directly what it is: a lover's horoscope, a little room, a ballot-bag environment, an album of Sound Poetry — An open purpose—our purpose, to explore contemporary, aesthetic by making art or poetry or what you will, by following whatever someone's tangent's, perhaps your imagination leads, if its lead should have us—And, once bored, we'll make the thing as it should be made; and rape, if rape we must, industrial design, produce, and process to help you do your, and us out; thing — We want, in short, to find old tricks in new media, new tricks in old media, new media themselves, new tricks—old tricks. We want, in short, to keep the arts, the oldest floating crap game in our culture, floating. In offer the (genuinely) pipe that blows the bubbles that float the dreams that drift, like the winds, as they will—We want in short, giving the artist's appetence as much rein as we can buy, to use what happens—And so, therefore our plans are these: to make books, trinkets, records, items of art that make some use and/or exploitation of those new poetics, still, willy-nilly happening to, and perhaps therefore not yet assimilated or appreciated by, us. Our immediately prospective books are three. THE PURPLE SAGE BOOK OF MODERN BRITISH POETRY, edited by John Matthias (whose inclusions — e. g. Basil Bunting and Ian Hamilton Finlay—and exclusions — e. g. Philip Larkin, and those critical introduction define the vital experimental line of modern British poetry that the American read ing public is too little aware of), and THE PURPLE SAGE BOOK OF CHILDREN'S ART AND WRITING, edited by Joanne Anania and Peter Michelson (the prima ry purpose of which is to delight and instruct Mr. Michelson's twin six year old daughters with next ing and art from their and immediately related generations rather than boring or corrupting them with writing and art from the Walt Disney Studios or the Whitman Publishing Company and the secondary purpose of which is to demonstrate what Mrs. Anania and others have shown in their grade school classrooms — that children can be gorgeous artists and writers, delighting in the spontaneity of their expression, which the editors will leave "unimproved", and instruct ing us with the honesty of their vision) and finally THE PURPLE SAGE BLACK BOOK, a study of race, sport and the university, growing out of the football debacles at the Universities of Indiana, Washington and Wyoming—We are making our record now, an album of Sound Poetry to include the likes, and noises, of Bob Cobbing (England), Henri Chopin (France), Ftransou Dufrene (France), Sten Hanson (Sweden), and others—And a varie cal party game (complete with beard, cards, dice)—BOURGEOISE, or CLEAN HANDS, THE AMERICAN GAME OF LIFE—invite a black anarchist poet home to meet your daughter—cost you money, but you'll gain morality points: get to have both to win the game—Trinkets we'll do, such items as CIGARETTE POEMS (Caution: Smoking Poetry May be Harmful To Your Health) by many hands, a joint venture, and from England D. M. Thomas' LOVER'S HOROSCOPE, a kinetic poster poem with spheres moving under the signs of the zodiac to inform lovers of these erotic postures prescribed by the harmony of the spheres (lovers under Capricorn may then be advised thus: "Touch ritually prick ye nipple kiss her lips, or butterfleyelash enter after sustainment meet her gate, or moan out obscene word none unexpectedly talk of the zodiac, crossed signs, the mysterious marriage")—And a series of environments, a 6 x 6 x 6   colltype   environment,

from   Karro Stern's 7 x 7 x 3'   oil
sept-tych   painting,   a room   to   assemble
within   a room,   a jog environment,   back
by   Container   Corporation of   America,
surrounding your   head   with   poetry
with   graphics   with such   sounds
as   your   larynx   is   moved
to   make,   And—   A Balloon   bag
environment,   permitting   safe free   fall
in space   space   and   freeing sense perception
according   to rapidly   changing,
visual   and   tactile   perspectives
And Richard Kostman's CHICAGO RIVER SPECTACLE COMPANY
(from, inexplicable, New York City) will do for   us
a   glacier   spectacle   in   the Wyoming Rockies
THE   PURPLE   SAGE,   the
subsidi.ed   University   of   Wyoming
unbelievable   as   that   might   seem
THE PURPLE SAGE
distributed   by   The Swallow Press
(1139 South Wabash Avenue,   Chicago   unbelievable
as   that   might seen)
technical advisors, collaborators and   confidants are
John Howard, designer (CCA) and sculptor, the Phyllis Kind Gallery
and the   Lawrence Levy Design Studio
all Chicago, unbelievable   as   etc.)
THE PURPLE SAGE   is edited   by
Peter Michelson   to   whom
at   the   address   below   and
accompanied   by
the   full   paraphernalia   of   return
mail,   you   may   send
your   musings,   your   blessings   your
manuscripts   or
with   or without   paraphernalia   be return
mail   your   dollars—
This   Purple   Sage   was
devised   by
Ernest Robuchon   THE PURPLE SAGE
is   dedicated
to   fellow-feeling   and
the   purple   voice   of   man
THE PURPLE SAGE   (alone")   has escaped—
to   tell   you
THE PURPLE SAGE   Boyt Ball   University
of   Wyoming   Laramie   82059

are so contemptuous of the faculty that they either ignore them—as was the case at Wyoming—or manipulate them into line—as at the University of Chicago in the *Chicago Review* affair. At Wyoming they basically wanted a magazine for window dressing. Even though we negotiated for a year and a half before I took the job, and in that time I distinctly emphasized how serious I was about the magazine's experimental character and had a "no censorship" clause written into my contract, they just didn't believe what I said. Or, more accurately, they didn't think it mattered what I said. For as a rule administrators also have a contempt for language. Like any bureaucrats, all they really believe in is the power of systems. What they wanted, it turned out, was to balance their heavy investments in science and technology with a flashy humanistic venture, and a magazine seemed a relatively cheap way of doing it.

The particular character of *The Purple Sage* didn't matter to them. In their heads it was a magazine and therefore interchangeable with the many other literary magazines that they also didn't know or care anything about. Being basically simple and cynical, they thought they could control it, which is to say castrate it and make it fit company for a proper college of arts and sciences. The political lesson here is that motives determine how much administrators will actively subvert the workings of a magazine. It's axiomatic that they won't help, so the question is how much they'll hurt. If they think you're causing them more trouble than you're worth, they'll do you in. When, as is usually the case, they have no aesthetic commitment, then you're really worth nothing to them, and so any trouble at all is more than you're worth. The "trouble" I was is worth checking into briefly. Wyoming suppressed *The Lover's Horoscope* on the grounds that it might antagonize the state legislature and thereby perhaps endanger budget allocations for the university. And there was probably some reality there. However, the university made no effort either to understand how the *Horoscope* fit into the aesthetic pattern of *The Purple Sage* or to check out the legislature itself. This latter is not so farfetched as it may seem. I had been told before I took the job that one of the trustees of the university knew my own writing and my proposal for the journal and supported both it and me. So it was not out of line to suppose there might also have been legislators similarly inclined. Clearly the *Horoscope* offended their own sense of propriety, and they were not about to confront the legislature with what they themselves found objectionable. Moreover, the Wyoming legislature met biennially, so it was highly problematical whether it would even be aware of the *Horoscope*. The point is that there was no trouble nor was any very likely; but the more chimerical the university's bureaucratic reasons for having the journal in the first place, the more their paranoid suppositions had the force of fact. However, as I said, the year had brought them heavy weather, and they were nervous. Consequently they were afraid of the "radical" possibilities of an uncensorable magazine, and they used the eroticism of *The Lover's Horoscope* as an occasion to either put the journal under their bureaucratic thumb or cashier it altogether.

The only amusing moment of the whole episode came on the day it all "broke," when Chicken Little—in the guise of Swallow Press, our distributor—called to tell me the sky was falling. During some bureaucratic business with the dean—who is the villain of this-here tale—I had casually and naively shown him a proof copy of the *Horoscope*. With equal casualness he asked if he might keep it over the weekend and return it on Monday, when we were to meet again. By Monday afternoon all the shit had hit the fan. I was walking to his office when my assistant called out the window that Swallow was on the phone and it sounded urgent. The crew-cut villain dean had been busy. He had got the university's legal adviser to contact the distributor and manufacturer of the *Horoscope,* both of whom were in Chicago, and with impeccably officious arrogance informed them that I was no longer empowered to contract for the university and that the *Horoscope* itself was to be shipped directly to the university president's office. I had in effect been fired without knowing it. Insane with rage and inspired by guerrilla theater, I went roaring off to what had been set up as an ambush in the dean's office, where a delegation of administrative types were waiting to browbeat me for smut mongering and general nastiness. They obviously did not expect me to be forewarned, and were astonished when I entered raving and threatened to bust the legal adviser, who had made the secret calls, in the eyes, ears, nose, and throat, crack his skull, and feed his flitweight brain to the coyotes. I ranted, cussed, pounded desks, and carried on in general like a red-blooded American maniac. Their eyelids clicked open like Barbie dolls. Great consternation, much hemming and hawing as I stomped

369

around the office. Then apologies for furtive behind-my-back goings-on, fidgeting and squirming; and from that point on, through four weeks of negotiation, the legal adviser, an unbelievable twirp, was carefully kept out of my sight. He would wait in adjoining offices while we negotiated, and the bureaucrats would shuttle back and forth to consult with him. It was a small but distinct victory over the good manners with which such folk ask you to please lift your chin as they prepare to cut your throat.

Meanwhile I asked the manufacturer to hold on to the *Horoscopes* until he heard from me, to which he agreed. He was in Chicago and not much impressed with the university's officiousness. The point of this was that I would at least have that card to use in trying to persuade the administrators to permit publication at a later time. Perhaps after a year or so the range of *Purple Sage* projects would show them that we were not in the smut business. We had a book of children's art and writing in nearly complete manuscript, likewise an anthology of contemporary British poetry (which subsequently became an issue of *TriQuarterly* and a book published by Swallow Press), etc.

Negotiations went their mindless way. No, the administrators said, under no circumstances could the *Horoscope* be published. Then the villain dean proposed an editorial board. Fine, I said. But what he really wanted was a censoring board. No, I said, under no circumstances. Besides they already obviously had censoring power, so it was a moot point. All through these meetings they were hangdog and nondirective. Except for the censoring of the *Horoscope* they just kept throwing the ball back to me. Yes, they wanted *The Purple Sage* to continue (at one pathetic moment the president, referring to the children's book, said, "I don't suppose you'd be content just to do that sort of thing . . ."). No, they didn't want to censor the journal. But also, no, the *Horoscope* could not be published any time. At one point faculty quislings were paraded in to tell me that my colleagues would most certainly not like it (and presumably therefore not support me) if their research monies, etc., were cut because the legislature got peeved. I replied that I did not choose to edit a journal according to the tastes of the Wyoming state legislature. So it went.

In the course of these meetings I called the legal director of the ACLU in New York. I explained the situation, the no-censorship clause in my contract, the general decorousness of the *Horoscope's* eroticism, etc. I asked if there was any reasonable hope of success-fully fighting the censorship in court. "Where did you say you were?" he asked. "Laramie, Wyoming," I said. A long pause at his end of the line. "That's the Wyoming District Court," he said, "and Judge X is a local Wyoming judge. Unless you're prepared to go to the Supreme Court you'll never win. Forget it," he said. Forget it, I thought; the flame's not worth the candle. I resigned. Back in Chicago, Max, so to speak, was waiting. I went there and finished my books, *The Eater,* and *The Aesthetics of Pornography.*

Some few thousand words ago I suggested that little magazines make up a kind of counter-industry, since for many people they are an alternative to the conventional business of life. And the conventional business of life is a bit like stupidity; it may or may not kill you, but it'll certainly make you sweat a lot. Even if you adapt to it like a healthy organism, your very health is often a mode of death. Or if you don't, you're locked up in a hospital or prison, or you destroy yourself and save them the trouble, or you find an alternative, some sort of compromise with which you can live. My grandfather had been locked up. My mother had destroyed herself. I have, at least so far, found an alternative, in and through the life of little magazines. Lenin called the Russian intellectuals of his day "shit." If, as seems to be the case, that attitude still prevails in Russia, small wonder that the Russian *samisdat* press is so active. In its relative way, the little magazine in the United States is analogous to the Russian *samisdat.* They are both an SOS by way of resistance to prevailing dogma—"mind the State" for Russians and "mind your Business" for Americans. Business—witness my grandfather Max—can be as lethal as the state. And the little-magazine world is largely powered by the will, at least, to resist the deadening aspects of the business ethos.

Jack Collom, editor and publisher of *the,* a mimeographed little magazine, is an example. Now in his middle forties, he has for the past fifteen or so years—while publishing his magazine, writing his own poetry, and earning an M.A. at night—supported himself and his family by working in a factory. When writer friends, sup-porting themselves at academic jobs, complained about their work, he would wonder if it was, after all, worth the effort. But he kept at it and finally finished the requirements for his degree, sustained by his editing and writing. Having marked time for many years, he quit his job as soon as he got the degree. He

371

managed to pay the rent for a while by working in the Colorado PITS program, at the same time continuing to edit and write. Then he landed a year's gig in Grand Island, Nebraska, as a poet-in-the-community. In short, after many years he extricated himself from industrial drudgery and had the satisfaction of working as a poet, of doing a job that more or less recognized and honored his spiritual energy. And he was happy at it. Whereupon, curiously, he decided to stop publishing his magazine. Now why, having borne it for so many years, did he stop at this point in his life? The reasons are, of course, complex—questions of money, of energy, etc. But he had found the money and energy before; why not now? A large part of the answer lies in his relation to his work. While in the factory he needed large doses of "other-level experience" just to keep alive, i.e. to survive the dissociations of industrial drudgery. With his work as a poet, more spiritually cohesive and satisfying, he no longer needed the symbolic activity of the magazine. His work and his being were integrated, so the magazine became in a sense superfluous.

Not that little magazines exist solely as some form of negative compensation for the otherwise drab lives of their editors. Not at all. They exist to satisfy what their editors see as a literary need. Of course, more than a few editors of littles earn quite livable salaries, though they are a minority in the industry. Nonetheless, even for careerists the prevailing little magazine energy connects with the spiritual need to do in life, with or without pay, something that makes one feel human. And often enough that carries with it a sense of cultural alternative. Alternative opportunity is what little magazines pride themselves on. To some extent that pride is based on a myth, but it's a healthy myth. Certainly, aiming to *challenge* your audience's expectations (as I think most little magazine editors intend) is healthier than simply aiming to please. We need not subscribe to the salvific hyperbole so characteristic of little magazine rhetoric to recognize that they make a significant contribution to the life of the culture, even though the cultural mainstream is largely unriffled by them. If literature matters, little magazines matter—and not simply because of the honor roll of great writers who may have gotten a start there. My guess is that great writers, or even good ones, are like fullbacks at the goal line, "not to be denied." Valuing little magazines as farm teams who feed the major leagues, however much that may happen (though it's probably a good deal less than is supposed), is just another way of plugging them into the GNP. And calling them the "furnace where contemporary literature is being forged" is dramatic but misleading. They're more like retail outlets. Whether bargain basements with plain pipe racks or some fancy import shop, all of them are marginal ventures (to whom the CCLM is the equivalent of the Small Business Administration). The furnace is the culture itself. Significant writing is forged by life, not magazines. What little magazines do is affirm that the written imagination matters. Their puny, inexhaustible voices encourage the collective imagination to articulate itself, and in that way they are part of the life that forges contemporary literature. Literature, they say, *is* part of life, however much commerce may discourage any but the most popular. Their importance, then, lies not in the success of their writers but in the quality of the life activity they exist to represent. Obviously some are better and some worse in terms of aesthetic quality. But that distinction is after the fact. A culture must be the healthier when it may choose from among the widest possible range of self-expression, i.e. when the existence of that range is itself regarded as a value. Little magazines matter not only for what they publish but also, perhaps more so, for the kind of generative activity they *are*.

When we insist that little magazines grow or die we are really demanding that they measure up to some mythically immutable standard. No one, not the most ingrown toenail of a mimeograph-magazine editor, will ever argue against good writing. On the other hand, Charles Bukowski, who ten or fifteen years ago was regarded as an illiterate drunk, is now practically a national hero. Modern literature is shot through with such anomalies. So there's no point in trying to bully people about "quality." "Quality" smacks of "success," and they both take care of themselves. Take, as examples of success, the dapper Edwardian image of the *New Yorker* logo and its evolution in caricature from *Esquire*'s white mustachioed old gentleman to *Playboy*'s snappy young would-be gentleman. Or the complementary transition of *Cosmopolitan* from purveyor of sturdy domesticity to chanteuse of sexy career girls. *The New Yorker,* as aesthetically serious and energetic as even the most austere of literary magazines, thrives to this day by huckstering urbanity in the forms of fancy food, drink, clothes, and hostelry. The others—with lesser but still prominent literary claims

—have flourished by adding the commodity of sex to the formula. This is not to say that they are all the same. But there is a sense in which they all succeed by catering the simple hedonism their readers associate with the good life: fancy food, drink, clothes, hostelry, and sex.

Now, take the following observation, that . . .

labour is external . . . , i.e. it does not belong to [man's] essential being; that in his work, therefore, he does not affirm himself but denies himself, does not feel content but unhappy, does not develop freely his physical and mental energy but mortifies his body and ruins his mind. [Man] therefore only feels himself outside his work, and in his work feels outside himself . . . it is the loss of his self . . . man [the worker] no longer feels himself to be freely active in any but his animal functions—eating, drinking, procreating, or at most in his dwelling and in dressing-up, etc. . . .

I cite this aspect of Marx's theory of alienation because I think it helps explain something important about the phenomenon of little magazines in our culture. Marx is describing here what Jung would call the transference of energy. Not being "freely active" in his work, where mind and soul are dissociated from body, we transfer frustrated spiritual energy to "animal functions—eating, drinking, procreating . . . dwelling . . . dressing-up." This is precisely what these successful magazines have understood, that their success depends upon playing fast and loose with the prevailing sociological rhythms that keep freedom of action domesticated within the bounds of simple hedonism. The more we keep focused on food, drink, clothes, hostelry, and virile or voluptuous Kewpie dolls, the more we keep the placid beat. *Playboy* has grown fat on pictures of decorously naked ladies. Is it an accident that Ralph Ginzburg went to jail for publishing in *Eros* more or less equally decorous pictures of a naked white woman and a naked black man embracing? Well, this is a bit facile and perhaps more than a bit evasive of the complexities of these magazines, especially *The New Yorker*. Still, one pretty certain road to success is a sophisticated use of soma. But it is to their credit that little magazines have by and large declined the gambit, even if a number of them do put us to sleep.

Serious writing has always been between a rock and a hard place. One of its duties, after all, is to sing out that the emperor is naked. Since social order depends on cultivating delusion, such singing has only occasional rewards. Unless, of course, being an

374

enfant terrible is it own satisfaction. And with regard to little magazines the emphasis has always been on *"enfant."* Even the big-money folks have their troubles in that respect. Newness, always a selling point, is really an analogue of infancy. Norman Mailer has been trying for twenty years to persuade people he's a grownup, but what made him the cultural object he is was his early promotion as an *enfant terrible.* To be taken seriously as an artist in the GNP ethos, it must first be demonstrable that one is a child and therefore need not be taken seriously.

But a good part of the raison d'être for little magazines is the outsider role itself, in which the moral kudos of fighting the good fight remains untainted by the corruptions of power (though the power structure of the little magazine world, too, grows apace). While many are acutely conscious of the irony of their situation— denouncing the power structure even as they apply to it for funding —what are they to do? What are any of us to do? Strum the blue guitar and sing of possibilities other than things as they are. In that there is at least the human dignity that goes with singing and dreaming. Moreover, it's fun, a pleasure beyond the slick placebos with which we're customarily anesthetized.

Meanwhile, Jack Collom's year as an official poet in Grand Island, Nebraska, is over, and he's back at the factory, happy to get the work. And my grandfather Max's poetry is still there to be read, if you look hard enough through old poetry magazines. And people like Len Fulton in Paradise, California, continue on their extraordinary way, carrying the torch for little magazines. As for me, when I finish this paragraph I'm going to write a review of Jerzy Kosinski's new book. In spite of the fact that I don't like it much—it's several cuts below *The Painted Bird*—it will doubtless sell many thousands of copies. After that I'm going to get the manuscript of my own new book ready for the printer. If I have extraordinary luck, it may sell a thousand copies. Then, if my luck holds, the publisher may run another thousand copies. Be that as it may, all you magazine editors, large and small, beware. Everybody knows about the little-man syndrome; we're feisty and persistent, like Snopeses. We'd as soon grind a shoeful of *Horse shit* on your new white carpet as anywhere else. One of these days you'll get my dog-eared manuscript in the mail. You'll know it by the name—the one you don't recognize.

ON TRACE
James Boyer May

Although James Boyer May lost more than $40,000 as editor of Trace, *his interest in little magazines has never wavered. His monograph* Twigs as Varied Bent *(published by Felix Stefanile's Sparrow Press in 1954) provides an overview of the state of little magazines on an international scale, though focusing primarily on English and American publications. Mr. May offers perspectives on the moral attitudes of little magazine editors after World War II, on the economics of small-press printing and distribution, as well as on the state of the art of the little magazine itself. He stresses the corrective potential of little magazines, their ability to lend cultural renewal to an essentially mechanized, artistically defeated age.*

Mr. May's ideology came to fruition in 1950 when he met John Sankey, the founder of the Villiers Press in England, and it was Villiers that published Mr. May's magazine, Trace. *In keeping with his belief in the importance of communication between the editors and contributors to little magazines, James Boyer May kept watch on American and English journals for eighteen years in his continuous "evolving directory" of little magazines—which alone made* Trace *one of the great formative journals of the fifties and sixties.*

Back when *Trace* was unnamed and nonexistent, its embryo, *Towards Print,* this editor's regular feature in *Matrix* in 1950 and 1951, was intended to aid new writers to find markets as well as to provide information for librarians and teachers. More so than today, there was a dividing line between old-line literary magazines (chiefly those sponsored by schools) and independent littles. Virtually nowhere, except in the latter, could unknowns find print unless they adopted somewhat commercial patterns or imitated prominent writers in accepted modes. At that time, largely because of this, what was to become an ever-augmenting increase in little

Revised and expanded by the author from editorials in *Trace* 68 and 72/73.

TOWARDS PRINT (an expanded continuation of the feature in MATRIX MAGAZINE, U.S.A., by the Editor of TRACE).

After a record postwar burgeoning of new literature—comprising what Australians prefer to call 'ajays' (viz. all amateur journalists, significant though a percentage of their writings invariably proves), the flight-conscious avant-garde, and also comprising solider reviews with paid circulations into the lower thousands—this once more is settling into categories which cut across these obvious classifications. At first, the attempt at a broad survey brings mainly confusion; for, in far the biggest group (many, poetry-only too) are those both eclectic and in part traditional and less-often essaying fresh departures. Their numbers cloudingly bewilder and render difficult to define even the brighter accomplishments of their own members. And yet, while three-fourths of these are less than semi-experimental in the usual meaning, and while typically just reflecting distinctive tastes and rebellions of their editors, each contains some symptom of the variant pioneering vitality most marked in more off-trail endeavors.

And since this attempt inescapably has to do with trends throughout the contemporary environment—not simply among small magazines nor solely in the literary domain—we oddly-seeming commence with one of two smallest groups. Fewer magazines than twenty years ago expound social reforms; and those which do chiefly preach in anarchistic or nihilistic terms. Less than a third stress Marxian concepts. Some on the surface appear actually reactionary. At least to the extent their exhortations obviously do encourage cultural-political modifications the reverse of those which were until the last couple of years regarded as progressive. Except for party-line leftists like MASSES & MAINSTREAM or NEW FOUNDATIONS, or some dwindling old-line socialistic publication like LAST CALL, providing little space for creative work anyway, these may not be said to foster any pat schemes for regimenting people into sundry enlightenments. Sounded not long ago, the editorial notes of most the others still sounding reform (and not a few have become comparatively neutral as re politics, like PARTISAN REVIEW) actually might have been pronounced ultra-conservative! But

the only reactive tone is that keyed by resistance to the proven stultifying effects of an urbanized rationale following over-rapid industrialization. In other words, there battles chiefly now a hardy little company championing individuality against the uniformities at last appreciated will ensue (however 'ideally') any rigorous centralized pattern for control. They battle all mass nostra—or, for that matter, mere mass suggestions. The latter almost have force of enactments, among populations conditioned by modern advertising. They also hint, for instance—to define them best from another phase—the desirabilities of restoring creativity not merely in the arts, but among lost handicrafts. Echoes of the protests grow, and not simply from lack of quality in machine products either. There's suggestion of relationship to agitations against assembly-line manufactures of such items as bread, neckties, and bedside tables—from humanitarian motives. Restoration of home- and community-shops and distributors quite logically might follow these pleas for independent morale to restore better purposive relationships within society—and not necessarily to be coupled with advocacy of community ownerships.

But, reverting to literary considerations, a large and less-demarcated group than the above contains nearly all true reactionarism. Contradictorily, these editors consider that they (and particularly, their own magazines—for often there's a warped, though understandable, perspectiveless arrogance) constitute the genuine 'advance;' yet scholarly restraints upon contributors continue enforcing reverences for one tradition or another. They let slip through scarcely any material which hasn't some supposition of precedent. The magazines usually are prepared with an eye to classroom use, a majority receiving partial college or university support. And the editorial boards may be heavy with 'names,' plus long rolls of editorial advisers. Slight wonder, what with numerous cooks, that the editorial broth at times fails of any tasty definition, that contents prove as eclectic as in the first-named group—yet, often lack faintest flavor of editorial policy to condone this. Few such straitened miscellanies—less-seldom than among the semi-traditional eclectics—contain significance. And when so, with dubious back-page smirks. They're apt to carry lesser samples from long-recognized authors, while little-known or first-printed authors just are imitators of the same.

Another larger group deliberately carries forward obsolescent traditions—not surprisingly with sturdier support (by reason of more paying subscribers who prefer familiar sentiment to disturbing originality) than any of the foregoing. Maybe a few of these shouldn't even be part of this survey—except they're links with past culture and don't belong with mass-entertainment magazines either. Surely, some do not live in anything resembling the sense of Paracelsus, observing over 400 years ago: "Learning is our very life, from youth to old age, indeed, up to the brink of death; no one lives for ten hours without learning." By this, some of these aren't simply expiring or deceased—they're but poor stuffed replicas of worthier museum mummies.

And many more of the above endure than of publications self-consciously fostering definable experimentalisms. This is the fifth group, the other smallest one. Yet these few may be expected to influence most important aspects of future writings. They, and the group powered by social scrutinies. Truly, the two are complementary, though strictly-literary editors dislike and even disdain 'messages,' and though socially-concerned editors call the others ivory-tower poseurs. Both at least do more, in their unique (and occasionally downright cranky) ways, and thus are the vital spirits of insurrection against any accepted literary 'attitude' which otherwise might set up exclusive worship of specially-evolved conformities adhered to by some advance-guarders surviving the Thirties.

Though they may not fairly be arrayed together, each magazine having a distinctive editorial line and distinguishing contents, the following hold sufficient in common to be grouped as having exhibited novel (and also definable) tendencies: CONTACT (Canada), THE GOLDEN GOOSE, IMAGI, INTRO MAGAZINE, MANDRAKE (Italy), NINE (England), ORIGIN, and WAKE. Those evincing social awareness (and in fair measure, if not entirely, composed of literary contributions) have been THE DELPHIC REVIEW (England), GOAD, THE GRUNDTVIG REVIEW, INFERNO, LAST CALL, PROTEUS QUARTERLY, PROTOCOL (Newfoundland), RESISTANCE MAGAZINE, RETORT, SUCK-EGG MULE, and UPSURGE. Two new ones, first issues of which at this writing haven't appeared, CITY (Australia) and FOUR WINDS (U.S.A.) seem from the editors' statements to belong here too.

Contrary to reasoning that magazines consistently publishing what's generally acclaimed quality work may be deduced 'best,' reconsideration suggests (besides the fact that art is not competitive) that future generations likely will discover more precedents among the less finicky magazines in the above two categories. And research not astonishingly confirms that nearly all early works of power and genuine originality have been published among their ancestors and relatives—very few by those whose editors toed academic marks. In other words, these projects in at least one important sense better justify the touted purposes of such endeavors, despite conceded excellencies of several individual magazines in other categories; for this is not to deprecate any meritorious publications—nor among those devoted to staider poetry, for instance, despite most of these finally may not gain credit except for having preserved minor work otherwise lost. Simply that real blazing does mark trail in magazines of emphatically unever timber (many with rank wild growths indeed!).

From Toronto, as example, the new and venturesome CONTACT already has been condemned by many. Yet, by very fact that the editors unmistakably explain intentions, significant things certainly will appear. They uphold poetry identified with immediate specific environmental problems, without censoring however almost-abstract contemplative and philosophical treatments in passages woven with quickening sensory imagery. Not only do these editors thereby define a trend direct from Sartre, but may be said to proceed along their own special self-conscious avenues concerning wider problems. Raymond Souster declares his interest in Irving Layton and other yet-obscure Canadian poets, but affirms they'll publish any good experimental work of purposes in the least relevant to the foregoing, no matter the divergent doctrine or the country of origin. So, within limits on this phase, a broader invitation is offered than among typical periodicals with sharply stated social views; and in fact, magazines stressing literary ingenuity usually display broader latitudes than those of emphatic social convictions.

Perhaps exceptional among the others is PROTEUS QUARTERLY. Editor Frederick C. Heckel's ideas do also take form from a literary bias—if such it can be named—an intense admiration for Goethe. If not markedly aware of questions of technique nor a standard-bearer among knights of

Above and overleaf: a manifesto from Trace, *Vol. 1, No. 1, by Editor James Boyer May (courtesy Northwestern University Library).*

literary theory, Mr. Heckel's belief in robustness and round-fleshed sentiment in general imparts a belletristic unity rare among magazines primarily devoted to message (versus expression). This grows clearer in recent numbers of PROTEUS, which have accentuated signs of tightening editorial awareness of form along with a continued unquenchable search after honest sentiments kindred to those of the editor in re the enigmas of man.

WAKE and MANDRAKE REVIEW are the only two in these groups, other than ORIGIN (which carries non-Anglo-American writing, but less of critical evaluations), extensively publishing translations and detailed appraisals of internationally prominent writers and schools. THE GRUNDTVIG REVIEW announces larger space in future for writers of other countries, both originals and translations. This WAKE (No. 11) contains new things by Conrad Aiken, together with essays about him by international figures, with Aiken bibliography and photographs. The same number contains Italian, French, and German sections—besides the editor's choices of significant contemporary U.S. writing.

Outstanding specimens (current) of the first and largest group, those printing all types both of prose and poetry, are the Canadian NORTHERN REVIEW, New Zealand ARENA, THE WINDOW, and THE WIND & THE RAIN (both England), and SHENANDOAH, published at Washington and Lee University. The British ADELPHI becomes not undeserving of inclusion here, for some of the recent fiction. Prominent eclectics among those restricted to poetry and articles about poetry have been THE BELOIT POETRY JOURNAL, CANADIAN POETRY MAGAZINE, EPOS.

Typical middle-ground belief appears to be that adoption of any 'ism' as editorial criterion may be dangerous and foster meretricious matter posing only illustrations of evanescent-spotlighted loci of the unceasing struggle between tradition and experiment. These aren't the exact words of any editor, but they summarize a position of some mainly guided by personal tastes and not consciously undertaking to drive toward definite selective synthesis. And there's justice in their charge that editors absorbed in exclusive theory of one sort or another—individual or that of a school—will publish much that just complies with over-special standards, and often (despite surface novelties) will

publish no more genuine spontaneity than deeply-conservative editors. With too closely prescribed prejudgments, this indeed would seem all but unavoidable. And yet, as remarked, 'one-track' magazines still give birth, among them, to more consequential material than the eclectics as a whole (exceptions both ways, naturally).

The best of that most carefully edited academic group which, in the professorial eyes, are the worthiest of all these 150 publications, perhaps are: THE ADELPHI (England), ACCENT, EPOCH, THE GEORGIA REVIEW, HUDSON REVIEW, KENYON REVIEW, MEANJIN (Australia), THE PACIFIC SPECTATOR, PRAIRIE SCHOONER, QUEEN'S QUARTERLY (Canada), SEWANEE REVIEW, UNIVERSITY OF KANSAS CITY REVIEW, THE VIRGINIA QUARTERLY, WESTERN REVIEW, and YALE REVIEW. Others falling in this category, but chiefly poetry and poetry criticism, include: CONTEMPORARY VERSE (Canada), CANADIAN POETRY MAGAZINE, POETRY (Chicago), and QUARTERLY REVIEW OF LITERATURE.

To name a few less-to-be-despised (by avant-gardists) of the near-outrightly traditional—FOLIO, POETRY CHAP-BOOK, WE OFFER (England) and WINGS. POETRY QUARTERLY (London) has published a wider selection than its Chicago counterpart, and recently may be declared to have better typified the original purposes of that long-pre-eminent endeavor.

Falling somewhat between stools are unique endeavors like FURIOSO, which while not eclectic, hasn't adhered to a consistently-definable logic in selections either. And then, the newer A. D. MAGAZINE, refusing to be regarded avant-garde, while announcing advocacy of a day-before-yesterday's notion among the then-advanced-persuasively-recognizable depictions of obvious realities as vs. the basic art-for-art's-sake idea that writers may create however-unreal worlds, to be 'understood' through their own curious distorting glasses. Also, as-yet less widely known: THE CALIFORNIA QUARTERLY, CAROLINA QUARTERLY, THE HOPKINS REVIEW, MEASURE, and PHYLON—all trending toward academism rather than experiment.

mags began. Already, there were more than in any earlier period, with the maximum activity in the U.S. A key paragraph of a *Towards Print (Matrix* number 32*)* nevertheless points to a predominance of conservatism:

Current literary magazines, especially those in some degree under the aegis of a school, betray a tendency to give more weight to technical finesse than to individuality of the sort to be expected from the advance guard. This may save them from printing an occasional callow mistake, but prevents printing much neoteric work . . .

However, I was in no sense campaigning, nor did I dream of founding *Trace.* This came about accidentally. I was simply serving a view expressed in my brief comments on periodicals.

The first "tracings," the small magazine listings appended to *Towards Print,* though not comprehensive, were geographically unlimited. I had established contacts with editors and writers in several countries, and it was comparatively easy to expand the listings into the international directories.

Initially, the main purpose was to provide a forum for information and discussion among little-mag people everywhere—to acquaint them with one another. Then, almost at once, it was seen that this "bridge," as some called *Trace,* enabled writers to find outlets in magazines far from their own national boundaries. The littles grew increasingly internationalized; writers from different lands, reading one another, were mutually influenced insofar as they were using English, the idioms of which varied from Canada to Australia, from South Africa to Scotland. Soon, too, there were many translations which otherwise never would have occurred.

Naturally, from the start, *Trace* appealed to teachers of liberal bent; and teachers were to comprise the biggest portion of individual subscribers. The standard quarterlies, much more than now, were devoted to writers already in the texts, and *Trace* supplied a guide to those who had not yet built reputations.

The story of the birth of *Trace* can be stated in a few sentences. I had cooperated with Whipple McClay in obtaining data for *Galley,* a bibliographical project in this field. He died in March 1952, rendering continuation improbable. (As it turned out, *Galley* did reappear in 1953 . . . then expired—but I had no advance knowledge of this.) My number 1 came into being in June of that year in response to many letters. For *Matrix*—which had endured since 1938—also was terminating. Editors Joseph Moray and S. E. Mackey had been unsuccessful in a search for some college or other institution to take over their project. My correspondents proposed that *Towards Print* be combined with a more adequate running survey similar to that maintained by *Galley,* with other contents limited to brief articles and letters.

I wrote to John Sankey, whose *Villiers Publications* had been founded in 1951. He had been editing *The Window,* one of the best British littles. He offered British printing at cost of labor and materials; and this is how it came about that *Trace* was published in London under *Villiers* sponsorship. I assumed responsibility for the financing of American circulation (about 90 percent of the total).

Trace was fortunate in gaining press notices. That summer, a couple of paragraphs by David Dempsey, in the "In and Out of Books" feature of the *New York Times Book Review,* brought 187 queries, accompanied by 347 dimes (the mag sold for 20 cents); and nearly a hundred joined *Matrix* supporters as subscribers. A few hundred other subscriptions were garnered by the end of the year. Number 1 sold out in weeks. There had been 300 copies produced on first estimates. The one typographical error corrected, an additional 300 were press run; and all of these also were sold.

Even with this propitious beginning, losses were sustained, as *Trace* grew in size (number 1 had just sixteen pages, but it finally averaged about 200). This growth always preceded, and never kept proportionate pace with, the increasing subscribership, which has been very gradual. Net increase was held to small figures by losses each year of approximately one-third of the roll (nonrenewing subscribers). Press runs have not been long enough to reduce per-copy cost sufficiently below the price obtained. It took eight years to approach a circulation of 2,000, and this turned out to be an average maximum.

The magazine would have broken even much of the time, however, had contributors not been paid. The deficit figures have just about matched the amounts paid them (losses eventually approached $3,000 a year). But I've insisted that authors be paid, as a matter of principle and to safeguard their rights without their having to apply individually for copyrights. And I think, too, that a higher caliber of material has been obtained.

Concerning contributors—from anywhere and, from early in the history, about everywhere—it should be noted that *they* came to *Trace*. Mss almost never have been solicited. The onrush (not "unrush," for we gave fast reports) has been read to the best of our abilities without regard to the authors' reputations or lack of reputations. Submissions from "name" writers frequently have been rejected because they broke no new ground or because they were found inferior as measured against their authors' best. No editorially preconceived ideas relating to comparative values of differing writing theories have been applied, and no "school" has been favored. I have tried to select on a basis of what I considered the degree to which writers accomplished what they were undertaking, in their *own* fashions.

Informed by *Trace,* scores of people have been led to found magazines. That they otherwise would not have considered this is attested by the letters we received. And scores of others, already determined to launch ventures (including small presses), have written for advice.

I don't maintain that this proliferation has been an unmixed good; yet, conceding that numerous publications have been of dubious worth, the opportunities afforded thousands who otherwise could not have found print, have—in the overall picture—influenced significant developments. The stream has been broadened and enlivened; not a few magazines have proven important in their own right. Critics who downgrade the little-mag movement cite mags which have merely been media to feed the vanities of their editors, those with eccentric or limited aims or devoted to cliques, those innocuously endeavoring to revive old traditions, and those in offensively bad taste. Such critics fail to see that the good outweighs the bad, that even cursory examination of the experiences of the writers forming today's quality vanguard verifies that little mags have been essential to an upsurge of creativity.

Evidence that unknown writers of probable significance have become known writers is part of the *Trace* story. In 1961, associate Gil Orlovitz suggested that we not only talk about new literature but publish examples of it. The "Creative Window" section was inaugurated; and now over half the content consists of poetry, fiction, literary experimentation of all types, plus graphic art. In eight years, more new writers have been introduced than in any other magazine.

And a few older writers of rather fading reputation have been aided. These had, for one reason or another (reasons having little to do with their works), fallen into disfavor, appearing scarcely anywhere until revived by print here. Related to this has been a policy of publishing articles, when available, about writers of the past who, I felt, deserved more attention than they were receiving. Preference has been given those whose influences were contemporary.

One way in which *Trace* has been different from nearly all other mags of its kind has been in its use of reviews and/or mentions of some books published by their authors, including some from vanity presses. This has not been to encourage people to pay for their own books (a most unsatisfactory nonsolution), and emphatically not to give comfort to unethical publishers, but because such books occasionally do have merit and the writers deserve recognition. I don't feel that talent should be penalized; and history reveals that many eminent authors have had to finance their early offerings. (It is this fact, by the way, which provides the potent lure to self-publication—the aspirants giving no thought to the added fact that only one in tens of thousands makes it in this way.)

The *Trace* editorial line mainly has been fixed by the editor—for most of the years solely by him. For about three years, there was an editorial board. If any one member was overwhelmingly impressed by a manuscript, it was accepted even though all the others did not much approve. The idea was to avoid falling into the pattern which results from majority rule: a leveling down to a common denominator, with nothing really inferior winning print, but nothing outstandingly offbeat winning it either. However, *Trace* began to lose direction, becoming more eclectic than eclectic. I again reserved all final decisions to myself.

Just the same, there has been no arbitrary one-man rule. Hundreds of subscribers have influenced me, as well as the many people who have come to my aid at various periods. Those who have helped *Trace* have been Marvin Bell, Mary Carol Bird, Guy Daniels, G. E. Evancheck, A. Fredric Franklin, Alexandra Garrett, Duncan S. Harris, Robin Johnson, Helen Luster, Carl Linder, Stuart Montgomery, Warren Netz, Gil Orlovitz, John V. Sankey, Geraldo Sobral, Lawrence P. Spingarn, Wai-lim Yip, and Curtis Zahn.

During 1960 and 1961, the directories were divorced from *Trace*. A separate project, *The International Guide*, was independently financed under direction of Miss Bird. I was merely an adviser, though I continued to maintain my own card files on the magazines, etc. With the collapse of the *Guide,* a complete directory again was carried in *Trace* (number 47). During those two years, *The Chronicle* had been limited to little-press books and pamphlets. Since number 47, each year's directories have been indexed so that the four (or three, now) comprised a workable inclusive reference for everything noted in the twelve months. These have been complete only so far as new or changing projects were concerned (together with a hundred or so of the more active regulars).

With 72/73, there have been 939 contributors, from most parts of the English-speaking world and from numerous other-language areas. As the years passed, the influx of submissions became larger and larger. A survey in 1965 showed that about 3 percent of these were accepted. This dropped below 1 percent in the intervening period. Manuscripts almost never have been solicited, and then only for a specific need. Yet this has not by any means been a major factor accounting for the comparative absence of well-known writers from these pages. "Name" authors have from time to time sent in work; but the policy has been to favor talented unknowns or those less recognized. When print has been given to established writers, this has been because the material was such that, for one or another irrelevant (from the literary view) reason, it might not be published anywhere else.

The editorial position has been to remain open to all types of writings and to judge these on the writers' degree of success in achieving their particular intentions—not to read with preconceived and set notions as to method. The result has been that, as mentioned in number 68—for better or for worse so far as the state of literature is concerned—*Trace* has introduced more new writers (especially in the sixties) than any other periodical. A policy of publicizing author-financed publications along with those from royalty houses also appears to have aided many beginners.

During the fifties, before the magazine was opened to original creative works, main emphasis was upon the littles and products of the small presses, and this coverage has continued to the very finish. And if less detailed descriptions and fewer and fewer reviews have since appeared, this has been due to the unbelievable proliferation of publications. Their numbers have made it impractical to much more than note their existence. The first directory (1952), limited to magazines, had but 152 entries; yet that was a fairly complete world coverage of littles in English. By 1956, 247 mags were listed along with 165 presses; and in 1963, the combined total had reached 747. But the huge acceleration began with 1964. The *incomplete* "Evolving Directory" in *Trace* 71 had 697 entries. Indexed projects and listings in this issue totaled 999.

In the early years, *Trace*—though carrying articles (some of them perhaps definitive) and critical reviews—was more a meeting place for other publications than a periodical in its own right. There were numerous exchanges of ideas and opinions among editors from all parts of the world. Number 4 (1953), for example, had letters from editors in England, France, and Australia,

383

as well as the U.S. In 1954, an attempt to get data on editorial *intentions* was less than successful. Only eleven editors were willing to express themselves frankly (a twelfth wrote for an ensuing issue). Still, scores of editors from time to time did reveal purposes quite honestly in the letters department.

In this same early period, there was a "first" statistical survey (number 5) derived from questionnaires concerning financing and management. Over seventy editors sent information for an article by John Sankey.

Trace helped in a general way to provide awareness of a *continuity* of literature developments through the two decades; and it had a decided share in the poetry revival. The editor wrong-guessed, in 1965, that what was then termed an unprecedented period of innovations was about to be succeeded by one of conservatism and "digestion." The opposite has been occurring, as every reader of new writings is aware—with ever more "far-out" matter. Not a few opinions with which the editor was in disaccord, and some poetry and creative prose not personally favored, were given print due to the wish to "trace" all types of possibly significant trends. From this, it was sometimes charged that *Trace* had no editorial direction. However, the editorial criticisms in *Trace* were outrightly biased and often strongly outspoken.

Among other prominent editorializings were those in which favor was expressed for more positive themes, as against a preponderance of negativism. It also was suggested—by example as well as comment—that a little mag, even though seeking newnesses of statement and publishing avant-garde material, mainly of interest to a limited audience, still might be entertaining to less prepared readers. Comparatively few editors have troubled themselves to try to make serious mags more enjoyable without catering to general public taste.

Since *Trace* emphasis always has been upon the individual and distinctively personal contributions, there has been editorial resistance to the concept of "movements." Rather than devoting sections or issues to this or that so-labeled trend, there have been features such as an autobiographical issue (number 58, 1965), a section of poetry derived from dreams (number 46, 1962), Chinese and Indian issues (number 54, 1964, and number 67, 1968), special numbers with emphasis on satire, humor, etc. Important in this connection was the *Trace* line of reaction to the dubious beginnings

384

of the "underground" in the late fifties. This was seen as—and so it *was*—an accidental and quite inconsistent and internally conflictive development. It was not foreseen that the beatnik attitude toward life and letters was to progress toward an organized political and literary persuasion—of late, under the hippie label. But I still hold to the argument of an essay in *Trace* number 34 (1959): that there are, betwixt and among and between the square conservatives and the posturing outsiders, the more significant individuals doing their own things.

Yet another matter, which has from time to time taken up many pages of this magazine, has been the conflict over comparative values of the creations of people connected with the "academy" and those not so connected—over the relative merits of things published in school-supported mags and things in independent mags. Again, so far as *Trace* has been concerned, this may be determined only by looking at particular *works,* disregarding academic connections (or their absence). It has not infrequently been charged that *Trace* has been anti the academy. This is patently ridiculous in view of the fact that far more than half the contributors to this magazine have been post-grad students and teachers, largely college professors. If more space has been given the "anti's" this has been because their contributions outnumbered the defenders. However, a large percentage of the "anti" arguments came *from* the colleges; and the real point of difference was not whether an author held degrees and made his living by teaching, but whether his work *therefore* was unoriginal and conservative. And, going back to the mags, unhappy pronouncements about independents have been as numerous as those about persons under school aegis.

Not only has considerable attention been given the probability that too many magazines have been publishing a great deal of inconsequential matter, but the question has been raised whether the enormous increase in publications has not brought about a progressive thinning of force and quality. At what point might not vitalizing diversification become senseless variegation? This sort of critical conjecture was not limited to the little-mag field, but extended to an examination of the entire overcrowded literary scene. Or *was* it really overcrowded, so much as weakened and muddled by increasing percentages of bloated semi-literacies?

Even more attention has been given to expression itself, to

possible language corruption (rather than healthy integral growth) and breakdown (where words often seemed no longer to be used for meaningful communication at any level). In 1962, the period was seen as one of nonconformism—some of it pertinent to possible major developments of expression, some of it superficial doodling. Earlier, there had been concern that so many serious writers were dealing with short-term specifics and disregarding long-term fundamentals. Then, after it was realized along in 1966 that the great explosion of experimentations had set up chain reactions which would continue into the seventies, the question was raised as to which kind of literary vehicle might best carry forward. The novel was looked upon with uncertainty, and the new poetries appeared to be communicating to increasing numbers of people. These and related factors were examined in numerous articles and interviews with prominent writers.

I have mentioned the part the magazine played in bringing writers in all parts of the English-speaking world together in print in many countries—and thus bringing about exchanges of influences that otherwise would not have occurred. Some of the littlest littles suddenly had contributors from far-scattered places. One gradual effect has been to lessen language differences. Another has been the breakdown of verbal reserve, the language of propriety. In the beginning, this was chiefly in the U.S., but today many writings in Britain, Canada, India, Australia, and New Zealand are as far out as any in the United States.

From the *Trace* view, to the extent that genuine originality (honest individual expression) has spread, this is to the good; but, to the extent that posturing abuse of expression and utilization of vulgarities for purposes of shock has spread, this is to the bad. This must not be interpreted as criticism of the use of four-letter words per se. Explicit consideration of specified works would be essential; and more weight should be given the achievement of an effective texture and style (*newly* and strikingly propounded themes) than to the inclusion or noninclusion of words which, until the last couple of decades, brought unquestioned censorship. The same holds true for what had been forbidden subject matter: not *what,* but *how,* and to what end.

This stance has been reflected in *Trace,* where all kinds of frankness have been permitted wherever the writings were judged to be of possible literary merit. From time to time, this has resulted in losses of subscribers who were offended. Precisely how many were lost, I cannot say; but I assume that for every one sending an indignant letter, there were many who silently allowed their subscriptions to lapse. From a "practical" view, *Trace* could have compensated for these many times over by becoming sensationally pornographic—as have certain magazines formerly in the literary category. But I should think it must have been clear long ago that *Trace* has not been edited to make money, or even to stop losing money.

Having firsthand experience of the financial problems of a little mag, as early as 1955 *Trace* pushed for grants for such projects. Apparently this was rather ineffective, more than ten years having passed before such aid began to flow after establishment of the National Endowment for the Arts. In the case of this editor, the probability of adequately substantial assistance for a comprehensive bibliographical project came too late. Since there have been many inquiries about this, it's fitting for me to state that considerations of health were the deciding negative elements.

The Wormwood Review

Winter 1960

Wormwood, *Vol. 1, No. 1, Winter 1960 (courtesy Marvin Malone).*

THE GALL OF <u>WORMWOOD</u> IN PRINTING OVER 66 ISSUES AND STILL CONTINUING
Marvin Malone

In addition to being a poet and the editor of The Wormwood Review, *Marvin Malone is professor of pharmacology at the University of the Pacific, the author of 167 research publications, editor of the* American Journal of Pharmaceutical Education, *co-editor of the* Pacific Information Service on Street-Drugs, *member of the editorial boards of* Lloydia: The Journal of Natural Products *and* Journal of Ethnopharmacology, *and an authority on the isolating and testing of drugs from higher fungi and plants.*

Mr. Malone is also a spare-time printmaker and an avid collector of little magazines. Frances Steloff of the Gotham Book Mart, H. E. Briggs of Books 'n Things, and Larry Wallrich of the Phoenix Bookshop were his original tutors in this regard. The earliest influence on Mr. Malone's notions of publishing was Eugene Jolas' magazine, transition. *His editorial philosophy is amply disclosed below.*

Let me be direct: for a little magazine to succeed it must have (1) a memorable title and a reasonably tidy publishing format; (2) one altruistic, well-read editor or editor in chief with extraordinary patience and persistence; (3) a budget which matches editorial aspirations with income; and (4) some sense of the absurd to offset the aura of high purpose which can clot around such a venture. Let me be realistic: the above items are listed in reverse order of importance.

A good little-mag title should be unique and have some poetic connotation(s). The "wormwood" of *The Wormwood Review* was not chosen because of the biblical star Wormwood heralding the oncoming apocalypse, not from *Screwtape,* not from oil of wormwood (the active ingredient in absinthe which is reputed to make "hearts grow fonder" but which in reality produces organic brain damage), and not from the classic bitter draft of wormwood and gall. The title derives directly from Wormwood Hill in East Connecticut, where artemisia grows abundantly and near the place where the first issue was printed. Artemisia tea "repels black fleas, discourages slugs, keeps beetles and weevils out of grain, and combats aphids." The word "wormwood" carries many connotations, all of which have some validity since all are based ultimately upon the reputation of the plant.

The editor is a professional pharmacologist, and as a result has been able to remain clear and independent of the politics, subpolitics, schools, subschools, factions, and subfactions of the nonliterary aspects of the literary culture and subculture of the past two decades. This has allowed him to focus available time and energy on the contents of the mag. The editor dictates the contents of *Wormwood*—rather than the audience (as in commercial magazines and the university quarterlies) or the contributors (as in the cult little magazines). Consequently *Wormwood* strives to educate and build an audience and to avoid cults.

Always a reader and a writer, the to-be-editor picked up on the *New Directions Annuals* during his first year in college. Then in rapid sequence he came across *transition, View, Poetry London, Horizon* (Connolly), *Golden Goose, Zero*—and then the world of the little magazine opened, with *Inferno* and *The Deer and the Dachshund.* The editor-to-be was hooked. The baptism was completed by the reading of the classic book *The Little Magazine: A History and a Bibliography,* by Frederick J. Hoffman, Charles Allen, and Carolyn F. Ulrich. He began collecting and reading, and the process continues undiminished. The collection is regarded as still the most comprehensive outside a university—beginning with complete sequences of Wyndham Lewis's *Blast* (1914–1915) and Margaret Anderson's *the little review* (1914–1929) and running through to this issue of *TriQuarterly.*

This catholic reading and collecting policy has forced the development of (1) a realistic perspective on what a little magazine can and cannot accomplish, (2) some editorial sense of what the sustaining influences are in Amerenglish literature, and (3) some editorial appreciation of what is merely sophomoric rediscovery, what is frankly imitative, and what is truly unique in regard to submitted manuscripts. All this has led to a modest philosophy for the mag, to suit its very modest budget. The editor has never focused his energy on seeking and printing "established" names. The policy is as follows: (1) to seek new names and to sustain them, (2) *not* to feature the work of the editor and his personal friends, and (3) to avoid all the subtle and not-so-subtle vanity aspects by making the mag pay its way completely. *Wormwood* is quite content to be a little magazine and not a big-little magazine, a little-big magazine, or a big magazine. It receives about 3,000 submissions (all unsolicited) for each issue; with this input, there is no problem in finding new names for each new number. *Wormwood* does "discourage slugs."

In early correspondence with the editor, Cid Corman indicated that it was useful to have each issue of *Origin* associated in the public's mind with one poet, i.e. the Charles Olson issue, the Creeley issue, etc. This concept appealed, and *Wormwood* instituted its yellow-paper center sections (8–24 pages) devoted to either one poet or one idea. Twenty to forty copies are signed, and half are retained by *Wormwood* to distribute to patrons and friends of the press, while the remaining half become the poet's property. This concept has been helpful to the poets and to *Wormwood*. The poets featured to date are John Bennett (issue 55), Harold E. Briggs (40), Charles Bukowski (16, 24, 53, 71), William S. Burroughs (36), Judson Crews (19, 58), John Currier (44), Sanford Dorbin (42), Ian Hamilton Finlay (14), Hugh Fox (32), Don Gray (26), Oliver Haddo (27, 28, 39), Alfred Starr Hamilton (61), Dick Higgins (25), Gloria Kenison (23, 26), Ronald Koertge (29, 35, 51, 63), Carl Larsen (11), Lyn Lifshin (47, 59, 65), Gerald Locklin (31, 50, 64, 67), Al Masarik (57), Ann Menebroker (54), Jack Micheline (37), Joyce Odam (49), Christopher Perret (21, 30), Ben Pleasants (38, 52), Bern Porter (41), Ray Puechner (27, 28, 39), Steve Richmond (43, 70), Kirk Robertson (60, 69), Walter Snow (46), Richard Snyder (56), Charles Stetler (48), Brian Swann (68), William Wantling (15, 36), Charles Webb (62), Jon Edgar Webb/*The Outsider* (45), and Phil Weidman (33). If you, the reader of these words, have never heard of 50 percent of these authors, then you are missing a certain section of living Amerenglish literature. Four are already deceased: Briggs, Perret, Snow, and Wantling. The ages, the personalities, the backgrounds, the writing styles of these four are disparate in the extreme—their only common denominator is that their best work appeared in *Wormwood.*

Possibly the most appreciated and dreaded award an author can receive today is the annual Wormwood Award "for the most overlooked book of worth for a calendar year." In his search the editor does not confine himself to a diet of scientific journals and little magazines. Certain of the awardees are no longer unappreciated and unknown, but they were at the time of the award. Here is the list. 1961: Alexander Trocchi, *The Outsiders* (Signet); 1962: Kurt Vonnegut, Jr., *Mother Night* (Gold Medal); 1963: James Drought, *The Secret* (Skylight); 1964: Russell Edson, *The Very Thing That Happens* (New Directions); 1965: Christopher Perret, *Memoirs of a Parasite* (Hors Commerce Press/Callahan); 1966: Stanley Crawford, *Gascoyne* (Putnam); 1967: Peter Wild, *The Good Fox* (The Goodly Co.); 1968: Ian Hamilton Finlay, *3 Blue Lemons* (Wild Hawthorne Press); 1969: Charles Bukowski, *Notes of a Dirty Old Man* (Essex); 1970: Lorine Neidecker, *My Life by Water* (Fulcrum); 1971: Jonathan Williams, *Blue & Roots/Rue & Bluets* (Grossman); 1972: Gerald Locklin, *Poop, and Other Poems* (MAG Press); 1973: Ronald Koertge, *The Father Poems* (Sumac); 1974: Steve Richmond, *Earth Rose* (Earth Press); 1975: Lyn Lifshin, *Shaker House Poems* (Tideline); 1976: Phil Weidman, *After the Dance* (Orchard Press); 1977: Joseph Nicholson, *The Dam Builder* (The Fault); 1978: Charles Webb, *Zinjanthropus Disease* (Querencia Press). One can regard this annual award as a public service function of *Wormwood.*

The editor receives inquiries at a rate of about once a month from individuals writing theses or taking polls/surveys relating to the little magazine scene. One of them asked for a list of the books that had most influenced the editor. The list was assembled hastily—but continues to be fascinating personally. Since it probably tells more about the philosophical slant of *Wormwood* than anything else which could be written, the list is reproduced here: Hugh Lofting's *Dr. Dolittle* books; Jules Verne's *The Mysterious Island;* Saki's *Beasts and Super Beasts* and *The Unbearable Bas-*

392

sington; Nathanael West's *Miss Lonelyhearts;* Walt Whitman's *Leaves of Grass* (especially the preface to the 1855 edition); Céline's *Journey to the End of the Night* and *Death on the Installment Plan;* Henry Miller's *Tropic of Cancer, Tropic of Capricorn,* and *The Books in My Life;* George Orwell's *Down and Out in Paris and London* and *1984;* William Sansom's *Something Terrible, Something Lovely;* D. H. Lawrence's *Birds, Beasts and Flowers;* Joyce Cary's *The Horse's Mouth;* William Carlos Williams's *The Autobiography of WCW* and *Collected Later Poems;* James Joyce's *Finnegans Wake;* Ray Bradbury's *Fahrenheit 451;* Kurt Vonnegut, Jr.'s *Mother Night;* James Drought's *The Secret* and *Gypsy Moths.* The sequence is roughly in order of reading and omits many of the editor's favorite authors/poets—a favorite book may not necessarily be an influential book. Certainly the editor's known predilection for the prose-poem should now be less surprising.

After the first three issues, *Wormwood*'s format has always reflected its income—the money necessary to put out four issues a year. The receipt of four issues annually pleases librarians, and the libraries are the stable backbone of our subscription list. The first issue was printed in 1959 in a barn by letterpress, on a machine owned by one of the founding editors (Alexander Taylor). Since the barn did not have adequate electrical wiring, the press was operated by having the other two editors (James Scully and Morton Felix) spin the flywheel by hand. The editors were fueled by gin, since the weather was cold and the barn drafty. The paper was obtained at cost via Sandy Taylor's father.

This operation was economically sound, but the manual aspects did not appeal to the founding editors. Consequently the subscription money was used to print the second issue commercially. This used up all available cash. The venture went eighty dollars in debt, and the magazine quietly folded, as all good little magazines are supposed to do. In September 1960, the present editor arrived in Storrs, Connecticut—brash from mimeograph publishing in New Mexico, where little magazines perennially thrive. The first day there, he found the second issue of *Wormwood* in the magazine rack of one of the two local drugstores. On the second day, he learned that the mag was defunct, and within the month it was apparent that *Wormwood* had been a sport, in the biological sense of the word. The academic and nonacademic locals did not look favorably upon modern literature, and the publishing of a little magazine was clearly neither sound nor right. With Sandy Taylor, *Wormwood* was resuscitated. The librarians received the balance of their one-year trial subscriptions and were pleased. The mag also had been critically accepted. Renewals came in. A policy was made to stay within the budget and adjust the format accordingly. This was not an easy choice, since many individuals consciously or subconsciously buy little magazines because of an attractive/exciting format—a format that will enhance coffee table decor.

With issue 5 other responsibilities took Sandy away from direct participation, and with issue 9 the present editor assumed full responsibility. To stay within the budget, he takes no money from the operation and puts every cent earned by the magazine back into its production. Any other names appearing on the masthead are pseudonyms (A. Sypher, Ernest Stranger, etc.); the magazine is a one-man operation. The editor reads all manuscripts, selects those matching the current editorial psyche, prepares camera-ready copy, designs the covers, maintains the mailing list, bills accounts, balances the books, addresses the envelopes, mails out the magazines. Currently, issues are mailed out two at a time to save effort in addressing, save the cost of envelopes, and cut the postal bill in half. The operation is tightly run: bills are paid on time and subscribers have guaranteed subscriptions. Only four bookstores in the U.S. have been found to be equally reliable in living up to their business obligations: Asphodel Bookshop (Burton, Ohio), Chatterton's Bookshop (Los Angeles, California), Either/Or Bookstore (Hermosa Beach, California), and Serendipity Books (Berkeley, California). This very sorry state of ethics explains why *Wormwood* is not to be found in more bookstores in more cities.

The bookstores are not the only ones at fault. The editor believes that the main reason why private individuals do not subscribe to little magazines in greater numbers is the sloppy business practices of the average little magazine. Speaking from much experience as a collector, the editor realizes no one wants to pay in advance for a four-issue subscription and receive one issue, knowing that two have been published (issue 1 reserved for libraries because too few copies were printed), and then have the magazine cease publication with the third issue (copies distributed only to friends of the press). No chance of a refund (there was a "closing" party and everyone left town)! After being burned this way several times in succession, only the true little-mag addict persists, and he too eventually begins to restrict subscriptions to DeBoer-circulated magazines. To combat this, *Wormwood* has a guaranteed subscription policy.

Wormwood prints only 700 copies. Approximately 100 are targeted as payment to contributors (two to six copies each or the cash equivalent), and 100 are designated as "exchange" copies for other little magazines (to keep communications open). If 300 copies can be sold regularly, then the magazine can survive with a decent format. The number of the remaining 200 copies sold determines the extra pages in the next issue and the luxuries of format that can be afforded. *Wormwood* retains its modest format because the magazine must operate within the limits of available money and available time. If 2,000 copies were to be printed, they could certainly be sold to bring in more money and to produce a more elegant look. However, the magazine could no longer be a one-man operation and a completely new and expensive set of operating procedures would be necessary—and the mag would probably not survive this "progress."

In July 1967 *Wormwood* received one of the first fifteen grants awarded by the Coordinating Council of Literary Magazines; the amount was $415. Two grants have been applied for and received since that time (1970: $500; 1973: $1,000). Each grant has been used to tidy up the format of the magazine and to consolidate the "gain" without departing from the modest philosophy and modest size. *Wormwood* continues without being dependent on grants for survival.

Every three years the editor rereads the magazine as he prepares the traditional three-year index and debates whether *Wormwood* continues to have a function; there is no wish for continuation as an end in itself. The responses of readers and contributors, the number of reprint requests, the relative number of new talents found, and so on, are considered. If this analysis is positive, sub-

395

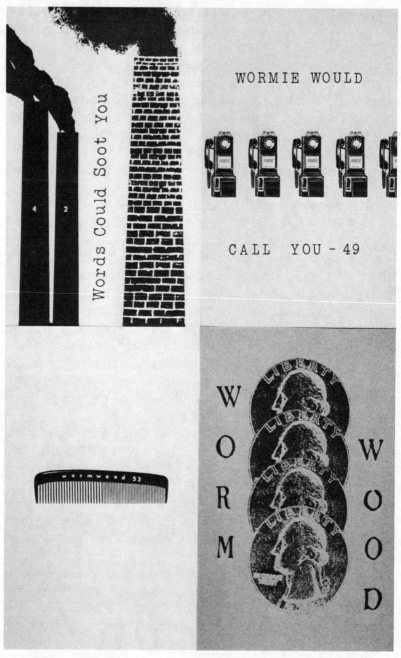

The Wormwood Review, *Nos. 42, 49, 53, 64 (courtesy Marvin Malone).*

scriptions are then guaranteed for the next three years. Issue 72 will carry the next announcement as to whether *Wormwood* continues or stops.

A sense of self-importance has stifled many little magazines. *Wormwood* has at least one apparent way of combating this phenomenon. The approach is somewhat sophomoric and has frustrated the librarians and put off certain serious scholars of modern literature—nevertheless the technique seems to prevent creeping pomposity. Since issue 32 the cover title of the magazine (supported by the cover art) has been some semantic corruption of the magazine's very high-poetry real name, e.g. *The Warm Wooly Review, Worm Oil on View, Wormwood Cuts Through, The Worm Would View You, Wormwood in You, The Worm Would Bite and Chew, The Worn World Raw View, The Warm Wood Tree View,* etc. In 1975 the masthead indicated that our beloved art editor, A. Sypher, had apparently been fired and a new editor, Ernest Stranger, hired. This allowed the ever considerate Editor-in-Chief Malone to adopt a subtitle for *The Wormwood Review.* The subtitle? "Incorporating *Malone-Stranger Review.*" The knowledgeable can only sigh and reply, "Heigh-ho, Silver!"

ROBERT KELLY
AN INTERVIEW ON
<u>TROBAR</u>
David Ossman

Robert Kelly, editor of Trobar. *Photograph by Gerard Malanga.*

Robert Kelly, one of the proponents of the blend of surrealism, imagism, and plain talk that characterizes the Black Mountain School and many of the Beat poets, called some of his poetic variants "lunes": "Lunes are small poems that spend half their lives in darkness and half in light. Each lune has thirteen syllables, one for each month of the moon's year. Along about the middle, the dark of the moon comes. The full moon is the approximate splendor of the whole lune, provided the clouds do not fall too heavily on that poem."

Mr. Kelly was co-editor of Trobar *magazine and Trobar Books in the early sixties. His publications comprise twenty-eight books of poetry—including* Armed Descent *(1961),* Flesh, Dream, Book *(1971), and* The Loom *(1975)—and three novels:* The Scorpions *(1967),* Cities *(1972), and* A Line of Sight *(1974). Mr. Kelly has taught at California Institute of Technology, SUNY-Buffalo, Tufts University, and currently teaches at Bard College.*

First of all, what is the relationship of the "Image" to Trobar?

With our first issue, we wanted poetry that qualified by being alive in one sense or another. We, in our own work and in our critical attention, grew more and more involved with the poetry of images.

Let me say this about the Image: if you want to divide all the ways of going into the poem, all the quanta and quotients of poetry, I think the division of powers that Ezra Pound made long ago, into three, is the best. His division was *logos*, or word—word-magic, word-development, the development of meaning; *melos*, the musical gist, the musical development—singing, really —sound; and third, *phanos*, literally "brightness," phanopeia equaling, for Pound, "throwing the image onto the mind." This is the intellectual and emotional tone of the poem.

Now, if poetry deals with word, word is its ground—you might call word the mystical hypostasis of all poetry, of all literary art. At the same time, music (*melos*) is the space-time of poetry—its line, extent, duration. These two approaches to poetry, or these two behaviors of poetry, have been well analyzed and well discussed for a number of years—I should say about 2,500 years at least. The third, *phanos,* the image, has gotten rather slighting attention. In the 30s and 40s we heard a lot about "metaphor," largely, I suppose, because Pound was talking about metaphor in the 10s and 20s; but we've also heard a little about image.

The Image Poetry that I'm talking about is not what Pound nowadays means when he speaks of the poetry *des Amy-gistes.* When I speak of Image Poetry, I'm speaking both of a way of looking at all poetry, and also, in our own time, of a particular

This interview is reprinted from a collection of interviews with modern poets by David Ossman called *The Sullen Art,* published by Corinth Books in 1963.

stance of the poet as regards his material; that stand generates a kind of poetry not necessarily dominated by the images, but in which it is the rhythm of images which forms the dominant movement of the poem. I'm not trying to say that all great poetry is essentially Image Poetry. I will say that all great poetry generates its images, both the Final Emergent Image of the work of art (Pound calls the *Commedia* a single image) and, more so, the image as prime generated material of the poem—the primal image—which can be expressed as it normally is—in the word—but can also be expressed, can cohere, in sound.

Now this all seems rather remote from *Trobar*, but what I've been saying records part of the sharpening process that went on in my mind and in the minds of my friends and associates. This sharpening of focus led us to try to make *Trobar* a vehicle for Image Poetry. I certainly don't say that that's the only place it can be found, or the only place it will be found, because the poetry of image is coming more and more to life in America. For confirmation, don't look to any tendentious little magazine whatever, but to the work itself or more and more poets. I think the revival of interest in poets like Lorca and Neruda—they're becoming almost "standard" poets now—is based very largely on the enormous dark sentiment of Lorca, that darkness that "surrounds" us in *things,* and on Neruda's celebrations and love of the things of the earth. In their work, image becomes the motive force of the poem: their voice is in the images as much as in the music. If they play, they play on some ground. Really, this revival had to come, this awakening to the fullness of poetry, after the dry wit and tricks of words that marred so much of the poetry of the 50s. This is a partisan statement, but the worst thing you can say about a poem, any poem, is that it's dull.

Do you think that a poetry concerned with the Image is likely to be a surrealist kind of poetry?

I think probably the first stage an individual poet would go through in trying to let Image emerge in his work would be a surrealist one. I really don't believe that surrealism and the Poetry of Image necessarily constitute more than a companionate marriage. Surrealism has its own technique at the heart—I think it is a technique—and I feel, rightly or wrongly, that the Poetry of Images

400

ANTIN

DUNCAN

ECONOMOU

ESHLEMAN

GREEN

KELLY

KUENSTLER

MENDELSON

ROTHENBERG

Trobar, *Vol. 1, No. 1, 1960 (courtesy Northwestern University Library).*

(stress on Poetry: it's not a technique) is essentially a mode of Vision. Vision is something of enormous importance in talking about poetry—we very rarely talk about it, perhaps because it's so indefinable. (Pound, for instance, leaves it out altogether in the *ABC of Reading;* that book is so good because it keeps to the discrete: you can't teach the other.) The use of images constitutes a part of the poet's Vision. It has nothing to do with technique. You can simulate a surrealist poem but you cannot simulate, in a true sense, an Image Poem. This is no real criticism of surrealism— it has its own concerns. But if it can be extrapolated and a technique formed on the basis of it, it's not what we're talking about. Image is a vehicle for Vision. Vision discovers. What some consider Blake's fancies are explorations of the real world, discoveries through perception. Remember what Stevens said: Surrealism invents; it cannot discover.

In your recent issue, you publish poems by Creeley, Duncan, and Snyder. How does their work in Trobar *differ from their work to be found in other magazines featuring them and the "new American poetry"?*

I don't believe it differs at all. I want to bring up again that I don't think that Image Poetry is the only kind of poetry. The poetry we publish, God knows, the poetry we write, is new and it is American; the important thing is that it gets written, that it stands.

I think Duncan is one of the greatest poets writing today in English. I think, as various people, notably Creeley, have said of him, that his work is enormously rich in technical solutions as well as in movement and meaning. I would think very little of a magazine that isolated itself from a poet such as Duncan merely because Duncan operates on all levels of poetic meaning. His *Venice* poem, his greatest work I've encountered, is very strongly built on the flow of Image, as well as upon space and measure.

With Creeley, there's a different consideration. Creeley, too, is an exceedingly fine poet, I think, if I can say so without anything at all except humble admiration of the man and his work—a man who's writing poetry of a beauty that I thought a few years ago impossible in this day and age—of an excellence I still think incredible. Again, for the magazine, similar reasons apply. Snyder is most relevant as far as the Poetry of Images is concerned. The most

402

recent book of Snyder's, *Myths and Texts,* is to my mind one of the strongest books published by an American since the *Pisan Cantos,* let's say. And it is, by my definition, Image Poetry. That's a tremendously important book, not just as an accomplishment and a measure, but as a direction.

The origin of a paper you have written, called Notes on the Poetry of Images, *was in seeing Eisenstein films and relating the Image in poetry to filmic montage. Do you still see Image Poetry in these terms?**

Since then, I've thought about something that might be a difference, might not be a difference. The film starts out with a *known* reality: the reality the camera faces—and when you're building up film montage with the sequences and the strips and the cuts and finally the frame itself, I think that you are in a different position altogether from the poet employing images. Different only because, while you don't know what the outcome is going to be, you at least know what you have to start out with. The poet doesn't. There is a Mystery in poetry, and I really mean this with a capital M, a darkness, an atmosphere in which the author composes the Images before he really knows what those Images amount to. Now, if you take one of the famous Eisenstein frames—a long line of troops seen far in the distance across a snowy field—whatever this Image may amount to in later development, it is something in itself. It is white and black and gray and the very thin line of soldiers and the whole horizontal motion—and the motion in depth. You can take it out and print it in a book, look at it, and know what you're seeing. It is a thing. The poetic Image is not a thing. It is process and a discovered identity. It discovers its being in its function.

*The paper referred to was privately circulated. A later version was published as *Notes on the Poetry of Deep Image* in *Trobar* 2 (1961). Before the printed version came out, the author benefited from a number of comments and criticisms generously and relevantly supplied by many people, especially Robert Duncan, Robert Creeley, Gary Snyder, Denise Levertov (whose critique was published in *The Floating Bear* No. 11), and Charles Olson, whose brief comment, "not imageS but IMAGE," was fundamental. Most of these comments took exception to the terms of the paper or their development; the names given above are in no way responsible for the printed version, which, it should be noted, paid much less attention to the film (R. K., 1962). David Ossman's comments on Kelly's paper, which pay considerable attention to the film, were also published in *The Floating Bear* No. 13.

I think there's that difference, and this is really why I bring in the question of rhythm. Image is the rhythm of poetry. I've said this over and over again in my paper, and I must say now, and give full credit, that this is a formulation that is not originally mine, though I've made use of it fully. Nicolas Calas, the surrealist writer and art critic, offers as a dictum (I really don't know in what context, since I've seen it only quoted) just this statement: "The combination of images constitutes the rhythm of the poem." Rather than talk of laws of combinations, I just want to say that the Image itself, in its development, constitutes the fundamental, basic rhythm of the poem, which all other rhythms—sound rhythms, stress rhythms, and so forth—must subserve.

Now here again I think you come back to the film, with its interspersal of one shot with another and (I don't know what Eisenstein calls it) the visual similarity, if not identity, of two successive images of different subjects—their formal, structural nature being the same. The intertranslatability of all things is fundamental to all poetry; it is perhaps more obvious in Image Poetry, and perhaps there there's a tie-in with the film. If it does tie up with film montage, it does so not so much from the point of view of the individual frame, as from the rhythmic point of view of what is done with the frame. The processes may be analogous; the modular units are different.

Is there any one experience, more than another, that prompts you to write a poem?

It's something that I do. I don't know how to stop writing them. I don't know what the impetus is—or, I guess, we can all say in one theoretical way or another what the impetus is and we all know in one real way or another what the impetus is, but can we verbalize them? Have any people succeeded in verbalizing that impetus? The conformation of necessities in the unconscious, the conformation of shapes and structures that demand expression—I think it is that, or sometimes the song—the sound of music of some kind.

404

EL CORNO EMPLUMADO, 1961-1969: SOME NOTES IN RETROSPECT, 1975
Margaret Randall

Margaret Randall, editor of El Corno Emplumado *(courtesy* Poetry *magazine).*

The birth of El Corno Emplumado, *and its maintenance throughout the eight years of its publication, came from a consciousness forged out of two quite different origins: Margaret Randall's own beginnings in the Beat and Black Mountain traditions in the United States during the late 1950s, and the work of a widely dispersed group of Latin American writers who emerged rather as iconoclasts but came to social consciousness as their life situations—and those of their countries and peoples—demanded. Writers whose work was important to Ms. Randall in her early days with the magazine included William Carlos Williams, Robert Creeley, Allen Ginsberg, and Gertrude Stein as well as Latin Americans Ernesto Cardenal (Nicaragua) and Octavio Paz (Mexico). "The development that went along with the making of the magazine changed our needs, tastes, in short our consciousness, literarily as well as socially, or literarily and socially at one and the same time." By 1969, when the magazine folded, it was possible to list the writers who had become vital to its growth. They were, with others, César Vallejo (Peru), Mario Benedetti (Uruguay), Violeta Parra (Chile), Walt Whitman, Hart Crane, William Carlos Williams, Roque Dalton (El Salvador), and Gabriel García Márquez (Colombia), and the newer Cuban poets and writers.*

During the years of El Corno's *publication, Ms. Randall maintained close ties with literary magazines on both continents: Cuba's* Casa de las Américas, *Mexico's* Pájaro Cascabel, *Venezuela's* Techo de la Ballena, *and Argentina's* Eco Contemporáneo, *among many more, as well as* City Lights, Trobar, I.Kon, *and others published in the United States. Ms. Randall has published twenty-three volumes of her own work—poems, essays, and stories. Much of her writing concerns women, including the study that led to the publication of* Cuban Women Now *(1974); a book about Nicaraguan women entitled* Somos Millones *(1977); a book of interviews with women living in the Democratic Republic of North Vietnam and the then-liberated zones of South Vietnam entitled* Spirit of the People *(1975); and a current project dealing with Chilean women in the resistance. Her short stories, poems, articles, interviews, essays, and translations have appeared in most of the major literary journals of the United States, Mexico, Cuba, and other countries.*

406

In the fall of 1961 I left New York and arrived in Mexico City with my small son; with a still to some extent individualized anguish, a consequently off-center rage, and the determination that everything would be different. I thought of myself primarily as Margaret Randall, a poet.

My spiritual baggage: middle-class and provincial America, an awakening in the Beat fifties, Ginsberg superimposed on Williams and Pound, hearing my own voice somehow out of Black Mountain and, more recently, Deep Imagery. Abstract Expressionism. Politics: progressive but unorganized; indignant but baffled.

In Mexico City the visionary Catholic poet Philip Lamantia had preceded me by some years. His apartment on Rio Hudson was a meeting place for other North Americans who, for one reason or another, had been exuded, expelled, or propelled from the metropolis: Ray Bremser, Howard Frankl, Harvey Wolin.

The Peruvian Raquel Jodorowsky and the Nicaraguan Ernesto Cardenal—later to become a priest—were other arrivals.

Of the Mexicans who frequented the apartment, read their poetry, and established with us—and we with them—the common need to know "what was happening to the south, what was happening to the north," there were Sergio Mondragón, Juan Martínez, Homero Aridjis, Jaime Augusto Shelley, Juan Bañuelos. The intense, complex, and silent painter Carlos Coffeen Serpas was there, his mother's wild shadow always drifting behind him. The English surrealist Leonora Carrington was a sometime part of our group. The great Spanish poet exiled in Mexico, Léon Felipe, was a mentor.

It would be difficult to recall a group of men and women who would later go in more diverse directions. For those of us who remain, it might be interesting to meet again one day, to assess together that moment in time. The sixties. Clearly, though most of us were grappling with very individualistic needs (or needs that did not yet fall into a social perspective in our heads and hands), the unifying factor was this realization: What did we, from the North, know of Vallejo, of Neruda, much less the expression of our more contemporary Latin American brothers and sisters? What did these poets and writers, whose medium was Spanish, know of our Williams, Pound, Creeley, Blackburn?

I remember long nights when most of us understood very little of what was being read. Our need to share, to experience each other's questions and answers, was expressing itself at that time all over Latin America and throughout the United States. It was the boom in the "little magazine."

El Corno Emplumado/The Plumed Horn (the jazz horn of the U. S. and the plumes of Quetzalcoatl) was simply an expatriate expression of that boom. In that sense it partook of the simple urge to speak, to be heard, to be felt—an urge characteristic of similar magazines that were born, lived, and died in many countries during those years. Its other dimension was the duality of language, the thrust toward breaking barriers which we knew were established by our enemy without yet understanding why or even how. Or even who the real enemy was.

In the United States *Black Mountain Review* was already a classic, to be drawn upon. We saw ourselves connected in one way or another to *Evergreen Review* before it became slick, *City Lights Journal, Trobar,* George Hitchcock's hand-wrought *Kayak, Kulchur,* the outer edges of *Poetry,* Robert Bly's *The Sixties* for his concern with the great Latin voices, and many, many others. The radius included *Duende* in New Mexico, d. a. levy's *Renegade Press* in Cleveland, *Elizabeth* in New Rochelle, and Leavenworth's *New Era* (written and run by prisoners).

South of the Río Bravo there was *El Techo de la Ballena* (*The Roof of the Whale*) in Caracas, *Eco Contemporaneo* and *Airon* in Buenos Aires, *Pajaro Cascabel* in Mexico, groups in Colombia, Peru, Nicaragua, Chile, Uruguay, Guatemala. And, increasingly, Cuba. We were in touch with all these groups—the letters back and forth, the poems, the dreams and plans shook with discovery and affirmation on a continental scale. From Canada, too, the feelers came. George Bowering had started up *Imago* to print the long poems. We communicated with poets, groups, magazines in India, Japan, Australia, Nigeria, England, Italy, France, the Soviet Union. At one time our exchange list numbered some 320—mostly "little"—magazines.

Sergio Mondragón, Harvey Wolin, and I launched *El Corno* in the last months of 1961. The first issue appeared in January 1962. It promised in its first editorial note to be ". . . a magazine of poetry, prose, letters, art from two Hemispheres . . . printed el corno emplumado the plumed horn el corno emplumado the plumed horn el corno emplumado the plumed horn el corno emplumado the plumed horn el corno emplumado the plumed horn el corno emplumado the plumed horn el corno emplumado the plumed horn el corno emplumado the plumed horn el corno

mejía sánchez - nieto - owens - shelley - randall - c
ardenal - frankl - lamantia - wolin - séjourné - der
meer - aridjis - jodorowsky - márquez - resnick - m
oudragón - glantz - clark - carrington - cofeen - soria
no - gavronsky - kelly - wulf - e. de kooning - león fe
lipe - cuadra - yllescas - mejía sánchez - nieto - ow

El Corno Emplumado, *Vol. 1, No. 1, January 1962 (courtesy Northwestern University Library).*

in Spanish and English . . . published in Mexico City out of the need for a NEW MAGAZINE . . . whose pages conform to the word instead of whose words conform to the pages . . . now, when relations between the Americas have never been worse . . . a showcase (outside politics) for the fact that WE ARE ALL BROTHERS . . . ."

We understood the alienation between two continents, but neither its colonialist nor its imperialist nature. We removed cultural expression from politics, falling easily into the enemy's trap of compartmentalization. The enemy—imperialism—that engages in cultural as well as economic and military penetration. The enemy that "brain drains," that has developed a thousand expert ways of ripping off people's culture and dangling the plastic and illusory dream called the "American Way of Life." For me, whose real history had been robbed from my life, the word politics had lost its real meaning. We were more concerned with form, perhaps, than we should have been, and we really thought we could all be brothers. (We didn't think, then, about being sisters. We were a few women, a minority among mostly men. Our intellectual pretensions took care of that ratio—women's consciousness was not part of us then.)

Now, holding *El Corno Emplumado* number 1 in my hands, rereading this editor's note after thirteen years, it's easy to see how we were then prisoners to a distorted, elitist, and even racist concept of art for art's sake. But there's a lot of solid searching, a lot of concrete discovery, a lot of brilliant, tactile, alive, and rebellious memory in the flashback. Whether we knew it or not (we didn't), and in spite of the idealistic nature of the moment, some of us at least were headed down roads that went in one direction only.

Looking through *El Corno* 1, I find Laurette Sejourne's wonderful *"El culto mágico de una virgen."* She deciphers the mysteries of Monte Alban, she who is without doubt one of the most penetrating, visionary, and dialectical of our anthropologists. I remember now how Laurette encouraged us from the beginning. She knew much more than the rest of us, always, but her greatness included knowing that we had to find out for ourselves.

Ernesto Cardenal goes back through the history of Nicaragua in *"El estrecho dudoso,"* denouncing the rape of land and people.

410

Léon Felipe speaks out in Spain's voice. Elaine de Kooning has contributed a strong drawing—one of her powerful bulls. Milton Resnick and Leonora Carrington stand out. In spite of ideological error, I am reminded how much really fine work the magazine offered.

Issue number 2: Allen Ginsberg for the first time in Spanish. Strong Clayton Eshleman, Paul Blackburn, Robert Kelly. Bruce Conner's asphyxiated sculpture. César Vallejo in English, though certainly neither well represented nor clearly appearing who or what he is.

In number 3 a long poem by Mario Benedetti appears in both Spanish and English. The Latin American poet dealing with New York City. A logical progression from Lorca. Kenneth Patchen and José Luis Cuevas yield the strongest visual expressions. Franz Kline's death is marked by two reproductions. Robert Kelly, Anselm Hollo, Kathleen Fraser, and others make statements worth remembering, and in that issue we began our policy (continued and expanded throughout the magazine's life) of presenting small anthologies of young work from different countries. Here it was Guatemala and Nicaragua.

The magazine became an institution. By that time—nearing the end of our first year—getting the money together to put out each issue was a task that consumed us. In the beginning it was an effort to collect the work, to convince writers and artists that the magazine was real, that it would appear, that it wasn't just another dream. By the end of the first year there was no problem getting material. Our correspondence grew and was richer every day. Funds were the problem—the story of all unofficial unbacked independent journals everywhere. I say "independent" with a bitter smile, for we maintained our independence with a fervor, we shouted it from the rooftops, and yet we had no consciousness of how tied we really were to our historic conditioning, to assumed attitudes and established institutions, even if those institutions weren't spelled with capital letters. We had been brought up in them. And yet we took a stand and, for where we were, it was an honest stand. In issue number 3 we could say (in our editor's note): "Our age—Cuba, Africa, Chessman, A-bombs, civil disobedience, abstract expressionism, electronic music, a million babies born every day—compresses the history we make to a madness which has fractured the light in which we move. . . ." If there was confusion, there was also awareness.

And who financed all this? Mexico's under secretary of state, José Goroztiza (once a great poet himself), New York bookseller Ted Wilentz, our parents, poets who contributed fifty pesos, occasional friends—Norman Mailer, Elaine de Kooning, Kurt Stavanhagan, etc.—who could give a hundred dollars. Poets got together and read to benefit the magazine. The first such reading, with poets of the stature of Ernesto Cardenal and Philip Lamantia, netted us six U.S. dollars! Later, painters offered their work, and several art shows in more than a few cities brought in considerable sums. Up to the last couple of years of the magazine's life, various agencies of the Mexican government—Bellas Artes, the Ministry of Education, the Secretary of the Presidency, etc. (this is common in Latin American countries)—provided subsidy. And our subscription list grew steadily, leveling off at around five hundred for most of the magazine's life.

Harvey Wolin, who was responsible for the magazine's name, dropped out after issue number 2. From then on it was Sergio Mondragón and me, for almost seven years. Sergio edited the Spanish side of the review and I the English. When we could (in issue 18, almost completely dedicated to Mexico, or in issue 23, totally dedicated to Cuba for that year's 26th of July), we presented bilingual facing-page translations. When we couldn't (which was much more often), it was Sergio's choice of work in Spanish, mine in English. During those years we also married each other, had children, created an institution of and around ourselves—an institution that both kept the project alive and came close to destroying us in our own lives.

Sergio's steady move toward the occult, the esoteric, the mystic and my just as steady move toward a Marxist-Leninist revolutionary consciousness began to create insoluble contradictions existing side by side between the magazine's front and back covers. There came a time when it was almost two magazines, within those covers—discernible only to the infinitely small percentage of our readership that digested both Spanish and English.

Throughout the magazine's history we took frequent stands, as did other publications of that kind, regarding issues of those times: the Vietnam war, support for the Cuban revolution, etc.

This never has been a problem in Mexico. The country has long been known for its libertarian stands on issues not directly affecting internal problems. However, when the 1968 student movement got under way, it was a different story. Our magazine, as well as many others, sided with the students in a movement for very basic and elemental human rights. Immediately, of course, official support was withdrawn. For most of our sister magazines, this meant instant death. However, perhaps because of *El Corno*'s bilingual nature, we had a possibility of support from outside the country. In answer to a letter we then sent to many friends in the United States, Europe, Latin America, and elsewhere, we received enough money to do another issue. We weren't willing to "go under" at the moment the enemy chose.

All this was heightened by the way things developed throughout the movement. The National University had been occupied by the students at the beginning of August (1968) and the army, complete with hundreds of tanks, etc., took it back on September 18. There were many deaths and many more people in prison. The 1968 Olympic Games were scheduled for October 12, at great political and financial cost to the country. On October 2, ten days before the Olympics, a peaceful demonstration in the middle of the city was surrounded by army, police, special troops, etc., and although the official death count was released as 26 (!), the real death toll has been calculated at between 500 and 1,000: men, women, old people, pregnant mothers, small children. No one will ever know for sure how many people died that afternoon because most of the bodies were incinerated and so simply "disappeared." For days those who loved them waited in endless lines in front of the Red Cross stations, before giving up hope.

So what was our situation in all this? What was the situation of *El Corno?* As individuals, we had taken part in the student movement. We weren't leaders; our roles were by no means important ones. We simply did what most honest people in Mexico City did at that time—helped the students, provided them with food, collected money, distributed propaganda, etc. At the same time, we had a magazine which, while not directly related to the student movement, supported it and took a radical stand, as it did on other problems. On top of that, we had not allowed them to do us in, as had been the case with several other similar

413

magazines. After their support had been withdrawn, we came out on schedule, as usual. This no doubt created resentment in some circles.

And *El Corno* kept on appearing: 1968 ended and 1969 began. I want to emphasize that our role was not particularly important, was not extraordinary in any way. But in those years in Mexico paramilitary groups were operating—either with or without direct cooperation from the government—and the prisons were overflowing. People were beaten up, clubbed to death; all sorts of methods were used (as are used everywhere when a system like capitalism feels threatened). By this time we had to change printers for each issue, because each printer we used would receive threats if he continued to help us publish. In July 1969, agents visited our house and stole my personal papers (passport, etc.). The first anniversary of the events of the year before was approaching. When harassment reached the level it did in July, we were advised to go into hiding. And that led to our eventually leaving the country. It wasn't that *El Corno,* as a magazine, was prohibited from appearing; it was simply that if the editors had to flee, who would do the magazine?

Thus the pressure, which produced its quota of struggle in 1966 and 1967, built beyond itself in 1968. Issue 29, corresponding to January 1969, was edited by me alone. The last two issues, 30 and 31, I co-edited with Robert Cohen. In mid-1969 the political repression that finally sent us into hiding and eventually out of Mexico forced the magazine out of existence. An era had ended. There was other work to be done.

As early as our first year, we hit upon the idea of dedicating each year's fourth issue (the magazine was a quarterly: January, April, July, and October) to a book of poems by an individual poet—one year from south of the border, the next year from north. These were completely bilingual facing-text enterprises which took a good deal of work and direction and love. The first year it was *Marsias & Adila* by the great Spanish poet, in exile in Mexico, Agustí Bartra. Elinor Randall (my mother) did the English translation. Our next such book, in issue 8, was Robert Kelly's *Her Body Against Time;* Sergio and I translated it into Spanish. In issue 12 was Raquel Jodorowsky's *Ajy Tojen,* and again the

414

translation (this time into English) was ours. Ditto for George Bowering's *Man in the Yellow Boots,* which was *El Corno* 16. The tradition stopped there; by that time *El Corno Emplumado* was publishing a series of books apart from the magazine itself, and so numbers 20, 24, and 28 were ordinary issues.

In our editor's note in number 5 we said, among other things, "Let us continue to destroy more boundaries in the race between atomic annihilation and man's spiritual emergence as an individual." In 6 we proclaimed: "From a Catholic seminary in the jungles of Colombia, a Buddhist monastery in Kyoto, from a carpenter in Nicaragua, a student of physics in New Mexico, a poet prophet wandering through the Himalayas, Trappist monk in Kentucky, professor of German in a college in upstate New York, bookseller in San Francisco, poets in London, Buenos Aires, Maine, Oslo, Montevideo, Cuba, New Jersey . . . comes the new poetry. A poetry new because it is of a new age, made by a new man. A man finding his voice in the new era."

That issue came out in April 1963. Two years later, in 1965, Ernesto Che Guevara would publish his *Man and Socialism in Cuba,* but his—the revolution's—new man (and woman) were

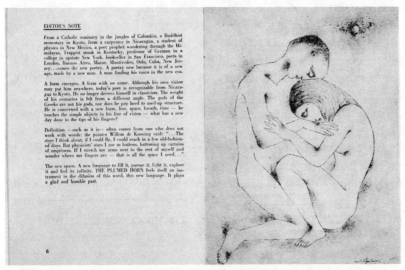

Editorial note by Margaret Randall and art work by Carlos Coffeen from El Corno Emplumado, *No. 6, April 1963 (courtesy Northwestern University Library).*

already perfectly defined: the man and woman who were committed to life, who were for justice, against exploitation. The ideologues of the Organization of American States (through its cultural body, the Pan-American Union) were also developing their "new man," the counter-image. Theirs, needless to say, was beyond politics. Like "art beyond politics." The two concepts were diametrically opposed.

In some muddled way we accepted both, though already we intuitively—if not clearly, analytically—suspected the OAS model and were moving toward Che's truth. It helped to be living in an underdeveloped Third World country whose culture, as well as its economy, was being raped by U.S. imperialism. Speaking in a personal sense, it helped to be delivering babies in the Mexico City misery belt. It helped to begin to develop our first contacts with young revolutionaries throughout the Continent. It helped to get our first letters from Cuba.

Our issue number 7, appearing in July 1963, presented a solid selection of new work from the "first free territory in America," headed off with fragments of Fidel Castro's "Words to the Intellectuals." It was an important offering; the U.S.-imposed blockade (again, cultural as well as economic) had thrown a curtain of silence around Cuba's literary production since the triumph of the revolution. Especially in the sister Latin American countries, and of course in the United States, you weren't free to read what was coming from Cuban poets. We were defiant in our offering, and proud to be making it.

In that same issue we said in our editor's note, "If Ernesto Cardenal . . . is right in saying 'the poets are the true Panamerican Union' and Miguel Grinberg in Argentina is promoting this vision into reality with his newly founded Inter-American League of Poets, the mirrors most publicly reflecting this common vision are the NEW MAGAZINES. . . ." Our sense of our own importance was overblown, to say the least. Poets throughout the Americas had already, many of them, laid down the pen and taken up the gun. The mirrors were not the new magazines, but lives forged in struggle. The mirror was the revolution, already under way. But the fact is, we *did* print the Cuban anthology, and we did, because of that, lose 500 subscriptions from the Pan-American Union in Washington. A specific attempt had been made to buy

416

us off. This taught us a lot; I guess you could also call it instinct. The road to hell is paved with good intentions, as they say, but our own were leading us in the right direction even when we didn't yet understand how or why.

In the editorial comment in our issue number 9 (January 1964) we were still grappling with the same problem. I quote it with great humility because my intention here is not to cover over false consciousness but to try, head on, to look at the road we took— twisted almost out of coherence by class distortions and the common mistake that intuition could or should take the place of analysis: "In eight issues we have . . . talked about a new era peopled by a new man. Many still ask us who this new man is and in what new age he lives . . . . Pisces/Aquarius. A spiritual revolution historically comparable to the industrial revolution(!). . . . It is a time for an art of the people which is not an 'art of the people.' . . . An individualism which includes everyone. A slice of bread buttered with vision and divided infinitely. . . ." How much was a question of semantics? How painful going back to this is! Well . . .

In 11 we picked up on sisters and brothers, saying that "any change must begin within you (me) . . . a single brush line can do more for man . . . than all the socially-morally conscious are . . ."—etc., etc. But by number 17 (January 1966), our cover showed the violence of U.S. Marines invading Santo Domingo. Our fourth anniversary was marked by an editorial note that spoke of 30,000 Vietnam war protesters marching in New York and was finally able to affirm that *"El Corno Emplumado* will continue to be the vehicle through which the other face of this struggle can be expressed, the interior aspect of what's happening, through the eyes of our poets." It was still inner, but the consciousness was developing that this inner manifestation was the reflection of the real, the outer, world.

By number 15 (July 1965), we had broken with our tradition of the purely typographical front cover (the continuous *El Corno Emplumado Plumed Horn El Corno Emplumado Plumed Horn* running back and forth along the top, and across the bottom a list of the contributors in a similar typographical style). From then on there were photographs, paintings, collages, poster art, cartoons, and covers specially designed by artists close to us. Among the most outstanding: Nacho López's photo of a police roundup of Mexican poor—faces of exploitation and defiance—on 15; "STOP THE WAR IN VIETNAM NOW!" running along one side of a detail from Picasso's *Guernica* on 18; a full-color Willem de Kooning painting on 19; Felipe Ehrenberg's special covers for 23 and 24 (Felipe was a close collaborator throughout the life of the magazine); on number 25, Larry Siegel's photo of young Harlem men hanging out; on 26, the great Cuban protest-song poster—the rose with the bloody thorn; and for 28, our own five-year-old daughter Sarah's cover drawing.

El Corno Emplumado was never just a magazine; it was never just a collection of words and images on paper, put together by two people (it was always only two people: editing, raising money, supervising the printing, handling the secretarial work and distribution). *El Corno* was a network—letters going back and forth between poets, between people. It was a meeting of poets like spontaneous combustion (some would sell books or "fly now—pay later" in order to make the trip) in Mexico City in February 1964. It was readings and art shows and contact between movements. It was young intellectuals throughout the Third World coming to terms with their role in revolution; it was U.S. intellectuals coming to terms with their relationship to their sisters and brothers in the world exploited and oppressed by "their" government.

Despite the broad base and the initially unclear focus—or perhaps, strangely, because of that—during the years *El Corno* lived we published some very great, very worthy work. Work that appeared for the first time in Spanish or for the first time in English. Work by unknown writers who would some day be known. Early drawings which today hold the clue to a particular artist's development. Photographs that reflect the sixties. Some extraordinary short stories. Looking through the thirty-one issues now, I can make a list of such work, tempered by my current vision and concerns. The list would have been different in 1965, when the magazine had gone only halfway through what was to be its natural life. It would have been different in 1969, when it died. For what it's worth, here are some of the things I now feel were particularly important:

The early (for outside the island) Cuban work in number 7; the primitive poetry and the drawings by Mexican Indians from the Guerrero mountains (10) and the long cry of anguish from an anonymous Colombian poet in the same issue; César Vallejo in English in 11; a selection of Finnish poets, Clayton Eshleman, Juan Rulfo, and Jerome Rothenberg in 14; Ginsberg's "Kaddish" in Spanish (17) and William Carlos Williams in Spanish (18); number 23 dedicated totally and bilingually to Cuba, with Nuez's incisive drawings; Ernesto Cardenal's "Zero Hour" in 25; Roque Dalton and Susan Sherman in 26; Roque Dalton, Michele Clark, and Richard Johnny John in 30; Bill Hutton's stories in 31.

There were those who were close to us, who were an integral part of *El Corno* during the sixties and who died in that decade. They met different kinds of deaths, and for that reason remain on the pages of the magazine like a special kind of monument. I want to honor them here:

Léon Felipe, *who died of old age and of Spain*
Paul Blackburn, *who died of cancer much too young*
Rosario Castellanos, *who died of electrocution in Israel*
José Cárdenas Peña, *who died of a lifelong affliction*
Waldo Frank, *his heart*
Otto-René Castillo, *tortured to death in the jungles of Guatemala while fighting with the FAR*
Kenneth Patchen, *dying such a long death in Palo Alto*
Franz Kline, *of drink and of being spent*
Pablo Neruda, *of cancer and of Chile*
Thomas Merton, *electrocuted in India while plugging in a fan*
William Carlos Williams, *age and life and paralysis*
Christopher Perret, *a sudden heart attack—too young—on the island of Majorca*
d. a. levy, *who shot himself*
Aldan Van Buskirk, *of a rare blood disease*
Elise Cowen, *who jumped from a tall building to her death*
José Carlos Becerra, *in a car crash in Italy*
Red Lane, *unknown and sudden*
Roque Dalton, *shot by traitors to his own revolutionary cause which was also ours*
Saul Gottlieb, *of lung cancer*
Javier Heraud, *shot down at the age of twenty-one in the middle of the Madre de Dios River, Peru*
Charles Olson, *of cancer*

Even when the distance between life and culture is wide, even when alienation has not been dealt with and contradictions not resolved—if there is honesty in the search, the distance inevitably narrows. As long as we at *El Corno* continued to protest the war in Vietnam from the relative safety of the other side of the river, as long as we spoke of a "new man" largely divorced from real cause and effect, as long as we lived (to a large extent) off Mexican government subsidy and believed ourselves independent, the contradiction was left unexposed and the magazine's contribution was limited pretty much to the publication of one or another beautiful poem, excellent short story, fine piece of graphic art.

But 1968 came along, and with it the social and political upheaval of the Mexican student movement. The student movement became a popular movement. We took sides. In our own backyard. Withdrawal of official support was immediate. Our artistic expression was forced by the circumstances of our life and struggle to define itself in a more relevant way. Our own experience helped us to understand the experience of others. The editorial note in number 29 read:

Beginning in July, the Mexican government has countered an authentic student strike with unreasoned brute force. The strike became a popular movement. In El Corno Emplumado #28 (October), our editorial was a protest against a repression which had not even then reached its high point. Immediately following that editorial, our government subsidy (accounting for approximately half of the magazine's finances) was cut off. . . .
We speak for the total revolution in mind/body/senses and social order. We are no longer subsidized by anyone but you, and our future issues depend on your response.

It wasn't something that happened all of a sudden. It had been a process, and the seeds were planted from the beginning. The editor's note in 26, I think, is worth quoting in full.

Our children will not see the world we know. The change is upon us, in our hands and in our mountains and in our cities—brute and sure. Vietnam, Korea, Guatemala, Guinea, Tierra Amarilla, Detroit. Artists and writers are no longer content to bear witness; looking to Debray, to Che, to Carmichael and Cesar Montes they are making their action a new kind of witness. In Cuba, the real mirror in which we care to see ourselves reflected, 600 intellectuals from 70 countries met in January and talked about THIS—*in all its details and faces. The "official" press everywhere is already engaged in its strategy of silence; but we are no longer on the defensive. Our offensive will be known—through our action, our eyes, the objects and lives we create and the news media, small press and little magazine, by which this reality goes out to you.*

420

In Havana, Uruguayan poet Mario Benedetti said: "The artist who resigns himself to be considered an ignominious article of luxury proves, in the last analysis, that the accusation is partly true in his particular case. On the contrary, the one who refuses to be considered a luxury of the revolution, the artist who defends his right to dream, to create beauty, to create fantasy with the same fury and conviction with which he defends his right to eat, to have a home, to safeguard his health, will be the only one capable of proving that his work is not a luxury, but a necessity not only for himself but also for his fellow man."

El Corno Emplumado *continues this witness which is action, this action which is poetry, this art which is life.*

As I've already said, number 31 was our last issue. Repression meant survival, reassessment, keeping on the move. The end of the magazine. The end of an era shared by many.

What would the magazine have become had we been able to continue it? It's pretty clear from the last two issues especially. The contents are less limited to the more formal literary forms: the poem, short fiction, etc. There is more emphasis now on letters, diaries, essays and articles, the interview. More direct testimony. And the poems and stories change, too, and grow.

A U.S. movement leader goes to Vietnam and reports back. A (necessarily) anonymous Mexican political prisoner draws what the cell feels like. An American woman shares her Cuban journal. An Iroquois Indian brother sings. A great Salvadorian poet makes poetry from the way the most marginal, the poorest of his countrymen finally settled accounts with the dictator responsible for thirty thousand working-class and peasant deaths. A young U.S. student participates in the Chinese cultural revolution. There is discussion of the Senoi dream community. Edmundo Desnois analyzes mass media. Karl Marx appears in comic strip format.

Form as well as content that more accurately reflects the struggle. Had we been able to continue, we would have hoped to move into some of the necessary political debates—on both Latin and North American terrain.

The importance of Latin America for the United States cannot be overemphasized, either from the enemy's viewpoint or our own. It's only a matter of time before Che's "two, three, many Vietnams" explode on the southern continent; events of subsequent years (in Chile, Uruguay, Argentina, Nicaragua, etc.) bear this out. Imperialism wields incalculable resources (the multinationals, military aid, media control, "education" and population control projects, etc. etc.) to keep the continent from bursting open. We too must coordinate our struggle—on the cultural as well as all other fronts. And the Latin American experience, inversely, is vital for the U.S. struggle; we must confront the real culture that emerges from beneath centuries of colonization. There are deep lessons there for us—and the roots themselves for vast sectors of our peoples: chicanos, Puerto Ricans, etc.

That exchange which is part of the struggle for a new society is what we didn't have time to extend and deepen. But others are doing it. Others are carrying it forward from where we left off.

Opposite: advertisement in Dust, *No. 17, for Len Fulton's* Directory of Little Magazines, Small Presses and Underground Newspapers *(courtesy Len Fulton).*

DUST: A TRIBAL SEED
Len Fulton

Directory of Little Magazines, Small Presses, & Underground Newspapers

Nyah-HA HA!

Kitchen

Typical Small Press Editors at Work

Seventh Edition, 1971-72

$2⁵⁰/copy ▬ $8⁰⁰/four-year sub.

dustbooks   Len Fulton, Editor & Publisher
5218 Scottwood Road, Paradise, Ca. 95969

The influences on Len Fulton's editorial methods extend back to 704 A.D.—the date, according to Mr. Fulton, of the oldest known printed work, a Korean religious scroll on woodblocks. In his Small Press Review, *he prints a monthly column, "The Small Press Chronology," which traces the evolution of the written and published word through the ages.*

Len Fulton, a onetime biostatistician and free-lance statistical consultant, founded and edited the magazine Dust *from 1964 to 1971. The journal gave rise to his publishing house, Dustbooks, best known for its yearly* International Directory of Little Magazines and Small Presses.

Mr. Fulton also founded the Committee of Small Magazine Editors and Publishers (COSMEP), and has served on the Literature Panel of the National Endowment for the Arts and on the Grants Committee of CCLM. He is the author of two books of fiction, The Grassman *(1974) and* Dark Other Adam Dreaming *(1975), and of an autobiography,* American Odyssey *(1975).*

I started *Dust* magazine in 1963 because I had the urge to do it— and because I had lain fallow long enough, thank you, under the largely self-inflicted notions that there were higher arbiters of taste. The quiet world of the fifties (actually more comatose than quiet) was falling in, and in Berkeley, California, where I lived and worked, the collapse was as big as they get. Mario Savio was making speeches about "putting your bodies on the wheels and on the gears to stop the odious machine," and the machine to which he referred, the University of California in Berkeley, was one with which I possessed intimate familiarity.

I had learned publishing early, and had learned it under the hard, bedeviled fist of Maine's icebound Yankee soul. A friend, Bob Fay, and I, new idylled from the University of Maine at Portland, started, with no more than some innocence and charm, a weekly newspaper at Kennebunkport in 1957. From that we embedded ourselves deeper yet into the Yankee soul upcountry at Freeport, where we purchased a letterpress print shop and two more local weekly papers. If it had worked (I was twenty-one), I might still be there, but it happened that the winter of 1957–58, riding in on sea winds that only a Melville could love, slapped us breathless. I strung south, working for a weekly in Massachusetts, and spent my last year east of the Mississippi (1958–59) on a daily just outside New York City. From there I returned to college at the University of Wyoming at Laramie, and moved to Berkeley in 1961 to work on a doctorate in psychology. Well before Savio and the Free Speech Movement (FSM) I had come to know and feel the insular and indurate heart of academe. Psychology was on the make everywhere for grants, crying out for a scientific name—and pulverizing those who resisted.

I resisted. I resisted because I had paid my price in austerity before the northern New England snows, and "experimental rigor" in the study of the human mind often reduced to absurdity the merest creative impulse. (We used to say of this experimental rigor that it had rigor mortis.) I had studied literature and done some writing, so I resisted because I sensed a more than chance connection between human behavior, language, and mind. Those Berkeley psychologists skirted that issue by using rats, monkeys, frogs, and other animals that did not confuse the issue with words. I proposed to study the literary roots of Freud for my dissertation; they handed me a faculty adviser named French, from Maine, with no r's in the soul of his language, and a herd of laboratory monkeys with their brains ablated. I proposed novels and poetry as the matter of my study; they proposed the English department—though my talent for statistics frustrated the clarity of this advice. "Symbols," I muttered to French one day. "It's all symbols." He looked up from my paper, written in the first person, active voice—a criminal thing in the academy. "You write that Freud *felt* a certain way about language. I doubt that many of us care how Freud *felt*," he said, leaning forward on that word as though he'd trapped the fingers of a heretic defiling a sacred fount. "Stated, postulated, yes—felt, no!"

Five years of academic psych plus a dime got you a cup of coffee in those days, and very little more. However, as an undergraduate at Wyoming I had been forced through a course in research statistics, something used to terrorize students in the social sciences. I found it in fact a quite sensible pursuit, took further studies in it, and when I went looking for work again in Berkeley I discovered I'd unknowingly gotten myself an ace in the hole. No one needed a psychologist, but every project in even the borderline sciences screamed out for a statistician, a person who could arrange raw and often carelessly acquired data into sophisticated tabular form, charts, graphs; one who understood "confidence" and "testing" and the use of computers. I was not long in landing good and steady employment with the California State Department of Public Health, a position I held until retiring in 1968, and without which there would've been no *Dust* and certainly no Dustbooks.

Dust magazine was founded in a breech. It was personal for me, and also spiritual, ideological in the social sense, a response to a new *Zeitgeist.* I found a number of others, too, with modest writing or publishing experience: Andrew Curry, black, brilliant, a product of Cleveland's Hough District, a psychiatric social worker, painter, poet, musician, dancer; George Kauffman, a staffer for the *Berkeley Barb,* a man from the thirties who'd never lost his angst or his consciousness of the world's dismal; Emil Strom, a composer—witty, good with language in a piecemeal fashion, an unruly conservative, like Kauffman a product of the thirties, who would argue that he'd "seen it all before"; Frank Lapo, a geneticist who couldn't find work precisely in his line and so took blue-collar jobs in defiance—a complex and unpredictable person

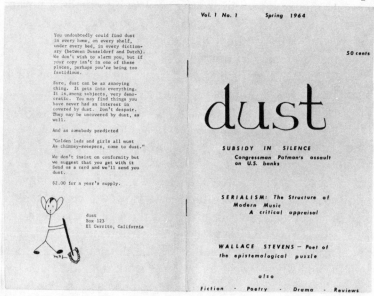

Dust, *Vol. 1, No. 1, Spring 1964 (courtesy Len Fulton).*

whom I understood least of all, given to an absolute distaste for conventional expression (Lapo was our "treasurer" and showed a transcending compulsion for the job); and Bob Fay, my old friend and partner from Maine newspapers, at that point an adman for a paper in Richmond, California.

Just before starting *Dust* in 1962, Kauffman and I had both been directors of a newspaper in Berkeley, a co-op weekly modeled on the food co-ops and titled *The Citizen*. By early 1963, with nothing published, the paper was already foundering in the wash of Berkeley's upper-middle-class liberality, reminding me more than anything else of academic rigor mortis. What wiped out *The Citizen*, however, was not the unending harassment by its reader-owners or by the California Corporations commissioner, or even the hostility of Berkeley's merchant class. What wiped out *The Citizen* was the *Berkeley Barb,* a hip, flip, and grainy harbinger of the underground press movement. The *Barb,* the *Los Angeles Free Press,* and New York's *East Village Other* all started circa 1963, and by the time they had organized the Underground Press Syndicate in 1965 there were some one hundred such papers in the country. It was a primal year for change.

Dust faced two struggles, fiscal and editorial, and both hit crisis proportions by the third issue (Fall 1964). At that time the "editorial board" had shrunk to four—Curry, Fay, Strom, and me. By the fourth issue Strom quit, and by the eighth, Fay. Curry, bless his magnificent soul, stuck with it through the thirteenth issue (Summer 1969), mainly as poetry editor, having given up all financial involvement in the magazine with Fay's departure in 1966. To this day I don't know whether the fiscal or the aesthetic/editorial problems were more to blame. Anyone who's tried it probably knows that a publishing operation with six editor-partners is a unique form of madness, and it is, in retrospect, marvelous that anything got out at all. Yet those first seven issues were regularly 64 to 88 pages, costing $600 apiece. This was prorated at $100 per partner—minus subscription receipts, which were boosted by having six people whose private circles of friends were as disparate as their artistic biases. By number 4 there were 518 paid subscribers, virtually all individuals, no institutions. Subscription fees covered roughly two of the first four issues; the other two cost those of us left about $250 each—a considerable

Dust, Vol. 5, No. 1 (17), 1971, the last issue (courtesy Len Fulton).

sum for a final product that was destined never to satisfy all investors. At our first renewal (with issue number 5) the real thunder of periodical publishing clapped me awake. Subscriptions plunged to 300. And with each succeeding issue more atrophy occurred, with huge gouges at numbers 8 and 12, which began new volumes. When *Dust* suspended publication in 1972, it had 290 paid subscribers.

The personal and editorial conflicts were simply inevitable— numerous and rending. Lapo, always unpredictable, dropped the records and bankbook on my doorstep one day and drove off forever into the sunrise. Kauffman, who thought we should publish only our own work and refused even to read unsolicited manu- scripts (which, with number 2, were pouring in), quit when we voted not to print one of his short stories. Strom objected to a lesbian poem titled "A Pretty Story" by someone named Lake Purnell from Kansas. We voted to print it anyway—and Strom withdrew the day number 3 was published. By number 7 Fay had amassed personal problems—and an obvious weariness for the repetitive process of periodical publishing, struggling through one issue only to get to the next. We agonized over this for a day, for neither of us took the other's plight lightly, but it was clear that he must leave.

And by then it was clear to me that though the founding deal had been a six-way split, the operant deal consisted of me and five others who had tentatively agreed to the thing as long as it pleased them. Everyone but me always thought of the magazine as ultimately mine, and as a result felt a certain freedom to walk away from it. At Fay's departure, Curry said he would edit the magazine as long as I would publish it. Faith, I must say, drove me after that. It was a faith in literature as an enduring human pursuit, a faith in the times—the sixties—as a sort of renaissance that neither I nor anyone then could precisely name, but being *in* those times was proof enough. It was a faith that measured the medicinal power of independence by the natterings of its many detractors, and a sense, somehow, of the intrinsic value and do- minion of the freedom of print. It was a faith in the essentially tribal spirit under which the small press functions—a spirit dwell- ing, on the one hand, outside the corporate octopus but, on the other, inside the cultural stream of real possibilities. And it was a faith, above all, in myself—as my father had known it in himself to survive the cold, blowing blizzards of the eastern north country.

I decided to be a publisher again.

Throughout the summer and fall of 1963 we had held many meetings, looking toward the first issue, planned for Spring 1964. We spent one of those meetings finding a name, which we came to after casting out the "journal of" stigma (stronger then than now, believe me), "quarterly of" (which was too entrapping in the periodical sense and also possessed some stigma), and Thales's four elements. I suggested *Dust* as something that existed in literature and life without regard to style, age, or place; and as a name under which we could maintain a sufficiently open (read "loose") editorial posture to accommodate all our aesthetic proclivities. We quickly began to use its literary references in ad copy, from "dust into dust" to "fear in a handful" of it. Issue number 1 carried a Shakespearean subscription pitch:

> *Golden lads and girls all must*
> *As chimney-sweepers, come to dust.*

We defined a "shovelful" ($3.50) as "four handfuls" (a dollar each), and when the mag died in 1972 one long-time subscriber wrote, "It is hard to believe that never again will another dust bite the day." Several scientific organizations subscribed, clearly planning to advance their laboratory knowledge of dust as a ubiquitous substance—but no one ever wrote back admitting an error, hanging on instead through four issues. We received, starting early, many poems and stories either titled "Dust" or about dust (I don't recall ever publishing one of these), and one day I found a copy of Yael Dayan's novel *Dust* lying on my desk with never an explanation as to how it got there. I became known in the post office as "Dusty," and once had a printer who would address my mail to:

> *Dirt Books*
> *Len Fulton, Chief Pornographer*

which did little, as you might guess, to alleviate suspicions of me in this cow county of Butte, where I came in 1969. Occasionally

430

even now bank clerks will look at me in that odd way, as though in fear of the information, and ask "What are *dust books* anyway?" I start by asking them to define "anyway."

In the early sixties, poetry was still struggling to escape the aesthetic regulations of the "formalists" (Eliot, Ransom, etc.). Language in general was still struggling for a full measure of freedom against suppressive social forces as well as academic ones. The Beats had made gains in both these matters in the fifties, but it truly remained for the little magazines and underground newspapers of the sixties to take up the cause with their sheer number and diversity. While they had been limited in number and located in either New York or San Francisco, these early efforts were easily isolated and harassed—as with, for example, "Howl" or Lenore Kandel's *Love Book*, or Miller's *Tropic of Cancer*, which was prosecuted in Marin County, California, in 1962. Once magazines, presses, and newspapers began to appear everywhere in the country it became a futile business to track them down—to say nothing of a demand for literacy that outran most county prosecutors. Furthermore, the Free Speech Movement at Berkeley in 1963, which drew masses of street-bodies to its cause, and the burnings in Watts and Detroit, soon created a perspective against which a free and open press looked least mean of all.

These small magazines, which began to proliferate in 1963–64, took up such causes as "concrete" poetry: a mix of visual and grammatical material in experimental form imported from Brazil, Switzerland, England, and Canada. This led to the whole testing of "intermedium art," wherein old structural genres were reworked in new, fluid, and functional ways. The "Meat" poets, who began as followers of Charles Bukowski, stretched the subject matter of poetry via their mimeo mags: "Every inch of the planet earth, every curse word, every thimble, every spot of dirt, every slam, bang, jing, every chug in the harbor is poetry" (Douglas Blazek in *Ole*, number 1). And dope, war, prison, race, ecology, and sexism all eventually worked their way into poetry as content which affected form, mostly by loosening it. Rhyme and meter in the old sense fell into final disuse as the "projective line" (that

431

of the natural breath) became dominant through oral presentation. When we started *Dust* there were two readings a week in the San Francisco Bay Area. Now, in the seventies, there are literally dozens.

In a way, *Dust* was a mini-cosm of the small magazine of its day. We published a little of everything and remained true to our founding goal of openness. We published Bukowski and Blazek, prison and dope poetry by William Wantling, socially satirical poems by L. C. Phillips, the street poems of Doug Palmer, translations from the Italian by Dora Pettinella, from the Japanese by Curry, and from the German by Gene Fowler. We published several hundred poets in the course of seventeen issues. For reasons unknown to my memory now, we did not publish much in the way of concrete poetry until Wally Depew took over as editor with issue 14 in 1970.

We set out early to publish interviews, and they, with some of the fiction, may be the most historically important features of the magazine. They covered modern poetry, black organizing, peace Berkeley-style, street poetry, small presses, Zen philosophy, and novel writing. Here are the people interviewed and the issues in which those interviews appeared: Alan Watts, Zen philosopher (numbers 2, 3; later published as a separate chapbook titled *The Deep in View*); Louis Simpson, Pulitzer poet (numbers 3, 4); Booker T. Anderson, black organizer (2); Doug Palmer, street poet (5); Gene Fowler, poet (6); Stephen Smale, anti-war activist (7); John Williams, novelist (7); d. a. levy, Cleveland editor-poet (12). We published thirty-five pieces of fiction in the first twelve issues, most of it experimental, including work by Ed Bullins, Gary Elder, Ed Franklin, Sinzer James, and Nigerian Babatunde Lawal. I worked with a writer named Gene Gracer (whom I have not heard from since) through five rewrites of his grimly colorful story, "Shadows of Dawn," before publishing it in number 7.

A year ago I met James D. Houston (*Native Son of the Golden West*), and as we shook hands I said, "I remember reading manuscripts of yours for a mag I once edited." I wondered how good his memory was.

"Dust," he said quickly with a smile. "You even published me!"

"No shit?" The trick was on me.

"Yeh—a play, I think."

"No shit! Really?"

Later he remembered the title: "Time to Kill."

We published work by two dozen artists, fifty letters ranging from hate to love, and several dozen reviews. We published an article by Strom on atonalism in music and Shakespeare's "Sonnet 50," which he'd set to piano music. This latter brought in a light-hearted complaint from a trumpet player who didn't "appreciate having to transpose his music from base to treble clef." Bob Fay wrote an article on Congressman Wright Patman's attack on the U. S. banking system, and Curry wrote several brilliant essays on Wallace Stevens, Issa, Hopkins, and James Baldwin. It was Fay who interviewed Booker T. Anderson one afternoon in Richmond, California, and Anderson had some unfavorable opinions about Richmond's black mayor. When the issue came out, the Richmond city manager called me and asked if he could photocopy the interview and reproduce it with the mayor's comments attached. I checked with Anderson, who was incensed. I offered the city of Richmond as many copies as they wanted at a buck each, but informed them that to copy the interview would violate copyright laws. They checked with counsel, then bought whole copies of *Dust*.

With the fifth issue (1965), we picked up a British editor named Cavan McCarthy, who published a little magazine out of Leeds titled *Tlaloc*. McCarthy contributed only one essay to *Dust*, a report on the obscenity-bust of British poet Dave Cunliffe over publication of a book called *The Golden Convolvulus*, but he figured critically in other Dustbooks publications later. In fact, McCarthy mined the entire European continent and Russia for listings for the second annual *Directory of Little Magazines* (1966) and set up for us a momentum to collect European information that is still going, though he quit in 1968 to disappear into Brazil and Nigeria. He was one of the best and brightest people I have ever worked with. (In March 1976, I was at the Gotham Book Mart in New York, promoting my new novel *Dark Other Adam Dreaming*. As the afternoon faded toward evening, a young man materialized in the gallery, grinning because we were about to meet and he didn't want the moment lost too quickly. It was McCarthy, eleven years later.)

I would venture to guess that most small-press editors active today have scarcely heard of *Dust* and certainly have never seen a copy. Yet they know of Dustbooks, and contribute monthly and annual data, advertising, goodwill, and ideas to its several information titles, most specifically the *International Directory of Little Magazines and Small Presses* and the *Small Press Review*. It is the case of the tree bearing no seeming resemblance to its original seed.

Early in the course of publishing *Dust*—perhaps before its second issue was out—we began getting exchange copies of other mags from everywhere in the country. As early as number 2 we printed reviews of Duane Locke's *Poetry Review* (Tampa) and Harry Smith's *The Smith* (NYC)—both of which, by the way, are still going. In 3 (1964) we listed thirty-six mags as having been received, and eight books, and we devoted five pages to reviewing them. In 4, this list of magazines received had grown to 67, and I began to be fascinated by the fact that with each one also came a story, a human drama not unlike the one behind the founding and publishing of *Dust* itself. The more I knew about it, the more taken I became with what was obviously a larger movement somehow related to ours by its literary and publishing spirit.

It was the first time in all my days that I'd found myself quite naturally and organically a part of something beyond the reach of my own hand, something that had not preceded me so much as it had simultaneously awakened with me, or I with it. I was drawn to it. At that point *Dust* receded in my interest and in the energy I would willingly give it. I devised the first of a multitude of forms for collecting information in 1965, and soon produced the first edition of the *Directory of Little Magazines*—40 pages, 250 listings, 500 copies, a buck each. A year later, in an effort to track the movement's accelerating action in a more dynamic and immediate way, I started the *Small Press Review* as a quarterly. (It is now a monthly with 3,000 paid subscribers and earns $5,000 a year in advertising. The *Directory* now lists 2,500 small presses and mags, is 500+ pages, prints 10,000 copies, and sells for $10.95.)

In 1967 an editor named Jerry Burns (*Goliards*) came to my home, and after we had talked and drunk and talked some more, he said:

"Let's join forces, man, a partnership!"

"I've done that one," I said—but he was wired.

"Then how about a meeting of little mag editors?"

A year later, almost to the day, we brought it off, Burns and I, in Berkeley on the U. of C. campus, which five years before had prodded its last rat through the maze of my academic life. We held the meeting, titled the Conference of Small Magazine Editors and Publishers (COSMEP), and attracted eighty editors like ourselves from everywhere in the country. I chaired a panel on distribution, which included Harry Smith (*The Smith*), Douglas Blazek (*Ole*), D. R. Wagner (*Runcible Spoon*), and Hugh Fox (*Ghost Dance*). It was out of that panel, the first of a thousand like it, in an effort to get funds for a catalogue of small press publications, that the Committee of Small Magazine/Press Editors and Publishers was born. By November 1968 it had 110 paying members and a self-appointed board of directors. (Burns and I fought furiously over whether those directors should be elected. By 1970 I had worn him down, and the first election was held at the Buffalo conference that year.) It was Burns who, after the conference in Ann Arbor in 1969, concocted the COSMEP *Newsletter*. We "hired" Richard Morris in late 1968 to help get out that first *Catalogue of Small Press Publications,* typeset by Burns and printed by Ben Hiatt (*Grande Ronde Review*).

In mid-1968 I retired from my work as a public health biostatistician under pressure from a nerve disease of still unknown origin or destiny. I broke with the urban madness and moved back to the mountains to spend time in the sun and the mud, and give the publishing and writing a chance to work its medicine. *Dust* had begun to be sporadic anyway in the flow of my other interests, and the move gave it a new setback. Number 11, published from the Bay Area, was dated Fall 1967; 12, published from Paradise,

435

was dated Spring 1969; 13, all fiction, was dated Summer 1969. At that point Andrew Curry, who'd been nothing if not a stolid co-editor and fast friend, quit—and I didn't blame him a whisker.

Finally, having quit gainful employment, I was running out of money and out of energy for a magazine which had cost me $7,000 in seven years, and some editor friends. It couldn't hold its subscribers (at number 4 there were 518; after 8 there were 129), and it worked in some devilish way against the rest of my operation, because it was forever unable to be as open spiritually as it needed to be to co-exist with the *Directory* and the *Small Press Review*—and with my chairmanship of COSMEP.

In late 1970, with subscriptions at 190, I hired Wally Depew to see what he could make of it. Depew was, along with Richard Kostelanetz and some others, one of the earliest and brightest experimenters in the U.S. in concrete art, games, probabilities and chance, series equations, permutations, and the like. He had started a magazine called *Poetry Newsletter* in New York in 1964, and I had published his chapbook *Once,* as the fourth in a series of "longpoems." Depew described his chapbook as "a contrapuntal, serially developed New Poetry longpoem using repetitive/progressive wood block series set against an expanding letter design." (The book remains in print today.) Depew edited four issues of *Dust* in 1970–71, one of which carried work by Folsom Prison poets and Canadians and one, the seventeenth, having four contributors, all experimental, including Kostelanetz, Alastair MacLennan, and Depew himself. I liked the "new look" of the magazine, the fresh and intricate designs by Linda Bandt, and the tight, no-nonsense editing by Wally Depew. I liked not having to decide on manuscripts and layout and wrestle with complaints from contributors and subscribers. Though Depew would confer with me on the general size and shape of each issue, those issues were always an enjoyable surprise. For the first time ever I was able to concentrate on what had become my first interest: small press information. I applied for a $1,500 grant for *Dust* from the Coordinating Council of Literary Magazines in New York, which had turned me down several times before.

But a magazine like *Dust,* as any editor can tell you, becomes the child of a life style, and you can partition it off no more easily than you can your personality or your face. I began to feel a vague, nagging sense that the all-fiction issue (13), Curry's last, had been somehow an organic end, that I had started a whole new contraption with Depew and it was a contraption which was not a part of me. I had become a financier, and was otherwise excluded from the continuity.

On New Year's Eve 1971 I walked with Depew, Gary Elder, and others along a pathway through the brush, watching the stars and hearing the wind across the live oak. Depew talked about the next issue, on baseball (a nonliterary interest we shared), and I knew in my heart it would never be. When, a few days later, the notice came from New York that *Dust* had gotten its first grant, enough money to see it through four more issues—enough, perhaps, under Depew's editorship, to reestablish the magazine as an important vehicle of experiment in the country, I replied to CCLM:

$1,500 is too little, and it is too late. I must turn it down.

But CCLM, unable to stop its wheels in time, sent the money anyway, and I put it in the bank. They stopped payment.

Dust had bitten its last day.

ON <u>KAYAK</u>
George Hitchcock

George Hitchcock, editor of Kayak. *Photograph by Gerard Malanga.*

The magazines that have influenced George Hitchcock include transition, Hound and Horn, Circle *(edited by George Leite in Berkeley), and Robert Bly's* The Fifties. *Mr. Hitchcock was brought up in the provinces (Oregon during the twenties and thirties) where, as he says, "the distant drums of surrealism, communism, and French decadence could be heard." His artistic masters were Georg Trakl, Max Ernst, Hans Arp, Federico Garcia Lorca, and Wallace Stevens. He spent one semester (1937) in the Berkeley graduate school, then dropped out and joined the working classes. For most of his adult life he has lived in San Francisco, working in shipyards and factories and writing during the winter seasons. According to Mr. Hitchcock, many San Franciscans of his generation thought of themselves as Europeans. This artistic alienation from America was reinforced by Red-baiting and political blacklisting. He has never supported himself by literary or magazine activity. Of late, lecturing at the University of California, Santa Cruz, has replaced shipbuilding and landscaping as his main source of income.*

George Hitchcock is the author of a novel, two plays, a book of stories, and seven books of poetry. He has edited The San Francisco Review *and* Kayak.

If there is any discernible trend in the publication of little magazines over the last decade, it is certainly only numerical: there are more and more of them. Because of the widespread availability of low-cost offset printing equipment and a newfound generosity on the part of the National Endowment for the Arts, small magazines have proliferated at an unprecedented rate. Is this boom growth a good thing? I am of two minds about that. Certainly from the political or social point of view it is preferable to have several thousand localized and generally anti-establishment voices, and any shift in that direction and away from the control of publishing by our great monopolies is desirable. Little magazines have come to be an integral part of the counterculture and, by their independence and intransigence, offer a really hopeful alternative to the increasing stranglehold the corporate marketing mind has over our traditional cultural outlets.

Yet at the same time I'm afraid the new wave of little magazines, by their very number and fundamental sameness, has created confusion and apathy. Who can possibly read more than a thousandth part of them? And isn't it probable that a sort of literary Gresham's Law has come into effect—bad writing driving out good, or at the very least inundating it in a surf of paper?

I have no real answers to these questions. Analyzing the state of the *Zeitgeist* has never much appealed to me. Artists are usually better off leaving such questions to the sociologists and historians of letters. In what follows I shall merely offer a few opinions based on twenty years of independent publishing, both of books and magazines, appending some caveats for those who may be considering a similar plunge into the unknown.

In the late fifties, encouraged by sparks from the bonfires of what was then called (in retrospect, a bit optimistically) the "San Francisco renaissance," I shared editorial responsibility in the newly launched *San Francisco Review*. The magazine was the creation of Roy Miller, a San Francisco lawyer whose impulses were, I suspect, as much sociological as literary. At any rate, he had gotten an article by Bertrand Russell and poems from the ever-generous William Carlos Williams and e. e. cummings with which to launch his first issue. There was also, I think, a prose poem by Bill Saroyan and a two-act play of mine that had been recently premiered by Jules Irving at the Actors' Workshop. It was because he admired this play that I was invited to sign on as associate editor (no salary, of course). That was more than twenty years ago, and, once hooked, I've never properly been able to get away.

The *San Francisco Review* was rather ambitiously conceived and, I'm afraid, never quite lived up to its initial promise. For one thing, it was letterpress printed in England and shipped to its editors via book post; consequently, there were vast and irksome editorial and publication delays. Even more important, there was a very substantial deficit for each issue. The deficit was made up by the editors but, I hasten to add, not by the associate editor. And in any case, it didn't run to such astronomical projections of red ink as were incurred by the other San Francisco literary magazine of that period, *Contact*, whose editors, Bill Ryan and Evan Connell, the grapevine tells me, contrived to drop around $70,000 in the five or six years of the magazine's existence.

But I soon learned the number-one law of little magazine pub-

440

lishing: no literary magazine in America can hope to break even without either financial subvention from a patron or the discovery of some way to beat the printer's bills. Another lesson I also learned was that collective editorship, even with the greatest initial enthusiasm, has dreadful drawbacks. In fact, I should be inclined to think that more initially promising publications have been ruined by the multiplicity of ladles in the literary broth than by any other single cause. The three of us at *San Francisco Review* (very shortly a third editor who was prepared to assist in the financing was added) regularly disagreed. Of course, that in itself is not a bad thing, and I look back upon many of our fiercer arguments with a certain retrospective relish. But what invariably happens with an editorial board of equals is that either—to borrow Orwell's phrase—one becomes more equal than the others, or the acceptance basket tends to become filled with submissions which have as their least common denominator the fact that no one objects to them very strongly. And I am afraid any magazine edited along these lines is ultimately doomed to a tepid eclecticism. In any event, soon enough the money ran out. Roy Miller, the founding editor, went back to the law; he is at present compiling a parliamentary guide for, I believe, the Library of Congress. June Degnan, on whose shoulders the lion's share of the financial responsibility had fallen, went on to greener pastures as financial consultant for Eugene McCarthy's presidential campaign. We had published twelve issues, some good authors, and a fair amount of rubbish, and had summed up the magazine by issuing, in collaboration with Jay Laughlin of New Directions, one paperback collection of which I am still quite proud.

But I had merely gotten my feet wet. I was convinced that the only effective way of publishing a little magazine was through an absolute dictatorship. This method of government, while certainly not to my taste in the commonwealth, seemed to me then, and still does, the only one that works in the world of art. An editor who is not prepared to be an autocrat in matters of literary taste, who is not ready to face with a smile the raucous cries of "Elitism!" would be better off somewhere else. Far too many editors or quasi editors lack the courage of their convictions. Many go into little-magazine editing with the psychology of correspondents of a Pen Pal Club or a society of clock collectors: they want to get letters; they want to be liked. A mistake. I have met others whose activities are ruled by the conviction that their chief function is a philanthropic one toward young writers. Of course, a certain amount of vaguely diffused benevolence *may* be a by-product of the publication of a good little magazine. But it should always be viewed suspiciously as a by-product and nothing else. An editor who is also publisher, and thus undertakes complete responsibility for all aspects of his magazine, should, I think, have first of all a responsibility to himself—that is, to please himself and to meet his own highest artistic standards. His second responsibility, I should like to argue, is to his readership, not to an amorphous, anonymous "public" but to a readership made up of individuals, with each of whom the editor can envisage an enjoyable conversation. If such a readership does not exist, then it's up to the editor to invent it, and in time nature may come to imitate art and provide him with it.

Somewhere very far down the scale of responsibilities comes the welfare of novice authors. And even there, let us remember that patronizing other human beings, and particularly bad writers, is a crime which should be punished by immersion in boiling— well, perhaps a boiling puree of old rejection slips.

In 1964, alone and armed by my experiences with the troika at *San Francisco Review*, I launched *Kayak*. The title was not accidental; in the initial issue I defined a kayak as

not a galleon, ark, coracle or speedboat. It is a small watertight vessel operated by a single oarsman. It is submersible, has sharply pointed ends, and is constructed from light poles and the skins of furry animals. It has never yet been successfully employed as a means of mass transport.

It was my intention to publish chiefly poetry showing certain tendencies which I admired and felt to be gravely underrepresented by the then existing poetry journals. These tendencies can, I suppose, be roughly defined as the various branches of contemporary romanticism. Romanticism is, of course, a very loose term, perhaps exclusively associated with Coleridge, Keats, Swinburne, Rossetti, and their epigoni. However, specifically modern romanticism seemed to me to be work in the imagistic and surrealist modes. In fact, I don't think it an overstatement to say that surrealism, in one or another of its forms, is the quintessentially

442

Above: Kayak, *Vol. 1, No. 1, Autumn 1964 (courtesy Northwestern University Library). Overleaf:* a Kayak *rejection slip (courtesy George Hitchcock).*

Sorry, but the editors of kayak feel that
your submission is not quite what we need
this season.   Thanks anyway.

modern guise of the romantic movement. At the same time that I was prepared to flaunt my own predilections for imaginative and subjective poetry of this sort, I didn't want to shut any editorial doors on romantic poetry in the English tradition where it was still alive. I thought when I started *Kayak,* for example, that I should prove a very poor and imperceptive editor if I were to turn down the work, let us say, of a younger Dylan Thomas or David Jones simply because it didn't measure up to some pre-established canons of surrealist taste.

Anyway, in practice no editor worth anything creates his magazine on the basis of a-priori considerations. Theories are interesting, but in artistic discrimination the viscera play an equally important part. So to the catalogue of preferences I've listed above I should add a list of my often irrational hates, particularly since by character and ancestry I have always been a rebel and tend to be provoked into action more by what I don't like than by positive affinities. Thus in 1964, listed in no particular order, I actively disliked neoclassicism, the neo-Hemingway "tough guy" posture, most of the New Criticism, the Vietnam war (already in its initial stages), the banal eclecticism of *Poetry* (Chicago), excessive academic analysis at the expense of feeling, our national administration, the pseudo poetics of Charles Olson and his Black Mountain disciples, the cliquish pretentiousness of many of the Beats, poets preoccupied with the trivia of suburban existence—in short, 90 percent of what was being written or done in my own time. Enough fuel to keep my critical fires burning for quite a while.

In the early sixties I was certainly influenced as well by Robert Bly and his rediscovery of what was then popularly referred to as "the deep image" of European and Latin American surrealist poetry. However, it was more than forty years ago that I first began to read Breton, Soupault, and Garcia Lorca, to mention but three, so what may have been a discovery to Robert Bly was not exactly a novelty to me. I think Bly performed a great service, though, with the early issues of his magazine *The Fifties*—to become in later decades *The Sixties* and *The Seventies*—and for a number of years it was certainly a model to me of what could be accomplished by energy and cantankerous individual taste. Since Robert has apparently lapsed into unforeseeable depths of

Four   **75c.**

THE
SIXTIES

A MAGAZINE
OF POETRY AND OPINION

Above: The Sixties, *No. 4, 1960, edited by William Duffy and Robert Bly
(courtesy Anania Community Trust). Opposite: Robert Bly, reading.
Photographs by Gerard Malanga.*

inwardness and Oriental mysticism, my own extrovert's empathies with him have diminished a bit over the years.

Still, if all this means anything it is that an editor or poet is capable of creating a magazine worth reading only if he feels passionately, if he brings to his work deeply held convictions and a taste founded upon something more committed than the desire for personal celebrity. And particularly in America, where getting ahead has been the major ideology for a century or more, this attitude is not found every day.

People sometimes ask me what they should do to make their forthcoming magazines successful. I think the only sensible answer I can give them is to start by forgetting about success. In our literary climate the only real successes are the honorable failures. Then, of course, they should read widely, learn about printing, and cultivate their own passionate prejudices. With these maxims in mind, they may find some joy in their work, and—who knows?—sooner or later they may earn the esteem of a few ardent readers. There are far too many magazines being published in America today that bring such stern joys to no one at all and fulfill no particular purpose unless it be to feed the editor's vanity or advance him up the ladder of academic promotion.

This of course brings me to the literary magazine spawned by a university English department or one or two ambitious creative writers within it. When editorial responsibility for such a magazine is turned over to students, it probably fulfills a sufficiently honorable pedagogical function and can be justified on those grounds. But when, as is more often the case, it is edited by a faculty committee with one eye fixed on the promotion and tenure committee and the other following the rise and fall of New York publishing reputations, then I for one can do without it.

Of course, there is nothing inherently wrong with university patronage of a literary magazine, but the university would be well advised to make sure that it is spending its money on the genuine living article rather than a mere eclectic grab bag and vehicle for faculty ambitions. I can think offhand of only two or three university-financed reviews in which the impact of a strong editorial personality has created a vital magazine. The examples that come to my mind are those of David Ray and the strong social-radical consciousness he has brought to the editing of *New Letters* for the University of Missouri at Kansas City; of the elegant and rather patrician standards James Boatwright has given to *Shenandoah* at Washington and Lee; and of Robin Skelton, who has brought such a distinctively international flavor to the *Malahat Review* at the University of Victoria in British Columbia. In all these cases the magazines appear to be run on the autocratic principle, and their achievements are counterbalanced by the dead, doughy weight of several score of other magazines—which shall here be nameless—edited by faculty committees.

Of course, if one is going to edit without patronage—and that has always been my personal choice—then the prerequisites must be sufficient mechanical and printing skill and a great deal of free time. I have no advice as to how to secure the latter, but offset printing equipment is today so readily available at a reasonable expenditure that I am inclined to think the chief prerequisite for any editor is to learn to print. Of course one doesn't have to approach printing with the zeal of a William Morris at Kelmscott, although it is certainly a nice thing to be able to do beautiful printing; but some knowledge of offset processes, or at least of typesetting and paste-up, seems to me to be absolutely fundamental. Besides which, I am with Morris and Blake in prizing the written word that you have designed and made with your own hands over and above the product of alienated labor. In a factory-ridden world, the little magazine can be one of the rare creations in which thought and labor meet without the intercession of the impersonal processes usual in our society. And as for *Kayak,* which is now publishing its forty-eighth issue, it is in its design and production— always with the freely given help of a sodality or brotherhood of poets—that the joy of the thing lies.

DOING <u>CATERPILLAR</u>
Clayton Eshleman

cover: Nancy Spero: "The Bomb"
1966 27 x 34

Caterpillar, *Vol. 1, No. 1, October 1967, back cover showing contents
(courtesy Northwestern University Library).*

Clayton Eshleman's aesthetic bent was early influenced by the jazz improvisation of Bud Powell, but when he was twenty-three Mr. Eshleman began to read and write seriously. The following year he began to edit the magazine Folio, *funded by the English department at Indiana University. After three issues in 1959–1960,* Folio *was discontinued because of adverse reaction to accepted work by Allen Ginsberg and Louis Zukofsky, which he was unable to publish. In 1965 Mr. Eshleman went to Lima, Peru, to do research on César Vallejo. There he was asked to edit a bilingual magazine funded by a Peruvian cultural institute, which turned out to be a front organization for the U.S. Information Services. The magazine was discontinued when he refused to withdraw some pastoral poetry by Javier Heraud, who was a member of the Communist Party. In 1967 Mr. Eshleman started* Caterpillar.

Clayton Eshleman has published thirty-six books, including his translations of Vallejo, Pablo Neruda, Antonin Artaud, and Aimé Césaire, as well as his own original verse. His co-translation (with José Rubia Barcia) of the complete poems of Vallejo will be published in 1979 by the University of California Press.

Mr. Eshleman teaches in a black ghetto high school in Los Angeles and gives private poetry tutorials. He will be traveling in France this year on a Guggenheim fellowship to do research on painted paleolithic caves.

I spent, on the average, around three hours a day on *Caterpillar* magazine during the six years that I published and edited it. Once *Caterpillar* was under way, there were generally four or five unsolicited manuscripts in the mail each day. I was never inundated, probably because the magazine had an exclusive look about it (although 168 different writers and artists appeared in its 4,000 pages) and also because it printed "difficult" poetry. Manuscripts that I was not interested in I sent back the day I received them and always wrote a personal note or letter, which at least showed that someone had actually read the submission. I always appreciate that personal note when another editor rejects my own writing, and I took it for granted, well into *Caterpillar's* run, that others did too. But it wasn't true. Many people became irritated when I wrote them that I did not like their writing well enough to print it and occasionally told them why. Gerard Malanga took one of my rejection notes, printed it at the top of a page, wrote his reaction under it, and mailed it out to people he thought would be sympathetic. An aggressive "gay" activist from Boston, Charley Shively, sent me a group of poems with a letter which he signed "gayly yours." I resent causes being used to push near-art, so when I sent back Shively's poems, at the end of my explanation as to why I was not printing them I wrote something to the effect of why did love have to be qualified by "gay"—what was wrong with simply love? A bit caustic, true—but that was the way his poems and letter made me feel. A couple of weeks later I received from Shively a ten-page attack on my own poetry, which I answered by saying that under the circumstances I would not deal with it. Both my letters became part of a mimeographed "Shively-Eshleman correspondence" packet which Shively, without my permission, mailed out to people. Amazing how these things proliferate. He mailed a copy to Richard Grossinger, who was writing an essay on androgyny at the time. Grossinger had previously written me about how much he admired a book of mine called *Altars,* in which my acknowledgment of Wilhelm Reich's work played a small but crucial role. The next thing I knew, Grossinger had lifted sentences out of Shively's attack and incorporated them in his essay in such a way that Reich and I were made to look like heterosexual chauvinist pigs—as if that is what both of us are about.

So doing *Caterpillar* was always lively, and there was meaningful conflict as well as the kind of flak I have described above. Such is inevitable if you do a magazine that gets under people's skins and makes a dent in the existing scene. Someone told Cid Corman, when he was preparing to start his magazine *Origin* in the early 1950s, that he should be willing to stick with it for at least five years or the magazine would have no real effect. Corman did, and I think that is true. When I began I committed myself to three years and/or twelve issues (having no idea how I was going to hold to that promise), and in this regard a bizarre thing occurred in the spring of 1970, after the eleventh issue came out. I was mailed a copy of a magazine called *The Smith,* edited by a Harry Smith, in which Smith had encircled a statement for me to note. I was advised that if I tried to publish *Caterpillar* after the twelfth issue, a group of (unnamed, of course) magazine editors would seek an injunction to prohibit me from doing so. On the one hand this was pretty funny, but on the other it reeked of self-hate and the yellow journalism by which Smith has tried to get his magazine known. When *Caterpillar* did not stop publication, there soon began to appear in *The Smith* vicious attacks on a number of people associated with it.

The main reason I began *Caterpillar* was that I did not feel poets like Robert Duncan, Diane Wakoski, Jerome Rothenberg, Frank Samperi, Cid Corman, Louis Zukofsky, and Paul Blackburn had a dependable and generous outlet for their writing. I hoped that these poets, along with perhaps a dozen more, would become regular contributors to the magazine and that around this core I could bring in eight to sixteen pages of art reproductions per issue as well as writing by younger and lesser known poets. I saw a poetry magazine as a granary of sorts, where writing could be stored until it was to be consumed or consummated in a book, a midpoint between its inception and its ultimate form. *Caterpillar* was useful to me in this way when I was working on *Altars*. On several occasions I put a fresh section or two into an issue of the magazine to test it in a context and see how it looked at that distance. I also hoped that if I got the magazine out regularly readers would be able to follow the development in regular contributors' writing. Looking back, I think that it was possible to do this in the case of Robert Kelly, Thomas Meyer, Kenneth Irby, and Gary Snyder.

Another thing that was on my mind when I started the magazine was poetry in translation. It seemed important not to push it to the exclusion of American poetry (as Robert Bly had done in *The Fifties* and *The Sixties*) because I was convinced that it was more important for us to read ourselves in 1967 than to give priority to translated poetry. On the other hand, the *quality* of translating was much on my mind, so I adapted Zukofsky's "test of poetry" and made it a "test of translation" and did the first two tests myself, on César Vallejo and Eugenio Montale. My idea was to set differing translations of a poem side by side and, with a minimum of comment, encourage the reader to measure them as articulations of the original poem. Behind this was a sense that we needed new translations less than we needed to know exactly what had been done in the past.

453

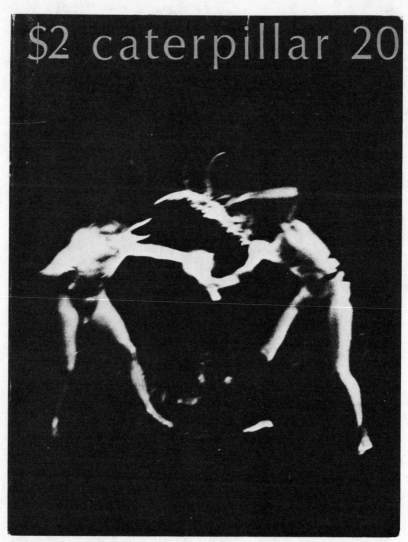

Caterpillar, *No. 20, the last issue, June 1973 (courtesy Northwestern University Library).*

I didn't print any of my own poetry in the first issue, but as I was putting the second one together I decided that something of mine should be in each issue. I felt that this would give the reader a kind of yardstick by which to understand and measure the editing, would put me on the line and involve me much more rawly with what I was printing than if I just edited. Since I was not trying to do an eclectic magazine, but was doing one with a definite point of view, I wanted this point of view to be immediately visible.

I also wanted to bring things that were not poetry per se to bear on poetry. I experimented with macrobiotic cooking for a year and in number 3/4 edited Georges Ohsawa's *The Book of Judgment* down to four pages and set it before a long poem by Theodore Enslin. In number 5 there was a scientology lecture, in 7 and 10 passages from the writings of Reich, and in 13 a statement by Billy McCune, a convicted rapist. The McMaster lecture on scientology looked suspicious almost as soon as number 5 was out. Putting it in *Caterpillar,* in a context with thoughtful writing, made its slovenliness evident to me, even though it had not been evident when I was sitting in the scientology offices on 32nd Street.

For the entire year before I started the magazine, I had been very much involved in protesting the American destruction of Vietnam. The first issue carried an edge of that protest and anger, but by the second issue I had realized that *Caterpillar* was not the place to take the matter up. Curiously, the first issue, with its exploding man on the cover, its bombs and helicopters, its N. O. Brown lecture and Margaret Randall essay on Cuba, got me a job a couple of years later at the California Institute of the Arts. On the basis of that issue, Maurice Stein, who was forming the Department of Critical Studies, decided that I was a poet-revolutionary, and, I guess, since he liked the idea of having at least one of those around he hired me. When my wife Caryl and I made the move to the West Coast in 1970—after the appearance of the twelfth issue, devoted mainly to Jack Spicer's early writing—and Stein and I got to know each other, he realized that the first issue was the least typical of all the issues that followed. It was never a matter of deciding that the anger was merely my own and should not be directed toward American genocide, but rather a realization that I did not want to use *Caterpillar* to "demonstrate" in. After

455

I printed those horrifying photos of twelve-year-old napalmed Vietnamese girls in 3/4 (photos which *Ramparts* refused to run when they did an article on war victims), I really didn't know what more could be said. I had them set right after the translation of a strong poem by Aimé Césaire, which opened:

> The heavy hit of machete red pleasure full
>   into the forehead there was blood & that tree called
> flamboyant . . .

to test those words of violence right up against the visualization of what violence in our time has become.

I had invited Robert Kelly to co-edit the magazine with me. Kelly wrote back accepting my gesture, but saying that he felt the magazine would be weakened by dual editorship. He did, however, offer to become a contributing editor and to send me his own writing regularly as well as collect pieces from others. We worked out an agreement whereby whatever he sent of his own, plus up to twenty pages of other writing, would go into *Caterpillar* without any editorial tampering on my part. This arrangement turned out very well. Besides bringing in material that I would not have otherwise solicited—or sometimes have been very sympathetic to—it made me stretch, to the point of allowing more to happen in the magazine than I probably would have allowed had I done it completely alone. At times I picked up Kelly's enthusiasms and invited someone who had previously been a Kelly contributor to send work directly to me, thus releasing space for Robert to fill in with new people. I had printed that long poem of Theodore Enslin's in 3/4 but did not feel any deep engagement with his work. Kelly sent me some short Enslin poems for the next several issues and urged me to think more about what he was doing. When Ted read his poems at Max's Kansas City in 1969, Caryl and I went, and both of us, Caryl especially, were moved by a section from a long work-in-progress called "Synthesis." The following week I reread everything by Enslin that I owned, and decided that Robert and Caryl were right. Beginning with the eleventh issue, I serialized sections of "Synthesis" to the end, printing around two hundred pages of it.

Having been in Reichian therapy, I should say something about the role it played in my doing *Caterpillar.* The therapy in itself was not a distraction from *Caterpillar,* for I only saw Dr. Handelman,

456

my therapist, an hour a week—but it flushed me out into the world, looking for people I could have real contact with, to such an extent that at times *that* was the focus. It was often difficult for me to acknowledge poems that were not involved with self-confrontation and contact in the way that I thought they should be. Of course, one has one's own set of priorities, and one must stick by them. And to the degree that therapy taught me how to free my intellectual energies I became a more discerning and severe reader. Kelly's poetry at this time was, in a number of ways, almost contrary to mine, especially in the way the two of us handled the self. Yet, although this may not be apparent for a while, our poems are deeply compatible.

Glancing back over the twenty issues in order to write this essay, I have found that a hundred pages or so of material now seems irrelevant to *Caterpillar* and does not support my own concerns at the time. Rather, it is material that I let get in when I allowed my attentions to go slack, or when I allowed myself to be influenced by friendship. This latter consideration, as everyone clearly knows, is a big determinant as to what gets in the little magazines and what does not. Michael McClure gave me some interesting visual poetry and a cover for number 6, then offered me a photograph of himself on his motorcycle to run in number 7. I remember being at the McClures' when this happened. We were sitting around the table having a good time, and Michael was saying that I should print photographs of all my contributors, for if some of the poets saw what they looked like they would write differently. That remark seemed funny at the time, but I wasn't convinced that it meant anything other than being Michael's way of slipping his photograph into *Caterpillar*. I humored him because I liked him and his writing, but in doing that I was wrong. Printing the photograph led to the following situation: Michael sent me some publicity on plays of his which had been produced in California and at the same time asked me to give his New York agent a free one-page ad. I wrote him back and said that if I agreed to do that I should also give free one-page ads to all the other contributors' publishers. I would, however, compromise: if he sent me a new unpublished play to print I would give the agent a free half-page ad. He never answered my letter and I have not heard from him since.

Another variation on the friendship problem came up with

Bernard Forrest. Bernard was a retired Lockheed accountant who had discovered art late in life and spent his days writing literally thousands of short poems and painting thousands of paintings in a beautiful redwood house in the Beverly Hills hills. Bernard was a very sweet guy who opened his house to hundreds of artists. There was one guest room, which was nearly always occupied by someone who needed a place to stay for a while or someone just passing through. I stayed with Bernard for a month in the summer of 1968, and since he read *Caterpillar* and was always showing me his poems, I knew that he wished I would print something of his in the magazine. Even though I did not think what he wrote was very interesting, I would always read what he showed me, hoping to find something that I could justify printing. One day I found four poems that almost made it as they were and that looked as if they could become acceptable with some cutting and revising. So I cut and revised them, and told Bernard that if he would agree to my changes I would run them in number 6. After the issue came out, I saw that the poems were odd hybrids and as such did not mean anything. I still think it is okay to rewrite someone's poems as a way of telling him what you see in what he has done—that seems more useful than mere descriptive criticism. But unless the original author can take the results and incorporate them in something that is ultimately his own, they really don't belong to anyone.

In spite of my moving around and being involved in other things besides *Caterpillar,* it was important to me to get the magazine out on time and to offer both authors and readers a sense of continuity. In fact, I think that continuity or the lack of it makes the difference between a magazine's being useful or not—especially to the authors. Yet I learned from Corman's *Origin* that not only should a magazine last for several years and appear at least quarterly, but it should be of real use to its contributors. *Poetry* (Chicago), during Henry Rago's editorship, seems to me to be a good example of a serious eclectic magazine in which you might very well have found a poem by James Wright facing a poem by Charles Olson. Yet even though Rago was generous to me—he printed my work once a year for four years—I never felt any connection with the magazine. I sent *Poetry* work because it had a good circulation and paid well. In contrast to this situation, when I was living in Kyoto and seeing Cid Corman a couple of times a week (in 1962–64 when he was editing his "second series" of *Origin*), I found that he was deeply involved with everything he published. He maintained a taut correspondence with some of his authors, and in turn some of his regular contributors could count on being featured at some point or other, when perhaps half of an issue would be given over not only to their poetry but to some of their correspondence. However, it also seemed to me that *Origin* had a central and severe limitation—the unvarying 64-page format—and that this limitation not only affected how much Cid could print of any one person's work, but also tended to prescribe a certain kind of poetry to be written. He backed the short poem to the exclusion of the longer, or "serial," poem which in the past couple of decades has become a direction in American poetry in a way that it had not been before the Second World War. While Corman began with Olson and printed sections from the beginning of the long "Maximus" sequence, and at the beginning of the "second series" printed a little of Zukofsky's "A," *Origin* was primarily a magazine for the short poem (which Corman himself has always written) in which the "self" has been omitted or resolved and is not seen as a part of the struggle unfolding in the poem itself.

Corman made his attitude clear to me in San Francisco in the summer of 1959 when he was planning whose work he wanted to print in the "second series." He told me that he wanted to present an alternative to "sick" poetry in *Origin,* and that he did not intend to publish such writers as Ginsberg, Burroughs, and McClure. What Corman seemed to oppose was anything that smacked of confession, subject matter which included drugs, and any detailed descriptions or thoughts about homosexuality or heterosexuality. While these concerns do not necessarily make a poem strong or weak, they have turned out to be elements in a gradual enlarging and deepening of materials to be dealt with in the poem. In seeking to "exercise [our] faculties at large," as Robert Duncan once put it in regard to the writing in his *The Opening of the Field,* many of us have attempted to eliminate the censorious mind in us which considers certain things not "proper" to poetry. By 1969 it was clear that Corman also included personal and historical mythology, when used as part of a poem's visible ener-

459

gies, in his evolving concept of "sick" poetry (see his review of *Maximus IV, V, VI* in Caterpillar 8/9). William Bronk and Corman-as-translator became the central figures of the "third series" of *Origin.* Olson, who at first represented the opposite pole of Corman's editorial tension, disappeared.

It seems to me that 1945 was the point when, to update two lines of Vallejo, "the winds change atmospheric needles / and the tombs change key in our chests." As soon as the concentration camps were opened in 1945, something in the air was felt by Charlie Parker and Jackson Pollock as well as Charles Olson. Whatever it was, it was connected with a much more complex and complicated sense of self, and the poetry that has been touched by this phenomenon is processual, longer, and more difficult than most pre–Second World War American poetry. In Hart Crane's *The Bridge* a mustang is haunted by a dream in which it is really a sonnet but, like Chuang-tze's butterfly, it does not know whether it is a sonnet dreaming that it is a mustang. Crane's dilemma could also be stated as that of a poet with a plan for a long poem, where certain procedures are to take place which don't seem to work once the poem is under way; and thus the plans, as they did to a certain degree in Williams's *Paterson,* became at odds with the veer the poem itself was taking.

In *Caterpillar* I wanted a magazine that was open-ended, in which the contributions, expected or unexpected, determined the nature and length of a given issue. Nothing was to be held over except work that was being printed serially. I always tried to keep an issue open right up to the time that I had to start typing the paper plates to get them to the printer at deadline time. I think that numbers 3/4 through 12 were most faithful to this intention; and they ran between 160 and 276 pages. After I moved to California I became less willing to do big issues—for one reason because I was so much in debt.

In 1970, when I was writing the introduction for *A Caterpillar Anthology* (published by Doubleday-Anchor in 1971 and pulped, without my knowledge, three years later), the phrase "a magazine organic to the ongoing needs" came to mind, and as I thought about the flexible issue size, I recalled the reasons for naming the magazine *Caterpillar.* That special word was given me by Will

Petersen on a Kyoto street corner in 1963, when he quoted Blake's couplet "The Caterpillar on the Leaf / Repeats to thee thy Mother's grief." When I was reading Reich in 1966, I came across a drawing he had made stressing

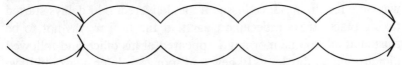

the peristaltic movement basic to all living creatures. In looking at photos of Vietnamese war victims, I would occasionally see a burned baby who looked like a black caterpillar, and in 1966–67, when I edited a series of books before starting the magazine, I used one of these black caterpillars on the colophon pages. I was also aware of the Caterpillar tractor used in earth moving as well as in tearing down old houses, so by the time I was ready to do the magazine, "caterpillar" seemed sufficiently complex to use as a name.

In the late summer of 1967 I wrote to about twenty people, telling them my plans and inviting them to send whatever they wanted. Most of them responded, although there were several disappointments. I telephoned Louis Zukofsky, since I was in New York City and had visited him several times in the past year. "How is the magazine to be printed?" he asked. "Photo-offset," I answered, and I heard him sigh. "Well," he said, "send me a list of who is going to be in the first issue and then I will make up my mind." If it had been anyone but Zukofsky I would probably have dropped the matter right there, but I did send him a tentative list. A few days later I received a postcard from Celia Zukofsky saying that Louis had decided not to send anything. Then, when I told Robert Creeley my plans, he seemed only irritated. He told me I did not have a group of poets and therefore it made no sense to start a magazine. That was it, as far as he was concerned. I borrowed from Margaret Randall an old *El Corno Emplumado* mailing list that had seven hundred names and addresses on it, wrote up a two-page statement on *Caterpillar,* mailed it out, and received around 150 one-year subscriptions.

I had $1,000 in the bank and a teaching job at NYU that paid $6,000 a year. For the first issue I went to a printing broker and put the entire production in his hands. He told me that 1,000 copies of a 140-page issue could be typed, printed, and bound, including stock, for around $700. After the first issue, I bought the old IBM typewriter that I still have and typed each issue myself. When it was time for the produced issue to be delivered, odd delays started taking place. It soon became clear that the broker was not to be trusted at all, so one morning I appeared at his office and followed him around all day long. I knew that sooner or later he would have to visit the binder, who had the issue, and then I would find out what was up.

The issue, carelessly produced, appeared a couple of months late and with it I received a bill for $1,400. When I refused to pay more than the original estimate, the broker took me to court. I went in alone and told the judge what had happened. The broker had a lawyer who kept repeating that the magazine had been perfectly produced and that, since unforeseen costs had come about, I should have to pay the difference. The judge picked up the specimen copy and saw for himself what it looked like. He then picked up a copy of the Bible and literally tossed it into the lawyer's lap, saying, "This is a perfectly produced book." I thought that I had won— and in a way I had. The judge ruled in the broker's favor but allowed him only $200 over his original estimate.

Two days before issue number 2 was to be delivered, I only had a few hundred dollars to my name and no idea as to how I was going to pay for it. That evening I was invited to Adrienne Rich's apartment to read some poems to her creative writing class. I got a lift back downtown from one of her women students and told her my plight as we rode along. She immediately offered to lend me the money for the printing bill and wrote out a check.

Once the first issue was out, I asked Andy Brown, owner of the Gotham Book Mart, if he knew anyone who might be interested in buying *Caterpillar* manuscripts and correspondence. He suggested I talk with Ted Grieder, the special collections librarian at NYU. I did—and lucked out. Grieder offered me $1,700 for the first year's material and a little more for the second and third years'. This helped a lot. If I had only kept the magazine small, and limited the press run to 1,000 copies per issue, then—what with subscription checks plus the dribble of income from bookstores— the magazine would have broken even, issue by issue. But in the seventh issue the number of pages jumped from 160 to 256 and I upped the press run to 3,500 copies, which was a real mistake.

After number 6 was published, Michael Hoffman of the Book Organization, which was then very new and based in NYC, decided his salesmen could sell *Caterpillar* along with the magazine and book titles from *Aperture, Jargon, Something Else,* etc. Mostly on the basis of *Aperture* sales, which seemed to have a very large circulation for a serious photography magazine, I ran off 3,500 copies of number 7 and spent around five hundred dollars on return subscription envelopes and ads in the *Nation,* the *New Republic,* and the *New York Review of Books.* All of a sudden *Caterpillar* had entered that no-man's land between the little magazine and the slick weekly or monthly. If I had had a large subscription base (as do little magazines like *Poetry,* which have been around for years and thus have many library subscriptions), or if I had had money to invest in real publicity, I might have been able to make it. But I didn't have either. I must have had around 400 subscribers at the time, and sold 200 copies of each issue in bookstores. After several months, the Book Organization salesmen, who probably didn't make enough commission off *Caterpillar* to push it, had sold less than a hundred copies!

Instead of dropping the idea of a larger distribution, I approached Eastern News Distributors, a national magazine distributor, and on the basis of being able to sell the *Paris Review* they agreed to take on *Caterpillar,* beginning with number 8/9—which meant I was stuck with about 2,700 copies of number 7 and was several thousand dollars in debt. What Eastern News did was to send a copy or two of *Caterpillar* to every newsstand they did business with, so the majority of the copies went to places that did not generally stock literary magazines (a friend once wrote me that he was quite surprised to find a copy of *Caterpillar* in a Birmingham bus station!). The issue sold fairly well. Of the 2,500 copies Eastern News sent out, I think only about 700 were returned. (I should say the covers were returned; they were torn off the unsold copies of the magazine to prove they had not been sold, and mailed back, at my expense, to the distributor.) But each subsequent issue did a little worse, and with number 15/16—a 304-page issue priced at $3.50 (not so much today, but overpriced at the time)—the bottom fell out. Only some 700 copies were sold, and most of the other 2,300 were destroyed before I could get them back.

At that point I was nearly $10,000 in debt and if my parents had not died I think 15/16 would have been the last issue. But my parents left me a little money, some of which paid most of the printing bill, and on a modest scale I did four more issues, spaced out over two years, cutting the press run down to 1,250 and using Serendipity Bookstore in Berkeley as the distributor. This worked out fine; in fact, the last four issues made a slight profit and I paid all contributors either $15 or $25, depending on the issue.

When I think back to the period covering issues 7 through 13 I don't know how I managed to keep myself going and turn out all those copies. In fact, after issue number 5 I quit my job at NYU. From then on, until checks from the California Institute of the Arts started coming in after the publication of number 13, I had no salary. I lived off the tiny royalties from my own books and some readings (which brought in very little), and sold a lot of my personal correspondence and work sheets to Grieder. If it had not been for him (and my Greene Street landlady, Anna Donovan, who kept my rent to $85 a month), it is doubtful if *Caterpillar* would have gotten beyond issue 5 or 6. Ted Grieder really went out on a limb for both me and the magazine, and I will always be grateful to him for doing so. During this period *Caterpillar* was awarded two small grants of $300 and $400 from the National Translation Center for the high quality of its translations, and two grants from the Coordinating Council of Literary Magazines— totaling $2,500.

So at this time a new thing that I got involved in was raising money. In New York City this meant following up every lead and wasting a lot of time at cocktail parties. Occasionally I got as much as a hundred dollars, and once Harold Wit gave me nine hundred, which was very generous of him. He was just starting his Croton-on-Hudson Press with Michael Perkins, so he also took out a few ads. When I told him I was going to see if I might have better luck on the West Coast in the summer of 1968, he suggested I look up an old friend of his whom I will refer to here simply as BK. Once I was settled at Bernard Forrest's, I called BK at his Wilshire Boulevard office—he was an investment broker—and made an appointment to talk with him the next morning at nine. I appeared, but no one else was there. I waited half an hour and when still no one showed up I asked a janitor if he knew BK. He did, and told me BK might be having breakfast at Nibblers, on the corner. With my little stack of *Caterpillars* I went in. There were lots of men eating breakfast, so I picked out one and asked him if he was BK. He was. He had forgotten, he said, that I was coming over; wouldn't I sit down and have some breakfast with him? In five minutes I knew that he had no interest in little magazines and that I was wasting my time. Out of the blue he asked me what I thought about LSD. I thought he was trying to find out something about me and was probably, like most people of his profession, against drugs. I told him I had taken LSD twice and while I had had interesting experiences, I did not think it had anything to do with the creative process as I understood it. (Note: I made that attitude up at the time for BK's benefit, but it is what I actually believe today.) He said that he disagreed, and it came out that he had been turned on to acid by a hooker a few months before, and now was experimenting with all sorts of things in all sorts of combinations. Somehow, in talking about LSD, I mentioned that I was in Reichian therapy, and that interested him too. He said, "Let's go back to my office and talk there." We did. He canceled all his morning appointments and we sat in his office talking, undisturbed, until noon. At a certain point he interrupted what I was saying to ask me how much money I needed. Like the LSD question, it came out of the blue. I thought, if I ask for too much he won't give me anything and if I ask for a pittance and get it I will be a fool for not asking for more. So I shot for something in between: "Ten thousand dollars," I said. He said, "OK, I'll give you half of that, but you must first raise the other five thousand from someone else." Then he said, "And be sure I get a tax writeoff." "Oh, sure," I said, stunned. Was this guy for real? The next thing I knew he was inviting me over to his house, so I followed his car in the one I had rented. He showed me around, and I saw that he had a small, uninteresting painting by about every twentieth-century master. After a brief tour of the house, we sat down at a coffee table in an alcove off the living room, and he offered me a joint out of an elegant wooden box in the same way, I imagine, that you would offer someone a Cuban cigar. We smoked that and I got high immediately. He then pushed what looked like a fat, ornate sugar

465

bowl toward me, took off the lid, and asked me if I had ever tried "that." There must have been a pound of cocaine in it, a drug I knew nothing about. We sniffed some and his daughter walked in, reminding him that he was supposed to go shopping and buy some new clothes for a trip to Europe the family was taking the following week. At this point he decided we should take off, get some lunch, and then go shopping. I waited out front while he went out back to get another car to drive. He appeared in what looked to me like a Stutz Bearcat, but that may have been a hallucination. We drove around the peaceful, leaf-mottled streets of Beverly Hills for half an hour, stoned out of our minds. Somehow he found Santa Monica Boulevard and the pizza restaurant he liked. I only remember eating an enormous amount of a house special at a rickety white metal table next to the parking lot. Then we drove off to Fred Segal's so BK could buy clothes. I was standing in a daze inside the door when he came over and said, "Go ahead, buy yourself some pants." I wandered toward the $12 corduroy rack, but BK came rushing over, exclaiming, "Hey, get yourself something nice!" So I found the leather rack and picked out a pair of gorgeous dark blue pants that cost $85. BK paid for our things from a fat roll of $100 bills. He had not found everything he wanted, so we went to a second Fred Segal's, and my head started getting funny. Without quite knowing what I was doing I walked in, picked out a $115 dark blue leather coat, and told the clerk that BK would pay for it. As soon as I did this I about fainted. Had I blown everything? Was anything at all going to come of this? Was it all a setup for him to put the make on me? BK found what he wanted, paid for everything without batting an eyelash, and drove me back to his house. He said that he had enjoyed our day together and that as soon as I raised the first $5,000 I should let him know.

When I got back to NYC several things became clear fast. I was not going to be able to raise that first $5,000. My day with BK had been an utter fluke, and I could not count on it ever happening again. And I desperately needed the $5,000 he had promised. So I wrote him and said that I had raised the money, and would he send me what he had promised. I told him that he could give it to *Caterpillar* via the CCLM, and that way he would get his writeoff. Two weeks later a check for $2,000 arrived. When I tried to call

466

him he was always out and never returned my call, so I had to start dealing with him through his secretary. She finally informed me that I would not get the other $3,000 until BK had been shown proof that I had actually raised the first $5,000. Then I had an idea. I called up a wealthy friend, told him my predicament, and borrowed $5,000 from him. He sent it to the CCLM as a *Caterpillar* donation, and as soon as it was in I asked the CCLM to write a letter to BK stating that the amount had been raised. They did, and weeks passed without the $3,000. So I then called up a friend who lived in Berkeley and told her that I would pay her way down to Los Angeles and arrange for her to stay at Bernard's if she would try to pry that $3,000 out of BK. She made the trip and was successful: the $3,000 came and I paid back the borrowed $5,000.

The upshot of all of this was more complicated than getting the money in the first place. Since the leather suit was the only terrific-looking thing I owned, I wore it everywhere, especially to Gotham Book Mart's four P.M. literary parties. Unknown to me at the time, rumors began to circulate that I was getting rich off *Caterpillar* (with the implication, of course, that the starving contributors were not even being paid). At the same time, some people who had been turned down for CCLM grants began to investigate the inner workings of the Council and were shown the financial report for the year. In an attempt to find any possible dirt, they disregarded the fact that the $10,000 which *Caterpillar* had received (of which I had only kept half, remember) had come from outside sources. In an article published in the *Nation* they stated that *Caterpillar* had received something like $12,500 from CCLM. This made me and *Caterpillar* appear very suspect, not just because only $2,500 been reported previously as the amount the magazine had been given by the Council, but because it appeared that I, a consultant, had been using that position to tap funds that should have been spread out among other magazines. I should have made a statement clarifying all this at the time it happened and printed it in *Caterpillar,* but I was never fully aware of how malicious people could be, and to what extent poets in NYC were jealous of me and my magazine. If I had been down and out, a junkie, or horribly unhappy, I imagine people would have let matters pass. But I was relatively healthy; I had bounced into

467

the city in 1966 and in a year had an impressive magazine going. It is hard to imagine the rancor that is shoveled from person to person in NYC unless you have lived there and had some of it dumped on you.

Rather than getting rich off *Caterpillar,* I was as broke as ever and got in deeper with each issue, because less and less money was coming back via Eastern News. Through a friend of Kelly's, I got in touch with a graduate student at Wagner College on Staten Island, a young man who had a private income and contributed his monthly graduate-assistant stipend to "worthy causes." He and I talked on the phone and he said that if *Caterpillar* was what he had been told it was, he would give me several hundred dollars. Before we got together, however, he made a trip to Boston and, while visiting the Temple Bar Bookstore in Cambridge, mentioned that he was planning to give some money to *Caterpillar.* When he returned to NYC he called me and said it was all off. When I inquired why, he said that a bookdealer by the name of Nunnalee was there, and when he mentioned the magazine, Nunnalee had told him that I was selling manuscripts to NYU for thousands of dollars a year, that I ate my meals at the Ritz, took taxis everywhere, and wore a fur hat! It happened that one of the charges was true: I did wear a fur hat—but so what? I pleaded with the student to come over to the loft and see for himself how I lived. He did, and went so far as to ask to see my checkbook. I had to show it to him, of course. I don't remember whether the rat was out that night or not, but after inspecting the place and listening to my refutation of all the charges—except the fur hat—he solemnly wrote me out a check for $200. Some of the charges were so incredible—I only remember four of what must have been eight or nine—that I asked him if he was sure Nunnalee had said all that. He was, he said, and had written them down in his notebook at the time. "Would you send me a copy of that?" I asked, and he agreed to. Since it never came, and since I called him several times and repeated my request, I am pretty sure he was at least exaggerating. What makes this story even stranger is that Nunnalee himself had called me long distance a year or so before and asked me if he could buy copies of issue number 2. I had told him that it was sold out, and we had discussed the possibility of his reprinting it. He finally decided that he could not make enough profit by doing that, and the matter was dropped. Of course, all along I assumed that he was interested in the magazine, and thus would have liked to see it continue, or he would not have called me in the first place. Nunnalee later wrote me and denied that he had bad-mouthed me or the magazine at all. So the whole thing remains a mystery.

The NYC printer whom I have referred to several times was David Miller, who probably still manages a large photo-offset business on West 19th Street. David was another of the generous people who made *Caterpillar* possible; he carried me for several years when I was unable to pay more than 30 or 40 percent of a bill when an issue was delivered.

A word about *Caterpillar's* subtitle, "A Gathering of the Tribes," which was dropped with number 11. It was never really true, and it took a personal incident for me to see just how untrue it was. My impulse to gather the poetic tribes under one cover came out of my desire to do a magazine that had a single point of view and was also eclectic. Some part of me wanted to believe that by printing poets as different, say, as Cid Corman, Diane Wakoski, Gerrit Lansing, and Jack Hirschman, and including writing and music by musicians Philip Corner and James Tenney as well as essays by the film-maker Stan Brakhage, etc., a symbolic "gathering of the tribes" could take place (and in 1967 that phrase still had a little zest left in it). And maybe it did, in a way. The falsity in the phrase lies in the fact that I did not print the Ashbery tribe, the Lowell tribe, or the Bly tribe, etc., which I would have had to do to make the phrase really stick. I had formulated it while reading an essay by Robert Duncan, "The Rites of Participation," which appeared in issues 1 and 2. When Duncan sent me the second half of his essay he asked me to send the typescript back after I had typed it for the issue. When I took the first batch of *Caterpillar* material over to Grieder, I told him that Duncan wanted the typescript. Ted said, "Why don't you xerox it and send him a copy?" I knew that Grieder wanted it as part of the *Caterpillar* archive, and since I was beholden to him I made a mistake and did what he suggested. Because Duncan did not say anything about it, I figured that it was okay with him. Afterward, I saw him several times. We were quite friendly, and he gave me material for issues 6, 7, and 8/9. Then in the fall of 1969 a couple of friends asked me, "Why did you do that to Robert Duncan?" Each person told me the same story: Duncan had told them that I had stolen a manuscript from him, that because of this he could not work on the book it was a part of, and that he wanted nothing more to do with me or my magazine. I knew the second charge could not be true if for no other reason than I had sent him a xerox of the typescript, but it also seemed bizarre that he would not have kept a copy of something he had mailed out (and, for that matter, had available in his copies of *Caterpillar* 1 and 2). But Duncan did have a point in his first charge. I had, against his wishes, turned his typescript into capital gain for the magazine, and this was a kind of theft. So I went over to NYU, told Grieder what had happened, and said I wanted to make another xerox of the typescript and to send the original back to Duncan. I did this, but I heard nothing from Duncan. The grapevine, for the little it is worth, continued to bristle with his ill will toward what *Caterpillar* and I represented. The incident upset me because, while I had made a mistake, I considered Duncan to be a friend. If he had really been my friend, he would have spoken up as soon as the xerox arrived, but the way he had handled the matter meant that he had never been a friend in the first place. Suddenly the phrase "a gathering of the tribes" looked ridiculous. Not only could poetic tribes *not* be gathered, but not even one tribe could be held together—and could *Caterpillar* even be thought of as a tribe? After issue 10 I decided it couldn't.

If I ever do another magazine (and I would like to, were someone to back it financially), I would insist on paying all contributors at least $50 per issue. Not only would they deserve that, but by doing so I could eliminate some of the complicated psychological dark that accumulates in hardly discernible ways between a little-magazine editor and his contributors. Without a contributor's fee, the contributor is made to feel that he is supporting the magazine more (in most cases) than the magazine is supporting him. True, the neophyte is overjoyed if a well-known magazine prints a poem and to him financial payment is a surprise. But if one reverses the implied age differences between a neophyte contributor and an older editor, a different picture results. The neophyte editor, while possibly doing a lot of hard work for others as well as for himself, is still building his reputation with the names of the older contributors whom he prints. If this so-called older contributor is someone like Robert Duncan, who has remained independent and has taken menial jobs to be able to do so, how must he feel when he is not only not paid for his writing but realizes that his unpaid-for writing is being converted into cash for something or someone else? Someone told me that Gilbert Sorrentino was furious when he heard that NYU was buying *Caterpillar* materials. My response to him was, "What a shame that Sorrentino did not make that kind of connection when he was doing *Neon*. He might have been able to do more issues, and at least the *Neon* archive would be all together in one place [for little-magazine editors do not send manuscripts back to contributors unless they are specifically requested to do so; they throw them out!] along with much of the correspondence as well." Who knows what triggered Sorrentino's anger? Had he just been fired from Grove Press and seen me in my leather suit? Perhaps the underlying pain is that all American poets share a cookie of a dividend that in the business world might sustain a few executives for a year. And given the sense of self-worth that a poet must daily raise in order to remain a poet in any meaningful way, one can see the enormous gap between sensed achievement and actual reward. And of course this is taking place in the wealthiest country the world has probably ever known, where most artists think nothing can be too good for them.

My greatest pleasure in doing *Caterpillar* was in the preparation of the manuscript for the printer. I held off typing up an issue until the last minute and then did it non-stop for two or three days, so that the material would coalesce in my mind as a typist-reader. That typing was engaging as well as grueling, for I would often see things in typed poems that I had missed when I read them in manuscript. Sometimes, in the case of regular contributors, when I was sure that I was going to print what had been sent, I held off reading the material until I typed the manuscript, allowing myself that special pleasure of reading it while it was becoming part of the issue. Once everything was typed, I paper-clipped the longer (more than one-page) pieces together and spread them out in a kind of fan shape around me on the loft floor, along with the artwork. Then I would start assembling two or three contributions at a time, to see how they would "set" next to each other. What piece would be best to open the issue? To close it? There was a potential rhythm in each issue, which assumed the kind of reader who would read it from beginning to end—though with a 256-page issue, such a reading was unlikely. Still, it was a stimulating challenge to get all of that work together in such a way that it cohered and made a whole image out of all its separate parts.

471

Blue Suede Shoes, *Vol.?, No.?, Date? (courtesy Northwestern University Library)*.

BLUE SUEDE SHOES, ISSUE 379 (THE BABE RUTH ESSAY)
Keith Abbott

Any discussion of the editorial and literary history of Blue Suede Shoes *must include mention of David Sandberg's* OR *magazine, which, although it existed for only two issues, was in some ways a model for* BSS. *According to Keith Abbott, the business of editing is a matter of saying yes and no. He cannot recall ever receiving any helpful comment from an editor about his work. Nor can he recall editing any individual poems, although when he has published a large selection of poems by a single poet he has explained the reasons for his choices.*

In addition to being an editor, Mr. Abbott is a poet and fiction writer. His work includes five books and pamphlets of poems, among them Putty, Erase Words, *and* 12 Shot; *and two novels,* Gush *and* Rhino Ritz. *His education as a writer has consisted primarily in learning how to live in the world as a writer, and he is indebted to Lew Welch, Philip Whalen, and Richard Brautigan for providing interesting examples.*

Steve Carey and I thought up the idea of *Blue Suede Shoes* while we were both living in San Francisco in 1968. What we wanted to do was a one-shot mimeo magazine and write all the material ourselves under various famous, ridiculous, or normal names. Although we saw each other frequently, we began to write each other letters, submitting material for the as yet unnamed magazine. This soon became part of the charade of naming the magazine: *Dear Cleat Habit, editor of Pantsed, . . .*

However, I think we arrived at the name *Blue Suede Shoes* just by chance or drugs or something. Anyway, we submitted cutups and parodies and regular poems and imitations to each other, and we soon had a completely crazed issue. Unfortunately Steve then moved away and took half the magazine with him. He also stopped writing letters.

Two years later I was walking into the Humanities building with the chairman of the English Department when I saw a janitor abandoning ten cartons of mimeo paper in the hallway. "Excuse me," I said to the chairman, and went over to the stack and put one carton on my shoulder. No one saw me leave.

Some friends of mine were running the student government and gave me access to a great new A. B. Dick mimeo machine. I took half of the original manuscripts that I had, and added a few more things, and published the first issue of *Blue Suede Shoes*.

But the impulse behind the magazine was different. I was now in the backwaters of literary endeavor, at Washington State, and I wanted to use the magazine to establish contact with the rest of the literary world. *Blue Suede Shoes* was also a great way to avoid the boredom of graduate school.

By stealing paper from the various departments and buying only my stencils, I managed to put out four issues of *BSS* and four mimeo books of poetry in the first year.

Certain things were retained from the first. Publishing poems under famous, ridiculous, and/or normal names became very amusing, as were the specials and editorials. Other poets soon were sending me work under fake monikers. In Michael-Sean Lazarchuk's case, I was so sure that he was a pseudonym of a friend that, after I accepted three of his poems, I tried to get him to admit that he was really someone else.

These little amusements led to more serious incidents, as when one Midwest editor, who seemed to take his position in literature quite seriously, wrote and said that the latest issue was "shit" except for Alvin Greenberg's "Modern Oven."

Somehow I managed to restrain myself from writing him and letting him know that the poem was a parody of Kenneth Koch and/or Allen Ginsberg by Steve and me, and that we had named the writer Alvin Greenberg because that was the name Kerouac had given Ginsberg in *The Subterraneans*.

474

About two years after that, I found out there was a Midwest poet called Alvin Greenberg.

Another thing I did was to play with the idea of a magazine. Fake contributors' notes, or notes that were a mishmash of fanciful and real information. Deranged pleas for funds, "Life in These Ignited States" specials, and "Statements of Ownership" that read like this: *Sweat spurted / as he struggled. / Blast and damn / marijuana anyhow*.

My favorite notes to the contributors ran like this:

Dear Contributor,

I wish I had time to comment personally on each manuscript submitted to Poetry Northwest, *but the large volume of submissions makes that impossible. The fact that you are receiving a form rejection slip is in no way a comment on the quality of your work. It simply means a knife in the white belly, for one of a large variety of possible reasons, including a shortage of space. We are only able to publish about 180 poems a year, and we receive approximately 40,000 poems a year in the mail. This rejection is not intended to discourage you from submitting further work at any time; we are dependent on your continuing interest and goodwill. I hate you as much as anyone else does, but they are indispensable; they have enabled* Poetry Northwest *to return your poem to you much faster than would have otherwise been possible.*

> *Sincerely,*
> *David Wagoner*
> *Editor*

Sorry to be saying no again. We're very crowded.

The contributor who receives the best note may wish to submit it to Blue Suede Shoes. *This month's winner of the* BSS *Notes to the Contributor wishes to remain anonymous; however, other work by Mr. Snyder appears in the pages of this issue.*

Translations were also big news then and so I took any cutups and/or collaborations that sounded like Char, Reverdy, Tzara, etc., and published them as being by them. So it came to pass that a hearty schizoid megalomania became the editorial policy for *BSS*. And all the editors agreed with it.

As for money, CCLM gave, and a few library subscriptions made their way through the maze of forwarding addresses. Very few unsolicited manuscripts too. Even though CCLM mailed the money to me, they always managed to have the wrong address on their grants list, and so I was spared writing too many rejection slips.

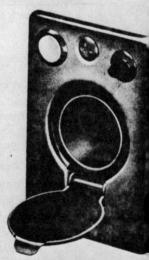
from Blue Suede Shoes, *the Board of Directors (courtesy Northwestern University Library).*

AN OPEN LETTER TO BSS SUBSCRIBERS

Dear Subscriber (or Casual Reader),

Most people in _____ are now getting ready
for Christmas. Christmas shopping for children and
relatives is well underway. Families are decorating
their homes and planning Christmas dinners. Everyone is
rushing to prepare for our most joyous celebration.

But for people in the hungry half of the world,
Christmas is just another day. Another day without
enough food, without medical care, without adequate
housing, and without dope.

Blue Suede Shoes is trying to change things. They
help a farmer improve his farming techniques so he can
grown enough drugs.

No matter how little you can afford to give, it will
be a big help.

Our Christmas has so much. Please share it with
others. Send your gift to Blue Suede Shoes today.[*]

                    Yours sincerely,

                    HUGH

                    Dr. Hugh Koolleyside
                    Editor, Blue Suede Shoes

---

[*] BSS is available in the Decimal Series for $1.00
from 1146 Sutter, Berkeley, Ca 94707. Complete sets
of BSS 1-15 are $35.00. A certain percentage of the
profits will go for the above research project.

My most enthusiastic response was at first from people in New York. Ron Padgett, Anne Waldman, Larry Fagin, and others were most supportive and encouraging. My writer friends from 1968 San Francisco had all zeroed out, with a few exceptions, and were into post-acid backpedaling. Many were not writing any more. So I didn't get too much positive feedback from there, even after I moved back to Monterey, with the exceptions of Philip Whalen, Clifford Burke, Richard Brautigan, and Pat Nolan.

There was no schedule for *BSS*. Basically I put everything I found or received in a folder and waited until I was going bananas from inactivity or too much activity (such as at the end of a prose writing spree) and then I would type up the stencils and run off two to four issues at a time.

I learned a lot about editing. How you could get the most out of a certain type of poem by following it with something that complemented it or contrasted with it. Sometimes the best thing to do for a group of poems was to put them between two neutral pieces, like a *BSS* "Special" and an editorial. Some poets' work was so different from the normal *BSS* fare, it was a pleasure to include them just to create new textures. Bruce Andrews was one such poet.

One of the things that bothered me about other magazines was that sense of stylistic claustrophobia. A Deep Dark & Delicious Surrealistic poem followed by another Deep Dark & Delicious Surrealistic poem. The virtues of any author's style tend to get blurred if he is surrounded by other authors too similar to him.

I think that from the experience of editing a magazine I learned to identify poems by their effects and/or style, and to put them together in pleasing combinations. I have since edited a couple of friends' books, and all of us were pleased with the results.

Another result of editing a magazine was an impatience with certain types of contemporary verse. From about 1970 on, the creative writing programs were turning out poets who were writing short and flat imagist poems which were, for all their brevity and opaqueness, also very sentimental and romantic. The poets would take an object, compare it to another object, and then

478

look out the window and see something mysterious, like a white horse.

Me arcane Magi poems, Drinkin' in the Alley poems, and what Clifford Burke has called the Lonely Cry in the Night poems. Eventually I became less and less amused by the various models, and I wrote a "Pre-digested Young American Poets Anthology."

Here I claimed to publish the poems without their authors' names, but with only their generic code names: "Just Tough Muscular Verse (Midwest Edition)," "Polite Buttoned-Down Surrealism," "The East & West Coast Sea Shore Agony Poem," "Every Day I Have the Blues (or Reds) Poem," etc. In *BSS* I published the parodies as straight poems sometimes with innocuous names attached and sometimes outrageous names like Al Chemical. Later I published the rest of the anthology in Steve Vincent's magazine, *Shocks*.

One genre interested me: the prose poem. My idea of a prose poem was one whose lines were so fast that you didn't want to slow the reader down with line breaks. Lots of velocity. Not lush description and none of that "of"-"of" prose where there's *lobsters of knives, napkins of oysters,* etc.

Sometimes a tiny story had the quality I thought of as being a prose poem. Where nothing could be replaced or changed but yet it was prose. The most interesting model for these was Max Jacob. His prose poems seemed to be almost language objects. Several other poets shared my interest in the prose poem, and so I came to publish Michael Lally, Richard Snyder, Bill Berkson, Jack Anderson, Michael Sowl, Bob Heman, and Pat Nolan.

Blue Suede Shoes would also publish collections of work as one issue. Books by Michael-Sean Lazarchuk, Steve Carey, Michael Sowl, Mary Carey, and Pat Nolan were originally submissions that seemed to me to be worthy of taking up an entire issue.

This practice led to the debacle of issues 16–20. Because I had received a huge grant for *BSS* from CCLM, I planned to produce two novels as *BSS*: *Gush* by myself and *The California Papers* by Steve Carey. But what to do while I waited for them to be done? Easy. I began the Decimal Series, taking *BSS* backward in time. The few libraries I had as subscribers became upset.

479

But then *BSS* had a history of library problems. Opal L. Nations and I switched issues once. He did number 11 of *BSS* and I did number 9 of his magazine, *Strange Faeces*. This created a wonderful amount of confusion among our library subscribers. But the Decimal Series was the last straw for some of my libraries. It was reported to me that at one library they refused to recognize my Decimal Series and were hand lettering each issue as it came in: No. 16, No. 17, etc.

I lost another library because they became hysterical when the .3141596265 issue came out; the number was too big to put on their index cards. (Alert readers will notice that this is the number for *pi*, only the decimal point has been placed incorrectly. This did not deter me, though, from calling it the *Pi* issue.)

The New York Public Library sent me an anguished letter, and I tried to convince them that this was a chance for true creativity and that they might arrange the issues any way they wanted, a chance not to be missed in the librarian's profession.

They canceled their subscription. *BSS* never did receive too much money from libraries anyhow, and basically the magazine was not sold but given away. The Decimal Series, besides providing a way out of the *Gush* problem, was an attempt to revive what I felt to be a flagging focus. I knew the maxim about no little mag going beyond twenty issues without going stale.

So I had a satori and began to write my manifestos of Syllogism. I explained that I had finally understood what sort of poems I *should* have been publishing all along, and so, instead of starting a new magazine, I went backward. I sent out letters to my friends, asking them for poems that they would have written in 1968 had they known about *BSS*.

I knew that I had to use as much reason as possible in order to smooth over the transition to the Decimal Series, so I tried to use *famous* decimals, such as Ted Williams' batting average, .406, the last time anyone hit over .400 in the major leagues, and Rogers Hornsby's equally celebrated .424, the highest batting average ever recorded.

As the Decimal Series continued, the plans for publishing *Gush* and *The California Papers* receded. The lean Republican years wiped that out. However, since then *Gush* has been picked up by Blue Wind Press and published, and I'm sure *The California Papers* will be eventually published too.

The one piece of praise which pleases me the most and which I have had most often is when people tell me that they read *BSS* from cover to cover. I always feel very good about that. *Blue Suede Shoes* has always attempted to be a totally engrossing magazine, cheerful and odd and surprising.

Selected Bibliography

Blue Suede Shoes, issues 1–15, edited by Keith Abbott and others.
Blue Suede Shoes, Decimal Series (9 issues), edited by Keith Abbott.
Abbott, Keith, *Putty* (Cranium Press, 1971).
Abbott, Keith, *Gush* (Blue Wind Press, 1975).
Abbott, Keith, *12-Shot* (Z Press, 1975).
Andrews, Bruce, *Corona* (Burning Deck Press, 1973).
Berkson, Bill, *Enigma Variations* (Big Sky, 1975).
Burke, Clifford, *Griffin Creek* (Cranium Press, 1973).
Carey, Steve, *Gentle Subsidy* (Big Sky, 1975).
Carey, Steve, *Smith Going Backward* (Cranium Press, 1968).
Lally, Michael, *Rocky Dies Yellow* (Blue Wind Press, 1975).
Nolan, Pat, *The Chinese Quartet* (Cranium Press, 1973).

Magazines of related interest: *Strange Faeces,* edited by Opal Nations; *The End (& Variations Thereof),* edited by Pat Nolan; *The Titmouse Review* (Canada), edited by Avron Hoffman.

Blue Suede Shoes is available in complete sets from Keith Abbott, 1020 Cornell, Albany, California 94706.

A HISTORY OF IO, 1964-1976
Richard Grossinger

Richard Grossinger and Lindy Hough, co-editors of Io. *Photographed by Gerard Malanga.*

Io is a series of book-length anthologies combining literature, anthropology, natural and physical science, and mythology in specific thematic issues that include, among others, "Alchemy," "Enthnoastronomy," "A Phenomenological Geography of Vermont," and "Baseball." Unlike most magazines, big or little, Io is, in Richard Grossinger's words, "a long accumulating poem, or myth, created by those who read it." Rather than collect and edit a number of manuscripts notable for their literary quality, Mr. Grossinger has concentrated instead on assembling a variety of texts to compose each issue, so that "the integrity of the individual pieces is less important than the coherence of the whole, either the issue or the set." "Set" here refers to the magazine's twelve-year run.

In addition to Io, *Mr. Grossinger also publishes North Atlantic Books. His own published work includes a volume of prose,* Solar Journal; *three collections of essays*—Mars: A Science Fiction Version, Early Field Notes from the All-American Revival Church, *and* Martian Homecoming at the All-American Revival Church; *and* The Cranberry Island Sequence, *in six volumes.*

Io was born by accident and then grew out of itself, changing subject matter, authors, and readership over the years. Although it has been most commonly regarded as a kind of poetic research project, *Io* is neither an intellectual poetry journal nor a collection of conventional scholarship. The actual text of the publication is very rough, with the appearance of a workbook more than a finished product. The individual pieces are often drafts or working notes, and the overall appearance is dense and continuous, like a long footnote broken by different type styles and illustrations from old texts. I know of no publication that preceded *Io* in the format of a handbook or catalogue interspersed with glyphs and landscapes from hermetic and scientific sources. The work in a journal like *Io* can afford to be daffy, extravagant, brilliant, sloppy, in some mélange or combination, because it has no authorities to serve, no elders except its own magic.

Throughout its history, *Io* has published major new works of poetry and prose—in the early issues, poems of Robert Kelly,

Edited and abridged by *TriQuarterly* with the author's permission.

Paul Blackburn, Diane Wakoski, Theodore Enslin, Kenneth Irby, and others; later on, such lengthy prose texts as Robert Creeley's "Presences," Gary Snyder's "Letters to Will Petersen," Michael McClure's "Wolf Net," and my own designations for the tarot deck. From the eighth issue on, in particular, *Io* has been responsive to new work from unpublished writers, much more so than have comparable magazines like *Kulchur* or *Caterpillar,* and it has introduced such authors as David Wilk, Charlie Walsh, John Moritz, Russell Gregory, John Thorpe, Anne Oswald, Paul Kahn, Irene McKinney, Don Byrd, Shepherd Ogden, and Jayne Anne Phillips.

Generally, however, *Io* has not been a source for individual gems; it is more nearly a long accumulating poem, or myth, created by those who read it. The integrity of the individual pieces is less important than the coherence of the whole, either the issue or the set. For twelve years now, the whole set has been kept in print, with old issues often enlarged in such a way that the response appears literally side by side with the original documents. Whatever weakness the journal has is a result of its commitment to text over literary value. Better writings are often not published when specifically relevant pieces fit into a given collection. Likewise, works are often used in a different way than was anticipated by the authors. Such attention to context is also, of course, *Io*'s strength.

I would date the beginning of *Io* from the merging of two events, one in the fall of 1964 and the other in the spring of 1965. In October of my second year at Amherst College, I gathered a group of people from Phi Psi—a fraternity that nourished artists, musicians, political radicals, nascent hippies, druggies, and bikies, as well as an odd assortment of people refused admission to other Amherst fraternities—and together we arranged a Halloween ceremony. For me it was a kind of inspirational celebration of occult and Jungian readings, and I wrote a very high-energy dedication speech. Charles Stein brought with him Josie Rosenfeld and Harvey Bialy. The speech found its way to Robert Kelly, who invited me to visit him and to begin studying with him. Later it appeared as the first piece in the first issue of *Io,* which was financed for fifty dollars as a "rushing publication."

Initially, then, *Io* was a fraternity magazine. When the fraternity

Io, *Vol. 1, No. 1, 1965 (courtesy Northwestern University Library).*

involvement was broken off, it was resurrected as a four-college magazine (Amherst, Smith, Mount Holyoke, and the University of Massachusetts), in order to get a wide editorial base and funds from all four colleges. Robert Bagge, a Phi Psi alumnus, was chosen as the University of Massachusetts editor; Lindy Hough, a poet friend, the Smith editor; and Susan Mohl, a painter, the Mount Holyoke editor. That particular constellation fell apart and was re-formed as a three-way editorship that held for the first two issues: myself, Lindy Hough, and Nelson Richardson, an Amherst student and poet. As the three of us talked over the project, we recognized our strong opposition to conventional school literary magazines and their coteries. *The Amherst Literary Magazine* was dominated by those who had taught writing at Amherst in recent years: Robert Frost, Rolfe Humphries, and Archibald MacLeish; it was, at the very least, literarily exclusive, but it was also socially elitist and commercially oriented.

Io was able to find very few local writers interested in an alternative publication, but we printed our own work and solicited work from friends. My affiliations brought in people like Charles Stein and Harvey Bialy, who have remained dominant. Nelson Richardson directed the graphics, and he and his friends in New York (Leandro Velasco and Philip Terry Borden) did the covers for the first four issues. By the time of the second issue in 1966, however, Lindy Hough and I had a falling out with Nelson over Robert Kelly, who had become our primary artistic and intellectual guide. Nelson had presented a chunk of work for the second issue, including that of Eduardo Zalamea, Aram Saroyan, and Edwin Denby, along with a letter from Saroyan advising us that there were "better and thinner poets than Robert Kelly." We were so offended by the letter that we argued with Nelson; eventually only the Zalamea was included, and Nelson resigned as editor, though he continued to send work to the journal.

The *Io* that appeared in two issues at Amherst was generally mocked by the literary establishment. It had a parapsychology-science-fiction bent, influenced by my Halloween speech, Nelson's surrealism, a few found documents, and a rather weak letter from Ray Bradbury. *Io* was named in a moment I have trouble remembering, except that we decided the title should be a heavenly body, preferably a moon, and probably the one with the shortest name.

486

Because of its astronomical origins, I stick to "eye-o" as pronunciation rather than the Greek "ee-o." We thought of the magazine as a one-shot deal, and I certainly never dreamed I'd be hassled for the next "x" years with letters and uncashable checks to *Lo, Ten, IQ, Id, Ion, I.O.*, or just (blank) *Magazine*.

What kept *Io* going past one issue was, first, the fact that we didn't use up all our funds while selling the magazine for a quarter; second, our interest in the work of the Aspen Writers' Workshop (summer 1965); and, third, a negative response from Amherst that was strong enough to arouse curiosity and interest. In fact, because I had become a sort of *bête noire*. I was able to command some administration attention. I visited the president, Calvin Plimpton, and received funds not only for the journal but also for a film and poetry series run by Phi Psi. We had visits from Stan Brakhage, Robert Kelly, Paul Blackburn, and Diane Wakoski, and we showed the films of Brakhage, Kenneth Anger, Harry Smith, and Bruce Conner. All this represented radical artistic innovations for the locale. People came from all four colleges, and we had something of a salon at Phi Psi.

Amherst nurtured *Io,* though *Io* never represented Amherst. Amherst's contribution was subtle—a kind of intellectual toughness and spirit of inquiry—and in its disdainful criticism (on both student and faculty level) of our work there was some grudging admiration. The second issue cost a dollar, and we sold several hundred on the long dinner lines. If copies were abandoned on the dining room chairs, Phi Psi members collected them, and they were sold again. In 1966 we moved to the University of Michigan, but Ann Arbor, on the surface much more worldly and artistically open, ignored *Io*. We tried setting up tables to sell copies, but we were in competition with SDS and other popular organizations. No one knew *Io* was there. Interestingly enough, however, after we moved to Maine in 1969, Ann Arbor became one of our better markets, and for several years we sold hundreds of every issue there.

During the years 1966–1969, *Io* had no niche in Ann Arbor. The English department dominated the literary scene so thoroughly that when Robert Kelly came to town, there was no place for him to read except in our living room. Of the visiting poets acceptable to the establishment, only Gary Snyder supported us and attempted

487

to gain us a hearing. The *Io* of this period was a continuation of Charles Stein's proposed magazine of Traditionary Science (*Aion*), which published only one issue, in 1964. Stein helped to guide our magazine away from literature toward hermeticism. During this time, *Io* published one issue (a thousand copies) a year for six years, and sold very few of them.

Io's 2 and 3 were younger cousins to *Yugen, Matter, Something, Floating Bear, Kulchur,* etc. Lita Hornick was *Io's* first subscriber. *Io* 3 was an American Indian issue that preceded the American Indian issue of the *San Francisco Oracle* and Rothenberg's anthologies. In fact, it was this issue that brought Rothenberg and David MacAllister together for the first time, initially in print, later in person. It led directly to the Indian material in later *Io*'s, which is one of the continuities: Cherokee in 4, Omaha in 5, Pawnee in 6, Eskimo in 7, Iroquois in 8, Hopi in 9, Tewa in 10, Osage in 14, Crow in 16, and Abenaki in 21. In a certain sense, this direction seems inevitable, since I was a graduate student in anthropology, but in another sense it was a continuation of my science-fiction and occult interests, and very different from Rothenberg's later invention of other Indians (which I have criticized so strongly in print). The Indian of *Io* 3 became the alchemist of *Io* 4. (The Amherst affiliation was continued by the submission of a poem the captain of the football team wrote on his helmet after the last game.)

Io 4 (1967), the first of the fat, bound issues, was born out of Robert Kelly's "Alchemical Journal." He submitted it, knowing it was long and hoping we might print some of it. But the piece moved me so much that it dominated my own work for a full year around 1966 and 1967. I began *Solar Journal* at that time (its "Alchemical Sections"); I made two hours of eight-millimeter alchemical films, the Michigan seasons as flux and alembic; and I used the surprisingly available alchemical section of the University of Michigan Library to find other texts to print beside the Kelly.

Io 5 (1968), called "Doctrine of Signatures," was a direct continuation of the "Alchemy" issue, moving from the field of minerals and salts to the domain of living things. I did most of the editing during a year of studying botany, ethnobotany, and ecology at Michigan, during which time I treated a text like Bold's *Morphology of Plants* as if it were Kelly's "Alchemical Journal."

I continued *Solar Journal* with "The Plant Book," and I entitled the issue "Doctrine of Signatures" after a passage in Foucault. At this point I was committed to subject-matter issues and had taken full control of the journal, mostly because of Kelly's physical distance and Lindy's lack of interest. "Doctrine of Signatures," "Ethnoastronomy," and "Oecology" (with the baseball issue in seed form) were all prepared together but came out in successive years because of the slow collecting of both work and funds. Thus *Io* 7, the "Oecology" issue, was a direct continuation of "Doctrine of Signatures," in a direction opposite to that in which it emerged out of "Alchemy."

The "Ethnoastronomy" issue, *Io* 6 (1969), was woven out of the science-fiction threads of *Io* 1 and the hermetic-scientific threads in *Io* 4, but it also included two events very important in the germination of *Io*. The first was Charles Olson's direct collaboration with *Io*, an influence equal to, and related to, Kelly's. Charles Stein had told me that Olson considered *Io* the most interesting magazine being published. Since I was editing a proposed ethnoastronomy collection, using part of his poem "The Praises," I wrote him and told him where I was. I got back not only a couple of essays but also letters of advice and the work of other people: a very useful poem discarded by Ed Dorn, and poems and translations by Mike Aldrich, Lewis MacAdams, and Charles Doria. For reasons not entirely clear to me, Olson's literary executors have tried to minimize his contribution to this issue and blame me for hustling out of him what he didn't want to say. This is foreign to my sense of the correspondence, and Don Byrd says it is because Olson's contribution stands in the way of a more purely Jungian interpretation of his intentions.

The second event explains the pure astronomy in the "Ethnoastronomy" issue. Originally, as part of the process (not usually successful) of interesting scientists in *Io,* we tried to get both astronomers and ethnoastronomers to contribute. There was topology in the "Alchemy" issue and much natural science in the "Oecology" issue. The ethnoastronomers we got in touch with were so paranoid about their scientific stature that they refused to publish in *Io* unless we eliminated the poetry. At the same time they tried desperately to get me to commit myself to a strictly scientific journal in their field. Thus the calendrics and star mythologies, promised in the prospectus, never appeared. The astronomer whose participation I sought was Kip Thorne, who had written an article in *Scientific American* on the gravitational collapse of stars. He rejected an offer to publish in *Io* or to be interviewed, but at that time I met Fred Haddock, a NASA-associated radio astronomer, through his secretary, who was a graduate student in anthropology. Haddock was cynical about appearing in the journal and was about to dismiss the possibility when he was struck with the significance of our name. "Io," it happened, was the moon of Jupiter he was studying at the time, and he could not pass up the opportunity to have the newest unpublished material on Io appear in a journal named after it. Eventually we did an interview with him and Haddock paid to have a hundred extras run off, and sent them to astronomers around the world. Later, when *Io* became popular (after we left town), Haddock became something of a cult hero in Ann Arbor, and his whole life was changed. When I returned five years later, I found him a bearded astronomer-mage.

To fulfill Olson's crystal-flower-star ratio, I got together with another anthropology student and called up the local crystallographer to request an interview. He was incredulous—even more so when we showed up at his office with a tape recorder, asked the relevant questions, and left. A rereading of that spontaneous interview shows it to be just as hot and lucid today as it was then.

Through the early years, *Io* was my own work. I did the editing as if it were writing—collecting in order to gain insight, always under the guidance of Kelly, Olson, Theodore Enslin, and others. When Clayton Eshleman returned from Japan and began *Caterpillar,* he took up the editorial mission of publishing new poetry in the tradition of *Origin* and *Kulchur,* and Kelly became his contributing editor. Meanwhile I was becoming more and more prone to pay attention to whatever in the local scene interested me. In Ann Arbor, it was the library and the scientists and anthropologists; on Mount Desert Island in Maine (where the "Oecology" issue was finished and published), it was the lobstermen.

A series of events, occurring from late 1970 through mid-1971, hastened the process of *Io*'s transformation and gave it an entirely new direction. Black Sparrow published my *Solar Journal: Oecological Sections* with an enthusiastic preface by Robert Duncan. This led to its listing in both the American and Canadian *Whole Earth*

490

Catalog (Almanac) and to an invitation from Robert Bertholf to read at Kent State with Duncan and Ginsberg on the anniversary of the Kent campus shootings. At the same time Book People, born with the *Whole Earth Catalog,* offered to distribute *Io.* In 1971 *Solar Journal* sold a large number of copies and aroused a curiosity about, and a demand for, *Io.* West Coast stores had never carried many copies, but Book People placed it there in such abundance that the first seven issues went out of print immediately (except for number 5, which lasted another year or two); they were reprinted with the money from the sales. Submissions increased; Lindy Hough and I were invited to do readings in many places. In the first seven issues we printed only one piece of unsolicited work (the poems of F. Paul Salstrom). After that, we received regular surprises. By the thirteenth issue, one-third of our subscribers had appeared in *Io,* having sent work with their subscriptions. For the first time the people who were buying the magazine and reading it were also writing it.

At the time the boom was happening, it was already ending. The forces that brought it about, almost from the start, were opposed to what it was. *Io* had its own obscure history, but by a coincidence it began to resemble the new ecological and spiritual publications from the West Coast. It was distributed with them and was seized upon with the same enthusiasm. Of course, this was not a coincidence; it was a general synchronous revival. When I complained to Robert Kelly about the misuse of Jungian interpretation in so many courses at Goddard College (Plainfield, Vermont) after I arrived there to teach, he said, "You have no one to blame but yourself." I thought at the time that this was too lofty a role for me and *Io.* Now I see that it was *Io*—in the sense that *Io* was very early and part of the tide that reached people in derivative forms. For instance, although *Io* was painstakingly accurate in its reconstruction of alchemy, it participated in a general fad of reinterpreting the occult sciences, and thus was indirectly responsible for some of the modernistic blurring and misuse of the subject. By making alchemical sources available for people to use metaphorically, loosely, psychedelically, etc., *Io* helped to make alchemy unavailable again, in a new way. *Io* has as little currency in Plainfield today as it did in Ann Arbor or Amherst; I take that obscurity to be the rule and *Io*'s brief flourishing the exception.

Io 8, the "Dreams" issue, marks the transition between the magazine's two periods. Contributors sent in dream material, which did not have to be verified or diligently argued. The later "Regions and Locales" issue permitted the same sort of personal response. *Io* 9 is the series' first book, a collection of rough, mainly discarded writing rather than finished work. I was working to evade the original integrity of the pieces and subject them instead to an editorial reordering. That I was the only author of the work in the issue seems incidental. I had felt the need of a science-fiction issue somewhere in the series, and since the unsolicited science fiction sent to *Io* was of low quality, I published *Io* 9 as a history of my own involvement with the planet Mars.

The "Baseball" issue was based primarily on an apocryphal connection between American Indian games of strategy and English field games. It fell very hollowly at first because *Io* was mainly reaching a Whole Earth and spiritualist audience, neither one of which had any use for baseball. In time, it developed a specialized readership having nothing to do with the rest of the series. I am now planning, with five other editors, a revived, enlarged baseball book, divided into sections: baseball, pastoralism, growing up, first love, totemism, landscape, strategy, numerology, autobiography, oral history, etc.

For the next publishing venture, a thousand pages of accepted material were divided into three batches titled, respectively, *Economics, Technology, and Celestial Influence; Regions and Locales;* and *Imago Mundi.* These appeared as the three Earth Geography Booklets. Then a much misunderstood project closed out the Maine period of publishing: *Io* #15, Frank Zero's book *Love Minus Zero.* We had already confused our readers, but this book on the Lama Foundation in San Cristobal, New Mexico, presented without explanation, brought outraged letters from subscribers who expected us to continue either with our Kelly–Black Mountain literary concerns and commitments or with our Whole Earth, geography, or hermetic-scientific emphases.

The sixteenth issue was the fourth Earth Geography Booklet, *Anima Mundi,* but it was really a collection of smaller issues. "Regions and Locales" and "Baseball" material, received after the publication of those issues, was included with a section on James Fenimore Cooper's novel *The Oak Openings* and a section based on Charles Olson's relatively obscure visit to Goddard in 1962 (from which tapes remained). The nineteenth issue, "Mind Memory Psyche," edited by Lindy Hough, with Robert Bertholf at Kent State as a contributing editor, was also a generally literary collection. She decided to push aspects of *Io* which had been dormant since the second issue, with sections on sculpture and photography indicating a clear, overriding sense of the artistic and aesthetic. There were plans to issue one literary issue of *Io* per year, with Bertholf, Victor Coleman, Pierre Joris, and Robert Adamson as contributing editors (the latter three representing Canada, England, and Australia). However, Bertholf began his own magazine, *Credences,* and Joris and Coleman had other editorial projects. At the same time, David Wilk, who had participated in *Io* as a writer and interviewer, remodeled his college mimeo magazine, *Truck,* after *Io,* and we turned over much of our unpublished work to him, since we planned no new issues for some time.

Charles Stein did number 17, a collection of his work called *Poems and Glyphs,* with a long cosmological preface constructed from tapes I made with him. Bialy did number 20, titled "Biopoesis," which proposed an exact correspondence between the genetic language (of the cells), which expresses us, and the poetic language (of the intelligence), by which we express our cellular and cosmic reality. The issue takes into account many synchronous systems: the I Ching, astrology, mathematics, memory, and embryology. In this issue Bialy, by now trained as a biochemist, was able to present his own arguments on matter and art and to combine the work of such familiar *Io* writers as Gerrit Lansing, Kelly, and Enslin with the four of us and Michael McClure. The issue was tight and read almost like a conference.

Stein and Quasha wrote an exchange on dream science for the enlarged "Dream" issue, and I collected much of Stein's unpublished *Aion* material and added it to a new alchemical essay of my own in doing a third edition of the "Alchemy" issue. I also collected, as number 18, many of my early writings on tarot, qabbala, Indians, angels, and general occult topics. All these simultaneous projects made for a very thorough reexamination and redefinition of earlier territory, and placed *Io* on firmer ground. Much of this work was done in connection with an Earth Mythology seminar at Goddard during the summer of 1974, in which I arranged to teach a course (with Stein, Bialy, and Quasha) on the emergence of biological and poetic form. After that we went our own ways: Bialy to Africa to work on native medicine, Stein and Quasha continuing to work together (see *America: A Prophecy,* co-edited by Quasha and Rothenberg, and the *Vort* issue on Robert Kelly).

Io's "Vermont" issue number 21 was assembled very gradually over the same three-year period as a collaborative writing and research project. It involved collecting current work done in Vermont as well as culling the historical records for precise and distinctive descriptions of the Vermont landscape and culture. These were then "sewn" together in a large, continuous diary (360 oversize pages, with photographs), to serve as a single Vermont image. The geographical-ecological remains one of the primary axes of *Io*, but much of that work has been taken up by Bob Callahan in the Turtle Island Foundation publications and *New World Journal.*

So *Io,* first series, is complete, having circled in on its own concerns and participated in numerous rebirths and the spawning and splintering of other publications and anthologies. The second series now takes the first into account, but sings in a different key. The scrambling, collecting, patchwork quality is no longer necessary. The first series stands as a twenty-one step initiation into a world view that might seem fragmented and discontinuous from without, but is entirely consistent in its germination and generation through the stages. It is now time to consider where that initiation has taken us. Past the nervous energy and the encyclopedia, there is an actual world to propose.

Postscript

This essay was written especially for the collection in which it appears. Since two years have passed between the writing and the publication, I will update it briefly. *Io*/22 and *Io*/23, entitled "Olson-Melville Sourcebooks," actually closed out the first full phase of *Io* in 1976. *Io*/22, "The New Found Land," dealt primarily with *Moby-Dick* in the context of North America—with a very detailed summary and analysis of Olson's uses of Melville. *Io*/23, "The Mediterranean," with an emphasis on the Pleistocene and ancient civilization, gave a historical and anthropological perspective to Olson's *Maximus Poems.* Together they were a restatement of the literary basis of *Io* itself.

494

Since then, we have moved to Oakland, California, and have included *Io* more actively in a cooperative network with other journals and editors (Bob Callahan, Ishmael Reed, Geoff Young, etc.). At the same time, we have continued the process of having the journal unfold from within, feeding off itself. Four of the themes are being repeated in new issues: baseball (already as a four-hundred-page anthology entitled *Baseball I Gave You All the Best Years of My Life)*, ecology (Ecology and Consciousness, at press), alchemy *(The Alchemical Tradition)*, and dreams. Meanwhile issues on homeopathy and astrology are being prepared by different editors.

Rereading this essay now, I am startled by my own sense then (two years ago) of *Io*'s continuous martyrdom and "outsider" status. The facts are accurate, certainly, but it is no longer how I remember it. The arguments have come to seem less important than the continuation of a process which is grounded in some real thing, and continues to emerge and shape our own world and the world of our readers. I would call the essay, as it now stands, a "social and anecdotal" history of *Io*—lacking, perhaps, the intimation of largeness and of something there, at the beginning of time and space and history, that sustains the interest and the work past any contemporary entanglements.

DISCUSSION OF LITTLE MAGAZINES AND RELATED TOPICS
Anne Waldman & Larry Fagin

*This conversation between the two editor-poets took place on
September 7, 1976, at the Boulder (Colorado) Recreation Center.
Larry Fagin had been participating in the summer program at the
Jack Kerouac School of Disembodied Poetics at the Naropa Insti-
tute in Boulder. Anne Waldman is the co-director of the School,
with Allen Ginsberg. For the past seven years, Mr. Fagin and Ms.
Waldman have worked together at the Poetry Project of St. Mark's
Church in the Bowery in New York City. The project holds poetry
readings and writing workshops, and owns the mimeograph machine
on which Anne Waldman's and Lewis Warsh's magazine* Angel
Hair *was printed from 1966 to 1969 and which now prints Ms.
Waldman's magazine* The World *(founded 1966) and Larry Fagin's*
Adventures in Poetry. *St. Mark's may be one of the only Christian
institutions to spawn a literary movement since T. S. Eliot became
an Episcopalian.*

Larry Fagin: The question was, "How do you edit a little magazine, run the Poetry Project and the Kerouac School, teach, and still find time to write?" And the answer is, "You do, that's all."

Anne Waldman: I have to make time. Actually there never is enough time. But the jobs get done. Little miracles. If I didn't have all these projects I'd probably write too much.

L. F.: How do you find time to do what you're doing this minute? (sunbathing)

A. W.: I've found I can write almost anywhere and at any time, not just a particular time slot—in notebooks, or using a tape recorder on an airplane, or in a car, or during some other project or activity. Frank O'Hara used to write in the middle of cocktail parties; Allen Ginsberg, too.

L. F.: I've seen Allen writing at someone else's poetry readings. Turned on.

A. W.: I think prose is another matter. You need a large block of time for prose. For long poems, too, and for open-ended writing where the idea is to collect material from all kinds of life situations and episodes. . . . Spontaneous performance and chant, too, where you're composing on the spot. . . . So there's more time than you'd imagine for your own work, despite everything else you have to do.

L. F.: Jack Spicer believed that a poet who had to write and simultaneously edit a magazine couldn't do both or either very well.

A. W.: There are no hard-and-fast rules. Reading work by my contemporaries inspires me in my own writing. But others may be distracted by that.

L. F.: I think editing *Adventures in Poetry* helped my writing. Seeing manuscripts I admire goads me to get busy. There was a time conflict with the Poetry Project, but even there I got feedback from the readings. It's all parallel, but maybe during a given period one aspect (writing, editing, administrating, or teaching) may suffer and another prosper.

Opposite: left to right: Gregory Corso. Anne Waldman, Gary Snyder, Allen Ginsberg. Photograph by Gerard Malanga.

Adventures in Poetry, *Vol. 1, No. 1, March 1968 (courtesy Northwestern University Library).*

A. W.: Sure, and it's always interesting if you accept a whole range of activities. . . . I've always found the best editors to be decent writers themselves.

L. F.: Right, I can't think of good editors whose work I haven't admired.

Fagin and Waldman compile a list of favorite postwar magazines:

Black Mountain Review (Creeley, Ginsberg)
Measure (Wieners),
Yugen (Jones)
Floating Bear (Jones, di Prima)
Poor. Old. Tired. Horse. (Ian Hamilton Finlay)
Joglars (Clark Coolidge)
Lines (Aram Saroyan)
Locus Solus (Schuyler, Koch, Ashbery, Mathews)
Art and Literature (Ashbery and others)
Kulchur (O'Hara, Berkson, Jones, Sorrentino, et al.)
Origin (Corman)
Once (Tom Clark's series)
Mother (Lewis MacAdams, Peter Schjeldahl)
"C" (Berrigan, Padgett)
Chicago (Alice Notley)
Angel Hair (Warsh, Waldman)
Big Sky (Berkson)
Juillard (Trevor Winkfield)
Fuck You (Sanders)
J (Spicer)
Open Space (Stan Persky)
0–9 (Acconci, Mayer)
Paris Review (Tom Clark only)

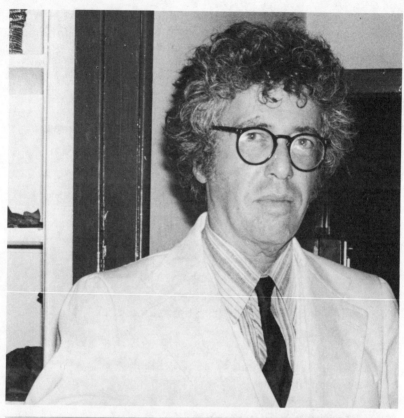

Winter 1961 $1.00

LOCUS SOLUS

I

Above: Locus Solus, *Vol. 1, No. 1, Winter 1964 (courtesy Northwestern University Library). Opposite: Kenneth Koch (below) and James Schuyler, editors (with John Ashbery and Harry Mathews) of* Locus Solus. *Photographs by Gerard Malanga.*

Top: John Ashbery (left) and Ted Berrigan. Photograph by Gerard Malanga. Bottom: Chicago, *Vol. 1, No. 1, February 1972, edited by Alice Notley (courtesy the Dauphine Foundation). Opposite:* C, a journal of poetry, *Vol. 1, No. 1, May 1963, edited by Ted Berrigan (courtesy Northwestern University Library).*

A
Journal of
Poetry

EDITOR   PUBLISHER

Ted Berrigan   Lorenz Gude

"The bachelor grinds his own chocolate"

Marchand du Sel

I

Manuscripts should be sent to Lorenz Gude,
319 West 100th St., New York City. C will
print anything the Editor likes, and will
appear monthly.

Above: Big Sky, *Vol. 1, No. 1, 1971 (courtesy Northwestern University Library). Opposite: Bill Berkson, editor of* Big Sky. *Photograph by Gerard Malanga.*

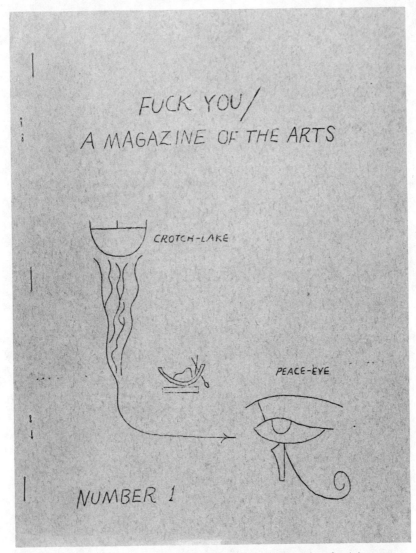

Above: Fuck You/A Magazine of the Arts, *Vol. 1, No. 1 (no date) (courtesy Northwestern University Library). Opposite: Ed Sanders, editor and publisher of* Fuck You/A Magazine of the Arts *and Peace Eye Books, and proprietor of Peace Eye Bookstore, N. Y. C. Photograph by Gerard Malanga.*

The World, *Vol. 3, May 1967, edited by Joel Oppenheimer, Lewis Warsh, and Anne Waldman (courtesy Northwestern University Library).*

A. W.: The weaker magazines, from my point of view, have been without a specific vision; those that have solicited anything from almost any well-known poet to get a little prestige.

L. F.: I don't mind the big quarterlies, though I hardly ever read them; once in a great while something interesting shows up. They seem kind of prehistoric, like mastodons. And there's no particular point of view except what's current or "important." *Contemporary Literature* and that enormous *Boundary* [*Boundary* 2] both have so-so articles on Frank O'Hara in recent issues. It's interesting to see a consideration of his work in a respectable, academic setting.

A. W.: Not that *The World* could ever be academic or respectable, but two anthologies were culled from issues over the years (both published by Bobbs-Merrill) and I'm working on a third collection now . . . more than twenty pages for the table of contents alone . . . a lot of variety. One misconception about this scene is that we're working out of one aesthetic only. Labels like "anti-academic" hardly apply now; Ginsberg's in the academy! I've published all kinds of exciting material—you, too. And when you come right down to it, it's the particular piece of writing (and not the writer) that's primary. Forget about the scene— and gossip! Interesting sometimes but, finally, irrelevant.

L. F.: Yes. Save the *auteur* theory for later. Meantime pay attention to what's on the piece of paper.

A. W.: Put John Wieners, Joe Brainard, William Burroughs, and Kathy Acker, say, together under one cover and you've got quite a mixture. Or Ron Padgett, Fielding Dawson, and Phil Whalen. The combinations, when editing, can be incredibly dynamic, though here I'm doing what I most dislike—describing authors' works by their names. Dumb. What I want to say is something about the variety of writing emanating from, or passing through, the Poetry Project and, recently, through the Kerouac School. There a journal of poetics is being put together based on a series of lectures by visiting poets, such as Robert Duncan, Robert Creeley, Michael McClure, Ted Berrigan, Philip Whalen, and others.

L. F.: Maybe you should briefly run through a history of the Project and *The World.*

A. W.: Paul Blackburn had the idea of moving the readings from Le Metro, a coffee house, to St. Mark's Church. In the fall of 1966 there was money from the Office of Economic Opportunity to structure a Poetry Project; to hold regularly scheduled open readings and paid readings by invited poets, and free writing workshops; and to print publications: *The Genre of Silence,* a one-shot affair, and *The World.* At first we sent out stencils to poets in the community on which they could type their own work, whatever they chose. Joel Sloman edited that first issue of *The World,* but nobody knew how to handle the stencils very well, and mailing them in tubes was troublesome. It was almost like a news sheet, carrying people's latest work (some of it still in progress), silly collaborations from the night before, and so on. Then an interaction between the magazine and the workshops developed, energized by the readings and by certain poets and artists in the Lower East Side community. The Poetry Project is in its eleventh year and *The World* has evolved and changed along with all other activities during that period. New energy kept coming in. Out of the workshops came other magazines and pamphlets, edited by Sam Abrams, Tom Veitch, Bernadette Mayer, Tom Weatherly, Charles North. . . .

L. F.: Most of whom cut their teaching teeth in those workshops.

A. W.: Then I did an all-prose issue, and later Ron Padgett guest-edited a special issue of translations, and Lewis Warsh did an issue of autobiographical writing. In a sense the magazine became more thematic, more specialized. The last two numbers, 29 and 30, are collections of reviews, commentary, and prose miscellany. All issues were graced with marvelous cover designs by artists Philip Guston, Larry Rivers, Alex Katz, Yvonne Jacquette, Joe Brainard, Mike Goldberg, Britt Wilkie, George Schneeman, and others—all gratis. There's always been terrific support from writers and artists, considering that contributors are not paid and the print run is never more than a thousand. We've survived mostly through CCLM grants and community team support—collating, for example.

510

L. F.: Aspiring writers are still starting little magazines for no particular reason. There are oodles of them and they're getting to seem . . .

A. W.: Redundant. Like the one you got last month. Suddenly another arrives with basically the same stuff, same people, and a couple of poems by each, so you don't get anything or anyone in depth . . . no substance.

L. F.: I started *Adventures in Poetry* in order to meet people.

A. W.: Good idea. Start corresponding, let them know you're there and interested. When I went to the Berkeley Poetry Conference in 1965 I met Lewis Warsh, and we decided to do *Angel Hair*. So we began by contacting Denise Levertov, Robert Duncan, and others.

L. F.: You build up a mailing list, a very particular readership, people who'll actually be *reading* what you've put together and who'll maybe notice how you've done it . . . the combinations, your style—rather than just going out and trying to sell it, or getting Robert Lowell to read it and maybe give you a crumb from his table. Or Robert Crumb.

A. W.: *Angel Hair* asked for specific work from specific people from the beginning. We weren't open to just anything arriving in the mail.

L. F.: A magazine might reflect a community of writers but I wouldn't want to keep it confined to that bunch. It doesn't matter who or where they are. The common denominator has got to be quality, not any particular style.

A. W.: *The World* does consistently publish the work, including reviews, of a group of writers whom I've followed for ten years, such as Michael Brownstein, Bernadette Mayer, and Ron Padgett. But also there have been many interesting newcomers.

L. F.: Sure. But if Mike Brownstein submitted a crappy poem you wouldn't use it.

A. W.: Of course not. But I've seen enough of their work to trust it in general.

511

L. F.: But editors still go out and ask a famous poet for manuscripts, and he may send in kaka. The editors know this, but they're trapped and they almost always lack the gumption (part of the vision) to refuse the said kaka. Of course, sometimes a famous poet's shopping lists are often more lively and more of a turn-on than most unsolicited manuscripts.

A. W.: I've encouraged young writers who ask me about publishing to start their own magazine, to publish their own work and that of their poet friends—say, three or four people who can be featured, presented in a big way. This instead of sending their poems out to all the big-time publications.

L. F.: Where the poems get buried. Magazines like *Poetry* are just as homogenized, antiseptic, democratic, and dreary as ever, but many of the little mags started by young writers are half-assed because they don't have a motive other than to make the writing scene. Maybe that's a good enough reason to get started, but somewhere along the way inspiration has to figure in it—passion, even a bit of coo-coo mania, to give the old rag that extra whatsis. Also, it's not such a great idea to have co-editors. Too often visions conflict, and you wind up hating each other.

L. F.: It's time for poets to start publishing books and pamphlets rather than magazines that can only give you snippets, little tastes . . . and it's the magazine that becomes the main thing, not individual works. But a month after it comes out the magazine winds up in a pile of magazines gathering dust under the sink, or the whole stack goes into cardboard boxes, gone and forgotten, thrown out entirely. Whereas if everyone who wants to publish or be published put together one book a year (say, anything from a $150 mimeo job to a $1,500 perfect-bound edition of 1,000), the publishing problem for poets would be solved. So GET ON WITH IT, everybody! . . . What a pipe dream.

L. F.: Helping a poet like Steve Malmude get going is really gratifying . . . encouraging the likes of Mary Ferrari or John Godfrey, wonderful poets already in their thirties and forties who need a little pushing. No big publisher is going to snap them up, no bright editor at Knopf or Random or Holt or Viking (who *are* those editors?) will "discover" them. So the small press is

512

there to start them. That's the reward if you have a small press: you're the intermediary.

L. F.: Jack Kimball's new magazine, *Shell,* looks promising. He seems to have something in mind, an interesting semi-abstraction shared by some of the contributors (Wieners, Ann Kim, Eigner, Elmslie, Donald Quatrale), rather than just collecting copy. It seems *edited,* anyway.

A. W.: Which is refreshing. I agree with you that the thrust should be toward books. That was the inspiration for our Full Court Press—to publish collections that wouldn't appear otherwise in a quality format, and really get them out there. For instance, Edwin Denby's work, long ignored, was the book we had most in our hearts.

A. W.: As for the question of the printed page versus poets' readings and performances, let a hundred flowers bloom, as they say. I see no problem, no contradiction. It's all working with the language.

VOL. I, NO. I

FICTION

50¢

New writing by JOHN ASHBERY   L.S. SIMCKES   THOMAS BERNHARD
JEROME CHARYN   MARVIN COHEN   JANE DELYNN   ROSALYN DREXLER
STANLEY ELKIN PETER HANDKE JOHN HAWKES   MAX FRISCH JEAN
GOLDSCHMIDT   JAMES KEMPTON ANTHONY KERRIGAN MARK MIRSKY

Fiction, *Vol. 1, No. 1, 1972 (courtesy Northwestern University Library)*.

ON FICTION
Mark Jay Mirsky

Mark Jay Mirsky began his professional career teaching in a public school in Boston. He became a staff writer for American Heritage *magazine in 1964, and then lectured at the City College of New York from 1965 to 1966. Mr. Mirsky taught at Stanford University for a year before returning to City College in 1967 as an associate professor of English.*

Educated at Harvard (B.A. 1961) and Stanford (M.A. 1962), Mark Jay Mirsky has been the recipient of a fellowship to the Bread Loaf Writer's Conference at Middlebury College, Vermont, and has served on the advisory board of the Coordinating Council of Literary Magazines (CCLM).

His published novels include Thou Worm Jacob *(1967),* Proceedings of the Rabble *(1971),* Blue Hill Avenue *(1972), as well as an edition of novellas,* The Secret Table *(1975). He has contributed short stories to* Partisan Review, TriQuarterly, New Directions Annual, Fiction, *and* Mosaic. *His articles have appeared in* The New York Times Book Review, *the* Washington Post, *the* Boston Globe, *and* The Village Voice.

I started *Fiction* out of desperation. One is supposed to be ashamed to admit such things. A friend, wife of a prominent New York publisher, recently accused me of being generous and ruthless by turns. But I've never seen myself as the latter—just desperate, a state which comfortable, lucky people often misunderstand.

Fiction was begun at a time when fewer and fewer magazines were taking stories for their pages, to say nothing of excerpting novels. I could accept my own dilemma and rage, all the while saying to myself, You're no good. In 1970 and 1971, however, when friends like Stanley Elkin and John Hawkes couldn't get their best fiction printed in periodicals, my selfish indignation passed into righteous fury. I railed against a whole kingdom of periodicals—*Esquire, American Review,* the *Atlantic,* bewailed the realm of dead issue, *Harper's Bazaar*'s discontinued fiction section, the defunct *Saturday Evening Post.* I cried out under a banner, and that banner was *Fiction.*

Several incidents provoked this flag waving. Stanley Elkin came to New York to read at City College. He recited a section of *The Dick Gibson Show* so funny that students were falling down in the hall, banging hands on the floor, against the walls, to try to stop laughing. I asked Stanley's friend, Gordon Lish, why *Esquire* didn't run the pages—a tall tale about a lady with an oversized private part, shopping under the eye of a lunatic pharmacist. Lish told Elkin to change the erotic key to the chapter and maybe he would consider it. No doubt Lish was under the yoke of *Esquire*'s puritan hangover, but it was an editorial attitude that put the book of Hosea beyond the pale of decency. *Esquire,* however, was a lamp unto my feet compared with *Playboy* or *Penthouse,* where one could be sure of reading a famous writer's worst fiction. The literary journals were not especially concerned with the short story or novel. Caroline Herron had brought some vital spirit to *Partisan Review*'s pages in this regard, but the critical essay still reigned supreme there and in the other serious reviews. *Paris Review*'s poetry kept abreast of what was happening, but its readers of fiction, who have since awakened, had fallen asleep for a moment in the nap time of the late fifties. I remember that once an editor there called me to ask the date of publication for a novel by Ronald Sukenick. They had a section they wanted to publish. With regret and a certain amount of malice (since they had told me that they didn't print excerpts in rejecting a manuscript of mine), I had to inform them that the book had been published two years before. Worst of all was reading the regional reviews from around the country. One was appalled by the difference between the discrimination they showed in selecting poetry and the hack stuff they represented as the experimental short story.

It was a bleak moment in which we were born, which probably explains some of our noisemaking: the fact that for an instant we were able to get national attention—the back page of the *New York Times Book Review, New York* Magazine's "Best Bets," a lot of newspaper coverage around the country. For a brief space it looked like a miracle. Let us pause at that second, enjoy its glow. I slyly hope that the attention we got did change, at least in the quarterlies and reviews, the attitude toward contemporary American fiction. Certainly at *TriQuarterly, Paris, Partisan,* and a host of smaller magazines, the situation is today much healthier.

Now I am forced to take the lamp from under my feet and shed the limelight on the features of one who habitually professes to detest it. *Fiction* owed its existence to Donald Barthelme. He kept ragging me when I came over to talk with him. "When are you bringing out that magazine? I'll do the layout for you." I had been trekking over to Donald's to listen to his talk about books and show him my own work. At one moment I had angrily threatened to bring out a magazine in pure spite at the vast conspiracy of indifference. He took me up on this vaunt during a late afternoon hour when I was well pickled in a friendly glass of Scotch. "When are you bringing it out?" he asked afterward, whenever I saw him, again adding the fateful words, "I will do the layout."

I used to meet Anne Waldman on street corners as I walked past Saint Mark's Church in the Bouerie, where we had both once worked in the theater. She and I would discuss *Angel Hair,* her mimeograph magazine *The World,* and the costs of printing, cheap and expensive. In the back of my mind was a conversation I had had years before with Rudy Wurlitzer over coffee in a dingy East Side luncheonette on Avenue B about the possibility of bringing novels out in newspaper format. Offset printing had briefly revolutionized publishing by cutting the costs of typesetting drastically. If one embraced the newspaper format, which was cheap to print, perhaps one could reach an enormous readership by distributing literature for pennies. Dreams of an underground audience of good readers began to haunt me. O vain illusion. O . . . but now the moment of the glow is fading and I promised to hold you in it for a while.

At this very instant, into my office at the City College English department walked a fireball named Jane DeLynn. Jane was looking for a teaching job. There was nothing, but as her legs and her tongue flashed I was moved by inspiration: "Why don't you become my managing editor?" I was outlining the hypothetical magazine as she snapped, "Absolutely." And we were off and running.

While Jane DeLynn hunted out the cheapest of printers, Donald Barthelme produced for us a handsome dummy page which was the basis for the first issue's design and layout. In the next few months, before we saw that issue, whenever my energy lagged I would look at the three elegant walls of type on the page, the collage which floated within them. I knew that if we never went beyond a single number of *Fiction,* it would be worth it, whatever the contents, just to hold the work of Donald's eye in my hands.

I had to hug the dummy many times. City College kept blowing hot and cold on the project. I felt that the financial support of the college was critical if we were to be able to open an office, send and get mail, answer telephones. I was blissfully ignorant of how much time *Fiction* would be stealing from my writing and teaching. In an English department committee meeting I had received a pledge from the powers-that-be to underwrite the magazine. But when I had the dummy in hand—stories in manuscript from Stanley Elkin, Donald Barthelme, John Hawkes, Max Frisch, Jerome Charyn, etc.—I was suddenly told that the funds were not there. I knew I couldn't wait. I swore silently. I collected pledges of financial support from friends. And when the issue went out to the typesetter, I went to the bank and withdrew the money from my savings account. Page after page appeared mysteriously before us—before me, a neophyte, as Donald bent expertly over the shoulder of the young man at the layout table. I trembled, holding the check from the bank in hand. Alas, we celebrated boisterously the paste-up of the final page—prematurely, it turned out, as someone spilled a glass of Scotch over them and it was a number of hours or a day or so (a happy alcoholic haze here obscures the details) until they were done.

Now, before the pandemonium starts, I have to mention a few more people. Donald Barthelme pulled me aside as we were assembling the issue at his apartment and said, "There's a woman downstairs who is willing to help you with the copy editing." It was Faith Sale, who quickly became a valuable member of the editorial board, joined by my close friend Jerome Charyn. Finally, the presence at this precise moment in New York of Max Frisch, the Swiss dramatist and novelist, and his wife Marianne (who was translating American writers into German), their enthusiasm for *Fiction,* their willingness to share their contacts with us, made

518

a large difference. The Frisches created something unique in that city for a few months—a European salon at which writers met each other, talked, quarreled, were introduced, scolded. One came in from the cold, lonely plain of America to a warm literary parlor. It was impossible in such an atmosphere not to talk about a second and third issue of *Fiction,* if only to bring the new names one was hearing about, discussing, together under the magazine's roof.

The efforts of all the editors, named above, and those of a publicist, Kathy Hartmann, who gave us her time and effort gratis, produced a sudden thunderclap of publicity. At one point, not only did we get attention from the newspapers already mentioned, and others—the *Washington Post, St. Louis Post-Dispatch,* etc., but the *Today Show* called. If we could produce one of our famous writers, they would be interested in having us on television.

In a "Guest Word" editorial in the *New York Times Book Review, Fiction* had asserted:

We simply cannot believe that people have tired of stories, that the ear of America has atrophied permanently and is now deaf to myth, fable, puzzle, paradox. . . . Literature is a mirror image of our own complexity—a necessity not a luxury. That is why we have spent a not inconsiderable amount of time and labor, plus a little money, in an effort to find new audiences. The 5,000 copies of our first printing melted away. Ten thousand more are just off the press and frankly we were amazed at the demand, stores like the Gotham Book Mart going through 250 copies in a few weeks. As we gather material for our second issue, we dream of reaching higher and lower, to the street-corner, to the benches of power, as Charles Dickens did with his cheap pamphlets. Illiterate workmen used to hire readers to recite Dickens to them as the chapters appeared. Can we live without fable? What a dreadful impoverishment.

. . . Writers must take matters into their own hands and search out the audience they believe is there. Gather the singular, the quixotic, the recondite, try even with the clamor of the bazaar around them to tell a curious tale. By going outside the marketplace (none of us at Fiction, *writers, artists or editors, have been paid) without grants or foundations, we have begun. As the Chairman says, seize the day.*

Brave words. Aye. For a moment the novelty of what we were doing, the newspaper format, the illusion that adult fable was as easy to read as a child's fairy tale, the newspaper, media attention, and some intangible historical freak did make those copies melt away. Most of them were never paid for, but that's another story—the wars of the newsstand deliverers, the piracy of distributors, the Mafia, etc. In a moment I will come to our sad *long march* through the vacuity of the American wasteland.

Was the intellectual premise of *Fiction* correct? Half a year later, Tom Wolfe attacked us in *Esquire*.

The idea that the novel has a spiritual function of providing a mythic consciousness for the people is as popular within the literary community today as the same idea was with regard to the seventeenth and eighteenth centuries in England. . . . Mark J. Mirsky writes a manifesto for a new periodical called Fiction *devoted to reviving the art in the 1970's and he says . . . quoting Thoreau, "In the mythos a superhuman intelligence uses the unconscious thoughts of men as its hieroglyphics to address men unborn."*

Nothing could be further from the minds of the realists who established the novel as the reigning genre over a hundred years ago. As a matter of fact, they were turning their backs, with a kind of mucker's euphoria, on the idea of myth and fable, which had been the revered tradition of classical verse and French and Italian style court literature. It is hard to realize today just how drenched in realism the novel was at the outset—realism pour le realisme! —all this is true of life! Defoe presents Robinson Crusoe as the actual memoir of a shipwrecked sailor. . . .

Esquire refused to give me space to reply. What nonsense! Wasn't *Tom Jones* a parody of *Oedipus Rex*, the old myth of the hero who sleeps with his mother? And in a clumsier fashion, this is the plot of *Moll Flanders* too. As for *Robinson Crusoe,* what really sold the book, then and now, was its magic, the fable of man returning to Eden. Defoe's far more realistic *Journal of the Plague Year* remains a deadly bore. Wolfe neatly had amnesia about the fantastic voyages in Swift's *Gulliver's Travels,* about Brontë's *Wuthering Heights,* Goldsmith's *The Vicar of Wakefield.* What I treasure in Dickens is the bizarre, the morbid, the grotesque, the fabulous and intricate fairy tale of his plots. But in most of the nineteenth-century masters there is room for realists and surrealists to plead their case.

Wolfe's distortions are a house of cards which any sophisticated English graduate student could huff down in a few minutes. What fascinates me about his article now is not the truth or falsity of his assertions but that his crowing about the New Journalism's having supplanted myth, fable, magic was in essence correct, as far as a serious audience was concerned. Cheap magic—*The Exorcist, Valley of the Dolls,* etc.—continued to be successful, but more intelligent readers were giving their attention to politics, sociology, psychology, journalism, in general to nonfiction. *Fiction* did not garner more and more readers as it became better and better. Its contents seemed too difficult and arcane to friends who were unprepared for contemporary fiction. The magazine aroused a rare enthusiasm among the few who already read, but that number, as the publishers had discovered, was woefully small and shrinking. All American artists are victims of the lemming effect. A certain panic, hysteria, begins, and everyone rushes out to buy something. Without that panic, one is dealing with the natural timidity of the crouching rodent. Pragmatic America wishes to take the mythos, the "unconscious," apart, much like a Model T, and so the how-to-do-it books about sex, personality, witchcraft are all more popular than the dream log in which you surrender to the hierogyphics rather than receiving a diagram on how to do it just as well. Woe when a serious artist like Norman Mailer is caught among the lemmings. Popularity again and again has proved a disaster, a siren that calls you to drown yourself in the great sea of American dribble. For a moment I almost tried to embark on it with *Fiction*. A distributor offered to spread 100,000 copies around the country. I looked at our treasury—nothing. The City College of New York was not about to foot big printing bills. My own small bank account would be depleted in one or two issues. I looked at the contents of our magazine. Thirty, forty thousand copies, perhaps, if we were very lucky; but that was too small for the distributor. And to the disappointment of some on my editorial board, I said no.

So in a sense the second premise, the commercial premise of *Fiction*—that one could bring the "quixotic, the recondite," to a large new audience—was never quite tried. Perhaps if I had closed my eyes and jumped, I would have swum to a great and successful future. At that moment, however, I trembled with light. I was a writer, not a publisher; without a paid staff, financial backing, professional promotion on a full-time basis, it would be suicidal to take the leap.

Still, short of taking on a commitment I knew would kill me, I tried. We printed a lot of copies of the first three issues: 25,000 of the first, 20,000 of the second, 15,000 of the third. Short of storage space, at one point we were storing them in a bedroom at Barthelme's, lugging them carton by carton up the stairs. I went from bookstore to bookstore opening accounts, trying to service them. Everyone on the editorial board was licking labels and stuffing envelopes. It was madness. Slowly we began to understand the problems that plague the literary magazine in this country: indifferent bookstores, surfeited subscribers, inefficient or impossible distribution systems. We slid down to the original number that we began with—5,000. Without reviews, media hype, heavy promotion, it was about average. I couldn't get from City College the kind of backing that *Partisan* or *TriQuarterly* receives: a managing editor, salary for a secretary. As the financial crisis bit into the college, they had to cut back my few privileges and increase my teaching load. I received a scholarship for a graduate student, office space, and some periodic help. Knowing the horrors that the whole city of New York was going through, I was grateful for this.

Where should the help have come from? The National Endowment, the New York State Council on the Arts, private patrons? All of these contributed meagerly. And so we limped along. (It never occurred to anyone in the grant establishment that writers and editors deserve to be paid at the minimum standard that an apprentice dancer or actor would receive for a week's work.) I continued to publish *Fiction* out of the same desperation with which I began it. Why? Because *Fiction* was more than a magazine for me. The banner we raised has been lowered, strung between poles, a shelter at half mast. *Fiction* kept me—and a few others, I hope—out of the cold.

It brought me into fellowship with South American and European writers. Publishing the frightening, obscure, unknown —stories by Alexander Kluge, Thomas Bernhard, a chapter of Manuel Puig's neglected masterpiece *The Buenos Aires Affair,* Bioy Casares, Benedetti, the River Platte school—I felt like Crusoe on his island. There is a taste of Eden in a book, a landscape whose shores you dream, with no one but a few faithful Fridays.

As for Americans, we bend tearfully to our unsolicited pile— hoping, taking risks, proudest when we have rescued something valuable from that dunghill. But America, my country, fills me with desperation. A terrible selfishness animates the establishment. I don't speak merely of my own generation; it is typical of the United States, like the slough into which Melville was consigned as his work grew more difficult. I don't see a literary community, even a quarrelsome school. I see only individuals who give easy lip service to fashion, are ready to appear, wherever there are flashbulbs, to protest a war, political prisoners, etc., but are unwilling to criticize, to encourage, to support, to join with younger and older writers. Instead, as always, they retreat into private rituals of self-destruction. Instead of the myth of what they have written, the myth of the writer becomes their testament. No wonder criminals like John Ehrlichman, in the wake of the New Journalists, step into the limelight to pander to the tangerine highs of America. The fantasist sits at his desk and walks in his dreams in order to see our future, understand the present, draw or set down a rhythm from the confusions of sight and sound around us. We are afraid of a moral literature because we are bent on quick, easy sensations and we fear that the thrill will be taken away from us. But it is precisely in reaching through the confusion for some idea of mastering it, if only in a dream for a second, that the thrill which is beyond the drab cake of the lotus eater lies. The self-excoriation of Heinrich Böll in *Katharina Blum,* of Márquez in *A Hundred Years of Solitude* is no different from the hair shirt of Dostoevsky in *The Brothers Karamazov* or of Dante in the *Comedy*—comparisons of mastery aside. But we are a poor country and the past few years have been a time of feeble chronicle and flash in the pan, crepe-paper genius. *Fiction* has published its share of this dreck; since it has passed through a generation publicly, it is impossible to be free of its sins. In the absence of a group of American writers who would sponsor magazines like *Fiction,* we have gone begging, threatening to shoot the periodical unless so and so contributed a piece. And this is the best I guess most of us can do: the stubborn begging to keep a house alive, hoping, knowing a few moments, perhaps, when the presence of something uncanny, unreal, holy(?) will alight before us.

ENTERPRISE IN
THE SERVICE OF ART
George Plimpton

George Plimpton, editor of the Paris Review *(courtesy* Paris Review*).*

Ernest Hemingway staged a bullfight in 1954 with George Plimpton as matador. Light heavyweight Archie Moore fought George Plimpton three rounds in 1959. Pancho Gonzales beat him at tennis 6–0. Mr. Plimpton has challenged championship swimmers, golfers, bridge players, major league hitters, and trapeze artists to compete with him, but has found "almost no pleasure in the actual moments of participation, because I invariably fail." He has tested his endurance and wit by joining professional football teams (from which came his book Paper Lion, *1966), a hockey team (the Boston Bruins), and the New York Philharmonic—and in so doing has raised the role of amateur to the pitch of art. Both as a writer for* Sports Illustrated *and the author of books on sports, George Plimpton has been praised for the literary excellence of his portrayals of the emotions of the athlete. Hemingway said of* Out of My League *(1961), "It is the dark side of the moon of Walter Mitty."*

In 1953, George Plimpton founded Paris Review, *which has not only discovered and published the work of Terry Southern and Philip Roth and maintained a consistent standard of somewhat unpredictable, angular, but undeniable artistic merit, but has also remained a magazine irrevocably, and properly, associated with the manner and personality and energy of its editor. It may also be one of the few little magazines to have a racehorse named after it, and one of the few to appear in advertisements for Peck & Peck and in* New Yorker *cartoons. Because of Mr. Plimpton's ingenuity, the Annual Spring Revel for the Benefit of* Paris Review *has become a news item; the galas have been held everywhere from a barge at the South Street port to Roosevelt Island, and, as we hear in the following essay, there have been* Paris Review *booths at World's Fairs. Mr. Plimpton has also tried to promote his magazine and his authors by a co-publishing venture with Doubleday (the Paris Review Editions), and by a remarkable series of Paris Review Posters with commissioned art by Andy Warhol, Roy Lichtenstein, Marisol, Jack Youngerman, Ben Shahn, Saul Steinberg, and Robert Rauschenberg.*

The short-lived American Literary Anthology *series of the mid-sixties was an attempt to bring before a wider public the best work from little magazines. George Plimpton secured a grant from the National Endowment for the Arts to publish the anthology and to*

525

recompense the authors and the little magazine editors whose work it contained. Unfortunately, when the fourth annual ALA was being prepared, a congressman from Iowa denounced the project by reading (or spelling) an Aram Saroyan poem on the floor of Congress. The National Endowment money was withdrawn.

Mr. Plimpton is currently at work on books about old-time tennis players, his reminiscences of Paris, and his experience as a goalie for the Boston Bruins. He continues his quest for rare birds. Although his most recent search for the Congo peacock closed without a sighting, Mr. Plimpton did meet a man who had eaten one the day before.

The Paris Review *booth at the New York World's Fair, Summer 1964–5 (courtesy* Paris Review*).*

I wonder if I could get you to describe The Paris Review *booth at the 1964–1965 World's Fair in New York. It sold little magazines, and thus has a certain distinction in little magazine history.*

I wish I could get you to say "literary" magazines rather than "little." I have never liked that appellative "little magazines" or, even worse, the collective "the littles." Dreadful. Midgets are said to prefer being called the "little people," which I can understand. But "little" referring to a magazine would by the same token, wouldn't it, refer to its *physical* dimensions—which suggests that a "little magazine" editor is responsible for those little fat numbers, two inches by two inches, that you ripple fast with your thumb, and you can see Carl Hubbell throwing a screwball (that dates me, doesn't it?) or, in the sleazier neighborhoods, Popeye doing something to Olive. No, no. "Literary magazines."

In deference to your feelings I'll try to do better. I was asking you about such commercial enterprises as The Paris Review *booth.*

Malcolm Cowley once described a direction *The Paris Review* took which was perhaps different from most little . . . *literary* magazines —that while the magazine hoped to present material that was new and uncommercial, it was willing to try commercial devices in order to get the contents read by people and talked about. He produced a motto which was appropriate enough: "Enterprise in the service of art." Some of the earliest decisions regarding the magazine were based on that—the design of the magazine, the use of artwork inside and on the cover. Even the instituting of the Art of Fiction series—interviews with distinguished writers on their craft—was done in part so as to be able to put a famous name on the cover to entice readers to buy the magazine and by indirection, having read the interview, to wander on and read the work of someone just starting off and with no reputation at all. In Paris, in the early days, we did all sorts of crazy things to promote the magazine—printing posters and pasting them up around the city on the *pissoirs,* even on the *défense d'afficher* walls, very late at night, in flying squads, and we never got into much trouble. I put one on the ceiling of the lavatory of the Café du Dôme in 1955 and it was there for a couple of years. This sort of enterprise has been kept up—in varying degrees, depending on the energies of the group running things—since the start.

A number of the writers living in Paris in late 1954 and early 1955 who contributed either to the Paris Review *or the short-lived publication,* Merlin. *Front row, left to right: Vilma Howard, poet; Jane Logue, the publisher of* Merlin; *Muffy Wainhouse, the wife of Austryn Wainhouse; Jean Garrigue, poet. Second row: Christopher Logue (with the cigarette), poet and* Merlin *editor; Richard Seaver, then associated with* Merlin, *and subsequently an editor of* Evergreen Review; *Evan S. Connell (with the moustache), novelist; Niccolo Tucci, essayist and novelist; the woman with the smile is unidentified; Peter Huyn, poet, translator, editor; Alfred Chester, novelist and story-writer; Austryn Wainhouse, novelist and translator. Third row: Eugene Walter,* Paris Review *editor and story-writer; George Plimpton,* Paris Review *editor, author (in the hat); William Pène du Bois,* Paris Review *editor, author and illustrator of childrens' books; James Broughton, poet and film maker; William Gardner Smith, novelist; and Harold Witt, poet (courtesy* Paris Review*).*

the PARIS REVIEW

1

E. M. FORSTER
an interview

Henry
de Montherlant

eight drawings
by
Tom Keogh

Short Stories

Poetry

Commentaries

Donald Hall
the Newdigate
prize poem

SPRING
1953

PUBLISHED BY "LA TABLE RONDE"

75 ¢   4/   200 frs

The Paris Review, *Vol. 1, No. 1, Spring 1953 (courtesy* Paris Review).

And one of enterprises was The Paris Review *booth. I believe it was known as "the smallest pavilion at the New York World's Fair."*

Quite right. It was at once the most ambitious and dismaying of our projects. It seemed such a good idea at the time. We got the franchise through a friend of mine whose firm was representing the corporation that owned the Pavilion of Paris. De Gaulle didn't want to have anything to do with the fair, and the Pavilion of Paris was a sort of ersatz substitution for a bona fide French pavilion. Through the terms arranged, we were permitted to put down (I think that's the proper designation) a structure outside the Pavilion of Paris on an avenue called the Harry S Truman, directly opposite Philip Johnson's New York State Building and down the road from the Astral Fountain and the "Vatican" where the *Pietà* was on display. The booth was designed by William Pène du Bois, our art editor—a charming, mushroom-like structure with a movable roof that raised up along a center flagpole, cranked up with a system of ropes and pulleys that one got at by crawling through a panel in the side of the booth and twisting a winch. It was built for us in Katonah, New York, at no great expense, by a firm of swimming pool specialists. It was made of wood, only ten by ten. But the booth had great style. There was a metal flagpole at each point of the roof, which was octagonal. It was decorated with blowups from pages of *The Paris Review*—both artwork and text —a chunk of Céline, Hemingway, Frost, and a line or two, I remember, from the interview with Evelyn Waugh:

Interviewer: What about Ronald Firbank?
Waugh: I enjoyed him very much when I was young. I can't read him now.
Interviewer: Why?
Waugh: I think there would be something wrong with an elderly man who could enjoy Firbank.

Sometimes the salespeople inside would spot a man slowly circling the booth, and they would appreciate that he was, as they put it, "reading the booth."

Who were the salespeople in the booth?

They were as decorative as the booth itself—a series of very young, pretty girls, a few of them French, all of whom were in love with the managing editor of the magazine at the time, Peter Ardery.

They would arrive early in the morning, crawl on hands and knees into the booth from the little side-panel, crank up the roof and set up the counters for the day's work, and then at closing time the roof would be cranked down and the girls would emerge like hedgehogs from a burrow onto the Avenue Harry S Truman. They were awfully pretty. On rainy days they would crank the roof down to protect the "goods," the edge of the roof just inches off the counter, and you could see the girls' eyes inside peering out from the darkness. On these days, when it was almost closed, or we gave up and it was closed completely, the booth looked like the turret on the *Monitor,* the "cheese box" of the "cheese box on a raft." When it was open, it looked too much like an information booth. In fact, on a fine day there'd be a thick ring of people around it, the ones in the back rising up on their toes and shouting over the heads of the others to get directions to the "Vatican."

And what was for sale? What were the "goods"?

By God, literary magazines. We wrote a form letter to every literary magazine in the country, with the heady news that what they had slaved over could be displayed on that busy boulevard and offered for sale. Everyone was intrigued. Cartons of magazines, back issues, broadsheets began to arrive, and I borrowed a station wagon and we took this tonnage out there and set it up on the counters of the booth. It was a brave display—not unlike what you see in the window of the Gotham Book Mart on 47th Street, except not as dusty. We kept a feather-mop duster in the booth, and sometimes a brisk wind swept down the Harry S Truman Avenue and rattled the pages.

Well, how did it do, the booth?

I have the figures here. The booth was open for the last five weeks of the fair's 1964 season—36 days precisely, or 413 working hours —by the end of which time the total gross sales had mounted to $379.70. That works out to a dollar of sales an hour. As I recall, our best day brought in thirty dollars, and the worst—a rainy Tuesday—a few cents more than a dollar. That was not very good. We came nowhere near that magic phrase in literary magazine financing, namely "breaking even." It was a melancholy time. The other day I was looking over the Common Book that we kept during the booth's operation. Two entries suggest how things were going. One of them: "The booth seems to attract more attention when closed than when open—is there anything we can do about this?" Another suggestion was that we try publicizing the booth by trying to get it referred to as "the smallest pavilion at the World's Fair"—as if somehow people would flock to see such a thing, as they might pay to get in to see a midget elephant.

Which of the little—I mean literary—magazines were the big sellers?

I was hoping you'd think of something else to ask. "Big seller" is not really an applicable term. Toward the end of that first year we had to sell other things. We brought in some books. The public bought an average of three and one-fourth books a day. Usually at least one of these was the *Tropic of Capricorn,* or *The Tropic of Cancer,* or Frank Harris' *My Life and Loves,* or Simone de Beauvoir's *The Second Sex* (with a photograph of a naked woman on the cover), or *Lady Chatterley's Lover. The Paris Review,* which took up one whole pie-section of the counter for those first five weeks, sold twenty-three copies. *The Realist* was the best seller among the other literary magazines. The cover was a cartoon of Senator Goldwater as a woman in a topless bathing suit. Four copies of *Yale French Studies* and four of *The Quarterly Review of Literature* were stolen. Our financial accountant was very accurate about such things, and kept excellent, if woeful, books.

But you didn't close down the operation when the fair went into its second season.

Good God, no! While a more prudent organization might have forgone that second year, we decided that an intensification of effort might bring better results. We expanded the booth into a complex by adding three bookstalls modeled after the bookstalls along the Seine. Enrique Castro-Cid, the Chilean sculptor, was persuaded to build and program a four-foot-tall weatherproof robot to stand in front of the booth, doing something to attract attention. No one ever saw what it looked like or what it was indeed programmed to do. Castro-Cid built it, but he was reluctant to part with what he had done. Somehow I recall that he once told me

532

it looked like a giant erect grasshopper. It had a voice box within, which would alarm passersby—at which point the grasshopper would wave an antenna-like arm at the booth. One of the minor despairs of the booth project was that the Castro-Cid sculpture never graced the Avenue Harry S Truman.

How did the booth do in its second year of operation?

Well, things went much more briskly. In a desperate attempt to recoup, we took over the operation of the French Book Center, which had failed for lack of profits in the great disaster of the Paris Pavilion next door. We took over its supply of French magazines (the fashion magazine *Elle* eclipsed *The Realist* as our big seller), records, books, little French flags on black wooden stands, French cigarettes, posters, Charles de Gaulle masks—God, what else?—tinny Eiffel Towers and Statues of Liberty, some fitted out with red light bulbs, just a tremendous glut of doodads and gimmickry. And in there somewhere, just a pie-slice of them now on the counter, were the literary magazines—*Hudson, Sewanee, Partisan,* the less known, the affairs of the heart, and *The Paris Review,* along with *Paris Review* T-shirts and sweat shirts that we thought might catch the fancy of at least a small segment of the people coming by, so that there might be some justification for what we were doing. Do you know what the big sellers were? Shopping bags! Truly. There was a big run on those damn shopping bags. It was an unexpected boon for us that one of the salespeople —one of the lovely girls doubtless—thought of selling those things. After we realized that we had a hot item, we draped them around the circumference of the counter. We bought them wholesale and stamped them "The Paris Review" with big rubber stamps (I remember doing that in the evening—*bang, bang, bang*) so that the people who purchased them could carry their souvenirs back from the fair brandishing this literary magazine's name around the New York City subway system. On the great days, on the weekends, we made $300, almost ten times as much as we had made on our best days the year before—the big sales being in shopping bags and French cigarettes. But somehow the evangelical fervor had gone. I didn't go out there much that second year. I couldn't bear the sight of all those Eiffel Towers with the red bulbs. I think we all felt that way. . . . I'll tell you something which epitomized that second year. One of the booth girls thought that the de Gaulle face masks might catch on, the way the shopping bags had. So she wore one. Besides, she was French. You can imagine what a sight it was to approach along the Avenue Harry S Truman and see a Charles de Gaulle (sometimes a pair of them if she had a friend working with her) peering out from the shadows of the booth. One day she saw someone coming down the avenue whom she recognized as a relative—I'd like to say it was her mother, but it wasn't actually; an aunt, or maybe a cousin—and the girl in the booth had the option of calling out through the mouth of the de Gaulle mask, "Hi, Genevieve," or whoever. But she didn't, you know. She just let that person cruise on by—past that strange little complex with all those crazy things for sale, which had started with such hopes—and she didn't utter a sound.

There is a certain
kind of woman who
reads Peanuts and
the Paris Review.
For this woman, there is
a certain kind of store:
Peck & Peck.

Enterprise in the service of art.

WE OBVIOUSLY F
CHANGES THAT WER
BUT AS A BOOKSELLER
BEHIND THE WRITER AN
THE PUBLISHER IS
I'VE FELT EXHILERA
OUR PUBLISHING
TO BE EXTREM

ON'T CAUSED THE
OING ON IN WRITING,
LWAYS WANTED TO BE
AHEAD OF THE READER.
THE ARTIST, BUT
BY THE FACT THAT
AS TURNED OUT
Y IMPORTANT.

—TED WILENTZ

STRIDENCY AND THE SWORD: LITERARY AND CULTURAL EMPHASIS IN AFRO-AMERICAN MAGAZINES
Eugene Redmond

While this essay concentrates on developments since 1950, black little magazines have actually been in existence for more than 140 years. Their continual rise and fall—even though they rarely merited being called "literary" in any exclusive sense—record the tumultuous life of Afro-American arts and letters. Beginning in 1838, David Ruggles' Mirror of Liberty, *a particular brand of cultural magazine that carried on antislavery warfare, formed the aesthetic and ideological spine of black thought and expression. During the antislavery era (1834–1861), the task was taken up by the* African Observer, Slavery in America, The National Anti-Slavery Standard, AME Church Magazine, Mystery, The North Star *(superseded by* Frederick Douglass' Paper *and* Douglass' Monthly), *and* Anglo-African Magazine. *The works of early race leaders, theoreticians, fiction writers, essayists, novelists, and poets, including Phillis Wheatley, Prince Hall, Olaudah Equiano (Gustavas Vassa), George Moses Horton, Maria W. Stewart, Jarena Lee, and Douglass, can be found in these journals; they published some of the best protest writing of the nineteenth century—literature in which the act of creation was synonymous with the act of liberation.*

Afro-American magazines, and their editors and writers, matured during the latter quarter of the nineteenth century. Among the new journals were The Southern Workman, National Baptist Magazine, Howard's Negro Magazine, Colored American Magazine, McGirt's Magazine, *and* Alexander's Magazine. *Faced with*

538

the task of having to create a black community out of the newly emancipated slaves, the new intellectuals and leaders founded black schools and colleges, and stressed skill development, especially reading and writing. Thus the new magazines not only had an immediate function to serve, but were assured of newer and larger reading audiences as these were produced by the schools. After the Civil War, writings by Afro-Americans became more consciously "literary." Led by authors like Paul Laurence Dunbar, Albert Whitman, Charles Chesnutt, Frances Ellen Watkins Harper, and James Weldon Johnson, both the older and the younger beginning writers made ample use of their new outlets. Without some notion of the longevity of the black little magazine in America, the particular tenor of the black magazines of the past three decades would, as Mr. Redmond indicates, be difficult to grasp.

Eugene Redmond has been a newspaper editor, publicist, and social worker in St. Louis and a theater director, poet-in-residence, and Afro-American scholar at Southern Illinois University, Webster College, Oberlin College, Southern University (Baton Rouge), and California State University at Sacramento, where he now teaches. He is the author of eight plays, eight volumes of poetry, and scores of articles on black writers. His critical history, Drumvoices: The Mission of Afro-American Poetry, *was published by Doubleday in 1976, his edition of Afro-American poetry in 1977. His arrangement of a novel by Henry Dumas,* Jonoah and the Green Stone, *appeared from Random House in 1976.*

Origins and evolutions

For the purpose of developing a contemporary peak from which to survey beginnings of the Afro-American literary magazine, we could select any year, but let us settle for the year 1968. That was when *Black Fire: An Anthology of Afro-American Writing*, edited by LeRoi Jones and Larry Neal, made its provocative appearance. In April of the same year, the world mourned the assassination of Martin Luther King, Jr., apostle of peace and one of the most influential Afro-American leaders in history. Less than two months later, Henry Dumas and Conrad Kent Rivers, premier poetic voices of the "second renaissance," were silenced—Dumas by the bullets of a New York transit cop and Rivers by an "impulsive" act. Earlier

539

in the decade, that missile-of-a-man named Malcolm X (*a.k.a.* Malcolm Little, Detroit Red, El-Hajj Malik El-Shabazz, "Black Shining Prince"), had been rammed by assassins' bullets at the Audubon Ballroom in Harlem. Black prophets and poets, activists and writers cried out, "If you talk too long and too loud about the hurt that's being put on you, you'll be long-gone." Hence Afro-American magazines such as *Liberator, Freedomways, Negro Digest, Dasein, Umbra, Soulbook, Black Dialogue, The Journal of Black Poetry, The Black Scholar,* and *Black Ascensions* became the cultural-literary offspring of the terrors and contradictions inherent in a society unable to practice what it preaches. *Black Fire,* in turn, was born of a disparate and far-flung, yet communalized, cultural spirit that completely remade the world of Afro-American arts and letters. Similarly, during the "renaissance" of the 1920s, Alain Locke's provocative *The New Negro* (1925), backdropped by Jim Crow laws, World War I, and lynchings, shored up the strength and perseverance of a kaleidoscopic battle line of black periodicals: *The Crisis, The Journal of Negro History, Southern Workman, The Messenger, Opportunity,* and others. This pattern was also seen in 1941, with the publication of *The Negro Caravan: Writings by American Negroes,* edited by Sterling A. Brown, Arthur P. Davis, and Ulysses Lee. *Caravan* performed what had become by then an important function of Afro-American editors and anthologists: to collect, at intervals, the best and most representative works from smaller black publications (journals, newsletters, pamphlets, broadsides, and newspapers) and put them into a substantial volume for posterity. Available to *Caravan's* editors was a rich new range of magazines and various periodicals, including *Challenge, New Challenge, Brown American, Journal of Negro Education, Negro History Bulletin,* and *Race.*

One sees in these and other new magazines of the thirties and forties—reflective as they were of the historical demands of the black struggle—an often part-time literary posture, since their primary function in each issue was to do battle with the forces of racism, oppression, and violence and to present basic usable data to Afro-American communities. The *Journal of Negro Education, Quarterly Review of Higher Education Among Negroes, Negro History Bulletin, Negro Digest,* and *Phylon: Atlanta University Review of Race and Culture* dealt with all areas of black develop-

540

SOULBOOK   #5

Soulbook, *Vol. 2, No. 1, Summer 1966 (courtesy Northwestern University Library).*

ment. On the other hand, a steady tradition of literary journal publishing had been established, as witnessed by magazines like the *Negro Quarterly, Challenge* and *New Challenge* (dedicated to the revitalization of black literature and art), *Negro Story,* and *Harlem Quarterly.* Often the editors and creative writers were one and the same. One found, for example, the following names on the editorial boards and in the tables of contents of these periodicals: W. E. B. DuBois, James Weldon Johnson, Wallace Thurman, Zora Neale Hurston, Langston Hughes, Countee Cullen, Claude McKay, Arna Bontemps, Ann Spencer, Angelina Grimké, Owen Dodson, Carter G. Woodson, Marcus Garvey, Margaret Walker, Horace Cayton, Richard Wright, Ralph Ellison, Gwendolyn Brooks, Robert Hayden, Melvin B. Tolson, E. Franklin Frazier, Chester Himes, and others.

Bearings and focuses: 1950–1960

Despite decades of vigorous effort to develop independent black literary and cultural magazines, these did not appear until the 1950s. Among the black literary journals to emerge at midcentury, *Free Lance* and *CLA Journal* have been the most influential, albeit for different reasons. Literarily speaking, the decade began auspiciously with several notable events: the reception of the works of Richard Wright (whose *Native Son* had been the first black-authored Book-of-the-Month Club selection); the establishment of several cultural and literary groups, such as the Harlem Writers' Club and the Committee for the Negro in the Arts; the awarding of the Pulitzer Prize for poetry (*Annie Allen,* 1950) to Gwendolyn Brooks; and the publication of the anthology *The Poetry of the Negro* (1949), edited by Langston Hughes and Bontemps— further indication of large publishers' growing interest in black literature. But it was an already-established journal, *Phylon,* that carried the literary and cultural weight of the black experience during most of the 1950s.

Phylon's 1940s format, designed by W. E. B. DuBois (and colleagues), continued into the next decade: a good balance between sociological-historical analyses and cultural-artistic curatorship. The most advanced indigenous Afro-American social theories and concepts were reflected in its literary content. For example, the fourth quarter 1950 issue of *Phylon* was devoted to

542

Afro-American literature and writers: "The Negro Writer Looks at His World" (William Gardner Smith, Ezra Bell Thompson, Langston Hughes, and *Phylon* editors); "Fiction and Folklore" (Thomas D. Jarrett and Sterling Brown); "Criticism and Literary Scholarship" (Ulysses Lee and Blyden Jackson); and "Poetry" (Margaret Walker and Arna Bontemps). In subsequent issues *Phylon* published "Contemporary French Negro Poets," "The Cuban Poetry of Nicholas Guillen" (Angel Augier, translated by Joseph Bernstein), an article by novelist René Maran (translated by Mercer Cook), and several pieces by the Dutch literary historian-anthologist Rosey E. Pool, including one on the "African Renaissance" (African writing in English). The poetry of Robert Hayden, Nanina Champney Alba, Hughes, Walker, Calvin C. Hernton, Ray Durem, Alvin Aubert, Raymond Patterson, Lance Jeffers, and James Emanuel also appeared in the journal along with short fiction by Hughes and Katherine Dunham ("Audrey"). In reviews and articles, writers waged critical wars, each adding to the wider portrait of the Afro-American literary legacy. Among books given extensive reviews in *Phylon* were all of Hughes's works, the autobiographies of Lena Horne and Ethel Waters, J. Saunders Redding's *On Being Black in America,* Wright's *The Outsider,* and Claude McKay's *Selected Poems,* Carl Rowan's *South of Freedom,* James Baldwin's *Go Tell It on the Mountain* and *Notes of a Native Son,* Gwendolyn Brooks's *Maud Martha,* Ann Petry's *The Narrows,* and George Lamming's *In the Castle of My Skin* (1953) and *The Emigrants* (1955). *Phylon's* book review pattern was reflected in almost all the black magazines of the fifties, including *Sepia* and *Ebony,* which irregularly published literary history and criticism. *Sepia* sustained a fine record for reviewing black literature, and both magazines carried in-depth stories on music and culture.

In 1953, *Free Lance* arrived as the first Afro-American literary journal destined to survive the handicaps and adversities usually visited on such efforts. Subtitled "A Publication of Free-Lance Poets and Prose Workshops, Inc.," this Cleveland-based little magazine played an as-yet-unsung role in the development of a multi-ethnic American literary underground, specifically the "Beat" movement in poetry, which prevailed between 1955 and 1965. *Free Lance* was directed by Casper Leroy Jordan, book reviewer and librarian at Wilberforce University, Ohio, and Russell Atkins, eccentric poet-composer and psycho-visualist. Early assistance also came from Helen J. Collins, Beatrice Augustus, and Helen Dobbins Dobbs. The first issues of *Free Lance* were hand done, so to speak, but it later took on a more professional look. Since it was devoted solely to the printing of short creative writings and occasional book reviews, the journal did not need the size or space of a *Phylon*. It became, by all definitions, a "little" magazine.

The first issue of *Free Lance* included work by Atkins, Augustus, Collins, Rose Green, Jordan, Budd Martin, Vera Steckles, Mott Wilson, and Jerry Davis. But the introduction—and the theme— were supplied by the literary father of all modern black writers, Langston Hughes:

Words are the paper and string to package experience, to wrap up from the inside out the poet's concentric waves of contact with the living world. Each poet makes of words his own highly individualized wrapping for life segments he wishes to present. Sometimes the paper and strings are more arresting than the contents of the package. Sometimes the poet creates a transparent wrapping revealing with great clarity and from all angles what is inside. Sometimes the word wrapping is clumsy and inept, and neither the inside nor the outside of the package is interesting. Sometimes the word wrapping contains nothing. But, regardless of quality or content, a poem reveals always the poet as a person. Skilled or unskilled, wise or foolish, nobody can write a poem without revealing something of himself. Here are people. Here are poems. Here is revolution.

Hughes was talking, it seemed, almost directly to Atkins. The introduction was stripped of racial intensity, since the older writer knew that Atkins, like William Stanley Braithwaite, Countee Cullen, and Hayden, had protested against being judged purely on the basis of race. Precocious and brilliant, he had studied music and begun to develop provocative ideas and concepts connecting sound, dance, mathematics, drama, psychology, and language. In a January 1973 *Black World* article on "Black Art and Artists in Cleveland," Leatrice W. Emeruwa referred to *Free Lance* as the "oldest Black literary magazine extant" and said that Atkins was "to poetic, dramatic and musical innovation and leadership what Coltrane has been to jazz and avant-gardism."

In addition to printing the works of black poets (such as Hughes, Dudley Randall, and LeRoi Jones), *Free Lance* also opened its pages to white bards: Robert Sward, the Canadian Irving Layton, Don Silberger, and Robert Creeley (also critic and editor of *Black*

544

Mountain Review). Stylistically, the poetry was traditional, experimental modern-formal, and offbeat; and much of it was iconoclastic, irreverent, pedantic, and didactic. Other writings ranged from a review of *Charles Waddell Chesnutt: Pioneer of the Color Line* to Philip Butcher's essay on Paul Laurence Dunbar and George Washington Cable, to Creeley's reflections on Hart Crane (including some letters of Crane). *Free Lance* also featured the fiction of Cleota Augustus, Adelaide Simon, Silberger, and Robert J. Shea. During the 1960s *Free Lance* would increase its review space, introduce some exciting new black poets to the public, and play an important role in the midwestern black arts scene.

CLA Journal appeared in 1957 as the brainchild of the College Language Association, formed in 1939 to protest the Modern Language Association's policy of excluding blacks. Its editor was Therman B. O'Daniel (Morgan State College); its associate editor, Blyden Jackson (Southern University); and its managing editor, Charles A. Ray (North Carolina College, Durham). Among its regional advisory editors were Hugh Gloster, Nathaniel P. Tillman, and Melvin B. Tolson. Contributing editors included Margaret Walker Alexander, Richard Barksdale, M. Carl Holman (of Clark College and editor of the *Atlanta Inquirer*), Redding, and Bertram L. Woodruff. Scholarly, erudite, and giving deference to linguistics and composition, the magazine's aims and objectives were stated by O'Daniel in the first issue: it would accept articles on "most languages." These languages, however, turned out to be "Greek and Latin, Old and Middle English, Modern English, and the Modern Foreign Languages." *CLA Journal,* as a black-based professional publication, was thus begun in something of a cultural limbo: it had no philosophical direction, no theoretical or conceptual framework with which to chart its direction, and hence no thrust that reflected, even from the magazine's high plane, the turbulence or beauty of the black sensibility that produced most of its staffers and contributors.

The cultural ambivalence of *CLA Journal,* born out of ideological tensions and conflicts that have historically mesmerized the black intelligentsia, was clearly seen in its allowance of twice as much space to writings on European and Euro-American culture as to African or Afro-American culture. Such a contradiction, hard to imagine when one recalls the social and racial factors that

545

prompted the founding of the journal, would become even more glaring in the sixties and seventies when many new black-consciousness journals were being born. Whereas *Phylon* unashamedly grounded itself in black and Third World cultures (relegating its European concerns to notes and excerpts), *CLA Journal* repeatedly printed articles on Congreve, Shakespeare, Alain Robbe-Grillet, Poe, Baudelaire, Swift, Hawthorne, Tennessee Williams, and hundreds of other European and Euro-American subjects and writers. In all fairness, however, the foregoing comments must be balanced by a consideration of *CLA*'s contribution to black literature. Its first issue, for example, did contain a review of Hughes's *Simple Stakes a Claim*. Later numbers of the quarterly carried articles on black authors and their work. During the sixties and seventies *CLA* would not be able to continue its immunity to the broad and intense cultural self-examination occurring in black communities. Like all other Afro-American publications, it would be substantially influenced by the social holocausts of the post–civil rights era.

Bob Kaufman, Ted Joans, LeRoi Jones, and Atkins come prominently to mind when one considers the "underground" movement. Kaufman, after an itinerant life, settled in San Francisco, where the West Coast pole of the Beat activity (Ferlinghetti's City Lights Bookstore) was centered. He published in *Beatitude* and numerous other little magazines, his work finally reaching France, where he became a literary sensation—occasionally being compared to Rimbaud and Baudelaire. Jazz poet Joans, trained as a painter, was among the first black artists to arrive in Greenwich Village, the East Coast center of the Beat school. Very early influenced by Hughes, he also published in many little magazines. The capricious LeRoi Jones was a central figure in the Greenwich Village movement (the New York literary underground), founding *Yugen* (1958–1961) with his Jewish wife, Hettie Cohen. Though Jones has always been irreverent and experimental in his posture and writing, the fact that he was black in 1958 was more or less incidental, since *Yugen* published mostly white authors. Occasionally, however, black writers were featured, as in the case of poets Allan Polite and Clarence Major. In addition to contributing to the avant-garde American poetry scene, these pioneers provided new experimental models for younger black poets tuned into the little magazine circuit.

Ascendancy's sharp mirror light: rear view to a future (1960–1978)

By 1960 Afro-American periodicals, and their faithful editorial staffs, were well seasoned from several decades of training and experience. During this exciting history, countless publications had been founded by sororities, fraternities, college literary workshops, community organizations, unions, social clubs, reading guilds, and private individuals. Many of these older organs also wound their way into the 1960s and 1970s: *Crisis, Negro History Bulletin, Journal of Negro History, Phylon, Negro Educational Review, Free Lance,* and *CLA Journal. Phylon* maintained its previous leadership, though some fatigue was beginning to show in the later sixties —the journal having witnessed the death or dispersion of many of its original founders and contributors. Fresh talent, which would have naturally gravitated toward it, was attracted to the new black publications and the white periodicals opening their pages to black writers. Nevertheless, *Phylon* continued to present a solid offering of essays, reviews, poetry, and some fiction. Among writers contributing articles to the journal during the sixties were Charles Hamilton (*Black Power,* with Stokely Carmichael), Eugene D. Genovese (*Roll, Jordan, Roll*), Eugenia Collier, John Henrik Clarke, Theodore L. Gross, Nathan Hare, Donald Henderson, B. I. Chukwukere (on African novelists), O. R. Dathorne (on Africa in West Indian literature), Charles Larsen, Addison Gayle, Jr., and Keneth Kinnamon. Older and newly discovered poets peppered the magazine's pages: Mary Graham Lund, Pinkie Gordon Lane, Dan Georgakas, Mari Evans, James Worley, Nanina Alba, George Douglass Johnson, James Emanuel, James Kilgore, and Julius Thompson. Of all the journals, *Phylon* in particular established an excellent record of good in-depth reviews.

On a smaller scale, but in steady pursuit of literary experimentation and freedom, *Free Lance* was realizing its goal of becoming a viable, if modest, alternative to the deaf ears and closed doors met by so many new young writers. *Free Lance* also upgraded its book review program and added a news column, "Occurrences." Among the black and white poets it published in the sixties were Major (editor, *The New Black Poetry*), Judson Crews, Charles Bukowski, Glen Grobos, Conrad Kent Rivers ("discovered" by *Free Lance*), Irene Dayton, Peter Jones (editor of *New Helios,* London), Hughes ("perhaps the only active link from the fabled period of the New York renaissance of the '20s"), David Rafael Wang (teacher at the University of Hawaii), Lewis Turco, L. S. Torgoff, Douglas Blazek, and Etheridge Knight (writing at this time from prison).

CLA Journal remained culturally adrift as the sixties unfolded. More than half of its space was still being devoted to the examination of European-American aesthetics. Granted the professional nature of the journal, with its emphases on composition and modern languages, one wonders why not even an experimental unit on Afro-American literary methodology was developed. The white-dominated MLA had established a Commission of Minority Literatures before the mid-seventies, but not until 1976 did *CLA Journal* begin its "Annual Bibliography of Afro-American Literature." Though hanging in a frustrating cultural limbo, it nevertheless published important articles on black culture, such as Jackson's "The Negro's Image of the Universe as Reflected in His Fiction," Barksdale's views on the teaching of poetry, Naomi Garrett's "French Poets of African Descent," Darwin Turner's "The Negro Dramatist's Image of the Universe, 1920–1960," Robert A. Smith on the folktales of Chesnutt, A. Russell Brooks's "The Comic Spirit in the Negro's New Look," and Arthur P. Davis' "The Black-and-Tan Motif in the Poetry of Gwendolyn Brooks" and "Gwendolyn Brooks: Poet of the Unheroic."

That a plethora of little magazines emerged during these years is obviously of more than mere incidental importance—even though so many were destined to a state of transiency or premature death. It is not always easy to record, or even locate, these publications. The most extensive listing of them, however, appears in various news and notes sections of *Negro Digest/Black World* (1961–1976), itself a product of the black cultural revival that swept the globe in the 1950s and 1960s. Other important magazines of the sixties were *Community, Dasein, Freedomways, Axiom, Approach, Adept, Negro Heritage, Floating Bear, Umbra, Harvard Journal of Afro-American Affairs, Soulbook, Vibration, Black Dialogue, Insurgent, Black America, Journal of Black Poetry, The Black Student, Echo, Negro American Literature Forum, Cricket, Shrewd, Issue: A Quarterly Journal of Africanist Opinion, Nommo, Pan-African Journal, Ex-Umbra, Newark Afro-American Magazine, The Feet* ("The Monthly Black Dance Maga-

548

THE JOURNAL OF THE OBAC WRITERS' WORKSHOP

NOMMO

VOL. I, NO. I $1.50 WINTER 1969

Nommo, *Vol. 1, No. 1, Winter 1969 (courtesy Northwestern University Library).*

zine"), *Black Theater, Echoes from the Gumbo, The Black Scholar, Pound, Confrontation: A Journal of Third World Literature,* and *Nkombo.*

Literally before our very eyes, these journals did cultural somersaults and demographic cartwheels: being born, often experiencing immediate death, then being reborn in another place with a refurbished staff and a new name. Most of them, however, responded to, and some grew in the shadow of, the glitter of *Negro Digest*—resurrected in 1961 after a publishing hiatus of ten years. Its helm was manned by Hoyt W. Fuller, an Atlanta-born journalist who had worked for several newspapers and had formerly been associate editor of *Ebony*. Since *Digest* was a Johnson publication, it offered little opportunity for free and open experimentation and exploration. Moreover, like *CLA Journal,* it initially could not take an official editorial stand based on cultural theories or ideological concepts. But Fuller sought to compensate for these built-in restraints by cautiously indicating his evolving aesthetic in book reviews, various notes, articles, and news items. He charted a course that took that journal from civil rights through black arts/black power and into its new pan-Africanist posture as *Black World* (1970–1976).

During the first five years of its new life, *Digest* followed somewhat in the path of its forties predecessor, publishing general articles about black life, with an emphasis on stars. It also ran reprints from various other (mostly white) magazines as well as poems and articles by whites. From its very beginning, however, it had more of a literary thrust than the earlier *Digest*. Articles on black history and culture were contributed by C. Eric Lincoln, Bontemps, John Hope Franklin, Benjamin Quarles, Frank London Brown ("Chicago's Great Lady of Poetry," about Brooks), Babs Fafunwa ("An African Student Looks at America"), participants in a symposium on "The Negro's Role in American Culture" (Baldwin, Nat Hentoff, Lorraine Hansberry, Hughes, Emile Capouya, Alfred Kazin), Nathan Hare ("The Black Anglo-Saxons"), Agnes Behling ("Father of Negro History," on Woodson), Casper Leroy Jordan (on Elizabeth Keckley, the black woman confidante to the wife of President Lincoln), Redding (interviewed by AMSAC on "An American Writer in Africa"), Kwame Nkrumah ("The Recovery of African History"), Louise Meriwether (on Baldwin), Horace

550

Mann Bond, Arthur Schomburg, Lomax, Hernton ("White Liberals and Black Muslims"), Elijah Muhammad, Rivers (on Hughes), J. Noel Heermance ("The Modern Negro Novel"), Thomas Echewa ("Africa vs. Afro-Americans," part of a series of debates involving John A. Williams and John Oliver Killens), and Hamilton Bims ("The Plight of the Negro Writer in a Segregated Society").

Bontemps opened the decade appropriately enough with his November 1961 article, "The New Black Renaissance." Since he had participated in the "first" renaissance, he was aptly qualified to make comparisons between the two. He noted that "the new crop of Negro writers in the United States show more traits in common with the writers of the Harlem Renaissance than with the famous WPA group who were their literary parents so to speak." Wright, Yerby, Motley, Walker, and Brooks, Bontemps felt, did not have progeny in the newest group of authors (Paule Marshall, F. L. Brown, Jones, Gloria Oden, Killens, Herbert Simons, and William Melvin Kelley). A possible exception was Hansberry (*A Raisin in the Sun,* inspired by Hughes's "A Dream Deferred"), who may have been related "in some fundamental literary ways" to Wright. Her work reflected the "increase of technical skills" expected of "a second or third generation of writers." Bontemps warned that there was, after Wright's heroic efforts to master form and language, no excuse for poor writing by black authors. Such an admonishment was to become a source of great irritation to the still newer writers waiting in the wings— some of whom assumed that it represented a broadside against the new *Black Esthetic.*

In June 1964 Fuller's article on "The Role of the Negro Writer in an Era of Struggle" explored Baldwin's frustration at being acclaimed as an essayist while the same attention had not been given his fiction. Fuller noted that in a time of social crisis, readers and critics perhaps find more meaning in social essays than in novels. Ralph Ellison, he observed, emphasized craft, while Hughes remained very committed to civil rights. Many other articles dealt with the problems of black authors. Bims examined "The Plight of the Negro Writer in a Segregated Society" in a January 1965 issue, and lamented, "The current Negro Writer who does not have an unshakable faith in himself is frustrated in looking about him for justification of himself, of his chosen profession." In April of the same year, a symposium undertook a look at "The Task of the Negro Writer as Artist" with contributions from Lerone Bennett, Jr. (author of *Before the Mayflower* and *Ebony* senior editor), Brooks, actor Ossie Davis, novelist William Demby, jazz critic Nat Hentoff, Hughes, Jones, Kelley, Killens, Redding, Harvey Swados, John A. Williams, Yerby, Hare, John Henrik Clarke, Rivers, Randall, Kristin Hunter, Bill Gunn, Lincoln, Ernest Gaines, Alex Haley (originator of *Playboy* magazine's famous "Interview" series, author of *Roots* and *The Autobiography of Malcolm X*), Lennox Raphael, Lomax, Hernton, playwright William B. Branch, Margaret Danner, Ronald Fair, and Emanuel. The committed Hughes remained basically true to his lifelong self, drawing away from the temporary *artiste*'s stance of his *Free Lance* introduction: "Contemporary white writers can perhaps afford to be utterly irresponsible in their moral and social viewpoints. The Negro writer cannot. Ours is a social as well as a literary responsibility."

Discussions and debates concerning the black writer's role had, in the mid-sixties, become an important arm of the black cultural enterprise, evidenced by the numerous conferences: AMSAC Student Editors Conference of Africans and Afro-Americans at Hampton Institute; a white literary luncheon in Chicago at which editors of *Digest* engaged in a touchy exchange with Roy Newquist over why his new book *Counterpoint* (featuring interviews with sixty-three writers) included no black authors; the Harlem Writers Guild–New School for Social Research symposium (Baldwin, Richard Gilman, Jones, Alice Childress, Sarah Wright, Marshall, Brown, Myrna Baines, Douglas Turner Ward, Killens, Gloria Oden, Allen, Walter Lowenfels, Loften Mitchell [*Black Drama*], Albert Murray, and others); and the Alabama A. and M. College Writers' Conference, where Rosey E. Pool, Hayden, Dodson, Evans, and Killens made presentations. Hayden, destined to figure prominently in the aesthetics controversy, talked about drama at the Alabama conference and labeled Baldwin's *Blues for Mr. Charlie* and Jones's *Dutchman* as "just bad plays." Notices of conferences and symposia were announced regularly in the columns of *Digest*—which developed into the best source of cultural news in black magazine history.

Jones and Major had been publishing in *Free Lance* and in

552

myriad white-dominated little magazines (*Beatitude, Blue River, Beat Coast East, Statements*). With Spellman, Jones also wrote exciting jazz criticism in more widely circulated magazines such as *Nation, Jazz,* and *Downbeat.* In the meantime, Ted Joans (the itinerant jazz poet), Kaufman (the irreverent and brilliant Beat poet), and Atkins (the genius-experimentalist) had begun separate but—hindsight shows us—related assaults on the language traditionally employed in the service of poetry. Their efforts and those of others, however, were not confined exclusively to the often black-influenced but white-controlled cultural and literary undergrounds. Writing and theater arts workshops began springing up all over black America. Following or preceding them were important social corollaries: political ideologies, religious sectarian theories, race pride philosophies, hero- and myth-makers, and an unprecedented consolidation of black activism (symbolized by freedom rides, sit-ins, and, most important, the 1963 March on Washington for Jobs and Freedom). It was not surprising, then, to find clusters of poets, writers, and activists developing their own journals: the Howard Poets and *Dasein;* "Liberation Committee for Africa" and *Liberator;* the New York activist-theoreticians and their *Freedomways;* the "Society of Umbra" and *Umbra;* the activist-writers workshops and their mirror-journal, *Soulbook* ("the Quarterly of Revolutionary Afro-America"); the Negro Student Association at San Francisco State College and *Black Dialogue;* the young poet-mystics who proudly announced their *Journal of Black Poetry* ("published for black people everywhere"); the Organization of Black American Culture's frank embrace of its Africanity in the name *Nommo* (Chicago); and the numerous others (most of them bearing names associated with the new mood and group spirit). It also goes without saying that because they took many and divergent ideological and cultural stances, they deserve more treatment than this essay can give them.

Dasein, one of the most consciously literary of the new journals, immediately established a link between the Harlem Renaissance and its progenitor of the sixties and seventies by organizing the following advisory board: Sterling Brown, Arthur P. Davis, Owen Dodson, and Eugene C. Holmes. Brought out by the Dasein Literary Society, the periodical was subtitled *A Quarterly of the Arts,* with Percy Johnston serving as publisher and Walter De-

553

Legall as editor. Al Fraser, Oswald Govan, Lance Jeffers, Leroy O. Stone, and Joseph White were contributing editors. Original and experimental in content, design, and layout, *Dasein* remains one of the truly beautiful cultural art survivals of the much-discussed sixties. Bebop, Zen Buddhism, black language and folk-lore, the Beat poetry of coffee shops, nuclear armaments. racism, and the threat of World War III all influenced the writings of *Dasein*'s contributors. Like *Free Lance*, the journal did not restrict itself to printing works by blacks. Among the poets were Clyde Taylor, Delores Kendrick, Jeffers ("My Blackness Is the Beauty of This Land"), William Jackson, Vernon A. Butler, Laura Watkins, Govan, Dodson, Fraser, Karl Darmstadter, R. Orlando Jackson, DeLegall, Johnston ("On Her Senility," "To Paul Robeson, Opus no. 3"), Stone ("Calypso"), Richard Eberhart, and Carl Smith ("The Little Red-Bellied Woman"). The usually strong essays of the early sixties included Kermit Keith's "Approaching Architecture as an Art"; and among the writers of fiction were Theophis Shine, Jeffers, White, Barbarossa ("The Avengers"), Helmar Cooper ("Elizabeth"), E. L. Robertson, and Mel Cebulash ("The Price of Fame").

The early sixties continued to witness an outpouring of cultural and literary magazines, but they also saw their share of new political journals, most of them avowedly nationalistic and devoted primarily to the struggle. Such was *Freedomways,* established in 1961 by Shirley Graham (editor), W. Alphaeus Hunton (associate editor), Margaret Burroughs (art editor), and Esther Jackson (managing editor). Initiated as a "Quarterly Review of the Negro Freedom Movement," the magazine later dropped the word "Negro" and broadened its scope to deal with Africa and the Third World. However, its service to poets and writers was more than incidental, since it regularly featured creative literature and commentaries on the arts. Moreover, it received a boost from two veteran activists and magazine developers, John Henrik Clarke and Ernest Kaiser, who wrote on "The New Afro-American Nationalism" in a 1961 issue. The title of the article set the political and cultural tone for *Freedomways.* Other articles looked at freedom, jazz, W. E. B. DuBois, challenges to black artists, blacks in films, black poetry, Paul Robeson, social justice, new civil rights heroes, the significance of Lorraine Hansberry, "The Negro Woman in

554

American Literature," and "The Free Southern Theatre." Handsome but rarely deviating from its basic design and layout, *Freedomways* soberly analyzed social and cultural developments, its pages reinforced by the fine art of Tom Feelings, Charles White, Elton Fax, and Lee Jack Morton. In 1963 the written and visual arts were combined in a special issue on "Harlem: A Community in Transition."

Taken together, the healthy group of black journals launched in the early sixties represented the Afro-American consciousness in all its many colors. It is to them that one must go to trace the weaving of black art and thought. They fashioned the new literary tapestry and published the new writers: Nathan Hare, Malcolm X, LeRoi Jones, James Emanuel, John A. Williams, Clarence Major, John Oliver Killens, Paule Marshall, Ernest Gaines, Jay Wright, Henry Dumas, June Jordan, Audre Lorde, Larry Neal, Frank London Brown, Herbert Simmons, Conrad Kent Rivers, and others.

Clarke, a regular *Freedomways* contributor, was also a founder of *Liberator,* along with L. P. Beveridge, Jr., and Evelyn Battle. *Liberator* brought the whole of black life into focus through its creative literature, social essays, reviews (books, plays, movies), cultural articles, photo-essays, and interviews. The first issue was dedicated to Patrice Lumumba: "a symbol of unity and freedom; the people know why he died and what he stood for. Lumumba has taken his place among millions of martyrs to 600 years of struggle against slavery and colonial exploitation in Africa." Because *Liberator,* like *Freedomways,* was born of struggle, it was hampered by none of the initial constraints imposed on *Negro Digest.* Very few subjects or styles were off limits—a fact that was much more obvious after 1963, when the magazine became financially stable enough to use color and to experiment with different designs and formats.

Each month *Liberator* expressed its message in cover photographs of the new and old black heroes: Baldwin, Dick Gregory, Marcus Garvey, Cassius Clay, Martin Luther King, Jr., Jones, Hughes, Malcolm X, Paul Robeson, Ornette Coleman, and Julian Bond. Following the example of *Crisis, Opportunity,* and *CLA Journal,* in 1965 the magazine sought to encourage writers by instituting a $100 short story contest. However, it had already begun publishing the fiction of Bims, Clayton Riley, Carlos Russell, Joseph White ("O'Grady Says"), Len Holt ("The Bug Feeder"), and Alfred Gray ("Any Other Reason"). Riley, the main critic of drama and film, wrote reviews of *Nothing but a Man, The Pawnbroker, China,* and numerous other works. Chief essayists were Larry Neal and Chester Fuller. The perceptive Neal reviewed Jones's *The Slave* and *The Toilet* in February 1965 and made this synthesizing comment: "Jones' plays are the verbal companions to the expressions that have reached their greatest intensity in the music of Coltrane, Ornette Coleman, and more lately Archie Shepp." One function of a journal like *Liberator,* Neal said in September of the same year, "is a passionate and sincere examination of the role of Afro-American culture, e.g. the arts, in shaping the spiritual foundation for revolutionary change." Indeed *Liberator* seemed to wear Neal's suggested role, attempting to bring all black art forms into an arena of reenergized fluidity.

The first literary magazines of the 1960s published exclusively for black writers and readers were *Soulbook, Black Dialogue,* and *Journal of Black Poetry. Umbra* ("shadow region"), which chronologically preceded them, presaged and shared the excitement they caused. Founded by the Society of Umbra, a workshop of musicians, poets, fiction writers, and visual artists, the journal was not, like the other three mentioned, a black nationalist literary organ. Aesthetically, however, it was born of the black struggle, as evidenced by this statement in its first issue: "*UMBRA* is not another haphazard 'little literary' publication. *UMBRA* has a definite orientation: (1) the experience of being Negro, especially in America; and (2) that quality of human awareness often termed 'social consciousness.' " Though concerned primarily with issues facing Afro-Americans as these were reflected in creative literature ("poetry, short stories, articles, essays"), *Umbra* warned, "We will not print trash, no matter how relevantly it deals with race, social issues, or anything else." Neither was the publication a "self-deemed radical," but "as radical as society demands the truth to be." Its "unequivocal commitment," the editor-founders noted, was to "material of literary integrity and artistic excellence." This stand, with its implied preference for art over politics, may have been an overreaction to the attitudes of *Liberator* and *Freedomways,* both

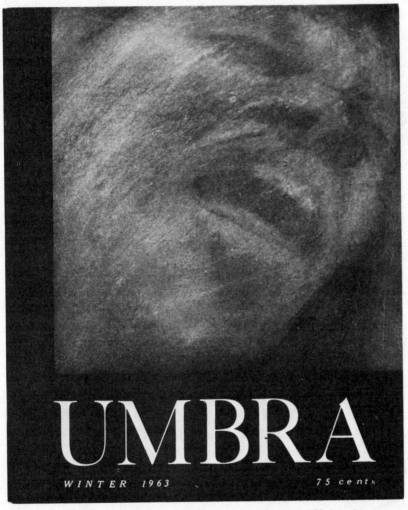

Umbra, *Vol. 1, No. 1, Winter 1963 (courtesy Northwestern University Library).*

published "uptown." Once one read *Umbra,* however, there was no question of the journal's involvement in the struggle—or of the need for a purely literary black magazine to serve as a forum and laboratory for new aesthetic experiments and analyses. Finally, like *Free Lance* and *Dasein, Umbra* had a particular interest in linking the post-Beat movement with the (often ill-termed) avant-garde. Considering the magazine's financial and spatial limitations, its achievements were quite substantial.

One important by-product of the founding of *Umbra* and its cousins (*Liberator, Negro Digest, Soulbook, Black Dialogue, Journal of Black Poetry*) was an effort to reformulate a vision of black artistic reality. The family of black artists and theoreticians who participated in this effort served as a nucleus out of which evolved the scope and design of most of the later magazines. In the persistent search for a synthesis of the artistic and the political consciousness, *Umbra* assembled a wide range of opinions, personalities, and attitudes: editor Tom Dent (freedom fighter and son of the president of Dillard University in New Orleans), assistant editors Hernton (sociologist-novelist-poet, a product of black colleges) and David Henderson (a poet and former student of writing at the New School for Social Research), and editorial assistants William E. Day, Rolland Snellings, Pritchard, and Nora Hicks. The first issue was divided into four parts: "Figurine of the Dream Sometimes Nightmare," "Blues and Bitterness," "Time and Atavism," and "Umbra Through Ethos." These titles, with their *Dasein*-like evocation of sensuality, mystery, psychology, and social consciousness, pretty much established the breadth of interest of *Umbra's* first contributors. Interestingly, one of the poets was Julian Bond.

None of the new magazines was developed in isolated, self-contained cultural centers, but each bore some evidence of regionalism. That the editors and contributors were aware of national literary activities is chronicled in the notes, titles of poems (and dedicatory inscriptions), reviews, and news. More important to this sense of black nationality, however, was the appearance of the same names in most of the publications. These writer-editors— Neal, Jones, Cruse, Clarke, Snellings, William Keorepetse Kgositsile, Henderson, Hernton, Dent, Major, Joans, Hughes, Ishmael Reed, Joe Goncalves, Atkins, Bob Hamilton, Lorenzo Thomas,

558

Ed Bullins, Jeffers, Donald Stone, Randall, and others—helped form the backbone of the new black periodicals. One finds this to be the case with *Soulbook, Black Dialogue,* and *Journal of Black Poetry,* all of which ironically, in view of their nationalistic orientation, sprang up in California, not in the compressed neo-African worlds of Chicago, Detroit, St. Louis, New York, or Washington, D.C. The on-again-off-again publication schedule of the journals attested to the problems they faced as the first black literary magazines in history to try sustaining themselves purely on black resources. The forerunner of these, *Soulbook,* "the revolutionary journal of Afro-America," came from the Afro-American Research Institution in Berkeley. Its focus was on black music, economics, black poetry, and anti-imperialism. With Hamilton as editor, the journal received editorial support from Wananchi Donald Freeman, Isaac Moore, Ernie Allen, Alvin Morrell, Ken M. Freeman, Carroll Holmes, and Leo R. Huey. Its major associates and contributors, however, reflected an East Coast influence: Kgositsile, Jones, Major, Doug Allen, Cornwell, Bullins, and Alfredo Peña. Among subjects treated in articles were Frantz Fanon and the Third World, racism and the socialist society, Egypt in history, "Blackness, That's Where It's At!" "Racism in France," and the whole of the African past. Africa began to figure prominently in *Soulbook* and other journals. *Soulbook,* for example, employed numerous African phrases ("Kitabu Cha Weusi"), ideas, concepts, drawings, maps, and names.

Black Dialogue and *Journal of Black Poetry* were low-keyed in that they, like *Soulbook* but unlike *Digest,* avoided taking on the whole of the black cultural experience. *Dialogue,* born in 1965 at San Francisco State College, featured some articles and essays, reviews, poetry, and fiction. Its founding editor was Arthur A. Sheridan, a San Francisco State student who had published his writings in *Canadian Sun, San Francisco Sun Reporter,* and *Liberal Democrat.* The East Coast editor was Edward Spriggs, brilliant poet and artist, while the editorial board consisted of Abdul Kaliem, Joe Howard, Aubrey Labrie, and Sidney Schiffer. Brought out by Ari Publications, *Dialogue* was expected to appear every two months as "a meeting place for voices of the Black community wherever that community may exist." It symbolized the youthful vigor of black America, publishing articles on "Revolutionary

Theatre," "Negritude Américaine," "The Future of 'Soul' in America," Santo Domingo, jazz, more on African negritude, revolutionary nationalism and the black artist, and Vietnam (by an eyewitness from Hanoi). Here the works of new young poets and occasionally those of older ones were printed: Al Young, Jon Lovett, Spriggs, Welton Smith, Neal, Conyus Calhoun, Alphonse Ngoma, Patricia Bullins, Goncalves, Senegalese David Diop, and Bisharo Al-Ausig. Here too were the fiction and drama of Marvin Jackmon ("Flowers for the Trashman"), Bullins ("How Do You Do"), Jane Clay (prize-winning author who had appeared in *New South* and *Negro Digest*), C. H. Fuller, and Melba Kgositsile. The talented, unpredictable LeRoi Jones led the roster of essay-article writers that included Saadat Ahmad, Romare Bearden, Neal, James T. Stewart, Bullins, and Eldridge Cleaver. The book review section, though sparse, was spiced with social undertones and ideological conflicts, as in reviews of *Glorious Age in Africa, Worth Fighting For, The Wretched of the Earth,* and *Manchild in the Promised Land.* There were also reviews of movies (for example, of *Uptight* by Nikki Giovanni) and the Afro-American Folkloric Troupe. The middle years of the sixties were given a particular twist and impetus by Jones, who wrote in a 1965 issue of *Dialogue:* "Revolutionary Theatre must Accuse and Attack anything that can be accused and attacked. It must Accuse and Attack because it is a theatre of Victims. It looks at the sky with the victims' eyes, and moves the victims to look at the strength in their minds and their bodies." In that year of Watts, a major jolt would be given the American social consciousness, and certainly not the least affected would be black cultural institutions, especially the literary magazines.

"Published for all black people everywhere," the quarterly *Journal of Black Poetry* was founded by Goncalves and had a great impact on black arts groups during the late sixties and early seventies. No other periodical before or since has rivaled its leadership in publishing the best of the newest poetry from the black world. Yet while it focused on poems and poets, the journal included incisive book reviews and excellent art and illustrations. Unlike some of its contemporaries (such as *Negro Digest, Freedomways,* and *CLA Journal*), it energetically sought to establish an unbroken relationship between typography, content, and ideol-

560

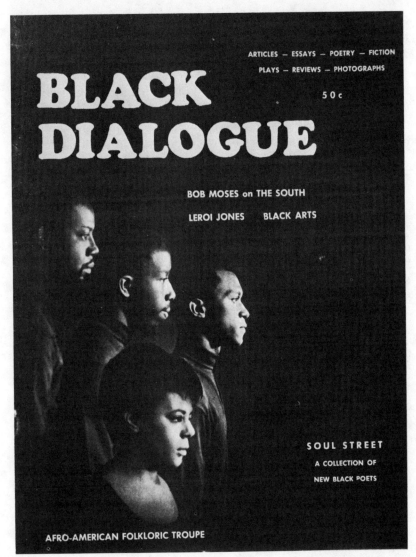

ARTICLES — ESSAYS — POETRY — FICTION
PLAYS — REVIEWS — PHOTOGRAPHS

BLACK DIALOGUE

50 c

BOB MOSES on THE SOUTH

LEROI JONES   BLACK ARTS

SOUL STREET
A COLLECTION OF
NEW BLACK POETS

AFRO-AMERICAN FOLKLORIC TROUPE

Black Dialogue, *Vol. 1, No. 2, July–August 1965 (courtesy Northwestern University Library).*

ogy. Following in the paths of *Soulbook* and *Dialogue,* it strove to achieve this synthesis by dismissing the Euro-American aesthetic and embracing neo-African criteria. An important component of this developing sensibility was the "new" music, which became increasingly important in the thinking of cultural philosophers, many of whom saw parallels between the ideas of Malcolm X and the "revolutionary" sounds. Goncalves' contribution to this vital breakthrough in black aesthetics was to provide a forum for the new poets and theoreticians. For over a decade this journal has remained the showplace for the best black poetry.

Part of the *Journal of Black Poetry's* appeal was in its cultural miscellany—a gumbo of criticism, reviews, news, and visual art. Articles, for example, covered such diverse subjects as Coltrane's music, black poetry from the Americas, "The Death of Yakub," "Toward a Purer Black Poetry Esthetic" (Crouch), "Letter to a Young Poet," "Black Magic" (on the new black poetry), "The Fire Must Be Permitted to Burn Full Up" (literary criticism), and "Black Arts Mexico" (Marvin X).

Battles over the new aesthetics continued to dominate the pages of *Journal* and other black cultural organs. One of the books contributing the most to this controversy was Cruse's *The Crisis of the Negro Intellectual*—a biting, searing indictment of black intellectuals and artists. It was simultaneously praised and attacked in all quarters. Two examples of staunch positions, pro and con, taken by contemporaries were poet-artist Edward Spriggs's endorsement of the work as the "most significant book of the decade" (*Journal of Black Poetry,* 1967–1968) and *Black Scholar* editor Robert Chrisman's condemnation of it as "The Crisis of Harold Cruse" in a later issue of his own journal.

A kind of "blackening" process—which, in *Digest,* for example, took the form of ceasing to publish or endorse white writers and changing its name to *Black World*—occurred in most of these new journals. The pattern was quite apparent in their names or subtitles, as witness this very incomplete list: *Afro-America, Black America, Negro American Literature Forum, Black Expression, Black Theatre, Nommo, The Black Scholar, Confrontation* (Troupe: Ohio University, Athens), *Echoes from the Gumbo, Proud* (St. Louis), *Revolt!* (Nat Turner Theatre, New Orleans), *Cosmic Colors, Nkombo, Cricket* ("New Ark"), *Deep Down in My Soul*

(Miami, Florida), *Spark* (Chicago), *Amistad* (John A. Williams and Charles Harris), *Black Academy Review* (A. Okechukwu, State University of New York, Buffalo), *Black Creation* (New York), *Black Review, Harvard Journal of Afro-American Affairs, The Mask* (Los Angeles), *Ex-Umbra, Chicory* (Baltimore), *Phat Mama* (New York, subtitled "Her Black Mind"), *Uptight* (El Paso), *Spirit* (London), *The Conch* ("Journal of Literary and Cultural Analysis"), *Rhythm* (Atlanta, African Expression, Inc.), *Black Lines* (Larry Coleman and Clarence Turner: Black Studies, University of Pittsburgh), *The Non-Aligned Third World Journal* (St. Louis), *Kushusu Vitabu* (Washington, D.C.), *Phase II* (Sarah Webster Fabio: Berkeley, "Journal of Black Art Renaissance"), *Onyx, Talking Drums* (London, monthly music magazine), *Yalode: Journal of Black Sister Poets* (Miami, Theatre of Afro-Arts), *Imani* (New York University, "Concepts of Education for Black People"), *Black History Museum Newsletter* (Philadelphia), *Roots* (Houston, Texas Southern University), *Hoo-Doo: A Journal of Black Arts* (later *Hoo-Doo Black Literature Series;* Up South–D.C. and Down South–DeRidder, Louisiana), *Transition* (later *Synergy;* D.C., Howard University Department of Afro-American Studies), *Pamoja Tutashinda* (Williamstown, Massachusetts), *Maongezi* (Detroit), *Renaissance 2: A Journal of Afro-American Studies* (Yale, Afro-American Cultural Center), *Watu* (Cornell University; "Journal of Black Literature and Art"), *Mwendo* (Coe College, Iowa), *The African Voice* (Camden, New Jersey, Black Cooperative Association), *Proud Black Images* (Ohio State University, Columbus; New World Arts Workshop), *Together Forever* (Chicago, Hirsch High School), *Poems by Blacks* (Lane; Baton Rouge and Fort Smith, Arkansas), *Shades* ("cultural, historical and literary magazine"), *Black Books Bulletin* (Chicago, Institute for Positive Education), *The Pan Africanist* ("quarterly of the international Black movement"; Claremont, California), *Black Music in Perspective* (Eileen Southern), *Blackstage* (Adesanya Alokoya, "a monthly magazine reflecting the development of Black art and culture"), *Living Blues: A Journal of the Black American Blues Tradition* (Chicago), *Identity* (Detroit, Rapa House Writers Association), *Drum: Journal of the Black Experience* (University of Massachusetts, Amherst), *Hambone* (Stanford, Committee for Black Performing Arts), *Obsid-*

ian: Black Literature in Review (Alvin Aubert; SUNY, Fredonia), *Studies in Black Literature, Movin' On in Space and Time* (Nora Bailey, Chicago: "Journal for the Fine Arts and Foreign Languages"), *Dues: An Annual of New Earth Writing* (Ron Welburn, New York), *Maji: A Journal of the Black Arts* (Philadelphia, The MAJI Collective), *Dark Waters* (Collen McElroy; Seattle, Washington), *Black Writers' News, Black Works* (New York), *Impressions, Spirit* (Jamaica, New York; Center for New Images, "A Black Arts and Communications Organization"), *Continuities: Words from the Communities of Pan-Africa* (Wilfred Cartey: New York), *BGI-18* (Black Graphics International, "Journal of Revolutionary Literature and Art"; Detroit), *Strive* (Montclair, New Jersey), *Gumbo: A Literary Magazine* (Yusef Komunyakaa), *Umoja: A Scholarly Journal of Black Studies* (Edward C. Okwu; University of Colorado, Boulder), *Blackprint* (Austin, Texas), and *Yardbird* (later *Y'bird*) (Reed and Young: Berkeley).

Many of these publications were patterned after their early and mid-sixties forebears. Some had radically new formats, reflecting the most advanced developments in print media technology; still others, like *CLA Journal* and *Phylon,* were more formal and academic in appearance. However, most were influenced by regional brands of black consciousness. This was particularly true of the Chicago-based *Negro Digest,* which, as the only national black literary magazine with a paid staff and a reliable publishing history, naturally assumed a position of leadership in the black arts movement. Until well into the seventies, Gayle, one of the most influential black aestheticians, dramatically aided Fuller in charting the journal's vision. He, along with Don Lee (Madhubuti) and Baraka (who later renounced *Black World*'s position), developed into a kind of axis force that monitored the evolution of the movement.

Of the other journals begun in the sixties, some, like *Dasein* and *Umbra,* changed paces and places. Others, such as *Liberator* and *Afro-America,* folded in the late sixties. Still others, among them *Freedomways* and *The Black Scholar*, remained strong and significant. Often the same editors simultaneously manned the staffs of several short-lived magazines. *Dasein,* which, like *Free Lance* and *Umbra*, had not been an exclusively black journal, reappeared in 1965 as a publication of the Dasein–Jupiter Hammom Press of

New York. With this shift had come a change in mood and format. It remained beautifully laid out with attractive color covers and fine-textured paper, but the obvious black context was gone, though all the black writers were not. The racially mixed contributors of poetry included Barbara Brown, Bruce Andrews, William Packard, Sue Abbot Boyd (white publisher of *Poems by Blacks*), Jeffers (who with J. William Meyers and Michael Winston had been added to the advisory board), Jack Crawford, and the talented young Jodi Braxton (*Sometimes I Think of Maryland*). Essays tended to be inspired by European-American academic ideas rerouted through an avant-garde consciousness. Very little fiction was published after the first two issues of *Dasein*, and there were few reviews. A current feature of the magazine is "The Young Writers' Salon," in which the work of new poets is introduced.

As nonliterary journals, *Freedomways* and *Liberator* nevertheless incorporated the essential black cultural spirit into their primary function. *Freedomways* opened its pages to dozens of poets. South African Bessie Head contributed short fiction ("Tao"), along with R. J. Meadough, Alice Walker, Loyle Hairston, Ann Shockley, and Mignon Holland Anderson. *Liberator,* with its larger size, made strategic use of visual arts and artists, featuring photo-essays on various black communities. Short fiction and plays were still its strong features in the late sixties, and its star-poet lineup was interspersed with occasional new names. However, publisher Daniel Watts and company were not able to keep *Liberator* in existence after 1970.

As for *Umbra,* the dispersion of its staff actually had a positive effect on the black literary world. Reed and Henderson went to Berkeley. Dent returned to New Orleans and, with the aid of Val Ferdinand (Kalamu Ya Salaam), organized two short-lived magazines: *Echoes from the Gumbo* and *Nkombo*. (Salaam, in turn, became a founding editor of *Black Collegian*.) In 1975 Dent joined Charles H. Rowell and Jerry Ward in establishing *Callaloo*, "born out of a specific desire to give expression to the new writers in the Deep South area." In the meantime, Henderson had revived *Umbra,* first in New York in the form of an anthology and later in California as a tabloid that has exerted considerable influence on Third World cultural programming. One of its most significant contributions was to bring together those writers and artists rarely published by the establishment with those from the black world.

Only Troupe's three-issue *Confrontation* and Reed's five-issue *Yardbird* seemed similarly interested in tapping this broader base of creative expression. Most new journals, while not completely ignoring other colored artists, rarely attempted to show relationships between cultural expression and political events occurring in Latin America, the Middle East, and Southeast Asia. A prototype format for dealing with wider issues of color had been developed by *Phylon* in the 1940s, but apparently the editors of the new journals were not aware of it.

The "survival of the fittest" axiom finally overcame both *Soulbook* and *Black Dialogue,* after the latter had been briefly revived in 1969 with a new editorial board. *Afro-American,* with its New York orientation, proudly advertised itself in a September 1966 issue of *Liberator* as a "new magazine dedicated to you of African ancestry. . . . We feature the new young Black poets and writers; we feature your history and heritage; we feature a review of current books about Africans and Afro-Americans." The *Afro-American Woman,* an *Ebony*-type publication brought out by the Negro Book Club, issued its first number in 1967. At Terre Haute, Indiana, Englishman John F. Bayliss of Indiana State University founded the scholarly *Negro American Literature Forum* "for school and university teachers." As a quarterly, which changed its name to *Black American Literature Forum* in the mid-seventies under the editorship of Hannah Hedrick, it has been a valuable source of reviews, criticism, and poetry. Its contributors have included Upward Bound and prison poets, members of the Watts Writers Workshop, John Lovell, Benjamin McKeever, Lloyd Brown, Daryl Dance, Abraham Chapman, Turner, and Tolson. In 1972 Redmond (*Drumvoices*) edited a special poetry number that presented the work of twenty-three black poets.

The black music magazine *Cricket,* an outgrowth of *Liberator* and other journals, carried the works of Sun Ra, Askia Touré, Caldwell, Neal, Baraka, Reed, Crouch, Kgositsile, Spellman, and Norman Jordan. Spellman later helped found *Rhythm* in Atlanta. Around the time *Cricket* appeared, *Nommo* arrived as the publications arm of Chicago's well-known OBAC, founded in 1966 by Rivers, Fuller, and Gerald McWorter. It came out irregularly and usually published works by members of the OBAC Writers' Workshop. Angela Jackson (*Voodoo/Love Magic*) became editor of

$3.95

YARDBIRD READER
VOLUME ONE

Yardbird Reader, *Vol. 1, No. 1, 1972 (courtesy Northwestern University Library)*.

the journal in the mid-seventies. The indefatigable Fuller oversaw these Windy City activities from his several-pronged position of editor, organizer, and father figure. His feminine counterpart, Gwendolyn Brooks, openly and unselfishly shared her resources with the new black writers in Chicago and elsewhere. With Randall of Broadside Press (publisher of *Black Position*), Fuller and Brooks, under the ever-hovering spirit of Baraka, formed a triumvirate that literally set the course of black creative expression during the late sixties and early seventies. This was achieved by rocketing to stardom their young poet-protégé, Lee (later Haki R. Madhubuti). In the meantime, Gwendolyn Brooks made a unique contribution to little magazine history by editing *Black Position,* wherein she promised to "present the music and the muscle of contemporary black pride as an excitement, a privilege, a responsibility." Mostly done in black and white, the magazine carried the writings of Randall, Fuller, Bennett, Lee, Curtis Ellis (Chicago bookstore entrepreneur), Neal, Francis and Val Gray Ward (of Kuumba Workshop), Carolyn Rodgers, Gayle, George Kent, and Kgositsile.

One of the most impressive literary periodicals to emerge from the Chicago and national scene, however, was Madhubuti's *Black Books Bulletin*. Though typographically imposing, with brilliant cover art and design, the journal's articles and commentaries were often of lesser quality. Part of *Bulletin's* problem was that its editor was simultaneously experiencing growing pains and occupying a vital leadership position in the Afro-American cultural sphere. Overpraised too early in his career, Madhubuti drastically simplified the most complex racial and social issues, then went on to quickdrawn conclusions. Nevertheless, the journal's service to black creativity remained invaluable, since it offered poetry contests as well as articles and essays by leading thinkers, and it became a leader in monitoring books by and about Africans. Still going strong in 1978, the *Bulletin* reflects, to use the words of poet Julius Thompson, "hopes tied up in promises."

The Black Scholar, founded in 1969 and now edited by Robert Chrisman, was established as a forum for social and political issues. However, its occasional literary criticism, book reviews, poetry, and short fiction have helped provide a platform for the new black literature. Most monthly issues have been devoted to the special concerns of black or Third World communities: Pan

568

Africanism, black psychology, the black soldier, black women, and fund-raising for the Afro-American community. There are essay and short story contests along with irregularly appearing reviews. One important service rendered by *Scholar* is its annual *Black Books Roundup,* and it has also devoted several issues exclusively to black literature and the arts.

While *Black Scholar* was establishing its base of operations in Sausalito, *Yardbird* was launched in the early seventies by Reed, Young, and associates in Berkeley. The journal resembled *Amistad* and Mel Watkins's *Black Review* (neither of which lasted very long). *Yardbird's* inability to tangle successfully with the various conflicts among its editorial ranks led to its death after only five issues. However, in its brief life the journal was more concerned—like its predecessors *Free Lance, Dasein,* and *Umbra*—with publishing literature than with discussing or reviewing it. Brought out by the Yardbird Publishing Cooperative, *Yardbird* reflected some of the best writing being done by Afro-American and Third World authors (and occasionally carried the work of non-colored writers). This practice of including some white writers was carried over into the new *Y'bird* (Reed and Young, 1977).

Nate Mackey, Sandi Richards, Charleen Rubin, and Gloria Watkins organized the magazine *Hambone* (in the mid-seventies), which is published by the Committee for Black Performing Arts at Stanford University. It featured poetry by Barra, Watkins, Henderson, Johnnie Scott, Halifu, David Jackson, Michael Harper, Fabio, and Reed. Drawings and photographs, interviews (Anthony Braxton), articles (Eckels and John Cochran), and fiction (Wandera Ogana, Fred Johnson) helped round out one issue of the attractive publication.

Historically the major centers of black little-magazine activity have been D.C., Atlanta, Cleveland, Chicago, New York, New Orleans, and Berkeley. Oddly enough, New York City has not been able to give continuous life to a single black literary periodical, though it has seen many come and go. Recently, however, encouraging signs have been appearing on the cultural horizon, and writers hope the phoenix cycle will produce an important New York–based black journal. In other parts of the state, as well as in adjacent states, various writing and arts workshops, studios, and social organizations have often joined Afro-American studies or English departments in repeated attempts to publish little magazines. When *Liberator,* the most literary of magazines in New York during its day, was on its deathbed, *Black Theatre* was ascending. As the official periodical of the black theater movement, it was based at the New Lafayette Theatre, founded in Harlem in 1966. It had hoped to publish six times a year but soon met all the familiar adversities. During its brief existence, however, it became a valuable source of cultural news, original short plays, interviews, reviews, and poetry. Bullins and Marvin X headed the staff of editors and correspondents that represented a national range and scope: Dent, Theodore Ward, Vantile Whitfield, Adam David Miller, Goncalves, Larry Miller (*Katibu*), Caldwell, Jones, Woody King, O'Neal, and Barbara Ann Teer (founder of the National Black Theatre of Harlem).

Black Creation, the brilliant prototype of a black cultural journal, appeared in the early 1970s. As a "Quarterly Review of Black Arts and Letters," it had much of the spirit and flavor of *Liberator,* except that its editors unashamedly announced that literature and the arts would be their main focus. Veteran and beginning artists and writers were given exposure in *Creation* which—like *Liberator, Black Theatre,* and other New York magazines—had regional editors in San Francisco (Cleveland Bellows), Detroit (Melba Boyd), New Orleans (Dent), and Paris (Lillian Barlow). Editor Fred Beauford was handily assisted by James Walker, John Flateau, and playwright Buriel Clay. The following claim by *Creation* was well documented in each issue of the colorful magazine: "We are one of the few magazines around where the heart beat of Black Americans can be felt with force; where young and old, male and female, come together in a community of creative expression." The entire spectrum of black expression was repeatedly seen in the journal: film and theater criticism, creative literature (fiction, poetry, essays), art, book reviews, in-depth interviews with authors and artists. One-time poetry editor was the gifted Elouise Loftin, who published her own poems as well as those of others. Editor Beauford published his own fiction along with that of Melvin Mitchell, Wesley Brown, Joe Johnson, Shelby Steele, King, Mignon Holland ("Gone After Jake"), and Ronnie Redd.

Bopp (earlier *BOP,* for "Blacks on paper") and *Black Works* were only two of several new magazines that showed promise in the mid-seventies. *Bopp,* originally conceived by students at Brown

570

University, is currently edited by Kambon Obayani, who is in the graduate writing program at the University of Iowa. Associate editors are Gayl Jones, Troupe, and Cannon; contributing editors include Charles Davis, Everett Hoagland, Rhett Jones, Major, and Mustapha (included in *Jumbalaya*). The future of *Bopp* is uncertain, but its present is bright.

Black Works, which made its first impact as a literary magazine published once annually, announced in 1977 that it would come out twice a year. Based at Long Island University, the journal has been reminiscent of *Liberator* in its practice of printing photographs of everyday blacks in natural surroundings. Poetry, stories, drama, and literary criticism accompany the visuals. Editors include Cecil Lee, Patricia Nichols, Wayne Dawkins, Gibson, Patricia Lee, and Grace Corbet. Gibson is also a member of Troupe's New York poetry workshop at the Frederick Douglass Creative Arts Center.

The struggle to bridge the gap between the academy and the streets was most notably seen in journals like *Phylon, Negro Digest/Black World, Liberator,* and *Black Scholar.* Within this frame of reference, one other New York State literary magazine deserves brief consideration. Although its future was not guaranteed (and it remained in need of subscribers in early 1978) *Obsidian: Black Literature in Review* appeared at mid-decade. Its attempt to avoid the tension between the streets and the academy, and to embrace the international black literary family, was seen in its list of contributing and advisory editors: Awooner, Lloyd Brown, Clarke, Arthur P. Davis, Nick Aaron Ford, Gaines, Gayle, Harper, Blyden Jackson, Kent, Arthenia Bates, Ezekiel Mphahlele, Redding, Rowell, and Douglas Turner Ward. *Obsidian* was described as being "devoted to the study and cultivation of Black Literature, featuring critical articles, book reviews, short fiction, poetry, interviews, very short plays." It is desperately needed as a review of literature—especially in view of the abdication of this position by *CLA Journal.*

At the same time, fine new journals like *Bopp* and *Hoo-Doo* are vital and important because they specialize in creative expression. The latter's peripatetic editor (Ahmos Zu-Bolton), who has been active on the little-magazine circuit (including the white network) for some time, made impressive strides in the mid-seventies, publishing a wide range of contemporary Afro-American poets and

571

devoting an entire issue to women writers. A southern flavor has pervaded *Hoo-Doo,* just as it has and does in such sister journals as *Echoes from the Gumbo, Roots, Nkombo, Pound, Deep Down in My Soul,* and *The Saracen.*

The excitement caused by black and other non-white interactions and struggles has spurred the development of Third World journal publishing. Early examples were *Tropiques, Présence Africaine,* and *Black Orpheus,* but these were followed by many others: *Abbia (The Cameroon Cultural Review), African Forum* (New York), *African Arts* (UCLA), *African Literature Today* (Sierra Leone), *Journal of New African Literature and the Arts* (Joseph Okpaku, New York), *Journal of Ethnic Studies, Lotus: Afro-Asian Writings* (Cairo), *African Studies Review* (New York), *Black Images* (Ontario), *Cavite* (Barbados), *African Language Studies* (London), *Voices from the Cave, African Theatre* (Kenya), *Jamaica Journal, African Review* (Dar es Salaam), *Gumbo: A Literary Magazine* (Yusef Komunyakaa), *Mazungumzo* (Michigan State University), *Calaban, Savacou* (Jamaica), *Insight and Opinion* (Ghana), *BIM* (Barbados), *Kairi* (Trinidad and Tobago), *Ufahumu, Busara, Caribbean Quarterly, Jonala, Harambee, Neworld* (Los Angeles), *Gigibori* (Papua, New Guinea), *Copesthetic* (Harryette Mullen), *Minority Voices, African Authors,* and *African Literature Association* (Pennsylvania). This list only samples the rich productivity occurring in worldwide circles of "color." Afro-American writers have become more involved in the Pan-African and Third World little magazine movement, and a healthy reciprocity has obviously emerged.

The "black world," as many now refer to the global existence of Africans, is the stage on which the drama of the black future will be played out. *Black World,* as name and new identity, was in fact born of this urgency. *First World*—a black-derived term to counter possible negative residuals in the phrase "Third World," and to suggest black leadership instead of followership in international life—adorned the masthead of a new magazine founded by Fuller, Parks, and associates in Atlanta. "An International Journal of Black Thought," *First World* has changed its location and format. However, despite its august editorial board (Samuel Allen, Maja Angelou, Houston Baker, Brooks, Clark, Cruse, Davis, Gayle, Madhubuti, and others), not much has been done to keep the journal alive. One of the best-looking of the new magazines, it offers criticism, poetry, reviews, and political analyses, and its shoestring existence is not unlike that of other black journals. At the same time, the journal's history has been fraught with controversy. During the mid- to late sixties and into the seventies, several writers and editors felt Fuller had allowed himself to be pushed into a myopic corner by proponents of the black aesthetic and black nationalism. This predicament, they maintained, aided in the circumvention of certain writers and their materials. So, when *Black World* folded in 1976, a number of supporters were less than eager to help Fuller develop another journal with the same editorial policies he had pursued in the last stages of *Negro Digest/ Black World*. One wonders, too, why Fuller, with both a knowledge of the journal's impending death and an international network of contacts, did not act sooner to conceive and implement the *First World* project.

The black little magazine has received indirect support from the big slicks (*Ebony, Essence, Encore, The Black Collegian, Players, Unique*) which, especially in the case of *Essence* and *Collegian*, feature creative expression and literary history. In publishing the works of little-magazine contributors, these bigger ones are helping to publicize the efforts of their less stable cousins.

For the black "littles," it has indeed been a long trek from instability to an uneasy stability, aided in part by wider reading audiences and various public or private grants. The same magazine (*Umbra-Yardbird-Y-bird, Gumbo-Nkombo-Callaloo, Shrewd-Confrontation-Bopp, Free Lance-Vibrations-Black Ascensions-Juju,* or *Liberator-Cricket-Black Theatre-Black Creation*) keeps being born within the spirit and letter of the African continuum. A healthy reflection is cast by the current state of the black cultural arts: strong, flexible, multidimensional/directional, proud, controversial, and life-giving. From this robust conflict is produced the stuff of future creative expression. The individual black journals have come and gone, but the idea that they are necessitated by life (art) will never disappear. *Callaloo,* one of the newest of these magazines, is, as its editors suggested in the inaugural issue, already in "a wretched financial state"—a desperate situation, to say the least. But hope abounds in the lead-off article, in which Lelia H. Taylor, preparing to examine the survival-food recipe that became the journal's title, flings a challenge and a lifeline: "Callaloo, anyone?"

Tom Montag's Concern/s, *Pentagram Press, Milwaukee, 1977. Photograph by Michael Tarachow (courtesy Tom Montag).*

THE LITTLE MAGAZINE SMALL PRESS CONNECTION: SOME CONJECTURES
Tom Montag

"If any single characteristic of many contemporary writers bothers me," says Tom Montag, "it is the pretension—the smug assumption that innovative writing is a more distinguished and honorable profession than farming or selling lumber." Thus he explains his decision in 1976 to leave Milwaukee, where he edited the Monday Morning Press *and the review magazine* Margins, *and become a country journalist in a central Wisconsin farm village.*

Mr. Montag's aversion to pretense is also manifest in his decision to use newsprint for twenty-four of the thirty large issues of Margins. *What* Margins *did in its four-year run from 1972 to 1976 was designed to be peripheral, "at the edge of serious literature."*

Tom Montag has published nine volumes of poetry (all with small presses), and two books of essays about small press books, poets, novelists, publishing, and literary journalism.

In the past, the study of American literary publishing has tended to center on the history, significance, and influence of the little magazine and to neglect the role of the small literary press. Works such as Frederick J. Hoffman's *The Little Magazine: A History and Bibliography* have been widely acknowledged and used as resources in the study of the dynamics of literature; other studies, such as the annotated bibliography included as part of *The Little Magazine in America, a Modern Documentary History,* serve to update and expand Hoffman's classic work and sometimes to emphasize the little magazine at the expense of the small press. Only recently, with the publication of Hugh Ford's *Published in Paris,* has any full account of particular literary presses (those in Paris earlier in this century) been readily accessible. Numerous studies of "fine presses" are available, but such books have been concerned primarily with the art of bookmaking rather than with the *dynamics* of literary publishing. Because Ford's *Published in Paris* presents considerable factual material about the operation of small presses (despite the boundaries of its concerns), the book will enable those interested in the processes of literary production to consider and assess the historical importance of the small literary press. Ford's book, we might hope, will spur similar research about past and present American literary presses.

To date, however, the intense interest in the little magazine has meant, largely, the neglect of the small press. In part, this may stem from the fact that the little magazine is more readily researched and studied than the press. A little magazine can be indexed; its editorial vision can be analyzed; its sphere of concern over a period of years can be assessed. By contrast, the nature, concerns, and editorial vision of the good small publisher may often be difficult to ascertain because, first, the small press editor does not have the convenience of "editorial notes" in which to set down his literary tenets; second, the publisher may present diverse kinds of writing, dissimilar in all respects except for that intangible called quality, something not easily described; and, third, students of literature generally seem more interested in the development of particular writers (and hence the bibliographies of particular writers) than in the larger dynamics of literature (to which the bibliographies or "lists" of publishers are relevant).

The editor of the little magazine can and often does explain his editorial position in the pages of his magazine; the small press editor can do so at the risk of irritating his readers, who buy a particular book in order to read the writer, not the writer's editor. In addition, an editor's concerns are more quickly apparent in a little magazine by virtue of the number of selections presented during a year's publishing; the book publisher usually presents considerably fewer writers, and therefore fewer examples of his editorial interests, in the same span of time. Further, the "lag time" between a decision to change editorial direction and the implementation of that decision is far shorter for the magazine than for the small press. The critical vocabulary necessary for discussing the common quality of several kinds of writing is available, but when a long-lived small publisher's list becomes extensive, such discussion may be highly intricate and complicated. Recurrent editorial patterns are more readily discernible for the magazine than for the press—again because the magazine presents a greater number of selections in a given period of time than does the press. Although the needed critical vocabulary may be available, we have only a limited understanding of the dynamics of literary interrelationships and influence; Hugh Kenner in *The Pound Era* presents the first comprehensive model for grappling with complex interactions of writers, writings, and emerging literary currents. Literature is studied so often in terms of writers alone, and so seldom in terms of processes, that we are not yet accustomed to considering the significance of the multifarious literary interrelationships that book publishing entails. We can, moreover, speak about the editor of the little magazine in terms similar to those we use for writers. We may discuss his vision, for instance, as we would talk about the vision of a novelist or poet. The editor of a good little magazine seems to be more visible (though not obtrusive, in the best cases) than the small press editor, although each may be exercising the same tight editorial control. Because researchers' interests have tended to focus on little magazines, the study of small presses has been neglected; hence the detailed factual information and the analysis needed for an understanding of the broader literary processes of which small presses are a part have not been gathered and made. The relationship between the small literary press and literature is only beginning to be examined. When factual material about literary publishing in America since 1950 is finally collected and analyzed, the significance of the small press might well prove greater than the current neglect by students of literary publishing would indicate.

That the editor of a little magazine is frequently also the editor of a small literary press should not surprise us. The concerns of the two enterprises, literature and readership, are similar and interrelated, however different the magazine and the press may be in practice. An editor may launch a little magazine only to discover that magazine format is confining and does not permit all the kinds of publishing he would like; in such cases the press is an outgrowth of the magazine. An editor may feel, for example, that one or more of the contributors to his magazine needs more substantial exposure than magazine publication would permit— i.e. that a particular writer would be better served by the presentation of a large collection of work in one place than by the publication of the same work in a number of issues of the magazine or in several different magazines. Such circumstances may serve as the most common impetus for founding a press out of a magazine. Depending in part on the editor/publisher's financial resources and in part on how frequently the editor sees the need, books may be an occasional or regular supplement to the magazine operation; the magazine itself remains the center of activity while books are viewed as adjuncts. For instance, *Gallimaufry* (formerly of San Francisco, now of Arlington, Virginia) continues as a literary journal on newsprint, but the editors have established the Gallimaufry Chapbook Series and are publishing 40-to-48-page collections of work by writers who have often been contributors to the magazine. *ManRoot* (South San Francisco, California) has also instituted a ManRoot Book series. Unlike *Gallimaufry,* however, *ManRoot* has been changing its editorial policies and scope of concern, to become less an eclectic gathering of work and more a tightly focused thematic publication. The *ManRoot* Jack Spicer issue (number 10) is evidence of this altered direction.

In some cases—more frequent in the past five years—the editor of a little magazine chooses to publish a book, the work of a single writer, and simply calls it a "special issue" of his magazine. The editor of *Road Apple Review* (Oshkosh, Wisconsin), for example, presented William Kloefkorn's *Alvin Turner as Farmer* in 1972 as volume IV, number 2, despite the fact that *Road Apple Review* and Road Runner Press are related enterprises. Windflower Press (Lincoln, Nebraska) reissued *Alvin Turner* as a book two years later. *Painted Bride Quarterly* (Philadelphia, Pennsylvania) recently published a title by John Giorno as an issue of that magazine. *December Magazine* (Chicago, Illinois) has probably made more frequent use of this type of special issue than most other little magazines. Since 1967 five novels and two books of stories (with another collection of stories forthcoming) have appeared as *December*s. The reason for such a decision could be financial—i.e. money is available for the magazine but not for the press. Or the editor could be attempting to conserve his energies by producing a book without interrupting the flow of his magazine-centered activities; he may fear, for example, that time and energy devoted to the production of a book will disrupt his magazine's publishing schedule. Or the editor may conclude that a book appearing as an issue of his magazine will have

Selected
Poems
Ballads
and Songs
of
Jack Micheline
1954–1975
—†—

Introduction
by
Jack Kerouac
—††—

Edited
w/a Preface
by
Paul Mariah
—†††—

240 pp

perfect bound $~~4.50~~ 5.95

Man-Root
Box 982
South San Francisco
California 94080

limited
signed
hardbound
edition $15.00

Publication date: Nov. 15, 1976

Flier for ManRoot *edition of* Selected Poems, Ballads, and Songs 1954–1975,
by Jack Micheline.

Above: Clown Wars, *Nos. 13, 14, 15, 16, 1977, edited by Bob Heman (courtesy John Jacob). Opposite:* The Painted Bride Quarterly, *Vol. 1, No. 1, Fall 1973, edited by Louise Simons and R. Daniel Evans (courtesy J&F Anania).*

THE PAINTED BRIDE
QUARTERLY

vol.1 / no.1
fall '73 / 1.00

BOOK

OF MAGAZINE VERSE

WHITE RABBIT PRESS   SAN FRANCISCO

Jack Spicer

POEMS

FOR THE NATION

FOR POETRY CHICAGO

FOR TISH

FOR RAMPARTS

FOR THE ST. LOUIS SPORTING NEWS

FOR THE VANCOUVER FESTIVAL

FOR DOWN BEAT

Above: Book, *a Jack Spicer spoof of* Poetry *magazine, featuring the* Poetry *format and logo (courtesy J&F Anania).* Opposite: Mojo Navigator(e), *No. 4, 1973, edited by John Jacob (courtesy John Jacob).*

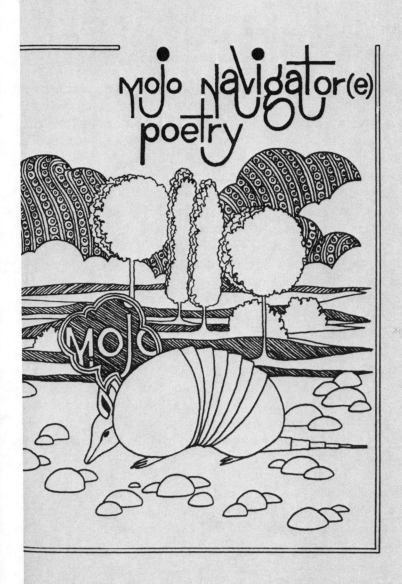

better distribution than otherwise. Subscribers to the magazine, at least, will receive a copy of the book immediately, while remaining copies can be promoted and marketed in the same way book publishers handle their titles.

A variation of the "special issue" book by one writer is the magazine appearance of what are essentially chapbooks by two, three, or more writers. Writers are sometimes allotted as many as 20 to 30 pages; depending upon the editor's selection skills and intent, the work presented may have the wholeness and integrity associated with a good chapbook or small book. *Salthouse: A Magazine of Field Notes* (Ann Arbor, Michigan) will soon be publishing an issue given over entirely to the work of two poets. *Stations* (Milwaukee, Wisconsin) devoted each of its first two issues to fairly lengthy selections from the works-in-progress of six writers, with extensive statements by each contributor about the work he is doing. Each issue of *Stations* is, in effect, a tightly edited and carefully orchestrated anthology. Other magazines, which may regularly have eclectic or grab-bag policies, have also been known to publish anthology-like issues containing large swatches of work by relatively few contributors. Thematic special issues, which present work by many writers around a single topic, also have the appearance of anthologies. The *ManRoot* Jack Spicer issue, mentioned previously, is one example: poetry, appreciations, and critical essays by a range of writers center on Spicer, with many contributors acknowledging literary debts to Spicer the poet. Both *Dacotah Territory* (Moorhead, Minnesota) and *Scree* (Fallon, Nevada) have published "Native American special issue" anthologies. *Dacotah Territory* also recently produced (as its number 11) a *Minnesota Poets in the Schools Anthology*.

The occasional special issue devoted to the work of a single writer, together with the anthology numbers of little magazines, indicates a strong impulse among magazine editors to produce titles which are characteristically booklike in terms of editorial stance and literary intent. The *Ironwood* (Tucson, Arizona) special issue devoted to George Oppen is a book, and is edited as such, regardless of its appearance in a serial sequence. The several issues of *Vort* (Bloomington, Indiana), each presenting essays and commentary on one or (more frequently) two contemporary writers, are also booklike collections of criticism. Although

584

subscriptions to *Vort* are encouraged, I suspect that the magazine's single-issue sales do better than individual subscriptions, simply because one might be particularly interested in some of the poets whose work is discussed but not in all of them. Two issues of *Truck* magazine (St. Paul, Minnesota)—number 13, *Landscape,* and number 14, *Explorations*—are also books centered on particular thematic considerations. A book, we might say, can stand alone with its own particular literary identity and a clear, self-sufficient reason for being, independent of any larger design on the part of the editor. With the eclectic magazines that seldom if ever publish special issues, the reader must become aware of the editor's (or editors') peculiar stamp—the special nature of the editor's vision which marks his magazine over the course of its existence. For unless a magazine that purports to publish "the best contemporary literature available" has a clear editorial intelligence behind it, it can easily end as a hopeless, unfocused hodgepodge of contradictions, a citadel of dullness. The grab-bag magazines are significant in one crucial respect: many of them are the first places where new, unknown writers can publish. But these magazines need a vitality, a unity, a vision that are too often lacking, to the detriment of the better pieces of work they present.

Some magazines steer clear of the hodgepodge effect by devoting themselves to particular kinds of writing. *Interstate* (Austin, Texas) is decidedly experimental in its emphasis; *Kayak* (Santa Cruz, California) is devoted to surrealistic poetry; *Alcheringa* (Boston) concerns itself with ethnopoetics; *Salthouse* presents historico-geopoetic work; *Assembling* (New York City) publishes "the otherwise unpublishable." The strength or weakness of magazines with clearly defined boundaries of concern lies in the skill of the editor, in the excellence of his eye. A magazine that publishes bad examples of experimental writing, for example, or one that presents the worst surrealistic poetry being written, does no service to the particular kind of writing it purports to be interested in, and no service to literature generally. By contrast, a well-edited magazine with special concerns benefits not just its particular kind of writing, but all writing. Further, such magazines frequently function as "continuing anthologies" or "active anthologies," and can be used in the same way that book anthologies are used.

585

The number of special single-author, thematic, or anthology issues of little magazines and of special-interest literary journals seems to have grown considerably in recent years. Where formerly an editor might have been content with a series of eclectic issues, more frequently now he seems to feel the need to produce singular issues with distinctive and clear-cut concerns. The magazine editor is beginning to view his role as similar to that of the writer, in terms of vision, balance, rhythm, and style in the work he is producing as editor. Any issue of a little magazine is becoming, more and more, a personal artistic statement on the part of the editor. Thus the magazine itself becomes a clearly stated aesthetic proposition, just as a well-written and well-assembled book of poems or stories or a novel is. The present tendency is to infuse each issue of a magazine with the wholeness, the unity or integrity we are accustomed to find in good works of art and good single-author collections or well-edited anthologies.

Historically, the impulse to edit and publish a little magazine frequently arose from the perception that an identifiable literary community needed a vehicle of expression. Little magazines were a means of communication and exchange among the members of particular groups of writers. By "identifiable literary community," however, I do not necessarily mean a school or clique of writers. Often the writers identified with particular magazines have been doing diverse kinds of work, although they might share common concerns. Such an influential promoter of new literature as Ezra Pound was interested in T. S. Eliot's *Waste Land*, James Joyce's *Ulysses,* and imagist poetry—and much more; others of Pound's time had similarly broad-ranging tastes.

The fact that magazines in the past tended to arise from, or to form around themselves, a community of writers served to give even the most grab-bag of them some measure of wholeness and unity. *Invisible City* (Fairfax, California), *Kayak, Wormwood Review* (Stockton, California), and *Vagabond* (Ellensburg, Washington) continue this tradition, serving identifiable communities. Other contemporary magazines, such as *Blue Cloud Quarterly* (Marvin, South Dakota), *Center* (La Honda, California), *Mojo Navigator(e)* (Oak Park, Illinois), and *Montana Gothic* (Missoula, Montana), are distinguishable and identifiable on the basis of each editor's interests and taste. Still other magazines, such as *Aspect* (Somerville, Massachusetts), *Caim* (Baltimore, Maryland), *Lake Superior Review* (Ironwood, Michigan), and *New Collage* (Sarasota, Florida), have no strong editorial presence and appear to serve no community in particular; magazines of this sort are often anonymous entities. All too frequently a would-be contributor makes no attempt to ascertain a magazine's intent, if indeed there is an identifiable purpose, and all too frequently the lack of any community of writers means that a magazine drifts aimlessly, selecting material almost at random and getting virtually no notice and readership. The trend toward issues of magazines that have the integrity of books is of course an encouraging sign. If a magazine is not useful to one particular community of writers, at least it can be of service to certain sets of ideas or kinds of writing (which implies, perhaps, a community of concerns).

Possibly one key distinction between a devoted magazine editor and a small press editor is this: the best little magazine editor situates himself within a literary community and uses his magazine to capture, reflect, and shape the energies of that community and to facilitate communication with those beyond the circle of writers. The small press editor, in contrast, is primarily interested, with each title he produces, in presenting a substantial, integral work by an individual writer (or, in the case of anthologies, a carefully edited selection of writings). Certainly the small press can serve a literary community, and many of them do. As with some magazines, however, there is the danger that small presses may publish only the clique of writers around them; other presses, especially those that are outgrowths of healthy magazine endeavors, serve a vibrant, already existing community. Perhaps the small press editor who brings out a highly influential and significant work intends, however slightly or secretly, to hitch his wagon to a star, to immortalize his name (or at least the name of his press) by being associated with a particular artist who comes to be regarded as a major writer. That the small press editor's impulse is necessarily any more aristocratic or elitist than the magazine editor's is doubtful; many magazine editors feel they are publishing the most select, excellent writers of a particular generation and are part of an aristocratic literary tradition. Indeed, the editors of some little magazines (*Partisan Review, Paris Review, Hudson Review, Iowa Review,* and many university quarterlies, with the notable exception of *New Letters* and *Cut Bank,* come to mind) are notoriously snobbish in their editorial selections, though not for any discernible literary reasons. Even magazines which are established to serve a particular literary community may be governed by aristocratic principles, if the group of writers being published is viewed as a special elite. Certainly the editors of some small presses, such as Black Sparrow Press (if we stretch definitions to count Black Sparrow a small press), the Fiction Collective, the Elizabeth Press, and others in varying degrees, seem interested in publishing that acknowledged first rank of poets and fictioneers—and intend the books they produce to endure as remarkable contributions to the literature of the world. This is not to say that the editors of less aristocratic small presses—e. g., New Rivers Press, Gallimaufry, Pentagram Press, Alice James Books, and others, believe they are publishing inferior writing. Rather, they may feel there is more exciting serious writing appearing today than we have been led to believe. We do not have many Walt Whitmans and Ezra Pounds among us these days, but then we are not living in an age of giants. Or at least there are many excellent small press editors, I'll wager, who will argue that the giants are extremely rare and that the task of the contemporary editor is simply to discover the best works of his generation, be they major or minor.

A distinction between the little magazine and the small press might be drawn in terms of the immediacy and topical characteristics of the magazine in contrast to the artifactual nature of the published book. Magazines can have an impact and topicality which bind them to a literary era, but if art is art it transcends those boundaries and endures. The best of the poems and stories in a little magazine will stand the weathering of time, although for a full sense of a particular poet or storyteller's range and vision we will need to see other work in other magazines or in full-length collections. Little magazines, by publishing single poems or stories, are perhaps issuing interim reports on the state of a writer's development or the progress of a particular extended piece of work. Yet more and more editors are turning to the small chapbook as a particularly useful way to present a writer's ongoing work, thus dissipating the immediacy of the magazine's "report." Some editors have gone so far as to issue boxed numbers of their magazines, the boxes containing various pamphlets and chapbooks by individual writers. Kirby Congdon's *Magazine* 5 (New York City, 1972) and issue number 7/8 of *Some* (New York City,

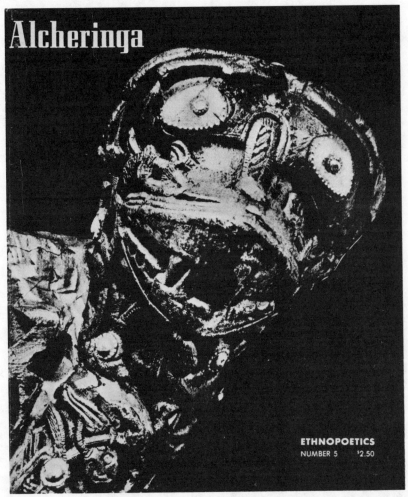

ETHNOPOETICS
NUMBER 5 $2.50

Alcheringa, *No. 5, Spring-Summer 1973, edited by Jerome Rothenberg and Dennis Tedlock (courtesy Anania Community Trust).*

Above: Some, *No. 3, Winter 1973, edited by Larry Zirlin, Alan Ziegler, Harry Greenberg. Opposite, left to right:* The Small Press Review, *Vol. 1, No. 4, December 1968, edited by Len Fulton;* The Sensuous President, *manufactured as a free supplement to* Fragments, The Little Magazine *(Vol. 6), and* The Minnesota Review *(New Rivers Press 3, Fall 1972);* December, *Vol. 10, No. 1, 1968, edited by Curt Johnson;* Field, *No. 12, Spring 1975, edited by Stuart Friebert and David Young (courtesy J&FAnania).*

VOL 1 NO 4   DEC 1968 $1.00

The
small press review

COSMEP
68

—SELLING TO LIBRARIES
—NEW ENGLAND SMALL MAGS, PRESSES
—30 PAGES MAG·PRESS·BOOK LISTINGS
—REVIEWS

The
Sensuous
President
by "K"

december

$2.00   a magazine of the
          arts and opinion

FIELD

L'amour de Pierrot

1976) are excellent examples of the melding of small press/little magazine concerns. We have the sense that these two boxed issues are balancing the magazine tradition and the press tradition, to initiate a new style of publishing. We have also seen, sometimes, that small presses offer subscriptions to broadside or chapbook series; the publisher may desire the extended contact with readers which magazine subscriptions provide. Some editors who have both a magazine and a press, such as John Judson of *Northeast/ Juniper Books* (La Crosse, Wisconsin), offer one subscription to the magazine alone and another subscription to the magazine plus the chapbook series. Others, such as the Alternative Press (Grindstone City, Michigan), provide copies of all work produced in the course of a year for a flat subscription fee. Some libraries have begun to deal with small presses the way they deal with little magazines, by providing standing orders for all of a press's work. This arrangement helps insure that the libraries will receive titles they wish to have without the risk that a book will be published and go out of print unnoticed. In such cases, each small-press book or chapbook retains its "artifactual" nature, yet the subscriber/reader perceives the series of which it is a part as an ongoing enterprise, similar to the little magazine. The combination of the chapbook and the subscription to a press's work lends small book publishers' lists some of the immediacy more often associated with little magazines. The pamphlet or small chapbook can also, of course, be used to present topical material. Literary history provides innumerable examples of this use of pamphlets, though the survival rate of such works, as art, is relatively low. Whatever distinctions are drawn between the magazine and the press begin to break down as magazine editors strive to create a sense of wholeness within each issue of a magazine and small press editors begin using little publications to provide ongoing reports on the state of literature.

Some magazines never develop an accompanying small press; the editors of such a magazine may not be responsible for the publication financially. University literary quarterlies, for instance, very seldom if ever set up small presses, although they may publish special issues devoted to individual authors. The vision behind such institutionally sponsored magazines may very well be that of a particular editor, and the publication may be clearly stamped with his concerns, but the economics of literary publishing do not permit that editor to extend his goals beyond prescribed limits. Those magazines from which we see small presses emerging are more frequently the work of an editor or group of editors who find themselves responsible for *all* aspects of the magazine's existence. Often the magazine and the newly founded press are serving a clearly defined literary community, the press being viewed as an added service to the member-writers. There are, certainly, magazines which are clearly intended to remain magazines, never evolving into a small press. Other magazines are at the service of what editors see as their most urgent needs; if a different kind of publishing seems appropriate to changing circumstances, the magazine operation can be adapted accordingly. Some small presses are clearly small presses only, designed to serve either a specific literary group or the more intangible interests of "literature." Theoretically at least, the editor of an existing small press can establish a magazine to facilitate communication with a larger literary community or to deal with certain situations he may face, but in my experience such an occurrence is rare. After some research, I remain unable to name a significant magazine which emerged from an established small press. A great deal more research needs to be done in this area, but as a general rule it appears that a little magazine and a literary press are founded simultaneously, or else the press emerges from the magazine operation.

Partly because factual material about the operation of small literary presses remains ungathered, a full examination of the role of small publishers cannot be made. We do not yet know enough to understand how publishing influences literature and how literary circumstances require the evolution of different kinds of publishing. Partly because researchers interested in literary publishing have studied the little magazine isolated from its small press counterpart, we have very little data on the interrelations between the two enterprises. The preliminary conjectures offered here are made in order to identify, and at least argue about, some of the correspondences binding the magazine and the press together as related and interdependent endeavors. Students of publishing now need to verify or disprove these tentative conclusions by collecting and analyzing sufficient information to allow the full examination which will provide insights into the dynamics of literature in America today.

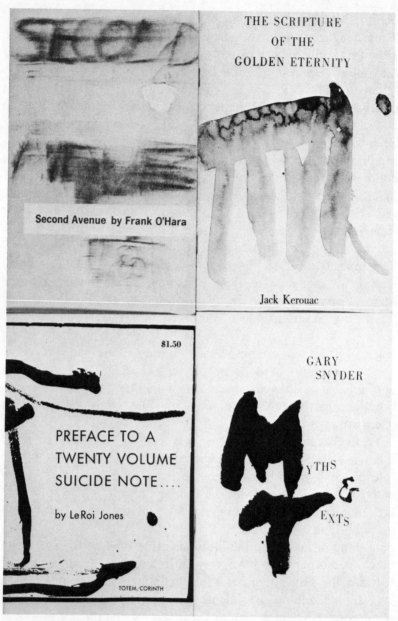

Four Corinth titles: Frank O'Hara's Second Avenue *(1960); Jack Kerouac's* The *Scripture of the Golden Eternity (1960); LeRoi Jones'* Preface to a Twenty Volume Suicide Note *(1961); and Gary Snyder's* Myths & Texts *(1960) (courtesy Ted Wilentz).*

BEHIND THE WRITER, AHEAD OF THE READER: A SHORT HISTORY OF CORINTH BOOKS
Ted Wilentz & Bill Zavatsky

Ted Wilentz has owned two bookstores. As a young man he and some friends started the first one in the Bronx after he discovered he could not get along with his father in the fur business. The second, the Eighth Street Book Shop, he opened with his brother Eli shortly after World War II ended. "The war changed everything," Mr. Wilentz writes. "I spent almost five years in the army, entering as a private and leaving as a captain. The army is a hard master, but I willingly served in the fight against a modern barbarism. In those years, the shock of realizing, emotionally as well as intellectually, that progress is not inevitable, that the Day of the Beast is always imminent, led me to a reexamination of my thoughts and beliefs, and affected my social, moral, and literary attitudes."

Soon after its opening, the Eighth Street Book Shop became a literary center, a gathering place for a variety of writers and poets. "Dylan Thomas was visiting America, his sonorous tones adding to his romantic image. Allen Ginsberg's voice began to be heard in the land. The New York School, the Black Mountain group, the Beats were emerging. Little mags and small presses came alive with a vitality and with new visions sometimes startling and shocking."

By the time Corinth Books was founded in 1959, Mr. Wilentz had become involved "personally, emotionally, and, to a degree, ideologically" with what Donald Allen would later call the New American Poetry *and the* New American Writing, *which included "a great range of social thought, mostly implicit, ranging from the philosophical anarchism of the Beats to what seems Art for Art's sake. . . . The wide variety of the books Corinth did indicates that*

595

*our editorial policies did not stem from a statement of principles.
I like to think that the overall list—the fiction, nonfiction, and
poetry—reflects our personal tastes and beliefs, and that Corinth
may be counted among the voices that sing 'the simple separate
person, yet utter the word Democratic, the word En-Masse.' "*

*In addition to being co-editor and co-publisher of Corinth
Books, Mr. Wilentz is a founding editor of the annual* Pushcart
Prize: Best of the Small Presses; *a member of the Literature Ad-
visory Panel of the National Endowment for the Arts; an associate
fellow of Silliman College, Yale University; and a member of
American MENSA.*

Bill Zavatsky has published a volume of poetry, Theories of
Rain and Other Poems *(1975), as well as two books with Ron Padgett:* The Poems of A. O. Barnabooth, *a translation of the work
by Valéry Larbaud (1977), and* The Whole Word Catalogue 2, *an
educational text (1977). He edits* Sun, *a little magazine, and publishes books from a press also called Sun. Mr. Zavatsky has taught
writing courses at the University of Texas, Austin.*

I've been co-editor and co-publisher of Corinth Books for seventeen years. Prosaic as this sounds, small press publishing is still
full of excitement for me. The same excitement I felt when I
read *The Little Review, Hound and Horn, transition,* and the
writers like Hemingway, Stein, Laura Riding, and the many
others who published their work in those pages. They filled my
memory as I became personally involved with the writers of the
fifties, sixties, and seventies whose works I published.

My brother Eli and I started Corinth Books in 1959. The
press grew out of our success with the Eighth Street Book Shop
in New York's Greenwich Village. The store had gradually become
a center for many writers of the fifties. Both of us were interested
in publishing, so we jumped in. For a while we thought we might
make Corinth into a full-fledged business, but that fantasy dwin-
dled as time went on. Our first publication was a book about
Greenwich Village which we commissioned Hal Bowser to write
—a fifty-cent guidebook that included photographs, a walking
map, and an essay by William Barrett. *The New Guide to Greenwich Village* was done with all the sophistication of Villagers.

My brother was always an art and architecture enthusiast, and made a perfect editor.

We knew a good many of the new writers during the fifties. I'm around Yale University now, where you often can't tell a student from a professor. But at that time even the clothing of these young people was disturbingly distinctive—and their beards! One of the factors that drew them into our bookshop was that we had empathy and respect for them when they weren't being well treated. And they appreciated it.

By this time I had practically stopped reading poetry. But these new poets brought an irresistible excitement with them. They were speaking for their time. They were where the action was. In their work they dealt with issues, though their poetry wasn't directly political—nothing like the proletarian poets of the thirties. But what they were saying in the fifties represented a social viewpoint altogether different from an accepted one. Theirs was a sensibility coming to grips with life as it had to be faced and lived after World War II.

In 1947, my brother and I bought a small Womrath's bookstore on MacDougal Street in the Village. It had the usual lending library, best-sellers, stationery, greeting cards, and so forth. We gradually threw out everything and changed the nature of the books. As I've said, both Eli and I had a feeling for the Village, a respect for writers and for the new. Once somebody tried to put me down by saying that I was a writer *manqué*. I knew that all the time. He wasn't putting me down. So in a very real sense my involvement with the writers came out of the fact that I've always believed writing is the highest form of art. The bookstore kept us close to the writers, and I think it's important to remember that most of the early American booksellers were also printers and publishers. And the number of writers who have worked in bookstores, owned them, and been involved in publishing is legion.

These new writers, then, began appearing sometime in the early fifties. They would come in the shop, often to leave their books—mostly on consignment because we usually couldn't sell them. I remember one guy who kept coming around and leaving five copies of his book, ten copies of his book. Every time he'd come in, we'd check on his last consignment—and it was always sold out. He had told us that the author of the book was a friend of his, but finally I faced him and asked, "Tell me, are you Gregory Corso?" "Well, well yes," he said, "but I felt embarrassed to be selling my own book." Which could only have been his first one, *The Vestal Lady of Brattle* (1955).

I think I met Ginsberg even earlier, but I can't recall exactly. Allen was a tremendous figure. Aside from the importance of *Howl* and his other writings, he has always been a catalyst. I remember in later years speaking to Lawrence Ferlinghetti and talking about what had been going on in San Francisco in the early Beat days. He said, "Well, everybody was writing and things were happening—of course. But it wasn't until Allen came that it *really happened*." Many years afterward I heard that same thing said again when I was in Berkeley with Al Young, whose book *Dancing* Joan and I published in 1969. We went to a nightclub to meet Ishmael Reed, who, as it happened, had told me about Al Young in New York. Every few minutes someone would rush up to the table to say hello: this one was a writer, that one did this or that. I said to Al, "Wow, what a lot of action!" And he replied, "Well, it didn't happen till Ishmael came." Ginsberg spread a great sense of brotherhood throughout the scene. And affection. During the anti–Vietnam war movement a peace demonstration was scheduled in Berkeley, and the Hell's Angels were going to break it up. Ginsberg went to see them and cooled them down. Allen has been a focal point for years, with a royal touch that I've seen bring solace and calm to many people.

There were many now-important writers whom I had the pleasure of working with and getting to know. LeRoi Jones, for instance, who today prefers to be known as Imamu Amiri Baraka. We began publishing books together in 1960. I met Roi when Hettie Jones, his first wife, worked as my secretary for a time. He was another of the young writers on the scene. But more about our association later.

During this period there was also tremendous activity in all the arts. The Living Theater, first uptown on New York's intellectual West Side and then in the Village on 14th Street, played a crucial role in our lives with its productions of plays like William Carlos Williams' *Many Loves* and Jack Gelber's *The Connection*. A number of important poetry readings were held on that stage.

598

In art, the New York School was emerging. We went to the Cedar Bar and numerous other watering places, such as the San Remo, which had displaced Minetta's by the early sixties. Then we went down to Louie's near the Circle in the Square, and of course the White Horse Bar, which Dylan Thomas made famous. But finally it was the Cedar. I first went there around 1951 or 1952 with Holly Beye, a poet and playwright who worked for me and who was married to the painter David Ruff. She was meeting David and other members of a workshop run by Stanley William Hayter near the Cedar Bar. You could sit in the back of the bar and have a ten-cent beer and nobody would disturb you. The owners were friendly and nice enough to let the artists alone. The Cedar emerged as a place where you could always go to meet people. Not only people you knew, but the friends your friends knew at other tables.

Naturally, no one had any money then. In fact I still recall the time when Ginsberg came to me and asked if I would lend him some money to bring Philip Whalen and Mike McClure to New York City for a reading. Ginsberg guaranteed the money, paid me back, and brought the poets to my house. I haven't met Gary Snyder more than ten times, but we share feelings of friendship—partly because Corinth published his *Myths and Texts,* but also because he was part of the circle. Robert Creeley was in Mallorca, and of course there was Olson in Gloucester. Jonathan Williams, at some point, used to pack books for us at the shop. His first work was printed by the same David Ruff I met at the Cedar Bar. These circles of writers and artists never stopped intersecting!

Our first co-publisher was Jargon, which was Jonathan Williams. Even as a young man, Jonathan had an extraordinary sense for new people of consequence, an amazing foresight I've come to treasure. For me, new writing is like a foreign language that only a few people can read until finally it becomes a daily language. Jonathan was one of the decoders, and his genius for recognizing first-class writing is reflected in Jargon's list—Olson, Creeley, Oppenheimer, Sorrentino, and writers like Mina Loy, Lorine Niedecker, and Louis Zukofsky.

We did four books with Jonathan, and published them under the Jargon/Corinth imprint. One was *1450–1950* by Bob Brown, who lived near me in the Village and who was then making his living selling cookbooks. His death, shortly before the publication of the book, saddened us all. That book had originally been published in 1929 by the Crosbys' Black Sun Press. Louis Zukofsky's *A Test of Poetry* was another reissue we did with Jonathan. Then we co-published *A Form of Women* by Robert Creeley. I didn't meet Creeley until after he had left Mallorca. When I first saw him he was reading at the YM-YWHA in New York City. He was up on the platform wearing that black eyepatch, and you could feel the tension pouring out of him, the same tension that characterized his poetry of that period. We kept *A Form of Women* in print until Scribner's was ready to publish Bob.

Then we published the first three books of *The Maximus Poems,* that great work of Charles Olson. Jonathan had published the first part three years before, when he was about nineteen. It was Roi Jones who introduced me to Olson in the flesh. At that time he looked like a German burgher—mustache, round face, a huge, solid person. Once on a visit to Gloucester we went looking for him in a poor section of town, perhaps a Portuguese fishermen's section. When we asked for Mr. Olson, the people said, "Oh yes, the big man!" When we published him he was living on very little, and did so knowingly, to continue his work. The irony is that later on all his papers were sold to the University of Connecticut for a large sum of money, which he never had the pleasure of enjoying during his career.

We didn't publish the rest of *Maximus*—not quite. We had the manuscript and had it set up in galleys, all ready to go. But we kept getting strange letters from Olson. (Anyone who knew him knows he would write letters that required a magnifying glass and an understanding of script to decipher, almost a scribble; and all kinds of additions covered the envelope.) The tenor of these letters was such that finally my brother and I threw up our hands and cried, *"What* does he *want? What* is *wrong?* What shall we do?" Olson kept writing to us saying, "Forget the money!" We finally wrote him a letter that said, "Dear Charles, we never said a word about the money! What *is* it?" Then after a time he went to Europe and the rumors began: this or that publishing house was going to bring out the book. Actually we could have stopped

Jonathan Williams, editor and publisher of Jargon Books. Photograph by Gerard Malanga.

publication. We had a contract, we had the galleys. But the book was ultimately published in England by Jonathan Cape. What was wrong with our printing, we found out partly from Olson and partly from others, was the spacing of the words on the page. To Charles this was extremely important. Here was a giant of a man with an epic view of the nation, and he wanted us to have a bigger page, more leading between lines, etc. He thought our standard-size page (which was slightly oversize but not really big) was too small. Some of the language he used in his letters to us was astounding: "This was no way to treat this poem!" But in his insistence on the point, Olson and many of the writers around him emphasized their sensitivity to, and their sense of, placement—the person particularized in place rather than lost in the abstract in an industrialized and dehumanizing society where the individual and the meaning of the earth are all too easily forgotten.

After we had published the Bob Brown and Creeley books with Jargon, and before *Maximus* came out, Fred McDarrah brought us a marvelous collection of his photographs and a pile of the new poetry. (Fred served as unofficial photographer of the avant-garde, would make *all* the scenes. Bumping into him anywhere meant you were at the event of the day!) Eli edited the material into an anthology. Some of the poets included weren't as good as others, but taken as a whole *The Beat Scene* (1960) presented a spectrum of what the young Village poets were up to at that time, and the general level of the work was very high. With good reason, the anthology has been called the family album of that generation.

Eli and I would work closely on the manuscripts, but he did more of the editing on the Greenwich Village guide and *The Beat Scene* than I did, and was mostly responsible for the layout and design. The wonderful thing was that, regardless of who did the lion's share, we were always in agreement.

In that same year, 1960, Corinth took three different directions. The first was its American Experience Series, a series of reprints based primarily on first-person narratives. This was fundamentally Eli's project, and it included classics such as Lewis Henry Morgan's *League of the Iroquois* and Owen Chase's *Shipwreck of the Whaleship Essex*, which figured so importantly in the making of *Moby-Dick*. We used Henry Bamford Parkes, the great

602

The Beat Scene *(1960), a Corinth Book edited by Elias Wilentz, with*
photographs by Fred McDarrah (courtesy Ted Wilentz).

historian at New York University, as a consultant. Once he knew what we wanted to do (and he liked the idea of the series), he supplied various ideas which we either accepted or rejected. As is usual with small presses, we didn't sell many of the twenty-one titles we republished in this series.

The second direction Corinth took was in the field of social ideas. In 1964 we brought out a paperback edition of a book written by Moses Richin and published by Harvard in 1962, *The Promised City: New York's Jews, 1870–1914*. (It's now a Harper paperback.) And we did a book that Dan Wakefield had written on the Puerto Ricans, originally published by Houghton Mifflin. We obtained the paperback rights and sold more copies than the hardcover edition. *Island in the City* is, I think, one of the best books on Puerto Ricans coming to New York, though it is unfortunately out of print. We also did a book that I'm still proud of—in 1962, before the civil rights movement had really gotten off the ground. We felt that writing about blacks was being done by white people, and that we should publish a book in which the young blacks would speak out. With the help of Dan Wakefield and others we found several writers, among them two young men— Glenford E. Mitchell and William H. Peace III—who had been involved in acts of civil disobedience. They commissioned articles on different phases of the movement from various young blacks. Unfortunately some of them weren't professional writers and never came through with the articles. Some of the pieces we did receive had to be rewritten. By the time we finally got the book together and published it, there was already a flurry of books of this type. Ours was called *The Angry Black South: Southern Negroes Tell Their Own Story*.

But the direction that most appealed to me, meant most to me, and I think we did the most with—in an original sense—was that of literature. We obviously hadn't caused the changes that were going on in writing, but as a bookseller I always wanted to be behind the writer and ahead of the reader. The publisher isn't the artist, but I've felt exhilarated by the fact that our publishing has turned out to be extremely important. A lot of the work we published we knew was a first book and that the writer might not develop as a talent. And if much of what we published turned out to become "Postwar American Poetry," part of the reason for that

604

were our co-publication ventures with Jonathan Williams and with LeRoi Jones, both of whom, in their different ways, were great editors.

One day Ginsberg came to me and said, "Y'know, you're publishing now, and here's Roi with his Totem Books. He hasn't got any money." (It cost a hundred dollars then to put out a book, but Roi had to pass the hat to pay the bill.) "Why don't you get together with Roi? Maybe you could publish together," Allen said. So I spoke to Roi, and he thought it was a good idea. I liked him very much and we got along very well. He had already published four books or so as Totem, including Olson's *Projective Verse.*

We got rolling in 1960 with four Totem/Corinth titles: *The Scripture of the Golden Eternity* by Jack Kerouac, *Myths and Texts* by Gary Snyder, *Second Avenue* by Frank O'Hara, and *Like I Say* by Philip Whalen. It cost us about $300 to produce each of these chapbooks. There was a royalty schedule. Our agreement with Roi was that he would submit manuscripts to us, and we were to say yes or no. If we said yes, we'd publish them. The heart of our editorial contribution was this judgment. Selection was up to Roi and he worked directly with the poets. We took the first ten selections he gave us.

At the same time, Eli and I were also originating projects. We had a strong feeling that Diane di Prima could write fine prose as well as poetry. (In my opinion Diane is probably the only woman writer who could be called Beat; her attitudes, her language, her whole approach was Beat.) She found writing prose very tough going, but finally came through with *Dinners and Nightmares* (1961), a book that catches the period with a hard, concise brilliance unlike any other writing from that time that I have seen. In 1973 we reissued the book with material that had been left out of the original edition.

In 1960, besides beginning our association with Totem and LeRoi Jones, we bought the rights to a delightful collection, *Irish Street Ballads.* One of our regular customers at the Eighth Street, Frank O'Connor, that "lovely" man and fine writer, wrote an introduction to it for a modest fee, being more interested in the material than in the money.

Our venture was filled with overlappings and intertwinings. For example, Jonathan Williams had published Joel Oppenheimer's first book; then LeRoi Jones later brought us *The Love Bit* (1962). Jonathan had also published *Maximus,* and Roi himself was very affected by Olson's poetics. When I first met Olson he was coming to New York and staying at Roi's. In fact, they came to me looking for a bed for Olson, and I had none big enough to fit him! We made do, though.

Another Corinth Book that happened by serendipitous chance was *Successful Love* (1961), the last collection of stories that Delmore Schwartz would publish in his lifetime. Delmore and I would often meet over breakfast, and at some point he mentioned to me that Doubleday had turned down his second volume of short stories. (The first was the remarkable *The World Is a Wedding,* published by New Directions in 1948.) I suggested to Delmore that we publish it—and we did.

In retrospect, David Ossman's *The Sullen Art,* a collection of short interviews which we published in 1963, seems to represent a summation of the period. David was doing radio interviews with poets, and at that period there were few places where one could find an expression of the ideas behind the poems of the time. Today, when Ginsberg is a kind of culture hero, it's hard to believe the scorn and ridicule that were heaped upon the new writers. Truman Capote, for example, stated that Kerouac wasn't a writer but a typist. Even though there are many different styles of poetry discussed in *The Sullen Art,* Allen's feeling of brotherhood, especially among these "alienated" writers, permeated the book.

We said no to the eleventh book that Roi gave us. It wasn't that the book was bad (nothing that Roi picked could have been bad); we just weren't excited by it. This came after we had published ten Totem/Corinth books, including collections by Ginsberg, LeRoi Jones himself, *Four Young Lady Poets* (which featured Carol Bergé, Barbara Moraff, Rochelle Owens, and Diane Wakoski), Ed Dorn, and Gilbert Sorrentino. We also published a collection of short stories that Roi edited, *The Moderns* (1963), which was strictly a Corinth Book. After 1964 Roi began to drift away from the scene and grew more and more involved with the black movement. I feel very strongly that one of his great contributions in that period was to really bring black writing onto a competitive level with writing done by whites. We all felt a great loss as he moved away. The better I knew Roi, the more I had

606

$3.50

The Moderns
edited with an introduction by LeRoi Jones

William Eastlake   Jack Kerouac
Robert Creeley   Paul Metcalf
John Rechy   William Burroughs
LeRoi Jones   Fielding Dawson
Douglas Woolf   Hubert Selby, Jr.
Michael Rumaker   Edward Dorn
Diane Di Prima   Russell Edson

The Moderns

THE SULLEN ART

Interviews by DAVID OSSMAN with modern American poets: Kenneth Rexroth, Paul Carroll, Paul Blackburn, Jerome Rothenberg, Robert Kelly, Robert Bly, John Logan, Gilbert Sorrentino, Robert Creeley, W. S. Merwin, Denise Levertov, LeRoi Jones, Edward Dorn, Allen Ginsberg

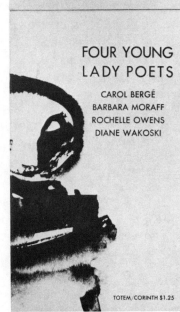

FOUR YOUNG LADY POETS

CAROL BERGÉ
BARBARA MORAFF
ROCHELLE OWENS
DIANE WAKOSKI

TOTEM/CORINTH $1.25

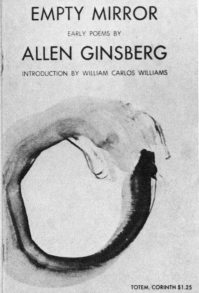

EMPTY MIRROR
EARLY POEMS BY
ALLEN GINSBERG
INTRODUCTION BY WILLIAM CARLOS WILLIAMS

TOTEM/CORINTH $1.25

Four Corinth titles: David Ossman's The Moderns *(1963);* The Sullen Art *(1963); LeRoi Jones' anthology* Four Young Lady Poets, *Carol Bergé, Barbara Moraff, Rochelle Owens, Diane Wakoski (1962) and* Allen Ginsberg's Empty Mirror *(1961); (courtesy Ted Wilentz).*

respected him and liked him personally. His new politics and racism shocked and saddened me.

My brother and I split up around 1968, and I took the press with me. We had never actually lost money (we must have sold 25,000 to 30,000 copies of LeRoi Jones's *Preface to a Twenty Volume Suicide Note*), but we never paid ourselves for our time and energy. My wife Joan and I directed the press after that. We were co-editors and co-publishers. Anything we published we must both agree on, and she has designed most of our subsequent titles.

After Joan and I took over the press, we were solely involved in the editing of the books. Often we found that there was material we didn't want to include in a volume, and our guide was always quality, never content. (I assure you that there's content in many of the books that I don't approve of!) We worked very hard with the authors—figuring out the order of the poems, challenging this poem or that, making suggestions. Naturally, as an editor/publisher, I feel more pride in the books that Joan and I edited ourselves, and part of the enjoyment in doing them has been in working with the younger writers we've published. As everyone knows, Donald Allen has busied himself for many years since the appearance of his seminal anthology, *The New American Poetry: 1945–1960,* with the definition of the "canon" of the Beat period,

Donald M. Allen, editor and publisher of Grey Fox Press and Four Seasons Foundation. Photograph by Gerard Malanga.

608

and I assume he will work on it until he's done all he can. The truth of the matter is that most editors get involved with a particular period, and it's very hard for them to get out of it. I once asked Don Allen why he didn't do a new anthology of the younger poets, and he said, "I can't keep up and I don't have the same feeling for them."

The first book Joan and I published was Barbara Guest's *The Blue Stairs,* in 1968. Barbara had also appeared in *The Beat Scene.* She's still one of our great friends, and an important part of doing the books is the friendships that develop. Not every writer is a likable man or woman, but certainly most of the people we've dealt with I would say awfully nice things about. Helen Frankenthaler, a friend of Barbara's, did a stunning cover for the book—one of our loveliest.

But by 1968 times had changed around the Village. A new group, referred to as the "second generation" of New York poets, had arrived: Ted Berrigan, Anne Waldman, Ron Padgett, Lewis Warsh, Peter Schjeldahl, and others. They had moved into the East Village. We published Peter Schjeldahl first, then Ted Berrigan, who doesn't like to be thought of as a second generation New York School poet. He actually spans the first generation, which includes such poets as Kenneth Koch, John Ashbery, James Schuyler, the late Frank O'Hara, and Barbara Guest, and the younger poets, and was born the same year (1934) as LeRoi Jones. In 1970 we were able to reprint John Ashbery's *Some Trees,* which had won the Yale Series of Younger Poets prize in 1957. At a couple of parties John mentioned to me that Yale was about to let the book go out of print. He didn't know what to do about it, and I assured him that Corinth would be happy to publish it. Eventually he called and we put out the book, minus the preface by W. H. Auden, which didn't seem to Joan and me to have much to do with anything. We asked Kenneth Koch to do a new introduction, but his schedule and ours didn't mesh.

We also published two books of translation. One I did with Eli—*Modern Poetry from Spain and Latin America,* edited and translated by Nan Braymer and Lillian Lowenfels (1964). It was a slim book, and included poets who were still unknown in the United States, even though Robert Bly was beating the drum of Spanish surrealism. But the book that really taught me about

609

translation was *I Am Listening to Istanbul* by Orhan Veli Kanik (1971). Of course, few of us knew anything about Turkish poetry, and I published the book after my good friend Erje Ayden—that mad Turk and author of *The Crazy Green of Second Avenue*—brought it to us in a translation by Talat Sait Halman. We looked at it and liked it immensely. Halman is a tremendously cultured man, but since he wasn't born here, his brilliant translation had a few rough spots. I learned what it meant to go to bed thinking about one word and how that word could be changed to catch the spirit of the original language.

One day we received a manuscript in the mail from a young woman named Brenda Herold, accompanied by the typical insufferable young person's letter. We wrote her back saying, "You're too good a poet to write a letter like that!" Although we weren't ready to publish her, we kept in touch. Our correspondence with her would fill a volume, for in it we worked on the development of a young writer. And we worked hard! Her book, *The St. Charles Gig,* came out in 1971. We had a similar experience with an earlier volume, *Julian the Magician,* a novel by Gwendolyn MacEwen that Eli and I published in 1963. The novel came to us "over the transom," and the book flopped, but I'm still pleased we published it. Gwendolyn is still writing, I believe, and at thirty-five is one of the better known writers in Canadian literary circles. (We never met her.) Some years later, Robert Duncan told me he had read the book and liked it very much.

It may have seemed to many of our readers that around 1969 we began publishing poets because they were black. We never did that. We published poets who were good, and in the late sixties the black poets were emerging. The trend began, naturally, with LeRoi Jones, and led to Tom Weatherly, Clarence Major, Al Young, and Jay Wright—four very different writers.

Joan and I became friendly with Clarence Major and his wife, and eventually he submitted a manuscript which we published as *Symptoms and Madness* in 1971. Strangely enough, when Ron Padgett started the *White Dove Review* in Tulsa at the age of fifteen or sixteen, one of the writers he published was Clarence Major. So in a roundabout way Clarence came to us as part of the second generation New York School.

I read some of Tom Weatherly's poems in a magazine, and learned that he was working as a cook at the Lion's Head, a Village literary hangout. Tom has a tremendous mind, and the vocabulary of his poems ranges from strictly black language to arcane nature words derived from plant names. I asked him for a manuscript, and we brought out *Maumau American Cantos* in 1970.

I asked Jay Wright for a manuscript, too. Tom Weatherly was working with me on an anthology of young black poets for Hill and Wang. In the course of editing *Natural Process,* Jay Wright's work turned up. Jay has been everything from a seminarian to a baseball player, and is very much involved in philosophy and anthropology. He's got a depth to him that is rare even for a writer.

For a time I was working at the Sierra Club, and one day Ishmael Reed came up to see me. Naturally we talked about writers. When I asked him who was new and good out west, he said, "There's this cat named Al Young." That's how *Dancing* (1969) came to us.

What unified our efforts at Corinth, in the midst of diverse schools whose poetry differed greatly, was the sense that all the writers whose work we became involved with were trying to write in a new language, with a new view and a new sense of America and of society. These writers joined together in sympathy and learned from each other.

Life is hard for anyone, and for an artist it is particularly hard. Simply to remain an artist creates so many problems—financial ones, especially. My dear friend, the late Cecil Hemley, summed it up in conversation this way: "Here you are at forty, a poet. If you're famous you wonder if it's temporary, and whether your poetry is really any good or not. If you're not famous, you wonder what you've been devoting your life to. If you're good, you'll never really know it." It makes for a difficult life, a life that by its very nature must be an extended act of faith. Someone once asked me to ask Delmore Schwartz why he wrote. I bumped into him at a party and blurted it out: "Delmore, someone asked me to ask you why you write!" "Ted," he answered, "I write because I have to write." And to me that was a perfect answer.

Corinth Books: A bibliography, 1959–1973

1959
The New Guide to Greenwich Village, Hal Bowser.
1450–1950, Bob Brown. (Jargon/Corinth)
A Form of Women, Robert Creeley. (Jargon/Corinth)

1960

The Beat Scene, edited by Elias Wilentz, photographs by Fred McDarrah.

The Maximus Poems, Charles Olson. (Jargon/Corinth)

Irish Street Ballads, collected and annotated by Colm O Lochlainn, introduction by Frank O'Connor.

The Scripture of the Golden Eternity, Jack Kerouac. (Totem/Corinth)

Second Avenue, Frank O'Hara. (Totem/Corinth)

Myths and Texts, Gary Snyder. (Totem/Corinth)

Like I Say, Philip Whalen. (Totem/Corinth)

1961

Empty Mirror, Allen Ginsberg. (Totem/Corinth)

Preface to a Twenty Volume Suicide Note, LeRoi Jones [Imamu Amiri Baraka]. (Totem/Corinth)

Dinners and Nightmares, Diane di Prima.

Successful Love and Other Stories, Delmore Schwartz.

The Hipsters, Ted Joans.

Island in the City: Puerto Ricans in New York, Dan Wakefield. (Paperback reprint of original Houghton Mifflin edition.)

The American Experience Series:

The Narrative of Colonel Ethan Allen

The Journal of John Woolman

The Life of Mrs. Mary Jemison, James E. Seaver

Brook Farm, Lindsay Swift

Four Voyages to the New World, Christopher Columbus

Journals of Major Robert Rogers

Harriet Tubman, the Moses of Her People, Sarah Bradford

Recollections of the Jersey Prison Ship, A. Greene

A New England Girlhood, Lucy Larcom

American Communities, William Alfred Hinds

1962

The Angry Black South: Southern Negroes Tell Their Own Story, edited by Glenford E. Mitchell and William H. Peace III.

The Love Bit, Joel Oppenheimer. (Totem/Corinth)

Four Young Lady Poets: Carol Bergé, Barbara Moraff, Rochelle Owens, Diane Wakoski, edited by LeRoi Jones. (Totem/Corinth)

The American Experience Series:

Intellectional Origins of American National Thought, edited by Wilson Ober Clough

League of the Iroquois, Lewis Henry Morgan

My Captivity Among the Sioux Indians, Fanny Kelly

Joutel's Journal of La Salle's Last Voyage

The Discovery, Settlement and Present State of Kentucke, John Filson

The Life and Remarkable Adventures of Israel R. Potter

Excursions, Henry David Thoreau

Father Henson's Story of His Own Life

1963

The Moderns: An Anthology of New Writing in America, edited with an introduction by LeRoi Jones.

Julian the Magician, Gwendolyn MacEwen.

612

After Appomattox: The Image of the South in Its Fiction, 1865–1900, edited with an introduction by Gene Baro.

The Sullen Art: Interviews with Modern American Poets, David Ossman.

Greenwich Village, text and photographs by Fred McDarrah, introduction by David Boroff.

The American Experience Series:

A Journal of the Pilgrims at Plymouth (Mourt's Relation), edited by D. B. Heath

Mutiny on Board the Whaleship Globe, William Lay and Cyrus M. Hussey

Shipwreck of the Whaleship Essex, Owen Chase, with Melville's Notes, edited by B. R. McElderry, Jr.

1964

Hands Up! Edward Dorn. (Totem/Corinth)

Black and White, Gilbert Sorrentino. (Totem/Corinth)

A Test of Poetry, Louis Zukofsky. (Jargon/Corinth)

New York, N.Y., Fred McDarrah.

The Promised City: New York's Jews, 1870–1914, Moses Richin. (Paperback reprint of original Harvard University Press edition.)

Modern Poetry from Spain and Latin America, edited and translated by Nan Braymer and Lillian Lowenfels.

Merz and More Merz, cartoons by Bob Merz.

1968

The Blue Stairs, Barbara Guest.

White Country, Peter Schjeldahl.

1969

Dancing, Al Young.

Many Happy Returns, Ted Berrigan.

1970

Giant Night, Anne Waldman.

Dreaming as One, Lewis Warsh.

Some Trees, John Ashbery. (Reprint, minus the Auden introduction, of the 1957 Yale Series of Younger Poets Prize book)

Emily Dickinson: Letters from the World, edited by Marguerite Harris.

Maumau American Cantos, Tom Weatherly.

1971

I Am Listening to Istanbul, Orhan Veli Kanik, translated from the Turkish by Talat Sait Halman.

The St. Charles Gig, Brenda Herold.

Symptoms and Madness, Clarence Major.

The Homecoming Singer, Jay Wright.

1973

Dinners and Nightmares, Diane di Prima, with a foreword by Robert Creeley. (Reprint, with added material, of the 1961 Corinth edition.)

ON PUSHCART PRESS
Bill Henderson

Bill Henderson is editor of the Pushcart Press and has recently published the 1978–1979 edition of The Pushcart Prize III: Best of the Small Presses. *Before establishing the Pushcart Press, Henderson worked at Doubleday (1972–1973) and Coward, McCann & Geohegan (1973–1975).*

Mr. Henderson's interest in self-publishing grew from a desire to encourage the small presses, and writers whose work might be discouraged by commercial publishing houses. In fact, three of the contributors to the first two editions of The Pushcart Prize— *Mary Gordon, Tim O'Brien, and John Irving—have all recently published successful novels.*

The author of The Galapagos Kid *(which he published in 1971 through his own Nautilus Press under the pseudonym of Luke Walton), Bill Henderson has guest-lectured on publishing at Harvard University, Sarah Lawrence University, and the University of Rochester. His work has appeared in* The Chicago Review, The New York Times Book Review, Publisher's Weekly, *and* Bookviews.

A publication party at the Gotham Book Mart, N. Y. C., September 28, 1976, for the first Pushcart Prize Anthology. Left to right: Barbara Damrosch, editor of Little Magazine; *John Ashbery; Bill Henderson (courtesy Bill Henderson).*

My first small press collapsed with the publication of my first novel—a funny book called *The Galapagos Kid*.

I had spent the better part of a decade in stoic devotion to every word of *The Galapagos Kid*. I thought such hard work had to pay off with fame, fortune, immortality, and a New York publisher's cocktail party where I would get heroically drunk and be propositioned by many women. That's how it went for Dylan Thomas, and he was very big in my youth. That's the way it was supposed to go in the very order of the universe—decent, diligent work paid off.

Not so.

At the end of a decade of writing, I entered my novel in the Harper and Row Prize Novel Contest for 1968. I waited months for a reply and steeled myself for disappointment by letting my hair grow long. If I was rejected, at least I'd *look* like a writer. One day, very hairy, I phoned the editor and was told that the manuscript had made it through all the first readers and was on his desk. He promised he would read it over the weekend.

I celebrated by getting a haircut. I was indeed a writer, and I didn't need my hair to prove it.

That was the last time I celebrated an editor's opinion of the novel. The rejection slip arrived in a few days. "We all feel that the novel is better than the average unsolicited manuscript." I wrote the editor back and asked where I should send it next. He replied: "The question you raise in your letter is that ancient and sad question of who publishes serious fiction these days. I would suggest that you try Farrar, Straus and Giroux; Viking; Little Brown; Houghton Mifflin; and Knopf, more or less in that order and good luck with the book."

"Serious fiction"! Such recognition, coming from a house notable for literary publishing, encouraged me through the next two years of rejections.

Farrar, Straus and Giroux neglected to confirm receipt of the manuscript. When I telephoned them they mistook my query and mailed the manuscript back the next day, special delivery. Viking sent a rejection slip. Little Brown did the same, and when I called them to ask just why, the managing editor fished a card out of his files. "Your characters are too fantastic," he said.

"What did they mean—that fantasy was unpublishable! Don't they realize that we live in a fantastic world!" I raged at my wife before heading for the local bar and the next rejection-slip bender. Houghton Mifflin sent a slip and Knopf's editor said, "I think you will have to find someone who responds to your very special kind of humor."

And so it went. Somewhere during that time I acquired an agent, who encouraged me at first (champagne lunches at his home) and tried all the usual channels without a whimper of success, and returned the novel to me.

At that time, 1970, I knew of only one other possibility—the vanity publisher. But desperate as I was, I resolved to do *anything* before that final humiliation.

A bighearted, adventurous uncle saved my mind and my novel. He agreed to publish a few other books if I paid for all the expenses of my novel, donated the income to the company—which we named Nautilus—and ran the entire operation.

"Self-publishing" at the time was thought to be for losers only. I didn't want to prejudice the chances of Nautilus—or of my *Galapagos Kid*—by admitting that the company's editor in chief was publishing his own book. Besides, I reasoned it would be easier to raise a lot of hoopla for the novel as its editor than as its author. So I tagged the author as "Luke Walton," after a Horatio Alger character, and used my own name as editor. In the role of Henderson trumpeting for Walton I managed to get quite a few advance quotes. The late Max Wylie's is my favorite: "Jonathan Swift might wish he'd said it all."

Being compared with a literary immortal was a heady trip for a twenty-eight-year-old rejectee. I upped my pre-publication printing to 2,000 clothbound copies and borrowed $4,000 from my mother and brother for advertising in the *New York Times Book Review*, the *New York Review of Books*, and *Publishers Weekly*. I did a lot of legwork to wholesalers and bookstore chains, teaching myself how to publish as I went along. I discovered that publishing was easy—at least getting the book into stores, stocking wholesalers, making an advertising racket, and putting reviewers on notice that an important literary event was afoot. What was tough was getting people to buy such literature. The responses to my ads brought only a mimeographed appeal for free books from a Maine charity, plus two letters from buyers of publishers' overstocks. In all, I sold about 500 copies and figured my losses at $10,000 for a decade of unpaid labor.

Of course the money wasn't important, and even the poor sales were respectable enough for the serious, underground sort of author Luke Walton now imagined he was. What really mattered was that my Great American Novel was finally published. It had even been reviewed in the *New York Times Book Review* ("an existential fantasy that does not have a frame of reference"). My mind was saved. I was purged of booze, dejection, and rejection. There was indeed a possible third way between commercial publishing and vanity house hopelessness.

I thought I should tell other writers about that some day. Nobody should have to suffer what I had suffered at the dictates of commerce. But first, since I was deeply in debt—and Nautilus had folded—I turned to commerce. Doubleday, thinking I was the sort of hustling young fellow they needed, hired me as an associate editor. I spent most of my time there hunting for fine literature. I discovered that the company, with Park Avenue rents to pay, wasn't particularly interested in unsalable literary stuff, and also that there really wasn't that much fine material around. I turned instead to founding and coaching the corporate softball team—a job almost as satisfying as poking through the slush piles.

It occurred to me that perhaps the reason so little good work was arriving at houses like Doubleday was not only that most commercial firms didn't want to publish it, but also that so much junk was being issued with big-bucks sound and fury that authors had stopped writing good books. Perhaps many of them had succumbed to the despair I felt after years of rejection.

Writers had to be wised up, I thought. They should know that they didn't need commercial publishers of any sort. And they needed a book to tell them that.

In my flirtation with vanity people, I had noticed their ads mentioned that various famous people had "paid to have their books published" (implying by inference that they had gone to vanity presses)—people like Thomas Paine, Edgar Allan Poe, Walt Whitman, Upton Sinclair, James Joyce, Anais Nin, and others. Noontimes I visited the Fifth Avenue Public Library and investigated the biographies of these writers who allegedly paid vanity houses. Not one had used a vanity house. All of them had issued their books themselves. A whole literary tradition lay buried in the phony claims of vanity houses.

Gradually a title evolved: *The Publish-It-Yourself Handbook:*

Literary Tradition and How-to. I had the title but I didn't have the book.

I started by writing a chapter about Luke Walton's bittersweet experiences and then a chapter on all the do-it-yourself literary history I had discovered during my lunch hours, plus a how-to section on my own learn-as-you-go publishing education.

I had the beginning, middle, and end of the book, but I wasn't confident that anybody else would get excited about the idea of *The Publish-It-Yourself Handbook.* I tried it out on New York publishing firms, but received only dull stares. The editors didn't understand what writers would need such a book; weren't all the commercial publishers listed in *Literary Market Place?* Every good book would find a home, they remarked. I realized if this title ever got off the ground it would have to be without a commercial publisher. At best it would be boring to such a publisher; at worst it would be insulting.

I asked a few other do-it-yourself publishers to join me with contributions to the *Handbook* and said if nobody else would publish the book, I'd damn well do it myself. One of the first people I wrote to was Anais Nin, who had done all her own work during the 1940s when she was a commercial outcast. She wrote back, "I'm too busy, but this summer I may not be and I will let you know." I took that for a no and shelved the project to concentrate on the slush pile and coaching the softball team.

I don't think there would have been a *Publish-It-Yourself Handbook* without Anais Nin. One day in summer, completely unannounced and unexpected, without a request for payment of any kind, and without any knowledge of who I was or if I knew a thing about publishing a book, her chapter arrived with a letter saying, "Your book is certainly needed."

The rest was easy. I wrote to thank her and she wrote back suggesting several other people who might be interested in contributing a chapter about their own publishing. It seemed that everybody I contacted had a friend (who in turn had a friend) who had self-published or published somebody else's book. The editor at Knopf who had rejected my novel suggested a sailor, Patrick Royce, who had published his own how-to sailing books, and a tailor-poet, Clarence Poulin, in New Hampshire, who issued his own poetry and also instruction books on tailoring. Stewart

Brand gave me permission to reprint his afterword in his *Whole Earth Catalog* (a catalog how-to). Barbara Garson, author-publisher of *MacBird,* consented to an interview about her play-publishing—but only after I argued with her agent, who thought the whole project sounded anticommercial and might be bad for Garson's career with commercial publishers. I picked up a chapter from Leonard Woolf's autobiography about the start of Hogarth Press—first publishers of T. S. Eliot, E. M. Forster, and others—and one by Alan Swallow on the history of Swallow Press. Irena Kirshman wrote about making a fortune through publishing her own cookbooks. And the small-press movement—then just catching on in an important and visible way—was represented by Len Fulton, Dick Higgins, Richard Morris, Daisy Aldan, Rochelle Holt, Adele Aldridge, Ricardo Sanchez, Richard Kostelanetz, Larry Rottman, Jay Bail, Frank Earl Andrews, Al Dickens, and others. There was even a fellow pseudonymous author, "Oliver Lange," who then had a novel on the *Times* best-seller list and admitted that his favorite was one of which he had published twenty-five copies at his kitchen table. The commercial people were more enthusiastic than I had first expected. A literary agent, Alex Jackinson, contributed a chapter. Martin Baron, an ex-vanity editor, slammed vanity publishing. And *Esquire*'s Gordon Lish knocked out a humorous piece about why the whole idea of the book was ridiculous—something about having lunch with Gordon Lish at fine New York restaurants and how, if you self-published, you didn't get to do that. A veteran of several memorial lunches with Lish, I admit that missing a lunch with him is a real drawback to do-it-yourselfing.

When I knew what I had to do—publish the book with my wife's help from our studio apartment in Yonkers, New York (more famous for horse racing and runner-up only to Philadelphia in city jokes)—I told Doubleday what I was up to, and prepared to say goodbye to the corporation, to our mutual satisfaction. Several editors there supported the book with suggestions, and two gentlemen, Sam Vaughan and Ken McCormick, were particularly helpful. *Publishers Weekly* gave the book a four-page send-off with an excerpt from my history of do-it-yourself publishing. *PW* later reviewed the book so well that I went reeling off to the Italian Pavilion restaurant, half in irony, half-seriously, because

CITY LIGHTS
BOOKSELLERS & PUBLISHERS
261 COLUMBUS AVENUE
SAN FRANCISCO, CALIF. 94133

May 16 1977

Dear Henderson:

Have been reading PUSHCART for 1976, and I think
it's the best collection of small press publishing
I've ever seen. Particularly liked the William
Eastlake Sun, Jack Spicer's Footnote to the Berkeley
Renaissance, and the Joyce Carol Oat.

I am wondering if you always just considered City
Lights press to be too big to be in the little press
category? If there is anything on the enclosed list
you'd like to see for next year's book, please let
me know.

And could you put us on your review list?

Light & Heat to you,

*Above: a letter from Lawrence Ferlinghetti to Bill Henderson. Opposite:
the first Pushcart Prize Anthology, 1976-77 (courtesy Bill Henderson).*

The Pushcart Prize: Best of the Small Presses

Edited by Bill Henderson
with the Pushcart Prize founding editors

that was where publishers often dined and I suddenly knew I was a publisher. (*PW* had said my Pushcart Press was "delightfully named," but for that I give credit to George Plimpton and others. Their Project Pushcart down Fifth Avenue, to protest publishers' ineptitude in getting books around, inspired the naming of Pushcart Press six months later, in 1973.)

Having been stung once (I still had about 1,250 copies of *The Galapagos Kid* stored in closets and under the bed), I was determined to be cautious no matter what the prepublication fireworks might be. The first printing of the *Handbook* was a mere 1,000 copies—100 in cloth and 900 in paperback. I spent almost our entire savings on printing, but saved some for advertising. It turned out we didn't need to advertise. More than a hundred newspapers and magazines serenaded the book. (Many reviewers are frustrated writers, as are lots of editors—rejected by New York and bound to be sympathetic.) Orders piled up faster than we could reprint. One mention in the *New York Times Book Review* by Victor Navasky, a paragraph buried in a longer article, brought in 400 prepublication orders. To date the *Publish-It-Yourself Handbook* has sold 22,000 copies and continues to sell strongly. Pushcart Press is now on something approximating a financial footing, and I am able to publish full time from a studio apartment—grantless, typing my own letters, and hauling my own mailbags.

The bad news is that I suspect many authors, while quite ready to buy a book about how to publish their own stuff, are far too reluctant to buy the works of other authors.

In order to give some sort of recognition to the more outstanding authors encouraged by the *Handbook* and by today's small press movement, in 1975 I asked several distinguished editors to help me start an annual prize anthology: the Pushcart Prize series.

Again Anais Nin was one of the first to respond to Pushcart's appeal. So were Buckminster Fuller, Charles Newman, Daniel Halpern, Gordon Lish, H. L. Van Brunt, Harry Smith, Hugh Fox, Ishmael Reed, Joyce Carol Oates, Len Fulton, Leonard Randolph, Leslie Fiedler, Nona Balakian, Paul Bowles, Paul Engle, Ralph Ellison, Reynolds Price, Rhoda Schwartz, Richard Morris, Tom Montag, and William Phillips.

In the first *Pushcart Prize: Best of the Small Presses* (1976–

1977) and in *Pushcart Prize II* (1977–1978) we have promoted the short stories, poems, essays, and literary whatnots of more than 140 small press authors as they appeared in 100 presses. *Pushcart Prize III* is now on sale, and *Pushcart Prize IV* will be receiving nominations around the time this issue of *TriQuarterly* appears.

The *Pushcart Prize* series is, first of all, publication and recognition for small presses and their authors who have done outstanding work in the previous calendar year. In the introduction to the various volumes we make a point of selecting "a" best. Obviously some "best" is not found in each book. The Prize series is only an attempt—but an attempt that receives more than 3,500 nominations every year from small press editors. Even with the help of some sixty contributing editors, and a constant influx of new editors each year, the Prize can be thought of as inclusive only if it is seen as a continuity of many volumes.

The Pushcart Prize is also a cooperation between a small press and a commercial publisher, Avon Books. Pushcart alone couldn't hope to make good each year in getting wide market recognition for other small presses and authors. So we do the elegant cloth-bound volume, and Avon sends the paperback around—with particular thanks to Avon's Walter Meade and to Peter Mayer. Mayer, now head of Pocket Books, is a weekend small-press person from his Overlook Press in Woodstock, New York.

Finally, the Pushcart Prize is a promotional event, a celebration by hundreds of small presses that says we seek meaning and excellence and are willing to take chances with the new and with young authors—kids like Luke Walton, and others with a lot more talent.

In the five years of Pushcart, I have published only four books, including the paperback edition of *The Galapagos Kid* (created by stripping the cloth binding off my remainders and rebinding them in paper). I doubt if I would have done more even if money was available. For Pushcart, and for other small presses, there is only one secret, and that secret has nothing to do with money: publish what you care about.

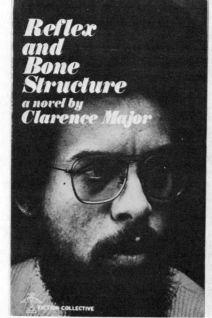

Four Fiction Collective titles.

WHO DO THEY THINK THEY ARE? A PERSONAL HISTORY OF THE FICTION COLLECTIVE
Jonathan Baumbach

It was Jonathan Baumbach's combative urge that led him, in the early 1970s, to make two of the most important gestures allowed American citizens: he defended himself in court and he became an entrepreneur. Mr. Baumbach acted as his own lawyer in small claims court over his demolished Mercedes, and he co-founded the Fiction Collective in order to right the wrongs created by the New York publishing "monopoly." In his essay, he explains some of the reasons why he and other writers thought an alternative press was needed, and how they went about getting support for distribution and publicity. George Braziller and the Fiction Collective have now published twenty-four volumes of fiction and two Statements: *anthologies of shorter fiction.*

Jonathan Baumbach has published one novel, A Man to Conjure With *(1965), with Random House; one with Harper and Row,* What Comes Next *(1968); and two novels with the Fiction Collective/George Braziller,* Reruns *and* Babble. *He is a professor of English at Brooklyn College.*

1

Reruns, my third and—at the time of its completion—best novel, was rejected thirty-two times over a period of three and a half years. It was circulated by Candida Donadio, a literary agent of the highest reputation, and so had every chance to find acceptance. (Only one other novel she had handled, she told me, had had more rejections than my book, and that was *Catch-22.*) During the years that *Reruns* was almost, if not quite, making connection—no small frustration in my life—I had difficulty getting into another novel. It is not an uncommon phenomenon, though by no means universal. My first two novels had been taken by major publishing houses on first and third tries, and had had their share of favorable attention. I had been spoiled in a modest way. The failure of *Reruns* to find a publisher was (and remains) a mystification to me.

I grudgingly began another novel. I began to talk with writers whose work I respected about alternative means of publishing fiction. We all knew that most publishing houses and their representatives were incapable of making real distinctions, but in the past we had been too self-interested to say it out loud. In addition to the old horror stories of how our books were not properly marketed, or how when the reviews came out there were no books in bookstores, were new ones about editors admiring manuscripts, keeping them on ice for five or six months, and then turning them back because the writer had a "poor track record" or because the book had limited sales potential. Sometimes books were accepted only to have that acceptance revoked at a higher level. The publication of fiction in America, with fewer and fewer exceptions (said the evidence), is a desperate transaction with the devils of greed. Something ought to be done, everyone said. On that point alone there was unanimity.

Here's where the story starts. A group of us, some eight or ten fiction writers mostly based in New York, began to meet regularly at my place or someone else's to explore the idea of a novelists' publishing cooperative. We were agreed on the necessity of taking the authority of publication into our own hands, although objections kept turning up. It was more expensive to publish books than we imagined, said one. It was difficult and time-consuming work, said another. Our business, after all, was writing books, and there was barely enough time to do that. We need capitalization to start, said K. A former theologian, K spoke eloquently on the accessibility of angels. Without a distribution arrangement, said L through the smoke of his cigar, we are dead before we begin.

We meditated on the death before life that was our present circumstance, persuaded ourselves against hope. Urgency kept us going, a sense of irony. It was hard to believe, having done nothing yet, that we had gotten as far as we had.

Between meetings, between exhilaration and despair, Peter Spielberg and I sought advice and information, went around together—each too diffident to go alone—talking to printers and distributors, representatives of foundations, anyone who knew

626

anything about the publication of books. We met with explicit encouragement for our idea and unspoken skepticism about its ever coming to pass. In the evenings, the two of us spent hours talking with each other on the phone (to the despair of our wives), sorting and analyzing information, reviewing alternatives, trading off anxieties, holding on as if the only thing that sustained our ephemeral project was each other's voice.

One afternoon I looked out the window to discover that someone had smashed into my parked car, a silver gray 1962 Mercedes for which I had a somewhat excessive affection. The owner of the car that had damaged mine (an owner of a bus company) was a slick operator, a fast-talking deadbeat, and led me a chase before I realized that he had no intention of making restitution. A new obsession governed me. I went to small claims court to present my case, studied law, interviewed witnesses.

My dreams confused the damaged Mercedes with my unpublished manuscript. In real life, I presumed to make distinctions. With each repair on the car, something new went wrong. The night after the day I won my hard-fought claim, the Mercedes was smashed into again, and this time the damage was irremediable. If it was an omen, I chose to overlook its implications.

At some point, Spielberg and I, both creative-writing faculty members at Brooklyn College, went with our ally, the dean of humanities, to see the provost and suggested the Fiction Collective —the name our group had selected from among other homely and unmemorable choices—as a forerunner of a Brooklyn College press. The provost was sympathetic to our idea, though vague about what he could do for us. Funds were out of the question. Space, he said, might be provided, some mailing privileges, and official connection with the MFA Program in Creative Writing (of which I was co-director). It would take time, eight months or more, to codify arrangements.

The talk at our meetings, now that we had a name to validate our existence, took a new turn. There had been a feeling in the room, inchoate and embarrassing to admit, that our collective authority lacked symbolic weight. The ritual of a publisher's acceptance satisfied us as our own improvised ritual—majority vote of writer-members—somehow didn't. (How important symbols were in our lives, we discovered.) It didn't matter that most editors couldn't distinguish original work from fashionable imitations or that most publishers could no longer afford to do any novel that was not "soon to be made into a major motion picture." A publisher's acceptance represented official sanction. For a sense of our worth, we were dependent, some of us, on an editor's approval. The more we denied the sway of establishment culture, the more we confessed it. The enemy, if there could have been said to be one, was as much within as without, whispering what was to become a familiar reproof: *Who do they think they are?*

R, one of our members in spirit only, wrote from California to say that he felt left out: "No one tells me what's going on." He and I had been exchanging letters almost daily. The time lag between the sending of a letter and its receipt (sometimes it took two days, sometimes a week) seemed to frustrate him. My four-year-old son, N, said he was sorry, but he hated the Fiction Collective.

Meanwhile H, who was in a subversive mood, suggested doing novels in throwaway editions.

Isn't the transience of commercial publishing the very thing we're resisting? said P.

Let's do something, said I, sometimes to myself, sometimes out loud, chronically impatient.

Finally, we decided unanimously—objections spoken under our breath—to do an anthology of new short fiction to be called *Statements,* and on the strength of that to apply for grants to do individual novels. The anthology, by dint of its breadth, would announce us as a collective.

A few weeks later, during one of our daily phone conversations, Spielberg said he was worried that by the time we got the anthology together—six months at least to do it right—the impetus we had to go ahead would have dissipated. We had already, in his opinion, been talking too long. After each of our meetings there seemed to be less enthusiasm for going ahead than before. (I had been thinking the same thing.)

After consulting with the others, we decided to postpone the anthology, which was after all an advertisement for the project and not the main event, and instead do the first series of novels for our opening publication. It seemed the only thing to do—the manuscripts had been ready to go into production for some time —if we were ever going to do anything.

The first series, the first three manuscripts that were accepted and ready to go, were *Twiddledum Twaddledum, Museum,* and *Reruns.* We broke the editing chores down in an informal way. Spielberg would edit *Reruns;* B. H. Friedman would do *Twiddledum;* I would do *Museum.* The only clear principle was to avoid reciprocity—that is, to avoid the potential conflict of interest in editing a book by the man who was editing yours.

At some time—so much was happening at once—Friedman asked a young designer friend to devise a uniform format for the series, something that would suggest a collaborative effort. One of his ideas, the one we decided on by majority vote, was to have the cover made up of a montage of faces, all in photographic negative except for the author of the particular book, who would be highlighted in positive. This format was used only for the first series (for the next three, each writer designed his own cover) though it has been picked up in diminution and used as an identifying symbol on the back cover of later books.

While editing *Museum,* while making last-minute revisions on *Reruns,* while getting together my case against the man whose car had smashed mine, while running the writing program at Brooklyn College, while teaching, while paying occasional attention to my family, I went around with Spielberg (and sometimes also with Mark Mirsky and Jerome Charyn) interviewing potential distributors.

The head of one distinguished publishing house, initially interested in the possibility of distributing our books, woke up one morning (so it was reported to us) furious at the idea. "Who do they think they are?" he said, or was reported to have said. "We publish all the good fiction that comes our way. There isn't any good fiction not getting published." It was an attitude we would encounter, directly and through oblique report, again and again.

To inspire such anger gave us a sense of weight and importance. We were—despite our expressed intentions not to (how mild and reasonable we thought ourselves)—challenging the way things were done. It made a lot of people uneasy with us. More than we knew, we were to discover; more than we meant.

An idealistic venture, we had been forever telling ourselves, ought to proceed idealistically. So we accepted the first publishing house to offer us distribution services. Two others were hanging fire at the time, procrastinating in their fashion. But we accepted

George Braziller's forthright offer without waiting to see what else was forthcoming. It occurred to us that the offer might be used as leverage to induce action elsewhere, but we were, for that moment at least, inured to temptation. George Braziller, Inc., announced our books in the centerfold of their catalogue.

The arrangement with Braziller, which continues to be mutually satisfying, was a turning point in our fortunes, a crucial piece of luck.

At the same time, before and after—the Collective obsessing us like a difficult love affair—Spielberg and I were checking out printers, comparing costs for various sizes of press run, evaluating reliability and convenience factors. A large printer in Michigan (with a sales office in New York City) gave us the lowest overall production bids, and we decided (a last-minute decision) to have the whole job done by them: typesetting, pages, binding, etc. We would use ten-point type for the first series, allowing forty-two lines (thirty-five is average) to a page—an austere choice. Austerity was one of the few vices we allowed ourselves. An attendant irony: the reviewer in *The New York Times Book Review* would reprove us for having an excess of blank space.

We moved from crisis to crisis, barely resolving one before the next was on us. X would call to say that I ought to know that V was bad-mouthing us. V, confronted (though sometimes confrontations were avoided), would insist that he had been misunderstood. Misunderstanding is the lot of most novelists. We write to perpetuate misunderstanding under the guise of making ourselves understood.

Despite the differences in the length of our novels, we agreed (Spielberg, Friedman, and I) to split costs and reimbursements three ways. All for one and one for all. There may have been private misgivings, jealousies (reviewers tended to make irrelevant comparisons among us), feelings of rivalry, but the sense of common bond—I still marvel at it—was transcendent.

When a writer has a novel come out, I've discovered (a discovery engendered by doing a book with the Collective), a variety of primitive feelings that have little to do with the book itself rise to the surface. A novel is sometimes (perhaps, at some level, always) an act of aggression toward the world at large. Unacceptable feelings toward parents, lovers, friends,

630

adversaries are revealed in, as it seems to the writer, transparent code. Such aggression engenders guilt. The childish association between wishes and deeds comes to the fore. On top of that (or on bottom) there's the murderous ambition of the writer to succeed, no small hostility in itself. A novel, in the melodrama of the heart, is like an assassination or a mass murder. I exist and am potent, says the book. Once I invade your life, you'll never be free of me. (When my first novel came out and I saw it in a bookstore with my picture on the back flap of the dust jacket, I had the sense that everyone in the city would recognize me, that my privacy would never again be my own.)

A publishing house mediates between the novelist and the rest of the world, serves (among other services, of course) as a symbolic protector. A publisher (or editor—I use the words interchangeably here) shares a writer's potency, takes it on himself by doing the writer's book, and at the same time shares responsibility for the murderous implication of that potency. A needful relationship on both sides, though traditionally rife with real and symbolic betrayals.

We were offering the writer—and I doubt that we understood it ourselves at the time—a new and less sanctifying relationship with his publisher. We were asking him to stand in for himself; to become, in the metaphoric sense I've been using all along, his own father.

2

Making ourselves known, getting press, was easier than we anticipated. We were news, a first (so said our publicity) of its kind in America. We believed what we read. The stories we read about ourselves were our own story returned to us through a variety of distorting mirrors.

We had books almost five months before publication date, and so we sent out paperbacks (we published in both cloth and paper simultaneously) in lieu of galleys as advance copies. It turned out that almost everyone who reviewed us—one of the mysteries of our experience—asked for books to be sent them again.

The first piece to appear about the Fiction Collective was in "Scenes" in *The Village Voice* (July 4, 1974). The representation was not notably inaccurate, was in fact sympathetic and fair; yet its publication embarrassed me. It was as if our private fantasies had been broadcast. How hard to see one's words, not always used as one meant them, stare back foolishly from the page. We would in time become inured to small and large inaccuracies in print, and to our own inability to answer interviewers' questions with sufficient public wit.

Next the reviews came in—the prepublication reviews—from *Publishers' Weekly* and Kirkus Services, sent to us in photocopy from Braziller. On the whole, we were treated respectfully, and in the Kirkus reviews with more than passing perception. It was just like, I remember thinking (another small irony), bringing out a book with a publisher.

On September 15, Ronald Sukenick published in the "Guest Word" of *The New York Times Book Review* something of a Fiction Collective manifesto, the closest thing to one. He had written it, given the kind of things we had been saying to each other about the publishing establishment in private, under the constraint of sweet reasonableness—though for reasons I had not foreseen the piece angered a number of people. Sukenick had presumed to say that the Collective was publishing (or would publish) quality innovative fiction—first-rate serious work—that was being "starved out" by the publishing industry. According to the establishment, such fiction was either not being written or was already being published in abundance. The word was that a good novel, no matter its specialty or difficulty, would ultimately find a publisher. It was impolitic, at the very least, to call conventional wisdom a liar.

The worst overall reviews the first series got were in *The New York Times;* for a long time they were the only bad reviews—though such is the influence of *The Times* that for many the book review's notice was all the news. The review itself represented an interesting phenomenon. The reviewer, a young novelist, had been messed over at one time by commercial publishing and had written a moving account of that unpleasantness in a magazine called *Intro*. His odd review of the Collective was informed by seemingly irrelevant outrage. The message of the review, behind the pretense of failed sympathy, was another version of *Who do they think they are?* No president of a publishing house could have been more patronizing in defense of the establishment. The former victim, in a not uncommon circumstance, had taken on the role of his victimizer.

Reviews of the Collective's books—and the obvious thing was to review them together—tended to set up invidious comparisons among them, playing them off against one another for rhetorical convenience. We had to remind ourselves that we were not in competition, as no writer really (outside the contrived arena of media) is competing with any other.

Most of the attention we received was generous. The Quality Paperback Club, just starting out, presented our first series as a Special Selection. *The New Republic* ran a long and highly favorable review of all three novels in the Fall Book Issue. Intelligent, affirmative pieces appeared in *Newsweek*, the *Los Angeles Times*, the *Village Voice*, the *Chicago Tribune Book World*, the *American Poetry Review*, the *St. Louis Post Dispatch*, among others. Something like forty-five periodicals throughout the country either covered the Fiction Collective as a news story or reviewed the books or both. The *Washington Post* listed *Reruns* as one of the notable books of the year. The first printing of all three novels was sold out before publication date. (Something of an illusion, since about 25 percent of the books placed in bookstores were later returned.)

Shortly after the first series of novels was published, we received a grant from the New York State Council for the Arts to hire a coordinator (a desperate need filled by the remarkable P. H.) and to publicize what we were doing. The following year, the NYSCA grant was renewed and the National Endowment for the Arts gave us funds to subsidize, in large part, eight new works of fiction.

There is material in the Collective experience for other fictions. I recently learned—it had been kept secret from me for reasons I've never understood—that someone (some unknown enemy) had been slashing copies of *Reruns* in a Greenwich Village bookstore. I wondered less who it was (though that too) than what it was I had written that had provoked the assault.

The rest is more of the same, or different, or less. By the time this appears we'll have twenty-four books in print (plus *Statements*, brought out by Braziller): a small shelf of the fiction of the seventies.

When the Fiction Collective started, I thought it would be

a way of pressuring commercial publishers into doing more innovative fiction, but I can see now that that's not going to happen. Publishers maintain they can't afford to publish fiction that sells fewer than eight thousand copies. (We need to sell about two thousand to break even.) Really good books will have large audiences, they tell us, pointing to Dickens and the latest middlebrow best-seller, and besides no one is buying serious fiction. The delusions necessary to keep a clear conscience make an ideology out of an unadmitted cynicism.

The Fiction Collective survives because it has to. Despite the unwieldiness of running a not-for-profit cooperative, despite continuing rumors of our demise, despite predictable problems with typesetters and printers and patrons and writers, we continue to bring out good-quality fiction in a reasonably presentable edition —a success (selling between 2,500 and 3,500 of each book) in terms that the publishing establishment is unable to appreciate and refuses to comprehend.

REPORT ON THE FICTION COLLECTIVE
Gene Lyons

"I write for fun and money," says Gene Lyons, who has supported himself entirely by literary and magazine writing since he left academe in 1976. He has been a columnist and fiction reviewer for The Nation *for the past two years, where he first discussed some of the Fiction Collective novels mentioned in his essay. He enjoys, he says, "giving the world a passing kick whenever I can."*

Mr. Lyons has taught at the universities of Massachusetts, Arkansas, and Texas, and has written for the following magazines: Shenandoah, Critique, The Progressive, The New York Review of Books, The New York Times Book Review, The Nation, Texas Monthly, Harper's, Moment, The Southwest Review, The New York Times Magazine, Intro, Bookletter, *and* Weekend *(Canada). He was a Ford Foundation fellow at the University of Virginia, and won a National Endowment for the Arts creative writing fellowship in 1976.*

> *The appetite for recognition, like the hunger for love and approval, is never satisfied. There isn't enough recognition in the world to satisfy even one cultivated appetite.*
> —George Garrett on writers and fame
>
> *Anything worth doing is worth doing badly.*
> —Anonymous

On the surface of things it is at least curious. Here we are devoting substantial chunks of the national treasure to something called higher education. Probably there are more literature professors proudly brandishing their "terminal" degrees than there were students of the subject forty or fifty years ago. Although the percentage of English majors is down somewhat from what it was when I was in college in the early 1960s, probably only Chicken

Little would make much of the fact. Back then, nobody worried much about making a living. Guns, butter, fellowships, and draft exemptions were all a part of the wartime economy. Teaching and other jobs were plentiful for college graduates, even in the liberal arts; within the American culture the prestige of imaginative literature was probably at an all-time high. To hear some people talk more recently, though, you might think it is now at an all-time low.

Part of the problem, we are told, is the publishing industry itself. Big business and the multinationals are taking over and flooding the bookstores with commercial sludge. Unless a novel has a Nazi assassination plot, a group grope, and two flying saucers somewhere in the first chapter, it doesn't stand a chance. Even so, according to Ronald Sukenick, a founding member of an organization called the Fiction Collective, "at the same time that publishing has been starving out serious fiction, the genre has experienced a resurgence of vitality and inventiveness." The group's answer has been to establish "not a publishing house, but a 'not-for-profit' cooperative conduit for quality fiction, the first of its kind in this country, in which writers make all business decisions and do all editorial and copy work."

Since its founding in 1974, the Fiction Collective has published more than twenty titles, for each of which the author has put up $3,000 or more of his or her own money to cover production expenses. Books are accepted or rejected by a vote of the membership, consisting of previously published writers. Copy-editing chores are shared.

Exactly what Sukenick meant by "not-for-profit" was unclear in the 1974 "Guest Word" column in the *New York Times Book Review* announcing the formation of the enterprise. The article also stipulated that each author "splits profits evenly with the Collective and gets 60 percent of its share of other rights." During its existence, the Fiction Collective has been variously supported by grants from the National Endowment for the Arts, a federal agency; the New York State Council on the Arts, a state agency; Brooklyn College, a public institution; and an organization called the Teachers and Writers Collaborative. Brooklyn College also helps out with office space, postage, and other small favors. That may be the key to the "not-for-profit" designation, since most public universities have regulations forbidding their faculty (which most members of the Collective are) from using their facilities for private gain. But that may be a quibble. More important to notice is what the group's members do not mean when they complain of being neglected and all but censored by something they call "The Establishment." They do not mean the governmental or educational establishments.

Almost everybody who knows and cares anything about serious fiction knows a few horror stories about agents, editors, and publishers. Having a book published, it seems, can often be an excruciating ordeal. Without promotion and distribution no book can succeed in attracting an audience in the short run; then corporate computers dictate remaindering or shredding long before word of mouth can create a demand for work that may have escaped early notoriety. There are also the tales about fine novels and short story collections which are never accepted at all by commercial houses. I confess to being of two minds about those. On the one hand, I have served as a reader in several literary competitions, including the National Endowment for the Arts Creative Writing Fellowships, and have never read—nor have I spoken to another judge who has read—unpublished fiction that we thought should be printed. I have read a great deal of "serious" fiction that I thought a waste of ink, and I have more than once directed friendly challenges to writers' groups to produce examples of such injustice, so I could promote them in a column on little magazines and small presses that I used to do for the *Nation*. I never got any takers. On the other hand, everyone knows that *Catch-22, From Here to Eternity,* and any number of other artistically respectable and commercially successful books were initially rejected by scores of publishers before finally being accepted, so perhaps it is best to temper one's skepticism.

In any case, most literary people are predisposed to accept arguments against both free enterprise culture and the vulgar herd —perhaps too easily. Almost everybody reading this magazine shares a common disdain for the average novel on the best-seller list. So when the Fiction Collective announces that it is selecting, printing, and distributing the "books of its peers on the basis of literary merit, free of the implicit commercial standards of the book business," and hopes by so doing "to open a path toward the maturity of the American novel," we ought to be interested. We ought also to be suspicious. For the Fiction Collective has done no such thing. Nor, from the evidence at hand, does it appear likely ever to be anything but what it is: a well-publicized, tax-supported vanity press. How and why the enterprise has failed, moreover, can tell us a good deal more about what is happening to the idea of serious fiction in our time than success could ever have done.

The fact that almost all of the Fiction Collective's organizers and authors are academics who teach creative writing is symptomatic. The institutionalization of creative writing as a permanent, degree-granting part of the academy has brought with it a permanent faculty. Since the M.F.A. degree is now considered sufficiently respectable so that one possessing it may gain tenure, many of that faculty are hothouse flowers like much of the rest of the faculty, i.e. persons who entered school in September of their fifth year and have never left it. Creative writing has become a specialty and, as such, is in a fair way to developing a kind of world view to protect itself from hostile scrutiny by outsiders. The components of that world view are not, thankfully, so widely shared by author-teachers as the following list may seem to imply, but I think it worthwhile, for the sake of clarity, to have them all in one place:

The need to "publish." Academic employment confers substantial benefits upon the young or would-be author, primary among them a decent salary and lots of free time. To keep getting them, he must compile a bibliography like any other assistant professor's. The result of the consequent frenzy is the same in literary magazines as it has been in scholarly journals for some time: an explosion of unread mediocrity. An article by Stephen Minot in the Spring 1977 issue of *North American Review* offers some exemplary statistics. In 1975 a magazine called *Field: Contemporary Poetry and Poetics* had 10,500 poems submitted to it by 1,875 authors. *Field* has 520 subscribers. Nor is that a freak. I have myself been present at a "writer's conference" and seen George Garrett wring a mass confession from a couple of hundred "poets" that *nobody in the room had purchased a single hardback volume of poems by one author for anything other than classroom use in a calendar year*. Minot reports, moreover, that in a considerable academic career he has never met a student or colleague who has either subscribed to a small magazine publishing poetry and fiction, or ever received one comment on work of his own published in such a magazine—not even when his college's library subscribed to and displayed the magazines printing his work. When it comes to fiction, there is no way that the centralized American literary marketplace can merchandise more than a fraction of what all those teachers and their students are writing, even if the work were of high quality generally, which most of it is not. An author can have a list of credits several pages long without being certain that anybody but editors has read his or her work. While the large number of outlets can in part be seen as an index of the health of our literary culture, for all their value in sustaining writers' hopes and accommodating their energies, too often they contribute to the every-man-an-artist-but-no-man-needs-to-read syndrome encouraged by large and promiscuous enrollment in creative writing courses.

Status frenzy. As a hierarchical bureaucracy, the American university rivals the Kremlin. Even if poets and fiction writers are employed everywhere in academe, they are only tenuously accepted there by the resident scholar-critics and are often regarded as presumptuous hacks. For some reason, the writing of unread criticism is considered an honorable pastime, while writing poems and stories is like mocking the gods of Parnassus. Literature professors themselves rarely trifle with contemporary work unless that happens to be their specialty. In many years of hanging around English departments I never heard the honorific adjective "brilliant" applied to a writer of fiction, although it is used quite freely otherwise. Mention to the average scholar that you have spent the weekend curled up reading Tom McGuane, Don DeLillo, or Lisa Alther and your reward will be a numb stare, as if you had confessed a passion for *Charlie's Angels* or professional wrestling, and a "From the reviews I shouldn't have thought . . ." If, that is, he has even read the reviews. Most Ph.D.s know and care less about contemporary fiction and poetry than your old man, and are fearful of being caught going ape over something posterity judges to be second-rate. Of course, most work is bound to be second-rate

639

by the standard the ages have set—as, at best, is most criticism. A writer who may begin with ambition, humility, and what Hemingway called a "good shit detector" often learns to suppress or conceal the two latter qualities in order to survive. Self-deprecation and modesty are the worst possible traits one can have in a generally humorless world where everybody has got the knives out. Hence organizations like the Fiction Collective and the Associated Writing Programs may be seen as essentially self-protective, like the Modern Language Association or the American Historical Association: job and prestige markets, the buddy system writ large, would-be determiners of professional tone, style, and prerogatives. You hire my protégé and I"ll publish your poems. I will read at your school's arts festival; you will serve on the staff of my place's summer writer's conference. The way of the world. Of course such groups are partly altruistic, and certainly necessary for maintaining the individual writer's dignity in an otherwise inimical climate, but that should not blind anybody to their primary function.

Academic values. Professors are interested in books that teach well, and that justify by their complexity the professorial mission. Not for nothing do Faulkner's *The Sound and the Fury* and *Absalom, Absalom!* sell hundreds of thousands of copies each year in campus bookstores, while the more accessible of his works are rarely required. That the average undergraduate at most American colleges and universities can scarcely grasp even the surface meaning of Joyce's works is precisely the reason so many of them are asked to read *A Portrait of the Artist as a Young Man* in their freshman composition classes. According to the English department, a novel is above all an encoded narrative, the understanding of which depends largely upon a system of hidden symbols requiring explication by a professional. Since the discovery of The Novel, there have been two main purposes for reading fiction in the academy: moral improvement and the demonstration of intellectual refinement. Such motives as pleasure and curiosity are rated quite low. Thus the most highly regarded sort of fiction is self-referential or "experimental" in nature. Anything traditional or too easily understood makes an academic fiction writer vulnerable to charges that he is a literal-minded simpleton or a shameless panderer to mass tastes. Once upon a time, part of fiction's appeal was in its bringing to a broad middle-class audience parts of the world—geographical, sociological, or what have you—remote from that audience's ordinary experience. But it is little recognized in the English department any more that a legitimate reason for reading a novel may very well be that one would like the vicarious experience of being a British policeman in Burma, sailing up the Congo in a flat-bottomed steamer, taking part in an abortive revolution in Shanghai, or smuggling cocaine from Colombia. For a writer to do actual "research" on a book, the way Harold Robbins and Irving Wallace do, is seen as a concession to the vulgarity of subject matter, which sophisticated novels no longer have.

Isolation. All these tendencies taken together only serve to magnify a fact of academic life so familiar that one who even brings it up is showing bad taste and can be accused of anti-intellectualism. One reason why classroom-oriented authors write the sort of claustrophobic, subjective, and willfully incomprehensible books they write is that they don't know enough about what goes on in the outside world to do anything else.

I wish that readers who think the foregoing a bit strong could have overheard a luncheon conversation I had a couple of years ago with several former colleagues just before departing on a magazine assignment to write about the Texas Prison Rodeo—an annual function put on in Huntsville by the Corrections Department, with volunteer inmates, in order to raise money for the system's recreation and education fund. None of those present had ever done more than drive across Texas, and none had ever been inside a prison or so much as seen a live rodeo. Nevertheless, neither had they, to a (wo)man, very much difficulty in converting the nouns *Texas, prison,* and *Rodeo* into abstract symbols, joining the symbols together and presenting me with the "meaning" of the experience I had not yet had in quite a neat package. Over the discussion hung the question that none knew me well enough at the time to ask: why would I give up tenure to do such tiresome, and tiring, things? As it was, the story took me almost two months and several drafts to write, and was perhaps not one of my best. Suffice it to say that the symbolic meanings offered by my well-intentioned academic friends were useful mainly in providing straw men to attack in the first draft, delaying for a time my getting anywhere near the real story. I should recommend as therapy to anybody suffering from hardening of the categories, or a sense of wonder atrophied by communing too long with adolescents and their mentors, a week or ten days interviewing inmates, guards, and wardens at their friendly neighborhood state pen. If that fails to cure the malady, it is probably terminal.

Now then. After all the above I must confess to never having been able to read any novel published by the Fiction Collective from beginning to end, although I have not tried all of them. As an example of why not I offer the following passage from *Althea,* by J. M. Alonso, who is also an editor of the *New Boston Review.* Generically speaking, the book is academic-sexual, the tale of "a wretched and paralyzed graduate student who never finished his thesis." The man's name is Muldoon, and as he is an Irish Catholic by birth and upbringing, naturally he despises and fears women, although like the man in the joke he can't seem to get along without them either. We come upon him in front of Harvard's Widener library, where he has been left by a fellow student who has gone inside to use the men's room. Ordinarily he avoids the place because he is afraid of meeting his faculty adviser.

So there I was, unknowingly positioned . . . in a most humiliating position before the Widener God, with my back turned, my face averted, practically cowering and reduced to cursing Ben (who, incidentally, was a pervert) for leaving me there.

Though not daring to look at the living Temple directly, I could feel the Widener God's life behind me with all its massive silent vibrations of obscene mental electricity. Sparking from books to minds and back again. All contained in the shadows of the stacks within the infinite creases, in the darkness deep beyond the cyclopic, glassed mouth behind me, with that low, dark, square mouth.

So, to protect myself, to undeify the living Temple, I tried thinking of the Widener God as just one more Harvard Corporation-owned factory, meshing stacks and stacks of minds with rows and rows of books. After all, professors author books which themselves author professors, and the Widener Factory God was in the business of producing both, which were sometimes barely distinguishable entities. Come to think of it, I knew many books that were far more perceptibly human, both in their affects and contents, than many a professor who had turned himself through his life's work into a walking thesis with hat and shoes.

642

Where to begin? With a "cyclopic" mouth, whatever that is, which in the same sentence is also "square"? With the barbarism of "author" used as a transitive verb not once but twice, the second time with "books" as an implied subject? With "undeify"? With "affects" used for "effects"? Or for something; the clause makes little sense either way. Alonso is equally apt at the coinage of adverbs. In other passages, *Althea* is a novel in which characters are "uncommentingly patient," and stand "homosapiently erect" while "looking Biblically up at the sky." Almost any selection of similar length from anywhere in the novel will yield such howlers. And this man is an editor! The daily newspaper, not to mention Harold and Irving, is better written.

Even more characteristic of the Fiction Collective's (pardon me) collective practices are the many paeans and asides Alonso's first-person narrator delivers to what he calls the "Unseen Mysterious Forces"—the UMFs for short. Essential to what the group calls "The New Fiction" is a sort of juvenile self-consciousness which demands that the author prate constantly about what he is doing, has done, or is about to do with his story—like a child learning to ride his bicycle with no hands. In Alonso's case the UMFs stand alternately for the wonders of the unconscious, for chance, and for coincidence. Every turn in *Althea*'s turgid plot must be explained as one or the other, or perhaps some mixture of all three.

A large part of the Fiction Collective's case against commercial publishers in fact rests upon its alleged hostility to, or incomprehension of, what is "new," or "innovative," or "experimental." In the organization's lexicon all of those words are good ones, as "traditional" and "commercial" are bad. Now, in America no one ever uses "new," as in the "new, improved lemon-scented Chevrolet Malibu," unless he is trying to sell us something. The word has virtually inescapable intimations of cant, never more than when it is being applied to ideas or attitudes, as in "new morality," "New South," or here in "The New Fiction." Were the Collectivists as a group not obsessed with irony about everything on earth except their own "voices" (another cant term), they might have spared us some of their claims to originality. In fact there is nothing

643

even remotely novel in the fictive practices of the group, and a good deal that is so tiresomely conventional in the contemporary fashion as to verge at times on self-parody. The best single place to verify the charge is in *Statements 2,* the Fiction Collective's most recent anthology. At the risk of seeming reductive, I should like to list, with representative examples from that book and a couple of others published by the group, the three main discoveries about prose fiction that the Collective and many of its academic allies seem to regard as daring:

1. Stories calling themselves "fiction" are not true. They are made up.

From Russell Banks's "By Way of an Introduction to the Novel, This or Any":

> *You know, it occurs to me that I really needn't bother with all this. Certainly not at this point. Perhaps later in the narrative such descriptions will be of significance, but here, now, I'm merely attempting to explain how I, Russell Banks, came to write a novel with a hero whose "real life" prototype is my friend, my own "hero," as a matter of fact. . . . I had reached a point in my relation to him where almost anything could happen and where whatever did happen would be believable to me. . . . In other words, the man had become sufficiently real to me that I could, and therefore should, write a novel about him—even if that "reality" were nothing more than a projection extruded by my unconscious life, even if it were no more than imaginary.*

More UMFs! One would think that Durrell's *Alexandria Quartet,* among forty or fifty others, had done this kind of thing to death.

2. Since stories are made up, it follows that the traditional beginnings, middles, and ends of retrograde, old-fashioned fiction are somewhat arbitrary and not to be confused with genuine necessity. Any story could have been told differently. The narrator, by entering his story as a "voice," demonstrates his advanced sensibility by pointing this out as often as possible.

The following passage is from Raymond Federman's Fiction Collective novel, *Take It or Leave It,* described on the back cover as a book in which "the narrator involves his listeners in digressive arguments about politics, sex, America, literature, laughter, death, and the telling of the story itself. Consequently as the story progresses it also deviates from its course and eventually cancels itself [whatever that means] as the voices in the fiction multiply . . . [and] makes a shamble of traditional fiction and conventional modes of writing, and does so with effrontery and laughter."

644

Why, when, where, how, why me, why then, who, and then, in which direction? How the hell do I know! . . . Dammit! If you guys keep talking all the time/and at the same time/we'll never get it straight! We'll never get there! Do you think it's easy to tell a story? Any story? HEY! Particularly when it's not YOUR story—a second hand story! Anywhere? To retell a story which was already told from the start in a rather dubious manner. Do you think it's easy to set it up so that it looks coherent? Or even readable? Not to mention credible? I tell you it's not easy.

Fearless innovator Federman also refuses to number the pages of his bulky text, and speaks of a "battle against the linearity of syntax," which he wages with the dazzling new weapon of creative typography.

3. Words and languages themselves are also made up, and may have a purely noumenal existence. It is this supposition that makes it impossible for any "real" writer to use the word "real," or any other that might imply metaphysical earnestness without the ironical quotation marks. Hence the flatulence of a writer like Federman indicates neither incompetence nor self-indulgent, lazy thinking and writing but extreme sophistication. At its furthest reaches, this skepticism about language compels the writer to demonstrate constantly that language is a kind of trapdoor through which all must fall. He does this through a kind of linguistic play (see Huizinga and other authorities on the seriousness of play) known as a "pun" or "play on words."

From B. H. Friedman's "P———: A Case History," a tale in which a horny middle-aged man has a case of priapism, or permanent erection, which turns out to be a symptom of terminal leukemia: "As he finishes dressing he wonders if he should call the office and tell them—what?—that something has come up. He smiles. That is just the sort of vague explanation his secretary gives. In his case it's precise, too precise." And later, "but the analogy won't stand up (another joke, another smile)," and again "he tells the nurse that this is an emergency. She says she will fit him in. P——— smiles. The world is filled with cruel jokes."

Not to mention juvenile ones. In Peter Spielberg's "The Hermetic Whore," about a government project to cheer up the elderly by encouraging masturbation that ends up so popularizing the practice that intercourse goes out of fashion and the birthrate plummets, there are more. Spielberg tells the one about

645

the crazy scientist who killed and cremated all the cats he could get hold of. Yes, cats. You know: kittens. Meow, meow! He sifted their ashes into empty coffee cans, or maybe it was baby-food jars, and tried to sell them to the hard-up dudes on 42nd street.

"Psst! Want a piece of the best stuff in town?" he would buttonhole a likely customer.

"Sure. Where is she? How much?"

"Right here in the jar. Five dollars a spoonful. Just add some hot water. My invention—instant pussy. . . ."

And so a one-liner copied from 25-cent vending machines in half the gas station men's rooms in America becomes a whole routine.

In *Take It or Leave It* Federman explains why his narrator has decided to travel across America by car (a daring new plot):

To penetrate you (all the way to the WEST COAST) because (up to now) I must admit I hadn't gone very far—very deep. Mostly stayed on the margin. Yes, dealing mostly in the CUNTFRONTATION. But now it was really going to be an enormous PENISTRATION. I couldn't wait to get going. AMERICA here I come!

When he is not altering the shape of literary perception Raymond Federman is a professor of comparative literature.

Not all of *Statements 2* or of the Collective's novels are so bald as the passages quoted. But I chose each of the writers above not only because his work was illustrative of what seems to me to be the Fiction Collective's guiding principles and general tone but also because he has a book in print with the organization and is therefore a member of its editorial board. The sexual obsessiveness of the last three is equally characteristic, as if a group of academically employed solipsists has no other subject matter available to it. Spielberg's "The Hermetic Whore" contains a carefully enumerated list of ways for men to masturbate, which seems just about right. Any of the three could easily make a living writing to the *Penthouse* Forum if they could forgo the puns for a while. But that would be commercial. It would not be art.

I find it puzzling that writers of genuine talent like Jonathan Baumbach, Russell Banks, and Ronald Sukenick seem content with the self-imitation of easy effects that their work in *Statements 2* shows. Reading too much of it is like watching a basketball game in which the players have gotten so cool that they have agreed true devotion to the sport requires that all shots be missed and the ball double-dribbled on purpose. I find it depressing to imagine the Fiction Collective version of contemporary literary "reality" becoming the currency of seminar tables all over the country—a gloom that is partially lifted by my knowledge of how little attention the most promising young writers will pay in the long run to any teachers. I emerge from my reading tempted to paraphrase Flannery O'Connor's remark on the effect of the American university on the national literature: if the publishing industry is stifling writers, it isn't yet stifling enough of them.

We have more mediocre fiction writers, poets, and critics than we need. What we lack is readers. Most of the Fiction Collective's members would do themselves and the rest of us a favor by knocking off the boasting and the bitching for a while and getting back to the classroom to train some.

The Sparrow, *Vol. 1, No. 1, June 1954 (courtesy Felix Stefanile).*

THE LITTLE MAGAZINE TODAY
Felix Stefanile

Felix Stefanile says that Cid Corman's Origin *taught him to value an editor's literary allegiances; that Robert Creeley's quirkiness in editing* The Black Mountain Review *taught him to respect his own eccentricities; that W. Price Turner's* The Poet *in England gave him a new view of eclecticism; and that Canadian poet Irving Layton* (Civ/n) *taught him arguing could be fun. The fifties were, says Mr. Stefanile, a marvelous time to be a young poet in. "There was a real and powerful establishment to fight. Because it deprived us, it gave us a vision of the Enemy that the new pluralism has taken away from young poets starting out now."*

Stefanile has taught creative writing and modern literature at Purdue University since 1961. Standard Oil of Indiana gave him an award in 1973 for being the best teacher in his school. He is the author of four books of poetry and has contributed to scores of little magazines. Mr. Stefanile is the editor at Sparrow Press (founded 1954), whose activities include the little magazine Sparrow, *now devoted to one poet per issue; Vagrom Chap Books; and the series of polemical pamphlets called* Black Rooster.

> *Now every week the mail brings in*
> *another braggart bulletin*
> *or newsletter straight from the heart*
> *of the National Endowment for the Arts,*
> *from Leonard Randolph, or Nancy Hanks,*
> *or some such pol, that offers thanks—*
> *in IBM Selectric Type—*
> *for the latest grant, the latest hype.*
> *—from* "The Sorrows of Pontifico"

For my own foray into the present discussion of the little magazine I shall not have much to say about my own poetry journal, *Sparrow* (now known, after twenty-four years, as *Sparrow Poverty Pamphlets*). The reader will find my modesty forward and articulate enough, however. At the not inconsiderable risk of expunging forever from the ranks of scholarly footnotes a fair history of the

649

efforts of my wife and me to publish poetry in our country, I begin by stating I have always thought of *Sparrow* as a publication in the second rank of independent literary publishers. Except in the lives of a few stalwarts, like Cid Corman or Frederick Eckman, whose first books, in poetry and criticism respectively, we were lucky enough to publish, our activities over the years have been stolid, almost dogged, hardly ever "crucial." We have broken no new ground. We have had to earn our taste. Our poetic vision has always been more often of the hindsighted, not the farsighted, kind. History will reveal, for the past generation, that the real comers in the land have been picked up first by *Origin*, or the *Hudson Review*, or maybe City Lights or Jargon Books, or some publisher of similar excellence. Because of our merely reliable performance, the fact that *Sparrow* has always been around, we have sometimes been the beneficiaries of spillage from these sources—resulting, say, in the special Eigner issue we published in 1956 or, for that matter, the charming Douglas Worth feature we were able to put out in 1975. Occasionally we have scored a minor critical coup, like publishing early Vassar Miller (even without credit from the Untermeyer or Meridian anthologies) or like having the reviewer at the *American Scholar* describe one of our small ventures in publishing literary criticism as the most knowledgeable thing of its kind. Given the context I have been attempting to establish for my magazine, it should be obvious that in calling us second rank I do not mean shopworn or secondhand. I suspect that the most amusing, and at the same time perhaps the most honorable, thing that can be said of Selma and me is that as poetry publishers we have *lasted* lo these many years. In this respect, and taking into account the often very proudly announced high casualty rate for little magazines, are we not then, in our own way, genuinely inimitable (apologies to John Martin of *BLACK Sparrow*)? We delight in observing, when the results of the latest Washington survey or librarian's questionnaire have been published, that we are always placed—even though anonymously, always as a cipher—among the "oldest" magazines. Forgive our little finger timidly raised, and pointing, not only at our modesty, with pride.

Things change. I quote from a note in the *Small Press Review* for October–November 1977 on Maurice M. Custodio, president

650

of Peace and Pieces Foundation: ". . . [the] Foundation was recently rejected by the National Endowment for the Arts Literature Program and the California Arts Council for 1977–1978 funding, and therefore cannot accept any manuscripts for books or its magazine until at least 1979." We see here, on the part of a fairly well-established organization with clear-cut social service and literary goals (Peace and Pieces serves prisoners, minorities, and other communities in a broad West Coast area), a wide-open implication that publication plans are being suspended until 1979, when, theoretically, the organization can once again apply for grants. The literary tie-in of an "alternative" publisher with government funding is, if not complete, at the very least tragically strategic. This writer could cite, at random and at a minimum, a score of similar examples of the connection, chilling to contemplate, between Big Uncle and a so-called alternative press. Yet the distinguished *Library Journal,* in its annual "Small Press Roundup" issue (December 15, 1977), has stories on little-magazine fortunes, one by Bill Katz and one by Michael Haldeman, that nowhere make mention of this ominous relationship. Though we are given facts and figures, lists, names and addresses, and all sorts of utopian prognostications of a bright future for independent publishing, there is not a single allusion to the National Endowment for the Arts. But the fact remains that for too many journals, like *Yardbird Reader* or *Gallimaufry,* a dependence on government funding seems to be the actual operative condition of their independence. I repeat—I have written of it elsewhere, and at length, and time and again—the most important thing to happen to the little magazine in the generation since the early days of City Lights and *The Fifties* is not the introduction of cheap offset technology, not the arrival of surrealism, not the education explosion of the sixties, which has resulted in a minor poetry audience, but government intrusion into the arts. It is *Sparrow*'s contention that we have yet to wrestle competently with that particular angel.

Not the least grim or the least dangerous result of this intrusion has been the rise of the poet as activist. Poets now run for office, on grant committees. Poets now proclaim their minority status, and *organize*. Where we once, in the more classical days, had an avant-garde, a group, an atelier, we now have the collective, the

651

community arts council, the neighborhood poetry cafeteria; what we now have is the poetry constituency. It is in the nature of all government arts budgeting and "service" in our country to have the burgeoning of conflicting "democracies" of the kind we are talking about here. As usual, the screamers run away with most of the loot. A high point in the democratization and politicization of poetry is the recent putsch brought off by the Fall 1977 Grants Committee of the Coordinating Council of Literary Magazines. The ladies and gentlemen involved, very much like a congressional ways and means committee, and by a majority vote of 3 to 1 (one timid and, I suspect, vapid soul abstaining), ruled that, with the exception of eighteen magazines excluded by some vague criterion, all 130 applicant magazines should share the money equally. It has never been clear to me what voting has to do with literature, but we must all admit this is democracy with big teeth. Note the ringing, manifesto tone of the majority statement: . . . *Therefore, some editors and writers have long advocated a populist approach, and the majority of this CCLM grants committee responsively votes to recommend an equal share of the public monies for every applicant which* [sic] *we have found to be qualified. We believe this position to be a practical alternative to the conventional system. We believe it accomplishes the greatest good for the greatest number. Sparrow* wonders what Plato would have had to say about that!

Irony of ironies, of course, and I hasten to make the statement, that the majority of little magazines do not, for one reason or another, apply for these grants. I do not mean to give the impression that we have all been caught in the director of the literature program's net. For the Fall 1977 Grants Committee's Jacobin pronunciamento to have made any egalitarian sense, the Charlotte Cordays and Robespierres of the group ought to have been speaking for *all* of us, and not just some of us. This, of course, is impossible: thereby proving, in today's Orwellian grants atmosphere (something that hardly troubles Washington), that although we are all created equal, some of us are more equal than others.

But grants *are* an ineluctable fact of the current literary scene, and we ought to be paying more attention to this fact. The director, who functions like a warring pope among the factions and constituencies—an Alexander VI, not a Paul VI—wields inordinate power in this "parlement" of benefit seekers. It is against this backdrop of factionalism that we must read his reckless statements, such as the one about seven hundred books having been published in 1976, with government help—the implication being, I assure you, that they all ought to have been published and were in truth dramatically rescued from oblivion. I am particularly struck by his proclamation, given to the editor of the "Book Ends" page of the *New York Times* for June 5, 1977, that government assistance to little magazines contributes to the lifting of "censorship by omission," by bringing before the public books heretofore threatened with extinction because of mere financial exigency. I wish he had also spoken, as others have, of "censorship by submission." There is indeed that negative censorship of what we must *not* do, and here, we see, Washington plays its cagey game, substituting for raw, negative censorship its own guideline: affirmative censorship of what, in order to obtain support, we *must* do, what we *must* publish. To cite but one example, this includes the numberless anthologies of the writings of children.

It seems clear, in today's advocacy enthusiasms, that the sonnet and other traditional poetry have effectively been eliminated from democratic privilege. (The director is notorious for his scornful public remarks about something he calls academic poetry.) Then there exists, for his own guidance, the statement of the National Council on the Arts—as quoted in *Publishers Weekly* for July 25, 1977, page 48—that the Endowment is "basically committed . . . to the support of future creativity rather than to the provision of cash awards for past work." With such official confidence in the future, who needs Shakespeare? What we seem to get, wherever we turn, is promises, promises, and the numbers racket.

The going little magazines (I mean journals like *Sparrow*) are effectively and in principle—especially when one considers that the past includes last year and yesterday—co-opted. The best indication of this bumping process, this co-optation in support possibilities, is the absence of any serious government program for the distribution of little magazines. There are the minuscule distribution projects that are funded, through a Ford Foundation grant, by the CCLM. *Sparrow* has had some decent luck here, often as much as a 50 percent return on consignments, but there ought to be many more such projects, and they ought to be more heftily funded. Unfortunately, distribution implies fulfillment, fulfillment implies performance, and performance-experience demands some kind of "past," which may all be a little too damn businesslike to serve the thinly masked social service strategies of the social engineers at the NEA. It is instructive to observe that the new executive director of the CCLM rushes to announce, in some of his correspondence, that he is a political scientist; and, as a matter of fact, from what I have read of a letter of his, he sounds like a welfare director, not a literary arbiter. He seems awfully worried about unsilencing "the silenced" (his phrase), and by the same token I am awfully worried that he and his ilk in Washington are perhaps also intrigued with the possibility of silencing the unsilenced, all sorts of people like me, with lack of interest or encouragement. Am I being paranoid? To get back to the pope, the latest thing I hear is that he has been admitted to the Poetry Society of America—his biographical notes identify him as an "assistant to a congressman"—and I shudder to think what designs he has on the club women of America.

We cannot leave this matter of censorship without also considering the self-censorship engendered by the total environment. I am grateful to Lingeman for quoting me, as well as Randolph, in his "Book Ends" story already alluded to, and there I specifically mention it. Felix Pollak writes me that self-censorship is a charge impossible to prove, and he is right. I can only depend on my own credibility-quotient among some trusting souls, and pray for a modest conversion here and there. With only that (admittedly tenuous) goal in view, I quote an unnamed "source," who recently wrote me in response to one of my more wearisome fulminations against the NEA in *Black Rooster* Newsletter. His words are a paradigm of one kind of correspondence I receive on the issue, even sometimes from the high and the mighty:

I may have to be one of your anonymous informants at this point—mute testimony to your assertion that there is fear and censorship. It is not that I'm afraid of sticking my neck out, but I'm very much identified with ———, and ——— does receive a publication grant from the NEA, and I would hate to see ——— penalized for my foolhardiness.

As the old saying goes, I didn't know whether to laugh or cry.

Some of the omens are good. We have Robert Brustein's long piece in the December 18, 1977, issue of the "Arts and Leisure" section of the *New York Times*. His article includes a report on conversations with Senator Pell, Livingston Biddle, our new NEA chairman, and Mrs. Joan Mondale, as well as other dignitaries, about the future of NEA activities. I enjoyed his identification of the pivot of the crisis under discussion here as a struggle between people interested in art and people interested in adult education. I would also add (Brustein does not refer to this forcefully enough) people interested in neither art nor adult education but in social engineering. His essay is too meaty to review here, but it is a healthy note that a person of his stature has decided to enter the fray, no matter how "impartially," and that his views have been presented on a national forum and not in some crazy little magazine. As nearly as I can tell, his is the first higher echelon voice to utter a demurrer on the whole arts binge. He has, of course, in subsequent letters to the editor, been called a "patrician" and a "snob" for his pains, but it is high time our more prominent writers and editors stood up to be counted on this all-important intellectual question; I for one hope Brustein's performance is not only symptomatic but prophetic. As things are falling right now, the Philistines are winning by default.

We must not omit our humor for the day. There is always the perennially trivial leadership of COSMEP (Committee of Small Magazine Editors and Publishers) to fall back upon for a good laugh. For a couple of years now, these unsturdy commissars of literature have been burning up the mails with their proposed van project: to bring in mobile form, much like our old peddlers, the little magazine to the boondocks of America, where a lot of good folks are. COSMEP is today—in essential, financial ways—an appendage of the NEA, and of course, under the literature program director's benign tutelage, has had no real trouble in obtaining a $30,000 grant for this purpose. There was an immediate falling-out between West Coast and East Coast partisans as to where the single van should operate. When the area of the Southeast was finally chosen as the base for the pilot project, charges of "sellout," and resignations, immediately followed. Do not think for a moment that President Carter—that wily southron —was exempt from accusation. One man wrote a book of poems explaining his secession from the mother organization. Then, after weary months of looking for the right vehicle to buy, drivers to hire, coordinators to appoint, the leadership sadly announced that the van had broken down, that the repair bill was $7,000, that the coordinator had resigned (I do not believe he wrote poems about his resignation), that the board of directors had voted itself $2,500 of the van money for a meeting, and that the directors must vote on the problem of the inclusion of anti-feminist material in the van. (There is a poem about it in a recent issue of the organization's newsletter.) As nearly as I can make out, Ken Kesey had nothing to do with any of this. Naturally, and to be expected, all this idealistic inexpertise bodes well for future creativity. Since the past does not count—the concept of "past work" having been abolished—COSMEP has been awarded, for the present fiscal year, not $30,000 but $40,000! Now that is what I call a real incentive system.

Sparrow's principle in all this is clear: we stay out of the game. We lack the financial buttressing of the university review, insecure and uncertain as that may be. (The *fat* university review is a small-press myth.) We have not developed the readership of solid institutionals, like *Partisan Review* or *Poetry*. We are not independently wealthy, as are the backers of some of our reviews. We earnestly feel that the better part of discretion, if not valor, is to keep lean, and depend only on ourselves. We're not exactly starving. We manage to get into the libraries. We have a sure, if not great, list of subscribers we can honestly call "hard core." We know where we're going. We too can—as can most serious little-magazine editors—truly point with pride to a bibliography here, a footnote there, a prizewinner now and then out of our ranks, poems in most of the major anthologies. We sense keenly and personally our by-now aging tradition: a tradition, for instance, that accommodates the inclusion of *Sparrow* poets in both pathfinder anthologies of a past exciting epoch—the Allen *New American Poetry 1945–1960* and the Hall, Pack, and Simpson *New Poets of England and America*. If *that* tradition, little as it is, doesn't have scope, I don't know what has.

Laboring as we do on the middle terraces of Olympus, neither among the establishment-view journals that feature essays by the Welleks and the Barfields of the acknowledged literary peaks, nor among the foothills of topicality and "movements" where the *small press revolution* lurks and ideologies and guidelines gather, we nurture our strong sense of portent, and endeavor to stand fast amid the buffetings and storms unleashed by the NEA pressure system. Once in a rare while, some name-poet sends us his castoffs, and the latest female vincitrix makes her browbeating inquiry about our attitude toward neglected literature. Our correspondence on such matters is always vigorously courteous and strategically brief.

Wanting to stay lean and to give government the slip, we are right now doing our best to retreat from the movement aspects of the little magazine. This is the main reason for our changeover from a traditional poetry miscellany to our pamphlet series featuring the work of a single poet. As we wrote elsewhere—our words were quoted in *Time,* of all places—it is impossible, this side of idiocy, *not* to get published these days. Thanks to the movement, we have magazines for all seasons, all gradations of talent and non-talent, and to get out of *that* game is not the elitist or antisocial act it might have been twenty years ago, before the era of poetry gamesmanship. Fortunately, the word is getting around, however slowly. In 1976—the first year of our change in policy—our manuscript mail was reduced by about 25 percent, a real work economy for us that made us feel very rescued. The reason for this reduction is simple: as our poet-in-the-school is quick to inform his or her charges, anybody can write a poem but not everybody can compile a genuine chapbook manuscript. *Sparrow* has changed the rules of the game, and a certain type of un-poet, or part-time poet, or one-shot workshop-poet is automatically cut out. The reader will note—with admiration, we hope —that a current requirement of the Yale Series of Younger Poets competition is a five-dollar submission fee. We wonder how many unspicy meatballs have been deflected in their course, in the mails, by such a simple fiat. To such lengths are conscientious editors brought in the continuing struggle to reduce the slush pile. A letter we wrote recently to a writer-in-residence of the South Carolina Arts Commission, in response to his request for donations, focuses sharply on this blight of poetry palaver, of poetry hordes that has overtaken today's little magazine, all in the name of future creativity. We rephrase in spots, to keep other people out of the discussion:

In all friendliness, and in all frankness as well, we feel we cannot oblige you in your request for copies of Sparrow *publications for your teaching projects, and in doing so we touch on a real social and intellectual problem that has already been discussed in the past by some well-known authors and publishers.*

657

I don't know how to put it, without sounding like a cannibal or some other kind of soulless literary golem, but Sparrow . . . *is the kind of magazine that can never be seriously interested in novice work. I am especially sensitive when it comes to prisoners because, with one or two exceptions, what has crossed our desk . . . bespeaks a truly tragic issue of identity and education problems, and we are quite simply a literary magazine, not a clinic, not a remedial institution. In other words, I don't see what purpose is served in telling these individuals that* Sparrow *is a market for them, when in utter fact* Sparrow *is not . . . and it seems to me, for the same reason, that it is a waste of effort to expose us to senior citizens, other novices, and kids. . . .*

Judging from the material we are now beginning to receive, we have lowered the boom still further. We give preference, and say so, to poets whose manuscripts are made up of mostly unpublished poems. This, we hope, will get the creative writing majors off our backs. There is one large school in the Midwest, just about all of whose MFA candidates, we sometimes feel, have sent us a typescript, with the duly cluttered acknowledgments page. Far be it from me to knock my own profession of teaching creative writing, but schools of this kind invariably harbor their own little magazines, stuffed with the work of their students, and token decorations from eminences like William Ginsberg or Allen Stafford. Aside from a general lack of adventurousness, what we detect in much of the work is the march of the syllabus—the poem addressed to Another Person, the poem that objectifies a person or personifies an object, the poem with the word "stone" in it, the backpack poem, and so on. While I am not prepared to argue that poems in these modalities cannot be good, I do come away from the manuscripts with the distinct feeling that to have read one such collection is to have read them all.

We ought not to overlook that in today's failing educational times creative writing is one of the disciplines bucking the declining enrollments trend, that composition and the new mass media programs are in our pedagogical future, and that these schools manufacture a product, just like other schools, and not poetry. All this is related once again, though at a different level, to the blight of poetry palaver. Accomplished literary competence may earn degrees and—I hope—get jobs, but its relationship to the classical tradition of the little magazine is nonexistent. A good little magazine is never after the merely correct, or publishable, or fashionable verse—the verse that is being "done" now. In this latter group there is a sameness of tone, a pedestrian exercise-development and gallop to the work that we do not intend to encourage. A good little magazine is very often after work that is *not* the "done" or going thing, that is not fashionable, not "in," and in fact some of these smart and talented degree candidates ought to be told to stop doing what comes to them so easily.

We seem to be arguing against the previously published poem, but this is not entirely true, and often enough we break our own rules. We are arguing against the Published Poem mind-set that freezes the insufficiently developed poem on the printed page. The magazines are full of these abortions. Granted the inevitability of eventual publication these days, we submit that *Sparrow*'s newfound prejudice in favor of the virgin manuscript places the responsibilities of art where they belong—on the artist, at the artist's own pace—and not on the interstices, drafty with the winds of fame, of an arts system riddled with sham, campy topicality, and "connection." We are, in other words, against the style of the times, and paradoxically our rigidity has elicited (as it was meant to), from out of the blue, work that is genuinely new. This comes especially from middle poets of sustained achievement, workmen who cannot claim to be new or young or current or innovative or underprivileged or needy or unemployed, and against whom the style of liberational novelty, with and without NEA and graduate school encouragement, militates to effectively shut them off from public attention. Again, our strategy is to refuse to fight the enemy on his terms, but to fight him on ours. *Sparrow* has, in effect, most unmilitantly abolished both the movement and the NEA.

In the single-poet idea—as anyone who has come across an issue of *Vort,* say the Guy Davenport number, will note—there is a philosophical challenge impossible to confront in most little-magazine publishing. The writer is truly up front where he belongs, in all his vulnerability and, in the case of a previously unpublished work, all his nakedness. Taste is at work, and vigorous choice—not enthusiasm, not educationist display, not cheap thrills. Audiences are being formed, no matter how small. Aim is being taken. This is the true job of little magazines. Of course nothing new has been said here, except, perhaps, that it is against the style of the times, the thematic anthologies, the discovered geniuses, the age-group choruses, the collections based upon issues and events, etc. We observe a trend that gives us pause to think: that more and more editors are devoting their efforts to the single-poet issue. One young fellow actually acknowledged in the *International Directory* that he got the idea from *Sparrow* and magazines like it. I'm sure the idea is around, and it is one way of combating the blitz. Also, more and more editors are publishing magazines that feature only work that has been solicited; as the saying goes, "Don't call us, we'll call you." Such self-protective gestures ought to rescue a certain type of little magazine from the general malaise of enthusiasm and future creativity that threatens to engulf us all like a flood. Once again, as in the single-poet issue, exclusivity places the burden of art where it belongs, on the individual, the editor as much as the poet, not on operation, gamesmanship, policy, production, guideline-fulfillment, publish-or-perish MFA degree requirements. Let us reflect soberly that it was precisely such editorial exclusivity that brought to us the superb poetry of people like J. V. Cunningham, William Bronk, Paul Metcalf—all nurtured through the years by their adoptive publishers. It may not be democracy, but it sure as hell is art! When such ideas and others like them catch on, as they very well may, I am sure that somebody on the literature panel of the NEA will come forth with the denunciation that these editors are being "elitist," or perhaps "unpopulist," and ought to be excluded from government grants.

In each of the categories cited—the movement, the schools, the government programs (I shall close with at least one well-aimed fling at PITS)—the mounting evidence of NEA influence is clear. By now literally millions of dollars have been given to the magazines. There exists a monolithic and automatic filtration system connecting the schools with CETA, PITS, and the Creative Writing Fellowships, still more and more millions of dollars. I have not so much been pointing out components on a grid as to one vast chaos of poetry palaver, misnamed renaissance: a veritable space program for the arts that involves children, state arts councils, neighborhood betterment projects, new education plans (a new star on the horizon is "arts education"), and so forth. Even our congressmen, usually suspicious of and hostile to art, have been bought off by the Washington decision to sink a hefty and regularized percentage of arts funds directly into the states, thus bringing the politics of the placement of an air force base or navy yard to a new level of finesse as state arts funds, or poetry as pork barrel. Next to the future creativity stress of the NEA— with its built-in exemption from critical scrutiny as the Now yields to the new Now annually, and the devil take the hindmost past— this is the most brilliant coup pulled off by our perilous benefactors, the social engineers. After all, with fifty states, how much more democratic can art get? What we really have is not poetry, but politics—the arts lobby, the arts caucus, committees and councils of poets and poetasters, constituencies including camouflaged quota systems; just check the sociological makeup of, especially, the smaller higher-echelon boards and panels—and Organization. The cult of plurality reigns, and the shit rains down on us all.

My favorite theory, for the present (one can never be sure when we are going to be hit over the head with another miracle from the NEA) is that Gradgrind is really in charge, and Gradgrind is bent on fostering and advancing, not literature, but hatred of literature. Hatred of literature has to be part of the present action because Gradgrind really wants literature as policy image, literature as social revolution, literature as statistics proving results. Something more important than literature, as most of us understand literature, is always going on. Such strategy of preconception and goals can only result, eventually, in suspicion of and mistreatment of the age-old, often aesthetic elements of the paradigm we have always accepted as art. I find here a frightening resemblance both to socialist realism and, with the committees, to the Soviet Writers Councils. As for the mystique of goals, of "700 books," it reminds me of Stakhanovism.

Surely a hatred of literature motivates any teaching that can result in the obvious victimization of individuals who send letters like the following to *Sparrow:*

Dear sir or madam:
I have enough pages for a book of poems of poetry, that will be for all ages. I think it is a two way street from the author and the publisher. I would like to know what I will receive, what type of paper they must be typed on and what type of typewritter ribbon. I am not a free lance writer, these poems is from observeation. I would like to have two books for copywrite purpose, also can I order additional books direct from you.

I have a poem I would like to be in the book. It has been acepted in the poetry press contest unpublished poetry, that ends in Dec. Do you want a sample or all at once. Will ga rentee [sic] postage back, I have a few more than necessary, will send for you to sort over.

661

At first my wife and I, on receipt of such letters, would suspect a joke. Today, we receive too many of them to doubt their sincerity. Note the mangle of teaching units, sticking out like bone splinters from the general mess; the reference to copyright; the implication of SASE in the return postage remark; the query tone of "sample." *This* is what is going on in the NEA world—grant-funded teaching, which can impel, out of dreadful innocence and stalwart misinformation, another letter to the poetry editor that begins, "Dear manager, I am 18 years old and have written 1200 poems. My teacher told me to send them to you . . ." We get this kind of query—there is also a category for the seventy-four-year-old who has written a "first" poem—about every third week. Being the sort of magazine we are, neither too high nor too low, we have a reputation for accessibility, and get all sorts of mail. Is *Sparrow* being cruel and insensitive to see—beyond the hope and innocence, the sweet temerity of inexperience, but equally as evident—the despair and loneliness of ignorance, the unready, absolutely vulnerable spirit unprepared for disappointment? Do I exaggerate? We too, like Gradgrind, keep statistics. Out of our first two hundred manuscripts for 1978 we noted that fully 12 percent came without a self-addressed, stamped return envelope. From 1965, the year the NEA was conscripted, this is a rise of about 1,000 percent for such manuscripts. Is the rise part of the renaissance? Let me momentarily lift the discussion out of its *Sparrow* context, and refer to a recent (November 1977) issue of *Indiana Writes,* where a poet-in-the-school attempts to answer William Jay Smith's charge that, by and large, people in the PITS program are not teaching the great lyric tradition to the kids, are not teaching them our classics, and above all are teaching them nothing about rhyme, language, and structure. He offers from his own experience the teaching (of all things) of a Neruda poem in a free verse translation; the main point of the lesson seemed to be to get the pupils to relate, out of their own lives, to the "theme"! What kind of answer to Smith was this? In terms of poetry, our general findings point to the existence of a burgeoning generation of educationally battered and abused children who can't spell, don't type, have never been taught the simple rudiments of manuscript preparation or the primitive ethics of paying for their return postage. These children—except (in the words

662

of another editor) for a pleasant bout with "recreational experimentalism"—have never been taught what writing or being published, in the larger environment of literature, really means or imports. This is not teaching, dear poet-in-the-school; this is child molestation.

I choose to close on this gloomy note in order to emphasize how rampant the plague of government policy in "supporting" poetry really is, affecting not only our magazines but, as the social engineers seem to want it to, our whole society. The condition is one that our writers, our critics, even our parents ought to be paying more attention to. It is truly a Big Deal, and I do not think it is going to readily go away. Gradgrind will not leave unless strongly invited to do so. In the meantime, funding gets bigger and better year after year. I used to think NEA-shenanigans were the greatest national joke since the popular self-help, "personal fulfillment" optimism, in the twenties and thirties, of Dr. Coué and his chortling band of enthusiast-imitators, like Harry Overstreet and Dale Carnegie. The equivalent slogan or meditation-words for NEA adherents would go something like "Every day in every way, my poems are getting better and better," or "How to win friends and influence poetry editors." I am no longer so offhandedly amused by the whole thing. What we have on our hands is a national hoax, perpetrated by government-funded brainwashing and boondoggle. The situation is a danger to us all. As the fellow said when the fight started on the train, "This is where I get off." This is where *Sparrow* gets off.

Felix Stefanile (courtesy Poetry *magazine).*

663

ALMOST EVERYBO
CARES ANYTHING A
KNOWS A FEW HORROF
EDITORS, AND PUBLI
PUBLISHED, IT
BE AN EXCRU

WHO KNOWS AND
UT SERIOUS FICTION
ORIES ABOUT AGENTS,
RS. HAVING A BOOK
MS, CAN OFTEN
TING ORDEAL.

—GENE LYONS

AN ANNOTATED BIBLIOGRAPHY OF SELECTED LITTLE MAGAZINES
Peter Martin

Peter A. Martin has published articles in The Arizona Quarterly, Studies in Short Fiction, *and* The Wisconsin Academy Review. *He has been working for some time on a comprehensive survey and bibliography of British magazines from 1919 to 1939, to be published by G. K. Hall. Mr. Martin teaches in the University of Wisconsin system.*

Note on the magazines

Although no one today doubts the importance of little magazines, there remains a frequently intemperate controversy regarding the boundaries of the little-magazine category. The broadest definition, and the one that creates the least controversy, suggests that a little magazine publishes creative work which for one or another reason is unacceptable to commercial magazines. Certainly few, if any, little magazines can be accused of commercial expediency. A narrower definition suggests that little magazines are limited in circulation and independent of outside funding, and that they not only avoid crass commercialism but focus principally upon new names and new literary techniques. This bibliography ignores the narrower definition and bases its selections on merit. To have excluded the more stable, better funded magazines would have meant passing over major works by many first-rank writers. At the same time it would be ingenuous to think that the really new and untried could be as consistently represented in *The American Poetry Review* or *The Hudson Review* or *TriQuarterly* as in *Wormwood* or in a little-little magazine with a dedicated but limited special readership. Therefore, the following list ranges from *The (New) American Review,* which tried to bring quality literature to a mass market through paperback anthologies, through a selection of university- and government-subsidized magazines, to little-little magazines such as *Vagabond* and *Blue Cloud Quarterly.*

This bibliography deals with the history of American little magazines since 1950. It includes a number of magazines that began well before 1950 (for example, *The Sewanee Review, Poetry, The Prairie Schooner, The Kenyon Review)* but have been an important part of magazine publishing since then. As with more recent university-sponsored magazines, omission of these periodicals would have eliminated much important writing by major literary figures. Also included for annotation are a few magazines that were not edited in the United States. These are either displaced American magazines *(Paris Review, Origin* in its Kyoto issues, *Locus Solus, Antaeus),* or magazines reflecting new international emphases that have been significant in American literary history *(El Corno Emplumado),* or magazines that have printed large amounts of significant English-language literature *(Botteghe Oscure).*

Selection of titles for this survey was made after consultation with a number of experts on American little magazines. Michael Anania, John Jacob, Marvin Malone, James Boyer May, Tom Montag, Felix Pollak, Marjorie Smelstor, S. C., Felix Stefanile, and Robert Wilson of the Phoenix Book Shop, among others, gave valuable advice on the choice of titles for annotations.

Special thanks go to John Jacob, Marvin Malone, and Marjorie Smelstor, S. C., who provided information which greatly facilitated the writing of a number of annotations; also to Gloria Prochaska, Darlene Safransky, and Ella Toigo for first-rate secretarial help; and to the highly efficient, knowledgeable, and invariably good-natured staff in the Special Collections room at the Northwestern University Library. I would also like to thank Bonnie Jo Sedlak for providing the information regarding magazine bindings.

A very brief checklist of sources for the study of American little magazines

Despite some occasionally erratic guesswork, the inevitable factual errors, and an unaccountable decision to include a hit-or-miss smattering of English magazines, Frederick J. Hoffman's *The*

667

Little Magazine: A History and a Bibliography is a comprehensive survey of American little magazines from 1891 to 1946. In addition to the 230-page discursive history and the 174-page annotated chronological checklist, this study also includes a list of references that forms a good starting place for an investigation of American little magazines up to the end of World War II.

A number of scholars and publishers have discussed updating the Hoffman book, but thus far no substantive study has appeared. The major inhibiting factor is the roughly 1,000 percent increase in the number of little magazines published over the past three decades. An immense post–World War II increase in the number of college-educated persons, combined with the accessibility of cheap mimeograph machines and inexpensive offset printing, has effected a phenomenal increase in the creation of small literary periodicals. Yet we are not without aids to the ordering of the welter of materials. For the fifties and sixties, a chronicle history of English-language little magazine activity is provided by the revolving directory of magazines in James Boyer May's *Trace* (see annotation below). The scope of the 1950s/1960s "mimeo revolution" is reflected in May's observation that his first directory (1952) contained 152 entries, "a fairly complete world coverage of littles in English," and the final directory (1970) included 999 entries. After the demise of *Trace,* May worked for some time on Len Fulton's *International Directory of Little Magazines and Small Presses,* an annual publication, now close to 500 pages, which lists several thousand magazines and small press ventures. The international directories, along with the ongoing accumulation of information in Len Fulton's monthly *Small Press Review* (a cumulative ten-year index is scheduled for 1978 release), helps provide for the 1970s an even fuller listing of little magazines than *Trace* offers for the 1950s and 1960s.

Among the other magazines which list or review current little magazines is Tom Montag's *Margins* (see annotation below), which offered intelligent, often comprehensive, reviews and commentary upon many small press books and magazines of the 1970s. Some persons find *Margins* too inclusive, too open to the new and the small, but it is an invaluable tool for the student of recent little magazine history. Harry Smith's *The Smith* (see annotation below) expresses a highly opinionated, often impolite, but interesting attitude toward both establishment and small press magazines; Smith also issues the *Newsletter on the State of Culture.* Noel Peattie's *Sipapu* is a good source of information on alternative and underground publishing, as is Peattie's *The Living Z: A Guide to the Literature of the Counter-Culture, the Alternative Press, and Little Magazines,* published in 1975 by Tom Montag as a Margins Book (an earlier version had appeared in *Margins* 10, February/March 1974). The bibliographic checklists in *The Living Z* are a logical starting place for anyone interested in recent little magazine history (especially regarding alternative press ventures). A good deal of information regarding details of publishing little magazines (funding, printers, formats, magazine exchanges, conferences, and the like) is found in the *COSMEP Newsletter,* edited by Richard Morris for the Committee of Small Magazine Editors and Publishers.

Fulton, Montag, and Peattie, like James Boyer May, are essentially concerned with the little-little magazines rather than, say, the substantial university-sponsored literary magazines and journals. Persons interested in the latter sort of periodical should consult the *Directory of Periodicals,* published by Swallow Press, a list of magazines printing articles on English and American literature and language. Designed for academics seeking to publish their articles, this guide naturally leans heavily toward establishment periodicals, but does list little magazines which carry critical articles. The *Fourth Directory* (1974), for example, includes *The Smith, Small Press Review,* and *December.* A number of periodicals regularly review other magazines and journals. Noteworthy is Bill Katz's "Magazines" column that has regularly appeared in *Library Journal* since January 1967. Although his primary purpose is to alert librarians to possible acquisitions, he maintains a strong and encouraging interest in little magazines, and his highly topical column is often of real interest.

Many of the magazines in the present checklist have been included in comprehensive little magazine indexes. Of primary importance is Swallow Press's *Index to Little Magazines,* begun in 1948 and later extended by increments through the 1960s. Excluding any title found in the *Readers Guide,* the *International Index,* or the *Social Sciences and Humanities Index,* the *Index to Little Magazines* offers a comprehensive guide to a selection of important little magazines (the *Index* for 1966–1967, for example, covers 49 periodicals, 20 of which are found in the present checklist). While a variety of compilers worked forward from 1948, Stephen A. Goode compiled a four-volume index of important little magazines covering the years 1900–1947. In 1976 the Kraus-Thomson Organization published Marion Sader's *Comprehensive Index to English-Language Little Magazines, 1890–1970*, Series One—an author index to one hundred selected little magazines. It has been estimated that only 15 to 20 percent of the titles here overlap the Swallow indexes.

Comprehensive Index to English-Language Little Magazines, 1890–1970, Series One. Comp. Marion Sader. Millwood, New York: Kraus-Thomson Organization, 1976.

COSMEP Newsletter [Committee of Small Press Editors and Publishers]. Buffalo, New York [then: San Francisco]. Vol. I, no. 1, Aug 1969+. Ed. Richard Morris.

Directory of Periodicals: Publishing Articles on English and American Literature and Language. [*Second Directory,* etc.]. Ed. Donna Gerstenberger and George Hendrick. Chicago: The Swallow Press, Inc., 1959, etc.

Hoffman, Frederick J., Charles Allen, and Carolyn F. Ulrich, *The Little Magazine: A History and a Bibliography.* Princeton, New Jersey: Princeton University Press, 1946.

Index to Little Magazines, 1948, etc. Denver, Colorado: Alan Swallow [then: Chicago], 1949, etc. [The years 1900–1947 are covered in 4 vol., comp. Stephen H. Goode, as *Index to American Little Magazines.*]

International Directory of Little Magazines and Small Presses [early editions: *Directory of . . .*]. Ed Len Fulton. El Cerrito, California: A Dustbook [then: Paradise, California], 1965, etc.

Katz, Bill, "Magazines," *Library Journal,* Vol. XCII, no. 1, 1 Jan 1967+.

Margins. Milwaukee, Wisconsin. No. 1, Aug 1972+. Ed. Tom Montag.

Peattie, Noel. *The Living Z: A Guide to the Literature of the Counter-Culture, the Alternative Press, and Little Magazines.* Milwaukee, Wisconsin: A Margins Book, 1975.

Sipapu. Winters, California. Vol. I, no. 1, Jan 1970+. Ed. Noel Peattie.

Small Press Review. El Cerrito, California [then: Paradise, California]. Vol. I, no. 1, Spring 1967+. Ed. Len Fulton.

The Smith. New York. 15 Feb 1964+. Ed. Harry Smith.

Trace. Hollywood, California. No. 1–72/73, Jun 1952–Autumn 1970. Ed. James Boyer May.

Guide to the Annotations

Wherever possible, the headnote information is taken directly from the magazine; first attention has been paid to the title page or masthead, then to the cover, and then to the rest of the magazine. Any information derived from sources other than the magazine itself is placed in brackets. A question mark (?) accompanies any item that is at all in doubt. Circulation and funding information, where not presented in the magazines themselves, was obtained from the editors and from CCLM, but is by no means complete.

Title. Place of publication

Changes of title or place of publication are given in chronological order.

Subtitles are listed when consistently used on cover and title page or masthead, or when they clearly explain the magazine's purpose.

Place of publication means the editorial office. The place of printing is not considered.

University or school affiliations are noted under place of publication when sponsorship is clearly indicated in the magazine. A number of magazines not so identified have received some support from such institutions. Other sponsoring or supporting agencies or publishing houses are not listed here (though often discussed in the annotation).

Volume numbers and dates. Frequency.

Wherever possible the use of volume, number, series, month or season, etc., follows usage in the specific magazine. Where any of these elements are not taken directly from the magazine itself, the matter appears in brackets.

Dates of first and last issues are listed. A plus sign (+) indicates that the magazine is still being published. A few magazines have not appeared recently but are considered to be in suspension rather than defunct (*The Seventies, Margins*). For these magazines no terminal issue is cited.

Simple changes in frequency are noted; multiple changes are listed as "Freq. varies"; publication at irregular intervals (including regular publication interspersed with frequent or extended periods of nonpublication) is listed as "Irreg."

Editors.

Editors are listed in chronological order according to when they first edited the magazine. The current editor is not always the last named (see *Poetry, The Massachusetts Review*).

Where no dates accompany an editor's name, that person is presumed to have edited every issue.

Where conflict exists, dates for changes of editor are based on internal evidence rather than upon outside testimony of editors and others.

Where editorship changes very frequently, the editors of issue number one are listed and the fact of frequent change noted. Later editors are listed only if especially important (see *Shenandoah*).

Contributing and guest editors, listed only when they strongly affect the magazine, appear in brackets.

671

Textual data.

Dimensions and pagination refer to normal issues and generally to recent issues. Many little magazines vary a great deal; therefore these figures should be taken as estimates.

"Illus." is cited only when illustrations are a regular and significant feature.

"Mimeo" is cited when most issues are reproduced by mimeograph machine.

"Stapled" indicates side-stapling; "stapled (folded)" indicates center-stapling in saddle-stitch position. "Perfect" indicates a spine to which cut signatures are glued; "sewn" indicates a spine to which sewn signatures are glued.

Indexes.

Indexes are noted where encountered in research. This is not an exhaustive list.

672

Magazines annotated

The Agni Review
Alcheringa
The American Poetry Review
Angel Hair
Antaeus
The Antioch Review
Aphra
Assembling
Audit
Bastard Angel
The Beloit Poetry Journal
Big Table
The Black Mountain Review
Blue Cloud Quarterly
Botteghe Oscure
Boundary 2
The Carleton Miscellany
Carolina Quarterly
Caterpillar
Center
Chelsea Review
The Chicago Review
Choice
Clown War
December
El Corno Emplumado
Epoch
Evergreen Review
Fiction
Field
The Fifties
The Floating Bear
Fuck You
The Greenfield Review
Hanging Loose
Hearse
The Hudson Review
Invisible City
Io
Kayak
The Kenyon Review
Kulchur

Lillabulero
Locus Solus
ManRoot
Margins
The Massachusetts Review
Mulch
The Naked Ear
Neurotica
New: American and Canadian Poetry
New American Review
The North American Review
Origin
The Outsider
Panache
The Paris Review
Parnassus
Partisan Review
Pembroke Magazine
Poetry
Poetry Northwest
The Prairie Schooner
Prose
Quarterly Review of Literature
Salmagundi
The Sewanee Review
Shenandoah
The Smith
The Southern Review
Spectrum
Story
Trace
TriQuarterly
Truck
Unmuzzled Ox
Vagabond
West Coast Poetry Review
Wild Dog
The World
The Wormwood Review
Yardbird Reader
Yugen
Zero

The Agni Review. Antioch College, Antioch, Ohio (no. 1–2, 1972–1973); Cranford, N.J. (no. 3–5/6, 1973–1976); Cambridge, Mass. (no. 7, 1977+). No. 1, 1972+. Irreg.
Ed. Askold Melnyczuk; David Ghitelman (no. 4–5/6, 1975–1976); Sharon Dunn (no. 7, 1977+).
5½" x 8½" perfect (no. 1–2: folded and stapled) 60–144 pp.

Askold Melnyczuk (with assistance from Eric Hoffman and Kim Connell for No. 1 and Hoffman and Thomas Bahr for No. 2) began *The Agni Review* at Antioch College, where he produced the opening issue at the college print shop. Then he moved the editorial offices to Cranford, N.J., where David Ghitelman served as co-editor, and later to Cambridge, Mass., where Sharon Dunn became the co-editor. With *Agni* No. 10, Dunn is scheduled to assume full responsibility for editing the magazine. *Agni* has become a sophisticated forum for both known and unknown contributors. Beginning with Robert Bly (a one-line poem) and Greg Kuzma in No. 1, *Agni* has printed a number of well-known poets, including Russell Edson, Ira Sadoff, George Hitchcock, Anselm Hollo, Paul Eluard, Susan Fromberg Schaeffer, Douglas Blazek, David Ignatow, Joseph Bruchac, Colette Inez, George Starbuck, and Carolyn Stoloff. *Agni* has published fiction by Hale Chatfield and Clarence Major and prose poems by Brian Swann, Russell Edson, and Carolyn Stoloff. At the same time it has also provided substantial space to less well-known writers. Beginning with No. 4 (1975), each issue has featured ten to twelve pages of work by a poet who has not yet published a full-length collection; these poets include Herbert Morris, John McKernan, Barbara Eve, Mekeel McBride, and Stuart Dischell. According to Melnyczuk, the one abiding characteristic of *Agni* over the years has been its "openness to anything of quality," from a photo-essay on spatial poetry by Timothy Cohrs, to a novella by David Bosworth, to poems by George Starbuck.
Starting with No. 5/6 (1976), *Agni* has received CCLM support. The current press run is 1,000 copies.

Alcheringa [no. 1–5: Ethnopoetics; new series no. 1+: A First Magazine of the World's Tribal Poetries]. New York, N.Y. [in association with Stony Brook Poetics Foundation] (no. 1–5, Autumn 1970–Spring/Summer 1973); Boston University, Boston, Mass. (New series, Vol. I, no. 1, 1975+).
No. 1, Autumn 1970+. 2/yr.
Ed. Dennis Tedlock; Jerome Rothenberg (Autumn 1970–1976).
8¼" x 9" (recently) perfect 132–152 pp. (recently).

Alcheringa (from the Arunta word for "dream time" or the act of dreaming) offers a format for tribal poetry in English translation. The manifesto that appeared in the first issue asserted the editors' intention "to assist the free development of ethnic self-awareness among young Indians & others so concerned, by encouraging a knowledgeable, loving respect among them & all people for the world's tribal past & present." *Alcheringa* has printed translations (and transcriptions) from oral traditions, explanations of new devices for rendering a strictly oral work into written English, and original work in English that attempts to reflect oral traditions.

To overcome the problems inherent in translating and then transcribing these oral-tradition works into English, *Alcheringa* contributors have experimented with punctuation, typography, and page layouts, as well as with patterns borrowed from concrete poetry and from emblem poetry. Collaborators on the transcriptions include Simon Ortiz, Robert Kelly, Nathaniel Tarn, Anselm Hollo, Kofi Awoonor, Clayton Eshleman, Diane di Prima, Charles Olson, Gary Snyder, Charles Doria, and W. S. Merwin. Some issues include disc recordings by Jackson MacLow, Armand Schwerner, Jaime de Angulo, and Anne Waldman.

The editors of *Alcheringa* are not interested in literal translations. Some versions synthesize a number of oral poems; others are the work of an English-speaking poet who develops a poem from a prose crib; occasionally a poet collaborates with an anthropologist, linguist, or classicist (e.g., the poet Milton Kessler and Egyptologist Gerald E. Kadish, who worked together on "Love Songs and Tomb Songs of Ancient Egypt").

New movements in art and literature may sometimes produce better manifestos than art; the opposite is true of *Alcheringa*, where the poetry is as a rule interesting and moving and the theoretical discussions muddled and jargon-ridden. Thus the special issue reporting on an ethnopoetics symposium at the University of Wisconsin at Milwaukee (edited by Michel Benamou and Jerome Rothenberg) addresses interesting topics in a way that makes the magazine dull when one compares it with earlier numbers that presented Indian poetry, black dialect, South Pacific oral poetry, and South American Indian poetry.

Alcheringa receives support from Boston University and CCLM. Circulation is 2,000 (600 subscriptions).

The American Poetry Review. Philadelphia, Pa.

Vol. I, no. 1, Nov./Dec. 1972+. 6/yr.

Ed. Stephen Berg; Stephen Parker (Nov./Dec. 1972–Nov./Dec. 1973); Rhoda Schwartz (Jan./Feb. 1973+); David Bonanno (Sep./Oct. 1973+); Arthur Vogelsang (1974+); Eleanor Wilner (1975–1977).

11¼" x 15" folded 40–72 pp. Illus.

With its circulation of 24,000 (15,000 subscribers), *The American Poetry Review* reaches a far wider audience than does the usual poetry magazine. At the beginning, in 1972, *APR* had two principal editors, a managing editor, three associates, and twenty-four contributing editors. By 1977 there were five principal editors, two editors-at-large, an assistant editor, and twenty-eight contributing editors. Although Stephen Berg and David

Ignatow have been associated with the magazine from the beginning (Ignatow resigned in 1977 after the magazine was cited for including too few women and blacks), *APR* does not bear any one individual's stamp. A major feature of *APR* has been the center supplement devoted to the work of a single poet (Czeslaw Milosz, Muriel Rukeyser, Pablo Neruda, John Berryman, Thomas McGrath, César Vallejo, Richard Hugo, Anne Sexton) or ethnic group (center pages of Eskimo, Hungarian, black poetry) or short anthologies of the work of younger poets selected by one other, better known, poet.

APR has also featured regular columns by Marvin Bell, Marge Piercy, Sonja Sanchez, Etheridge Knight, and Stanley Plumly. Other frequent contributors include Donald Hall, Clarence Major, June Jordan, Robert Bly, Charles M. Fair, Adrienne Rich, Ralph J. Mills, Jr., and Joyce Carol Oates.

APR appears in tabloid format on newsprint, which, especially for large-circulation magazines (the early *Fiction,* for example), substantially reduces production costs. *APR* has received funding from the National Endowment for the Arts.

American Review: see New American Review

Angel Hair. New York, N.Y.
No. 1–6, Spring 1966–Spring 1969. Irreg.
Ed. Anne Waldman; Lewis Warsh.
9¼" x 12½"　stapled (folded)　24–64 pp.

Angel Hair was a well-designed serial poetry anthology. Its issues concentrated strictly on poetry and prose-poems to the exclusion of criticism, reviews, letters, manifestos, and the like. *Angel Hair* developed its identity by focusing on late-sixties work by the poets often grouped under the term "the New York School." Of the twenty-seven poets anthologized in the *Anthology of New York Poets* (1970), edited by Ron Padgett and David Shapiro, all but Harry Mathews, David Shapiro, and Ed Sanders appeared at least once in the six issues of *Angel Hair*. Although there are great differences between the poets in this school (compare John Ashbery with Aram Saroyan), and although many of them are not native New Yorkers, a strong link of acquaintanceship ties them together, and they often appear together in other anthologies and periodicals. Other frequent *Angel Hair* contributors were Ron Padgett, Anne Waldman, Ted Berrigan, Dick Gallup, Peter Schjeldahl, Michael Brownstein, Lewis Warsh, John Perrault, Jonathan Cott, Tom Clark, and Clark Coolidge.

Circulation of *Angel Hair* was between 350 and 500 copies. See also the annotation for *The World* (below).

Antaeus. Tangier, Morocco (no. 1–4, Summer 1970–Winter 1971); Tangier, London, New York (no. 5, Spring 1972+).
No. 1, Summer 1970+. Qy.

Ed. Daniel Halpern.

6½" x 9" (varies)   sewn   96–272 pp. (double numbers to 416 pp.)

Index no. 1–20, 1970–1975 in no. 21/22, Spring/Summer 1976; no. 21–28 in no. 29.

Among magazines that began in the 1970s, *Antaeus* is one of the finest repositories for the work of the literary mainstream. Like John Lehmann's *New Writing* anthologies in the mid and late 1930s, the *Penguin New Writing* published in the 1940s, and the magazine *ZERO* of the 1950s, *Antaeus* is cosmopolitan and maintains an interest in international arts and letters. Where *Penguin New Writing* was uniformly anti-Nazi, however, and where Lehman concentrated on special interests like the Spanish Civil War and working-class writing, *Antaeus* reflects the political eclecticism of the 1970s—some Vietnam contributions, some translations of work by political radicals, but generally no fixed intellectual or political position.

Antaeus has published a number of special issues: a fifty-poet British anthology in Winter 1973; a double fiction issue in Spring/Summer 1974; two translation issues, Autumn 1974 and Winter 1975; a special essay issue, double number Spring/Summer 1976; and a popular fiction issue, double number Spring/Summer 1977.

Antaeus is much more concerned with established figures than with new writers. Featured interviews, for example (a favorite device), have been conducted with Gore Vidal, Edouard Roditi, Cyril Connolly, W. H. Auden, Andrei Voznesensky, and Stanley Kunitz, Jorge Luis Borges and Pablo Neruda, John Berryman, Gabriel García Márquez, Alfred Hitchcock, and Pier Paolo Pasolini. But such a list also typifies the geographic and artistic breadth of *Antaeus*.

Antaeus, published by Ecco Press, has a circulation of 5,000. It has received grants from CCLM.

The Antioch Review. Antioch College, Yellow Springs, Ohio.

Vol. I, no. 1, Mar. 1941+. Qy.

Editorial Board for no. 1: J. Donald Kingsley, W. B. Alexander, Paul Bixler, Freeman Champney, George R. Geiger, Lincoln R. Gibbs, Herman Schnurer [edited by committee until Vol. XXVII, no. 2, Fall 1967]; then Ed. Victor Ayoub (Vol. XXVIII, no. 4, Winter 1968/1969); Lawrence Grauman, Jr. (Vol. XXIX, no. 1–Vol. XXXII, no. 4, Spring 1969–Nov. 1973); Paul Bixler (Vol. XXXIII, no. 1–Vol. XXXV no. 2/3, Spring 1975–Spring/Summer 1977); Robert S. Fogarty (Vol. XXXV, no. 4, Fall 1977+).

5½" x 8½"   perfect   128 pp. (varies widely).

Indexed by volume.

From its inception in 1941, *The Antioch Review* has been a liberal intellectual magazine. On the eve of the Second World War, the magazine published pleas by liberals for greater involvement of Americans in sociopolitical activities. The lead article in the first issue called for a new application of scholarship to the solution of social problems, and added that "this is our purpose in founding a magazine."

During the war years, *Antioch Review* was run by an editorial board dominated by social scientists; most of the articles printed were concerned with social issues and written by economists, political scientists, and political activists. The magazine published some literary criticism but no poetry and practically no fiction. After the war, the editorial board was made up of more humanists and fewer social scientists. Finally, in 1967, the system of editing by committee came to an end, and *Antioch Review* entered a period during which it was influenced by individual editors. These included Victor Ayoub, Lawrence Grauman, Jr., and Paul Bixler. Bixler has been with the magazine from the beginning, when he was librarian at Antioch College. His own remarks on the magazine in its twenty-fifth anniversary issue give a useful survey of its publishing history.

In recent years, special issues have become an important feature. The long history of *Antioch Review*'s interest in social and literary issues is reflected in the Fall 1967 discussion of the Watts Writers Workshop. Other special issues have included "The Politics of Scholarship" (Fall 1969), "The Role and Rule(s) of Law in Contemporary America" (Summer 1970), "The Rediscovery of Cultural Pluralism" (Fall 1971), and an Ohio bicentennial issue (Summer 1976). Many fiction writers and poets have also appeared, including Alvin Greenberg, Annie Dillard, Jane Kenyon, Heather McHugh, Daniel Halpern, and Ira Sadoff.

Current circulation is about 3,200 (2,500 subscriptions). Support has come from Antioch College and the Ohio Board of Regents.

Aphra. Springtown, Pa. (Fall 1969–Winter 1970); New York (Autumn 1971+).

Vol. I, no. 1–Vol. VI, no. 3/4, Fall 1969–Spring/Summer 1976. Qy. Ed. Elizabeth Fisher [Co-editors have included Gerry Sachs, Vivien Leone, Ellen Harold, Ravelle Brickman, Dorothy Hage, Yvonne, Margaret Lamb, Sandy MacDonald, Terry Hinte, Leah Zahler, Dana Biberman, Jane Augustine, Daphne Patai, Edith Konecky, Claire Sawitzky Reed].
6¾" x 8½" stapled (folded) 72 pp.

In its first issue, the editor of *Aphra* (named for Aphra Behn, "the first woman professional writer") stated that in a patriarchal society the magazine would be "free of ulterior motives, interested only in giving women a chance to express themselves and to see themselves." Editor Elizabeth Fisher vowed to emphasize "art, not ideology." *Aphra* has frequently printed work about women that had been rejected by male-dominated magazines. Fisher discusses this policy in *Margins*, No. 7 (August/September 1973).

Almost all contributors to *Aphra* are women—some who write poetry, fiction, and essays, and some who come from conventional magazines, journalism, New York publishing, and so on. Among the prominent contributors have been Ellen Glasgow, Kate Millett, Muriel Rukeyser, Christina Stead, Marge Piercy, Colette Inez, Carolyn Kizer, Käthe Kollwitz, Erica Jong, Jean Garrigue, Adrienne Rich, Lyn Lifshin, Carol Bergé, and Sheila Delaney.

Aphra published a "Whore Issue" in Spring 1971, and another special issue in Winter 1970 to try to answer the question, "Can women and men live and work together in fairness?" The framework for the issue is a study of the lives of three "Couples from History"—Zelda and Scott Fitzgerald, Virginia and Leonard Woolf, and Harriet Taylor and John Stuart Mill.

Aphra has received grant money from CCLM. Circulation was 4,500 in 1974.

Assembling: A Collection of Otherwise Unpublishable Manuscripts. Brooklyn, N.Y.
?1970+. Annual.
Ed. Henry Korn; Richard Kostelanetz.
8½" x 11"   stapled   varies up to 300 pp.   Illus.

Assembling comes close to being a periodical that is more interesting to read about than to read. Its aim is to "help stave off the coming end of imaginative writing by putting into print what would otherwise remain unpublished." Arguing that no established literary magazine and no agency (not CCLM, nor the National Endowment for the Arts, nor any private foundations) has any real interest in the avant-garde (especially visual poetry), Richard Kostelanetz asserts that "our ultimate aim is nothing less than the creation of a literary situation open enough to allow good innovative writing to be published and yet discriminating enough to insure that it gets recognized." The *Assembling* procedure calls for approved contributors to submit 1,000 copies of up to four pages (later three pages) of any subject matter, printed in any manner on 8½" by 11" paper of any sort. *Assembling* binds the submissions in alphabetical order and sends three copies to each contributor, the remainder going to a limited number of subscribers and to single-copy purchasers.

After examining *Assembling,* one can easily agree with Kostelanetz that nearly everything printed in the collection "would be rejected by every art-literary magazine in America." Whether the work is as fertile and consequential as Kostelanetz might hope is an open question. *Assembling* does show, however, that in much recent verbal art there is a strong trend toward the use of print for nonlinear, nonverbal messages. The editors' call for "poetry, fiction, graphic art, designs, architectural proposals, or any other ideas adaptable to print" has resulted in a publication full of mixed media, visual and concrete poems, collages, and typographic experiments of all sorts. *Assembling* has received grants from CCLM. There are 1,000 copies of each issue.

Audit [Some individual issues are titled Audit/Poetry or Audit/Fiction; Vol. V, no. 3, May 1969, has cover title Audit 3]. Buffalo, N.Y.

Vol. I, no. 1, 22 Feb. 1960+. Irreg.

Ed. Ralph Maud (Vol. I, no. 1-Vol. II, no. 8, 22 Feb. 1960-Winter 1963). [Special fiction issues Vol. I, no. 8, 12; Vol. II, no. 4, 8, ed. David D. Galloway, Richard M. Koffler]; David D. Galloway (Vol. III, no. 1-2/3, Spring 1963–Summer/Fall 1963); Michael Anania (Vol. IV, no. 1-3, 1964–1967); Charles Doria (Vol. IV, no. 1-3, 1964–1967); Edward Kissam (Vol. V, no. 1-3, Spring 1968–May 1969); Mac Hammond (Vol. VI, no. 1-2, 1972–1973; Vol. VIII, no. 1, 1975+); Wayne Andrew Howitt (Vol. VI, no. 1-2, 1972–1973); Charles Baxter (Vol. VII, no. 1-2, 1973–1974).

Format varies widely; recent issues 6″ x 9″ stapled 32-56 pp.

Audit has undergone radical policy changes since its inception in 1960. Founding editor Ralph Maud, drawing on his twenty-two "staff writers," intended to hold an "audit . . . a significant reckoning of the pros and cons of the twentieth century." The result was, for a time, a small magazine that published some poems, reviews, and literary essays, along with many more essays on morality, civil defense, modern technology, and similar issues. Special fiction numbers did, however, become a regular alternating feature; these were edited by David Galloway and Richard M. Koffler.

Major changes began in 1964 with Vol. III, No. 1, when Ralph Maud stepped down and *Audit* became more consistently a literary magazine emphasizing fiction. With Vol. 4 Michael Anania and Charles Doria became the editors and began publishing poetry, which has been the central focus of the magazine since then. From 1964 to 1969 five issues appeared at irregular intervals. Anania and Doria edited special issues of work by Frank O'Hara and Robert Duncan. Edward Kissam edited a John Koethe issue and, in 1969, an anthology of fifteen poets including Anne Waldman, Theodore Enslin, Peter Schjeldahl, and Anselm Hollo. *Audit* did not appear again until 1972, when editors Mac Hammond (who had appeared in the first issue of the magazine) and Wayne Howitt established the current policy of featuring two poets in every issue (poets Alan Feldman and Mike Finn were the first pair). Only chapbook-length manuscripts by poets who have not yet published a book are considered. Other poets in this series include Gary Margolis, William B. Hunt, John Howell, Richard Pearse, Gail Fischer, Thomas Frosch, Paul Genega, Margaret Savides, Anne Pitrone, Tom Centolella, and Ron McFarland.

Audit has received support from SUNY-Buffalo, the New York State Council on the Arts, and CCLM. Recent circulation has been listed at 600. Frequency of publication and magazine format have varied widely.

Bastard Angel. San Francisco Cal.

No. 1, 1972+. Irreg. ("when funds allow").

Ed. Harold Norse.

8½″ x 11″ stapled (folded) 52–65 pp. Illus.

Bastard Angel No. 1 announces that it will "present new and established writers, with emphasis on the experimental and non-conformist in poetry, stories, excerpts from diaries and novels." Editor Harold Norse has recently described the noncomformist contents of *Bastard Angel* as "Beat. Surrealist. Cut-up, Raw Meat." The magazine, though it appears at irregular intervals, is a good source for anyone interested in the 1970s work of the Beat writers. Besides a number of previously unpublished poems by Jack Kerouac, *Bastard Angel* also carries poems, autobiographical notes, and recent experimental work by Bob Kaufman, Allen Ginsberg, Peter Orlovsky, Lawrence Ferlinghetti, William Burroughs, Michael McClure, Diane di Prima, Nanos Valaoritis (a contributing editor), and others. Issue No. 3, Fall 1974, featured "Beat Generation Poets: The Prints of Peter LeBlanc." This issue was used as the catalogue by the DeYoung Museum, where the prints were exhibited.

Two of the three issues have been supported by matching grants from the National Endowment for the Arts (one of which came from the DeYoung Museum through the NEA). Circulation is about 1,200 copies, with many single-copy sales.

The Beloit Poetry Journal. Beloit College, Beloit, Wis. [With Vol. VIII, no. 4, Summer 1958 connection with Beloit College ended].
Vol. I, no. 1, Fall 1950+. Qy.
Ed. Chad Walsh (Fall 1950–Summer 1964); Robert Glauber; David M. Stocking (Fall 1952+); David Ignatow (Fall 1952–Fall/Winter 1958); Marion Kingston Stocking (Winter 1956+); John Bennett (Spring 1961–Fall/Winter 1971/1972); David Palmer (Spring 1966–Winter 1966/1967); Brian Dibble (Spring 1970–Winter 1972/1973).
5½″ x 8½″ stapled (folded) about 40 pp.
Twenty-Five Year Index (Vol. I–XXV, 1950–1975) available separately.

The Beloit Poetry Journal's editors indicate that the magazine's editorial policy has not changed since 1950: "independent . . . publishing the best poems it receives, without preconceptions as to form, content, length, or allegiance. It also tries to keep its readers abreast of new directions in today's poetry." They substantiate their claim of ongoing concern for "new poets, the growing tip of contemporary poetry," by pointing out that *Beloit Poetry Journal* has been "the first or among the first to publish Galway Kinnell, James Dickey, Anne Sexton, Adrienne Rich, David Ignatow, David Shapiro, Erica Jong, etc."

In 1958, *Beloit Poetry Journal*'s independence and freedom from allegiances led to a significant development. Beloit College, which had sponsored the magazine since its inception, ceased to support it because of a special issue devoted to the British "movement" and the United States "underground" (Winter 1957/1958). Since then the editorial board has been solely responsible for the magazine's finances.

Over the years *Beloit Poetry Journal* has published a number of less controversial special issues and chapbooks (issued as regular numbers of the

681

magazine). Chapbook anthologies have been dedicated to Walt Whitman, Robert Frost, and William Carlos Williams; others are collections of folk songs, contemporary Asian poetry, concrete poetry, longer poems, and Western Australian poetry. Chapbooks in translation have presented work by García Lorca and Kaoru Maruyama; chapbook American poets have included Galway Kinnell, Anthony Ostroff, Winfield Townley Scott, and Suzanne Gross. A *Discoveries* chapbook, published under a matching grant from the Wisconsin Arts Foundation and Council, presented new poets recommended by established figures (among the new writers were Dennis Saleh, David Steingass, and Peter Wild). In general, the Wisconsin influence on *Beloit Poetry Journal* is slight. The magazine consistently prints a wide range of poetry by contributors, some new and some well known, from a broad geographical area.

In more than twenty-five years of publication, the format of *Beloit Poetry Journal* has changed very little. The usual size is about 40 pages. Twelve hundred copies is an average printing, with about 150 copies usually left over —a pattern which, the editors indicate, has remained remarkably stable over twenty-seven years, except for a steadily growing list of subscribing libraries. From 1950 to 1958 the magazine got "a few hundred dollars a year" from Beloit College; since then the only outside sources of support have been three grants from CCLM and one from the Wisconsin Arts Council for a special issue.

Big Table. Chicago, Ill.
[Vol. I], no. 1–Vol. II, no. 5, Spring 1959–1960. Qy.
Ed. Irving Rosenthal (no. 1, Spring 1959); Paul Carroll (no. 2, Summer 1959+).
5½" x 8"   sewn   120–158 pp.

The first number of *Big Table,* edited by Irving Rosenthal, advertised the fact that it contained "the complete contents of the suppressed Winter 1959 *Chicago Review.*" Rosenthal, who resigned at *Chicago Review,* said that the trouble there began with a *Chicago Daily News* article by Jack Mabley in the fall of 1958 called "Filthy Writing on the Midway." When the University of Chicago administrators saw the contents of the proposed winter issue (contributions by Jack Kerouac and Edward Dahlberg and excerpts from William Burroughs's *Naked Lunch*), pressure was exerted on Rosenthal to scrap the issue. Six of the seven editors, Rosenthal included, resigned. *Big Table*'s first number, with the suppressed contents of the *Chicago Review* number plus three poems by Gregory Corso, was itself banned in March 1959, and more than four hundred copies were impounded by the Post Office. In a lawsuit in which the American Civil Liberties Union defended *Big Table,* the magazine won. Judge Julius J. Hoffman quoted part of the Judge Woolsey *Ulysses* decision of 1933 in presenting his favorable judgment on July 5, 1960.

Paul Carroll became editor with *Big Table* No. 2. The second issue published a long section from Edward Dahlberg's *Because I Was Flesh* (further excerpts from the Dahlberg autobiography appeared in each subsequent issue of *Big Table*); an excerpt from Burroughs's *In Quest of Yage;* Allen Ginsberg's "Kaddish"; poems by Gael Turnbull, Brother Antoninus, Paul Blackburn, Lawrence Ferlinghetti, and André Breton; and essays on Burroughs by Alan Ansen and Paul Bowles.

Two facts distinguish *Big Table* from magazines like *Chicago Review*. First, it was a professional-looking magazine; because of the quality of its physical appearance and the huge quantity of advertising it carried, *Big Table* had more in common with commercial magazines than with most shoestring literary journals. Second, it began as a controversial magazine, publishing suppressed material, but did not shift its emphasis or settle into a less incendiary editorial policy. In issues subsequent to the two numbers mentioned, *Big Table* published the work of Kerouac, Burroughs, Blackburn, Bowles, Artaud, Dahlberg, Corso, and Ginsberg as well as work by Denise Levertov, John Ashbery, Robert Duncan, Ed Dorn, Peter Orlovsky, Jean Genet, Frank O'Hara, Norman Mailer, Michael McClure, James Wright, John Rechy, Kenneth Koch, Diane di Prima, Philip Lamantia, Gary Snyder, LeRoi Jones, Charles Olson, Paul Carroll, Bill Berkson, Pablo Neruda, John Updike, and Alain Robbe-Grillet. From Spring 1959 to the middle of 1960, *Big Table* presented a concentrated package of non-establishment literature.

The Black Mountain Review. Black Mountain College, Black Mountain, N.C.
Vol. I, no. 1–7, Spring 1954–Autumn 1957. No. 1–4: qy; no. 5–7: irreg.
Ed. Robert Creeley.
No. 1–4: 6⅜" x 8½" sewn 64 pp. Illus.
No. 5–7: 4¾" x 6⅝" sewn 224–240 pp. Illus.

Because he believed that the poetry magazines of the early fifties were either "dominated by the New Critics . . . or else . . . so general in character that no active center of coherence was possible," Editor Robert Creeley—with help from Charles Olson, Kenneth Rexroth, Irving Layton, and Paul Blackburn—founded *The Black Mountain Review*. It was an extension of magazines like Cid Corman's *Origin,* and in some respects (especially because of the "chunky" size of the last three issues) a prototype of magazines like *Caterpillar.*

Creeley's magazine was built in part around the faculty and students of Black Mountain College. Charles Olson was then college rector; Robert Creeley, Richard Hillman, and Robert Duncan had all taught there; Jonathan Williams, Joel Oppenheimer, Fielding Dawson, Ed Dorn, Michael Rumaker, and Tom Field either had been or still were students. But *Black Mountain Review* did not draw exclusively on the college. The seven issues of the magazine also published work by C. G. Jung, Jorge Luis Borges, William Carlos Williams, William Lee, Jack Kerouac, Allen

Ginsberg, Herbert Read, Paul Goodman, Lorine Niedecker, James Purdy, Louis Zukofsky, Hubert Selby, Jr., and Judson Crews.

Robert Creeley has also indicated the extent to which *Black Mountain Review* was founded to supplement the poetry published in magazines like *Origin*. "One possibility did seem to me lacking in *Origin*, despite occasional notes and reviews, and that was the ground that an active, ranging critical section might effect." Despite some interesting essays, however (Jung's "The Mass and the Individual Process," Zukofsky's "Bottom on Shakespeare," frequent aggressive reviews by Martin Seymour-Smith—one of which, an attack on Theodore Roethke, caused Kenneth Rexroth's resignation as a contributing editor), *Black Mountain Review* was primarily a poetry magazine whose attempts at critical "grounding" were always a sidelight.

Black Mountain College provided funding. The print run was from 500 to 750 copies.

Blue Cloud Quarterly. Marvin, S.D.

Vol. I, no. 1 [?1954] +. Qy.

Ed. Brother Benet Tvedten, O.S.B. [Editorship of pre-literary magazine issues undetermined—see below].

5¾" x 8¾"   stapled   12–24 pp.   Illus.

Blue Cloud Quarterly specializes in American Indian literature. Begun as a parochial newsletter intended for members and benefactors of the Benedictine community at Blue Cloud Abbey, it gradually shifted emphasis under the editorship of Brother Benet Tvedten and by 1971 had evolved into an exclusively literary publication offering "prose and mostly poetry on Indian themes." It is from the time of this transition that *Blue Cloud Quarterly* is of interest to students of small literary magazines.

Blue Cloud Quarterly is a clean, spare, elegantly produced magazine; some issues are mini-anthologies, but many issues focus upon the work of a single writer. Within the boundaries of American Indian literature *Blue Cloud Quarterly* is open and eclectic. It offers translations of anonymous tribal songs (Vol. XX, No. 1, n.d., versions by David Cloutier of Northwest coast songs; Vol. XXII, No. 3, 1976, translations by Jim Heynen of Sioux songs), writings by American Indians who have appeared in general literary magazines (Norman H. Russell, Wendy Rose, Buffy Sainte Marie), and a good deal of poetry and commentary by young writers of varied Indian ancestry (one issue, Vol. XV, No. 3, n.d., printed poems by Pueblo, Ute, Seneca Seminole, Navajo, and Nez Percé poets). If there is any particular emphasis in *Blue Cloud Quarterly* it is perhaps a focus upon the Sioux, a tribe with whom the Blue Cloud Abbey has immediate connections. Volume XIX, No. 1 (n.d.), for example, presents "Two Legends of the Sioux," narrated by Wamdi Wicasa and sponsored by the American Indian Cultural Research Center of Blue Cloud Abbey.

Current circulation is about 3,250. The chief source of funding is the Benedictine Missionaries.

684

Botteghe Oscure. Rome, Italy.

Vol. I–XXV, Spring 1948–Autumn 1960. 2/yr.

Ed. Marguerite Caetani [with various assistants].

5½" x 9" perfect (may have been sewn) 240–622 pp. (usually over 450 pp.).

Index Vol. I–X issued separately in 1953; complete index by Wesleyan University Press, with introduction by Archibald MacLeish.

After she had run the French quarterly *Commerce* for almost a decade 1924–1932), Marguerite Chapin (Princess Caetani) decided to found a multilingual magazine. A relative of hers, T. S. Eliot, advised her not to; he didn't believe a multilingual publication could be successful. But *Botteghe Oscure,* founded in 1948, did succeed despite the fact that it did not originate in one culture, nor were its contents restricted to the work of any one literary movement. *Botteghe Oscure* published a diverse group of poets in half a dozen languages; during twelve years of publication, 650 writers of thirty nationalities appeared in its pages.

Caetani took particular care with the magazine's format, so that the poems in different languages had a distinctive appearance. She also preserved the multilingual interest of her enterprise by printing foreign-language versions of English poems. Robert Lowell's "Quaker Graveyard in Nantucket" and John Keats's "Ode on a Grecian Urn," for example, were translated into Italian.

Among the poets who published their work in *Botteghe Oscure,* one finds Wallace Stevens, e. e. cummings, Marianne Moore, William Carlos Williams, Randall Jarrell, Leonie Adams, James Merrill, Theodore Roethke, Stanley Kunitz, Anthony Hecht, Richard Wilbur, Archibald MacLeish, Robert Penn Warren, Dylan Thomas (the first draft of *Under Milk Wood,* "Do Not Go Gentle . . ."), W. H. Auden, Walter de la Mare, Kathleen Raine, Edith Sitwell, Roy Fuller, Louis MacNeice, Elizabeth Bowen, Thom Gunn, Robert Graves, Charles Tomlinson, Paul Valéry, Albert Camus, André Malraux, Antonin Artaud, Ingeborg Bachmann, Heinrich Böll, Uwe Johnson, Eugenio Montale, Natalia Ginzburg, Carlos Fuentes, Octavio Paz, and Jorge Guillén.

Botteghe Oscure was funded by Marguerite Caetani. Circulation has been estimated at about 5,000 copies.

Boundary 2: A Journal of Postmodern Literature. SUNY-Binghamton, Binghamton, N.Y.

Vol. I, no. 1, Fall 1972+. 3/yr.

Ed. William V. Spanos; Robert Kroetsch.

5¾" x 8¾" sewn 230–350 pp. Illus.

Indexed by volume.

While *Boundary 2,* subtitled "A Journal of Postmodern Literature," has been a significant outlet for experimental fiction and for recent poetry, "especially that in the Pound-Williams-Olson-Creeley line," this magazine is most closely associated with postmodern literary criticism and theory:

"criticism, theoretical and practical, with an awareness of post-New Critical, post-Structuralist phenomenology and hermeneutics." Special issues have been devoted to Charles Olson, Martin Heidegger, Jack Spicer, Canadian literature, Greek writing, and "The Oral Impulse in Contemporary American Poetry." Supplements have been devoted to David Ignatow, Nathaniel Tarn, Robert Bly, and "Contemporary American Fiction" (with discussion centered on Barthelme, Barth, Pynchon, Nabokov, and Sukenick). The 330-page Winter 1977 issue includes papers from a symposium on postmodern literary theory held at SUNY-Binghamton on March 25–27, 1976.

According to the editors of *Boundary 2*, its "central critical focus is derived from the temporally oriented philosophy of Heidegger and existential phenomenology. A key point of attack therefore becomes the spatial, object oriented perspective of, for example, New Criticism and Structuralism." In "Modernism and Postmodernism: Approaching the Present in American Poetry" in the first issue (Fall 1972), David Antin discusses modernist literature in terms of collage (with pieces selected and arranged by the artist) and contrasts postmodernist creativity, which is based upon perceptions of a phenomenological reality that "is 'discovered' and 'constructed' by poets" and which is "part of a great Romantic metaphysic and epistemology."

In "From Symbolist Thought to Immanence: The Ground of Post-Modern American Poetics" in the Spring 1973 issue, Charles Altieri explains that modernist, symbolist writers stress the creative faculties of the poet as observer (Coleridgean view), while postmodern writers stress the immanent power of perceived objects (Wordsworthian view). The development of *Boundary 2* has involved an "issue-to-issue attempt to help define postmodern literature and criticism, as well as to 're-read' key Modernist texts."

Contributors to *Boundary 2* have included essayists and critics Edward W. Said, Ihab Hassan, Ralph J. Mills, Jr., Nathan A. Scott, Jr., Jerome Rothenberg, and Dennis Tedlock; creative writers Arlene Zekowski, David Ignatow, Susan Fromberg Schaeffer, Greg Kuzma, Eli Mandel, Clayton Eshleman, John Tagliabue, Theodore Enslin, and Yannis Ritsos.

Boundary 2 has been aided by SUNY-Binghamton as well as by CCLM and the New York State Council on the Arts. Subscriptions, a major source of funds, are at about 500 and slowly rising.

The Carleton Miscellany. Carleton College, Northfield, Minn.
Vol. I, no. 1, Winter 1960+. Freq. varies.
Ed. Reed Whittemore (Winter 1960–Summer 1964); Erling Larsen (Fall 1964–Summer 1970); Wayne Carver (Summer 1971–Fall/Winter 1976/1977); Keith Harrison (Winter 1977/1978+).
6" x 8½" perfect 96–176 pp.
Indexed by volume.

The *Carleton Miscellany* is a continuation of Reed Whittemore's *Furioso* (1939–1952), a magazine of verse, fiction, and cultural comment. The characteristic "Department of Culture and Civilization" column in *Furioso*, for example, had criticized the Book-of-the-Month Club, discussed the dangers of the hydrogen bomb, and satirized academic rhetoric. In *Carleton Miscellany* Whittemore continued this social critique in featuring Wayne Booth's satiric column, "Department of American," and more pointedly in the symposiums, which treated topics like "The City and Its Planners" (Summer 1962); "Foundations and Magazines," with essays by Allen Tate, Dwight Macdonald, Henry Rago, Robie Macauley, and Paul Carroll (Spring 1963); "What to Do About the *New York Times Book Review*" (Winter 1963); what's wrong with graduate training in the humanities (Winter 1964); a retrospect on the 1930s, with poems, essays, and reminiscences by Jack Conroy, David Ignatow, Nelson Algren, and Malcolm Cowley (Winter 1965); a symposium on little magazines (Spring 1966); a "Challenges to Reason" issue in which Wayne Booth discussed the rhetoric of the public media (Fall 1967); and a symposium on the state of the liberal arts in universities (Winter 1970). The symposiums indicate *Carleton Miscellany*'s interest in the role played by politics in communication and art.

Carleton Miscellany has also published the poetry, fiction, and essays of writers like A. R. Ammons, William Stafford, Diane Wakoski, Stephen Spender, Joyce Carol Oates, and Howard Nemerov.

Major funding for the magazine has come from Carleton College.

Circulation is about 1,000 copies.

Carolina Quarterly. University of North Carolina, Chapel Hill, N.C.

Vol. I, no. 1, Fall 1948+. 3/yr.

Ed. no. 1: William Sessions [changes frequently].

6" x 9" perfect 120 pp. Illus.

Index with Kraus reprint edition.

Carolina Quarterly is proud of the fact that it is part of a great tradition and frequently advertises itself as the fourth manifestation of a University of North Carolina journal which has previously appeared as *North Carolina University Magazine* (1844), *North Carolina Magazine* (1861), and *New Carolina Magazine* (1920). As the opening issue's editorial indicates, *Carolina Quarterly* commenced in 1948 with a strictly regional goal: to be "a quarterly which would ultimately represent the intellectual and artistic endeavors of students here, of people of thought and feeling throughout the state and region." Ten years later, however, the tenth birthday issue (Fall 1957) announced that in addition to creative writing and literary criticism it would begin to publish book reviews as well. A concomitant policy shift came with the inclusion of more and more works from experimental and non-southern writers, so that *Carolina Quarterly* has developed into a cosmopolitan little magazine with a general readership. A thirtieth anniversary issue (Winter 1978) includes John Tagliabue, George Hitchcock, and Albert Goldbarth. Among the many other 1970s contributors have been poets Doug Blazek, Peter Wild, Greg Kuzma, Arthur Vogelsang, Howard McCord, John Hollander, Kate Jennings, Lyn Lifshin, Andrei Voznesensky, William Stafford, Annie Dillard, Philip Dacey, Ira Sadoff, Danny L. Rendleman, Susan Fromberg Schaeffer, Stanley Cooperman, Joyce Carol Oates, and Raymond Carver. Fiction has been contributed by Anthony Burgess, Joy Williams, Michael Jennings, Jerry Bumpus, Joyce Carol Oates, Donald Barthelme, Barry Hannah, Annie Dillard, Rosellen Brown, Don DeLillo, and Ursule Molinaro.

The financial status of the magazine has been helped by a patronage program in which funds from donors are matched by grants from CCLM and the North Carolina Arts Council. Circulation is approximately 1,500.

Caterpillar [no. 1: a magazine of the leaf, a gathering of the tribes; no. 2–12: a gathering of the tribes]. New York, N.Y. (Oct. 1967–Jul. 1970); Sherman Oaks, Cal. (Oct. 1970+).

No. 1–20, Oct. 1967–Jun. 1973. Qy.

Ed. Clayton Eshleman.

5½″ x 7″ perfect (4 issues sewn) 128–256 pp. (double numbers over 300 pp.) Illus.

The original *Caterpillar*, edited by Clayton Eshleman, was a series of chapbooks by Louis Zukofsky, Paul Blackburn, David Antin, Eshleman, and others, published from 1966 to 1967 by Jim Lowell of Asphodel Books. Eshleman began the magazine *Caterpillar* in the same format (the distinctive, squat 5″ x 6″ trim size) as the last few issues of *Black Mountain Review*. As Robert Bertholf suggests in *Caterpillar* 20 (June 1973), Eshleman owed more than trim size to Robert Creeley's journal; it was "an extension of *Origin* and *Black Mountain Review*, in the sense that it provided a place for the writers of that generation to publish."

Caterpillar was, however, more than an extension of Cid Corman's and Creeley's magazines. As Eshleman has indicated, it published writers as different in craft and attitude as Diane Wakoski, Frank Samperi, Norman O. Brown, Jackson MacLow, Jerome Rothenberg, Cid Corman, Kenneth Irby, Carolee Schneemann, and Stan Brakhage. As some of the names indicate, Eshleman was for some time interested in translations, and published many of his own translations of César Vallejo. Early issues carried a series called "A Test of Translation," featuring two or more translations of a work in a foreign language with several commentaries assembled by the "collector" of each exercise. Some of the works tested were by Vallejo, Aimé Césaire, Akutagowa Ryunosuke, Antonin Artaud, and Paul Celan. After the first four issues, Robert Kelly joined *Caterpillar* as a contributing editor and was responsible for a section in each issue.

Because it contained three to four times as many pages as most privately printed literary magazines, *Caterpillar* was able to devote thirty to forty pages to single poets. July 1970 was a special issue devoted to work by

Robin Blaser and Jack Spicer. Number 15/16 (1971) contained 75 poems by Stephen Jonas. Number 19 (October 1972) contained ninety-nine pages by Gary Snyder as well as work by Robert Kelly, Theodore Enslin, César Vallejo, Thomas Meyer, and Eshleman. *Caterpillar* also published regular reviews by Frank Samperi and Stan Brakhage, artwork, movie stills, and works in progress.

Caterpillar received three CCLM grants. Print runs varied from 1,000 copies for Nos. 1 and 2 and 17–20, to 3,500 for Nos. 3–16. Library subscriptions never numbered more than 60. Doubleday-Anchor published *A Caterpillar Anthology* in 1971, drawn from issues 1 through 12.

Center. Woodstock, N.Y. [place varies].

1970+. Irreg.

Ed. Carol Bergé.

8½" x 11" stapled (folded)   80–100 pp. (recent issues) reproduced from typewriting.

"*Center* wants to see short non-form prose from known writers—exciting work unacceptable in the usual media. Many resemble previous forms, but we are not involved in formal-concept writing. See contents for clues." The contents of this irregularly issued periodical do indeed validate the statement that introduces issue No. 1. Almost all the contributions are limited to one or two typed pages. The writing is relatively unanchored and "experimental," but strictly in prose format—no collages/visual prose poems/concrete patterns. The contributors include Jonathan Baumbach, Raymond Federman, Ronald Sukenick, Fielding Dawson, Ed Sanders, Theodore Enslin, David Antin, Jackson MacLow, Arlene Zekowski, Stanley Berne, Joseph Bruchac, John Jacob, Carol Bergé, Clarence Major, Gayl Jones, Richard Kostelanetz, Joe David Bellamy, Alta, and Jack Micheline. Editor Carol Bergé refuses almost all first-person contributions. "My stance is that I deplore confessional writing as not being 'art,' and I believe diaries and journals are miles behind the competent writer; very few writers are interesting enough to create/sustain first person." Poetry is never published in *Center*. Summarizing the magazine's special interests, the editor says that she publishes "sections from letters, from novels in progress, 'articles' about innovative or experimental lifestyle material (astrology, biorhythms, new educational techniques, psychic phenomena, etc.)." *Center* is at present undergoing a change in emphasis from one- or two-page selections to longer chapbook-size contributions.

Center's print run is 450 to 500. There are no subscriptions or advance sales and no bookstore sales. CCLM has provided partial funding (allowing nominal payments to authors).

Chelsea Review [no. 6, Winter 1960+: Chelsea]. New York, N.Y.

No. 1, Summer 1958+. Irreg.

Ed. Robert Kelly (no. 1–5, Summer 1958–Summer 1959); Ursule Molinaro (no. 1–17, Summer 1958–Aug. 1965); Venable Herndon (no. 2–17, Au-

tumn 1958–Aug. 1965); George Economou (no. 2–5, Autumn 1958–Summer 1959); Sonia Raiziss (no. 6, Winter 1960+); Alfredo de Palchi (no. 6–24/25, Winter 1960–Oct. 1968); David Ignatow (no. 24/25–29, Oct. 1968–July 1971).
5½" x 8½"   sewn   70–245 pp.   Illus.

Chelsea ("Review" was dropped from the title after five issues) began under the editorship of Robert Kelly and Ursule Molinaro, with George Economou as European editor. In five regularly issued quarterly numbers, the editors presented a cosmopolitan selection of literature that included fiction by Martin Buber, Raja Rao, Nathalie Sarraute, and Cecil Hemley (*A Folly to the Greeks,* serialized as the Chelsea Novel of 1958) and poetry by Daniel Berrigan, Paris Leary, Armand Schwerner, Jerome Rothenberg, David Antin, Blaise Cendrars, and Boris Pasternak. Number 4 (Spring 1959) contained a selection of contemporary African poetry. After No. 5 (Summer 1959), Robert Kelly and George Economou left with Joan Kelly to form *Trobar,* while Ursule Molinaro, Sonia Raiziss, Venable Herndon, and Alfredo de Palchi formed a new editorial board which continued the international flavor of the magazine (perhaps even increasing the number of translations). Special issues have been devoted to French (No. 13, June 1963) and to Italian (No. 18/19, June 1966) literature; No. 9 (March 1961) contained an interesting special unit on workshop poetry; No. 12 (September 1962) carried several pieces by and about Laura Riding, a fairly regular contributor. *Chelsea* also has been one of the few little magazines that regularly prints plays.
Since its change in editorship, *Chelsea* has appeared irregularly (about two issues a year including double numbers). It has kept up with developments such as pattern poetry and the prose poem. Some issues have had guest poetry editors (e.g., A. R. Ammons, Michael Benedikt), and through the 1960s *Chelsea* published dozens of the most active and best known practicing poets.
Editorial control has changed periodically, with Sonia Raiziss remaining the constant factor. A typical print run of 900 to 1,400 copies is widely circulated. Size has varied from 94 pages to 245-page double numbers. Some aid has been accepted from the National Endowment for the Arts, and from CCLM and the New York State Council on the Arts.

Chicago Choice: see Choice.

The Chicago Review. Chicago, Ill.
Vol. I, no. 1, Winter 1946+. Qy.
Ed. no. 1 Carol Dillard, Radcliffe Squires [changes frequently].
5¾" x 8¾"   perfect (early issues stapled–folded)   160–230 pp.
Indexed by volume.

The Chicago Review is edited by graduate students at the University of Chicago, and has thus been that sort of university magazine which changes

690

editors very frequently, often with each school year. The editors try to mix student and local writers with better known literary figures. Beginning as a small, indifferently produced paper, containing student work buttressed by an occasional professional piece by a Chicago writer such as James T. Farrell or by University of Chicago faculty members, *Chicago Review* grew steadily in size and scope until by Vol. IX (1955) it had become a genuine literary and cultural magazine of national scope. Aside from some overzealous defense of Chicago humanists and the occasional puffery of R. S. Crane and Elder Olson, the early *Chicago Review* established an attitude of youthful exuberance and positive faith in new directions that has characterized the magazine throughout its history. The Spring 1958 issue was particularly influential (see the annotation on *Big Table,* above).

In recent years *Chicago Review* has been a supporter of experiments in poetry, such as concrete poetry and *Poesia Visiva* (the next step after concretism), which is the special subject of Vol. XXVI, No. 3 (1974), edited by Thomas Joyce. In fiction, too, much space has been given to such "new writers" as John Mella, Gilbert Sorrentino, David Zane Mairowitz, Blaise Cendrars, and John Jacob. Though the 1940s tendency to puff the Chicago humanists is recapitulated by a 1970s willingness to permit (to cite one example) rather uncritical backslapping of (and at times by) Ronald Sukenick, Jonathan Baumbach, Jerome Klinkowitz, and the Fiction Collective, *Chicago Review* remains a vital source for new thrusts in fiction and poetry, both American and foreign. Recent issues have printed translations of Robbe-Grillet, Nathalie Sarraute, Jorge Luis Borges, Roland Barthes, and others, while special issues have been devoted to modern Japanese poetry and Latin American writing (a bilingual issue). Total paid circulation of *Chicago Review* is about 2,000, with mail subscriptions accounting for 1,470 copies. Funding is largely from sales revenues, a University of Chicago subsidy, and grants from CCLM and the Illinois Arts Council. The German government has contributed toward a special bilingual issue of postwar German language writing.

Choice [no. 1: Chicago Choice]. Chicago, Ill.
Vol. I, no. 1, Spring 1961+. Irreg. ("occasionally").
Ed. John Logan; Aaron Siskind (no. 2–6, 1962–1970); Milton Kessler (no. 9, 1974+).
8¼″ x 9″ sewn (no. 7+: perfect) 112–243 pp. (double number 326 pp.). Illus.
Index no. 1–6 in no. 6, 1970.

Choice is an attractively produced, representative blend of new and well-known poets. Numbers 1 through 6 included close to three hundred poets. Editor John Logan claims first publication of Shirley Kaufman, Stan Rice, Marvin Bell, William Hunt, Dennis Schmitz, Bill Knott, Naomi Lazard, Jessie Kachmar, and others. *Choice* No. 1 alone contained an impressive roster of seventy-three poets, among them A. R. Ammons, Robert Bly, Hayden Carruth, John Ciardi, e. e. cummings, James Dickey, Galway Kinnell, Denise Levertov, W. S. Merwin, Howard Nemerov, Jerome Rothenberg, Dennis Schmitz, and James Wright.

In No. 2 Aaron Siskind became co-editor, with special responsibility for photography and graphics. From that issue on, *Choice* has played a major role among little magazines in combining poetry, photography, and graphics.

With No. 9 the editors announced a change in strategy: unsolicited manuscripts would no longer be accepted, and the magazine would concentrate solely on chapbooks of solicited material. For a magazine that has often published as many as a hundred poets in one issue, this decision has been a major policy shift.

Despite its concentration on the poem itself, *Choice* has managed to include an occasional controversy. In the opening issue, Marvin Bell attacked Donald M. Allen for including all those "pseudo-hipsters" in the anthology *The New American Poetry*. Controversy escalated with No. 2 when John Logan printed a Robert Bly article that had been "originally commissioned by the *Hudson Review*, and later withdrawn . . . when they refused to print certain sections." When the editor of *Hudson Review,* Frederick Morgan, publicly denounced *Choice*, John Logan took the matter to a CCLM meeting.

Choice has had grants from CCLM, and both SUNY-Buffalo and SUNY-Binghamton have contributed funds. Current circulation is about 1,000 (down from a peak of 3,000 copies for numbers 2 through 6).

Clown War. Brooklyn, N. Y.

No. 1, Feb. 1972+. Irreg.

Ed. Bob Herman [Co-founder Stephen Fairhurst is co-editor of some issues].

5″ x 7″   stapled   32–40 pp.

Clown War offers an outlet for short experimental poems, especially in the new surrealist mode, and for experimental graphics. Despite the magazine's small size, the index to Nos. 1–12 includes 110 contributors, among whom are Keith Abbott, Douglas Blazek, Ray Di Palma, Russell Edson, Albert Goldbarth, Richard Kostelanetz, Michael Lally, Lyn Lifshin, Opal L. Nations, Marge Piercy, Rochelle Ratner, Ron Silliman, and Keith Waldrop.

With No. 13 (1977) Heman decided to distribute the magazine free of charge. The first free issue included the work of John Jacob, Paul Colinet (tr. Rochelle Ratner), Richard Kostelanetz, Francis Picabia (tr. Rochelle Ratner), and others. Editor Heman has also issued *Clown War Extras,* usually odd-size artworks that would not fit the magazine. (A. F. Caldiero, Rochelle Ratner, and B. Solomon, as well as Bob Heman, have been featured in *Extras*.) Special issues have been devoted to prose poems by

692

the Belgian surrealist Paul Colinet and to the rubber-stamp art of Leavenworth Jackson.

Clown War is an open, unpredictable magazine in which poets can experiment freely. Heman currently distributes 1,500 copies (mainly through selected bookstores and art galleries) within Manhattan, and intends soon to expand to 2,500 copies. CCLM has provided grants.

December: A Magazine of the Arts and the Opinions. ?Iowa City, Iowa (Vol. I–II, 1958–1959); Chicago, Ill. (Vol. III, 1960+; local address occasionally changes).

Vol. I, ?1958+. Irreg.

Ed. Richard Schechner, Deborah Trissel, and Louis Vaczek (Vol. I, ?1958); Jeff Marks (Vol. II–IV, 1959–1963) [with various co-editors]; Curt Johnson (Vol. V, 1963+) [with various co-editors].

5½" x 8½" no. 1–10: sewn; no. 11+: perfect 100–388 pp. Illus.

Although *December* began in 1958 with three editors, who were soon succeeded by two new editors, the magazine is now largely identified with editor Curt Johnson and with his predilection for short fiction and novellas. Johnson has attacked cronyism in government-supported art (in articles in the *San Francisco Review of Books* and *The Smith*), and his publishing policy indicates that he has no particular regard for names or reputations. In Vol. XIV, No. 1 (1972), he summarizes the contents of fifteen years of *December*: (1) one novel (*Anaconda* by Jerry Bumpus), (2) one chapbook (*The Fake Revolt* by George Legman), (3) 125 short stories, (4) 41 articles about film, (5) 728 poems, (6) 94 book reviews, (7) 59 general articles, (8) two plays, (9) six interviews, (10) 173 pages of photos, and (11) 182 pages of graphic art. He concludes by saying that the editors have read 200,000,006 manuscripts.

Most of the recent issues have been devoted to a single long work—for example, Curt Johnson's *Nobody's Perfect* and Jay Robert Nash's *On All Fronts* in 1974; Matthew Hochberg's *Sweet Gogarty* and Robert Wilson's *Young in Illinois* in 1975; and John Bennett's *The Night of the Great Butcher* in 1976.

In 1972 Curt Johnson reported 238 subscribers (170 of them libraries). Contributing editor Robert Wilson estimates that cash gifts to *December* during the first nine years of publication amounted to $4,066 ($3,050 from CCLM), and the overall cash loss was $10,000.

El Corno Emplumado. Mexico City, Mexico.

No. 1–31, Jan. 1962–Jul. 1969. Qy.

Ed. Margaret Randall; Sergio Mondragon (Jan. 1962–Oct. 1968); Harvey Wolin (Jan. 1962–Apr. 1962); Robert Cohn (Apr. 1969+).

5½" x 8" (some 7½") no. 1–19, 24: sewn; no. 20, 26–27, 31: perfect 100–256 pp. Illus.

El Corno Emplumado began in 1962 as a magazine of international and interracial unity, publishing many translations of poems from English to

Spanish and vice versa, often with the original *en face*. As the sixties progressed and the magazine's liberal aesthetic attitude became increasingly politicized by the civil rights movement and the war in Vietnam, its content became more radically anti-war and anti-establishment. This shift was reflected in an editorial in No. 17 (January 1966): "We will be sharper, harder in our choice of publishable material, try to get further to the roots of what's happening. We plan to devote more space to the long, significant poem [and] also plan a series of translations of important major works from both languages. Allen Ginsberg's 'Kaddish' in this issue being the first." (The Ginsberg poem appeared in a Spanish translation by Ernesto de la Peña.)

Early issues of *El Corno Emplumado* had special sections for translations into English and Spanish of poetry from Guatemala, Nicaragua, Argentina, Ecuador, Uruguay, Cuba, Colombia, Canada, the Netherlands, Finland, and Russia. The Mexican anthology (No. 18, 1966) was the first extended bilingual edition. The large Cuban anthology in No. 23 (July 1967) was also bilingual. *El Corno* published Spanish translations of the work of T. S. Eliot, Allen Ginsberg, Robert Creeley, Lawrence Ferlinghetti, William Carlos Williams, and Ezra Pound. For the first four years, the last issue of each year was devoted to the work of a single poet: Agusti Bartra in October 1962, Robert Kelly in October 1963, Raquel Jodorowsky in October 1964, and George Bowering in October 1965.

In the issue for January 1969 the editors revealed that the Mexican government had cut off the magazine's subsidy; they were able to continue publishing only until the July issue.

Margaret Randall writes that *El Corno Emplumado* "was mainly funded by Mexican government grants, individuals, benefits, art sales." Average circulation was 3,000 copies per issue.

Epoch. Cornell University, Ithaca, N. Y.

Vol. I, no. 1, Fall 1947+. Qy. (now 3/yr.).

Editor-in-chief Baxter Hathaway (Fall 1947–June 1976) [a shifting list of co-editors served with Hathaway]; Walter Slatoff, Alison Lurie, Robert Morgan, William J. Harris, and Thomas Johnson (Fall 1976); James McConkey, Walter Slatoff, Alison Lurie, Ken McClane, William Harris, and Thomas Johnson (Winter 1976); Walter Slatoff and James McConkey (Spring 1977+).

5" x 9"   perfect (early issues stapled)   96 pp. (recently)

Complete index 1947–1964 in Winter 1964; also, regular biennial indexes.

Editor Baxter Hathaway announced in the first issue of *Epoch* that the magazine would "print a lot of fiction and poetry" and not much criticism; in the early postwar years many felt that literary criticism had forced original work out of magazines entirely. For thirty years *Epoch* has followed its original plan and, despite the accusation that it is too "establishment," has maintained a reputation for publishing good work, especially short stories. The Spring 1959 issue, for example, included the first published stories of Thomas Pynchon ("Mortality and Mercy in Vienna") and Ronald Sukenick ("The Sleeping Gypsy"). Other fiction writers who have often appeared in *Epoch* are Joyce Carol Oates, Jack Matthews, Cyrus Colter, Ray Bradbury, and William Carlos Williams. Also published has been poetry by William Dickey, A. R. Ammons, Chad Walsh, e. e. cummings, Daniel Berrigan, and John Haines.

In the winter of 1971 *Epoch* began to appoint an editor for prose and one for poetry for each issue, so as to expedite the handling of manuscripts and to economize on editorial responsibility.

Epoch currently prints 1,200 copies per issue (600 to libraries, 150 to individual subscribers). It has received grants from CCLM.

Evergreen Review. New York, N.Y.
Vol. I, no. 1–Vol. XVII, no. 97, Jan./Feb./Mar. 1957–Summer 1973.
Freq. varies.
Ed. Barney Rosset; Donald Allen (Jan./Feb./Mar. 1957–Spring 1959).
No. 1–31: 5¼" x 8" (varies) 158–260 pp.
No. 32+: 8¼" x 11" about 96 pp.
Binding varies: sewn/perfect/stapled Illus.
No. 97 is tabloid on newsprint.
Index to Evergreen Review (1957–1970), by David A. Bower and Carol Campbell Strempek, Scarecrow Press, Inc., 1972.

In its early issues (during the time when Donald Allen was Barney Rosset's co-editor), *Evergreen Review* was a literary magazine hospitable to the New York poets, the San Francisco writers, and international writers of a sort likely to appeal to Grove Press, Inc. With sponsorship by a publishing house and with a much larger operating budget than most literary magazines, *Evergreen* was able to print in issue No. 1 such established writers as Jean-Paul Sartre and Samuel Beckett, along with Michael Hamburger, Henri Michaux, Harold Feinstein, James Purdy, and Mark Schorer. Other contributors to early issues included Albert Camus, William Carlos Williams, Eugène Ionesco, Alain Robbe-Grillet, Karl Jaspers, Federico García Lorca, St. John Perse, Boris Pasternak, e. e. cummings, and Robert Lowell. From the beginning, though, *Evergreen* had little interest in first publications. Many of the contributions from the writers named above had originally appeared elsewhere, often in Europe, and were subsequently printed in *Evergreen.*

Issue No. 2 (April/June 1957) was in effect a special San Francisco number and contained the work of Kenneth Rexroth, Brother Antoninus, Robert Duncan, Lawrence Ferlinghetti, Henry Miller, Michael McClure, Gary Snyder, Jack Kerouac, Allen Ginsberg, and others, as well as a Ralph J. Gleason article on the San Francisco jazz scene, some Harry Redl photos of San Francisco poets, and Dore Ashton on the "San Francisco School" of art.

As time went on, *Evergreen,* widening and popularizing its contents, added jazz columns and then articles on various aspects of popular culture while concentrating more and more on second or later publication of much material, until by the early 1960s it had become a kind of *Reader's Digest* of literary magazines.

In another shift of emphasis, *Evergreen,* which had always welcomed controversial writers and questioned the censors (No. 1 contained an article by Mark Schorer on *Lady Chatterley's Lover),* got into the business of nude photo-essays, and articles and stories of graphically sexual content. Thus it completed its modulation from literary magazine to *Reader's Digest* to the *Playboy* of literary magazines. It did, however, continue to print well-known and respected writers and to make new writings available to a wider audience; for example, *Evergreen* printed the text of Michael McClure's *The Beard* and of Tom Stoppard's *Rosencrantz and Guildenstern Are Dead.* When *Rosencrantz and Guildenstern* appeared in *Evergreen,* it had already been discovered at the Edinburgh Festival, brought to London where it became a success, and then staged in New York to further acclaim. *Evergreen* wasn't making any discovery, but it was making available to a magazine audience a new play by an important new playwright. This process was typical of *Evergreen* throughout the 1960s and until its demise as a tabloid in 1973. Therefore, though it was important as a genuine literary magazine only for eight or ten issues, it retained a certain significance to literary history throughout its run of ninety-seven issues.

Fiction. New York, N. Y.
Vol. I, no. 1, Nov./Dec. 1972+. Freq. varies.
Ed. Mark Mirsky.
Vol. I–II: 11½ " x 16" (varies)   folded   24–32 pp.   Illus.
Vol. III–V, no. 1: 10" x 14" (varies)   folded   32–36 pp.   Illus.
Vol. V, no. 2/3: 6" x 9"   perfect   256 pp.

Partly because of the cost of paper, print, and layouts, the short story has lagged behind poetry in little-magazine publication during the sixties and seventies. Mark Mirsky's *Fiction* tries to reduce the odds somewhat by printing only fiction—no criticism, reviews, or poetry and no correspondence. Originally a tabloid (until Vol. III, No. 1, in 1974), and then an outsize format with uncomplicated layouts, *Fiction* has been able to print fiction by a dozen or more contributors in each issue.

Fiction has also been important in keeping both serious readers and major New York publishers apprised of new work by serious novelists. A significant part of each issue is devoted to excerpts from novels. The first fourteen issues contained contributions from Stanley Elkin, Donald Barthelme, John Hawkes, John Barth, Samuel Beckett, Anthony Burgess, Joyce Carol Oates, and James Purdy. Editor Mark Mirsky's affiliation with the City College of New York is reflected in the table of contents. He also publishes work by members of the Fiction Collective and by John Ashbery (prose poems), Kenneth Koch, Howard Moss, and Michael Benedikt. Mirsky's eclectic taste also allows him to offer work by a range of writers, from Flann O'Brien to Ishmael Reed, Gayl Jones, and Clarence Major, and by newer writers like Robert Stone and Thomas McGuane.

Another special feature of *Fiction* has been the translation of works by Peter Handke, Heinrich Böll, Günter Grass, Nathalie Sarraute, Roland Barthes, Louis-Ferdinand Céline, Alfred Jarry, Yuri Olesha, Ilya Ehrenburg, Kobo Abe, Isaac Peretz, Halldor Laxness, and Julio Cortázar. In Vol. V, No. 1 (1976) there is a special tribute to *Marcha,* the Uruguayan weekly, with work by "H. Bustos Domecq," Felisberto Hernandez, Carlos Martinez Moreno, Mario Benedetti, and Juan Carlos Onetti.

Fiction has received support from CCNY, the Longview Foundation, Herbert Lehmann College, CCLM, and the New York State Council on the Arts.

Field: Contemporary Poetry and Poetics. Oberlin College, Oberlin, Ohio.
No. 1, Fall 1969+. 2/yr.
Ed. David P. Young; Stuart Friebert (no. 11, Fall 1974+).
5¼" x 8½"   perfect   74–112 pp.
Index no. 1–10 in no. 10, Spring 1974.

Field, sponsored by Oberlin College and edited by David P. Young (with Stuart Friebert as co-editor commencing with No. 11, Fall 1974), is especially interested in contemporary American poetry, translations (generally of contemporary poets), and poets' prose statements about poetry. Short poems have been well represented in *Field,* with a good deal of space devoted to "deep image" poets such as Robert Bly and surrealist and neo-surrealist poets such as Benjamin Peret or Charles Simic. Other well-known contributors have included Margaret Atwood, Marvin Bell, Michael Benedikt, Philip Booth, Hayden Carruth, Robert Creeley, Ian Hamilton Finlay, John Haines, Donald Hall, Louis Hammer, Richard Hugo, David Ignatow, X. J. Kennedy, Galway Kinnell, Maxine Kumin, Al Lee, Denise Levertov, John Logan, W. S. Merwin, Cynthia Ozick, Kenneth Rexroth, Adrienne Rich, Dennis Schmitz, Louis Simpson, Robin Skelton, Gary Snyder, William Stafford, James Wright, as well as (in translation) Rafael Alberti, Gunter Eich, Osip Mandelstam, Eugenio Montale, Pablo Neruda, Rainer Maria Rilke, Georg Trakl, and César Vallejo.

Many issues have included one or two essays by poets on the craft of poetry. A recurring theme in these essays involves personality in poetry, especially with respect to the self and the need to universalize individual experiences and perceptions. Editor David Young sees a crucial con-

697

trast between two kinds of recent poem: one kind is "*selfish,* receding into a childish and fearful ignorance. The other is *selfless,* moving toward maturity, acceptance, understanding" ("The Bite of the Muskrat: Judging Contemporary Poetry," No. 7, Fall 1972). Elsewhere Young advises that the creative discipline of the translator be primarily directed not to external form but "to the feelings themselves, to the experience on which he draws" ("Second Honeymoon: Some Thoughts on Translation," No. 11, Fall 1974). In general he seems to speak against formal considerations and in favor of re-creation of emotion and experience, against the personal case history and in favor of universalized particulars. If there is a central purpose in collecting the hundreds of poems that have appeared in *Field,* it seems to develop out of these ideas constructed by Young and discussed from different angles by other contributors. See especially the article by Galway Kinnell, No. 4, Spring 1973, on recent poets' attempts to break out of "the closed ego" and transcend isolated experiences. Adrienne Rich, replying to Kinnell, offers her own suggestions toward a new poetry that escapes the mere "I" in favor of common experience (No. 7, Fall 1974).

Circulation of *Field* is approximately 2,700 copies. Subscriptions are evenly distributed geographically, with more individual than institutional subscribers. The editors have received support from Oberlin College, CCLM, the Ohio Arts Council, and "occasional private individuals."

The Fifties: A Magazine of Poetry and General Opinion [then The Sixties; The Seventies]. Pine Island, Minn. (no. 1–3, 1958–1959); Madison, Minn. (no. 4, Fall 1960+).

No. 1, 1958+. Irreg.

Ed. Robert Bly; William Duffy (no. 1–5, 1958–Fall 1961).

5¼ " x 8½ "   sewn (The Seventies: perfect)   52–104 pp.

The Fifties (later *The Sixties* and *The Seventies*) is a little magazine closely identified with its editor, Robert Bly (although William Duffy served for a time as co-editor). Bly has never been afraid to take sides and, in an advertisement for *The Sixties* No. 7, promises never to publish anything that sounds as if it were written by Norman Mailer, Leslie Fiedler, LeRoi Jones, Allen Tate, Bennett Cerf, or William Burroughs. In No. 10, Bly announced that he was canceling the subscriptions of thirty-one universities known to have accepted money from the CIA or the armed forces for research on chemical germ warfare. The criticism published by Bly is frequently a blending of undergraduate humor (often parodies) with more precise critical arguments. Typical are regular features like "Madame Tussaud's Wax Museum," in which are placed, for their lack of poetic images, writers like Yvor Winters and Allen Ginsberg, and the "Order of the Blue Toad," awarded to Gilbert Highet, Norman Cousins, Jacques Barzun, Cleanth Brooks and Austin Warren, and Arthur Mizener.

698

Committed to "deep image" poetry, *The Fifties* features many poems in translation (with some bilingual presentations); often the editor propounds the curious thesis that the mainstream of English-language poetry proceeds from Spanish and French poetry. Louis Simpson and Gary Snyder are esteemed for their poetic practice, with some praise going also to Robert Creeley, Donald Hall, W. S. Merwin, John Logan, James Dickey, James Wright, Denise Levertov, W. D. Snodgrass, and Jerome Rothenberg, most of whom have also published their poems in *The Fifties*. Typical of Bly's magazine is its attitude toward Robert Creeley and *Black Mountain Review:* the magazine is too un-international, and Creeley too often fails to use images, is not truly avant-garde in linking up with French and Spanish poets. (Elsewhere Charles Olson's *Maximus Poems* are rated the worst of the year.)

The Fifties and its successors have published some special translation issues: French poetry in No. 5 (Fall 1961), German poetry in No. 8 (Spring 1966), and Norwegian poetry in No. 10 (Summer 1968). Circulation has varied between 2,000 and 4,000 copies.

The Floating Bear: A Newsletter. New York, N.Y. [no. 25, Nov. 1962/ Mar. 1963: Topanga, Cal.].

No. 1–37, 1961–1969. Irreg.

Ed. Diane di Prima; LeRoi Jones (no. 1–25, 1961–1962/1963) [guest editors include Billy Linich (Oct. 1963); Alan Marlowe (June 1965); Kirby Doyle (Feb. 1966); John Wieners (Feb. 1967); Bill Berkson (Jan./July 1969)].

8½″ x 11″ stapled 8–36 pp. mimeo.

Reprint edition with complete index and notes: Laurence McGilvery, La Jolla, Cal., 1973.

The subtitle "A Newsletter" is the key to *The Floating Bear*'s chief contribution to literature of the 1960s; it *was* a newsletter, a speedy line of communication between experimental poets. Diane di Prima, in the introduction to the reprint edition of *Floating Bear,* recalls Charles Olson's tribute to the magazine: "The last time I saw Charles Olson in Gloucester, one of the things he talked about was how valuable the Bear had been to him in its early years because of the fact that he could get new work out that fast. He was very involved in speed, in communication. We got manuscripts from him pretty regularly in the early days of the Bear, and we'd usually get them into the very next issue. That meant that his work, his thoughts, would be in the hands of a few hundred writers within two or three weeks. It was like writing a letter to a bunch of friends."

One is apt to think of a literary newsletter as a device for talking *about* poetry but not as a means for transmitting the poem itself; in *Floating Bear* most of the space was given over to primary work. The first twenty-five issues (up to the point when LeRoi Jones resigned as co-editor) were published over a two-year period and comprised 284 pages of poetry, creative prose, and comment. Among the more frequent contributors to *Floating Bear* during those first two years were Charles Olson, Robert Creeley, Frank O'Hara, Joel Oppenheimer, William Burroughs, Ed Dorn, A. B. Spellman, and George Stanley, as well as editors Diane di Prima and LeRoi Jones.

After 1963, *Floating Bear*'s function as a swift communicator among poets seems to have diminished (Nos. 29 to 37 appeared over a period of five years). Size and frequency varied widely: No. 27 had 36 pages and included a 19-page section of poems by Philip Whalen; the following number had 16 pages and included work by eight authors. The range of contributors widened somewhat during this time, perhaps because a number of guest editors assumed partial responsibility for the magazine's contents. Billy Linich, Alan Marlowe, Kirby Doyle, John Wieners, and Bill Berkson each appeared on the masthead as guest editor for one of the magazine's last dozen issues. One last issue (No. 38) appeared in 1971 as a joint issue with *Intrepid* (its No. 20), and was edited entirely by Diane di Prima.

Floating Bear was supported solely by contributors; it was never offered for sale. Circulation ranged from 117 to 1,250 copies over its eight-year span.

Fuck You: A Magazine of the Arts. "Edited, Published & Printed by Ed Sanders at a Secret location in the Lower East Side, New York City, USA."
[1962]–June/July 1965. Irreg.
Indexed in *Serif*, Vol. VIII, no. 3, pp. 23–28.
8½" x 11"   stapled   12–83 pp.   mimeo (one side only).

"I'll print anything" is Ed Sanders's boast in this 1960s protest magazine. *Fuck You* was a prototypical journal of the new era of freer sexual expression, more vehement antiwar and anti-bomb sentiment, and the urge (and freedom) to print shocking material of a kind highly offensive to the middle-class establishment. An editorial statement in No. 1 announced that *Fuck You* was "dedicated to pacifist, unilateral disarmament, national defense through nonviolent resistance, multilateral indiscriminate apertural conjugation, anarchism, world federalism, civil disobedience, obstructers and submarine boarders, and all those groped by J. Edgar Hoover in the silent halls of Congress."

Fuck You is a record of several kinds of anti-establishment thought and expression. Its anarchistic policies so offended Dorothy Day that she fired four writers from the *Catholic Worker* because their work had appeared in Sanders's magazine. The pacifism wavered from the standard sort of diatribe to the lampoon; Sanders threatened to publish a Quaker version to be called *Fuck Thee*. He also initiated the era of mimeograph publishing. *Fuck You* was batted out in an incredibly sloppy way; one often saw footprints on the paper. The numbering system was impossible to follow: the magazine published five numbers, but in No. 5 alone one finds nine volumes—exactly contrary to ordinary procedures. The prevalence of sexual and scatological expressions became a sublanguage that many considered a "new realism."

As it pursued its erratic course, *Fuck You* managed to publish a number of well-known writers, among them Charles Olson, Joel Oppenheimer, Paul Blackburn, Peter Orlovsky, Philip Whalen, Allen Ginsberg, Diane Wakoski, Julian Beck, Robert Creeley, Gary Snyder, Robert Duncan, William Burroughs, Gregory Corso, Norman Mailer, Antonin Artaud, Philip Lamantia, Lawrence Ferlinghetti, Ted Berrigan, W. H. Auden, and Gilbert Sorrentino.

The Greenfield Review. Greenfield Center, N.Y.

Vol. I, no. 1, Spring 1970+. Irreg. (recently two double numbers/yr.).

Ed. Joseph Bruchac III.

5½" x 8½" (varies) stapled/perfect 48–206 pp. (varies widely).

Although *The Greenfield Review* has printed a wide variety of poets, including a number of new names, the magazine's chief interest has been in native American poets, prison poets, and Third World writers. Volume I, No. 4, 1971; Vol. II, No. 3, Fall 1972; Vol. III, No. 4, 1974; and Vol. V, No. 3/4, Winter 1976/1977, have all been special African poetry issues. Volume III, No. 2, was a special "NCAE Writers Workshop Issue," based on a workshop for ethnic writers conducted by Ed Burrows at the University of Wisconsin at Stevens Point for the National Center for Audio Experimentation. Volume VI, No. 1/2, Spring 1977, was a "Special Asian American Writers Issue," edited by Garrett Kaoru Hongo. Volume I, No. 2, Fall 1970, featured "Some Poets Who Happen to Be Women," a presentation of nine poets. Much of the special issue work supports Editor Joseph Bruchac's efforts to provide exposure and outlets for international writing, particularly Third World poetry. Bruchac is coordinator of the COSMEP Prison Project, which makes literary magazines available to prison inmates.

Current circulation ranges from 750 to 1,000; many issues are exchanged or distributed free to Third World writers and readers and to prisons. *Greenfield Review* has been supported by CCLM.

Hanging Loose. New York, N.Y. (no. 1–5/6, Fall 1966–1968); Brooklyn, N.Y. (no. 7, Summer 1969+).

No. 1, Fall 1966+. Irreg.

Ed. Dick Lourie; Emmett Jarrett; Ron Schreiber; Bob Hershon (no. 4, Winter 1967+); Miguel Ortiz (no. 9–22, Winter 1970–Winter 1974).

7" x 8½" (varies) Summer 1975+: stapled (folded) 72–80 pp. (recent issues).

Separate indexes for no. 1–12 (Fall 1966–Fall 1970) and no. 13–24 (Winter 1971–Winter 1974/1975).

Hanging Loose, a magazine of "poetry, songs, fiction," edited by Dick Lourie, Emmett Jarrett, and Ron Schreiber—joined in No. 4 by Bob Hershon and later by Miguel Ortiz—takes its title from the fact that its first twenty-four issues, covering a ten-year period from 1966 to 1975, consisted of loose sheets of paper delivered in an envelope bearing a cover design. This format was meant to imply a "stance" toward literature: "Poems are not artifacts to be bound and someday carefully studied but living expressions that aid and exalt us as we try to live our lives now. If you liked a poem among our loose pages, you could always tack it to the wall or carry it in your pocket; if you hated a poem you could always throw it away and still retain most of the magazine" (No. 25).

Like most other small literary magazines, *Hanging Loose* has claimed an interest in printing some known writers, while also providing space for new talent. In this instance the editors have genuinely demonstrated their "continuing interest in work by new writers" (the first twenty issues contained the work of almost two hundred different authors). One regular feature has been a special section devoted to work by high school students. Some of the young poets appear once only, while others, such as Katy Akin (Ma Prem Madhuri), have become regular contributors and developed with the magazine. For No. 21 (Winter 1973) Denise Levertov, a contributing editor, put together a special supplement featuring ten young poets. As a way of promoting exchange of ideas, criticism, and encouragement, especially for the young contributors, *Hanging Loose* includes with the table of contents the addresses of all contributors.

Among the more established poets appearing in *Hanging Loose* have been Earle Birney, Douglas Blazek, Robert Bly, George Bowering, Victor Contoski, Clayton Eshleman, Dan Georgakas, John Gill, Denise Levertov, Lyn Lifshin, Ron Loewinsohn, Marge Piercy, Margaret Randall, Ron Schreiber, John Tagliabue, Joseph Bruchac, Rochelle Ratner, Susan Fromberg Schaeffer, Lynn Sukenick, and Al Young.

Beginning with No. 25, *Hanging Loose* has been bound and now is hanging together. Since the editors have found themselves printing more long poems, they have shifted to a format that "seems friendlier" to extended pieces.

Hanging Loose maintains a fairly steady circulation of about 1,200 copies distributed nationally, with peaks in New York, California, and Massachusetts. More individuals than libraries are subscribers. Essentially an independent magazine, it has received aid from CCLM and the National Endowment for the Arts.

Hearse: A Vehicle Used to Convey the Dead. Eureka, Cal.
No. 1–17, [Sept. 1957]–1972; [suspended publication between 1961 and 1969]. Irreg.
Ed. E. V. Griffith.
5½" x 8½"   stapled (folded)   16–88 pp.   Illus.

702

E. V. Griffith's editorial policy is expressed in the continuing sub-title, "An irreverent quarterly, carrying poetry, prose, artwork, and incidental cadaver to the Great Cemetery of the American Intellect." He sets the tone for each issue with a pair of quotations on hearses or coffins printed inside the front cover. *Hearse* No. 1 quoted Flannery O'Connor's *Wise Blood*—"Cash Parnum's dead," Haze said. "He got cholera from a pig"—and John Faulkner's *Men Working*—"Well, paw. What are we going to do now?" said maw. "I just hadn't thought about it," said paw. "Seems like we maybe ought to get some kind of a coffin together fer him." *Hearse* proves to be one exception to the general rule that little magazines become more moderate and sedate with time.

Hearse No. 1 presented poetry by Joel Oppenheimer, Raymond Souster, Louis Dudek, Robert Creeley, Judson Crews, Barriss Mills, Jonathan Williams, Larry Eigner, Gil Orlovitz, Langston Hughes, David Cornel DeJong, and James Boyer May, among others, and featured a painting by Lawrence Ferlinghetti and a college poem (one of the continuing specialties of the magazine) by Kenneth Lawrence Beaudoin. Early issues contained such diverse names as Charles Bukowski, Kenneth Rexroth (sections deleted from the New Directions edition of *The Dragon and the Unicorn*), Richard Brautigan, Paul Blackburn, Allen Ginsberg, LeRoi Jones, Clarence Major, and Robert Sward.

After *Hearse* No. 9 (1961), publication was suspended until 1969. In 1965, midway through the hiatus, there appeared one issue of *Coffin,* a similarly uninhibited satellite magazine consisting of forty-one broadsides and booklets loosely inserted into a printed folder (in a print run of 150 copies). This collection is frequently pirated for two booklets now considered to be collector's items: Fielding Dawson's *The Canoe* (dated 1/19/59) and Charles Bukowski's *The Paper on the Floor.*

In 1969 *Hearse* resumed publication. In eight issues between 1969 and 1972 it printed an impressive number of poets, among them Winfield Townley Scott, Charles Bukowski, Lyn Lifshin, Theodore Enslin, Harold Witt, Marge Piercy, Felix Stefanile, Victor Contoski, Gene Fowler, Diane Wakoski, Douglas Blazek, Robert Mezey, H. L. VanBrunt, Charles Wright, Rochelle Owens, Charles Simic, Michael Benedikt, David Antin, Greg Kuzma, David Ignatow, Robert Hershon, John Haines, James Schevill, Felix Pollak, John Gill, Stuart Friebert, John Judson, Larry Eigner, Raymond Di Palma, Peter Schjeldahl, James Tate, Carolyn Stoloff, Marvin Bell, Adrien Stoutenberg, Peter Wild, Philip Booth, David Wagoner, Sonya Dorman, Joseph Bruchac, John Unterecker, William Witherup, Hale Chatfield, Rochelle Ratner, Dan Georgakas, Harold Norse, X. J. Kennedy, Russell Edson, Philip Dacey, Colette Inez, Ron Padgett, and Yevgeny Yevtushenko (tr. Irina Zheleznova). In these issues of *Hearse* the aim seemed simply to be the setting forth of as many poems from a wide range of poets as limitations of space would allow.

703

In 1973 Griffith (at one time editor of *The Minnesota Quarterly*) launched a new magazine in tabloid format. This venture, *Poetry Now,* was much less irreverent than *Hearse* and *Coffin* and soon won a much larger audience. In the birth process, *Hearse* died.

Circulation for issues 1 through 9 was 100 to 275 copies, for issues 10 through 17, from 1,500 to 2,500 copies.

The Hudson Review. New York, N.Y.
Vol. I, no. 1, Spring 1948+. Qy.
Ed. Frederick Morgan; William Arrowsmith (Spring 1948–Summer 1948; Autumn 1951–Winter 1959/1960); Joseph D. Bennett (Spring 1948–Winter 1965/1966); Mary Emma Elliott (Spring 1960–Winter 1965/1966); Paula Dietz (Summer 1975+).
6½" x 9½" perfect about 150 pp.
Indexed by volume.

"The editors are committed to recommend those strategies and disciplines which hold experience within an objective frame and which prevent the dissolution of aesthetic constructs into anarchic sensation. It is the function of a responsible quarterly not simply to provide outlet, but to channel the manifestations of the contemporary creative imagination into the mainstream of traditional insights and universal perceptions. . . . Necessarily, the *Review* must be critical, eschewing political or philosophical commitment. . . . It must be on guard against the vagaries attendant upon a constant quest for novelty and timeliness." With these opening comments *The Hudson Review* began in 1948 its tenure as a leading literary and intellectual review. Contributors to the opening issue were R. P. Blackmur, Wallace Stevens, Joseph D. Bennett, Alex Comfort, W. S. Merwin, Herbert Read, Josephine Miles, Mark Schorer, D. S. Savage, e. e. cummings, and Frederick Morgan.

In the Spring 1968 twentieth anniversary issue, the editorial referred to the socially disruptive Vietnam conflict and added: "Of what use are literature and the arts at such a time? They will serve best if they perform their traditional function—which is, putting it only in part and much too simply, to keep our minds and sensibilities alert and honest, and our imaginations free." Among the contributors to this anniversary issue were E. M. Cioran, Anthony Burgess, Isaac Bashevis Singer, James Merrill, Anne Sexton, and A. R. Ammons, with Herbert Read, Josephine Miles, and W. S. Merwin returning from the first issue. From these statements and lists of contributors one can clearly see the extent to which the *Hudson Review* actually has represented and reflected the intellectual and creative mainstream. Now, in the mid-seventies, the *Hudson Review* is printing John Gardner, Joyce Carol Oates, Samuel Hazo, Anthony Hecht, William Stafford, Hayden Carruth, Charles Tomlinson, Michael Benedikt, John Hollander, and Colette Inez.

Without slighting the importance of all the significant writers who have contributed to the *Hudson Review*, one can argue that the liveliest aspect of the magazine, as well as a central means of both being in and helping direct the mainstream, is the review section, led in recent years by Roger Sale, William H. Pritchard, and especially Marvin Mudrick. In addition, John Simon conducts a spirited "Theatre Chronicle," while Robert S. Clark does the same for music. Vernon Young is a contributing editor for film, but ranges widely in seeking subjects for his acerb, highly opinionated reviews. Charles W. Millard is the regular art critic.

While it seems to have done quite well at receiving grants, the *Hudson Review* prides itself on its independence from affiliation with any university or publishing house.

The magazine has received grants from CCLM. Circulation in 1976 was 3,200 copies.

Invisible City. Fairfax, Cal.

No. 1, 1971+. Irreg.

Ed. Paul Vangelisti; John McBride.

11½" x 17" folded together 16 pp. (double and triple issues to 56 pp.).

According to its editors, "*Invisible City* is a collection of poetry, statements and reviews, published by the Red Hill Press whenever enough material is available." Translation from many languages and countries has been a major feature of every issue, with a great deal of the work being done by Jack Hirschman and Paul Vangelisti. Hirschman has been responsible for translations from several languages, his most sizable and notable contribution being the whole *Issue of Work* by Antonin Artaud (No. 6, July 1972). Vangelisti has produced translations from recent Italian poets for almost every issue of *Invisible City,* a practice which has contributed greatly to the particular tone of the magazine. A special characteristic of *Invisible City* translations is that, while they have included French surrealists, Spanish Civil War poetry, and such current favorites of American translators as César Vallejo, Rafael Alberti, and Julio Cortázar, they also have included many interesting poets whose poems are not often seen in English translation, such as Adriano Spatola, Corrado Costa, and Giulia Niccolai.

Invisible City appears in an 11" by 17" tabloid format on heavy stock. A typical sixteen-page issue, featuring one to three columns of as many as ninety lines on each page, contains more than seventy-five poems, some very short and others quite long. A poet is frequently represented by ten or more poems. A leftist socialist viewpoint, asserted by Editor Paul Vangelisti in the opening issue, is apparent in many of the selections, especially in translations of poets like René Depestre, but it never becomes overbearing; the magazine remains primarily a literary anthology. Circulation is 1,500 copies; grants have been received from CCLM.

Io. Amherst, Mass. (no. 1–2, ?1964–Feb. 1966); Ann Arbor, Mich. (no. 3–6, Winter 1966/1967–Summer 1969); Somesville, Me. (no. 7, Winter 1970); Cape Elizabeth, Me. (no. 8–15, 1971–1972); Plainfield, Vt. (no. 16, Winter 1972/1973+).

No. 1, ?1964+. Irreg.

Ed. no. 1: Phi Alpha Psi Society, with "special thanks for help to Rich Grossinger, Nels Richardson, Marty Bickman, Randy Gingiss, and Lindy Hough"; then Ed. Richard Grossinger (Feb. 1966+); Linda Hough [Grossinger] (Feb. 1966+); Harvey Bialy (1974).

Format varies (mostly 6" x 9" or 8½" x 11") perfect (no. 1–3: stapled folded) 94–385 pp. (varies widely). Illus.

Io No. 1 was "put together by the members and friends of the Phi Alpha Psi Society" at Amherst. The first three issues, small stapled affairs, established the early format. Themes for the issues were drawn from "science fiction, parapsychology, magic, comets, psi" or from "the works of photon and electron; cosmological essays." Editor Richard Grossinger has also been interested in ethnic poetry.

Beginning with No. 4, the magazine has been square-backed and substantial in size, often running to more than 200 pages. Each issue carries a special area title, such as Alchemy, Doctrine of Signatures, Ethnoastronomy, Oecology, Oneirology, Mars, SciFi, Baseball, Earth Geography (Nos. 12, 13, 14, 16), Mind/Memory/Psyche, Biopoesis. According to promotional material, "the entire series is a growing and evolutionary cosmology; the individual numbers are not disposable or dated, as magazines; they are more prophetic than topical." *Io* abandons traditional literary magazine criticism and investigation in favor of a search into sources of poetic sensibility and the springs of poetic expression. By the seventh issue, Grossinger was able to state that "*Io* has served as our own education in the source material of New American Poetry."

Io is made increasingly interesting by the fact that, as it ostensibly searches out the wellsprings of creative action, it draws contributions from many widely published recent writers. Among them are Jorge Luis Borges, Theodore Enslin, Michel Foucault, Gerrit Lansing, Clayton Eshleman, Kenneth Irby, Charles Olson, Ed Dorn, Paul Mariah, Thomas Merton, Anselm Hollo, Gary Snyder, Allen Ginsberg, David Wilk, Robert Creeley, Dennis Tedlock, Gilbert Sorrentino, George Bowering, Jack Spicer, Stan Persky, Fielding Dawson, Robert Duncan, Kenneth Anger, R. Buckminster Fuller, George Quasha, Nathaniel Tarn, Osip Mandelstam, John Wieners, Joe Brainard, Lenore Kandel, and Charles Doria.

Recent concentration seems to be upon Grossinger's and Lindy Hough's North Atlantic Books venture. One large book is *Baseball I Gave You All the Best Years of My Life,* edited by Kevin Kerrane and Richard Grossinger, which also serves as *Io* No. 24. Among the contributors are Jack

Kerouac, Donald Hall, Lewis Warsh, Roger Angell, Gilbert Sorrentino, Philip Roth, Richard Hugo, Ron Loewinsohn, Tom Wicker, Charles Stein, Joel Oppenheimer, Paul Blackburn, John Updike, Anne Waldman, Bernadette Mayer, Tom Clark, Fielding Dawson, Rolfe Humphries, and Jack Spicer.

Io funding is estimated as 75 percent from sales and 25 percent from grants, including grants from CCLM. Circulation varies widely but averages about 1,000 per issue. In keeping with the conviction that *Io* is a growing, organic publication, the editors make all back issues available for purchase.

Kayak. San Francisco, Cal. (no. 1–20, Fall 1964–1969); Santa Cruz, Cal. (no. 21, 1970+).
No. 1, Fall 1964+. Irreg. ("more or less quarterly").
Ed. George Hitchcock.
6½" x 8½" stapled (folded) 56–72 pp. Illus.

Like most other good little magazines, *Kayak* strongly and uniquely reflects the tastes of its editor. George Hitchcock's *Kayak,* "operated by a single oarsman," begins with a set of unabashed preferences:

Kayak will print what its editor considers the best poets now working in the United States.
Kayak is particularly hospitable to surrealist, imagist, and political poems.
Kayak welcomes vehement or ribald articles on the subject of modern poetry.

Starting with the Autumn 1964 issue, Hitchcock has published *Kayak* "more or less" quarterly. Most issues run to sixty-four pages and include found poems and collages as well as space for scores of poets, many new and many quite well known. Hitchcock has published the work of Louis Simpson, A. R. Ammons, George P. Elliott, Paul Blackburn, Robert Bly, W. S. Merwin, Hayden Carruth, David Ignatow, Margaret Randall, Carol Bergé, John Logan, James Merrill, X. J. Kennedy, Robin Skelton, Robert Mezey, Charles Simic, Donald Justice, David Wagoner, Josephine Miles, Gary Snyder, Donald Hall, Anselm Hollo, Anne Sexton, Diane Wakoski, Evan S. Connell, Jr., Karl Shapiro, Carolyn Kizer, John Unterecker, and Kenneth Rexroth.

From the beginning, Hitchcock has decorated the magazine with drawings from Victorian illustrated texts of all sorts. The verse in *Kayak*—referred to somewhat dubiously as surrealistic, perhaps because it is frequently inward and sometimes employs dislocated images—covers all areas of human experience, perception, and emotion but has a tendency toward personal communion with nature as manifest in harvests, woods, and animals. *Kayak* No. 2 was "dedicated to America's Underground Channels and Seams," but the underground seems to be psychological rather than political, emotional rather than geographic. By 1966, though,

707

the war in Vietnam had induced a type of poetry that was more overtly and specifically political regarding both the war and society in general. At one point in 1968, Hitchcock used some money from an award to run a poetry contest on the "Life or Death of Che Guevara."

While poetry provides the bulk of each issue, *Kayak* also publishes reviews and prose essays, which range from a Louis Hammer article on recent American poetry (No. 2) to John Haines's reviews and essays on the work of well-known poets. In No. 6, Haines calls Olson's "Projective Verse" essay "Mainly hogwash, with its pseudo-scientific terminology (a poem is a 'high-energy-construct,' etc.)." Since this opinion, and the manner of its assertion, agrees with Hitchcock's own stated viewpoint, it stands as a good example of the sort of criticism often found in *Kayak*. Robert Bly, Robert L. Peters, and Robin Skelton are among the other contributors of testy, outspoken essays and reviews. Victor Contoski (No. 17) caused some controversy by attacking the "curiously negative" James Dickey; John Haines (No. 20) aroused letter writers with his argument that American poetry is in decline; and John Herschel raised hackles by his attack on Diane di Prima and her fellow social protesters for their paranoia. *Kayak* also publishes critical reviews of work by contributors.

Other than one award from CCLM to pay authors, Hitchcock reports that *Kayak,* with a circulation of 1,400, is "entirely self-supporting through subscriptions and sales."

The Kenyon Review. Kenyon College, Gambier, Ohio.
Vol. I, no. 1–Vol. XXXII, no. 1, Winter 1939–Issue 1, 1970. Qy. (Jan. 1966+: 5/yr.).
Ed. John Crowe Ransom (Winter 1939–Summer 1958); Robie Macauley (Autumn 1958–Mar. 1967); George Lanning (June 1967+); Ellington White (Nov. 1967+).
5½" x 8½" sewn about 196 pp. (1966+: 5/yr. of 144 pp. each).
Annual index; 25-year index (1939–1963) by AMS (compiled by Elizabeth Browne).

Throughout the 1940s and 1950s, founding editor John Crowe Ransom developed *The Kenyon Review* into a leading organ for the "new critics." An AMS twenty-five-year index to *Kenyon* lists more than 300 non-fiction prose contributors, many of whom appeared a number of times. Among these contributors were many of the best known new critics— Ransom and Allen Tate, Cleanth Brooks, R. P. Blackmur, Robert Penn Warren, Austin Warren, and William Empson—as well as a mixed bag of critics familiar to English professors and their students. Paul Goodman, Kenneth Burke, Benedetto Croce, Leslie Fiedler, Northrop Frye, Frederick J. Hoffman, Marshall McLuhan, Herbert Read, Lionel Trilling, Harry Levin, and Stephen Spender indicate the range and quality of

Kenyon Review criticism. Selecting out some poets whose work has frequently been discussed in the magazine, one finds the names of many writers whose poetry is especially suited to new critical readings; John Donne, T. S. Eliot, Gerard Manley Hopkins, Wallace Stevens, and W. B. Yeats are all subjects of multiple essays.

Under Ransom, *Kenyon* featured literary criticism but also printed fiction, poetry, and essays on art and film (Parker Tyler contributed a regular "Movie Letter" for some time). When Robie Macauley took over the editorship in 1959, the emphasis shifted from criticism to poetry and especially to fiction. The new direction is immediately seen in Vol. XXII (1960), which features fiction by John Barth, William Eastlake, Flannery O'Connor, Thomas Pynchon, and others.

In 1966 George Lanning took over the editorship and guided the magazine until its demise in 1970 (Ellington White joined him as co-editor). In its last issues the magazine ran a four-part series, "The Short Story Today."

Circulation of *Kenyon Review* peaked at about 6,000 in 1965–1966, with single-copy sales reaching 400. Besides the support of Kenyon College, in the 1950s the magazine also received aid from the Rockefeller Foundation.

Kulchur. New York, N.Y.

No. 1–20, Spring 1960–Winter 1965/1966. Qy.

Ed. Marc D. Schleifer (Spring 1960–Summer 1962); Lita Hornick ("Managing Editor," Summer 1962–Winter 1963; Editor, Spring 1964+) [guest and contributing editors: Gilbert Sorrentino (Poetry/Guest/Book Editor, 1961–Summer 1963); Joel Oppenheimer (Guest Ed. Spring 1962); LeRoi Jones (Music Editor, Spring 1962–Spring 1964); Frank O'Hara (Art Editor, Summer 1962–Spring 1964); Joseph Le Seuer (Theatre Editor, Fall 1962–Spring 1964); Bill Berkson (Film Editor, Fall 1962–Fall 1963)].

5½″ x 8½″   sewn (no. 1 stapled, 52 pp.) 96–104 pp.   Illus.

The first issue of *Kulchur* (edited by Marc D. Schleifer) was a good example of the range of essays and critiques published throughout the magazine's twenty-issue history. For this issue Charles Olson wrote a four-page meditation on perception; John Fles praised the poetry of Robert Creeley; William Burroughs published an excerpt from the manuscript version of *Naked Lunch* (not in the published version and not available elsewhere). Allen Ginsberg's short poem "Paterson" also appeared here, along with articles by Erick Hawkins on dance; by Donald Phelps on Lenny Bruce, Don Martin, Ernie Kovacs, and the "Muck School" of comedy; and by Martin Williams on television. Films were reviewed and discussed by Louis Zukofsky (Charlie Chaplin's *Modern Times*), Parker Tyler, Pauline Kael, and Richard Kraft.

With the support of both Martin Williams and LeRoi Jones (who was jazz editor for a time), *Kulchur* made coverage of jazz one of its strongest points. Another strength was its focus on modern art. The "Art Chronicle" was regularly written by Frank O'Hara and then by Bill Berkson, with less regular contributions by Gilbert Sorrentino and Carl Belz. *Kulchur* also published articles on many aspects of popular culture: pornography, drugs, William Reich, the Kama Sutra, Freud, civil rights, L. Frank Baum and the *Oz* books, blues singers, Hollywood's ten best social protest movies, and the dangers of hipness.

Poetry and fiction were published, but not in great quantities. The typical *Kulchur* contributor already had outlets for creative work in *Floating Bear, Yugen,* and allied publications. *Kulchur* adhered fairly closely to its goal to become "the only vanguard magazine devoted principally to Criticism and Commentary—essays on literature, art, jazz, politics and pop culture by leading poets." *Kulchur*'s contributions to literary criticism in the 1960s included Charles Olson on projective verse, Robert Duncan on the meaning of form, Jerome Rothenberg and Robert Creeley on "deep images," and Louis Zukofsky's "5 Statements for Poetry." The temper of many reviews was vitriolic; LeRoi Jones, in reviewing Robert Bly's and William Duffy's magazine *The Sixties,* wrote, "I suspect Mr. Bly and Mr. Duffy are ignorant fools." Among other frequent reviewers were Fielding Dawson, Jonathan Williams, Walter Lowenfels, Allen Ginsberg, and Denise Levertov. *Kulchur* would occasionally print the odd, unexpected piece by writers like Paul Goodman.

Kulchur, entirely funded by Lita Hornick, reached a peak circulation of about 1,400.

Lillabulero: Being a Periodical of Literature and the Arts. Published and edited at Chapel Hill, N.C. by Lillabulero of the Whigh Court [no. 6, Fall/Winter 1968+: Lillabulero: A Journal of Contemporary Writing, Northwood Narrows, New Hampshire].

Vol. I, no. 1–no. 14, Winter 1967–Spring 1974. Irreg.

Ed. Russell Banks; William Matthews (no. 4, Fall 1967+); Newton Smith (no. 4–5, Fall 1967–Winter 1968).

No. 1–2: 9" x 14½" stapled (folded) 30, 56 pp. + portfolios.

No. 3–5: 8½" x 13" stapled (folded) 54, 66, 80 pp. + portfolios.

No. 6–14: 6" x 9" perfect 90–188 pp.

Lillabulero's interests included "contemporary American poetry and fiction, including interviews, reviews, occasional criticism."

The first series, Nos. 1–5 in folio format, contained the work of William Stafford, O. B. Hardison, Jr., Evan S. Connell, Jr., Nelson Algren, David Madden, Dabney Stuart, John Hollander, Malcolm Cowley, Stanley Cooperman, Greg Kuzma, Douglas Blazek, Margaret Randall, Peter Wild, Howard McCord, and others. A special feature of Nos. 1–4 was loose-leaf portfolios (tucked into a pocket in cover iii) of artwork by

Peter Schlaifer (No. 1), Daniel Patterson (No. 2), Arturo Esquerra (No. 3), and Chris Parsons (No. 4).

The second series added many new contributors, among the best known being A. R. Ammons, Andrei Codrescu, Vern Rutsala, Charles Simic, Wendell Berry, Anselm Hollo, Diane Wakoski. No. 12, Winter 1973, was a special Paul Metcalf issue, edited by Russell Banks and containing contributions from Howard McCord, Theodore Enslin, Ronald Sukenick, Lindy Hough, Richard Grossinger, Jonathan Williams, and others. Upon occasion, single poets were the recipients of "Appreciations" in which several poems by the honored poet were followed by a prose critique: W. S. Merwin (No. 6), Gary Snyder (No. 7), Robert Creeley (No. 8), A. R. Ammons (No. 10/11).

The editors, by prearrangement, terminated *Lillabulero* after No. 14. Once established, the magazine had maintained a constant circulation of about 1,000 copies. Aid had been received from CCLM, the New York State Council on the Arts, and "three generous, anonymous patrons."

Locus Solus. Lans-en-Vercors (Isère), France.

No. 1–5, Winter 1961–1962.

Ed. John Ashbery, Kenneth Koch, Harry Mathews, James Schuyler.

4¾" x 7¼" (varies slightly)   sewn   168–204 pp. (296 pp. double issue).

Locus Solus appeared in five numbers over a one-year period and was edited by John Ashbery, Kenneth Koch, Harry Mathews, and James Schuyler, with individual editors alternating special responsibilities, at least for some issues. This magazine offered no apologies, no explanations; it simply tried to provide an attractive format for poets whom it respected and honored.

Locus Solus No. 2, Summer 1961, edited by Kenneth Koch, was titled a "Special Collaborations Issue." Asserting that "the act of collaborating on a literary work is inspiring, I think, because it gives objective form to a usually concealed subjective phenomenon and therefore it jars the mind into strange new positions," Koch then gave a cursory history of verse collaborations by ancient Chinese and Japanese poets, Provençal troubadours, Renaissance English dramatists, seventeenth-century French surrealists, and contemporary writers like Burroughs and Corso. The text of this volume consisted of close to 200 pages of collaborations by poets from each era mentioned in his history.

Locus Solus No. 3/4, 1961, edited by John Ashbery, was a "Double Issue of New Poetry," consisting of some 250 pages of poems by more than forty poets. The general focus of this volume is indicated by a partial listing of contributors: Michael Benedikt, LeRoi Jones, Bill Berkson, Larry Rivers, Robin Blaser, Diane di Prima, Jean Boudin, Frank O'Hara, George Stanley, Paul Carroll, Daisy Aldan, Kenward Elmslie, James Schuyler, Gerard Malanga, James Merrill, John Ashbery, Barbara Guest, Anselm Hollo, Kenneth Koch, and Harry Mathews.

Koch, Schuyler, Ashbery, and Mathews, along with Barbara Guest and Frank O'Hara, also appeared in *Locus Solus* No. 1, Winter 1961, and in No. 5, 1962—a pair of poetry anthologies edited by James Schuyler, who also called upon such other New York poets as Ebbe Borregaard, Edwin Denby, and Ted Berrigan.

Locus Solus, with its unusual size (150–250-page issues), its concentration upon the poem itself, and its concern with appearance, was a periodical that resembled a book and anthologized the work of an impressive number of contemporary poets.

ManRoot. South San Francisco, Cal.

No. 1, Aug. 1969+. Irreg.

Ed. Paul Mariah; Richard Tagett.

Format varies (recently 5⅜″ x 8⅜″)   no. 1–4: stapled (folded); no. 5+: perfect   96–200 pp.   Illus.

ManRoot, edited from its beginnings by Paul Mariah and Richard Tagett, is a poetry magazine open to a wide range of writers, but with a specific emphasis upon homoerotic poetry. Editor Paul Mariah states that only one-third of the contributors have been homosexuals, though they are responsible for 58 percent of the total pages. The magazine developed from a workshop devised by Paul Mariah and Robert Duncan and sponsored by the Society for Individual Rights (SIR).

ManRoot is a large magazine (over the last five years of irregular publication, individual numbers have averaged more than 150 pages) which takes advantage of its size by allowing generous amounts of space to individual poets and to particular themes or types of poetry. Each issue has devoted at least 30 pages to a featured poet, in some cases a writer the editors feel has been ignored by other publications. Featured poets thus far have been Gerald Fabian, Lynn Strongin, Paul Mariah, Richard Tagett, Richard Grossinger, Paul Eluard and Nanos Valaoritis, Allie Light and Lynn Lonidier, Victor Borsa, Jack Spicer and Robert Duncan, Stephen Kessler, and Michael Finley.

ManRoot has also produced special issues devoted to such topics as womanhood, Greek poetry, and the poetry of Jack Spicer (a 200-page commemorative issue). A 192-page "Surreal Issue," No. 6/7 (April 1972), contained 25 pages by Paul Eluard and 30 pages by Nanos Valaoritis, with other contributions (all in English) by André Breton, Robert Desnos, René Char, Hans Magnus Enzensberger, Arthur Rimbaud, and Jack Spicer. No. 11 (Spring/Summer 1977) is a "New Voices" special issue.

ManRoot is a large, offset-printed magazine with a print run of 1,000 (120 subscriptions). CCLM is the only significant outside funding source. though small donations have helped compensate for the editors' personal financial losses. *ManRoot* has only 17 library or university subscriptions. The editors plan to suspend publication after No. 12 and concentrate upon their line of ManRoot Books.

Margins. Milwaukee, Wisc.

No. 1, Aug. 1972+. Freq. varies.

Ed. Tom Montag; David Buege (Aug. 1972–Dec. 1972).

8¼" x 10¼" (no. 1–3: 8½" x 13") stapled (folded) 72 pp. (varies widely).

Margins was begun as a bimonthly newsletter in response to the proliferation of small-press books and magazines; its purpose was to "put small press materials before a buying audience." *Margins* was to be distributed free to "some 400 libraries and bookstores who have expressed an interest in such small press materials."

With No. 4 (1973), *Margins* shifted to a magazine format, principally to allow "more space for essays and reviews, a broader coverage of little magazines, small press books, and projects and activities of interest." As *Margins* grew in scope and size, Editor Tom Montag eschewed comprehensive bibliographic listings of small-press publications in favor of more detailed critical and descriptive essays on a large but selective number of small-press books and magazines.

Besides articles and special features on all aspects of editing, producing, and marketing small-press publications, *Margins* reviews a large number of books and magazines (sometimes offering two or three reviews of a given piece). Especially interesting are the "Focus" sections, featuring collections of essays on women's writing (No. 7, 1973), native American writing (No. 8, 1973), the role of the review journal and the small-press reviewer (No. 9, 1973/1974), prison writing (No. 12, 1974), gay male writing and publishing (No. 20, 1975), lesbian feminist writing and publishing (No. 23, 1975); and special symposiums on Michael McClure (No. 18, 1975), Rochelle Owens (Nos. 24/25/26, 1975), William Wantling (No. 27, 1975), and Diane Wakoski (Nos. 28/29/30, 1976). These special features are remarkably comprehensive, running in some cases to well over fifty double-column pages and including contributions from important figures in small-press publishing.

The nature of some of these topics has made *Margins* at times controversial, as has the inclusion of essays by writers such as Victor Contoski and Richard Kostelanetz (whose *End to Intelligent Writing* appeared in excerpts in several issues of *Margins*). The major criticism of *Margins* seems to have been the charge, especially regarding early issues, that it has favored midwestern presses and writers, even though this interest seems legitimate. More to the point, the reviews don't indicate how to distinguish the good books from the bad.

Margins has received funding from CCLM.

The Massachusetts Review: A Quarterly of Literature, the Arts and Public Affairs. University of Massachusetts, Amherst, Mass.

Vol. I, no. 1, Oct. 1959+. Qy.

Ed. F. C. Ellert (Oct. 1959–Summer 1963); Sidney Kaplan (Spring 1961–Summer 1963); Jules Chametzky (Autumn 1963–Autumn 1969,

Autumn 1971–Winter/Spring 1974); John Hicks (Autumn 1963–Summer 1972, Summer 1973+); Francis Murphy (Autumn 1965–Spring 1967); Robert G. Tucker (Summer 1971, Autumn 1972+); Lee Edwards (Summer 1974+); Mary Heath (Summer 1974, Winter 1975+).
5¾" x 8¾" sewn about 200 pp. Illus.
Indexed by volume.

While interested in literature and the arts, *The Massachusetts Review* has always managed to present a very current picture of public affairs— a remarkable feat for a quarterly periodical. The first issue featured an Edward L. Katzenbach article on U.S. military policy; the second (February 1960) published a controversial assessment of Fidel Castro and other Latin American leaders. Special issues and supplements in *Massachusetts Review* tend to involve areas where literature and social criticism merge. The Winter/Spring 1972 number, an issue on women, published essays, creative work, and documents by many writers, artists, and even politicians: Bella Abzug, Anais Nin, Angela Davis, Maxine Kumin, Audre Lorde, Rochelle Owens, Crystal Field, and Rosalyn Drexler. Other special numbers or supplements have featured the Paris Commune of 1871 (Summer 1971), Latin America and the Caribbean (Winter/Spring 1974), the problem of New York City (Summer 1973), William Carlos Williams (Winter 1973), Afro-American literature (Autumn 1977), and a four-part "Bicentennial Gathering" beginning in the Summer 1977 issue.

Along the same lines, essays in recent issues have discussed Indian women in America, twentieth-century European social thought, developmental psychology and the arts, the IRA, the 1950s, Frantz Fanon, and Claude Lévi-Strauss. The literary essays, however, tend to be eclectic and nonpolitical.

Among the dominant characteristics of the early issues of *Massachusetts Review* were the special, separately paged sections on the visual arts, introduced in the third issue with work by Ernst Barlach. Printed on fine colored papers at the Gehenna Press or the Meriden Gravure Company, these sections frequently contained the wood engravings of Leonard Baskin, printed directly from the block.

Funding of *Massachusetts Review* comes primarily from the Five Colleges, Inc. (Smith, Mount Holyoke, Amherst, Hampshire College, and the University of Massachusetts). Circulation is 2,500, with 1,000 single-copy sales.

Mulch. New York, N.Y. (Vol. I, no. 1–Vol. II, no. 1, Apr. 1971–Spring 1972); Amherst, Mass. (Vol. II, no. 2–Vol. III, no. 2, Winter 1973/1974– Winter/Spring 1975); Northampton, Mass (Vol. III, no. 3–Vol. III, no. 4/Vol. IV, no. 1, Fall 1975–Spring/Summer 1976).
Vol. I, no. 1–Vol. III, no. 4/Vol. IV, no. 1, Apr. 1971–Spring/Summer 1976. Irreg.

Ed. David Glotzer; Basil King; Harry Lewis.

5″ x 8″   perfect (no. 1: sewn)   70–226 pp.   Illus.

Just as the proper mixture of organic matter will replenish the soil, so this collection of aesthetic and intellectual "mulch before the hard freeze" is intended to fertilize the sensibilities of its readers. The diversity of *Mulch* is suggested by the names of the writers whose quoted statements introduce each issue—Albert Camus, Colette, William Carlos Williams, and Basil King—and by the editor's statements on subjects like raising pigeons and eating Spam, and on more serious subjects like the politics of survival. Some of the most interesting experimental materials in the magazine are by Allen Ginsberg, Paul Blackburn, Joel Oppenheimer, and Paul Metcalf (guest editor for No. 7, Fall/Winter 1975). Provocative materials of a more traditional nature included an anonymous letter (No. 5, Fall 1974) written in 1741 about a Negro plot in New York which resulted in multiple executions of both blacks and whites, and an article in the Spring 1972 issue entitled "A Conspiracy Theory of Poverty."

Among the other contributors to *Mulch* are Nicolas Guillén (tr. Paul Blackburn), Theodore Enslin, Toby Olson, Vladimir Mayakovsky (tr. H. Lewis, L. Hellegers), Russell Banks, John Wieners, Diane di Prima, Jaime de Angulo, and George Economou.

Mulch has been supported by CCLM. Peak circulation was 1,000 copies.

The Naked Ear. Ranches of Taos, N.M.

No. 1–11 [Winter 1956–Jan. 1959]. Irreg.

Ed. Judson Crews.

4¼″ x 5½″   stapled (folded)   12–20 pp.   Illus.

The Naked Ear, edited by Judson Crews, fits the popular conception of the prototypical *little* little magazine as a periodical with one editor/publisher/distributor, operating on a shoestring budget and publishing only highly original and/or controversial talents. The magazine—short poems and photographs—was directed to an audience of practicing poets and to other little-magazine editors, who, in turn, mailed their copies on to other poets and little-magazine editors. Because of their scarcity—copies invariably got worn out or lost—and because they contain early work by a number of now-established poets, all issues have become collector's items. An inveterate little-magazine editor, Crews built this magazine on its predecessors (*Suck-Egg Mule: A Recalcitrant Beast,* Nos. 1–5, November 1950–March 1952; *The Deer and Dachshund,* Nos. 1–6, 1952–1954); and even earlier versions (*Vers Libre, Motive, Taos*). One can consider them one continuing magazine with differing names and formats, corresponding to the passage of years and the state of Crews's personal finances.

The initial number of *Naked Ear* featured four poems by Robert Creeley and a cover reproduction of a Henry Miller watercolor. Other poets were Wolcott Ely, Crews, Max Fenstein, Hyacinthe Hill, and Cerise

Farallon. Subsequent issues included such diverse names as Mason Jordan Mason (Jason Gordon, a continuing contributor to Crews-edited magazines), Wendell B. Anderson, Stuart Z. Perkoff, Larry Eigner, Norman Macleod, Robert Sward, Alfred Dorn, Charles Bukowski, Michael McClure, LeRoi Jones ("Preface to a Twenty-Volume Suicide Note"), and Diane di Prima.

Crews-edited magazines are remarkably free of editorial statements or manifestos—the implication being that the published work can speak for itself and needs no interpretation. Crews evidently was convinced of the value of the Bill Heaton statement which gave the magazine its title: "The naked ear will hear the sound of the waves we make."

The circulation of *Naked Ear* was from 100 to 200 copies.

Neurotica. St. Louis, Mo. (no. 1–4, Spring 1948–Spring 1949); Stamford, Conn. (no. 5, Autumn 1949); New York (no. 6–9, Spring 1950–Winter 1952). Irreg.

Ed. Jay Irving Landesman (no. 1–8, Spring 1948–Spring 1951); Gershon Legman (no. 9, Winter 1952 [?1951]).

6¼″ x 9½″ stapled (folded) 48–80 pp. Illus.

Index no. 1–8 (1948–1951) in no. 8.

In its first issue the editors described *Neurotica* as "a literary exposition, defense, and correlation of the problems and personalities that in our culture are defined as 'neurotic.' It is said that if you tie a piece of red cloth to a gull's leg its fellow-gulls will peck it to pieces: and *Neurotica* wishes to draw an analogy between this observation and the plight of today's creative 'anxious man.' We are interested in exploring the creativeness of this man who has been forced to live underground, and yet lights an utter darkness with his music, poetry, painting, and writing." Further, in issue No. 5: "We define neurosis as the defensive activities of normal individuals against abnormal environments. We assume that human beings are born non-neurotic, and are neuroticized later. We do not agree that it is the measure of social intelligence and psychiatric health to adapt to, and rationalize for, every evil. . . . *Neurotica* is the first lay-psychiatric magazine. It is our purpose to implement the realization on the part of people that they live in a neurotic culture and that it is making neurotics out of them. The practitioners have their own journals. *Neurotica* is for the patients—present and future." Among the persons lacking their own journals, according to *Neurotica,* are free-spirited, non-clique poets whose serial outlets have been co-opted. "As we see it, the little literary magazine is dead. The 'little mags that died to make verse free' have been replaced by subsidized vehicles for clique poetry, critical back-scratching, and professorial piddle, served up with a certain transparent overlay of regional or radical futilitarianism. Having embraced the preciosity and academicism that the little mag was raised up to fight, the current types find themselves wholly without purpose and practically without audience."

716

Neurotica tries to serve the true literary community by publishing such writers as Kenneth Patchen, Leonard Bernstein, Chandler Brossard, Anatole Broyard, Lawrence Durrell, Clellon Holmes, Allen Ginsberg, Peter Viereck, Larry Rivers, Mason Jordan Mason, David Cornel DeJong, Harry Roskolenko, Judith Malina, Charles L. Newman, and Ernest Jones. But the reputation of *Neurotica* really rests upon the provocative essays which set the tone for every issue: Rudolph Friedman, "The End of Feeling," No. 1, Spring 1948; William Krasner, "The Psychopath in Our Society," No. 2, 1948; Gershon Legman, "The Psychopathology of the Comics," No. 3, Autumn 1948; Legman, "Institutionalized Lynch—The Anatomy of the Murder Mystery," No. 4, Spring 1949; Legman, "Rationale of the Dirty Joke—The Castration Complex," No. 9, 1952; Marshall McLuhan, "The Psychopathology of *Time* and *Life*," No. 5, Autumn 1949; McLuhan, "The Folklore of Industrial Man," No. 8, Spring 1951; Alfred Towne, "The Myth of the Western Hero," No. 7, Autumn 1950; Towne, "Sexual Gentleman's Agreement," No. 6, Spring 1950.

One noteworthy *Neurotica* by-product was the publication in 1949 of Gershon Legman's *Love & Death: A Study in Censorship*. Two of its four essays had appeared in *Neurotica*, while the remaining two ("Avatars of the Bitch" and "Open Season on Women") were prepared for the magazine but never appeared there. Fervently praised (Leslie Fiedler in *New Leader*) and equally fervently damned (Robert Warshaw in *Partisan Review*), this 104-page book appears to have been one of the most influential "underground" books of the past three decades in its impact on the national consciousness. Demand for back issues of *Neurotica* and *Love & Death* was sufficient for Hacker Art Books to issue reprints in 1963. Before that time, reprinting of little/literary magazines was thought to be financially unfeasible.

Neurotica attained a circulation of 5,000 copies.

New: American and Canadian Poetry [no. 22/23, Fall/Winter 1973/1974+: New]. Trumansburg, N. Y.
No. 1–27/28, Sep. 1966–Fall 1975. Sep. 1966–Spring/Summer 1973: 3/yr.; Fall/Winter 1973/1974+:2/yr.
Ed. John Gill.
No. 1–20: 6½″ x 8¼″ (varies) stapled 30–100 pp.
No. 21+: 6″ x 9″ (varies) perfect 80–144 pp. (double no. 224 pp.).

Beginning with a special interest in the midwestern and Canadian poets (Earl Birney, Al Purdy, Alden Nowlan, Raymond Fraser, John Newlove, and Irving Layton, all of whom appeared in early issues), Editor John Gill soon increased the scope of *New* so that it included a wide range of poetry from a great many poets. Special issues have been important. Gilles Cormier edited a "Special Bilingual French/Canadian Issue" (No. 14, December 1970), with translations by Gilles and Linda Cormier. Elaine Gill edited the "Special Review Issue: What's New in American and Canadian Poetry" (No. 15, April/May 1971), featuring twenty-two essays by poets and editors in the United States and Canada (including Robert Bly, George Hitchcock, Douglas Blazek, Daryl Hine, Richard Morris, Ron Schreiber, Victor Contoski, and Dick Lourie). Michael Lally edited "None of the Above: New Poets of the U.S.A." (No. 27/28, Fall 1975, the final issue of *New*), featuring thirty-one poets, with a photo of each.

Especially in later issues, *New* made room for longer pieces (such as Marge Piercy's "The Tarot Poems" in No. 19, Fall 1972) and for substantial sections by individual poets (Robert Sward and Keith Abbott in No. 20, January 1973; Howard McCord and Mike Finley in No. 21, Spring/Summer 1973; Michael Lally and Tom Wayman in No. 24, 1974; Joel Deutsch in No. 25/26, 1975).

After ten years of publication, *New* was suspended in order to allow John Gill more time for operation of his Crossing Press. *New* received support from CCLM, and its circulation rose from an initial 300 to a peak of 1,000 copies.

New American Review [no. 16, Feb. 1973+: American Review: The Magazine of New Writing]. New York, N. Y.
No. 1–26, Sep. 1967–Nov. 1977. Freq. varies.
Ed. Theodore Solotaroff [Poetry Ed. Stanley Moss (Sep. 1967–Aug. 1970); Richard Howard (1971–Nov. 1977)].
4¼" x 7" perfect 224–290 pp.
Index no. 9–24 in no. 24 (Apr. 1976); index no. 1–26 in no. 26 (Nov. 1977).

New American Review (later *American Review*) was a large-circulation magazine featuring established as well as lesser known writers. It was produced in paperback format in print runs of from 25,000 to 100,000 copies, and published fiction, poetry, and essays.

Theodore Solotaroff's headnotes to early numbers set forth the goals of *New American Review*. Regenerating the spirit of *New American Library*—an earlier paperback literary periodical which, in Solotaroff's opinion, had avoided cult and coterie literary publishing and had extended hospitality to all good creative writing—*New American Review* broadened this focus so as to generate "more explicit and topical connections between contemporary literature and the culture-at-large." Observing that "there is a great deal of creative expression in America today that does not flow in strictly literary channels," Solotaroff included in *New American Review* numerous topical essays that frequently belong within the definition of New Journalism.

In the "Editor's Note" to No. 11 (the issue with which Simon and Schuster replaced New American Library as publisher), Solotaroff pointed out that a large-circulation literary periodical stands or falls according to the degree to which it fulfills its "particular purpose and value—that of bringing an abundance of significant writers, often relatively unknown ones, to the attention of a wide audience." For the editor and publisher, the problem involves getting a paperback little magazine to compete in volume sales with other mass-market and trade paperbacks. Despite staggering economic pressures, *New American Review* brought a considerable number of talented writers and poets to a new, much wider audience.

According to Solotaroff, in its first seven years the magazine printed "almost 500 different contributors, at least 90 percent of whom have been American." One finds fiction by John Barth, John Hawkes, Robert Coover, Ralph Ellison, Richard Brautigan, Doris Lessing, and Malcolm Lowry; poetry by every major American poet from John Ashbery to Robert Penn Warren; and essays by Norman Mailer, Theodore Roszak, Benjamin DeMott, and Frank Kermode.

Issues 1–10 of *New American Review* were financed by New American Library/Signet Books; issues 11–15 by Simon and Schuster; issues 16–26 by Bantam Books.

The North American Review. Cornell College, Mount Vernon, Iowa (Mar. 1964–Nov./Dec. 1968); University of Northern Iowa, Cedar Falls, Iowa (Spring 1969+).
New Series, Vol. I, no. 1 (Old Series, Vol. CCXLIX), Mar. 1964+. Qy.
Ed. Robert P. Dana (Mar. 1964–Nov./Dec. 1968); Robley Wilson, Jr. (Spring 1969+).
8½″ x 11″ stapled (folded) 64–96 pp. Illus.
Annual index.

The *North American Review* began in Boston in 1815 and developed into a leading American journal of opinion on current issues. In 1940, the magazine's one-hundred-and-twenty-fifth year of publication, it came to an abrupt conclusion when its editor, Joseph Hilton Smyth, who had written some impassioned isolationist editorials, admitted to being a paid agent of the Japanese government. In 1964, Robert P. Dana revived the magazine with a vow to return to an impartial discussion of current issues. Robley Wilson, Jr., took over in 1969, emphasizing environmental matters in addition to poetry, fiction, and reviews.

In Dana's first issue, the presence of essayists like Julian Huxley and Paul Goodman forecast the wide range and lively nature of things to come. Later issues covered everything from the 1964 elections, pornography laws, and moon shots to highway deaths and the war in Vietnam. A good deal of space was given to civil rights issues. At the same time, *North American Review* printed poetry by John Logan, James Dickey, David Ignatow, William Stafford, Louis Simpson, Dennis Saleh, and many others. But fiction was probably the center of the magazine, with twenty-five or more stories appearing each year, many by new writers.

719

Under Wilson, *North American Review* has printed poetry by Rochelle Ratner, Susan Fromberg Schaeffer, John Taggart, Stephen Dobyns, Samuel Hazo, Colette Inez, Douglas Blazek, Felix Pollak, Greg Kuzma, Rosellen Brown, and Philip Dacey. The long list of fiction contributors includes Paul Theroux, Gail Godwin, Flannery O'Connor, Raymond Carver, and Annie Dillard. *North American Review*'s catholicity of taste is indicated by the fact that Jerome Klinkowitz and George V. Higgins have both been frequent contributors in recent years. The Summer 1977 issue contained an interesting feature, "Inside the Iowa Writers' Workshop," with Steve Wilbers interviewing Donald Justice, Marvin Bell, and Vance Bourjaily.

Aside from the support first of Cornell College and later of the University of Northern Iowa, *NAR* has received some grant money from CCLM and, since 1969, from the Iowa Arts Council. Circulation has grown from about 650 in 1968 to about 2,700 (1,600 mail and 900 newsstand copies). The current press run is 3,700. Libraries account for about 1,000 subscriptions.

Origin [Series I: A Quarterly for the Creative; Series II: Response; Series III: Center]. Dorchester, Mass. (Ser. I, no. 1–11, Spring 1951–Autumn 1953); Ashland, Mass. (Ser. I, no. 12–20, Spring 1954–Winter 1957); San Francisco (Ser. II, no. 1–4, Apr. 1961–Jan. 1962); Kyoto, Japan (Ser. II, no. 5, Apr. 1962+).
Ser. I, no. 1–Ser. III, no. 20, Spring 1951–Jan. 1971 [a fourth series is planned]. Qy.
Ed. Cid Corman [guest editors include Paul Blackburn (Spring 1953), Denise Levertov (Summer 1954), Irving Layton (Winter/Spring 1955)].
6″ x 8⅜″ (varies)   stapled (folded)   54–68 pp.

In a note to the Kraus reprint of *Origin*, Editor Cid Corman tells how Evelyn Schoolman suggested the magazine and paid for the early issues of Series One, which ran from Spring 1951 to Winter 1957 (twenty issues). Corman at that time was conducting a weekly poetry reading on a Boston radio station. In the first series he printed occasional essays, reviews and letters, and some fiction, but the real emphasis was on poetry. Corman introduced some new poets, got new work from some established poets, and printed translations of Artaud, Gottfried Benn, René Char, Lorca, and Ungaretti. Of the many poets appearing in the twenty issues of Series One, the most frequent contributors were Paul Blackburn, William Bronk, Paul Carroll, Cid Corman, Robert Creeley, Wade Donahoe, Robert Duncan, Larry Eigner, Theodore Enslin, David Galler, Irving Layton, Denise Levertov, Samuel French Morse, Charles Olson, Gael Turnbull, and William Carlos Williams. Number 8 was Charles Olson's book, *In Cold Hell, in Thicket*, printed by Robert Creeley's Divers Press on Majorca.

A fourteen-issue second series, running from April 1961 to July 1964, and a twenty-issue third series, running from April 1966 to January 1971, carried many of the poets who had figured prominently in the first series. In each issue of Series Two and Three a generous amount of space was devoted to a particular featured poet (occasionally a group). The best way to describe *Origin* is simply to list the featured writers issue by issue. In Series Two, there were special concentrations of work from Louis Zukofsky, Gary Snyder, Zeami Motokiyo, Margaret Avison, Robert Kelly, Ian Hamilton Finlay, Gael Turnbull, Cid Corman, Robert Duncan, Francis Ponge, Perse, Dadelsen, Frank Samperi, Roberto Sanesi, and Basho. In Series Three, Corman featured work by himself, Lorine Niedecker, André du Bouchet, Kusano Shimpei, William Bronk, Douglas Woolf, Seymour Faust, Josef Albers, Francis Ponge, René Daumal, Chuang-tzu, Denis Goacher, Jean Daive, John Taggart, Paul Celan, Daphne Marlatt, Philippe Jaccottet, Jonathan Greene, Frank Samperi, and Hitomaro.

One thousand copies of *Origin* No. 1 were printed; thereafter the print run was much smaller. For the second series, 300 copies per issue were printed, and 200 per issue for the third. Financial help seems to have come mainly from individual patrons. An anthology, *The Gist of Origin, 1951–1971,* was published by Grossman/Viking in 1975 with an introduction by Cid Corman. Corman plans to inaugurate a fourth series.

The Outsider. New Orleans, La. (no. 1–3, Fall 1961–Spring 1963); Tucson, Ariz. (no. 4/5, Winter 1968/1969).
Vol. I, no. 1–Vol. II, no. 4/5, Fall 1961–Winter 1968/1969 (Mar. 1969).
Irreg.
Ed. Jon Edgar Webb.
6" x 9"   no. 1–3 stapled; no. 4/5 perfect   102–196 pp.   Illus.

While Jon Edgar Webb was incarcerated in a midwestern reformatory, he was discovered, championed, and published by Whit Burnett, editor of *Story* (see the February 1936 issue). Webb's gratitude for this recognition was a major factor in his launching of *The Outsider* many years later. His perspective as a social "outsider" in turn shaped his editorial policy, as he made clear in No. 3, Spring 1963. There he spoke of working toward a "representation that would not be just what serious writing was happening cross-country today but what, specifically, talented outsiders were doing. And most of the clique-minded writers, no matter how good they are, or validly vital by academic standards, are not especially our kind of writers. Which doesn't make *us* a clique at all— outsiders are totally outside of cliques."

A catholic approach characterized the first issue, which featured such diverse authors as Russell Edson, Diane di Prima, Gary Snyder, Charles Olson, Langston Hughes, Cid Corman, Robert Creeley, Kay Boyle, Charles Bukowski, Robert Sward, Colin Wilson, William Burroughs, Judson Crews, G. C. Oden, Jonathan Williams, Gregory Corso, Gael Turnbull,

Ed Dorn, Allen Ginsberg, Peter Orlovsky, Gilbert Sorrentino, Walter Lowenfels, Lawrence Ferlinghetti, Ray Bremser, Mike McClure, Henry Miller, LeRoi Jones, Marvin Bell, Paul Carroll, James Boyer May, Paul Blackburn, Clayton Eshleman, Tuli Kupferberg, and Barbara Moraff. The Henry Miller/Walter Lowenfels letters were serialized in Nos. 1–3. A survey on jazz by Richard B. Allen, Sam B. Charters, E. L. Borenstein, and others appeared in Nos. 2–3. Charles Bukowski's "outsider of the year" special section highlighted No. 3, Spring 1963, and the very moving Kenneth Patchen homage (with contributions by Norman Thomas, Brother Antoninus, Allen Ginsberg, James Boyer May, Harold Norse, Hugh Mac-Diarmid, Kenneth Rexroth, Lawrence Ferlinghetti, David Meltzer, and Henry Miller) appeared in No. 4/5. Although the later issues featured established authors (Jean Genet, Jack Kerouac, Thomas Merton, Lawrence Durrell, and others), a generous number of pages was set aside for then relatively unknown authors (William Wantling, Ian Hamilton Finlay, Clarence Major, Dick Higgins, Emmett Williams, Kay Johnson, Marcus Grapes, Richard Morris, and others).

The Webbs, working as a husband-and-wife team, laboriously set and printed the copy by hand on a Chandler & Price 8″ by 12″ press. After successfully completing three yearly numbers, they ventured into the production of fine printed books. In 1967 they were given the Type Directors of New York Award for Typography, Type Direction, and Design for a Henry Miller work titled *Order and Chaos Chez Hans Reichel* —an endeavor which seriously depleted their limited energies and finances. Five years off schedule, the final double issue was released in 1969. Available in hard cover, it was made possible by donations from friends and two small grants from CCLM and the Fidelis Foundation. The death of Jon Webb in June 1971 terminated all activities of the press.

An issue of *The Wormwood Review* (No. 45) commemorates *The Outsider* and contains an informative essay by Charles Bukowski which details the Webbs's editorial devotion and the difficulties under which they labored.

The Outsider reached a peak circulation of about 3,000.

Panache. New York, N.Y. (no. 1/3, 1965–1969); Princeton, N.J. (no. 4–13, 1970–1974); Sunderland, ass. (No. 14, 1975+).

No. 1, 1965+. Irreg.

Ed. Rosalie P. Frank (no. 1–13, 1965–1974); David R. Lenson (no. 14, 1975+).

Format varies (recently 5½″ x 8½″) stapled (folded) 64 pp. (some longer).

No. 6, Ed. Richard Kostelanetz, is 8½″ x 11″ and 176 pp.

In a tribute to the late founding editor, Rosalie B. Frank, her successor David R. Lenson pointed out that "she invested—and lost—thousands of dollars of her own in order to pay contributors, print generous quantities of

722

each issue, and still keep the price of the magazine down," while publishing the work of George Chambers, Raymond Federman, Gayl Jones, Richard Kostelanetz, Charles Aukema, Gary Goss, and Maura Stanton.

David Lenson's current plan to produce one issue each year devoted to poetry and one devoted to fiction is a continuation of Frank's policy. Numbers 4–8 (Summer 1970–1972) all dealt exclusively with new fiction, most of it experimental. Number 6 (1971) was an oversize number (8½" x 11" and 176 pages), edited by Richard Kostelanetz and featuring a sampling of visual and nonlinear fiction. *Panache* No. 10 (Summer 1972), co-published with *December* magazine, was a perfect bound edition of George Chambers's novel *The Bonnyclabber*.

During David R. Lenson's tenure as poetry editor, the poetry issues of *Panache* included contributions from Robert Coover, Raymond Federman, Richard Kostelanetz, Edwin Brock, John Koethe, Philip Dacey, Edwin Honig, Gayl Jones, Lyn Lifshin, Kenneth Rexroth, Lawrence P. Spingarn, and others. One interesting characteristic of the poetry issues is the presence of contributions from authors primarily associated with fiction and experimental fiction.

Panache has received aid from CCLM and the Massachusetts Council on the Arts and Humanities. Recent circulation is 700 (down from a peak of 1,000).

The Paris Review. Paris, France (no. 1–46, Spring 1953–Spring 1973); New York, N. Y. (no. 57, Spring 1974+).

Vol. I, no. 1, Spring 1953+. Irreg. (now qy.).

Ed. George Plimpton; Peter Matthiessen (Summer 1953+); Donald Hall (Summer 1953+); Harold L. Humes (Summer 1953–Autumn 1953); William Pène du Bois (Summer 1953–Summer 1954); Robert B. Silvers (Spring 1956+); Blair Fuller (Spring 1958+); Maxine Groffsky (Winter 1971+); Lawrence M. Bensky (Spring 1966–Summer 1968); Peter Ardery (Fall 1968–Spring 1973) [the continuing editors do not all appear in every issue].

5¼" x 8½" no. 1–56: sewn; no. 57+: perfect 120–224 pp.

Index 1953–1963 in Winter/Spring 1964 (10th Anniversary Number).

Paris Review was founded in 1953 on the premise that creative performance has primacy over criticism. From the beginning, the magazine has printed poetry and fiction as well as "portfolio" reproductions and photos of artwork by Picasso, Zev, Kokoschka, Giacometti, Chagall, and Pierre Soulages, among others. Even the nonfiction prose has tended more toward notebooks and reminiscences or interviews or biography than toward critical essays.

The poetry editorship of *Paris Review* has undergone interesting changes. Donald Hall held the post from 1953 to 1961, with X. J. Kennedy replacing him and filling the position until No. 31 (Winter/Spring 1964). Kennedy's last issue, the tenth anniversary number, contains a "Portfolio of New Poetry" by some poets who are "among those writers whom this magazine has helped make known"—John Hollander, Christopher Middleton, Donald Justice, X. J. Kennedy, Elizabeth Jennings, James Wright, Louis Simpson, Robert Pack, James Dickey, Charles Tomlinson, Adrienne Rich, George Mackay Brown, Robert Bly, Geoffrey Hill, W. S. Merwin Robert Mezey, Henri Coulette, Donald Hall, Philip Booth, Donald Petersen, and Robert Layzer. From 1964 to 1974, Tom Clark was poetry editor and the New York poets dominated the magazine (even, at times, the fiction section). From 1974 to 1978, Michael Benedikt was poetry editor; he continued the New York emphasis but with special focus upon the prose poem. In 1978, Jonathan Galassi, an editor for Houghton Mifflin, took over the poetry editorship.

The most popular features of *Paris Review,* and certainly the elements which most people associate with the magazine, have been the regular interviews with novelists, poets, and playwrights. Beginning with an E. M. Forster interview in No. 1, discussions with novelists (less frequently with poets), have been published in every issue. These *Paris Review* interviews have been collected in several volumes (four by mid-1977) and published by Viking Press.

Paris Review has a circulation of 8,000 to 10,000, with single-copy sales of 2,500. According to the editors, "Funding is derived from state and national grants, subscriptions, advertising in the magazine, patrons, and proceeds from the sale of a series of poster prints the magazine commissioned in 1966." *Paris Review* has also received grants from CCLM.

Parnassus: Poetry in Review. New York, N. Y.
Vol. I, no. 1, Fall/Winter 1972+. Semiannual.
Ed. Herbert Leibowitz.
6″ x 9¼″   sewn/perfect   200–550 pp.
Index Vol. I–II (Fall/Winter 1972–Spring/Summer 1974) in Vol. II, no. 2; index Vol. III–IV (Fall/Winter 1974–Spring/Summer 1976) in Vol. IV, no. 2.

In the fifth anniversary issue of *Parnassus,* Editor Herbert Leibowitz, explaining his decision to print only criticism and commentary and no original poems, describes his view of *Parnassus* as "a kind of Hyde Park Corner where poets and critics of all persuasions—the solemn advocate, the debunker, the passionate idealist, the scholar, the crank, the rehabilitator of a neglected reputation—can gather and discuss with freedom, wit, partisanship, and objectivity issues, trends, and new and old books." The files of this bulky magazine (a typical issue carries more than twenty review essays, most of them substantial in length and depth) perhaps constitute the best key we have to the range of interests of 1970s poets and critics. Emphasis is overwhelmingly on discussion of individual poets or groups of poets linked according to nationality, race, or language: Aztec, Swedish, Greek, Russian, American Indian, Chinese, Yiddish, Latin American, African, black American, and English.

In 1976, the American bicentennial year, the Fall/Winter issue printed reviews (some from the past and from such unlikely sources as *Time* magazine) of Poe, Emerson, Thoreau, Whitman, Emily Dickinson, T. S. Eliot, Ezra Pound, Wallace Stevens, William Carlos Williams, Hart Crane, Edna Millay, Randall Jarrell, Sylvia Plath, Robert Duncan, W. S. Merwin, James Merrill, Kenward Elmslie, and Weldon Kees, as well as the blues, black poets, and the prose-poem in America. More often, though, the central tendency of the magazine is toward reviews of new work by the regularly practicing American poets who are generally known to readers of contemporary poetry: Diane Wakoski, John Hollander, Denise Lever-tov, Howard Nemerov, and Robert Creeley, among many others.

Since poets generally are committed readers of new poetry, it is not sur-prising that many of the *Parnassus* review essays are written by poets. These poet reviewers include Colette Inez, William Meredith, Muriel Rukeyser, Richard Howard, Hayden Carruth, Adrienne Rich, Diane Wakoski, John Ashbery, X. J. Kennedy, John Hollander, Anselm Hollo, and Howard Nemerov.

Parnassus has featured occasional special sections, notably the "Garland for Charles Ives" (100 pages by ten authors in Spring/Summer 1975) and the "Tribute to Virgil Thomson on His 81st Birthday" (125 pages by fifteen contributors, including Thomson, in Spring/Summer 1977, the fifth anni-versary issue). In this same anniversary issue, Editor Herbert Leibowitz suspended his usual policy and printed poems by authors who had con-tributed review articles to *Parnassus*.

Parnassus has received aid from CCLM, the New York State Council on the Arts, and CUNY–College of Staten Island.

Partisan Review. New York, N.Y. (Feb./Mar. 1934–Summer 1963); Rutgers University, Rutgers, N.J. (Fall 1963–Summer 1978); Boston University, Boston, Mass (Fall 1978+).

Vol. I, no. 1, Feb./Mar. 1934+. Freq. varies (now qy.).

Editorial board for no. 1: Nathan Adler, Edward Dahlberg, Joseph Free-man, Sender Garlin, Alfred Hayes, Milton Howard, Joshua Kunitz, Louis Lozowick, Leonard Mins, Wallace Phelps, Philip Rahv, and Edwin Rolfe [edited by committee until Oct. 1936, then reorganized Dec. 1937: Ed. F. W. Dupee, Dwight Macdonald, Mary McCarthy, George L. K. Morris, William Phillips, and Philip Rahv; then continues with some shifts; Rahv was an editor until 1969; Phillips remains an editor in 1978].

6" x 9"   Feb./Mar. 1934–May 1948: sewn; Nov. 1948+: perfect   about 160 pp.

Annual index; index 1934–1965 by Elizabeth Wright in AMS reprint edition.

Partisan Review's most distinguishing feature in the late forties, the fifties, and the early sixties was its essentially eclectic view of literature as well as a liberal socialism, and later a liberal academic stance, in politics. Its original editorial board after the first issue (Philip Rahv, William

Phillips, F. W. Dupee, Mary McCarthy, George L. K. Morris, and Dwight Macdonald) was amended in 1943 when Macdonald was replaced by Delmore Schwartz. Schwartz served on the editorial board until 1946 and then was associate editor until 1955. Under Schwartz's influence *Partisan Review* moved more toward literature—though still strongly eclectic. Against the background of literature and alienation emphasized by Philip Rahv, *Partisan* published poetry and prose by Wallace Stevens, William Carlos Williams, Lawrence Durrell, Elizabeth Bishop, Jorge Luis Borges, Franz Kafka, Randall Jarrell, W. H. Auden, Vladimir Nabokov, and Saul Bellow, and political, social, and cultural essays by Arthur M. Schlesinger, Jr., Irving Howe, Stephen Spender, Ernest Nagel, and C. Wright Mills. Contributions by Sidney Hook, F. O. Matthiessen, Nigel Dennis, Ernest Simmons, André Gide, George Orwell, Eric Bentley, Newton Arvin, and F. R. Leavis all indicate the range *Partisan* presented before 1960.

Harold Rosenberg's art criticism first appeared in *Partisan,* which was also the first magazine in the United States to publish T. S. Eliot's *Four Quartets* ("East Coker" in Vol. VII, No. 3, May/June 1940, and "The Dry Salvages in Vol. VIII, No. 3, May/June 1941). *Partisan Review* was also important for its continued focus on political comment. Articles on "The Future of Socialism" by Arthur Schlesinger, Jr., in 1947 (Vol. XIX, No. 3), "The Leninist Myth of Imperialism" by Raymond Aron in 1951 (Vol. XVIII, No. 6), Hannah Arendt's "Understanding Communism" in 1953 (Vol. XX, No. 5), a 1954 review by Dwight Macdonald entitled "McCarthy and His Apologists" (Vol. XXI, No. 4), and a series of anti-Stalinist articles titled "The Crisis in Communism," with commentary by Hungarian, Polish, and French critics (Vol. XXIV, No. 1, Winter 1957)—all give a clear indication of *Partisan Review*'s close watch on the politics of the fifties.

Political awareness has remained strong in recent issues of the magazine. The extent of this concern in recent years is shown by a 1964 critique, "Some Comments on Senator Goldwater" (Vol. XXXIV, No. 1) and the following symposiums: "The Cold War and the West" in 1962 (Vol. XXIX, No. 1); "What's Happening to America" in 1967 (Vol. XXXIV, No. 1); "Black Power: A Discussion" in 1968 (Vol. XXXV, No. 2); and "Art, Culture, and Conservatism" in 1972 (Vol. XXXIX, No. 3).

Another aspect of *Partisan*'s significance was the fact that it served as a meeting ground, a common denominator, for a notable New York literary coterie of the fifties that included Larry Rivers, Frank O'Hara, Bill Berkson, Kenneth Koch, and John Ashbery.

Several *Partisan Review* anthologies—*The Partisan Reader* (1946), *The New Partisan Reader* (1953), and *The Partisan Review Anthology* (1962) —offer an excellent survey of the magazine's blend of poets, short story writers, and essayists on literature and the social sciences. As recently as 1977, *Partisan* was printing fiction and poetry by both the old guard and

726

the new, many of them writers who had already been certified by other publications: Delmore Schwartz, Donald Barthelme, Harry Mathews, Michael Brownstein, Frank O'Hara, and Robert Duncan, as well as John Hollander, William Stafford, and Richard Elman. (Guest editors are now responsible for much of the poetry published, among them Michael Anania, Paul Zweig, and, more recently, John Ashbery.) *Partisan* also continues to carry a wide range of provocative articles: on Freud, on films and literature, on Norman Mailer and Henry Miller, on John Berryman and booze, and on communism at Harvard—plus symposiums on popular art and culture in New York .

Circulation is about 8,500. *Partisan Review* has received grants from CCLM.

Pembroke Magazine. Pembroke State College, Pembroke, N. C.
No. 1, 1969+. Annual.
Editorial director: Norman Macleod.
6" x 9"   perfect   48–372 pp.   Illus.
Cumulative index for no. 1–4, 1969–1973.

Pembroke Magazine is interested in ethnic and regional literature and art with an emphasis on American Indians, black Americans, and North Carolina writers and artists. Among the American Indian poets in *Pembroke* have been Grey Cohoe, Duane Niatum, R. C. Gorman, Ray Young Bear, and Norman H. Russell. No. 3 printed nine poems by the Acoma poet Simon J. Ortiz; No. 5 contained a substantial "Conversation with Frank Waters on American Indian Religion." Editor Norman Macleod has also published poets from the British Isles—Hugh MacDiarmid, J. F. Hendry, and W. S. Graham; biographical materials on Robert McAlmon and Norman Holmes Pearson; a special Scottish literary supplement edited from Edinburgh, Scotland; and a sizable collection of letters from William Carlos Williams to Macleod.

In addition to university support from Pembroke State University, *Pembroke* has received grants from CCLM and the North Carolina Arts Council. Circulation is 1,500.

Poetry. Chicago, Ill.
Vol. I, no. 1, Oct. 1912+. My.
Ed. Harriet Monroe (Oct. 1912–Oct. 1936); Morton Dauwen Zabel (Nov. 1936–Oct. 1937); George Dillon (Nov. 1937–Aug. 1942; Vol. LXVIII, Apr.–Sep. 1946–Vol. LXXIII, Oct. 1948–Mar. 1949); Peter DeVries (Sep. 1942–Vol. LXVII, Oct. 1945–Mar. 1946); Jessica Nelson North (Sep. 1942–June 1943); Marion Strobel (Apr. 1943–Vol. LXXIII, Oct. 1948–Mar. 1949); Margedant Peters (Vol. LXVIII, Apr.-Sep. 1946–Vol. LXIX, Oct. 1946–Mar. 1947); John Frederick Nims (Vol. LXVIII, Apr.–Sep. 1946–Vol. LXXI, Oct. 1947–Mar. 1948; Jan. 1978+); Hayden

Carruth (Vol. LXXIV, Apr.–Sep. 1949–Jan. 1950); Karl Shapiro (Feb. 1950–Sep. 1955); Henry Rago (Oct. 1955–June 1969); Daryl Hine (July 1969–Dec. 1977).

5½" x 8" (Mar. 1971+: 5½" x 9") sewn (Aug./Sep. 1970+: perfect 70 pp.

Indexed by volume (semiannual); index Vol. I–LX (Oct. 1912–Sep. 1942); index Vol. I–C (1912–1962) compiled by Elizabeth Wright for AMS reprint edition.

Poetry has continued its unbroken monthly publication since 1912, and has presented work by every major American poet from Ezra Pound and Wallace Stevens to John Ashbery, Robert Lowell, Richard Wilbur, and Louis Zukofsky. It has produced a number of special issues on the poetry of France, Italy, Greece, Japan, India, and Israel, on the dissident poets of the U.S.S.R., and on poetry against the war in Vietnam. The magazine has continued its policy of printing reviews as well as poetry.

Poetry is supported primarily by subscriptions and by its board of trustees. It has also received support from various foundations (Ingram Merrill, Bollingen, and others), as well as from the National Endowment for the Arts, the Illinois Arts Council, and CCLM. Circulation is currently between 7,500 and 8,000 (single copy sales from 500 to 600). An index of Volumes I to LX appears in *Poetry* itself. AMS has also published an index of volumes I to C, 1912–1962. Houghton Mifflin recently brought out an anthology of poems selected from *Poetry* (1912–1977) by former editor Daryl Hine.

Poetry Northwest. Seattle, Wash.

Vol. I, no. 1, June 1959+. Qy.

Editorial board for no. 1: Errol Pritchard, chairman; Nelson Bentley, Richard Hugo, Carolyn Kizer, Edith Shiffert [from no. 2 the board underwent changes; then Ed. Carolyn Kizer (Spring 1964–Summer 1966); David Wagoner (Autumn 1966+)].

5½" x 8½" stapled (folded) 48–56 pp.

Poetry Northwest has had, in effect, only two editors: Carolyn Kizer (as part of an editorial board) and, beginning with Vol. VII, No. 3 (Autumn 1966), David Wagoner. Each issue contains 48 or 56 pages of poetry by a dozen to a dozen-and-a-half poets. *Poetry Northwest* does not feature essays, reviews, or fiction; it has printed verse in translation and a good deal of English poetry. Very rarely does it print poems of extended length. Some of the poets included in recent issues are Joyce Carol Oates, James B. Hall, Ray Young Bear, John Unterecker, Harold Will, Arthur Vogelsang, Robert Pack, Naomi Clark, Felix Pollak, Samuel Hazo, Constance Urdang, Philip Dacey, Albert Goldbarth, Sonya Dorman, and Philip Booth. Since 1962, the *Poetry Northwest* Helen Bullis Prize has been awarded to Hayden Carruth, John Logan, Donald Finkel, Mona Van Duyn, Richard Hugo, Winfield Townley Scott and Katie Louchheim,

728

Sandra McPherson and Gwen Head, Eugene Ruggles, Will Stubbs, Kenneth O. Hanson and Jack Tootell, Lewis Turco and Tom Wayman, Richard Hugo (again), Adrien Stoutenberg and Lisel Mueller, Dan Masterson and Paul Zimmer, John Allman, Greg Kuzma, John Taylor, and Diana O Hehir. Some winners of the magazine's Theodore Roethke Prize have been Richard Hugo, William Stafford, Carolyn Stoloff, John Woods, Philip Booth, Mark McCloskey, and Greg Kuzma, while the Young Poet's Prize, initiated in 1973, has been given to Greg Kuzma, Joseph di Prisco, Thomas Brush, Judith Small, and Stephen Jaech.

Circulation is approximately 2,000. Since 1966, the magazine has been partially supported by the University of Washington Graduate School. Other support has come from CCLM.

The Prairie Schooner. University of Nebraska, Lincoln, Neb.

Vol. I, no. 1, Jan. 1927+. Qy.

Ed. Lowry Charles Wimberly (Jan. 1927–Fall 1956); Karl Shapiro (Winter 1956–Winter 1962/1963); Bernice Slote (Spring 1963+) [for Spring 1963 Frederick L. Christensen, Virginia Faulkner, and Lee T. Lemon were members, with Bernice Slote, of a board of editors].

6¾" x 9¾" perfect 96 pp.

Indexed by volume.

The Prairie Schooner began as "an outlet for literary work in the University of Nebraska and a medium for the publication of the finest writing of the prairie country," but it soon found itself a national publication both in readership and in contributors. Lowry Charles Wimberly, editor from 1927 to 1956 and the man most closely identified with the magazine, decided not to maintain strict local boundaries. The magazine has, however, tried to remain essentially national rather than international in scope. In its first thirty years, *Prairie Schooner* presented the first published work of over 300 writers, including that of Weldon Kees, Jesse Stuart, and Jessamyn West.

Later editors Karl Shapiro (1956–1963) and Bernice Slote (1963 to the present) have maintained the mixture of national, and sometimes international, literature with more local midwestern concerns. In recent years *Prairie Schooner* has done special issues on such themes as children's poetry, little magazines, and women and tragedy, and special numbers on Willa Cather and Wright Morris. Volume XL, No. 4 (Winter 1966), the fortieth anniversary number, presented a number of selections from early issues of *Prairie Schooner*.

Prairie Schooner is supported by the University of Nebraska English department, the University of Nebraska Press, and private grants. Circulation is 1,500.

Prose. New York, N.Y.

No. 1–9, [Fall] 1970–Fall 1974. 2/yr.

Coburn Britton, publisher.

5½" x 8¾"   sewn   159–251 pp.
No. 4–9 contain cumulative indexes.

Prose was a beautiful magazine—spare and elegant in appearance, with an unfailingly urbane tone which frequently made its contents seem a transcription of impossibly brilliant conversation. There were essays on fashionable topics (neuroses, the American liberal/intellectual establishment); on artistic culture, high and low (Stephen Orgel's "Inigo Jones on Stonehenge," Donald Phelps on Dick Tracy); and on the special interests one might find among a group of educated people (writing dictionary definitions, electronic music, ancient Anglo-Saxon cures and remedies). A good deal of space in *Prose* was given over to memoirs, autobiography, and reminiscences of such persons as Margaret Anderson, Glenway Wescott, Sanche de Gramont, Daryl Hine, Allen Tate, Paul Bowles, Elizabeth Hardwick, Jack Sullivan, Alfred Kazin, Donald Davie, Paul Horgan, Charles Newman, Annie Dillard, Richard Howard, and Edouard Roditi. Then there were general essays by interesting prose stylists like Djuna Barnes, Reynolds Price, and Edward Dahlberg (who appeared in eight of nine issues), essays on art and literature by Richard Howard, Kay Boyle, Howard Nemerov, Harold Rosenberg, Robin Magowan, Henri Peyre, Virgil Thomson, John Hollander, and Howard Moss. Finally, there were essays on specific artists and literary figures and their works: W. H. Auden on G. K. Chesterton, Harold Bloom on Wallace Stevens and on Browning's "Childe Roland," Anthony Burgess on Shakespeare's marriage, Parker Tyler on Ronald Firbank, John Hollander on Thomas Cole, Marius Bewley on Disraeli's writing, Robert Payne on T. E. Lawrence's prose, Donald Phelps on Melville's *Pierre*, Paul Schmidt on Rimbaud, Richard Howard on Emily Dickinson, James Kraft on Henry James, Edward Foote on Ezra Pound, Stephen Koch on Andy Warhol, Donald Phelps on Edith Wharton, Wallace Fowlie on Jean Cocteau, Paul Metcalf on Charles Olson, Howard Hussey on Joseph Cornell, Howard Nemerov on Dante. The emphasis in most of these essays was upon biographical and societal factors impinging upon the artist, thus bringing us back to the autobiographical contributions mentioned earlier and completing a unified, organic collection of essays, always urbane and sophisticated and never dull. *Prose* was a magazine whose simple elegance in appearance suited the familiar ease and accomplishment of its contents.

Quarterly Review of Literature. Chapel Hill, N. C. (Autumn 1943–Summer 1944); New Haven, Conn. (Fall 1944–1947); Bard College, Annandale-on-Hudson, N. Y. (1947–1968); Princeton University, Princeton, N. J. (1969+).
Vol. I, no. 1, Autumn 1943+. Qy.
Ed. Warren Carrier (Autumn 1943–Summer 1944); Theodore Weiss (Winter 1944+); Renée Weiss ([1946]+).
5¼" x 8¼"   perfect   no. of pp. varies (double nos. about 250 pp.).
Index by volume for Vol. I–XV, 1943–1968.

Quarterly Review of Literature was begun at the University of North Carolina in 1943 by Warren Carrier. After a year of publication, Carrier left for the war in Europe and Theodore and Renée Weiss took over permanent control of the magazine, which published poetry, fiction, essays, and reviews. According to Theodore Weiss in the 1974 retrospective issue (Vol. XIX, Nos. 1–2), his interests as editor were set on "stimulation and innovation rather than on consolidation, evaluation, and scholarly taste-making." Also eschewed were "the overtly political and the social." A significant modification of policy occurred in 1949 when, in reaction against a common opinion that this was an era for secondary and critical work rather than creative production, *Quarterly Review of Literature* turned its pages over entirely to poetry, fiction, and drama (except for whatever critical-biographical matter might be included in special issues).

Quarterly Review of Literature's expressed areas of interest are poetry, fiction, and special issues devoted to major writers like Franz Kafka, Ezra Pound, Giacomo Leopardi, Friedrich Hölderlin, Paul Valéry, and Eugenio Montale, who are felt to be "inadequately known or understood." For more than thirty years, the magazine has made a point of printing novellas, plays, long stories, and large selections of an individual writer's work, thus providing an outlet for a good deal of longer work that simply could not be produced by many small magazines. For a time it managed to do this by printing two double issues each year, one for prose and one for poetry.

Persons interested in the achievements of *Quarterly Review of Literature* should consult the three large retrospective issues covering poetry, fiction, and special authors—the three special concerns of *Quarterly Review of Literature*: Vol. XIX, Nos. 1–2 (1974), which is devoted to poetry and reprints 146 contributors; Vol. XIX, Nos. 3–4 (1975), which reprints prose selections from 31 contributors; Vol. XX, Nos. 1–2 (1976), which includes large chunks from the special issues devoted to major writers; and Vol XX, Nos. 3–4 (1977), a 345-page eclectic retrospective with 32 authors.

Aside from some matching-funds grants, *Quarterly Review of Literature* has at times received support from the Ingram Merrill Foundation. Circulation varies from 1,500 to 3,000 copies, according to the issue. The editors' present intent is to shift to "larger publication," by which is meant "whole volumes of poetry, poetic plays, novellas, translations, etc. in each issue."

Salmagundi: A Quarterly of the Humanities & Social Sciences. Flushing, N. Y. (Fall 1965–Spring 1969); Skidmore College, Saratoga Springs, N. Y. (Fall/Winter 1970+).
Vol. I, no. 1, Fall 1965+. Qy.
Editor-in-chief Robert Boyers.
5¼" x 8¼" sewn about 150 pp. (double issues over 300 pp.).
Index no. 1–30 (Fall 1965–Summer 1975) issued separately.

Robert Boyers began *Salmagundi* at a time when many writers and intellectuals were intensely interested in politics and in the politics of culture. The subject index to issues 1–30 (Fall 1965–Summer 1975), indicates how various that interest has been, listing items under such headings as aesthetics, art works, books in review, contemporary culture, culture criticism, film, history and sociology, literary criticism, memoirs, poems, philosophy, plays, politics, psychology and psychoanalysis, stories. Special numbers, issued about once each year, have focused upon subjects as diverse as "The Legacy of the German Refugee Intellectuals," "R. D. Laing and Anti-Psychiatry," "Contemporary Poetry in America," "Dance," and "On Liars and Lying," among others.

In a preface to the tenth anniversary issue (Fall 1975), Christopher Lasch stresses *Salmagundi*'s sympathy for the political left and the spirit of scrupulous detachment in the face of calls for militant engagement. He contrasts the magazine's championing of critical thinking with the "familiar academic evasion," false objectivity, and modish "obscurantism" of more mandarin journals similarly catering to professor-intellectuals. In its willingness to argue issues and to demand that positions be taken, *Salmagundi* has invited a wide range of responses without pretending to be equally taken with every new voice and every passing ideological fancy.

Despite the intermittent emphasis upon the social sciences and upon their relationship with the humanities, broadly defined, *Salmagundi* has been fundamentally a literary magazine. At least half the categories in the subject index can be subsumed under the heading "Literature and the arts," while many of the entries in other areas refer to topics and figures often associated with literature, literary criticism, and the arts. There are some 65 entries under "Literary Criticism" and over 200 poems by 79 poets in the "Poems" category. Since the subject index was published in 1975, *Salmagundi* has revealed a stronger commitment to publish younger poets along with discussions of their work.

Especially interesting is the number on "Contemporary Poetry in America" (No. 22–23, Spring–Summer 1973), a 315-page anthology with essays by Howard Nemerov, John Bayley, M. L. Rosenthal, and others; long interviews with poets like Stanley Kunitz, W. D. Snodgrass, and Galway Kinnell; and new poems by Robert Lowell, Adrienne Rich, Robert Penn Warren, A. R. Ammons, et al. The most recent (Spring 1977) of the two special issues on Robert Lowell includes close readings by Helen Vendler, Robert Hass, G. S. Fraser, and others, and a reply to his critics written by Lowell shortly before his death. The issue on Saul Bellow features a long interview with the novelist in which he discusses not only his writing but the cultural climate in general, and his attitudes toward psychoanalysis and a variety of contemporary controversies. Whatever its focus, *Salmagundi* regularly manages to see the literary occasion as closely related to other "modern occasions."

Circulation is 2,500–3,000 for general issues and 3,000–6,000 for special

732

issues. Though it began as a private journal, since 1969 *Salmagundi* has been funded by Skidmore College.

The Seventies: see The Fifties.

The Sewanee Review. University of the South, Sewanee, Tenn.

Vol. I, no. 1, Nov. 1892+. Qy.

Ed. Telfair Hodgson (Nov. 1892–Aug. 1893); William P. Trent (Nov. 1893–July 1900); Benjamin W. Wells (Jan. 1897–?1898); J. B. Henneman (Oct. 1900–Jan. 1909); B. J. Ramage (Oct. 1900; then Assoc. Ed.); John M. McBryde, Jr. (Jan. 1910–Oct. 1919); George Herbert Clarke (Jan. 1910–Oct. 1925); Seymour Long (Jan. 1926–?Apr. 1926); William S. Knickerbocker (Jan. 1926–July/Sep. 1942); Tudor S. Long (Acting Ed.: Oct./Dec. 1942–July/Sep. 1944); Allen Tate (Oct./Dec. 1944–July/Sep. 1946); J. E. Palmer (Oct./Dec. 1946–July/Sep. 1952); Monroe K. Spears Oct./Dec. 1952–July/Sep. 1961); Andrew Lytle (Oct./Dec. 1961–Oct./Dec. 1973); George Core (Jan./Mar. 1974+).

5½″ x 8½″ sewn 175–200 pp. (varies widely).

Indexed by volume; index Vol. I–X (Nov. 1892–Oct. 1902) in Vol. X.

After eighty-five years of publication, *The Sewanee Review* remains a leading American critical journal. In 1974, the present editor, George Core, expressing a determination to continue *Sewanee Review*'s "established commitment to humane letters in the Western world," defined the ongoing general subject areas of the magazine: "By and large the focus will be upon Anglo-American literature from 1500 to the present, with the emphasis on modern literature and with latitude for classical and European letters." Although *Sewanee* would continue to publish fiction and poetry, "the accent will remain critical (with slightly greater stress upon literary history than in the immediate past)" (Winter 1974).

The accent on criticism noted by Core had grown increasingly important during the editorship of Allen Tate, when *Sewanee Review* was most influential as a new critical journal. A clear statement of some of its fundamental attitudes is found in a seventy-fifth anniversary year article, "An Earthen Vessel" by William Ralston (Vol. LXXV, No. 3, July/September 1967): "We are doing everything we can to provide a place where the unity and the continuity of writing in English can be celebrated—in verse, in fiction, and in criticism. . . . We intend to publish writing which in any form affirms the traditional and familiar meaning of words." Thus the close readings associated with the new critical approach to literature are tied to a respect for traditional forms and their continuous adaptation to new demands in new times.

In 1977, critical essays in the *Sewanee Review* still discuss Matthew Arnold and T. S. Eliot, Ezra Pound, and Kenneth Burke as well as southern writers (John Crowe Ransom, William Faulkner, and others). Along with selected poetry and fiction, recent issues have carried essays and comments by distinguished literary critics such as Samuel Hynes, Denis Donoghue, Wylie Sypher, William Walsh, and Louis D. Rubin, Jr.

Shenandoah. Washington and Lee University, Lexington, Va.

    Vol. I, no. 1, Spring 1950+. 3/yr (then qy.).

    Ed. no. 1: J. J. Donovan, D. C. G. Kerr, and T. K. Wolfe, Jr.; then frequent changes until Ed. James Boatwright (Autumn 1962+).

    6" x 9" stapled (folded)/sewn/perfect about 100 pp. (up to 175 pp.).

    Annual index; Vol. I–IX index in Vol. XI, no. 1, Autumn 1959.

In Spring 1950 Washington and Lee University published the first issue of *Shenandoah,* very much an academic literary magazine. Editors J. J. Donovan, D. C. G. Kerr, and T. K. Wolfe, Jr., divided the issue into three short stories, three poems, and a few essays and reviews. Contributors included John Dos Passos, B. S. Ford, and John Bowen; reviewed were T. S. Eliot's *The Cocktail Party* and Francis Fergusson's *The Idea of a Theatre,* although most of the contributions were by students and advisers to the magazine.

Shenandoah achieved editorial stability with the Autumn 1962 issue when, after a period that had seen a new editor for each issue, James Boatwright became permanent editor. During his tenure, the magazine, while maintaining its special interest in southern literature, has offered a cosmopolitan selection of essays, poems, and fiction. Special issues have ranged from Yeats and Ireland to Greek literature and culture. Especially interesting are the Winter 1967 "Tribute to W. H. Auden" on his sixtieth birthday and the Winter 1976 "Symposium on Fiction," with comments by Donald Barthelme, William Gass, Grace Paley, and Walker Percy.

Some indication of the magazine's quality is gained by examining the twentieth anniversary issue (Vol. XXI, No. 3, Spring 1970), which includes fiction by Joyce Carol Oates and Guy Cardwell; poems by twenty-two authors including W. H. Auden, Philip Booth, Richard Eberhart, Richard Howard, Maxine Kumin, William Meredith, James Merrill, Howard Nemerov, Robin Skelton, Stephen Spender, C. P. Cavafy, Dabney Stuart, Julian Symons, Peter Viereck, and John Wain; essays by Roy Fuller, Hugh Kenner, Monroe K. Spears, G. S. Fraser, and Cleanth Brooks; a notebook by Theodore Roethke; and three plays by Peter Taylor. All these contributors had appeared previously in *Shenandoah.*

Shenandoah has received grants from CCLM and the Virginia Commission of the Arts and Humanities, as well as support from Washington and Lee University and individual benefactors. Circulation in 1967 was 1,600.

The Sixties: see The Fifties.

The Smith. New York, N. Y.

    15 Feb. 1964+. Irreg.

    Ed. Harry Smith.

    Format varies (often 6" x 9") stapled/sewn/perfect up to 250 pp. (varies).

Although *The Smith* has asserted certain defensible preferences—for the work of the "generalist" opposed to that of the specialist; for a populist poetry both generally understandable and yet aesthetically valuable; and for an organic aesthetic leading to a constantly changing magazine rather than a static in-group journal—one comes away from most issues remembering chiefly the ornery attacks on, apparently, just about everyone. The "generalist" stance seems to set *The Smith* against all the groups and schools. Robert Bly and all who are associated with him are attacked as vigorously as the Beat poets and the New York School. At times the attacks are vitriolic (as when Diane Wakoski is called "banal, mediocre") and almost libelous (as when Bly is called "Hitlerian"). Yet there is usually a genuine critical stance behind the sensational evaluations. Given its own orientation, it is reasonable for *The Smith* to attack the murky, oddly located "deep images" of Robert Bly. Also *The Smith* and H. L. VanBrunt are exceptionally good at isolating the most muddled and laughable lines from volumes of poetry. This talent gives many of their reviews a concrete quality that is quite convincing.

The poetry in *The Smith* is unassuming. Issue No. 12 (1971), "The Smith Poets," is a 262-page volume featuring the work of Gene Fowler, Sam Cornish, Irene Schram, Theodore Sloan, Charles M. Wyatt, Karen Swenson, and Jonathan Morse. Issue No. 17 (February 1975) is an anthology of "Eleven New Poets" (Charles Potts, T. E. Porter, Richard Morris, Bill Costley, Frank Rios, Jared Smith, Gary Livingston, James Ryan Morris, Stephen Philbrick, Reginald Berry, and Rod Townley). Probably *The Smith*'s principal contribution to literature is the rediscovery of James T. Farrell in 1965.

The magazine has carried a number of interesting attacks upon methods used in recent government funding of magazines. H. L. VanBrunt wrote scathing attacks upon the parochialism and arrogance of the editors of the *American Literary Anthologies* I and II, financed by the National Endowment for the Arts, while summarizing the contents as "the sorry product of a clique of mediocrities." Curt Johnson, editor of *December*, contributed a twenty-five-page essay on the program of aid to magazines through the NEA and its organ, CCLM. Elsewhere Harry Smith attacks the institutionalization of magazine editing, even among the underground presses, so that common cause deteriorates into absorption by the establishment. Anyone interested in *The Smith*'s stance on issues in this area should consult its subsidiary publication, *The Newsletter on the State of Culture,* which often features the witty observations of Sidney Bernard.

Circulation of *The Smith* varies from 1,700 to 2,500 on regular issues; there are about 1,000 subscribers, half of them institutional. Revenue from sales and individual contributions through The Generalist Association, Inc., accounts for all funding of the magazine.

The Southern Review. The Louisiana State University, Baton Rouge, La.
New Series, Vol. I, no. 1, Jan. 1965+. Qy.
Ed. Lewis P. Simpson; Donald E. Stanford.
6½" x 9¾" sewn/perfect 225 pp.
Yearly index.

Co-editors Lewis P. Simpson and Donald E. Stanford, with Associate Editor Rima Drell Reck, revived *The Southern Review* in 1965, some twenty-three years after its predecessor had ceased publishing. Although the magazine has printed a substantial amount of new poetry and fiction (in 1966, for example, the short-story version of John Gardner's *Nickel Mountain* and several sketches from N. Scott Momaday's *House Made of Dawn* appeared), its central feature has been literary criticism and essays, particularly by academic critics. Among the essayists and reviewers contributing to New Series Vol. I were Graham Hough, Austin Warren, Malcolm Cowley, T. R. Henn, Milton Hindus, Glauco Cambon, Marius Bewley, Cleanth Brooks, David Daiches, Donald Davidson, James F. Feibleman, Robert B. Heilman, Frederick J. Hoffman, Hugh Kenner, Max Lerner, Harry Levin, Samuel French Morse, Kathleen Raine, Allen Tate, Leonard Unger, Robert Penn Warren, and Eudora Welty. In 1977 *Southern Review* still featured solid academic critical writing (by such writers as William Arrowsmith, Cleanth Brooks, Malcolm Cowley, Richard Eberhart, C. Hugh Holman, Martin Turnell, Ian Watt, and René Wellek), supplemented by verse from such established poets as Elizabeth Daryush, Roy Fuller, Thom Gunn, and Robert Penn Warren and short stories from writers such as Carolyn Gordon and David Madden. The magazine's southern heritage has revealed itself in some of the special issues and features, notably the April 1975 poetry issue, which was slanted somewhat toward southern poets; the January 1975 "Essays on Self and Society" by Robert Penn Warren, Walker Percy, and others; and the series "Writing in the South," which has run in five separate issues. Less localized special issues or features in recent years have focused on Mark Twain, W. B. Yeats, Wallace Stevens, French literature, the sixties, the twenties and thirties, the outsider, and fiction.

Southern Review has prepared cumulative indexes for the years 1965–1971 and for the earlier Robert Penn Warren–Cleanth Brooks–Charles W. Pipkin incarnation of the magazine (1935–1942). Recent circulation of *Southern Review* has been about 3,000. It receives support from Louisiana State University and CCLM.

Spectrum. University of California, Santa Barbara, Cal.
Vol. I, no. 1, Winter 1957+. Freq. varies.
Ed. no. 1: James Bell [changes frequently].
6" x 9"   perfect   42–74 pp.
Index Vol. I–XV issued separately.

A separately issued index to *Spectrum*, Vols. I–XV, announced that Vols. XIV and XV had been "awarded first place prize by Coordinating Council of Literary Magazines as best collegiate literary mag. in nation." The selection was certainly a defensible one. For twenty years *Spectrum* has combined student and faculty work from the University of California, Santa Barbara, with material from well-known outside contributors. One

736

feels that *Spectrum* has benefited greatly from having a highly involved faculty Advisory Board which, by the third issue, included Donald Davie and Marvin Mudrick as well as founding advisers Ashley Brown and Hugh Kenner. According to later testimony in the magazine, Hugh Kenner was especially responsible for *Spectrum*'s early success. During his half-dozen years with *Spectrum* the magazine carried several of his contributions, along with the work of such other UCSB professors as Marvin Mudrick, Donald Davie, and Edgar Bowers, as well as a number of distinguished outside contributors including Charles Tomlinson, Ezra Pound, William Carlos Williams, Jean Cocteau, and Jules Supervielle. At all times *Spectrum* mixed the contributions of these authors with those of UCSB students in a way that enhanced the competent student writing without detracting from the professional work.

Among the many other contributors to *Spectrum* are David Antin, Raymond Carver, Clark Coolidge, Thomas Cornell, Robert Creeley, Guy Davenport, David Cornel DeJong, Stephen Dobyns, Richard Eberhart, Raymond Federman, Jim Harrison, Robert Kelly, John Knoepfle, Konstantinos Lardas, Denise Levertov, Wyndham Lewis, Leconte de Lisle, Ron Loewinsohn, Howard McCord, David Meltzer, Deena Metzger, Josephine Miles, George Oppen, Gilbert Sorrentino, Lucien Stryk, Paul Vangelisti, Philip Whalen, Peter Wild, and Howard Warshaw.

Circulation of *Spectrum* is about 750 copies.

Story [no. 1–54: (The only magazine) devoted only to the Short Story; no. 55+: The Magazine of the Short Story]. Vienna, Austria (Apr./May 1931–May/June 1932); Palma (Majorca), Spain (Aug. 1932–Feb. 1933); New York, N. Y. (Apr. 1933+).
Vol. I, no. 1–Vol. XXXVI, no. 142, Apr./May 1931–Oct. 1963 [publication suspended between Summer 1948 and Spring 1960]. Freq. varies.
Ed. Whit Burnett; Martha Foley (Apr. 1931–Oct. 1941); Hallie Burnett (Spring 1948–Oct. 1963); Eleanor Gilchrist (Spring 1948–Summer 1948); William Peden (Spring 1960–Nov. 1961); Richard Wathen (Nov. 1960–Nov. 1961).
No. 1–129: 6¾" x 9½"   80–148 pp.   no. 1: mimeo.
No. 130–142: 5½" x 8¼"   98–128 pp.
Indexed.

From the outset *Story* was recognized as a magazine of distinction. Edward J. O'Brien selected four stories (by Kay Boyle, Whit Burnett, Oliver Gossman, and Martha Foley) from its first issue for *The Best Short Stories of 1931*. Then, in the preface to the 1932 anthology, O'Brien singled out *Story* as "now the most distinguished short story magazine in the world"—an accolade difficult to challenge in the 1930s and 1940s.

Editorial intent was defined in the first number: "The only purpose of *Story* is to present, regularly, from one place, a number of Short Stories of exceptional merit. It has no theories, and is part of no movement. . . .

737

It is not an anthology, but a sort of proof-book of hitherto unpublished manuscripts. Some of the stories will doubtless appear later in other, perhaps more permanent pages, and the rights remain vested in the authors. . . . Thus the magazine is withheld by the editors from public sale in England and the United States, but may be obtained in Vienna, Paris, Nice, Budapest and Berlin." With the August 1932 number the magazine was made available in the U.S. and England.

Contributors to the first volume included Laurence Vail, James T. Farrell, José García Villa, Eugene Jolas, Erskine Caldwell, Ralph Manheim, William Carlos Williams, Manuel Komroff, and Alvah C. Bessie. By the end of Vol. V, December 1934, *Story* had printed Carlton Brown, William March, Conrad Aiken, H. E. Bates, Nelson Algren, William Faulkner, Malcolm Cowley, Sherwood Anderson, William Saroyan, Ivan Bunin, August Derleth, Malcolm Lowry, James Laughlin, and Jerome Weidman. The next ten volumes, January 1935–November/December 1939, were characterized by the discovery of new writers: Peter DeVries, Gloria Kenison, Jesse Stuart, Jon Edgar Webb, Ludwig Bemelmans, John Cheever, Eric Knight, Wallace E. Stegner, Carson Smith (McCullers), Mark Shorer, Howard (Melvin) Fast, Richard Wright, Budd (Wilson) Schulberg, Tennessee Williams, and Mark Harris. A history of the first five years of *Story* appeared in No. 45, April 1936. From 1940 through the war years and afterward, the discovery rate for major new talents sharply decreased. Nevertheless, this period saw the appearance in *Story* of Vivian Connell, J. D. Salinger, Mary O'Hara, Norman K. Mailer (age eighteen), Charles Bukowski, Robert Lowry, Truman Capote, Joseph Heller, John D. MacDonald, William Sayres, and others. Issue No. 91, September/October 1941, was entirely devoted to homage to Sherwood Anderson.

With No. 119, May/June 1946, *Story* shifted to the use of pulp paper. The July/August 1947 issue was dropped, and quarterly publication was instituted. Soon, however, publication ceased. A series of books titled *Story: The Magazine of the Short Story in Book Form* was started in 1951, and other book ventures were attempted—for example, *Sextet: Six STORY Discoveries in the Novella Form* (1951). Sponsored first by the University of Missouri and then by the University of Cincinnati, *Story* was reactivated as a periodical in 1960, but the spirit of the early volumes was absent and the magazine was quietly discontinued. During this period, the editors were instrumental in setting up the Association of Literary Magazines of America (ALMA), the first organization of literary magazine publishers in the United States. ALMA was succeeded by the Coordinating Council of Literary Magazines (CCLM), which still functions. The preamble and statement of principles of ALMA appeared in *Story*, No. 134.

Trace [no. 1–39: A Chronicle of Living Literature; no. 40+: Living Literature]. Hollywood, Cal.

No. 1–72/73, June 1952–Autumn 1970. Qy.

Ed. James Boyer May.

5¼" x 8⅜" 1952–1961: stapled (folded); 1961–1966: sewn; 1966/1967+: perfect 12–340 pp. (varies widely).

James Boyer May originally intended *Trace* as a meeting place where little-magazine editors and writers might exchange ideas. The most important feature of his new periodical was a revolving directory of magazines published in English. A summation in the final issue of *Trace* (No. 72/73, Autumn 1970, pages 417–421) details the growth of the listings from 182 magazines in the first directory (1952) to a combined listing of one thousand magazines and small presses in 1970. The directory, patterned on the mimeo magazine *Galley* (1949–1953), was taken up during and after *Trace*'s last years by Len Fulton (the annual *International Directory of the Little Magazines and Small Presses*).

In 1961 *Trace* began to publish poetry, fiction, and graphic art. Its selection policy was broadly eclectic. Almost no work was solicited, and established writers were evidently discouraged as often as encouraged by Editor May. The broad-based policy was both the strength and the weakness of *Trace*. May introduced close to eight hundred new writers and brought forward older writers who had been overlooked and underestimated. At the same time, however, *Trace* was open to a charge of extreme unevenness and of editorial laxity.

The chief significance of *Trace* is the forum it provided for little-magazine editors and contributors. Beginning in 1952, *Trace* anticipated the "mimeo revolution" of the later 1950s and 1960s and promoted discussion of small magazines and presses at a time when they received little other attention. Over the years *Trace* grew from 16 pages to more than 200 pages per issue. Circulation in its later years averaged around 2,000.

Tri-Quarterly [new series no. 10+: TriQuarterly]. Evanston, Ill.

Vol. I, no. 1–Vol. VI, no. 3, Fall 1958–Spring 1964; [new series] no. 1, Fall 1964+. 3/yr.

Ed. Edward B. Hungerford (Fall 1958–Spring 1964); [new series]: Charles Newman (Fall 1964–Winter 1975); Elliott Anderson (Spring 1975+).

No. 1–12: 6½" x 10" perfect/sewn 96–288 pp. Illus.

No. 13+: 6" x 9¼" perfect (a few are sewn) 140–640 pp. (avg. 256 pp.). Illus.

Index [new series] no. 1–3 in no. 4; index no. 4–10 issued separately; index no. 1–22 issued separately.

After a number of years as a Northwestern University magazine chiefly produced by and for local faculty and students, *TriQuarterly* was reborn in 1964, beginning again with an issue No. 1, augmented in size and scope, with a new editor and a truly international range of interests and contributors. (No. 1 contained work by Stephen Spender, W. B. Yeats, Koz'ma Prutkov as well as Leslie Fiedler, Lionel Trilling, Richard Brautigan, and William Stafford.) The new *TriQuarterly* soon began publishing special features; early issues carried sections on "The Quest of Zen," "Humanism vs. Behaviorism," "The Case of James T. Farrell," "Creativity in the Soviet Union," "New African Writing." Then it moved to special issues; No. 4, 1965, concentrated on two subjects, "The W. B. Yeats Centenary" and "New French Writing," while No. 7, Fall 1966, was a special "Womanly Issue," with one hundred pages devoted to "The Art of Sylvia Plath." Number 9, Spring 1967, featured Eastern European literature, and No. 10, Fall 1967, was an "Under 30" issue. From this point on, *TriQuarterly* has frequently invited the cooperation of guest co-editors who are experts in special subjects; José Donoso co-edited No. 13/14, Fall/Winter 1968/1969, "Contemporary Latin American Literature" (a supplement to this issue appeared in No. 15, Spring 1969). Alfred Appel, Jr., guest-edited a Nabokov issue (Winter 1970) and shared with Simon Karlinsky the co-editorship of the "Russian Literature and Culture in the West" issue (Spring 1973). Jonathan Williams co-edited the Edward Dahlberg issue (Fall 1970). Lawrence Levy and John Perreault prepared the "Anti-Object Art" issue (Winter 1975). Other guest editors included John Matthias: "Contemporary British Poetry" (Spring 1971); George Gomori: "A Leszek Kolakowski Reader" (Fall 1971); George Abbott White: "Literature in Revolution" (Winter/Spring 1972); Mary Kinzie: "Prose for Borges" (Fall 1972); Lucien Stryk: "Contemporary Asian Literature" (Fall 1974); David Hayman: "In the Wake of the *Wake*" (Winter 1977). The Fall 1977 number culminated a six-issue survey, "Ongoing American Fiction," which anthologized scores of stories by active writers. These fiction issues, like the guest-edited special numbers, are characterized by breadth of coverage.

TriQuarterly is a large magazine, usually running well over 200 pages and sometimes surpassing 500 pages. As a result, most of the special issues are remarkably comprehensive. The wide range of special topics, coupled with the broad coverage of each, makes it difficult to select names of chief contributors. An index to *TriQuarterly* 1–22, roughly half the issues thus far published, includes close to 600 contributors.

TriQuarterly receives support from Northwestern University and has been awarded grants by CCLM and the Illinois Arts Council. Circulation is 5,000 copies.

Truck. Calhoun College, Yale University, New Haven, Conn. (no. 1–10, 1970–Summer 1972); Putney, Vt. (no. 11, Late Spring 1973); Enosberg Falls, Vt. (no. 12, Early Fall, 1973); Carrboro, N. C. (no. 13, Spring 1974+) [Editorial office has moved to St. Paul, Minn.].
[1970]+. Irreg.
Ed. David Wilk [with various co-editors, including Steve Benson, Kit

Robinson, Michael Waltuch, Hetty Wood, Jay Dougherty].
No. 1–10: 8½ " x 11" stapled.
No. 11+: 6" x 9" perfect 96–225 pp. (recently).

Begun by a group of Yale undergraduates, *Truck* became, with issue No. 8, the sole responsibility of David Wilk. Although the first ten issues of *Truck* carried contributions from Paul Mariah, Mike Finley, Paul Metcalf, Nathaniel Tarn, Richard Grossinger, Ken Irby, Paul Blackburn, and others, it is the second series, beginning with No. 11 (Spring 1973), that, in the words of the editor, "marks its maturation in terms of content and production." For the new series, *Truck* shifted from a stapled 8½ " by 11" format to a 6" x 9" perfect binding. Issues were built around special themes: a Vermont issue, a landscape issue, an exploration issue featuring Richard Grossinger and Lindy Hough, Michael McClure, Daphne Marlatt, and others. Space was allocated with an eye toward overall mood and tone. Especially interesting are the 224-page *Poesis* issue (Spring 1975), "the last of the regular poetry issues, a gathering of voices the magazine cleaves to," among whom are Ken Irby, Michael Rumaker, Paul Metcalf, Clayton Eshleman, Robert Kelly, and George Quasha; and the 150-page Lorine Niedecker issue (Summer 1975), featuring poems and letters by Lorine Niedecker, commemorative poems by Carl Rakosi and others, and essays by Cid Corman, Jonathan Williams, Morgan Gibson, and others.
Truck has been supported by CCLM grants. Circulation is about 600 copies an issue (sometimes less).

Unmuzzled Ox. New York, N. Y.
No. 1, 1971+. Irreg.
Ed. Michael André.
5" x 8" perfect (no. 1–4, 7: stapled; no. 8/9: loose sheets boxed; no. 12: sewn). 64–148 pp. Illus.

Michael André, aided by Tom Wayman, began *Unmuzzled Ox* as a vehicle for the fusion of avant-garde artwork with poetry and poetry criticism in New York City. One aim, the presentation of multimedia art, is well illustrated in a special issue, No. 8/9, 1974. This consists of a boxed set of loose sheets of poetry and sketches by Gregory Corso which the reader may paste end to end to form one long pattern. Other special features that have appeared in *Unmuzzled Ox* include a suite of poems by Daniel Berrigan in No. 4, Autumn 1972, with proceeds from a 100-copy special signed edition going to the antiwar effort; a 35-copy special signed edition featuring Gregory Corso (No. 5/6, 1973); and a 77-page issue (No. 12, 1975) devoted to Kenward Elmslie's *Tropicalism*. Exposition of interdisciplinary views of artistic postmodernist expression is pursued in a series of interviews conducted by André with Robert Creeley, Gregory Corso, W. H. Auden, James Wright, James Dickey, Allen Ginsberg, Daniel Berrigan, Nhat Hanh, Eugene McCarthy, Robert Duncan, and Andy Warhol.

Although *Unmuzzled Ox* has reproduced art by R. Crumb, Willem de Kooning, Gerard Malanga, Andy Warhol, Hannah Wilke, and Claes Oldenburg, art criticism by Hannah Green, and fiction by Ed Sanders and Robert Creeley, the breadth and depth of coverage of its poetry best reveals this magazine's openness and interdisciplinary nature. Enhanced by well-conceived layouts and accomplished graphics, the poems in *Unmuzzled Ox* cover a range best illustrated by a partial listing of contributors: Diane Wakoski, Charles Bukowski, Douglas Blazek, Daryl Hine, Richard Kostelanetz, Gary Snyder, James Wright, Allen Ginsberg, William Burroughs, Robert Bly, Marge Piercy, Lyn Lifshin, Peter Wild, Harold Norse, Ted Enslin, Gilbert Sorrentino, Denise Levertov, Margaret Atwood, Clarence Major, Ron Loewinsohn, Rochelle Owens, Judson Crews, David Ignatow, Cid Corman, Jerome Rothenberg, Irving Layton, Michael Benedikt, Isabella Gardner, Russell Edson, Carol Bergé, Charles Olson, Robert Creeley, Barbara Guest, Anne Waldman, Adrienne Rich, Rosalyn Drexler, Joel Oppenheimer, Paul Goodman, and William Stafford. Some emphasis is given to New York poets John Ashbery, Kenneth Koch, and Frank O'Hara, and to poets whose work frequently shares the same journals with them (such as Bill Berkson, Kenward Elmslie, Ron Padgett, Bill Knott, John Giorno, Bernadette Mayer, Clark Coolidge, Ed Sanders, and James Schuyler).

Unmuzzled Ox has been assisted by CCLM. Circulation has grown from 800 to 4,000.

Vagabond [no. 1: A Literary Quarterly of Poetry; no. 2–3; A Literary Quarterly]. Munich, Germany (no. 1–5, Jan./Mar. 1966–Summer 1967); New Orleans, La. (no. 6–7, 1968–1969); San Francisco, Cal. (no. 8–11, 1970–1971); Redwood City, Cal. (no. 12–16, 1971–1973); Ellensburg, Wash. (no. 17, 1973+).
No. 1, Jan./Mar. 1966+. Irreg.
Ed. John Bennett, Jr.
6¾" x 8½" stapled (folded) size varies (72–120 pp. recently) some issues mimeo.

Vagabond, a successful example of the mimeo magazine, was begun by John Bennett, Jr., in Munich, Germany, and followed him to New Orleans and Ellensburg, Washington, its current address. For some time it proudly announced itself as produced on a "1917 A. B. Dick Mimeo." By the time *Vagabond* issued its twenty-fifth number (1977), it could count among its contributors Heinrich Böll, Stefan Andres, Charles Bukowski, Curt Johnson, Douglas Blazek, William Wantling, Stephen Spender (an interview), D. A. Levy, A. D. Winans, Hugh Fox, Lyn Lifshin, Jerry Bumpus, Ron Koertge, Nelson Algren, Alicia Ostriker, Jack Micheline, Gerda Penfold, Marvin Malone, Rich Mangelsdorff, and Felix Pollak.
In No. 14 (1972), Bennett expressed his distrust of much that passes for avant-garde writing; in 1977, he said that he wanted to publish fiction that

would "counter . . . 'experimental fiction.' " Said Bennett: "All good fiction is and always has been that."

Vagabond is a genuine "little" magazine. Though it has received some CCLM support, it is essentially John Bennett's personal responsibility (he estimates a current annual loss of $1,000). Circulation is about 1,000 copies.

West Coast Poetry Review. Reno, Nev.

Vol. I, no. 1, Summer 1971+. Irreg. (2/yr. promised).

Ed. William Ransom (no. 1–3, Summer 1971–Spring 1972); J. Glaser (no. 1, Summer 1971); William L. Fox (Vol. I, no. 4/Vol. II, no. 1, Summer/Fall 1972+).

6" x 9" no. 1–11, 13–15, 17: stapled; no. 12, 16, 18: perfect 44–180 pp. No. 9: 8" x 8¼".

Index Vol. I–IV, no. 1–16 (1971–1975).

West Coast Poetry Review is currently in its third phase. William Ransom, who edited three issues before his resources were exhausted, printed such poets as William Childress, Susan Fromberg Schaeffer, Harold Witt, Mark McCloskey, Hale Chatfield, Danny L. Rendleman, Ann Stafford, and Richard Wilbur (translations of Yevtushenko in Nos. 1–2). The shift to phase two was clearly exhibited in the double number for Summer/Fall 1972, in which Editor William L. Fox produced two separate sections: an anthology edited by William Ransom (with work by forty-two contributors, including Gottfried Benn, Lucien Stryk, Sam Hamill, Christine Zawadiwsky, Jascha Kessler, and Patricia Goedicke) and an anthology edited by William Fox (ten contributors, including Fox himself, Morton Marcus, Greg Kuzma, Miller Williams, and J. Michael Yates). In the third phase, the magazine began to feature visual and concrete poetry. In issue No. 9, Fall 1973, Fox commenced printing visual poetry by Ian Tarnman, and in No. 12, Summer 1974, he was deeply involved in visual experiments with the "Extensions of the Word" special issue—advertised as "a workbook of current experiments in poetry with concretes, post-concretes, minimals and UFO's." Among the contributors were Ian Hamilton Finlay, Emmett Williams, Jane Augustine, Alison Sky, Peter Finch, Bob Cobbing, Peter Mayer, Aaron Marcus, Mary Ellen Solt, Nick Zurbrugg, Richard Kostelanetz (his work was accompanied by an article on him by Hugh Fox), and others.

Number 13/14, Fall 1974, exemplified Fox's attempt to strike a balance between conventional forms and visual experiments. This issue carried visual poetry by Patricia Elliott, Lawrence Lewis, Alison Sky, Venantius Fortunatus, Gerald Lange, John Kallio, Loris Essary, and Ian Hamilton Finlay (a group of photographs), and also non-concrete work by Albert Goldbarth, Ross Talarico, Duane Ackerson, Stuart Peterfreund, and Harold Witt.

Fiction, a minor element in *West Coast Poetry Review,* is edited by Bruce

743

McAllister. The most ambitious project in fiction thus far has been Ronald Arias's *The Road to Tamazunchale*, a chicano novel which was later nominated for a National Book Award.

West Coast Poetry Review has received aid from CCLM, the National Endowment for the Arts, and the Nevada State Council on the Arts. "Our regular issues generally lose money; our special ones pay for the magazine as a whole. . . . Our greatest sales come from mass buys—like the NEA purchasing 2,000 copies of No. 8, which was a special on poetry-in-the-school before anyone else was talking about it." Circulation has risen from 500 to 1,000, with special issues running as high as 4,000 copies.

Wild Dog. Pocatello, Ida. (no. 1–9, Apr. 1963–18 July 1964); Salt Lake City, Utah (no. 10–12, Sep. 1964–1 Dec. 1964); San Francisco, Cal. (no. 13–21, 12 Jan. 1965–1 Mar. 1966).
Vol. I, no. 1–Vol. III, no. 21, Apr. 1963–1 Mar. 1966.   Irreg.
Ed. Geoffrey Dunbar (Apr. 1963); John Hoopes (May 1963–Jan. 1964); Drew Wagnon (Jan. 1964–Mar. 1966); Ed Dorn (Apr. 1964–July 1964); Gino Clays (Sep. 1964–July 1964); Joanne Kyger (June 1965–July 1965); Terry Wagnon (Dec. 1965–Mar. 1966).
8½ " x 11"   stapled   26–66 pp.   mimeo.

Although *Wild Dog* was originally conceived as a local literary magazine associated with Idaho State College, the second number indicated "independent" publication, and the third number emphasized "no affiliation" with Idaho State College. Quite possibly this disaffiliation stems from Robert Kelly's frank essay in No. 1 on the loyalty oath required of state college faculty members by the Idaho legislature. This first number announced that:

> *Wild Dog* is prose, poetry, non-fiction / and other things.
> *Wild Dog* is not for Everyone / or by Someone.
> *Wild Dog* is for people who read, / by people who write.

This editorial purpose was maintained faithfully through several relocations and rearrangements of editors, while the magazine's scope, circulation, and reputation grew from local to international. In No. 7, April 5, 1974, the basis for this growth was defined: "It is our one highfalutin idea that this magazine, given its frequency, may be a kind of clearinghouse for notations from far places. . . . Contributions may be of the nature of calculated correspondence."

Wild Dog No. 1 featured Douglas Woolf, Robert Kelly (instructor in English at Idaho State College), and Ed Dorn, among others—plus, "by direct wire," Caliph John's inside–New York City literary letter, a feature which was continued in subsequent issues. By the completion of its fifth issue, *Wild Dog* had published Black Mountain authors Fielding Dawson, Charles Olson, Larry Eigner, and Louis Zukofsky along with LeRoi Jones, Judson Crews, Denise Levertov, George Bowering, and others. With the next five issues the magazine's literary horizons were widened to include Margaret Randall, Allen Ginsberg, Tom Raworth, Miguel Grinberg, Ron Loewinsohn, Diane Wakoski, and others. The diversity of still later issues is suggested by the following contributors: Christopher Perret, Stan Brakhage, Charles Bukowski, R. Buckminster Fuller, Gary Snyder, Gerard Malanga, Richard Brautigan, Robert Duncan, Robert Sward, Clark Coolidge, Bill Hutton, Victor Contoski, Stuart Friebert, Ed Bullins, and Clarence Major.

Wild Dog is an excellent example of the fully edited mimeographed periodical, as distinguished from the minimally edited or nonedited mimeographed journal of writings—a form all too common in the time of the "mimeograph revolution in literature." Much of the credit for the continuing high quality of *Wild Dog* can be assigned to editors Drew Wagnon and Ed Dorn. Wagnon functioned continuously as an editor from No. 5 forward; Dorn appeared in the first issue, acted as co-editor for Nos. 7–9, and was contributing editor for Nos. 10–18. Financed by donations and a limited number of subscriptions, this cheaply produced magazine consistently showed signs of care in production. The text was always legible and neat, and frequently the covers were exemplary illustrations of design triumphing over the medium (e. g. the covers for Nos. 17–20 by Bill McNeil, Joyce Barkett, and Fielding Dawson).

Wild Dog's circulation ranged from 200 to 500 copies.

The World [no. 1–11: A New York City Literary Magazine]. Poetry Project at St. Mark's Church in the Bowery, New York, N. Y.

No. 1, Fall 1966+. Irreg.

Ed. Joel Sloman (Fall 1966–Mar. 1967); Anne Waldman (Mar. 1967+) [Guest editors include Lewis Warsh, Joel Oppenheimer, Sam Abrahams, Tom Clark, and Ron Padgett].

8½″ x 14″   stapled   25–112 pp.   mimeo.

Since the mid-sixties, *The World,* the mimeo magazine of the Poetry Project at St. Mark's Church in New York City, has constituted a kind of record of the work of a sizable number of the New York poets. Typed and reproduced on 8½″ by 14″ paper (except for No. 7), this irregularly issued magazine (30 issues from 1966 [?] to 1977) counts the following poets among its many contributors: Allen Ginsberg, Peter Orlovsky, Tom Clark, Michael Brownstein, Joel Oppenheimer, Michael Benedikt, Ted Berrigan, John Giorno, Ron Padgett, Clark Coolidge, Phillip Lopate, Gerard Malanga, John Ashbery, Bill Berkson, Edwin Denby, Bernadette Mayer, Frank O'Hara, John Wieners, Raymond Di Palma, Ed Dorn, Aram Saroyan, Ray Bremser, Ed Sanders, James Ratner, Gary Snyder, David Antin, Clayton Eshleman, Harry Mathews, Donald Hall, Anselm Hollo, Greg Kuzma, Diane di Prima, Lita Hornick, Fielding Dawson.

In the mid-seventies, the emphasis shifted somewhat away from the poem itself. See, for example, the autobiographical issue guest-edited by Lewis Warsh (No. 28, May 1973) or the 123-page issue of April 1974 (No. 29), which featured reviews, commentary, and interviews. Anne Waldman has had chief editorial responsibility, with help at times from Lewis Warsh, Joel Sloman, Ted Berrigan, and Joel Oppenheimer. Other guest-edited issues are No. 6 (Sam Abrams), No. 22 (Tom Clark), and No. 27 (the translations issue, edited by Ron Padgett).

See also the annotation for *Angel Hair* (above).

The Wormwood Review [no. 57+: Incorporating Malone-Stranger Review]. Storrs, Conn. (no. 1–34, Fall 1959 [cover date incorrect]–Aug. 1969); Stockton, Cal. (no. 35, Nov. 1969+).

No. 1, Fall 1959+. 4/yr.

Ed. Morton Felix (Fall 1959–Winter 1959/1960); Jim Scully (Fall 1959); Alexander Taylor (Fall 1959–1962); Marvin Malone (June 1961+) [Guest Ed. Allen DeLoach (May 1965); George Montgomery (Aug. 1969)].

5⅜" x 8½" stapled (folded) 28–48 pp.

Index no. 1–12 in no. 12; no. 13–24 in no. 24; no. 25–36 in no. 36; no. 37–48 in no. 49–60 in no. 60; no. 61–72 in no. 72.

The Wormwood Review has printed a wide range of poetry by hundreds of poets, some of whom are fairly regular contributors. If there is a principle of selection, it is a negative one involving avoidance of cliques and groups. *Wormwood* is "non-beat, non-academic, non-sewing circle and non-profit. *Wormwood* is interested in quality poems and prose-poems (proems) of all types and schools—the form may be traditional or avant-garde-up-through-and-including-dada—the tone serious to flip, the content conservative to utter taboo. A good poem should be able to compete with the presence of other poems. *Wormwood* is not afraid of either intelligence or wit—both are rare qualities."

Wormwood's open-arms policy has led to the inclusion of many kinds and degrees of parody and spoof, as well as concrete poems, prose poems, collages, and number games. Poets who contribute fairly regularly include Charles Bukowski, Lyn Lifshin, Ronald Koertge, Gerald Locklin, and Phil Weidman. Each issue has a colored center section featuring a single poet or theme. Among the roughly three dozen poets featured in center sections, the following have made multiple appearances: Charles Bukowski, Judson Crews, Oliver Haddo, Gloria Kenison, Ronald Koertge, Lyn Lifshin, Gerald Locklin, Christopher Perret, Ben Pleasants, Ray Peuchner, and William Wantling. In addition, a few issues have been devoted to a single author: No. 59 (1975), Lyn Lifshin, *Paper Apples;* No. 63 (1976), Ronald Koertge, *Cheap Thrills;* No. 67, Gerald Locklin, *Pronouncing Borges.* Occasionally issues have dealt with single themes: No. 45 was a memorial to Jon Edgar Webb, editor of the magazine *The Outsider.*

Another *Wormwood* special feature has been an award to the "most over-looked book of worth published within the calendar year." Winners during the fifteen-year period from 1961 to 1975 included Alexander Trocchi, Kurt Vonnegut, Jr., James Drought, Russell Edson, Christopher Perret,

746

Stanley Crawford, Peter Wild, Ian Hamilton Finlay, Charles Bukowski, Lorine Niedecker, Jonathan Williams, Gerald Locklin, Ronald Koertge, Steve Richmond, and Lyn Lifshin.

Except for small CCLM grants, *Wormwood*'s funding is entirely from subscriptions. Of the 700-copy print run, 300 copies go to subscribers, approximately 100 copies each to authors and to other little magazine editors, with 100 copies for individual sales and 100 copies as reserve. One peculiarity of *Wormwood* is that it usually appears two issues at a time.

Yardbird Reader. Berkeley, Cal.
  Vol. I–V, 1972–1976. Annual.
  Ed. Ishmael Reed (1972); Al Young (1973); Shawn Wong and Frank Chin (1974); William Lawson (1975); Ishmael Reed (1976).
  5½" x 8½" (varies)   perfect   184–326 pp.
  then: Y'Bird Magazine. Vol. I, no. 1, 1978+. Ed. Ishmael Reed.
  5½" x 9"   perfect   204 pp.

The first volume of *Yardbird Reader* begins with a preface by Chester Himes and three separate introductions. In the first, Ishmael Reed, exposing the exploitation of black writers by the establishment, both black and white, explains the founding of the Yardbird Publishing Cooperative to "publish the finest work by Afro-American artists without regard to ideological or aesthetic affiliation." Al Young, in the second introduction, reaffirms the existence of "a non-white establishment." Cecil Brown, in the third, again summarizes the forms of black exploitation and brings together all three introductions: "Mr. Reed speaks of the need of individuality among black writers; Mr. Young of returning us to a freedom as stimulating as the old barbershop; I have spoken of inexpressiveness as metaphor for the enslavement that the Afro-American writer finds himself in. We are talking about the same thing, defining it in our own *individual* ways. *Yardbird Reader* will reveal how this critical attitude can also be exemplified in the sphere of creative imagination."

Yardbird Reader's shifting editorship helped it maintain its diversity. Volume II was edited by Al Young, Vol. III by Shawn Wong and Frank Chin, Vol. IV by William Lawson, and Vol. V by Ishmael Reed. Volume I divided its space equally between prose and poetry. Among the prose contributions were a John A. Williams travel article on Granada (refused by the *New York Times*) and Claude Brown's discussion of pressures on him after publication of *Manchild in the Promised Land*. Poems by some twenty contributors ranged from exercises by Sarah Fabio in the transcription of black dialect to violently anti-white verse by O. O. Gabugah, and proceeded from African poetry through Hoo-Doo to American verse in both black and "edited American English" dialects.

Volume II (1973), dedicated to Arna Bontemps, contained contributions from Afro-Americans, Chinese-Americans, Japanese-Americans, Colombians, Puerto Rican-Americans, Filipino-Americans, Franco-Americans, Anglo-Americans, North Africans, Kenyans, and Caribbeans. In Vol. III (1974), guest editors Shawn Wong and Frank Chin set out to meliorate the obscurity of yellow fiction and poetry. They selected works from three generations of Asian-American writers, to produce one of the most singular and interesting anthologies in years. For Vol. IV, Editor William Lawson selected contributions from a wide range of African and American writers, including material on Chinua Achebe, Camara Laye (a Guinean novelist), and Clarence Major. Volume V (1976) featured some strong attacks against other interpreters of black culture. O. O. Gabugah, John A. Williams, Amiri Baraka, and Ishmael Reed all ripped *Black World,* while Ishmael Reed and Stephen Henderson lambasted a Robert Moss article published in *Saturday Review.* Ishmael Reed also defended the multicultural *Yardbird Reader* against a charge that it was merely integrationist.

Yugen [no. 1: a new consciousness in arts and letters]. New York, N. Y.
No. 1–8, 1958–1962. No. 1–5: qy.; no. 6–8 irreg.
Ed. LeRoi Jones; Hettie Cohen (from no. 6, 1960, "Assistant Editor").
5½ " x 8½ "   stapled (folded)   24–36 pp.

LeRoi Jones's *Yugen* published Allen Ginsberg, Jack Kerouac, and Gregory Corso as well as Robert Creeley and Charles Olson (the *Black Mountain Review* had ceased publication in 1957), while introducing such poets as Peter Orlovsky (his first published poem appeared in *Yugen* No. 3), Kenneth Koch, Rochelle Owens, and David Meltzer, At the same time, *Yugen* served as an outlet for the work of a number of writers identified with Jones's Totem Press and with *Floating Bear* and *Kulchur,* among them Diane di Prima, Gilbert Sorrentino, Ray Bremser, Robin Blaser, Frank O'Hara, Fielding Dawson, Paul Blackburn, Joel Oppenheimer, John Wieners, Michael McClure, Barbara Guest, and Ed Dorn.

Most readers prefer later issues of *Yugen* because they are more professional in appearance and less erratic in content (e. g. No. 4, with McClure, Olson, O'Hara, Gary Snyder, Kerouac, Creeley, Ginsberg, Corso, Sorrentino, and with interesting pieces by Peter Orlovsky, Fielding Dawson, Ray Bremser, Joel Oppenheimer, and John Wieners, as well as LeRoi Jones himself). Still, there is something to be said for the rougher opening issues, which Jones co-edited with Hettie Cohen. The poetry in No. 1 was embarrassingly personal and self-indulgent (only three of about twenty-three poems failed to use first-person pronouns), and yet it convincingly transmitted the disaffection of the late fifties.

In Spring 1960, *Kulchur* began as a professionally printed, full-sized journal with a general interest in jazz, film, comics, and popular culture as well as in the work of poets appearing in *Yugen.* Then in February 1961 *Floating Bear* was started as a newsletter to enable new ideas, experiments, and achievements to be quickly communicated among a circle

748

of interested poets, most of whom were also involved with *Yugen* and *Kulchur*. Of these three interrelated publications, *Kulchur* was the most substantial and professional and *Floating Bear* the most immediate—a real poetry newsletter—but *Yugen* came first, the start of the venture.

Circulation of *Yugen* was 1,000. It was supported by personal funds and subscriptions.

Zero: A (Quarterly) Review of Literature and Art. Paris, France (no. 1, Spring 1949); Tangier, Morocco (no. 2–6, Summer 1949–July 1954); New York, N. Y. (no. 7–8, Spring 1956–Winter 1956).

No. 1–8, Spring 1949–Winter 1956. Irreg.

Ed. Themistocles Hoetis; Albert Benveniste (no. 1–3/4, Spring 1949–Autumn/Winter 1949/1950).

No. 1–4, 7: 5½" x 8" sewn 76–166 pp. Illus.

No. 5–6: 9" x 11" stapled 12–14 pp. Illus.

No. 8: 5½" x 8½" sewn (hardcover) 240 pp. Illus.

Index no. 1–6 in no 7.

As an introduction to the first issue of *Zero*, the editors proposed that the magazine act "as a raw and basic channel for creative assumptions, affiliating itself to all and to no techniques: conscious and unconscious, erudite and untutored, therapeutic and unpragmatic, right, left, with only the one major stipulation incumbent upon its use: that it be relevant to the principle of ZERO/zero itself, primarily honest in its use of the basic meaning of creative expression and communication; a meaning which does not allow for any forms of obscurantism in its literal sense (i.e. ideas in stasis, without volition)."

The initial issue was expatriate in tone and spirit, but with subsequent numbers the magazine became truly international in every respect. In 1955, for example, the magazine was printed in Mexico and editorial offices were maintained in Tangier, Madrid, Paris, Cornwall, and Flushing, New York. Despite its internationalism, some readers tended to identify it with the exotic locale of Tangier. As interest in psyche-modifying drugs increased in the United States, pilgrimages of writers (William Burroughs, Allen Ginsberg, Alfred Chester, among others) to Morocco were common, and the magazine became associated secondarily, and perhaps unfairly, with the so-called "kif cult."

Zero continues to be remembered for its focus on the prose poem, myth/ fables, and the short story. Appearing in the first number, along with the editors, were Wallace Fowlie ("Three Masks of Mallarmé"), Kenneth Patchen, William Carlos Williams ("All That Is Perfect in Woman"), Christopher Isherwood, Richard Wright, James Baldwin, and Mason Hoffenberg. Subsequent numbers featured Paul Bowles ("The Delicate Prey" in No. 2, Summer 1949), Federico García Lorca, Dorothea Tanning, Klaus Mann, Jean Garrigue, Octavio Paz, Gore Vidal, Colin Wilson, Samuel Beckett, Ursule Molinaro, Marianne Moore, Robert Kelly, and others. The art presented was generally surrealistic (tipped-in plates in No. 3/4, Autumn/Winter 1949/1950), the artists ranging from the well-established Max Ernst to the first-appearing Bruce Conner (No. 8, Winter 1956).

Zero's artistic progression culminated in No. 8, a 240-page volume (available in hardcover) which included such well-known literary figures as Jean-Paul Sartre, Colin Wilson, Marianne Moore, Samuel Beckett, Federico García Lorca, Samuel French Morse, Paul Bowles, Gore Vidal, Ahmed ben Driss el Yacoubi, Hart Crane, Ursule Molinaro, Constantine Cavafy, Kenneth Patchen, and Bruce Conner. Also included was "A Selection of Nine Young American Poets": Venable Herndon, Smith Oliver, Storm de Hirsch, Joseph Awad, Sanora Babb, Dachine Rainer, James Parsons, George H. Morse, and Robert Kelly.

A

751

752

754

Moss, Howard, 151–2, 182
Moss, Stanley, 158
Mother, 499
Mudus Artium, 41
Mulch, 714
Murray, Henry A. 162
Musil, Robert, 178
Myers, Frank, 127–8

N

Nabokov, Vladimir, 137, 159
Naipaul, V. S., 76
The Naked Ear, 715
National Endowment for the Arts
(NEA), 9, 18–9, 186, 194, 209, 278,
387, 439, 522, 633, 636–7, 651,
654–6, 660–3
Nations, Opal, 480–1
Neal, Larry, 539, 555–6, 558, 560, 566
Negro American Literature Forum,
548, 566
Negro Digest/Black World, 540, 548–
51, 555, 562, 564, 571–3
Negro Educational Review, 547
Negro Heritage, 548
Negro History Bulletin, 547
Neidecker, Lorine, 173, 392
Nemerov, Howard, 65, 104, 106–7, 160,
176
Neon, 298–311, 314–5, 319, 328, 471
Neruda, Pablo, 98, 419
Netz, Warren, 382
Neurotica, 100, 716
New, 717
New American Poetry, 1945–1960 (Al-
len), 11, 608, 656
New American Review, 40, 718
The New Anvil, 127–8
New Boston Review, 642
New Collage, 587
New Directions, 334, 350, 441
New Directions Annual, 253, 390
New Era, 408
New Helios, 547
New Letters 49, 129, 448, 587
The New Masses, 121, 126, 133
New Orleans Poetry Journal, 40

New Republic, 362
New Rivers Press, 588
New World Journal, 494
New York State Council on the Arts
(NYSCA), 522, 633, 636
Newberry Library, 202, 206, 208, 228,
231–2
Newman, Charles, 362, 622
Newton, Race, 150, 152, 154
Nicholson, Joseph, 392
Niebuhr, Reinhold, 360
Niedecker, Lorine, 306, 599
Nims, John Frederick, 222–3, 234
Nin, Anais, 275, 618, 622
Nkombo, 550, 562, 565, 572
Nolan, Pat, 478–9
Nommo, 548, 553, 566
Norse, Harold, 12
North, Charles, 510
North, Jessica Nelson, 222
North American Review, 638, 719
North Country Anvil, 129
Northeast, 35, 592
Northern Light, 117
Northern Review, 256
Northwest Mounted Valise, 14
Northwest Review, 29, 38, 352
Notley, Alice, 499
Nouvelle Review Francaise, 252
Nugget, 335

O

Oates, Joyce Carol, 76, 97, 178, 181,
622
Obayani, Kambon, 571
Obsidian, 571
O'Connor, Bill, 207
O'Connor, Flannery, 74, 76, 189
O'Connor, Frank, 76, 605
O'Connor, Philip, 97
Odam, Joyce, 391
O'Daniel, Therman B., 545
O'Faolain, Julia, 76
Ogden, Shepherd, 484
O'Hara, Frank, 11, 199, 268, 270,
274–7, 284–93, 305, 307, 313, 319,
327, 335–6, 353, 497, 499, 605, 609

763

Riesman, David, 348
Rivers, Conrad Kent, 539, 547, 555
Rivers, Larry, 264, 270, 286, 510
Road Apple Review, 578
Robertson, Kirk, 391
Roberts, Michael, 220–1
Robinson, Charles, 27–33
Robson, W. W., 98
Roditi, Edouard, 225
Roethke, Theodore, 137, 201, 214, 225
Rogers, John, 154
Rolfe, Edwin, 119, 125–6
Rolling Stone, 52, 65
Roots, 572
Rosenberg, Harold, 137
Rosenfeld, Isaac, 326
Rosenfeld, Paul, 152
Rosenthal, Irving, 307, 328, 350–1
Rosenthal, M.L., 176
Ross, David, 297
Rosset, Barney, 334
Rothenberg, Jerome, 284, 419, 453
Rottman, Larry, 619
Royce, Patrick, 618
Rubin, Jerry, 329
Rubin, Louis D., 97
Rudnick, Charles, 181
Rudnick, Raphael, 173, 181
Ruff, David, 599
Rukeyser, Muriel, 225
Rulfo, Juan, 419
Rumaker, Michael, 259–60, 287, 305–8
Runcible Spoon, 435
Russell, Bertrand, 440
Ryan, Bill, 440

S

Said, Edward, 64
Sale, Faith, 518
Salinger, J.D., 128
Salmagundi, 13, 50, 61–5, 731
Salstrom, Paul F., 491
Salthouse; A Magazine of Field Notes, 584–5
Samperi, Frank, 453
San Francisco Oracle, 488

San Francisco Review, 348, 351, 440–2
Sanchez, Ricardo, 619
Sandberg, David, 473
Sandburg, Carl, 220
Sanders, Ed, 499
Sanford, Marvin, 123
Sankey, John V., 379, 382, 384
The Saracen, 572
Saroyan, Aram, 296, 486, 499
Saroyan, William, 440
Sartre, Jean-Paul, 137
Savage, D. S., 137
Savio, Mario, 424
Schjeldahl, Peter, 499, 609
Schleifer, Marc, 281–5, 310–3
Schlesinger, Arthur, 137
Schneeman, George, 510
Schorer, Mark, 162
Schubert, David, 183
Schulman, Grace, 180
Schuyler, James, 270, 305, 499, 609
Schwartz, Delmore, 73, 134, 200, 225, 326, 606, 611
Schwartz, Horace, 253
Schwartz, Rhoda, 622
Schwerner, Armand, 295–7
Scope, 123
Scree, 584
Scully, James, 393
Scwartz, Delmore, 136
Seaver, Richard, 254
Seay, James, 97
Secession, 42
Seferis, George, 73, 98, 163, 179–80, 271
Seigel, Alfred, 302–3, 306
Sejourne, Laurette, 410
Selby, Hubert, 260, 282, 302–10, 312, 327, 329, 335,
Serpas, Carlos Coffeen, 407
Settle, Mary Lee, 174
The Seven Arts, 49
The Seventies (see *The Fifties*)
Sewanee Review, 86, 93, 188, 211, 319, 326, 357, 358, 533, 733
Sexton, Anne, 180
Seymour-Smith, Martin, 254

769

Wolf, Dan, 335
Wolfe, Tom, 327, 336, 520
Wolin, Harvey, 407–8, 412
Woolf, Douglas, 255, 286, 308
The World, 509–11, 517, 745
Worley, James, 547
Wormwood Review, 389–97, 586, 746
Worth, Douglas, 650
Wright, James, 76, 176, 180, 353, 611
Wright, Richard, 127
Writers in Revolt: The Anvil Anthology,
1933–1940 (Johnson), 118
Wurlitzer, Rudy, 517

Y

Yale French Studies, 532
Yardbird Reader, 564, 566, 569, 573,
651, 747
Yeats, William Butler, 220
Yerby, Frank, 128
Yip, Wai-Lim, 382
Yorke, Ruth, 273, 275
Young, Al, 560, 569, 598, 610
Young, David, 180

Young, Geoff, 495
Young, La Monte, 287
Young, Thomas Daniel, 97
Young Guard, 7
Yugen, 307–11, 315, 319–23, 328, 351,
354, 488, 499, 546, 748

Z

Zabel, Morton Dauwen, 221
Zahn, Curtis, 382
Zalamea, Eduardo, 486
Zaturenska, Marya, 152
Zavatsky, Bill, 595–613
Zazeela, Marian, 284, 313
0–9, 499
Zero, 390, 749
Zero, Frank, 492
Zimmer, Paul, 279
Zinnes, Harriet, 268, 275
Zobel, Fernando, 151
Zu-Bolton, Ahmos, 571
Zukofsky, Louis, 167, 173, 211, 220,
258–9, 282–4, 301, 306, 312–3, 451,
453, 459, 461, 599–600